Communications
in Computer and Information Science   471

T0241202

Jerzy Mikulski (Ed.)

Telematics – Support for Transport

14th International Conference
on Transport Systems Telematics, TST 2014
Katowice/Kraków/Ustroń, Poland
October 22-25, 2014
Selected Papers

Springer

Volume Editor

Jerzy Mikulski
Silesian University of Technology
Faculty of Transport
Krasińskiego 8
40-019, Katowice, Poland
E-mail: jerzy.mikulski@polsl.pl

ISSN 1865-0929   e-ISSN 1865-0937
ISBN 978-3-662-45316-2   e-ISBN 978-3-662-45317-9
DOI 10.1007/978-3-662-45317-9
Springer Heidelberg New York Dordrecht London

Library of Congress Control Number: 2014951756

Typesetting: Camera-ready by author, data conversion by Scientific Publishing Services, Chennai, India

Printed on acid-free paper

Springer is part of Springer Science+Business Media (www.springer.com)

Preface

Welcome to the proceedings of the 14th Transport Systems Telematics Conference (TST) held in Katowice/Kraków and Ustroń, Poland.

This was the 14th time that the Polish Association of Transport Telematics, together with leading Polish universities as well as representatives of leading companies in this field, organized the most important scientific event for the sector of intelligent transport systems.

Each year the conference gathers more and more participants from Poland and other EU countries. And every year it attracts presentations and discussions on topics relating to all four modes of transport.

The TST 2014 conference was organized under the patronage of leading institutions associated with the development and implementation of advanced technologies in transport. The cluster is formed by the Ministry of Infrastructure and Development, Parliamentary Team for Intelligent Transport Systems, Transport Committee of the Polish Academy of Sciences, ITS Europe (ERTICO), Association of ITS Poland, and the Polish Chamber of Information Technology and Telecommunications.

The conference is primarily aimed at: elaboration of the concept of the development of modern transport systems, supporting the development and innovation in the field of transport telematics solutions, formulation of the transport policy, assessment of the effectiveness and providing support to the presented solutions in the field of ITS, popularization and increasing the knowledge on the subjects of intelligent transport systems.

TST 2014 was an excellent opportunity to learn more about the latest trends and specific achievesments in the ITS field as well as to intensify cross-border coordinated implementation of telematics solutions.

The articles published in this volume met the Scientific Program Committee's criteria for high quality. Each article was reviewed by two independent reviewers (double-blind review). In addition, a Scientific-Editorial Special Committee was appointed to work on the final qualifying items.

October 2014   Jerzy Mikulski

Organization

Organizers

- Faculty of Transport, Silesian University of Technology
- Polish Academy of Sciences, Transport Committee
- Polish Association of Transport Telematics

Co-organizers

- Faculty of Economics, University of Economics in Katowice, Poland
- Faculty of Finance and Management, Wroclaw School of Banking, Poland
- Faculty of Transport and Electrical Engineering, University of Technology and Humanities in Radom, Poland
- Faculty of Transport, Warsaw University of Technology, Poland
- Faculty of Navigation, Gdynia Maritime University, Poland
- Faculty of Navigation, Maritime University of Szczecin, Poland
- Faculty of Social and Technical Sciences, Silesian School of Management, Poland
- UNESCO AGH Center

Organizing Committee

Chair

J. Młyńczak

Members

A. Białoń
P. Gorczyca
J. Łukasik
T. Sabuda
S. Surma

Secretary

R. Skowrońska

Scientific Program Committee

J. Mikulski – chairman	Silesian University of Technology, Polish Association of Transport Telematics, Poland
A. Bujak	Wroclaw School of Banking, Poland
R. Bańczyk	Regional Centre of Road Traffic, Katowice, Poland
M. Bukljaš Skočibušić	University of Zagreb, Croatia
T. Čorejová	University of Zilina, Republic of Slovakia
W. Choromański	Warsaw University of Technology, Poland
M. Dado	University of Zilina, Republic of Slovakia
A. Dewalska-Opitek	Silesian School of Management, Katowice, Poland
J. Dyduch	UTH, Radom, Transport Committee, Polish Academy of Sciences, Poland
A. Fellner	Silesian University of Technology, Poland
M. Franeková	University of Zilina, Republic of Slovakia
V. Gavriluk	Dnipropetrovsk National University of Railway Transport, Ukraine
T. Gugała	General Command of Branches of Armed Forces, Poland
M. Holec	Gdynia Maritime University, Poland
A. Janota	University of Zilina, Republic of Slovakia
J. Januszewski	Gdynia Maritime University, Poland
Z. Jóźwiak	Maritime University of Szczecin, Poland
U. Jumar	ifak, Magdeburg, Germany
A. Kalašová	University of Zilina, Republic of Slovakia
J. Kisilowski	UTH, Radom, Poland
J. Klamka	Polish Academy of Sciences, Katowice Branch, Poland
B. Kos	University of Economics, Katowice, Poland
S. Krawiec	Silesian University of Technology, Poland
O. Krettek	RWTH Aachen, Germany
J. Krimmling	TU Dresden, Germany
A. Križanová	University of Zilina, Republic of Slovakia
A. Lewiński	UTH, Radom, Poland
J. Lewitowicz	Air Force Institute of Technology, Warsaw, Poland
M. Luft	UTH, Radom, Poland
B. Łazarz	Silesian University of Technology, Poland
Z. Łukasik	UTH, Radom, Poland
A. Maczyński	University of Bielsko-Biala, Poland
M. Michałowska	University of Economics, Katowice, Poland
G. Nowacki	Military University of Technology, Warsaw, Poland

T. Nowakowski	Wroclaw University of Technology, Poland
Z. Pietrzykowski	Maritime University of Szczecin, Poland
B. Piotrowski	Silesian Inspectorate of Road Transport, Katowice, Poland
A. Prokopowicz	Intermodal Transport Center, USA
K. Rástočný	University of Zilina, Republic of Slovakia
M. Siergiejczyk	Warsaw University of Technology, Poland
M. Sitarz	Silesian University of Technology, Poland
J. Spalek	University of Zilina, Republic of Slovakia
R. Srp	ERTICO - ITS Europe, Belgium
Z. Stotsko	Lviv Polytechnic National University, Ukraine
W. Suchorzewski	Warsaw University of Technology, Poland
M. Svítek	Czech Technical University in Prague, ITS&S Czech Republic
J. Szpytko	AGH University of Science and Technology, Poland
E. Szychta	UTH, Radom, Poland
R. Thompson	University of Melbourne, Australia
R. Tomanek	University of Economics, Katowice, Poland
A. Tomasik	The Upper Silesian Aviation Group (GTL), Poland
R. Wawruch	Gdynia Maritime University, Poland
W. Wawrzyński	Warsaw University of Technology, Poland
A. Weintrit	Gdynia Maritime University, Poland
B. Wiśniewski	Maritime University of Szczecin, Poland
E. Załoga	University of Szczecin, Poland
J. Ždánsky	University of Zilina, Republic of Slovakia
J. Żak	Poznan University of Technology, Poland
J. Żurek	Air Force Institute of Technology, Warsaw, Poland

The Scientific–Editorial Special Committee

M. Dado	University of Zilina, Dean of Electrical Engineering Faculty, Republic of Slovakia
J. Dyduch	President of Transport Committee, Polish Academy of Sciences, Poland
W. Wawrzyński	Warsaw University of Technology, Dean of Transport Faculty, Poland
O. Krettek	RWTH Aachen, Professor Emeritus, Germany
R. Thompson	University of Melbourne, Professor, Australia
A. Prokopowicz	Intermodal Transport Center, Professor, USA
M. Svítek	Czech Technical University in Prague, Dean of Transport Faculty, Czech Republic

Table of Contents

Road Surface Degradation –
Measurement and Visualization

Marián Hruboš and Aleš Janota

University of Žilina,
Faculty of Electrical Engineering,
Univerzitna 2, 01026 Žilina, Slovak Republic
{marian.hrubos,ales.janota}@fel.uniza.sk

Abstract. The paper presents the designed algorithm capable of creating the 3D road surface model based on measured data. This model can be used to calculate severity of degradation of road infrastructure manifested by cracks, pot-holes, rutting and shoving, deterioration, local deformations or beaten longitudinal tracks. The algorithm may also be used to calculate amount of material needed for repair of road surface deformations. It can provide data on GPS position of individual distresses together with visual information. In future information about positions of road surface deformations could be integrated into road databases and via I2C communication sent to drivers in the form of early warnings.

Keywords: point cloud, 3D model, road surface, degradation, data processing.

1 Introduction

The ever-increasing intensity of road transport has adverse effects on the quality of communications. Different types of disturbances resulting from road surface damages such as cracks, potholes, longitudinal and transverse bumps, wavy surface, local declines or beaten longitudinal gauge have adverse effect on ride comfort and cause increased damage of certain parts of motor vehicles.

To measure the deformation of road surface many methods and measuring equipment have been developed so far. One large group of measuring devices used for measuring the deformation of road surface are laser measuring systems. They use contactless measurement methods based on measurement of the laser pulse time of flight. With these methods we can measure a distance between the laser measuring device and the road surface.

One of the basic characteristics of the surface is roughness. Roughness ensures concurrence between the road surface and the wheels. Roughness, from the geometric point of view, is expressed as a road surface texture. It affects the interaction between the road surface and the tyre footprint. To provide adequate skid resistance road texture need to be measured and provided. It can be classified, based on the amplitude and wavelength, to several basic groups of textures (Fig. 1):

J. Mikulski (Ed.): TST 2014, CCIS 471, pp. 1–10, 2014.
© Springer-Verlag Berlin Heidelberg 2014

- Microtexture (wavelengths shorter than 0.5 mm);
- Macrotexture (wavelengths from 0.5 mm up to 50 mm);
- Megatexture (wavelengths from 50 mm up to 500 mm);
- Uneveness (wavelengths > 500 mm – 50 m).

Microtexture is a property of the individual pieces of aggregate making up the road surface – it controls the contact between the tyre rubber and the road surface and results from a material's crystallographic parameters and other aspects of microstructure such as morphology, including size and shape distributions; chemical composition; and crystal orientation and relationships. The macrotexture of road surface refers to the coarser texture defined by the shape of the individual aggregate chips and by the spaces between them [8].

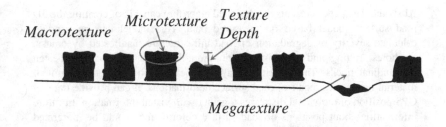

Fig. 1. Microtexture, Macrotexture and Megatexture [4]

In our work we focus just on measurement of macrotexture up to uneveness using a laser measuring device by which we are able to measure road surface and thus create a 3D model of road surface formed by the point cloud. After processing all the points we get a model of road surface on which we can apply the texture. Generally, point clouds are acquired with stereo cameras, monocular systems or laser scanners. There are many methods and approaches available such as e.g. [1], based on extraction of so called "feature points"; or [2], which defines the surface as the isosurface of a trivariate volume model, or many others.

1.1   Equipment Used in Slovakia

At present the Slovak Road Administration uses similar equipment as can be found in many other neighbour countries: Profilograph GE [4] - a multifunctional measuring device designed to measure road surface degradation, with well-known technical parameters. To measure road surface degradation this device uses 16 laser scanners. Its movement is recorded by three accelerometers and two gyroscopes. The measuring device is able to measure road surface in width 2.7 m. Distance between laser scanners and road surface is about 30 cm. Movement of the girder is recorded using the inertial navigation system (INS) with two gyroscopes and with three accelerometers. Software Profilograph for Windows can calculate dimensions of road surface and display the result in the form of the (Fig. 2). Subsequently data can be exported into the output file of the .pg2 type.

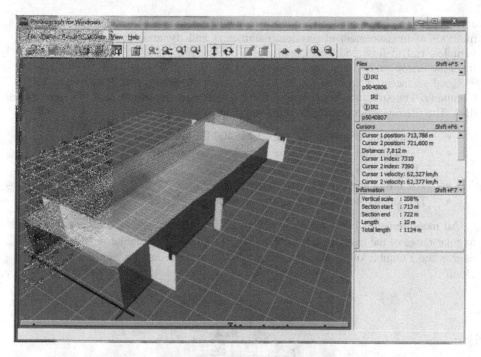

Fig. 2. A Sample model of road surface generated by Profilograph GE [4]

1.2   Concept of Our Measurement Unit

The concept of our measurement unit is based on getting and fusing data obtained from different devices and their fast processing. The primary data are obtained by the two-dimensional (2D) laser scanners. The control program is based on the calculation algorithm that depends on the used measurement method. In our work we use fusion of sensory data obtained by different equipment integrated in the mobile measurement platform which consists of two 2D lasers scanners, seven cameras, GPS receiver, server, switch and UPS (Fig. 3). Laser scanners are used for accurate measurement of space around the mobile measurement platform. The angular range of the first laser scanner is 360 degrees and distance which we can measure is about 250m. We use this scanner to measure an area surrounding the road. The second scanner is used to measure the road itself. Its angular range is 70 degree and the measurement distance about 2.4 m. Gathering visual information is ensured by a set of cameras installed in the front part of the measurement platform.

We use the SPAN CTP navigation system to get precise position of the measurement platform. It is a combination of a classical GPS receiver providing basic position data, corrected with position data received from the OMNISTAR satellites and the inertial navigation system. So the SPAN CTP navigation system evaluates its current location just on the basis of the classical position determined from the GPS with OMNISTAR correction, but this position is also corrected based on real motion sensed by a set of accelerometers and gyroscopes [3], [5].

The research project whose partial results are presented here is entitled "Study of interactions of a motor vehicle, traffic flow and road". Practical experiments were carried out on the equipment acquired under the project ITMS-26220220089 "New methods of measurement of physical parameters and dynamic interactions of motor vehicles, traffic flow and road conditions", i.e. the project which has been financed from the European regional development funds.

Road surface is measured by the laser scanner LMS-400, produced by the SICK Company. The structure of the output file consists of a file header and the measured data. The file header contains the following pieces of information:

- Type of the laser scanner, e.g. „LMS400 Data Recorder",
- The date and time when the record was made, e.g. „Tue Nov 12 12:12:11 CET 2013",
- The initial angle, e.g. „Start Angle[°] 55.0",
- The angle resolution, e.g. „Angle Resolution [°] 0.25".

All measurements follow this head part. Each line consists of one measurement. The angular range of the laser scanner LMS400 is 70 degrees. The angular resolution is 0.25 degree and a number of measured points is 280. From these data we can generate a point cloud.

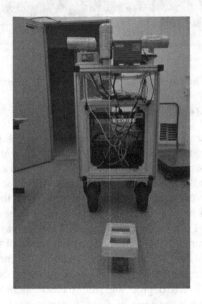

Fig. 3. Mobile measurement platform captured during measurement process in the laboratory conditions [own study]

2   The Algorithm for Detection of Degradation of the Road Surface

For points cloud processing we use our own algorithm that incorporates a real position of the measurement equipment and tilts in all axes. To be compatible with various visualization equipment we use *.OBJ format of the output data file. It is suitable for display of objects in the three-dimensional space. Another advantage of that format is its compatibility with multiple imaging software environments. The internal structure is freely available and the process of data storage is simply algorithmizable.

2.1 The 3D Model of Road Surface

To calculate a cloud of points (Fig. 4) we use our own algorithm (1) [4] utilizing the equations proposed on the base of received data analysis. These equations enable to fuse data obtained by the laser scanner, GPS receiver and INS. Similar equations for calculation of trajectory were used in the publication [6]. We are able to calculate trajectory of the mobile measurement platform using video information. More details about this method could be found in the publication [7].

$$x'_{in} = d_{in} * \sin\left[\frac{(\alpha_{0n} + i * \Delta\alpha_n + \alpha_{rn} + 90) * \pi}{180}\right] * \cos\left[\frac{\beta_{rn} * \pi}{180}\right] + x_{0n}$$

$$y'_{in} = d_{in} * \cos\left[\frac{(\alpha_{0n} + i * \Delta\alpha_n + \alpha_{rn} + 90) * \pi}{180}\right] + y_{0n}$$

$$z'_{in} = d_{in} * \sin\left[\frac{(\alpha_{0n} + i * \Delta\alpha_n + \alpha_{rn} + 90) * \pi}{180}\right] * \sin\left[\frac{\beta_{rn} * \pi}{180}\right]$$

$$r'_{in} = \sqrt{y'^2_{in} + z'^2_{in}}$$

$$\gamma'_{in} = \arccos\left[\frac{y'_{in} * 180}{r'_{in} * \pi}\right]$$

$$x_{in} = x'_{in}$$

$$y_{in} = r'_{in} * \cos\left[\frac{(\gamma_{rn} + \gamma'_{in}) * \pi}{180}\right]$$

$$z_{in} = r'_{in} * \sin\left[\frac{(\gamma_{rn} + \gamma'_{in}) * \pi}{180}\right] + z_{0n}$$

(1)

Data obtained by the laser scanner are:

- Initial angle α_{0n},
- Serial number of the current point i,
- Angle resolution $\Delta\alpha_n$,
- Distance between an object and the laser scanner d_{in}.

Data obtained by the GPS receiver:

- Position of the mobile measurement platform x_{0n}, y_{0n} and z_{0n}.

Data obtained by the GPS receiver:

- Rotation of the mobile measurement platform in each axe α_{rn}, β_{rn} a γ_{rn}.

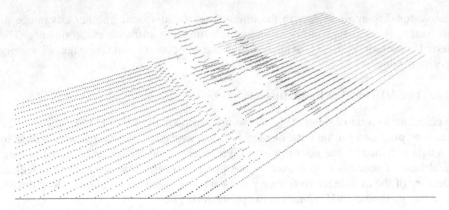

Fig. 4. Model of road surface with a real object (from Fig. 3) on it – point cloud form [own study]

2.2   Algorithm for Road Surface Creation

This algorithm is used to create surfaces of objects defined by a cloud of points (Fig. 5). Generally, there are many methods designed for creation of a surface based on known points of individual objects. The method utilized in our algorithm is designed in such a way that three points are necessary to create surface. In this way it is possible to reach better interpretation of final objects thanks to smaller dimensions of individual surfaces. The surface is generated from metadata as follows. The point "n" is connected with the point "$n+1$" and with the point "n" in the next plate. If we use the above mentioned settings we connect points "1", "2" and "281". In the next step the point "$n+1$" is connected with the point "$n+1$" in the next plate and with the point "n" in the next plate. In this step we connect points "2", "282" and "281". Algorithm continues until all areas of the building are not generated.

Results of sequentially performed steps can be found in Fig. 5 up to Fig. 7 and confronted with a real photo of the scanned object lying on the laboratory floor taken in (Fig. 3) together with the measurement platform.

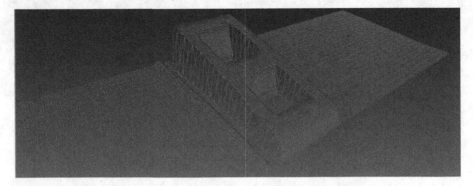

Fig. 5. An object with its own surface [own study]

After processing of all the points in this part of our algorithm we get a model of road surface on which we can apply the texture. Gradually we receive texture (Fig. 6) from individual images of the road surface using cameras.

Fig. 6. Texture of the measured object [own study]

This texture can be applied to the final model of road surface (Fig. 7).

Fig. 7. The final model of road surface with real object on it [own study]

2.3 Searching of Road Surface Degradation, Calculation of the Volume of Material, and Statistical Calculation of Changes

The first of the basic tasks performed by this algorithm is finding the coordinates that represent a found place of degradation of road surface. The second task is calculation of the volume of degradation. The following values are used as inputs to the algorithm:

- Distance between the laser scanner and the object: 108 cm (height „c" reference value);
- Distance between points in one plate: 0,54 cm (width „d");
- Distance between each scanned plate (depth „z") - this value depends on velocity of mobile measurement platform movement.

The distance „c" between the laser scanner and road surface has been set to the value 108 cm based on experimental measurements; deadband of measurement in the algorithm has been denoted as the quantity „a". The actual search is then carried out in a very simple form:

$$if(c + a <= y \parallel c - a >= y)$$

Subsequently, these results are written to the output file.

The calculation itself is divided into two sections according to whether it is a calculation of the stroke or a decrease by applying the integral calculus.

Calculation of volume of stroke:
```
if (y < c)
{
Oz = (c - y) * d * z;
output << Oz << endl;
}
```

Calculation of volume of decrease:
```
if(y > c)
{
Op = (y - c) * d * z;
output << Op << endl;
}
```

We can apply statistical methods of data processing on data obtained from the model. In our work we focused on calculation of the gradient of individual changes. The gradient of the function of two variables, $F(x, y)$, then has been defined as:

$$\nabla F = \frac{\partial F}{\partial x}\hat{i} + \frac{\partial F}{\partial y}\hat{j} \tag{2}$$

and can be thought of as a collection of vectors pointing in the direction of increasing values of F.

In the picture (Fig. 8) we can see results of our analysis.

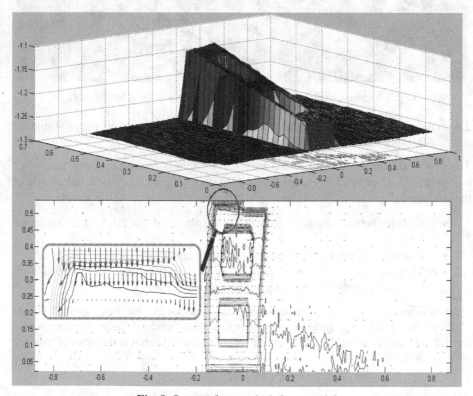

Fig. 8. Output of our analysis [own study]

In the Matlab environment the problem can be solved in the following way:

```
subplot(2,1,1);
surfc(Xv,Yv,Zv)
colormap hsv
[px,py] = gradient(Zv);
subplot(2,1,2);
contour(Xv,Yv,Zv)
hold on
quiver(Xv,Yv,px,py)
hold off
```

3 Conclusion

This work has introduced our designed and tested algorithm which makes possible to measure road surface degradation. If we measured road surface regularly with a certain frequency, we could also calculate and provide the rate of degradation of the road surface in time. The proposed approach seems to be better than provided by commercial measuring equipment since our solution also provides higher resolution (the number of measured points per scan) and application of texture of road surface. Increase of the number of measured points in our approach, compared with the device Profilograph GE, is 17.5 times. Sampling has been increased from the original 25 cm to 0.54 cm while we have enable simpler visual detection of potential road surface deformations through a texture applied to the model.

Acknowledgment. The paper was elaborated with support of the Slovak grant agency VEGA, grant No. 1/0453/12 "Study of interactions of a motor vehicle, traffic flow and road."

References

1. Toll, B., Cheng, F.: Surface Reconstruction from Point Clouds. In: Olling, G.J., Choi, B.K., Jerard, R.B. (eds.) Machining Impossible Shape. IFIP, vol. 18, pp. 173–178. Springer, Boston (1999)
2. Huang, A., Nielson, G.M.: Surface Approximation to Point Cloud Data Using Volume Modeling. In: Data Visualization. The Springer International Series in Engineering and Computer Science, vol. 713, pp. 333–343 (2003)
3. Halgaš, J., Janota, A.: Technical Devices Cooperation to Obtain Data for 3D Environment Modelling. In: Mikulski, J. (ed.) TST 2011. CCIS, vol. 239, pp. 330–337. Springer, Heidelberg (2011)
4. Hruboš, M.: Nástroj na zistenie stavu degradácie vozovky v čase (A Tool to Detect Status of Road Degradation in Time). MSc. thesis No. 28260220122010, Dept. of Control & Information Systems, University of Žilina, Slovakia, p. 77 (2012)
5. Halgaš, J., et al.: Determination of Formulas for Processing of Measured Points Representing Road Surface Deformations. Archives of Transport System Telematics 5(1), 7–10 (2012)

6. Šimák, V., Nemec, D., Hrbček, J., Janota, A.: Inertial Navigation: Improving Precision and Speed of Euler Angles Computing from MEMS Gyroscope Data. In: Mikulski, J. (ed.) TST 2013. CCIS, vol. 395, pp. 163–170. Springer, Heidelberg (2013)
7. Bubeníková, E., Franeková, M., Holečko, P.: Security Increasing Trends in Intelligent Transportation Systems Utilising Modern Image Processing Methods. In: Mikulski, J. (ed.) TST 2013. CCIS, vol. 395, pp. 353–360. Springer, Heidelberg (2013)
8. Feighan, K.: Pavement Skid Resistance Management. In: Fwa, T.F. (ed.) The Handbook of Highway Engineering, pp. 21-1–22-51. CRC Press (2006) ISBN 0-8493-1986-2
9. Mikulski, J. (ed.): TST 2011. CCIS, vol. 239. Springer, Heidelberg (2011)
10. Mikulski, J. (ed.): TST 2010. CCIS, vol. 104. Springer, Heidelberg (2010)
11. Mikulski, J.: Introduction of telematics for transport. In: Proceedings on 9th International Conference ELEKTRO 2012, Rajecke Teplice, IEEE Catalog Number CFP1248S-ART, May 21-22, pp. 336–340 (2012), http://ieexplore.ieee.org

Modeling of ETCS Levels with Respect to Functionality and Safety Including Polish Railways Conditions

Andrzej Toruń[1], Andrzej Lewiński[2], and Paweł Gradowski[1]

[1] Railway Traffic Control and Telecom Unit, Railway Institute
J. Chłopickiego 50, 04-275 Warszawa, Poland
{atorun,pgradowski}@ikolej.pl
[2] Faculty of Transport and Electrical Engineering, University
of Technology and Humanities in Radom, Malczewskiego 29, 26-600 Radom, Poland
a.lewinski@uthrad.pl

Abstract. Authors deal with functionality and safety problem of three levels of ETCS. To such analysis the stochastic processes are used to build appropriate models giving the possibility of estimation both probabilistic and time parameters related to efficient application of such solutions in the conditions of existing and planed railway infrastructure and assuring the required safety level corresponding to EU standards and recommendations.

Keywords: ETCS levels, stochastic processes modelling, functionality and safety, EU railway standards.

1   Introduction

The railway control devices according to existing type of signaling are typical dissipated systems with old fashion technology in many working solutions. such situation enforces the EU administration to introduce the requirements of unambiguous consolidated technical specifications for whole railway control market [9]. The assumed aim of designed control equipment using such recommended methods may assure the achievement of high level of competition in accordance to other types of transport with satisfaction of safety planning with coordinated strategy of migration. The all tasks connected with such strategy including the advantages of digital control techniques may be assured by ERTMS (European Railway Train Management System). The tasks are divided into two parts, first ERTMS/ETCS (European Train Control System responsible for processing of all signaling data (both for train side and train side), and second ERTMS/GMS-R (GMS for Railway) related voice and data transmission between devices. Such closed co-operation of both parts allows to concentrate the terrestrial data transmission system with eurobalises and Radio Block Centre (RBC).

The introduction of ERTMS/ETCS as a obligatory radio transmission system may assure as main aim the high level of functionality and inter-operability for passenger trains including control and monitoring of high speed railway (HSR) lines [6].

J. Mikulski (Ed.): TST 2014, CCIS 471, pp. 11–18, 2014.

The basic questions connected with ETCS are related to:

- improvement of safety (monitoring the train driver),
- increasing the capacity of railway lines, especially of HSR lines,
- implementation of new communication standard such GSM-R and in future the more efficient radio-transmission standards including LTE or WiFi.

Now ERTMS is implemented not only in HSR lines (at first assumed for this system) but in 6 main freight railway lines in EU corridors.

2   The Basic Model of Train Control

The drive of train from control point of view may be presented by stochastic process approach. In many papers [1,3,4,8] the homogeneous, stationary and ergodic Markov process is very convenient from description the transition between states corresponding to typical behavior of the train. The presented model is simple, because in this stage of research the safety and functionality of introduction of ETCS may be shown assuming the basic parameters of train control (in the next stages the multi state models with semi Markov approach will be examined).

On the Fig. 1 the control process of the train is presented [3,7]. The introduced states corresponds to following situation:

0. state of correct drive according to last received information, the locomotive driver works corresponding to last drive permission up to next information about train movement,

1. state o proper realization the control procedure (corresponding to semaphore lights or deck computer recommendations),

2. state of emergency stop or reducing the speed after lost of control (emergency breaking caused by ATP systems – in PR condition – SHP system class AWS).

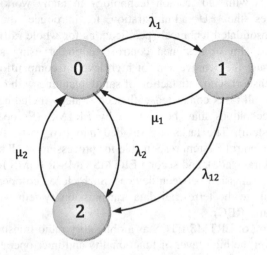

Fig. 1. The basic model of controlled drive of the train [3,7]

The transitions between states are related to typical parameters of railway control procedure. We assume maximal length of block section as 1500m (minimal length as 1300m is nor required) for maximal speed V=160 km/h, and:

- λ_1 – intensity of events connected with departure of train to signal or MA and receiving the information about next drive procedure
- λ_{12} – intensity of event connected with faulty reaction of locomotive driver or inproper action of ATP system,
- λ_2 –intensity of events connected with Emergency signal, implementation of service breaking (without driver) to total stop of train,
- μ_1^{-1} – mean time necessary for show the driver the information about next action – procedure of train driving with respect to safety conditions,
- μ_2^{-1} – mean time necessary for driver to next start after automatic stop of train.

The differential equations describing the transitions between states of the system are corresponding to [3,7] to assumed Markov model the Fokker-Planc (Kolmogorov) equations are derived:

$$
\begin{cases}
\dfrac{dP_0(t)}{dt} = -\lambda_1 \cdot P_0(t) + \mu_1 \cdot P_1(t) - \lambda_2 \cdot P_0(t) + \mu_2 \cdot P_2(t) \\
\dfrac{dP_1(t)}{dt} = \lambda_1 \cdot P_0(t) - \lambda_{12} \cdot P_1(t) - \mu_1 \cdot P_1(t) \\
\dfrac{dP_2(t)}{dt} = \lambda_{12} \cdot P_1(t) - \mu_2 \cdot P_2(t) + \lambda_2 \cdot P_0(t)
\end{cases}
$$

$$P_0(t) + P_1(t) + P_2(t) = 1$$

where:

P_0, P_1, P_2 – probabilities of occurrence in the state 0, 1,2,

λ_1 –   intensity of events connected with departure of train to signal or MA and receiving the information about next drive procedure

λ_{12} – intensity of event connected with faulty reaction of locomotive driver or inproper action of ATP system,

λ_2 – intensity of events connected with Emergency signal, implementation of service breaking (without driver) to total stop of train,

μ_1^{-1} – mean time necessary for show the driver the information about next action – procedure of train driving with respect to safety conditions,

μ_2^{-1}– mean time necessary for driver to next start after automatic stop of train.

(1)

The linear equations (1) after Laplace transform have a form (2) .

$$
\begin{cases}
s \cdot P_0 - 1 = \mu_1 \cdot P_1 - \lambda_1 \cdot P_0 - \lambda_2 \cdot P_0 + \mu_2 \cdot P_2 \\
s \cdot P_1 = \lambda_1 \cdot P_0 - \lambda_{12} \cdot P_1 - \mu_1 \cdot P_1 \dots \dots \dots \dots \dots \\
s \cdot P_2 = \lambda_{12} \cdot P_1 + \lambda_2 \cdot P_0 - \mu_2 \cdot P_2 \dots \dots \dots \dots \dots
\end{cases}
$$

(2)

Using the Mathematica software we can estimate the boundary values of probabilities of occurrence in defined earlier states. $P_i(t)|_{t\to\infty}$. The solution is as follows (3):

$$P_0 = P_0(t)|_{t\to\infty} = \frac{\mu_2 \cdot (\lambda_{12} + \mu_1)}{(\lambda_{12} + \mu_1) \cdot (\lambda_2 + \mu_2) + \lambda_1 \cdot (\lambda_{12} + \mu_2)}$$

$$P_1 = P_1(t)|_{t\to\infty} = \frac{\lambda_1 \cdot \mu_2}{(\lambda_{12} + \mu_1) \cdot (\lambda_2 + \mu_2) + \lambda_1 \cdot (\lambda_{12} + \mu_2)} \tag{3}$$

$$P_2 = P_2(t)|_{t\to\infty} = \frac{\lambda_1 \cdot \lambda_{12} + \lambda_2 \cdot (\lambda_{12} + \mu_1)}{(\lambda_{12} + \mu_1) \cdot (\lambda_2 + \mu_2) + \lambda_1 \cdot (\lambda_{12} + \mu_2)}$$

In the existing railway control systems based on fixed block distance (determined by occupancy the sequence of rail section) the green signal permitting the drive is generated with the information about occupancy signals of the 2-3 following train sections.

The sense of above values is obvious. The P2 may be treated as operational (functional) coefficient responsible for efficiency of control. (It means how control of train regards the capacity of railway line according to occupancy of rail sections in front of the train.

We assume the same maximal length of block section as 1500m but now the maximal speed is V=160 km/h, and the parameters for Markov model from Fig. 1 are:

- λ_1 – intensity of drive requirements for permission of drive equal to $106{,}67 h^{-1}$ (corresponding to time of request of train for signal 33,75s),
- μ_1 – intensity of typical service equal to $300\ h^{-1}$ (reciprocal to mean time of service 12s),
- λ_2 – intensity o faulty requirements (failure rate) equal to $0{,}000227687\ h^{-1}$ (related to request of emergency drives 2 per year),
- λ_{12} – intensity o faulty requirements (failure rate) $0{,}005952381\ h^{-1}$ related to time emergency drive but during permission for drive, 1 per week
- μ_2 – intensity of emergency service equal to $72 h^{-1}$ (reciprocal to mean time of service 50s)

For Fixed Block Distance method such value is equal to: $P_{2FBD} = 2{.}401 \cdot 10^{-5}$

3   ETCS Models

The ETCS is an intelligent overlay on the existing fail safe railway control and management systems. The complete descriptions of ERTMS levels contains the SRS ERTMS/ETCS Class 1 [2,6].

The all trains not equipped with deck ERTMS/ETCS devices will receive the Permission for Drive (PfD) via side rail signaling. The traction vehicles equipped with deck ERTMS/ETCS devices of Level 2 will receive the PfD from Radio Block Control (RBC) via safety transmission network ERTMS/GSM-R, but for railway lines of Level 1 after passing the balises situated near light signaling devices. The traction devices may have an ability of work in different schedules (levels and routines) according to compatibility of deck devices with side rail devices. The existing rule of co-operation of deck devices with respect side rail devices is defined as "top down" compatibility, i.e. train equipped with level 2 devices may drive in lines assigned to Level 2 and Level 1, but train equipped with Level 1 devices may drive only in Level 1 lines.

The trains equipped with ERTMS/ETCS deck devices will be informed about No of ERTMS level controlled in given railway area in the moment of passing the group of balises informing about approach to given area assigned to appropriate ERTMS/ETCS level.

The deck devices (according to compatibility of deck and side rail parts) after receiving the information about entry to area switches on the control to ETCS Level defined in design of appropriate system [3,7].

3.1   ETCS Level 1

The Level 1 is a overlay on to station and line devices treated as a dissipated railway control system. The ERTMS/ETCS level 1 devices assure that the monitored train does not pass outside off point restricted by se and approved route way, and does not exceed permitted speed in each section of route way. The track equipped with level 1 devices use the eurobalises, both with swich on or non switch on circuits. In addition the track may be equipped with euroloops or radio used for up-dating the information transmitted by eurobalises or two way communication rail vehicle for pre processing the information by side rail devices [2].

We assume the same maximal length of block section as 1500m but now the maximal speed is V=250 km/h, and the parameters for Markov model from Fig. 1 are:

- λ'_1 – intensity of request before balise (semaphore) equal to $\lambda1=166,67h^{-1}$ (related to 21.6s),
- μ'_1 – rate (intensity) of service equal to 360000 h^{-1} (related to max 10ms) with assumption the mean time of synchronization is related to 1m way of drive,
- λ'_{12} – intensity of faulty receive the message from balise leading to stop of the train equal to $0.33*10^{-9}/h$,
- λ'_2 – intensity of failure of deck devices equal to $1x10^{-9}$ according to THR for deck devices (Tolerable Hazard Rate according to PN-EN 5012x requirements and remarks [7]),
- μ'_2 – intensity of switch on to mode assigned to not equipped train equal to 0,03333h (connected with mean time of implementation the drive with mode of not equipped train120s).

For ETCS L1 such value is equal to: $P_{2ETCS\ L1} = 3.003 \cdot 10^{-8}$

3.2   ETCS Level 2

The Level 2 of ETCS is a railway control with continuous, digital two channel radio transmission. The track is equipped in addition (besides the eurobalises) with radio control centers RBC. It is related with elimination the semaphores from the track and application the eurobalises with non switch on circuits. The parameters for Markov model from Fig. 1 are:

- λ''_1 – equal to 14.173h^{-1} (related to maximal time of request the RBC 254s – T_CYCLOC variable in ETCS),
- μ''_1 – rate (intensity) of service the telegram in RBC equal to 3600h^{-1} (related to mean time of service 1s)
- λ''_{12} – intensity of RBC leading to stop of train, THR for Radio Block Center – RBC 0.67*10^{-9}/h (Tolerable Hazard Rate according to PN-EN 5012x requirements and remarks [7]),
- λ''_2 – intensity of deck devices fault, THR for deck devices 1x10^{-9} (Tolerable Hazard Rate according to PN-EN 5012x requirements and remards [7]),
- μ''_2 – rate (intensity) of implementation of emergency mode 30h^{-1}, such for Level 2

For ETCS L2 such value is equal to: $P_{2ETCS\ L2} = 3.407 \cdot 10^{-11}$

3.3   ETCS Level 3

The Level 3 is a an evolution of Level 2 by transfer the monitoring of track occupation from side rail devices to vehicle deck devices. It allows to control of train succession with respect to Changeable Block Distance (CBD) without of rail circuits and axe counters.

The parameters for Markov model from Fig. 1 for this levels are the same such for Level 2 with exception :

- λ'''_1 – intensity of request MA (Movement Authority) is above 70h^{-1} (related to maximal time of request 2s).
- μ'''_1 – rate (intensity) of service the telegram in RBC equal to 3600h^{-1} (related to time of service 1s)
- λ'''_{12} – intensity of RBC leading to stop of train, THR for Radio Block Center – RBC 0.67*10^{-9}/h (Tolerable Hazard Rate according to PN-EN 5012x requirements and remarks [7]),
- λ'''_2 – intensity of deck devices fault, THR for deck devices 1x10^{-9} (Tolerable Hazard Rate according to PN-EN 5012x requirements) and remarks [7],
- μ'''_2 – rate (intensity) of implementation of emergency mode 30h^{-1}, such for Level 3

For ETCS L3 such value is equal to: $P_{2ETCS\ L3} = 3.695 \cdot 10^{-11}$

4   Conclusion

Now we can resume the results of control efficiency in traditional control of train with respect to proper occupation of rail section in the procedure of Fixed Block Distance with three levels of ETCS. The Table 1 contains the results obtained using (3) for estimation the probabilities of each states in our model.

Table 1. The probabilities of states 0, 1, 2 in analyzed Fixed Block and three levels of ETCS

Probability	Fixed Block	ETCS Level 1	ETCS Level 2	ETCS Level 3
P_0	$7.376 \cdot 10^{-1}$	$9.995 \cdot 10^{-1}$	$9.960 \cdot 10^{-1}$	$9.809 \cdot 10^{-1}$
P_1	$2.622 \cdot 10^{-1}$	$4.627 \cdot 10^{-4}$	$3.921 \cdot 10^{-3}$	$1.907 \cdot 10^{-2}$
P_2	$2.401 \cdot 10^{-5}$	$3.003 \cdot 10^{-8}$	$3.407 \cdot 10^{-11}$	$3.695 \cdot 10^{-11}$

All parameters corresponds to official ETCS data and signaling [2,6,9]. In all presented models (Fixed Block, ETCS Level1, ETCS Level2, ETCS Level3) the probability of state 2 is important from system non availability (the state 2 corresponds to uncontrolled, emergency stop caused by faulty signaling or automatic control devices.

We can remark that each next level of train control decreases the probability of P2, thus the availability of whole system is better. It is related with idea of ETCS: better capacity, availability and in consequence better parameters of train traffic including High Speed Trains [2,6].

Presented model is rather simple but gives some possibilities of modeling and verification of assumed parameters using computer simulation methods (till now we have no experimental test results].The next stage will be building more sophisticated models with greater number of states and more complicated distribution (not only exponential) leading to semi-Markov processes.

References

1. Lewiński, A., Bester, L.: Additional warning system for cross level. In: Mikulski, J. (ed.) TST 2010. CCIS, vol. 104, pp. 226–231. Springer, Heidelberg (2010)
2. Interoperability-related consolidation on TSI annex A documents, ERA Subset-108, version 1.2.0
3. Lewiński, A., Toruń, A.: The changeable block distance system analysis. In: Mikulski, J. (ed.) TST 2010. CCIS, vol. 104, pp. 67–74. Springer, Heidelberg (2010)
4. Lewiński, A., Toruń, A., Bester, L.: Methodsof Implementation of the Open Transmission in Railway Control Systems (Sposobyrealizacjitransmisjiotwartej w systemachsterowaniaruchemkolejowym). Logistyka (March 2011)
5. Norma PN-EN 50159: 2011. Zastosowania kolejowe. Systemy łączności, sterowaniaruchem i przetwarzania danych – Łączność bezpieczna w systemach transmisyjnych
6. System Requirement Specification, UNISIG Subset-026, wersja 2.3.0
7. Toruń, A.: The method of train positioning in railway control process, Ph D. dissertation, University of Technology and Humanities in Radom (December 2013)
8. Toruń, A., et al.: Szacowanie funkcjonalności i bezpieczeństwa systemów sterowania ruchem kolejowym. Prace Naukowe Politechniki Warszawskiej, Transport z. 96. Międzynarodowa Konferencja Naukowa TRANSPORT XXI WIEKU 2013, Ryn (2013)

9. Załącznik do Decyzji Komisji z dnia 26 kwietnia 2011 r. (2011/291/UE) w sprawietechnicznej specyfikacji interoperacyjności odnoszącej siędo podsystemu "Tabor – lokomotywy i tabor pasażerski" w transeuropejskim systemie koleikonwencjonalnych

10. Rástočný, K., Nagy, P., Białoń, A., Mikulski, J., Młyńczak, J.: Prvkyzabezpečovacíchsystémov, Žilinskáuniverzita v Žiline (2012)

11. Białoń, A., Gołębiewski, M., Młyńczak, J.: Wprowadzenie do układów kontroli niezajętości. Infrastruktura Transportu 6 (2011)

Traffic Data Collection
Using Tire Pressure Monitoring System

Nemanja Savić[1], Marek Junghans[1], and Miloš Krstić[2]

[1] DLR (German Aerospace Center), Berlin, Germany
{nemanja.savic,marek.junghans}@dlr.de
[2] IHP, Frankfurt (Oder), Germany
krstic@ihp-microelectronics.com

Abstract. In this paper we present initial results in utilization of TPMS (Tire Pressure Monitoring System) for collecting traffic data and deriving traffic information, i.e. travel times. The obtained results show that current detection ratio is less than 5 % and the obtained travel times are in consistency with referent data. The experiment is performed on DLR test track in Berlin. In particular, architecture of TPMS receiver is proposed. Next, the algorithm for reducing data redundancy and for deriving traffic information is introduced. Finally the obtained results are presented.

Keywords: Tire pressure monitoring system, traffic data collection, travel time, traffic detection.

1   Introduction

Traffic and transportation management is of significant importance for ensuring and improving the mobility of the people in our cities. With this respect the most important issues are: efficiency, safety and environmental concerns. The process of collecting data from the traffic is the base for deriving traffic information, further processed to augmented traffic information and finally used for traffic control. However, there is a long-standing interest in developing novel technologies, which are able to provide higher quality traffic data with lower implementation and maintenance costs. Classical technologies applied for data collection are for instance: inductive loops, laser scanners, radars, etc. These technologies are not able to provide identification of the vehicles and thus cannot be used for deriving route based information, e.g. travel times, origin-destination (OD) matrices, routes, route paths, etc. To obtain such spatial information, other measuring principles and technologies are required, e.g. video based ANPR (Automatic Number Plate Recognition), RFID, Bluetooth and WiFi. ANPR and RFID provide direct identification of the vehicles while, on the other hand, Bluetooth and WiFi are used for indirect identification. ANPR systems adopt cameras that automatically detect the number plates of the vehicles under different viewing angles. Currently, these systems achieve an accuracy of up to 98% [1-2]. Direct detection technologies usually suffer from privacy concerns and they require specific hardware used only for detection purposes. Indirect

J. Mikulski (Ed.): TST 2014, CCIS 471, pp. 19–28, 2014.

detection relies on detecting devices that are not meant to be used for these purposes. These devices are equipped with a wireless communication protocol such as Bluetooth or WiFi which makes their detection and identification possible using a unique identifier, i.e. MAC address. Indirect detection based on Bluetooth and WiFi are described in [3] and [4], respectively. The base for indirect Bluetooth detection is large scale usage of smart phones, tablets, hands-free devices, etc., which can lead to equipment ratios of 20% to 40% [5]. Currently, the DLR is working on a novel approach for the mobile detection of Bluetooth and WiFi devices [6-7], which combines the classical FCD (floating car data) and FCO (floating car observer) approaches.

One of the technologies able to fill the gap between the direct and indirect principles is TPMS (Tire Pressure Monitoring System). We assume TPMS can provide direct detection based on wireless technology with the simplicity typical for indirect approaches. TPMS utilization for traffic data detection was first discussed in [8-9].

Until now, no practical results of deriving traffic information using TPMS have been published. In this paper, we will present our initial results in this field. Section 2 gives an overview of TPMS operation. The basic principles of the approach are given in Section 3. In Section 4 we explain the methodology used in our experiment which concerns the following: learning about TPMS sensors by performing reverse engineering, designing a receiver for TPMS signals and finally installing receivers on the gantries at the test track. The processing of the collected data is presented in Section 5. There, we provide a solution solution for the problem of data redundancy. Finally, in Section 6 the results of deriving travel times on a test track are given.

2   Tire Pressure Monitoring System (TPMS)

TPMS is an electronic system used for measuring and monitoring air pressure inside pneumatic tires. Although safety concerns were the primary reason for the usage of TPMS, they can also improve the efficiency of fuel consumption and the lifetime of the tire. TPMS became mandatory for all new vehicles as of September 2007, while in the EU, all new models since November 2012 as well as all new vehicles from November 2014 must be equipped with TPMS [10]. The regulations in other countries South Korea, Russia, Indonesia, etc., will also request obligatory usage of TPMS in the future [10]. There are two principles of measuring tire pressure: indirect and direct. Indirect principle, iTPMS, derives pressure value using ABS sensors for angular speed of the wheel. As iTPMS does not perform any wireless activity, it cannot be used for collecting traffic data and thus will be not in the focus here.

Direct TPMS, in the following text referred only as TPMS, use the sensors that are measuring absolute pressure and temperature values inside the tires. The operation of TPMS has already been described in [8], [10] and only brief description will be given here. The sensors are installed on the rim, usually inside the tire. The connection between sensors and ECU (Electronic Controlling Unit) is established via receiving unit, using radio link. Sensors transmit their data periodically. The typical value of the transmission period is about 60s, but it can differ from manufacturer to manufacturer. TPMS intended for usage in the EU uses 434 MHz ISM band, while in the US, it is also allowed to use 315 MHz band. The data sent from sensors to the receiving unit is organized in frames. Every data frame consists of the following fields: preamble, sensor ID, pressure, temperature, status and error correction data. The receiving unit decodes messages sent from the sensors and provides corresponding information to the ECU, which informs the driver about the state of the pressure. The structure of TPMS is shown in Fig. 1.

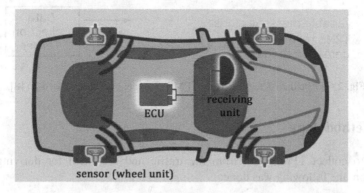

Fig. 1. Structure of direct TPMS. Source: own study based on [10].

3   Basic Principles of Traffic Detection Using TPMS

TPMS based traffic data detection relies on receiving TPMS signals externally and using information about sensor ID as an identifier of the vehicles. This idea is described in [8], while the practical results on eavesdropping TPMS is presented in [12]. For deriving traffic information using TPMS we assume sensor ID is unique, and it can be used for vehicles identification. The assumption is based on the fact that sensor ID is 32-bit number, which allows 2^{32} unique values. This value is much bigger than the number of produced vehicles in the in the period of the lifetime of the sensor which is usually reported as ten years.

There are several benefits of using TPMS collecting traffic data. First, as stated earlier, TPMS usage will become mandatory for all new vehicles in the EU and many other countries in the near future, which means that no additional in-car hardware will be required. Second, the usage of TPMS is limited only to vehicles, and faulty detection of cyclists and pedestrians is not possible like with Bluetooth detection [13]. Third, weather conditions do not have negative influence on the detection as in ANPR technology. On the other hand there are several limitations of TPMS approach. First, the strength of the radiated signal is constrained by the strict EMC regulations. Second, there is no standard for communication between sensors and the receiving unit which results in many different realizations of TPMS. The principle of TPMS detection is shown in Fig. 2.

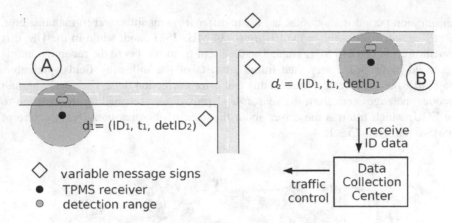

Fig. 2. Traffic data detection using TPMS. Source: own study based on [8].

4   Methodology

In order to collect TPMS data from the traffic and use them for deriving traffic information, the following was done:

- Analyzing TPMS sensor operation
- Designing receiver of TPMS signals
- Performing field test setup on the test track
- Processing collected data

4.1   Analyzing Operation of TPMS Sensors

The operation of TPMS sensors is presented in [8]. However, we performed further investigations and gained additional information about various others TPMS sensors. Our investigations are based on reverse engineering of the sensors operation. The procedure consisted of recording raw signals transmitted by the sensors followed by post processing using DSP approach. The raw signal is first demodulated and the bits were extracted. Next, the utilized encoding scheme was determined. Since the ID of the sensor was known, the first step was to find ID field inside the frame. After extracting ID the byte boundaries are set and the rest of the bytes were extracted. The positions of other fields, such as, pressure, temperature and error correction code were extracted using brute force method.

As a result the frame formats of seven different sensor types from three most dominant vendors on the market have been obtained. The sensor types are particularly selected for covering a significant number of vehicle models from different car manufacturers.

4.2   TPMS Receiver

Based on the analysis of the sensor's operation, the prototype receiver of TPMS signals was designed. One of the main challenges here was performing simultaneous reception of signals from the different TPMS sensors. Rouf et.al [12] have shown that TPMS signals could be received from a static sensor at the distance of approximately 40 m, but also from the sensor in motion at the speed of 35 km/h. For designing the prototype, the software defined radio approach was chosen, meaning that high frequency radio signal is down converted to baseband in hardware and after digitization sent to general purpose computer, where demodulation, decoding, checking and extracting of the data are accomplished. This approach provides high flexibility and possibility to implement parallel processing chains for different sensor types without multiplication of hardware. For this purpose, USRP device from Ettus Research [14] was used as radio frontend, while the software is based on GNU Radio framework [15]. The block diagram of the receiver is shown in Fig. 3. As can be seen, there are two main processing paths based on modulation type. One processing path is used for sensors which utilize ASK modulation, while the other is used for FSK modulation.

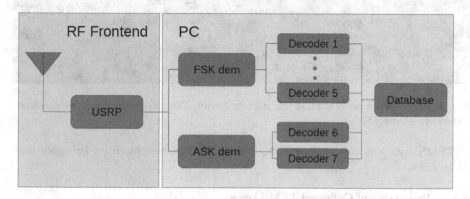

Fig. 3. Structure of the prototype TPMS receiver [own study]

Our receiver is capable of receiving signals from seven different types of TPMS sensors and measured range is around 100 m when directional antenna is used. Upon correct signal reception, receiver ID, sensor ID, sensor type and time stamp are stored in a database for post-processing.

4.3   Test Setup

The experiment for collecting TPMS frames from the traffic was conducted on the DLR test track in Berlin, called UTRaLab.

The UTRaLab (Urban Traffic Research Laboratory) is located at Ernst-Ruska-Ufer, Berlin, Germany (Fig. 4). It has a length of about 1 km and is equipped with two gantries that have a distance of 850 m. These gantries provide sensors for overhead detection, e.g. cameras, laser scanners, and sensors for wireless communication technologies, i.e. Bluetooth, WiFi and TPMS detectors. The loops are placed before and after each intersection to guarantee reliable measurements. Furthermore, the environmental sensors, e.g. visual-range meters, weather stations, ground sensor are also installed.

The experiment consists of two prototype receivers placed on two gantries as shown in Fig. 4. In this setup we used directional Yagi antennas with the gain of 9 dBi. The antennas point towards the intersections in order to raise the number of detected sensor, due to the fact that many vehicles are forced to stop there. The intersections are located west of the west-bridge and east of the east-bridge, respectively, as in Fig. 4.

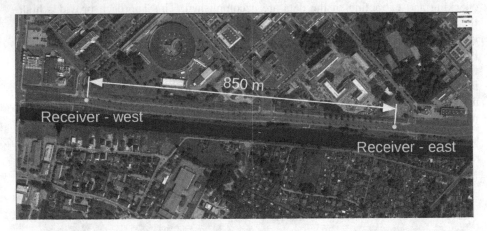

Fig. 4. Experimental setup at DLR test track in Berlin. The red triangles depict the antenna radiation patterns [16].

TPMS data was collected over the course of three months, from February until May, 2014.

4.4   Processing of Collected TPMS Data

The data collected at the test track need to be processed in order to derive traffic information, such as for example travel time. The main issue in processing TPMS data is dealing with data redundancy. Namely, the data redundancy exists due to the fact that every vehicle is usually equipped with four TPMS sensors. This implies that the number of detected sensors can be up to four times higher than the actual number of the vehicles. We assume that such redundancy would not introduce a significant error if, for example, only travel times are required. For extracting precise OD and routes information, the tracking of the sensors is not enough, and the tracking of vehicle is required. For this purpose an algorithm able to discover a group of sensors which belong to the same vehicle was designed. This allows us to couple sensor information to the vehicle information and enables vehicle identification. The algorithm is based on calculating probabilities of detecting different sensors of the same type at the same time on the same place.

The procedure of processing the data consists of the following stages: grouping sensors from the same vehicle, assigning the group to a generated virtual vehicle ID, and, finally, deriving traffic information based on the information about detected vehicles.

In the following section, the results of our experiment will be presented.

5   Results

In our experiment, over the period of three months, around 11000 unique sensors IDs were collected. The main drawback in the evaluating obtained results is inability to estimate the total number of vehicles equipped with TPMS on the test track. As a consequence, we are not able to perform precise estimation of the efficiency of our receiver.

5.1   The Influence of Sensor Type on Detection Rate

One of the first things we realized was the influence of sensor type on detectability of the sensor. The sensors can differ with respect to various parameters, but it is assumed that most dominant factors with respect to detection probability are: radiated power and message transmission period. Radiated power directly influences detection range, and test reports from different sensor types suggest that they radiate almost the same power. Transmission period specify how often sensors transmit their signal. The probability of signal reception rises with decreasing the value of transmission period. The contribution of every sensor type in the total amount of detected unique sensor IDs is shown in Table 1. Additionally, the available information about the number of models where sensor type was utilized, modulation, transmission period and radiated power is given. For confidentiality, sensor types are given generic names (A-G).

Table 1. Amount of detected sensor types

Sensor type	Number of models [17]	Modulation type	Measured peak power @3m [dbμV/m]	Transmission period [s]	In use since [17]	Relative number of detections [%]
A	14	FSK	66.8 [17]	5	2004	47.6
B	7	FSK	55.9 [17]	15	2005	23.9
C	9	FSK	53.8 [17]	30 [17]	2010	3.4
D	9	FSK	55.3 [17]	54 [17]	2009	3.5
E	29	FSK	39.8 [17]	54 [17]	1999	5.8
F	22	ASK	83.0 [17]	60 [17]	2007	9.7
G	13	ASK	N.A.	N.A.	2005	6.0

As can be seen from Table 1, sensor type A has the lowest transmission period and this type was 47 % of all detections, which shows very widespread use of this type. The capability of detecting types C and D is added later in the experiment to the receiver's chain and therefore the detection percentage is not giving the realistic figure of their application. If we take types A and B for example, they have been both in use since 2006 and they were utilized in 14 and 7 car models, respectively. The number of models implies that there should be twice as much vehicles equipped with type A than with type B.

5.2   Traffic Detection: TPMS vs. Inductive Loops

As mentioned above, test track is equipped with inductive loops which can provide precise information about the number of vehicles in the range of TPMS detectors. Using this information detection ratio can be derived. Detection ratio is defined as the ratio of the number of detected vehicles and total number of vehicles.

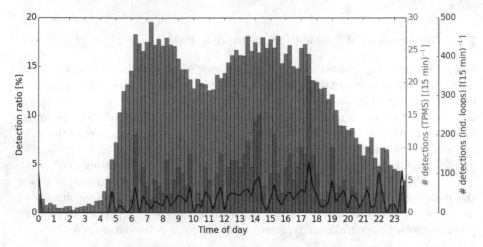

Fig. 5. Number of detected vehicles on 10.04.2014 using TPMS (red bars) and inductive loops (blue bars), and detection ratio (black line), averaged over 15 minutes [own study]

The results of single day measurements are shown in Fig. 5. Detections from inductive loops (blue) and TPMS (red) are aggregated over 15 minutes and detection ratio derived (black). As can be seen, the detection ratio is less than 5 %. We assume that this number will gradually rise in the future as the effect of more pervasive use of TPMS in vehicles. However, according to [18-19], with FCD/XFCD approach, equipment ratio of around 3 % is already enough to ensure good LoS (Level of Service) and traffic breakdown detection 10 minutes time interval.

5.3   Deriving Travel Times Using TPMS Data

Travel times are derived by calculating time difference between identification of the vehicle at one detector and re-identification at another detector. At one detector, vehicles are usually detected more than once due to the facts that there are four sensors per vehicle and because sensors can transmit a few frames per session. Having previous in mind, in order to minimize error in travel times for vehicles traveling from west to east, the last detection at west detector and the first detection at east detector are considered. The procedure is analogous for travel times from east to west. The obtained values are compared to the reference data. Reference travel times are derived by applying correlation method on inductive loops data. This method is described in [20]. The travel times are shown in Fig. 6. Due to the small sample size, travel times are aggregated in time intervals of 20 minutes and averaged over the period of 3 months.

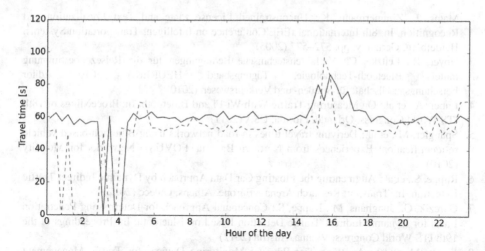

Fig. 6. Travel times measured with TPMS (solid) and inductive loops (dashed) [own study]

As can be seen from Fig. 6, travel time derived with TPMS is very close to the reference value. Between midnight and 5 a.m. the number of vehicles on the test track is low thus some values from that interval are missing. If we compared derived values, the difference is usually between 5 s and 10 s. The afternoon peak around 4 p.m. is detectable with both technologies.

6   Conclusion

In this paper we presented the first experimental results of collecting traffic data using TPMS and deriving traffic information, i.e. travel times. The experiment is conducted using two TPMS detectors installed on two gantries on DLR test track in Berlin. For the purpose of experiment a prototype receiver of TPMS signals is designed, as well as the algorithm for processing collected data. The results of our first experiment show that current value of detection ratio using TPMS is less than 5 %. In the second experiment, travel times are calculated using TPMS data. The obtained results correspond to the large extent to the reference data.

Regarding our future work, we will focus on deeper analysis on sensor types and their impact on detection ratio. Next, the receiver will be optimized in order to improve reception efficiency and sensor types will be added into receiving chain. Additionally, optimal position and antenna type of the receiver will be investigated.

References

1. Hsieh, C.-T., Juan, Y.-S., Hung, K.-M.: Multiple License Plate Detection for Complex Background. In: Proceedings of the 19th International Conference on Advanced Information Networking and Applications, vol. 2, pp. 389–392 (2005)

2. Matas, J., Zimmermann, K.: Unconstrained License Plate and Text Localization and Recognition. In: 8th International IEEE Conference on Intelligent Transportation Systems, Heidelberg, Germany, pp. 572–577 (2005)
3. Hoyer, R., Leitzke, C.: Verfahrenstechnische Bedingungen für die Reisezeitbestimmung mittels Bluetooth-Technologie, Tagungsband HEUREKA 2010, Editor Forschungsgesellschaft für Straßen- und Verkehrswesen (2010)
4. Luber, A., et al.: On Measuring Traffic With Wi-Fi and Bluetooth. In: Proceedings of 18th ITS World Congress, Orlando, Florida, USA (2011)
5. Spangler, M., et al.: Deriving travel times in road networks using Bluetooh-based vehicle re-identification: Experiences from Northern Bavaria. FOVUS - Networks for Mobility (2010)
6. Ruppe, S., et al.: Augmenting the Floating Car Data Approach by Dynamic Indirect Traffic Detection. In: Transport Research Arena – Europe, Athens, Greece (2012)
7. Gurczik, G., Junghans, M., Ruppe, S.: Conceptual Approach for Determining Penetration Rates for Dynamic Indirect Traffic Detection Based on Bluetooth. In: Proceedings of the 19th ITS World Congress, Vienna, Austria (2012)
8. Krstic, M., et al.: Applying Tire Pressure Monitoring Devices for Traffic Management Purposes. In: International Symposium on Signals, Systems and Electronics, ISSSE 2012, Potsdam, Deutschland, October 3-5, vol. 10, pp. 2012–2015 (2012)
9. Schulz, J., Junghans, M.: Deployment of Tire Pressure Monitoring Systems for Traffic Monitoring And Safety Purposes. In: Proceedings of 18th ITS World Congress, Orlando, Florida, USA (2011)
10. Hoppe, U., et al.: Reifendruckkontrollsysteme (2013)
11. TPMS mandatory in even more countries (2011), http://www.niradynamics.se/scripts/newsletter.php?id=55 (date of access: June 09, 2014)
12. Ishtiaq Roufa, R.M., et al.: Security and privacy vulnerabilities of in-car wireless networks: A tire pressure monitoring system case study. In: 19th USENIX Security Symposium, Washington DC, pp. 11–13 (2010)
13. Cragg, S.: Bluetooth Detection–Cheap But Challenging (2012)
14. Ettus Research, LLC, http://www.ettus.com (date of access: June 09, 2014)
15. GNURadio, http://www.gnuradio.org (date of access: June 09, 2014)
16. Google. Google Maps (2014), http://maps.google.de (date of access: June 09, 2014)
17. Tecma, http://www.tecma.de/tpms/ (date of access: June 09, 2014)
18. Breitenberger, S., Gruber, B., Neuherz, M.: Extended Floating Car Data–Potenziale fur die Verkehrsinformation und notwendige Durchdringungsraten. Straßenverkehrstechnik 48(10), 522–531 (2004)
19. Gössel, F.: Informationsentropische, spektrale und statistische Untersuchungen fahrzeuggenerierter Verkehrsdaten unter besonderer Berücksichtigung der Auswertung und Dimensionierung von FCD-Systemen. Ph.D. Thesis, Dresden University of Technology (2005)
20. Unbehauen, Rolf. Systemtheorie 1: Allgemeine Grundlagen, Signale und lineare Systeme im Zeit-und Frequenzbereich. Mit 148 Aufgaben, vol. 1. Oldenbourg Verlag (2002)

Portable Electronic Devices
on Board of Airplanes and Their Safety Impact

Marek Turiak, Alena Novák-Sedláčková, and Andrej Novák

University of Žilina,
Univerzitná 1, 010 26 Žilina, Slovakia
{marek.turiak,alena.sedlackova,
andrej.novak}@fpedas.uniza.sk

Abstract. Paper deals with the use of portable multimedia devices for VFR flights. It explains the basic terms concerning the use of portable electronic devices on-board aircraft. It analyses the relevant international and national legislation for the use of portable electronic devices on-board aircraft. It includes a survey of the available devices, accessories and software on the market. An analysis and comparison of the devices, based on their technical specifications is included as well. The paper also deals with various aspects of the use of portable multimedia devices for a flight school. It reviews the whole process of selecting a suitable operating system, device, accessories and software with an example of calculation of the required financial expenses. A comparison of the devices based on the battery life in relation to the selected aircraft is also included. Furthermore, the paper considers the mounting options of the devices in the cockpit, points out the required changes in the operational procedures within the flight school and highlights the potential assets which could the use of portable electronic devices bring.

Keywords: EFB, Electronic flight bag, Tablet, VFR, AMC 20-25, Application, iOS, Android.

1   Introduction

Technological progress of the mankind is unstoppable and it penetrates types of industries. Air transport is no exception. Throughout its history it has recorded several breakthrough milestones. Apart from the advancement in the areas of aircraft engines and airframes, lately we were witnesses to significant changes in the field of avionic equipment of aircraft.

While classic analogue dials were once an essential part of any cockpit, nowadays they are more likely a relic and their function is being taken over by multifunctional displays (glass cockpit) that we can find in many general aviation airplanes.

Similar fate also awaits the paper documentation necessary for flight. Nowadays it can be substituted by electronic devices with a characteristic name Electronic Flight Bag (EFB) without any problems. Goal of this paper is to summarize and analyse the issue of portable electronic devices usage aboard the aircraft with an emphasis on utilization for VFR (Visual Flight Rules) flights.

J. Mikulski (Ed.): TST 2014, CCIS 471, pp. 29–37, 2014.

Fig. 1. Tablet usage during a flight [14]

2   Electronic Flight Bag

2.1   History

The beginnings of the EFB stretch back to the year 1991 when the FedEx Company as a first started to utilize ordinary laptop computers to compute operational parameters directly on-board the aircraft. In year 1996 a German company Aero Lloyd introduced a system called Flight Management Desktop (FMD). It consisted of two laptops that enabled the calculation of operational parameters and they dispose of the database of aeronautical charts. Aero Lloyd Company has after agreement with a German Aviation Authority as a first in the world certified a so called paperless cockpit – a cockpit with no paper communication. The evolution of EFB has advanced very rapidly and more and more companies were equipping their aircraft with it. Nowadays this system is widely recognized and used in the air transport. [3][4]

Usage of EFB was at the beginning narrowly oriented to the commercial air transport. It took more than 20 years of IT technologies development to get such devices aboard the aircraft of general aviation. The situation has changed rapidly in 2010 when first tablets were introduced. They become very accessible in a very short time and they found an application in the general aviation.

3   Division of Devices by Hardware

3.1   Portable EFB

Portable EFB is defined as a device that provides a host platform for software equipment. It is used in the aircraft cockpit but is not a part of certified equipment of the aircraft.

Additional characteristics:

- Device can be used aboard the aircraft as well as away from it,
- Device is a host platform for software application types A and B as well as additional applications (that are not a part of EFB),
- Device is a Portable Electronic Device (PED). PED is characterized as any electronic device usually (but not always) appertaining to the category of consumer electronics brought aboard the aircraft by crew members, passengers or as a part of the cargo load and it is not included in the list of aircraft's certified equipment. This category includes all devices that consume electric energy. This energy can be supplied either by an built-in battery (rechargeable or not) or the device can be plugged-in to a specialized socket,
- Weight, dimensions, shape and placement of the EFB must not compromise the flight safety,
- Device can be supplied from the aircraft network through certified socket,
- In case the device is mounted in a holder easy and tool-free removal by crew must be possible. Securing device in the holder does not present an action of maintenance,
- Device can be a part of the system that includes built-in EFB sources that are part of aircraft's certified equipment,
- Built-in components of EFB system are part of aircraft's certified equipment with an intention of mounting of the portable EFB into the mount and/or connection to other systems,
- If the device belongs to T-PED (with intentional broadcasting) category the terms for broadcast use are listed in the approved Aircraft Flight Manual (AFM). In case these are not included in the AFM the broadcast is only permitted during the non-critical phases of flight,
- Device can be used in all flight phases if it is mounted in the certified mount or is places differently in a way that ensures its normal usability,

Devices that don't meet the above mentioned characteristics have to be safely stored (not used) during the critical phases of the flight.

- Portable EFB devices belong to group of controlled PEDs. This means that they are a subject of administrative check of the user. This includes, inter alia, the allocation check to specified aircraft or personnel and making sure that no unauthorised changes to hardware, software or databases were carried out,
- Every EFB component that is inaccessible by crew in the cockpit or is non-removable has to be installed within the framework of aircraft's certified equipment with a corresponding Type Certificate (TC), changed Type Certificate (changed TC) or supplement Type Certificate ((S)TC).[1][2]

3.2   Built-in EFB

Built-in EFB is defined as a device that provides a host platform for software equipment, it is installed in the aircraft and it is a part of aircraft's certified equipment which is a subject of Certificate of Airworthiness. [7]

Additional characteristics:

- Device is operated on the grounds of aircraft type configuration,
- Device can be apart from type A and B equipped by other certified applications provided that the EFB in question fulfils the requirements for these applications including a warranty that the uncertified applications cannot have malignant influence those that are certified. As an example for ensuring the independence between certified and other applications is a mechanism of robust formatting.

4   Software Applications for EFB Systems

4.1   Type A

Type A applications are those, whose failure or incorrect use does not have an influence on safety. Additional characteristics:

- Can be used on portable as well as on built-in EFBs,
- Do not require certification,
- Have to be in line with the appendix D.
  Note: Appendix D gives a detailed analysis of human – machine interaction from the Human Factor perspective. It provides various requirements for EFB (e.g. text readability under all lightning conditions, method of crew warning in case of malfunction of any part of EFB, etc.)

Application examples:

- Certificates and documents displayed by a browser (e.g. Registration Certificate),
- Interactive applications (e.g. crew rest calculator).[4]

4.2   Type B

Type B applications are those, whose failure or incorrect use can cause a minor malfunction and those that by any means do not substitute or replace any system or function required by the regulations of the air space and operational regulations. [8]
Additional characteristics:

- Can be used on portable as well as on built-in EFBs,
- Require operational examination,
- Do not require to be included in Airworthiness Certificate.

Application examples:

- Handbooks and documents displayed in browser (e.g. Operating Handbook)
- Electronic aeronautical charts with options to zoom, scroll, turn, centre etc., however without indication of aircraft's position (e.g. approach, sectional, aerodrome aeronautical charts),
- Applications that indicate the position of the aircraft in real time (AMMD).

- Applications that utilize internet or other aeronautical communications for reception, processing and distribution of data (e.g. information about unscheduled maintenance),
- Applications utilizing algorithms for calculation of flight parameters (e.g. take-off runway calculations, aircraft weight and balance).[6][9]

4.3   Complementary Applications

Complementary applications are those that do not directly relate to EFB or activities of flight crew.

5   Legislation Relating to Usage of Multimedia Devices On-Board the Aircraft

Legislative background for usage of EFB in Europe stretch back to year 2004 when the list of temporary directives TGL 36 has been issued. This document defined the characteristics of devices, their system equipment as well as the method of their usage. However this document had predominantly informative function and not binding character. This has changed on February 2nd, 2014 when by the decision of EASA 2014/001/R the acceptable means of compliance demonstration AMC 20-25 came into effect. These fully cover the issue of EFB and its usage on-board the aircraft. [10][11]

6   Usage of EFB during VFR Flight

Flight under visual meteorological conditions (VMC) is a flight whose necessary condition is the visibility of the ground because the navigation is carried out primarily by visual reference. Task of the EFB during a VFR flight is therefore not a provision of navigational information for the pilot according to which he will carry out the flight. Pilot is however able to quickly verify the flown track in case his device is equipped with a GPS receiver and a corresponding application. The most valuable contribution of the EFB for a pilot will be in the phase of pre-flight preparation or in the phase of flight analysis. Prior to every VFR flight the pilot has to gather and evaluate significant amount of information such as meteorological information, flight route, fuel consumption calculations, weight and balance calculations, etc. Exactly for this flight phase the EFB – Tablet provides the ideal solution because it can gather and provide all abovementioned information. Nowadays a large number of devices and applications covering needs of complete VFR flight are available in the market.

7   Analysis of Available Devices, Applications and Accessories in the Market

Currently a wide spectrum of various devices that fulfil the requirements for EFB functions exist. Multiple producers supply a range of smartphones and tablets in different price categories. For VFR flight needs the most suitable option is a tablet which thanks to its large display and high performance provides a wide range of possible use. Two most dominant operating systems are iOS and Android. For both platforms a wide range of aviation applications exists.

For evaluation of individual devices we utilize analytical method supplemented by a comparison of devices based on technical specifications and price. Analysis considered 21 different tablet models from different producers (figure 2). Parameters that had an influence on final assessment were the following:

- Display resolution
- Display size

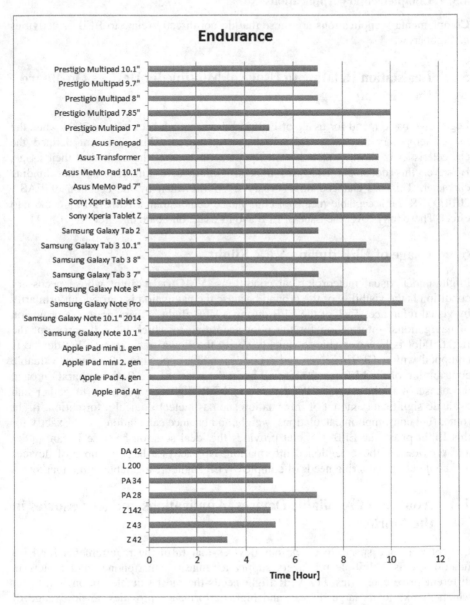

Fig. 2. Tablet battery life and endurance of aircraft used in the pilot training in Flight school of University of Žilina [own study]

- Processor performance
- Application support and OS stability
- Battery life

After analysis the tablets from Apple and Samsung proved to be the most suitable. They are equipped with superior displays with sufficient resolution. Samsung tablet series Galaxy Tab offers devices with Android operating system that are affordable and of excellent built quality. They are therefore very popular among users as they are powerful enough and price is reasonably set. Battery life is 7 to 10 hours which is sufficient for inflight use.

Regarding the accessories we were reviewing and analysing stands and knee pads that are necessary for fitting the tablets in the cockpit. All used devices had to fulfil requirements for safe mounting in the cockpit. From other accessories we focused on charging options through a mains socket of the aircraft as well as the possibility to utilize external battery.

8   Software Equipment of Tablets and EFB

Operating systems iOS and Android have several integrated applications that are utilizable in the aviation. For example the compass, calculator or current location indication. However there are many other specialized applications that are specifically designed for use in the aviation. In the following paragraph we will analyse few selected applications, their features, availability and price.

Air Navigation application offers a bundle of several useful functions for use in VFR flight. It offers integrated database of basic charts which can be extended for a fee. Database includes all air spaces for given area (TSA, TRA …) with depicted boundaries on the map. Very useful are information regarding the airports such as elevation, runway system or all corresponding frequencies. During flight it provides the pilot with his current position. Pilot can also select to view other information such as ground speed, heading or alternatively classic analogue Horizontal Situation Indicator (HSI). Obviously it can provide function "Direct – To" which draws a shortest route to the destination on the map.

9   Requirements for Portable Electronic Devices for Flight School

In this part we will analyse the possibilities of usage of portable electronic devices for usage in flight school. We will discuss basic requirements in process of suitable model selection. It is mainly these requirements:

- Hardware equipment
- Operating System
- Display size

9.1   Device Hardware Equipment

One of the most important features for our needs is the connectivity. Nowadays all tablets have access to the network via Wi-Fi, however only few are equipped with data modem and allow connection to the network without Wi-Fi availability. Data transfer is not inevitable condition for usage of tablet for VFR flights purposes however it brings valuable advantage in possibility to obtain METAR messages any time as well as possibility to determine exact position in cooperation with GPS module. For Air Training and Education Centre (ATEC) the most advantageous option would be a device with 3G/4G modem. Requirement of internal memory capacity of at least 32GB stems from the need to store large data files such as maps. Therefore the option of 16GB that majority of devices have is an insufficient for comfortable coverage of EU region.

9.2   Operating System

Prior to selection of suitable device it is necessary to determine the priority of operating system. In case of iOS and Android it is not that easy. In the past the Android has suffered stability issues which the iOS was able to exploit and established itself as stable OS. Currently both systems are fairly comparable in all aspects. According to the latest research the Android version 4.0 and higher are even more stable than iOS. According to the research carried out by Crittercism that was carried out on one billion devices the probability of failure of Android 4.0 Ice Cream Sandwich, 4.1 – 4.3 Jelly Bean and 4.4 KitKat was only 0.7%. On the other hand the probability of failure of iOS 7.1 was 1.6%.

9.3   Device Display Size

Another important aspect in selection process that it is necessary to consider is display size. Devices on the market are available in various diagonal sizes of the display ranging from 7" to 12.2". This presents a wide range of options as the difference between the smallest and the largest display is 13cm in diagonal. If we consider VFR flights we need a device that can under all conditions display relevant information clearly and at the same time it will not interfere with the crew activities. Device will be primarily used to display static data such as METAR messages. For this purpose a device with smaller dimensions is sufficient. To display charts a larger screen would be required. Nevertheless the integrated browsers as well as stand-alone chart applications have a zoom function which enables comfortable portrayal of charts even on smaller screens. From the evaluation we can conclude that for the purposes of VFR flights a device with diagonal screen size of 8" would be the most suitable.

10   Conclusion

Popularity of multimedia portable devices has an increasing tendency from their introduction. Modern tablets have become an everyday part of our lives and they found their application in many industries. Aviation is one of them. Tablet can significantly ease the work of the pilot. This paper analysed basic parameters and requirements for equipping flight schools with tablets or more precisely EFBs. This paper covers all key areas that relate to the issue of usage of portable multimedia devices for VFR flights and in flight schools. We have reached a conclusion that equipping the aircraft with tablets would bring several advantages such as increased safety. Safety is the single most important factor in air transport and within the context of flight school its level is an indicator of quality. Usage of tablets could help divert dangerous situations such as flight of students into the restricted areas during solo flights. Equipping the aircraft with tablets would also increase the image of the flight school towards the public and it would be a clear sign that the flight school follows modern trends and it is trying to implement them into its operations. Usage of tablets would also help the instructors and students to adapt to touch screen controls that the producers of avionic systems are starting to use and we can also expect that in the relatively short time these systems will form standard equipment of aircraft used in general aviation.

References

1. Starr, A., Hoogeboom, P.: Future trends in flight deck equipment. Springer, Heidelberg (2007)
2. Civil Aviation Authority of New Zealand. Electronic Flight Bags. In: Vector (2012)
3. Hengi, B.I.: Airlines Wordwide. Midland Publishing (2000)
4. Kratochvíl, P.: EFB - Electronic Flight Bag. In flyMag (2013), [cit. 2014-5-3] http://www.flymag.cz/article.php?id=9208 (date of access: May 10, 2014)
5. Ogg, E.: What makes tablet a tablet. In Circuit Breaker (2010), [cit. 2014-13-3], http://news.cnet.com/8301-31021_3-20006077-260.html?tag=newsLeadStoriesArea.1 (date of access: February 20, 2014)
6. Stallings, W.: Operating Systems: Internals and Design Principles. 7. vyd. Pearson Education, Inc. (2012)
7. Joint Aviation Authorities. TGL 36. Approval of electronic flight bags (2004)
8. European Aviation Safety Agency. Acceptable Means of Compliance 20-25 (2014)
9. European Aviation Safety Agency. Acceptable Means of Compliance and Guidance Material to Part-CAT (2012)
10. European Aviation Safety Agency. Certification Specifications and Acceptable Means of Compliance for Large Aeroplanes CS-25 (2011)
11. European Aviation Safety Agency. Acceptable Means of Compliance and Guidance Material to Part-ORO (2012)
12. Letecká Informačná Služba Slovenskej Republiky. L6 Prevádzka lietadiel. II časť. Všeobecné letectvo (1998)
13. Jeppesen Mobile Flitedeck VFR, http://jeppdirect.jeppesen.com/main/corporate/m-fc-landing-page.jsp (date of access: May 10, 2014)
14. Aviatorshop. Kneeboard i-PiLOT, http://www.aviatorshop.eu/en/kneeboards/211-kneeboard-i-pilot-for-regular-ipad.html (date of access: May 10, 2014)

Modeling of Reliability and Safety
at Level Crossing Including in Polish Railway Conditions

Lucyna Bester[1] and Andrzej Toruń[2]

[1] Faculty of Transport and Electrical Engineering,
University of Technology and Humanities in Radom,
26-600 Radom, Malczewskiego 29, Poland
l.bester@uthrad.pl
[2] Railway Traffic Control and Telecom Unit, Railway Institute,
04-275 Warszawa, J. Chlopickiego 50, Poland
atorun@ikolej.pl

Abstract. The paper presents a proposal to improve safety at unguarded level crossings, class C and D, by using an additional warning system in conditions of the current PKP railway infrastructure. In order to estimate reliability and safety of the proposed system, the authors carried out mathematical modeling based on stationary, homogeneous and ergodic Markov processes. They also carried out a hazard analysis and risk assessment using the FTA method, and calculated the MTBF coefficient using the Windchill Quality Solutions software.

Keywords: stochastic process modelling, EU standards, functionality and safety, level crossing systems.

1 Introduction

Traffic Security Systems for level crossings are designed to facilitate safe control of train traffic as well as of vehicular traffic participants. The introduction of ICT into these systems makes it possible to extend system functionality and make traffic control easier. Depending on the class of a given level crossing, users of vehicular roads are warned by road signs B-20, G-3, G-4 (class D), traffic lights (class C) and traffic lights plus barriers (class B and A) [7]. The key to safety at level crossings lies in the degree of their automation and reliability of level crossing equipment. Taking into account the risk level at level crossings in class C and D, it is necessary to focus on factors such as: working condition of the crossing, traffic volume and the human factor, i.e. car driver's behavior while approaching the level crossing. This is also the reason why the main reason of accidents at level crossings are mistakes made by participants of the vehicular traffic who infringe traffic regulations, fail to pay attention when they cross a railroad or fail to comply with signals sent by the crossing's safety equipment. The safety level at a crossing is also directly influenced by high failure frequency or early activation of the railroad safety equipment. This decreases drivers' trust in its proper operation and in consequence they try to cross the railroad anyway.

J. Mikulski (Ed.): TST 2014, CCIS 471, pp. 38–47, 2014.
© Springer-Verlag Berlin Heidelberg 2014

Considering the above, one should consider whether or not the warning system for road users at level crossings is sufficient, and if not, then what changes should be introduced in order to improve safety at level crossings, especially the unguarded ones.

A solution to this problem could be to link the crossing's automatic traffic protection equipment and wireless data transmission, e.g. in the manner described in detail by the authors in the paper [4], [5], [6].

The concept of an additional warning system at unguarded level crossings is based on radio data transmission. A car driver near the level crossing concerned would be informed about an approaching train, warning messages would be sent directly to the car and displayed by the on-board computer. It would be desirable to use normalised standards to transmit such warning messages so that they are supported by vehicle computer systems.

In future, it is planned to integrate information about approaching trains with smart geolocation systems based on dynamic broadcast to vehicles using the Internet, just like it happens e.g. with information about accidents or traffic jams.

The paper presents an idea for implementing an additional warning system at level crossings in the conditions of the existing PKP infrastructure. The system has been designed to improve safety at unguarded level crossings in class C and D. In order to prove the rationality of implementing the system, a number of analyses had to be carried out. The objective of the analysis in this paper, was to estimate reliability and safety of an additional warning system. To provide it, the authors used mathematical modelling based on stationary, homogeneous and ergodic Markov processes, which made it possible to carry out the probability-related part of the analysis, and in order to carry out the reliability analysis, a risk assessment and evaluation by means of the FTA method (*Tolerable Hazard Rate*) has been carried out and MTBF parameters (*Mean Time Between Failures*) have been calculated [4], [5], [6].

2   Safety Level Determination through Probabilistic Analysis of Level Crossing Models with and without an Additional Warning System

The objective of the modelling was to form an opinion about improving safety at level crossings and to gather information about new methods that could improve safety at level crossings.

Due to the fact that in Polish conditions statistically the highest amount of accidents happens at unguarded level crossings, this paper only takes into account models of unguarded crossings (class C and D) and a model of an unguarded crossing with an additional driver warning system.

In order to carry out the probabilistic analysis, we created analytical models which describe typical situations that can happen on an unguarded level crossing. Consideration of individual incidents included: analysis of causes, analysis of consequences and probability of occurrence. Limit probability of an incident occurrence was adopted as the measure of safety level at unguarded level crossings. For modelling the actual behaviour of traffic participants approaching a level crossing, we adopted homogenous, stationary and ergodic Markov processes, which made it possible to estimate limit values of probability of dangerous situations. The main indicator characterizing the level of safety at level crossings is the probability of a catastrophic situation, i.e. collision between a car and a train in this case.

The basic model for the analysis of safety at level crossings is a model of a D class crossing. In Figure 1 it is presented together with a description of situations that can occur at this type of crossings.

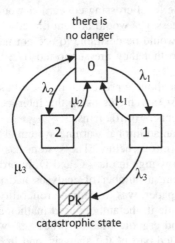

Where:

State 0 - a condition in which there is no danger
  • the train appeared but the car didn't
  • the car appeared but the train didn't
State 1 - the driver didn't stop before the level crossing
State 2 - the driver stopped before the level crossing
State Pk - catastrophic state, the driver drove into the approaching train
$\lambda_1, \lambda_2, \lambda_3$ - intensity of transition to state 1,2 and Pk
μ_1, μ_2, μ_3 - intensity of return to the state without danger "0"

Fig. 1. Model of a classical level crossing in D class without an additional driver warning system [own study]

From the perspective of safety analysis, the most important state in this model is the catastrophic state Pk. After solving a system of equations and calculating the limit for t→∞, we obtained the limit probability of the Pk state, described by equation (1)

$$P_k = \lim_{t \to \infty} P_k(t) = \frac{\lambda_1 \lambda_3 \mu_2}{(\lambda_3 + \mu_1)(\mu_2 + \lambda_2)\mu_3 + \lambda_1 \mu_2(\lambda_3 + \mu_3)} \tag{1}$$

For the mathematical analysis was assumed a traffic movement of 10 000 at a D class level crossing, and assuming typical values of μ and λ parameters accordance with conditions of calculating the traffic movement coefficients as is it defined in Ordinance [7].

According to calculations, the probability of a catastrophic state is Pk= $7.6 \cdot 10^{-5}$. Based on this probability, we calculated the safety value B for the level crossing in class D model, which for t→∞ is (2):

$$B = 1 - P_k = \frac{\lambda_2 \lambda_3 \mu_3 + \lambda_1 \mu_2 \mu_3 + \lambda_3 \mu_2 \mu_3 + \mu_1 \mu_2 \mu_3}{\lambda_1 \lambda_3 \mu_2 + \lambda_2 \lambda_3 \mu_3 + \lambda_1 \mu_2 \mu_3 + \lambda_3 \mu_2 \mu_3 + \mu_1 \mu_2 \mu_3} \tag{2}$$

B= 0.99994838086989

The next analysed model was a level crossing in class C, the model is presented in Figure 2. A probabilistic analysis was carried out to compare safety levels on level crossings in class C and D.

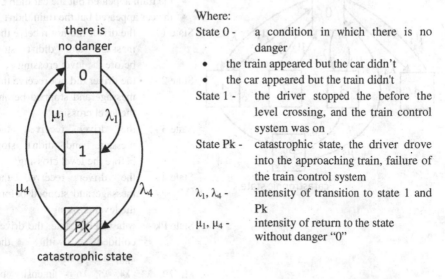

Where:

State 0 - a condition in which there is no danger

- the train appeared but the car didn't
- the car appeared but the train didn't

State 1 - the driver stopped the before the level crossing, and the train control system was on

State Pk - catastrophic state, the driver drove into the approaching train, failure of the train control system

λ_1, λ_4 - intensity of transition to state 1 and Pk

μ_1, μ_4 - intensity of return to the state without danger "0"

Fig. 2. Model of a classical level crossing in class C equipped with traffic lights [own study]

Just like above, after substituting the adopted values of parameters λ and μ, we obtained the probability of catastrophic state Pk for the C class model, which is Pk = $4.9 \cdot 10^{-6}$ and determined the safety of the system B, which is described by the following equation (3):

$$B = 1 - P_k(t)\,|_{t \to \infty} =$$
$$= 1 - \frac{\lambda_4 \mu_1}{\lambda_4 \mu_1 + (\lambda_1 + \mu_1)\mu_4} = \frac{(\lambda_1 + \mu_1)\mu_4}{\lambda_4 \mu_1 + (\lambda_1 + \mu_1)\mu_4} \tag{3}$$

B= 0.99999337364

To present and justify the introduction of solutions aimed at improving safety at level crossings, a model of a D class level crossing with an additional driver warning system was developed, as shown in Figure 3. The model of a level crossing with an additional warning system can apply both to class D and C because both classes include unguarded level crossings.

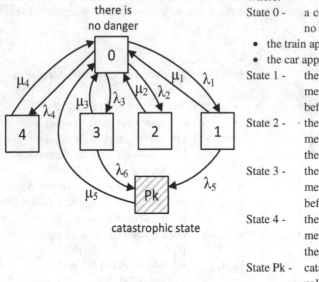

there is
no danger

catastrophic state

Where:

State 0 -   a condition in which there is no danger
- the train appeared but the car didn't
- the car appeared but the train didn't

State 1 -   the driver did not receive the message and didn't stop before the level crossing

State 2 -   the driver did not receive the message and stopped before the level crossing

State 3 -   the driver received the message and didn't stop before the level crossing

State 4 -   the driver received the message and stopped before the level crossing

State Pk -   catastrophic state, the driver collided with the approaching train

$\lambda 1$, $\lambda 2$, $\lambda 3$, $\lambda 4$, $\lambda 5$, $\lambda 6$ - intensity of transition to state 1,2,3,4 and Pk

$\mu 1$, $\mu 2$, $\mu 3$, $\mu 4$, $\mu 5$ - intensity of return to the state without danger "0"

Fig. 3. Model of a system with an additional driver warning system at level crossings in class C or D [own study]

Limit probability for t→∞ of the catastrophic state Pk is represented by the following formula (4):

$$Pk = Pk(t)_{t\to\infty} = \frac{\mu_2(\lambda_3\lambda_6(\lambda_5+\mu_1)+\lambda_1\lambda_5(\lambda_6+\mu_3)\mu_4)}{\lambda_1\mu_2(\lambda_6+\mu_3)\mu_4(\lambda_5+\mu_5)+(\lambda_5+\mu_1)((\lambda_6+\mu_3)(\lambda_4\mu_2+(\lambda_2+\mu_2)\mu_4)\mu_5+\lambda_3\mu_2\mu_4(\lambda_6+\mu_5)))} \quad (4)$$

Having carried out the analysis for a traffic moment of 14 400, which fits in the traffic moment range according to the [7], and having adopted appropriate λ and μ values, we calculated that the probability of a catastrophic situation amounted to Pk = $1,1 \cdot 10^{-7}$. Then, system safety B was determined and it amounted to B=0.999997007.

Based on a probabilistic analysis for level crossing models in class D and C without an additional warning system and for a level crossing model with an additional driver warning system, one can state that the implementation of such a system at level crossings may improve the safety of unguarded level crossings.

3   Reliability Analysis of an Additional Warning System at Level Crossing

In order to prepare a concept of technical solutions, it is necessary to estimate the degree of reliability of the designed object and decide whether or not the proposed system will fulfil the expectations of the future user.

Due to the fact that a reliability analysis can only be carried out in relation to a specific system structure and its modules with specific reliability characteristics, in the paper we propose an example of structure of an additional warning system. The structure is presented in Figure 4.

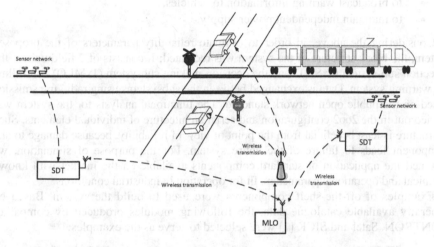

Fig. 4. Structure of an additional warning system – functional and logical modules. Source: own study based on [8].

The authors assumed that the system will consists of the following logical modules:

- SDT – Rolling Stock Detection System – Its task is to detect a train approaching a crossing and to transmit this information the Logical Warning Module (MLO), which makes the decision to broadcast a warning message for vehicles.
- MLO – Logical Warning Module, based on information about approaching or departing trains, it makes the decision to start or stop broadcasting a warning message for vehicles.

Taking into account the basic tasks fulfilled by individual functional modules, the authors adopted a general block structure, which facilitates meeting the functional requirements, and decided to apply in the system public open transmission standards in order to ensure communications and data exchange in the system. In view of the above, the following tasks were assigned to:

SDT:

- to detect rolling stock (for this purpose, the application of sensor networks was assumed),
- to transmit information about train detection to the decision-making module, to encrypt information and send it to MLO,
- to maintain independent power supply.

MLO:

- to receive information from SDT about a train approaching a level crossing,
- to make decisions about broadcasting warning messages,
- to broadcast warning information to vehicles,
- to maintain independent power supply.

Considering the above, in order to estimate reliability parameters of the proposed system, the block structure of the system was recreated: It consists of 2 field units – the detection sub-system (2xSDT) and the decision-making subsystem (1xMLO) controlling the warning system. Data is exchanged between the subsystems using radio transmission based on the public open network standard. The functional analysis for the system was carried out in the 2oo2 configuration and serial architecture of individual elements. Such a structure is least beneficial from the point of view of reliability, because damage to any component leads to failure of the entire system. For the purpose of simulation, we assumed the application of standard components available on the market with known technical and operational parameters, fit for operation in industrial conditions.

Examples of off-the-shelf components were used to build the system. Based on generally available catalogue data, the following modules produced by companies KONTRON, Satel and SICK [1] were selected to serve as the examples:

- SR-EBC1 – processor board for the management of SR box/boxes with installed object cards type SR-xxx,
- SR-IO2 - universal output card for controlling devices and continuity of external systems circuits.
- SR-IO3 - universal input card for gathering information about states of devices from relay contacts, optoisolation or other forms of signal distribution,

and commercially available standard:

- radio transmission modules by Satel – Satelline -2ASxE,
- sensor networks using proximity sensors by SICK (DML-40-2 fit for detection in the 0.5m - 1200m range).

To estimate the reliability of the system defined above, we used a computer package supporting reliability calculations Windchill Quality Solutions (better known under its old name Relex), which makes it possible work in the Microsoft Windows environment. The package has been developed by ReliaCore. The software consists of 11 instruments for reliability predictions, which among others facilitate the following analyses: FTA, FMEA, determination of reliability indicators THR and MTBF. (programme [6] in its demo version is available under www.reliacore.eu).

To determine parameters for individual modules of the system, we applied the TelCordia SR 2.3.2, 2nd edition, which is equivalent to the MIL-217F-HDBK standard.

Based on assumptions made for the sake of calculations and using the FTA analysis effective in evaluation of the system [3], we adopted the serial architecture of the system and assumed that every error will lead to system failure and make the system go to the repair state. Due to the modular structure of the system and the application of the "hot-swap" technology in production of the components, which makes it possible to replace a damaged package or module without turning off power supply, we assumed that the maximum repair time, including travel time of the repair team and error removal, would by 8 hours.

In order to estimate functional properties of this example of technical implementation of an additional driver warning system at level crossings, two basic reliability parameters were determined for the system: MTBF (mean time between failures) and technical readiness index Kg, which expresses the system's ability to fulfil its tasks. In the theory of reliability, the generalised readiness co-efficient is defined as the probability of an event in which the system is operational at any moment in time t in compliance with the adopted model of reliability. For the purposes of this paper, we adopted the stationary form of this indicator expressed by the following equation (5):

$$K_g = \frac{T_{pp}}{T_{pp} + T_{on}} \tag{5}$$

Where:

T_{pp} – time of correct system operation (to simplify matters, we took the mean time between failures, MTBF)

T_{on} – time of waiting for failure removal, in calculations for the analysed system we used 8h,

As a result of calculations, we obtained the following damage levels coefficients, which make it possible to determine the MTBF rate and the technical readiness index Kg in a simple analytical way:

a) for a single detection unit – SDT (because of identical architecture and components used), the following failure rate was obtained:

$$\lambda_{SDT} = 29.010878 \cdot 10^{-6} \ [h^{-1}]$$

whereas the controlling computer system in the 2oo2 configuration was characterised by a failure rate equal:

$$\lambda_{SDT} = 20.153735 \cdot 10^{-6} \ [h^{-1}]$$

b) for the decision-making unit – MLO, the following failure rate was obtained:

$$\lambda_{MLO} = 20.852397 \cdot 10^{-6} \ [h^{-1}]$$

whereas the controlling computer system in the 2oo2 configuration was characterised by a failure rate equal:

$$\lambda_{MLO} = 11.519064 \cdot 10^{-6} \ [h^{-1}]$$

Applying the equation (6):

$$MTBF = \frac{1}{\lambda_s} \qquad (6)$$

We determined individual mean times between failures MTBF (in case of the analysed system – any failures):

a) for a single detection unit:

$$MTBF_{SDT} = 34\ 470\ [h]$$

whereas the controlling computer system in the 2oo2 configuration was characterised by a failure rate equal:

$$MTBF_{S1-1,3-1} = 49\ 619\ [h]$$

b) for the decision-making unit – a united referred to as subsystem S2 in the programme, the following failure rate was obtained:

$$MTBF_{S2} = 49\ 756\ [h]$$

whereas the controlling computer system in the 2oo2 configuration was characterised by a failure rate equal:

$$MTBF_{SDT} = 86\ 813\ [h]$$

In consequence, for the proposed system consisting of 2 field detection units (SDT) and one decision-making subsystem (MLO) arranged in the 2oo2 configuration and connected by a radio transmission network, we obtained λ_S and MTBFS rates equal:

$$\lambda_S = 78.874153 \cdot 10^{-6}\ [h^{-1}]$$

$$MTBF_S = 12\ 678\ [h]$$

It means that mean time to occurrence of a failure for the proposed system amounts to ca. 1.5 years. It is noteworthy that such an error does not lead to a dangerous situation threatening the safety of traffic control yet, it only decreases availability of the system until the error is removed. Due to the fact that the analysed system is an additional warning system for level crossings, a technical readiness level of $3 \cdot 10^{-4}$, ($Kg = 0.999369$) is considered sufficient.

4   Conclusion

Models of level crossings in class C and D and a model of an unguarded level crossing with an additional driver warning system presented in this paper made it possible to estimate the safety level at the level crossings concerned. The safety level is defined by the probability of a catastrophic situation. The results obtained in the proposed form are an important source of information, which is necessary in the process of selection of the best indicators to examine the accident rate at level crossings, which in turn makes it possible to determine the safety level status. The number of accidents at level crossings is also indirectly linked to the growing number of wheeled vehicles, therefore also this situation requires a general introduction of modern system solutions in the PKP network that can considerably improve safety at level crossings.

A reliability analysis for an example of a system built on the basis of freely available components and modules showed that it is possible to build a system with satisfactory reliability parameters, which due to the applied components can be an economically attractive alternative for improving safety at level crossings.

In is noteworthy, that the objective of the calculations and analyses was to confirm certain assumptions concerning an additional warning system. They also made it possible to answer the question whether or not the selected direction for improving safety at D class level crossings is reasonable.

References

1. Catalogue cards for components by Kontron, Satel, Sick
2. Dąbrowa–Bajon, M.: Podstawy sterowania ruchem kolejowym. Oficyna Wydawnicza Politechniki Warszawskiej (2002)
3. Jaźwiński, J.: Ważyńska – Fiok K. Bezpieczeństwo systemów. Wydawnictwo Naukowe PWN Warszawa (1993)
4. Lewiński, A., Bester, L.: The Analysis of Transmission Parameters in Railway Cross Level Protection Systems with Additional Warning of Car Drivers. In: Mikulski, J. (ed.) TST 2012. CCIS, vol. 329, pp. 124–131. Springer, Heidelberg (2012)
5. Lewiński, A., Bester, L.: Additional warning system for cross level. In: Mikulski, J. (ed.) TST 2010. CCIS, vol. 104, pp. 226–231. Springer, Heidelberg (2010)
6. Ordinance of Minster of Transport and Maritime Economy of 26 February 1996 on technical conditions applicable to crossings between railways and public roads as well as their locations (Journal of Laws, No. 33. Item 144)
7. Relex 7 Visual Reliability Software – Reference Manual
8. Toruń, A., Bester, L., Siergiejczyk, M.: Szacowanie funkcjonalności i bezpieczeństwa systemów sterowania ruchem kolejowym. Prace Naukowe Politechniki Warszawskiej, Transport z. 96. Międzynarodowa Konferencja Naukowa Transport XXI Wieku, Ryn (2013)
9. Białoń, A., Gołębiewski, M., Młyńczak, J.: Wprowadzenie do układów kontroli niezajętości, Infrastruktura Transportu 6 (2011)
10. Rástočný, K., Nagy, P., Białoń, A., Mikulski, J., Młyńczak, J.: Prvkyzabezpečovacíchsystémov, Žilinskáuniverzita v Žiline (2012)

Utilization of Mobile Applications
for the Improvement of Traffic Management Systems

Stanisław Iwan[1], Krzysztof Małecki[2], and Damian Stalmach[2]

[1] Maritime University of Szczecin, 11 Pobożnego St., 70-507 Szczecin, Poland
s.iwan@am.szczecin.pl
[2] West Pomeranian University of Technology, Dept. of Computer Science,
52 Żołnierska St., 71-210 Szczecin, Poland
{kmalecki,dstalmach}@wi.zut.edu.pl

Abstract. In recent years, the utilization of telematics systems using the concept of Cloud Computing still increases. Also mobile phones have ceased to be the tools for conversation only. Additionally, the proliferation of new devices, such as smartphones and tablets, makes such solutions become even more useful. The paper is focused on utilization of mobile devices to assist traffic control systems. The application designed for Android, which is used for the presentation of the content of the traffic control system in Szczecin is introduced. The paper shows the concept of it, the method of its preparation and the results of experiments that demonstrate the usability of the tool in the context of reducing the negative environmental impact of the transport system.

Keywords: urban freight transport, city logistics, environmental impact of transport, telematics systems, sustainable development, efficiency of transport systems.

1   Introduction

The need to support the transport and distribution of goods in urban areas with telematics solutions results mainly from the complexity of these processes and the need to optimize the implementation of transport by ensuring adequate availability of linear and nodal infrastructure, while reducing the adverse impact of the transport system on the environment. A constant increase in demand for transport make city authorities turn to solutions of Intelligent Transportation Systems (ITS), which are the basis for the design of intelligent transport networks. Their importance is highlighted, inter alia, in one of the classic definitions of urban logistics, proposed by E. Taniguchi, RG Thompson, and T. Yamada, according to which "city logistics is the process for totally optimising the logistics and transport activities by private companies with the support of advanced information systems in urban areas considering the traffic environment, its congestion, safety and energy savings within the framework of market economy" [1].

In recent years, the increasing importance has been gained by V2V (Vehicle-to-Vehicle), V2I (Vehicle-to-Infrastructure) and I2V (Infrastructure-to-Vehicle) systems,

J. Mikulski (Ed.): TST 2014, CCIS 471, pp. 48–58, 2014.

which are a direct implementation of the concept called "Cloud computing" in road transport systems. Under an increasing dominance of information technology in most areas of life, their further expansion and increased importance of telematics systems should be expected also in relation to urban freight transport.

2   Urban Transport Telematics

2.1   Areas of Telematics Application in Urban Transport System Assistance

The purpose of the use of telematics in urban logistics is to optimize access to logistics hubs and linear infrastructure. Its use implies, among other things [2]:

- reduction of freight distribution costs
  - increase in productivity of local delivery vehicles;
  - increase in reliability of commercial vehicle operations;
  - increase in safety;
- increase in the capacity of urban freight systems (without providing additional traffic infrastructure).

Telematics solutions support many aspects of urban transport systems, including vehicles, infrastructure, and organization and freight management. Among the solutions developed in recent years in the world, particularly important are [3]:

- Traffic Management Systems – task of telematics systems is to control "working" vehicles by responding to any changes in communication processes;
- Systems for Classifying and Weighing Vehicles – classification systems allowing for counting vehicles and their distribution depending on the speed of movement and length, as well as systems for weighing vehicles in motion providing a variety of parameters (e.g. pressure on the axles, weight, distance between vehicles, classification by length and weight, speed) without interfering the safety and behaviour of drivers;
- City Cards – modern and multi-functional medium for electronic products and services, the implementation of which in transport systems simplifies toll systems for urban services (such as entry into the restricted traffic zone);
- Park-and-Drive Systems – parking systems, designed for people commuting from greater distances, enabling quick change to the means of public transport;
- Variable Message Signs – road signs and boards showing information on a given road section and at given time which changes depending on circumstances, such as speed limits, diversions for traffic, delays, functioning of public transportation, available parking spaces, warning of the road dangers, etc.; they can be shown using a variety of technologies (e.g. LED, electromechanical systems, liquid crystal displays); their use improves the level of road safety and increases the efficiency of transport management;

- Passenger Information Systems – are among the most modern transport solutions, enabling for a rapid delivery of information using video and audio signals for passengers; major components of these systems are aggregated timetables, information boards at bus stops, clocks;
- Toll Collection Systems for Entry to the City Centre – the likelihood of transport congestion increases in the realities of dynamic growth in the number of vehicles within urban areas, which is a consequence of the weak "expansion" of urban infrastructure. These systems belong to the administrative solutions improving the situation in this respect; automatic toll collection systems are based on the use of solutions for the diagnosis and classification of vehicles.

The main task of telematics solutions as tools to enable effective support for urban freight transport is the management of information flows generated within this transport, and the most important result of this process is to improve the quality of functioning of the urban logistics system by enhancing the ability to control and impact on the present data flows [6, 7, 8]. Among the many practical solutions, there are three main categories, which are based directly on telematics and where the use of ICT tools determines their proper functioning:

- systems directing commercial vehicles entering downtown on scheduled routes, e.g. by setting specific traffic signs (usually signs and Variable Message Signs - VMS) or providing maps of planned routes for trucks with relevant traffic information;
- intelligent systems for managing transport routes, integrating the planned route and information for vehicles with navigation software, where the data obtained from trucks on their location, load and planned destinations can be linked with data on road traffic in real time;
- integrated logistical tools, which are solutions based primarily on the use of web technologies (mainly the Internet and websites) that allow combining and coordinating producers, buyers and logistics operators in terms of placing orders for optimization of logistics flows.

In addition, many other solutions in the field of urban freight transport use telematics systems as additional support tools to improve their effectiveness.

2.2   Variable Message Signs as a Key Technology Supporting Traffic Control

Particularly important in technical solutions used in telematics systems are Variable Message Signs (VMS), which next to traffic light, are key tools for traffic control. For a specific road section and time VMS can display information varied and dependent on the current traffic situation, such as: speed limits, diversions for traffic, delays, functioning of public transportation, parking available, warning of the road dangers, etc. Information is presented in the form of text or symbols, using special screens or rotating drum signs (solution, which is used less).

VMS can be run by an operator or by an automatic control system. In the second case, the combination of VMS with motion detection subsystems enables for a full implementation of the idea of intelligent transport systems. The system configured in such way includes three key elements (Fig. 1):

- data acquisition subsystem (motion detection) - is a key element deciding on the accuracy of the presented information, and elimination of the human factor (operator) and reduces susceptibility to errors; its task is to transfer data to the information control subsystem concerning e.g. traffic on selected road sections;
- data processing and communication subsystem - is responsible for carrying out data analysis and determining the messages transferred to the information dissemination subsystem;
- information dissemination subsystem - based on VMS, which provides information to road users being a result of the analysis of data from the detection subsystem.

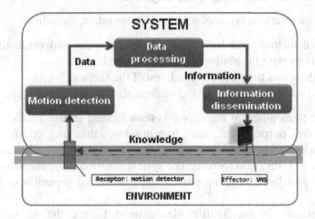

Fig. 1. Interaction of key subsystems in an intelligent traffic control systems [4]

In this context, there are four fundamental processes in the system which should be highlighted (Fig. 1):

- inputs, which are system supply, by which the system interacts with the environment (motion detectors);
- outputs, which show the results of operation of the system and through which the system interacts with the environment (VMS);
- transformation, including the processes within the system, providing transformation of input signals into output signals;
- feedback, being the foundation of system control processes, which is the influence of the final signal (output) generated by the effectors of the system, on the reference signals (input), received by the receptors.

3   Intelligent Traffic Control System in Szczecin

The main objective of the implementation of the traffic management system in Szczecin was to increase the flow of traffic on the approach roads to the city centre within the existing transport corridors along Gdansk Route, by providing road users with real-time information about the current overcrowding and projected states as well as information about traffic incidents or possible alternative routes. As part of this project, its authors designed, supplied, installed, integrated and commissioned ITS technology elements compromising the system, which allows to actively manage traffic in the area of implementation with the impact on the area of the Szczecin Metropolitan Area. The system consists of two main layers:

- application layer, which consists of Urban Transportation Management System (UMTS) with the individual subsystems designed to monitor and manage traffic actively.
- executive layer, consisting of VMS, which allow for the presentation of complex information, signs and diagrams.

The system uses various types of sensors to collect data, including:

- video detectors used for segmental measurement and evaluation of traffic conditions with the ability to determine travel times;
- laser detectors to assess the condition of the surface;
- optical sensors for adaptive traffic control.

All data are transmitted to the server system located in the Traffic Management Centre. For the purpose of data transmission, the project includes mixed communication system based on wired communications - fibre and wireless communication of GPS / UMTS type. The system is powered by the urban grid and in the data centre part by the backup power based on UPS / generator of the Szczecin Town Hall.

System operators in the Traffic Management Centre define, implement and configure parameters which, thanks to special system algorithms and after processing the measurement data, are used e.g. to provide real-time information to road user about road conditions, including overcrowding, the average travel time on individual road sections and weather conditions. Additionally, it is used to identify traffic incidents and other situations that may affect the traffic, such as mass events.

The system has the functions of traffic forecasting, based on the traffic model, which allows for generating forecasts useful in the planning of routes for certain time intervals. Operators have access to a specialized engineering and simulation tools to support traffic management functions. The system includes cooperation of fully adaptive traffic control algorithms by which it is possible to increase traffic flow at selected intersections in situations where the drivers use the alternative route.

An important element of the system is a web portal, consisting of a few key modules that cover most of the system command and control operations, several external interfaces, and several independent modules for functions that are implemented independently. The portal core consists of:

- a common graphical user interface (CGUI), which displays data on the system using GIS data provided by the GIS module;
- data collection module that is used to collect data from the field devices and store them for later processing;
- road network module, which allows for dynamic changes in the network;
- traffic forecasting module that uses data collected by the data collection module and road network model in order to provide proper forecasts for road traffic;
- video monitoring module, which allows to display real-time video images of specific devices in a common graphical user interface (CGUI), and also to control video cameras remotely;
- VMS module to manage VMS installed in the system;
- external interface subsystem, consisting of three main elements:
  - WWW web interface, which is used by Internet users of the system
  - DATEX and RDS / TMC interfaces, used to communicate with other systems;
- GIS module, which is responsible for managing geographic data as well as the presentation of data on demand;
- module for recording and storing video, which is responsible for recording and storing video signals from the video cameras.

The software is designed on the basis of an open architecture using several free software and publicly available products. The system is developed in J2EE technology based on the free ESB (Enterprise Service Bus) software implementation. As a general feature of the system, all modules are integrated in ESB, allowing for flexibility in the future expansion.

Currently, there are 19 electronic signs in Szczecin, 5 of which show travel time between selected sections on the map of the part of the city (mapped to the needs of navigation systems) and inform about traffic. These signs inform drivers about the actual travel time between the signs and target points (Most Długi, Trasa Zamkowa, Rondo Uniwersyteckie and the A6 motorway in the case of exiting the city), and between control points (e.g. between Szosa Stargardzka and intersection of Struga and Granitowa streets). The signs show information in real time, calculated on the basis of data read from the license plates of passing cars on two points of detection. The other information communicated to drivers via VMS shows the traffic flow on given sections and is based on colour codes, representing respectively: green – information about free traffic on the given road section, yellow – slow down of traffic, red – significant traffic problems. Moreover, signs inform about the traffic restrictions, surface condition or weather conditions.

The major part of the system functionality has been confirmed by analyses conducted by the Szczecin Town Hall. The research was conducted on measurement sections associated with the choice of an alternative route for getting to the centre. On the basis of measurements and calculations comparing the state prior to the implementation of the system (as of October 2011) with the state after its implementation (as of November 2012), the average travel time in analysed sections was reduced despite of the increase in traffic, which led to the increase in traffic flow by 36%.

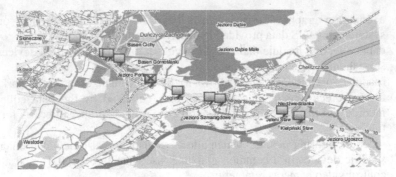

Fig. 2. Map of Variable Message Signs in Szczecin [5]

As part of the analysis carried out during the C-LIEGE project, further assessment was conducted for the possibility of using a mobile application that would allow for even bigger system improvement.

4   Mobile Application Supporting Traffic Control System in Szczecin

4.1   General Assumptions of Application

Szczecin Traffic Manager application has been developed to support the needs of drivers traveling around Szczecin, particularly in terms of early display of messages shown on each variable message sign installed within the city as part of the above-described Traffic Management System for Szczecin. Proper operation of application requires constant access to the Internet, both in terms of packet data transmission and Wi-Fi connection. It also requires GPS module. Additionally, the device supporting the application (smartphone or tablet) must be equipped with an accelerometer and magnetometer. Application uses class diagram in UML modelling (Figure 3) in order to illustrate the scope of the types of objects used in applications designed for a user. Its key components include:

- DistanceCalculator - is responsible for checking and calculating a distance from the signs. If the current location is within the sign, class object Sign is captures;
- Sign - is responsible for the storage and handling of sign data collected from XML;
- ApiClient - is responsible for the connection to the server and includes a method of connecting to the server using headers and SSL;
- SZRApiClient - support class, ApiClient class, calls the ApiClient class with additional parameters such as the server address;
- GoogleMapManager - class responsible for managing map, includes methods for initializing markers and animating map;
- XMLParser - class responsible for parsing XML data, captures a hash table with table images.

Additionally, the application includes two additional classes that should be emphasized:

- ManualMode – class responsible for the manual mode of application, which calls the method initializing map and the method connecting to the server, which captures table images. It also has an internal class CustomInfoWindow Adapter, the task of which is to place image in the cloud called after clicking on the symbol on the map;

- AutomatMode – class responsible for the automatic mode, implementing interfaces such as: LocationListener, LocationSource and SensorEventListener. The first interface is responsible for listening for the current GPS position, using the events:

  - onLocationChanged() – called after the change in location;
  - onProviderDisabled() –called when the GPS is turned off;
  - onProviderEnabled() –called when the GPS is turned on;
  - onStatusChanged() –called at the change in status.

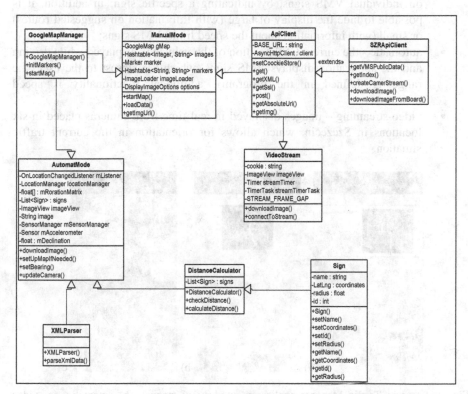

Fig. 3. Class diagram for the Szczecin Traffic Manager application [own study]

The application is equipped with a special LocationSource interface which includes a method associated with activation and deactivation of the map. SensorEventListner module listens to changes associated with the motion sensor. Additional important features are provided by the following modules:

- VideoStream, downloading the images from the video cameras in the form of frames, calling cyclic clock, which captures a single frame from the video camera at equal time intervals;
- VideoStreamList, containing a list of video cameras available in the application.

4.2   Application Functioning

The application is available on the Android platform. The proper functioning of the application requires constant access to the Internet (for both packet data of the phone and Wi-Fi) and GPS receiver switched on. In addition, the smartphone must be equipped with an accelerometer and magnetometer.

The application can operate in three basic modes (Figure 4):

- manual - giving the opportunity to get familiar with the information provided on individual VMS signs, by indicating a specific sign; in addition, it is possible to hide the display of large (with information on suggested routes) or small (with information about the speed limit) VMS signs;
- automatic - the current GPS position of the vehicle is displayed while driving and the application displays VMS signs, which are closest to the user (the range is defined in the program); additional functionality is speed measurement;
- video-streaming – images displayed in real-time from cameras placed in six locations in Szczecin, which allows for orientation in the current traffic situation.

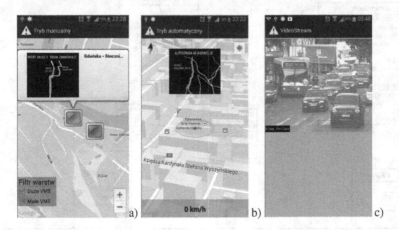

Fig. 4. Szczecin Traffic Manager application modes: (a) manual, (b) automatic, (c) video streaming [own study]

The program uses Google Maps API, access to which is based on a library of Google Play Service. Presentation of data is based on collecting data from the Variable Message Signs system and their presentation on the map using features available in Google Maps. The application runs on multiple threads executed asynchronously. Querying is supported by Asynchronous Http Client library that allows querying outside of the main thread of the program by which all happens concurrently. Information from electronic signs is presented in XML format on the site called UMTS, which are parsed (translated) using the built-in DocumentBuilderFactory library and displayed in designated areas.

The application has access to cameras via AssyncHttpClienta and properly set thread using cyclic timer, which collects and returns the image of the 6 cameras in Szczecin.

The program has also the ability to track the user and display the characters appropriate to its location. The GPS, which is built in phone, tracks user's location and then displays the closest, electronic board located within a radius of 1,000 m. Moving the phone rotates camera on the "z" axis plane by using compass function of the phone. Additional feature is speed measurement determined by the changing GPS location.

5   Conclusion

As demonstrated by the example of Szczecin, the use of ITS solutions can significantly reduce the negative impact of road transport on the urban environment. By improving traffic flow and reducing congestion effect, it is possible to significantly reduce fuel consumption and hence emissions. Usability of such systems increases even more in the era of developing solutions based on the use of mobile devices.

Through the use of applications designed for mobile devices, it is possible to plan and choose a route well in advance, which allows for the shortening of the travel time. Given the prevalence of the use of this type of devices, the applications become easy to use and do not require additional technical solutions.

It should be emphasized that the combination of systems based on the use of typical telematics solutions, such as motion detectors, Variable Message Signs and data processing systems concerning traffic information in real-time with solutions focused on mobile technologies extends their capabilities and usability.

Acknowledgment. This paper was financed under the project "Analysis of information needs of heterogeneous environment in sustainable urban freight" by the Polish National Science Centre, decision number DEC-2012/05/B/HS4/03818.

References

1. Taniguchi, E., Thompson, R.G., Yamada, T.: Recent Advances in Modelling City Logistics [w:] red. E. Taniguchi, R. G. Thompson, City Logistics II, Institute of Systems Science Research, Kyoto (2001)
2. Taniguchi, E., et al.: City Logistics. Network Modelling and Intelligent Transport Systems, Pergamon, Oxford (2001)
3. Mikulski, J.: The Possibility of Using Telematics in Urban Transportation. In: Mikulski, J. (ed.) TST 2011. CCIS, vol. 239, pp. 54–69. Springer, Heidelberg (2011)

4. Iwan, S.: Wdrażanie dobrych praktyk w obszarze transportu dostawczego w miastach, Wydawnictwo Naukowe Akademii Morskiej w Szczecinie, Szczecin (2013)
5. https://szr.szczecin.pl/utms/index (date of access:June 4, 2014)
6. Oskarbski, J., Jamroz, K., Litwin, M.: Inteligentne Systemy Transportu – Zaawansowane Systemy Zarządzania Ruchem, I Polski Kongres Drogowy Lepsze drogi – lepsze życie, Warszawa (2006)
7. Karoń, G., Mikulski, J.: Transportation Systems Modelling as Planning, Organisation and Management for Solutions Created with ITS. In: Mikulski, J. (ed.) TST 2011. CCIS, vol. 239, pp. 277–290. Springer, Heidelberg (2011)
8. Kalasova, A., Krchova, Z.: Telematics applications and their influence on the human factor. Transport Problems 8(2), 89–94 (2013)
9. http://www.itspolska.pl/ (date of access May 16, 2014)
10. https://developers.google.com/appengine/docs/java/sockets/ (date of access:October 22, 2013)
11. http://developer.android.com/ (date of access:November 26, 2013)

Selected Issues of Reliable Identification
of Object in Transport Systems
Using Video Monitoring Services

Piotr Łubkowski and Dariusz Laskowski

Military University of Technology,
Gen. S. Kaliskiego 2, 00-908 Warszawa, Poland
{plubkowski,dlaskowski}@wat.edu.pl

Abstract. The process of ensuring the security of monitored objects and material goods requires access to the information from sensors located in different points of monitoring and data acquisition systems. Therefore, they are becoming widely used in the transport services where they are needed for the administration of car fleet or the visualization of selected functions of transport processes. In each of these applications, the reliability and quality of the processes of supervision and monitoring is an important issue. Unfortunately, transmission of data from multiple video sensors may lead to degradation of video quality and reliability of identification. The paper presents a study of selected QoS (Quality of Services) supporting mechanisms and components elaborated for provision of reliable video monitoring services. The results of research have been presented as well which show the efficiency of the developed mechanisms in the process of reliable identification of objects in the transport system.

Keywords: dependability, surveillance services, video data identification.

1   Introduction

Video surveillance systems have been used for many years to enhance the safety of citizens and the protected objects. We encounter video surveillance in both public and national utility facilities, in commonly available places and in the areas with limited access. Monitoring systems are a combination of video recording (sensors), transmitting, storing and reproducing devices in one integral unit. They enable observation of people or objects in real time as well as event recording for later analysis. Modern transport systems use highly developed technology to perform the functions of monitoring, supervisory and management of transport processes. In each of the mentioned applications, the reliability and quality of the supervision and monitoring processes is an important issue.

The detection and identification of objects is one of the primary advantages offered in the modern surveillance systems. Automatic detection and recognition of objects is an active area of research covering different fields of science [1]. Complete image analysis system should be able to search for and identify the object and to provide

J. Mikulski (Ed.): TST 2014, CCIS 471, pp. 59–68, 2014.

information about its condition, multiplicity or dislocation. At the same time, the monitoring system records events in the object surroundings creating the possibility of gaining access to the relevant video recordings based on date, time or other searching criteria. An efficient video surveillance system in combination with the current and efficient database can become an element of an integrated system solution with the ability to recognize vehicles, traffic monitoring, collection and processing of data used in forecasting the traffic or planning repairs of roads and streets. There is also a need to monitor the state of the system in terms of the above-mentioned resources, which by changing their values may also change the dynamic characteristics of the system thereby reducing its safety [2].

However, in order to obtain such functionality several factors that affect the efficiency of the process of analysis, detection and identification of objects require consideration. The impact of environmental and sensor technical factors on reliability of the detection and identification processes has been discussed in [3] and [4]. The parameters of techniques used for data transmission (wired or wireless), and in particular the available bandwidth are not without significance. Therefore, in the paper, we have investigated the problem of reliable objects identification in the real-time monitoring system taking into account the available bandwidth.

The paper presents also the QoS platform that is composed of QoS Streaming Server and Resource Broker modules and QoS-aware Client module. It is a part of the solution developed under INSIGMA (*Intelligent Information System for Global Monitoring, Detection and Identification of Threats*) characterized by the possibility of notification of QoS requirements in order to support video monitoring services with a user-specified level of quality.

2   Methods of Object Identification

The process of detection and identification of objects in a digital image is related to advanced processing and recognition of images. Detection and identification of complex objects is a difficult process performed using complicated algorithms when taking into account the essential features of a digital image. Very often, this type of process uses several methods at the same time, which improves their efficiency, but may also result in increasing the complexity of the algorithm operation. Combining of algorithms causes also difficulties in proper identification of methods used by a specific application.

Objects can be identified and detected in an image using software and hardware tools. In the case of software tools, there are many more possibilities connected with the use of a more extensive set of transformations, but the processing of image takes significantly more time. Hardware tools are based on a smaller number of algorithms used and they allow identification of an object in a shorter time. However, these solutions are restricted by the processor capacity and the operating system used.

In image processing aimed at detection of certain objects, segmentation is commonly applied which consists in image division into fragments corresponding to objects visible in the image. Therefore, this is an image processing technique allowing separation of regions that meet certain criteria of homogeneity. The segmentation process is associated with the labelling process (indexation) as a result of which all pixels belonging to a certain object are marked using the same labels, which facilitates their later identification.

The most popular methods used in digital image processing associated with identification of objects comprise methods based on image fragmentation and methods using colour or texture. The image analysis techniques using segmentation can be divided into two basic types: segmentation by region partitioning and region growing [5]. Segmentation by partitioning consists in successive divisions of a larger region into smaller ones until a region is obtained where the pixels are characterized by properties significantly distinguishing them from the remaining regions. On the other hand, in the region growing segmentation, the pixel degree of similarity is tested, which is the criterion for qualifying them into the given region. An example for a method using fragmentation commonly used in applications connected with object retrieval is the line detection method that is a type of edge detection method.

Methods using line detection algorithms detect straight line segments located on the image object edges [6]. They are supported by region detection algorithms [7]. Line detection process is based on detection of short line fragments that are combined into longer segments (Fig. 1). In most of the cases, it is sufficient to identify an object. An example for such an approach may be detection of solid or broken lines separating traffic lanes. Apart from detection of the lines occurrence place, the algorithm discussed specifies their direction, which significantly facilitates detection of large objects.

Fig. 1. The effect of line detection algorithm [10]

Another group of methods includes those, which use object colour [7]. These methods are used for detection and identification of objects of indeterminate shape or objects whose shape is complex or time-varying. An example for such an object is the human face whose shape changes depending on the point of observation and elements such as headgear, hair, make-up or glasses are important obstacles in detection and identification of such type of objects. The common feature for objects such as face is colour which, although it can be different for various human races, is a feature that enables detection. Face detection is not the only area of application of the colour-based method. It can be successfully used for detection of objects whose colour is different in relation to the environment, e.g. a product moving on a conveyor or a customer livery truck on a highway. In order to detect and identify an object based on the colour it is necessary to identify the colour in request and the range of its variability. Most often the process is implemented by manual colour sampling from a certain region of the model image which is the basis for detection algorithm. Colour variability range is determined by identification of the colour average value for the specified region of the model and permitted deviation of colour coordinates. Unfortunately, methods based on colour use are not those that are most accurate due to the fact that any change in the lighting hinders correct detection. The problem is also to define the range of the colour pallet used.

In the case of the third object detection method based on texture, it is assumed that image regions exist where repeatable (regular) points or elements are found. In the method, information on the element or point colour is used. When detecting objects, in the first place sampling of object texture and colours is performed which are the model for the object detected.

In the image analysis process, a technique of moving objects detection is used, whose application in logistic processes is of great importance. These processes are often characterized by high dynamics of changes associated with moving objects where sensors of the video monitoring system can identify objects and track changes in the object or product. Objects moving relative to other objects can be detected based on the analysis of differences in the content of the successive frames of a film. As the image is known before a new object appears, it is easy to specify its location. During its movement, the differences between the successive frames allow tracking its movement.

3   Risk Assessment of Correct Identification

Modern technology offers access to increasingly cheaper and more efficient image capture devices, creating the possibility of common use of the above mentioned methods for object detection and identification in everyday use. However, creation of an algorithm which detects objects in such a manner a human does is not an easy task. At present there is no method that would guarantee hundred percent efficiency of any object recognition process. It results from the fact that the images processed representing various objects are similar due to image components and their location. Another factor hindering correct identification is the variability of features that can be identified in images representing the same or similar objects and that are the result of external factors such as differences in lighting or viewing angle. Hence, in the reliable identification analysis, the following threats related to reliable data identification should be taken into account: lack of proper object lighting (insufficient sensitivity of the transducer) or no infrared operation mode, too long distance between the object and the camera (no proper selection of the focal length), no possibility of object specification (insufficient sensor resolution) or no extraction possibility (low resolution, sensitivity). These threats can lead to the following problems associated with the reliable identification process (Fig. 2):

- false rejection - an object that has its model in the database is unrecognized and rejected due to the fact that it does not have its counterpart,
- misclassification - an object that has its model in the database is not properly assigned to other model in the database,
- false acceptance - an object that does not have its model in the database is assigned to a model that already exists in the database.

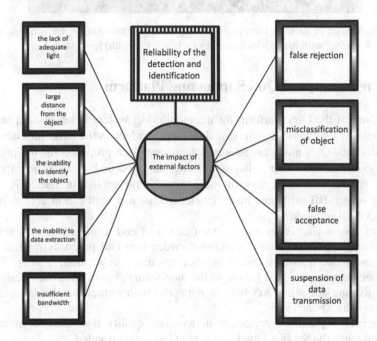

Fig. 2. The Bow Tie risk assessment of object identification [own study]

As already mentioned, the impact of environmental factors has been discussed in [3] and [4]. However, a significant threat is caused by lack or decrease in the available bandwidth which, along with others, may result in misstatements in the process of detection and identification of objects (Fig. 3).

The video transmission requires sufficient bandwidth and small delays, but tolerates partial packet losses. Lack of bandwidth is often the reason of large packets delivery delay (round trip time), large jitter and considerable percentage of packet loss.

Thus, in relation to monitoring systems, it appears to be necessary to ensure an adequate level of Quality of Services of video sequences in order to provide correct identification. That requires application of a quality supporting platform equipped with movement control mechanism for handling video traffic transmitted by the system. The QoS supporting platform presented below is characterized by the possibility of notification on QoS requirements in order to support the implementation of video monitoring services with a reliability level determined by the user.

Fig. 3. The impact of lack of bandwidth on the identification process (A - image without distortion, B - image with distortions caused by lack of bandwidth) [own study]

4   The Concept of QoS Supporting Platform

The structure of the QoS platform for the monitoring system is based on a standard video monitoring network including quality support which is the basis for elaboration of the individual QoS modules. Solutions that have been proposed for the presented platform cover a signalling subsystem using the modified Real Time Streaming Protocol, stream admission control mechanism implemented in the STR mobile streaming server, BB resources management module and application able to interact with the QoS IP network.

Network monitoring is seen as a specification of end terminals, access networks and backbone networks. Communication between two end points is realized using packet transmission for which communication resources are secured.

QoS mechanisms proposed for use in the monitoring system have been designed in view of ensuring adequate QoS both in networks with limited bandwidth and those with oversize backbone.

In order to implement services with required quality between the monitoring network domains the Service Level Agreement has been provided.

As already mentioned, the proposed QoS supporting platform consists of the QoS-Aware client application module, STR mobile streaming server and BB resources management (Fig. 4).

The QoS-Aware streaming application client is equipped with a dedicated RSTP signalling module allowing transmission of the guaranteed service request to STR. Each request contains information on the service class (represented by the expected bandwidth) and video stream priority. STR is responsible for informing the BB manager on the QoS requirements transmitted from the client application. The BB manager monitors available resources of the output access router interface of the monitoring domain and, according to the QoS requirements transmitted by STR, maintains the required resources for the selected video stream. If the resources available at the BB manager level do not allow handling the new stream, it sends an appropriate message to STR.

Following such an action, the STR server rejects the possibility of handling the new video stream in the guaranteed service mode. Functional elements of the presented platform have been described in detail in [9].

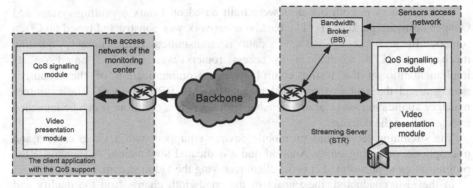

Fig. 4. Functional diagram of the QoS platform [own study]

5   Test Environments for Identification in the Monitoring System

For the experiment, the existing infrastructure of the laboratory monitoring network has been used (Fig. 5) [8, 9]. Reasoning about the correctness of network components specification as regards data transmission reflecting information from the monitoring system is based on a statistical estimation of reliability of the software and hardware platform forming the service chain. The presented infrastructure is also a result of our experience gained when designing a laboratory network environment, as well as the conclusions of the analysis of the literature [14-17].

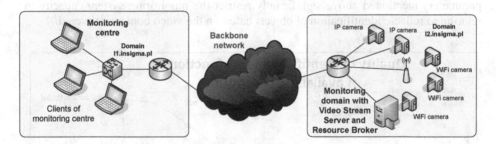

Fig. 5. Diagram of the test bed environment with implemented elements of the QoS platform [own study]

Products of renowned suppliers of hardware and software for both the systems and applications are the components of the test platform. Therefore, it appears reasonable to conclude that the specified measuring system is a correct and highly reliable testbed.

In the monitoring domain, 3 streaming servers were launched (mobile user), while traffic from these servers was received in client applications in the management centre domain.

Access routers in both domains were built based on Linux operating system and Quagga software packet [11]. The backbone network was constructed based on Cisco routers. In a backbone network, data is transmitted using priority queuing mechanisms. HTB mechanism in access routers was launched based on its implementation in the traffic control packet. Communication of the resources manager and the router is provided using the XML-RPC protocol. The resources manager application was elaborated using Java language, therefore it can be launched in any node in the domain.

The streaming server runs on mobile devices equipped with a video camera and microphone, operating under Android and a dedicated application. A standard VLC programming application [12] is the client receiving the video stream.

In the tests conducted, the impact of the bandwidth changes on the quality and reliability of video transmission in the presence of the proposed QoS mechanisms was evaluated. The impact of packet loss on transmission quality was tested as well. In the process of quality evaluation, single stimulus method compliant with ITU-R BT 500-11 recommendations was used [13].

During the first test, video transmission from two sources was realized. The first source included implemented QoS mechanisms, while the second source was not provided with these mechanisms. The value of the available bandwidth varied within the range of 1 Mbps - 54 kbps. The results of bandwidth measurement show that the video stream with QoS support is handled without any interference when the resources are reserved. However, in the case of a stream without QoS support, video information loss occurs due to the lack of available throughput.

The next figures (Fig. 6 and Fig. 7) present the impact of bandwidth and packet losses on the identification process quality. It can be noticed that the network parameters mentioned above significantly restrict the monitoring system capacity in relation to reliable identification of objects based on the video content delivered.

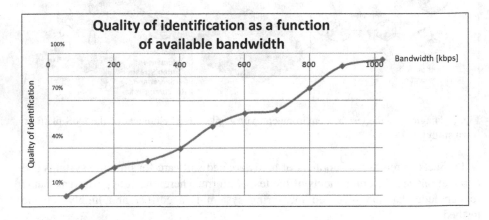

Fig. 6. Impact of bandwidth on identification quality [own study]

It can be easily noticed that application of the proposed quality support mechanisms based on the QoS platform can support the process of data identification in the monitoring system.

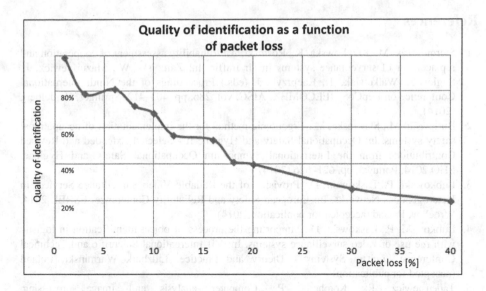

Fig. 7. Impact of losses on identification quality [own study]

6   Conclusion

Testing results presented here confirm that the elaborated QoS mechanisms work correctly in conditions of changing the throughput of the transmission channel. From these results, we can see that video monitoring can be ensured using proposed QoS platform.

The results obtained show also that the provision of reliability and quality of the supervision in monitoring processes preserves the continuity of service without significant deterioration of image quality. This enables to use the functions of monitoring, supervisory and management in transport processes.

Furthermore, one can determine the suitability of the monitoring system, taking also into account different technical and environmental conditions, for recognition of vehicles, monitoring of traffic or collecting and processing of data used in forecasting the traffic or planning repairs of roads and streets.

In summary, it should be noted that although there is no monitoring system that gives 100% guarantee of reliable identification, however, the use of specific mechanisms, presented in this article would lead to achieve the desired "high" degree of reliable identification. The obtained results are determinant for further studies in the area of reliable object identification and monitoring systems.

Acknowledgement. The work has been supported by the European Regional Development Fund within INSIGMA project no. POIG.01.01.02,00,062/09.

References

1. Siergiejczyk, M., Krzykowska, K., Rosiński, A.: Reliability assessment of cooperation and replacement of surveillance systems in air traffic. In: Zamojski, W., Mazurkiewicz, J., Sugier, J., Walkowiak, T., Kacprzyk, J. (eds.) Proceedings of the Ninth International Conference on DepCoS-RELCOMEX. AISC, vol. 286, pp. 403–412. Springer, Heidelberg (2014)
2. Butlewski, M., Sławińska, M.: Ergonomic method for the implementation of occupational safety systems. In: Occupational Safety and Hygiene II - Selected Extended and Revised Contributions from the International Symposium Occupational Safety and Hygiene, SHO 2014, Portugal, pp. 621–626 (2014)
3. Lubkowski, P., Laskowski, D.: Provision of the Reliable Video Surveillance Services in Heterogeneous Networks. In: European Safety and Reliability Conference, ESREL 2014, Wroclaw, Poland (accepted for publication, 2014)
4. Lubkowski, P., Laskowski, D.: Supporting the process of object identification in logistic with the use of video surveillance systems. In: VII International Scientific and Technical Conference Logistic Systems - Theory and Practice, Lidzbark Warminski, Poland (accepted for publication)
5. Tadeusiewicz, R., Korohoda, P.: Computer analysis and image processing. Telecommunications Advancement Foundation Publisher, Krakow (1997)
6. Gonzalez, R., Woods, R.: Digital Image Processing. Prentice-Hall, New Jersey (2002)
7. Russ, C.: The image processing handbook. CRC Press, Boca Raton (2007)
8. Łubkowki, P., Laskowski, D.: Test of the multimedia services implementation in information and communication networks. AISC. Springer, Switzerland (accepted for publication in, 2014)
9. Lubkowski, P., Laskowski, D.: The end-to-end rate adaptation application for real-time video monitoring. In: Zamojski, W., Mazurkiewicz, J., Sugier, J., Walkowiak, T., Kacprzyk, J. (eds.) New Results in Dependability & Comput. Syst. AISC, vol. 224, pp. 295–305. Springer, Heidelberg (2013)
10. Borawski M.: The detection of objects in images (paper in Polish), http://it.rsi.org.pl/dane/artykul_Borawski.pdf (date of access: May 10, 2014)
11. Quagga Routing Suite, http://www.nongnu.org/quagga (date of access: January 20, 2014)
12. VLC media player, http://www.videolan.org/vlc (date of access: February 01, 2014)
13. ITU-R Rec.BT 500-11 Methodology for the subjective assessment of the quality of television pictures, Geneva (2006)
14. Nowosielski L., et al.: The Methods of Measuring Attenuation of Thin Absorbent Materials Used for Electromagnetic Shielding, PIERS. Marrakesh Marocco. Progress in Electromagnetics Research Symposium book series, pp. 870–874 (2011)
15. Przesmycki, R., et al.: Small Chambers Shielding Efficiency Measurements. In: PIERS 2011. Marrakesh Marocco. Progress in Electromagnetics Research Symposium Book Series, pp. 875–879 (2011)
16. Lenarczyk, P., Piotrowski, Z.: Parallel blind digital image watermarking in spatial and frequency domains. Telecommunication Systems 54(3), 287–303 (2013)
17. Rozanowski, K., Piotrowski, Z., Ciolek, M.: Mobile Application for Driver's Health Status Remote Monitoring. In: 9th International Wireless Communications and Mobile Computing Conference (IWCMC), pp. 1738–1743 (2013)

Evaluation of Safety of Highway CCTV System's Maintenance Process

Mirosław Siergiejczyk[1], Jacek Paś[2], and Adam Rosiński[1]

[1] Warsaw University of Technology,
00-662 Warsaw, Poland
{msi,adro}@wt.pw.edu.pl
[2] Warsaw Military University of Technology,
00-908 Warsaw, Poland
JPas@wat.edu.pl

Abstract. Issues of highway CCTV systems used in transport telematics systems were presented in this paper. Because those systems feature a vast range of electronic systems, they need to be tightly "packed" i.e. placed next to each other very closely. On one hand, integrated circuits bring down considerably dimensions of electric devices (and could also decrease power consumption), but on the other "packaging" them together in substantial amounts creates a danger of mutual interference (internal and external electromagnetic compatibility). Therefore, design of highway CCTV system needs to assure it both does not produce but also is resilient to external and internal electromagnetic interference (including overvoltage induced by atmospheric discharge).

Keywords: Electromagnetic compatibility, transport, Closed Circuit Television.

1 Introduction

Highway CCTV systems could be used as part of transport telematic systems. In that arrangement they assure safety during travel, which among other is the service provided by transport telematic systems [10], [19]. This functionality is delivered by systems installed at permanent structures of airports, railway stations. logistics bases, handling terminals as well as by the systems installed in moving objects (e.g. vehicles). Consequently, the security level of both the travellers and cargo increases [14]. In terms of reliability analysis of those systems there are already numerous publications (concerning both the entire system [6], [17], as well as its constitution elements e.g. power supply [13], [16] and transmission media [15]), thus they will not be discussed.

Highway telematics entails using various IT systems along highways in order to considerably increase safety during travel and commercial transport. A range of other positive effects are generated i.e. lower environmental impact, higher efficiency of transport processes through traffic solutions, better use of road infrastructure, stronger economic validity of highway operator business [8], [18].

J. Mikulski (Ed.): TST 2014, CCIS 471, pp. 69–79, 2014.
© Springer-Verlag Berlin Heidelberg 2014

Among highway telematics' elements are centres controlling transport, passengers, vehicles (cars, coaches etc.), drivers and cargos. Intelligent Transport System, subsystems managing roads, vehicles, drivers and transport service based on real time telecommunications create a logical sequence capable of managing moving people, vehicles and cargo under changing environmental conditions. Once of its subsystems is highway CCTV system. Among other is enables to assess highway conditions by locating the area where an accident has taken place and detecting its type. It can also determine the length of any consequent traffic jams (Fig. 1).

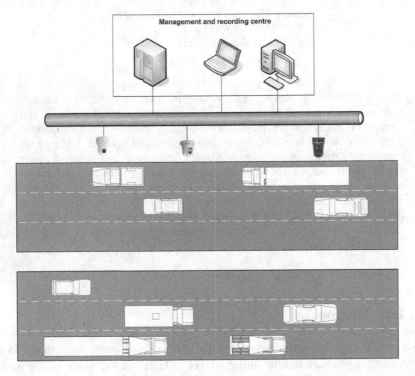

Fig. 1. Highway CCTV system [own study]

Highway CCTV systems are classified as transport safety systems. Their status may vary across different operational states [1], [3]. Those sets of states may be divided into subsets by particular chosen criteria. The following subsets of states apply to transport surveillance systems:

- subset of operational states including the state of full ability, partial ability and reached operational ability;
- subset of availability states including state of continuous availability, full availability and non-availability;

- subset of safety states including the state of safety, "perception of impendency over safety", impendency over safety, unreliability of safety, failing working order (Fig. 2).

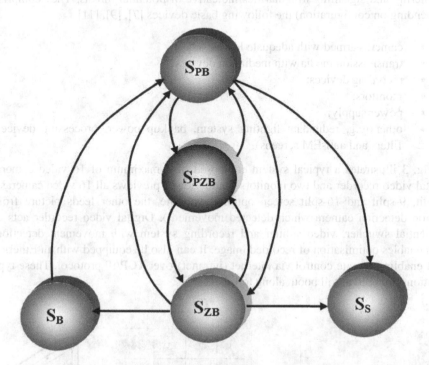

Fig. 2. Diagram of safety states of transport surveillance system, where: S_{PB} – state of safety, S_{PZB} – state of perceptive impendency over safety, S_{ZB} – impendency over safety, S_B – state of unreliability of safety, S_S – state of failing working order [own study]

Above subsets are not disjoint sets and many different states of reached operational capability, safety sates and states of unreliability of safety could occur simultaneously at given time in a system. The aforesaid states may be temporary (e.g. testing) or absorbing state (state of failure). The system transitions from temporary state into a different state with probability greater than zero. The system does not transition into other states from absorbing states. By default, states like the state of full ability, state of safety are temporary whilst the state of reached operational capability, state of unreliability of safety are often perceived as absorbing states.

Currently there are many key solutions being implemented at visual monitoring systems concerning constructional design and organisation. Hence it is important to analyse existing systems in terms of electromagnetic interference [2], [4], [12]. Issues of assessing safety of CCTV maintenance process were presented in this paper.

2   Highway CCTV Systems

CCTV (*Closed Circuit Television*) is used as part of transport telematic systems. It is a system of technical and software measures intended for observing, detecting, registering and signalling irregularities indicative of potential threats. They comprise (depending on configuration) the following basic devices [7], [9], [11]:

- cameras armed with adequate lenses;
- transmission media with mediation devices;
- recording devices;
- monitors;
- power supply;
- other (e.g. redundant lighting system, backup power, processing devices, filters and anti-EM screens).

Fig. 3 illustrates a typical system composed of a maximum of 16 video camera, digital video recorder and two monitors (multi viewer previews all 16 video cameras - 4-split, 9-split and 16-split screen options available, the other feeds picture from motion detection camera which detected movement). Digital video recorder acts as sequential switcher, video splitter and recording system with movement detection. This enables optimisation of recorded image. It can also be equipped with an Ethernet card enabling remote control via internet (intranet) over TCP/IP protocol. These type solutions are used at toll booth along toll roads.

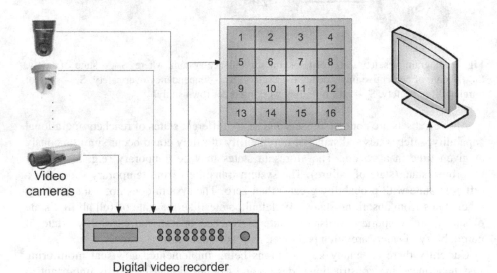

Fig. 3. Example Highway CCTV system [own study]

Digital video recorders from different toll plazas can be connected via optical fibre with the central highway agency control centre. Advantages of this solution are: low attenuation, resilience to external magnetic and electric fields, confined energy radiation. It is used at facilities located in considerable distance from one another. It requires converter devices to transform electric signals into optical and reverse.

3   Evaluation of Safety of Highway CCTV Maintenance Process

In order to evaluate safety of CCTV system maintenance process, different types of systems in production will need to be analysed. Interference free conditions will be simulated first and then interference will be introduced. Hence it will become possible to determine probability of analysed systems staying in particular operational states.

Analysis of CCTV system concluded its structure is mixed. Malfunction of the management and recording centre causes the entire system to exit the state of full operational capability $R_O(t)$ and enter the state of failing security $Q_B(t)$. Failure of any video camera causes the system to transition from the state of full ability $R_O(t)$ into state of impendency over safety $Q_B(t)$ [5]. Transitions into state of full ability are also possible, but they will not be considered. Fig. 4 illustrates relations - in terms of security - within the system in question.

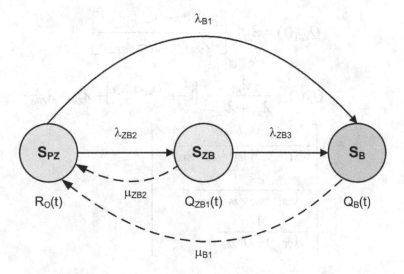

Fig. 4. Relationships within CCTV system [5]. Where:
$R_O(t)$ – the function of probability of system staying in state of full operational capability,
$Q_{ZB}(t)$ – the function of probability of system staying in state of the impendency over safety,
$Q_B(t)$ – the function of probability of system staying in state of unreliability of safety,
λ_{B1} – change rate of the management and recording centre
λ_{ZB2} , λ_{ZB3} – transition rates of video cameras,
μ_{B1} – intensity rate of restoring the state of full ability and recording,
μ_{ZB2} – intensity rate of restoring the state of full ability of video cameras.

The system illustrated in Fig. 4 may be described by the following Chapman–Kolmogorov equations:

$$R_0'(t) = -\lambda_{B1} \cdot R_0(t) - \lambda_{ZB2} \cdot R_0(t)$$
$$Q_{ZB1}'(t) = \lambda_{ZB2} \cdot R_0(t) - \lambda_{ZB3} \cdot Q_{ZB1}(t) \tag{1}$$
$$Q_B'(t) = \lambda_{B1} \cdot R_0(t) + \lambda_{ZB3} \cdot Q_{ZB1}(t)$$

Given the initial conditions:

$$R_0(0) = 1$$
$$Q_{ZB1}(0) = Q_B(0) = 0 \tag{2}$$

and after rearranging:

$$R_0(t) = e^{-(\lambda_{B1}+\lambda_{ZB2})\cdot t} \tag{3}$$

$$Q_{ZB1}(t) = \lambda_{ZB2} \cdot \left[\frac{e^{-(\lambda_{B1}+\lambda_{ZB2})\cdot t} - e^{-\lambda_{ZB3}\cdot t}}{\lambda_{ZB3} - \lambda_{B1} - \lambda_{ZB2}} \right] \tag{4}$$

$$Q_B(t) = \frac{\lambda_{B1}}{\lambda_{B1} + \lambda_{ZB2}} \cdot \left[1 - e^{-(\lambda_{B1}+\lambda_{ZB2})t} \right] + \lambda_{ZB2} \cdot \lambda_{ZB3} \cdot$$
$$\cdot \left[\frac{e^{-(\lambda_{B1}+\lambda_{ZB2})t}}{(\lambda_{B1}+\lambda_{ZB2})\cdot(\lambda_{B1}+\lambda_{ZB2}-\lambda_{ZB3})} - \right.$$
$$- \frac{e^{-\lambda_{ZB3}\cdot t}}{(\lambda_{B1}+\lambda_{ZB2}-\lambda_{ZB3})\cdot\lambda_{ZB3}} +$$
$$\left. + \frac{1}{(\lambda_{B1}+\lambda_{ZB2})\cdot\lambda_{ZB3}} \right] \tag{5}$$

Fig. 5 shows relationships occurring within CCTV system exposed to electromagnetic interference in context of safety. Transitions into state of full ability are also possible, but they will not be considered.

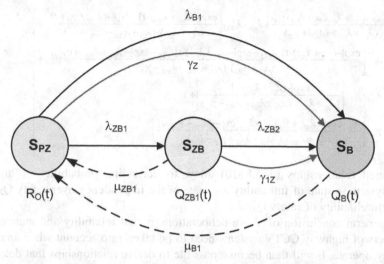

Fig. 5. Relationships within CCTV system exposed to electromagnetic interference [5]. Where:
$R_O(t)$ – the function of probability of system staying in state of full operational capability,
$Q_{ZB}(t)$ – the function of probability of system staying in state of the impendency over safety,
$Q_B(t)$ – the function of probability of system staying in state of unreliability of safety,
λ_{B1} – change rate of the management and recording centre
λ_{ZB1}, λ_{ZB2} – transition rates of video cameras,
γ_Z, γ_{1Z} – indicators determining influence of electromagnetic interference,
μ_{B1} – intensity rate of restoring the state of full ability and recording,
μ_{ZB1} – intensity rate of restoring the state of full ability of video cameras.

The system illustrated in Fig. 5 may be described by the following Chapman–Kolmogorov equations:

$$R_0'(t) = -\lambda_{B1} \cdot R_0(t) - \gamma_Z \cdot R_0(t) - \lambda_{ZB1} \cdot R_0(t)$$

$$Q'_{ZB1}(t) = \lambda_{ZB1} \cdot R_0(t) - \lambda_{ZB2} \cdot Q_{ZB1}(t) - \gamma_{1Z} \cdot Q_{ZB1}(t)$$

$$Q'_B(t) = \lambda_{B1} \cdot R_0(t) + \gamma_Z \cdot R_0(t) + \gamma_{1Z} \cdot Q_{ZB1}(t) + \lambda_{ZB2} \cdot Q_{ZB1}(t)$$

(6)

Given the initial conditions:

$$R_0(0) = 1$$ (7)

$$Q_{ZB1}(0) = Q_B(0) = 0$$

and after rearranging:

$$R_0(t) = e^{-(\lambda_{ZB1} + \gamma_Z + \lambda_{B1}) \cdot t}$$ (8)

$$Q_{ZB1}(t) = \lambda_{ZB1} \cdot \left[\frac{\exp[-(\lambda_{B1} + \gamma_Z + \lambda_{ZB1}) \cdot t] - \exp[-(\lambda_{ZB2} + \gamma_{1Z}) \cdot t]}{(\lambda_{B1} + \gamma_Z + \lambda_{ZB1} - \lambda_{ZB2} - \gamma_{1Z})} \right]$$ (9)

$$Q_B(t) = \begin{bmatrix} \dfrac{\lambda_{ZB1} \cdot \lambda_{ZB2} + \lambda_{B1}\lambda_{ZB2} + \lambda_{ZB1} \cdot \gamma_{1Z}}{(\lambda_{B1} + \lambda_{ZB1}) \cdot (\lambda_{ZB2} + \gamma_{1Z})} + \lambda_{B1} \cdot \lambda_{ZB2} \cdot \left[\dfrac{\exp[-(\lambda_{B1} + \lambda_{ZB1}) \cdot t] - \exp[-(\lambda_{ZB2} + \gamma_{1Z}) \cdot t]}{(\lambda_{B1} + \lambda_{ZB1}) \cdot (\lambda_{B1} + \lambda_{ZB2} - \lambda_{ZB1} - \gamma_{1Z})} \right] + \\[3mm] + \lambda_{B1} \cdot \left[\dfrac{\exp[-(\lambda_{B1} + \lambda_{ZB1}) \cdot t] \cdot \lambda_{ZB2} - \exp[-(\lambda_{B1} + \lambda_{ZB1}) \cdot t] \cdot \lambda_{B1} - \exp[-(\lambda_{B1} + \lambda_{ZB1}) \cdot t] \cdot \lambda_{ZB1}}{(\lambda_{B1} + \lambda_{ZB1}) \cdot (\lambda_{B1} + \lambda_{ZB1} - \lambda_{ZB2} - \gamma_{1Z})} \right] + \\[3mm] + \lambda_{ZB1} \cdot \gamma_{1Z} \cdot \left[\dfrac{\exp[-(\lambda_{B1} + \lambda_{ZB1}) \cdot t]}{(\lambda_{B1} + \lambda_{ZB1}) \cdot (\lambda_{B1} + \lambda_{ZB1} - \lambda_{ZB2} - \gamma_{1Z})} \right] + \\[3mm] + \gamma_{1Z} \cdot \left[\dfrac{\lambda_{B1} \cdot \exp[-(\lambda_{ZB2} + \gamma_{1Z}) \cdot t] - \lambda_{ZB1} \cdot \exp[-(\lambda_{ZB1} + \gamma_{1Z}) \cdot t]}{(\lambda_{B1} + \lambda_{ZB1}) \cdot (-\lambda_{B1} + \lambda_{ZB2} + \gamma_{1Z} - \lambda_{ZB1})} \right] \end{bmatrix} \tag{10}$$

Obtained relationships ($3 \div 5, 8 \div 10$) allow to determine probability of highway CCTV system in state of full ability R_O, state of the impendency over safety Q_{ZB} and state of unreliability of safety Q_B.

The general conclusion of above deliberations is that reliability and maintenance parameters of highway CCTV systems need to be taken into account when analysing how they operate. It will then become possible to derive relationships that determine probabilities of analysed system staying in particular states.

Above analysis was summarised and generalised by an algorithm for evaluating safety of CCTV system maintenance process (Fig. 6). Step one is to decide whether evaluation criteria for the system need to be determined. If yes, serviceability and ability to repair the system is verified. Electromagnetic interference may also be included, which affects the system.

Fig. 6 presents the algorithm for determining evaluation criteria for safety of CCTV systems' maintenance processes.

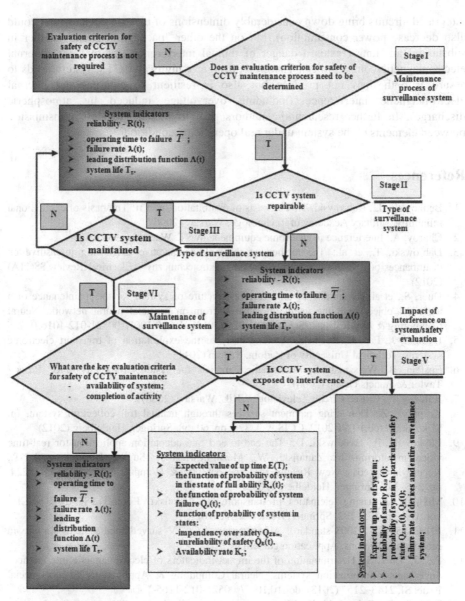

Fig. 6. Algorithm for determining evaluation criteria for safety of CCTV systems' maintenance processes [own study]

4   Conclusion

Issues of highway CCTV systems used in transport telematics systems were presented in this paper. Because those systems feature a vast range of electronic systems, they need to be tightly "packed" i.e. placed next to each other very closely. On one hand, integrated circuits bring down considerably dimensions of electric devices (and could also decrease power consumption), but on the other "packaging" them together in substantial amounts creates a danger of mutual interference (internal and external electromagnetic compatibility). Therefore, design of highway CCTV system needs to assure it both does not produce but also is resilient to external and internal electromagnetic interference (including overvoltage induced by atmospheric discharge). In further research the authors plan to include wireless transmission between elements of the system under real operational conditions.

References

1. Będkowski, L., Dąbrowski, T.: The basis of exploitation, part II: The basis of exploational reliability. Military Academy of Technology, Warsaw (2006)
2. Charoy, A.: Interference in electronic equipment. WNT, Warsaw (1999)
3. Dabrowski, T., et al.: The method of threshold-comparative diagnosing insensitive on disturbances of diagnostic signals. Przeglad Elektrotechniczny - Electrical Review 88(11A) (2012)
4. Duer, S., et al.: Designing of an effective structure of system for the maintenance of a technical object with the using information from an artificial neural network. Neural Computing & Applications 23(3-4), 913–925 (2012), doi:10.1007/s00521-012-1016-0
5. Dyduch, J., Pas, J., Rosinski, A.: The basic of the exploitation of transport electronic systems. Technical University of Radom, Radom (2011)
6. Epstein, B., Weissman, I.: Mathematical models for systems reliability. CRC Press / Taylor & Francis Group (2008)
7. Kałużny, P.: Closed Circuit Television. WKiŁ, Warsaw (2008)
8. Kasprzyk, Z.: Delivering payment services through manual toll collection system. In: Mikulski, J. (ed.) TST 2012. CCIS, vol. 329, pp. 60–68. Springer, Heidelberg (2012)
9. Lubkowski, P., Laskowski, D.: The end-to-end rate adaptation application for real-time video monitoring. In: Zamojski, W., Mazurkiewicz, J., Sugier, J., Walkowiak, T., Kacprzyk, J. (eds.) New Results in Dependability & Comput. Syst. AISC, vol. 224, pp. 295–305. Springer, Heidelberg (2013)
10. Mikulski, J.: Using telematics in transport. In: Mikulski, J. (ed.) TST 2010. CCIS, vol. 104, pp. 175–182. Springer, Heidelberg (2010)
11. PN-EN 50132-7:2003 standard: Alarm systems. CCTV surveillance systems for use in security applications. Application guidelines
12. Paś, J., Duer, S.: Determination of the impact indicators of electromagnetic interferences on computer information systems. Neural Computing & Applications 23(7-8), special Issue: SI, 2143–2157 (2013), doi:10.1007/s00521-012-1165-1
13. Rosinski, A., Dąbrowski, T.: Modelling reliability of uninterruptible power supply units. Eksploatacja i Niezawodnosc – Maintenance and Reliability 15(4) (2013)
14. Siergiejczyk, M., Paś, J., Rosiński, A.: Application of closed circuit television for highway telematics. In: Mikulski, J. (ed.) TST 2012. CCIS, vol. 329, pp. 159–165. Springer, Heidelberg (2012)
15. Siergiejczyk, M., Rosiński, A.: Reliability analysis of electronic protection systems using optical links. In: Zamojski, W., Kacprzyk, J., Mazurkiewicz, J., Sugier, J., Walkowiak, T. (eds.) Dependable Computer Systems. AISC, vol. 97, pp. 193–203. Springer, Heidelberg (2011)

16. Siergiejczyk, M., Rosiński, A.: Reliability analysis of power supply systems for devices used in transport telematic systems. In: Mikulski, J. (ed.) TST 2011. CCIS, vol. 239, pp. 314–319. Springer, Heidelberg (2011)
17. Stapelberg, R.F.: Handbook of Reliability, Availability, Maintainability and Safety in Engineering Design. Springer, London (2009)
18. Sumiła, M.: Selected aspects of message transmission management in ITS systems. In: Mikulski, J. (ed.) TST 2012. CCIS, vol. 329, pp. 141–147. Springer, Heidelberg (2012)
19. Wydro, K.: Telematics - significance and definition of the term. Telecommunication and IT. Publishing House of National Institute of Telecommunications, Warsaw (2005)

E-Navigation Revolution – Maritime Cloud Concept

Adam Weintrit

Gdynia Maritime University, The Faculty of Navigation
81-345 Gdynia, Poland
weintrit@am.gdynia.pl

Abstract. The International Maritime Organization (IMO) has decided that e-Navigation should be 'User Need' led and take into account the Human Element. In this paper the Author, which is a member of the IMO expert group on e-Navigation, will describe the Maritime Cloud, communication framework enabling efficient exchange of electronic information between maritime stakeholders, in terms of their benefits, core components, applicability to the prioritized e-Navigation solutions, considerations related to governance, impact on legal and operational issues, benefits compared with existing alternatives, administrative burdens, cost and options for implementation.

Keywords: e-Navigation, IMO, Information Exchange, Transport Telematics, ITS, Marine Navigation, Safety of Sea Transportation, Marine Communication.

1   Introduction

The IMO (International Maritime Organization) has defined e-Navigation as "the harmonized collection, integration, exchange, presentation and analysis of marine information on board and ashore by electronic means to enhance berth to berth navigation and related services for safety and security at sea and protection of the marine environment" [3].

The last decades have seen huge developments in technology within navigation and communication systems. Sophisticated and advanced technology is developing rapidly. Mariners have never had more technological support systems than today and therefore there is a need to coordinate systems and more use of harmonized standards. Although ships now carry Global Satellite Navigation Systems (GNSS) and will soon all have reliable Electronic Chart Displays and Information Systems (ECDIS), their use on board is not fully integrated and harmonized with other existing systems and those of other ships and ashore.

At the same time it has been identified that the human element, including training, competency, language skills, workload and motivation are essential in today's world. Administrative burden, information overload and ergonomics are prominent concerns. A clear need has been identified for the application of good ergonomic principles in a well-structured human machine interface as part of the e-Navigation strategy [7].

J. Mikulski (Ed.): TST 2014, CCIS 471, pp. 80–90, 2014.

2   Development of E-Navigation Strategy

The combination of navigational errors and human failure indicate a potential failure of the larger system in which ships are navigated and controlled. Accidents related to navigation continue to occur despite the development and availability of a number of ship- and shore-based technologies that promise to improve situational awareness and decision-making. These include radio navigation, Automatic Identification Systems (AIS), Electronic Chart Display and Information Systems (ECDIS), Integrated Bridge Systems (IBS), Integrated Navigation Systems (INS), Long Range Identification and Tracking (LRIT) systems, Automatic Radar Plotting Aids (ARPA), Vessel Traffic Services (VTS) and Global Maritime Distress Safety Systems (GMDSS) [6].

It is believed that these technologies can reduce navigational errors and failures, and deliver benefits in areas like search and rescue, pollution incident response, security and the protection of critical marine resources, such as fishing grounds. They may also contribute to efficiencies in the planning and operation of cargo logistics, by providing information about sea, port and forwarder conditions.

2.1   An E-Navigation Cultural Change

The roll-out of ECDIS across the merchant fleet is now well underway. Despite some early missteps, the signs are that more and more ship owners are getting to grips with the practical aspects of implementation – partly due to a realisation that successful electronic navigation depends on more than just technology. Instead, it requires shipping companies to instigate a 'cultural change', which, among other things, includes a joined-up approach to training, revised bridge working practices and a robust plan for ongoing navigation software and hardware maintenance [8].

2.2   Collective Effort

However, even the most well-organised and progressive ship owner can only achieve so much by themselves. Issues remain that need to be tackled collectively, at an industry level, pooling the shared experience and wisdom of everyone in the e-Navigation value chain, not least, equipment vendors and chart suppliers, hydrographers, authorities and regulators. Any forum that can pull together such a diverse population of stakeholders should to be applauded. Last year's conferences on e-Navigation Revolution, eNavigation, RIN NAV and TransNav got as close as any to achieving that aim to reflect the evolving nature of electronic navigation.

Scenarios painted included the potential for ships' teams to work in closer partnership with shore agencies, further integration of bridge and wider ship systems, the implications for positive control of shipping in complex sea spaces and the expanding use of unmanned vessels. More immediately, the e-Navigation conferences considered whether IMO standards have set a bar that is too low to ensure comprehensive understanding of and training for ECDIS, and particularly the complex issues surrounding the user/machine interface.

2.3   Positive Reinforcement

In terms of corporate culture, the message was clear that a successful ECDIS strategy needs the buy-in of management and leadership from the top. Owners should avoid 'cutting corners' for short-term financial savings. There should be an emphasis on reinforcing good practices, not just knocking out the bad. Concerns were raised about the difficulties of accomplishing this in a business often based on short-term contracts. Cultural change was also explored from the perspective of those actually working on ships. Officers, regardless of rank, should feel empowered – that is to say, not afraid to confront authority if bridge management is going wrong. This can be difficult particularly for sea-staff who lack assertiveness due to their cultural background. It was suggested that a framework for anonymous reporting would serve as a pragmatic solution, whilst sidestepping any anxieties about blame culture.

It is accepted that ECDIS is about more than just high-tech bridge consoles. Consequently, owners have paid due attention to the needs of end-users – the officers who have to interact with this hardware to perform their job. The next step will be to consider the implications of electronic navigation - and how best to embrace it – from various sides and levels.

One of considered option is that the existing as well as new communication links may serve to provide information exchange using the Maritime Cloud.

2.4   Prioritized E-Navigation Solutions

The e-Navigation Strategy Implementation Plan (SIP) sets up a list of tasks and specific timelines for the implementation of prioritized e-Navigation solutions during the period 2015-2019. The SIP focuses on five prioritized e-Navigation solutions, as follows [9]:

- S1: improved, harmonized and user-friendly bridge design;
- S2: means for standardized and automated reporting;
- S3: improved reliability, resilience and integrity of bridge equipment and navigation information;
- S4: integration and presentation of available information in graphical displays received via communications equipment; and
- S9: improved communication of VTS Service Portfolio.

S1, S3 and S4 address the equipment and its use on the ship, while S2 and S9 address improved communications between ships and ship-to-shore and shore-to-ship.

The work on an e-Navigation Strategy Implementation Plan has been broken down into several clear phases: assessing user needs, constructing an open, modular and scalable architecture and completing a series of studies: a gap analysis, cost-benefit analysis and a risk analysis.

The Maritime Cloud is to be considered as part of the e-Navigation Strategy Implementation Plan (SIP) and, more specifically, as a communication infrastructure supporting the five prioritized solutions for e-Navigation, as well as other non-prioritized potential solutions to be developed in the future.

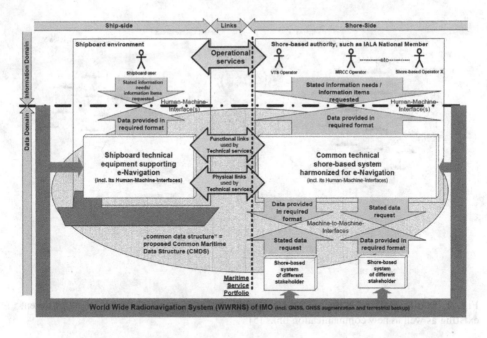

Fig. 1. Overarching e-Navigation architecture on ship and shore sides [4]

3 Overview of the Maritime Cloud Concept

The Maritime Cloud is defined as: "A communication framework enabling efficient, secure, reliable and seamless electronic information exchange between all authorized maritime stakeholders across available communication systems" [5].

3.1 Brief Introduction to the Maritime Cloud Concept

The Maritime Cloud is a dynamic concept derived from a user-driven process based on experience gained from several e-Navigation testbed projects. It is a scalable enabler of seamless information exchange between a variety of available systems and across different physical communication links in the Maritime Domain, as explained graphically in Fig. 2.

The Maritime Cloud is not to be confused with a "storage cloud" containing all information about every ship, nor does it refer to "cloud computing" (computing that involves a large number of computers continuously connected through a communication network such as the internet, or the ability to run a program or application on many connected computers at the same time). Rather, it acts as an open gateway between different authorized stakeholders who participate in the dynamic exchange of information, enabling guaranteed data integrity, confidentiality and authenticity.

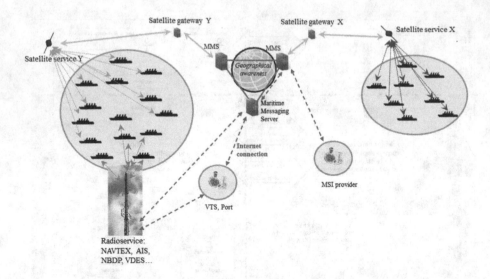

Fig. 2. Maritime Cloud supporting e-Navigation through seamless integration of different existing as well as new communication links [5]

Specifically, the Maritime Cloud consists of standards, infrastructure components, and service reference implementations of standardized information services.

Based on an appropriate governance regime, the Maritime Cloud is an effective enabler of efficient exchange of information between qualified maritime stakeholders via interoperable information services. It supports the utilization of highly automated interfaces to different secure communication options, enabling better communications related to berth-to-berth navigation and related services for safety and security at sea and protection of the marine environment, in support of an efficient and sustainable maritime transportation system.

The implementation of the Maritime Cloud is envisaged as an evolutionary process based on a gradual transition towards a service-oriented information exchange infrastructure. The adoption of the Maritime Cloud will be flexible, fostering increased levels of collaboration within business domains and enabling supporting systems to interoperate based on open standards.

3.2   Stakeholders and Benefits

In order to achieve seamless communication, a compelling need for a supporting infrastructure was identified in the original IMO e-Navigation strategy. Stakeholders to the Maritime Cloud are ships, shipowners and operators, charterers, agents, ports, VTS, MSI providers, HOs, Met offices, MRCCs, flag States, coastal States, port States, AtoN providers, other relevant maritime authorities, and potentially many others requiring interaction with maritime stakeholders.

The benefits of the Maritime Cloud include [5]:

- verification of authenticity of origin and content of information as an additional service (not generally required);
- availability of prioritized messaging queuing systems for addressing mobile actors;
- ability to reuse existing communication systems, while communicating seamlessly across different digital systems, and further facilitating transition to new technologies and systems;
- automatic quality assurance of communication links and information delivery through requests for automated acknowledgements, when using the maritime messaging service;
- enabling automated access from one shipborne single window to multiple national single windows for reporting, further enabling a reduction in the administrative burden and cognitive load on mariners;
- enabling the development of a unified communication terminal able to switch automatically between a multitude of different channels to identify and address a specific actor, thereby reducing the complexity in choosing the right communication system depending on purpose of use;
- facilitation of the future definition of new and improved information services, based on an open architecture allowing alternatives for distribution of information storage or service points;
- a framework enabling secure ship-to-ship and ship-to-shore data exchange, as well as shore-to-shore data exchange between MRCCs, VTS, ports, agents, national single window systems for reporting, etc.;
- further facilitate logistics chain integration with other modes of transport, promoting an efficient and sustainable maritime transportation system;
- secure private and public communication links supported by the Maritime Cloud, taking into account issues of cyber security.

3.3   How Can the Maritime Cloud Support E-Navigation?

Existing as well as new communication links may serve to provide information exchange using the Maritime Cloud. Provision of mandatory information services, such as the Maritime Safety Information (MSI) service under the Global Maritime Distress and Safety System (GMDSS), is currently provided using the Navtex and SafetyNet communication services. However, the Telex-based Navtex and SafetyNet technologies do not allow the distribution of S-100 structured data [1], which can be presented on geographically oriented display systems. Mandatory reporting for the purpose of interaction with VTS may utilize VHF voice communication and AIS. Application Specific Messages via AIS or a future VHF Data Exchange System (VDES) could support such functions, and these communication services should remain cost free for ships.

Non-safety related communication is currently conducted using commercially available systems such as internet satellite connections, allowing the distribution of e-mail. These communication links are non-mandatory and many options exist. Their bandwidth, availability and cost can be selected based on the specific business need of the ship owner concerned.

The Maritime Cloud is capable of delivering a Geocast MSI Service, using Application Specific Messages via no-cost datalinks such as AIS, backed up by already available commercial datalinks. Such a system will be capable of achieving a quick introduction of an MSI service providing machine-readable and geographically representable MSI, while providing automatic quality assurance of information delivery, where two-way datalinks are available.

A new technology called NAVDAT has already been approved at ITU, which will be tested in the coming years, to demonstrate the ability to introduce a modernized broadcast system in the same frequency band as Navtex. The same physical infrastructure can be reused to deliver higher bandwidth broadcast of an MSI information service using S-100 structured data.

Coastal mobile broadband communication links (3G or 4G) could further provide high-rate data transfer between ship and shore. A prerequisite for combining most of these options is, however, an underlying communication infrastructure, unless each shore-based actor is required to have its own radio network. The Maritime Cloud Geocasting service will allow for the gradual introduction of future systems such as NAVDAT and VDES, and for the provision of mandatory services intended to be cost free for the users, while utilizing commercially available internet services as a backup and thus providing additional resilience.

3.4 The Maritime Cloud and the Specific E-Navigation Solutions

Different e-Navigation solutions would benefit from the Maritime Cloud as follows:

S1: Improved, Harmonized and User-Friendly Bridge Design

The Maritime Cloud supports the provision of harmonized information services to mariners, enabling integration of navigation and communication systems and allowing ship designers to introduce more user-friendly bridge designs. Through methods like the Almanac, easy checking of updated contact details of ships nearby, ports, pilot contact points, VTS, MRCCs, etc. will enable user-friendly communication as well as automatic discovery of information services and automated transfer of data/information.

S2: Means for Standardized and Automated Reporting

Today information flows are at a point midway between signed and authorized paper documents, still often painfully filled in by hand, and the computerized handling of information. Most documents produced by computers are still sent manually to the other involved party (and often re-entered manually into another computer). Excessive manual procedures which carry the risk of taking the attention of navigators away from their primary task of safe navigation should be avoided. The world of internet, e-mail and electronic exchange of information where data is sent from computer to computer with minimal human intervention is rapidly developing.

The timely arrival of information is a vital component in international transport. The electronic transfer of structured data through EDI, and in general electronic business [2], has none of the disadvantages of paper documents and brings substantial benefits and savings to the companies implementing it. Accuracy (data are received directly from computer files and are not re-entered manually), speed and savings (on the cost of copying, filing, distributing and capturing data) are some of the obvious advantages.

The e-Navigation solution S2 is specifically targeted towards enabling the automated electronic exchange of such information, based on the recommendations of the IMO, as well as local and regional harmonization of electronic reporting systems.

Existing single window systems for reporting do not have to be abandoned. Instead, an evolving process of automating integration gateways as alternatives to manually entering data in a web form will be facilitated.

Where and how the reportable information is stored and maintained will be a business decision of the individual operators. A captain may maintain all reportable information on board his ship and push it through to the relevant authority or single window system at the required time – or the shipping company may choose to trust a service provider/agent with the task of maintaining and storing most of the information, only requiring limited synchronization of information from the ship at regular intervals, in order to facilitate the reporting of relevant information on time.

S3: Improved Reliability, Resilience and Integrity of Bridge Equipment and Navigation Information

The Maritime Messaging Service will allow for the introduction of future information services, based on the utilization of several different communication links backing up each other seamlessly. This will provide reliability and resilience in communication. Based on the request for acknowledgements when providing messaging via the Maritime Messaging Service, a basis is provided for automated quality assurance of information delivery. Through the regular updating of the position of mobile actors, quality assurance measures may provide qualitative reports related to the coverage areas or the availability of specific communication services, or quantitative reports on the quality performance of individual radio installations.

S4: Integration and Presentation of Available Information in Graphical Displays Received via Communication Equipment

One example of an information service which may be improved through definition of S-100 data structures [1] (or Application Specific Messages), integration of communication equipment and graphical displays is the promulgation of MSI. Such development of data structures could soon be extended to include Temporary and Preliminary Notices to Mariners, which it will be possible to provide through the same communication infrastructure.

Global services such as the World-Wide Navigational Warning Service (WWNWS), as well as local services can be supported by a geocasting service. By retaining one or more broadcast components in this regime, the basic MSI service becomes available to the GMDSS-compliant as well as the non-SOLAS segment. The participants in the Maritime Cloud will become part of a regime of quality assured MSI delivery, based on structured data that can be presented on graphical navigation displays.

S9: Improved Communication of VTS Service Portfolio

The Maritime Service Portfolio concerns a combination of a shore-based functional and technical service to be provided by a competent authority or recognized maritime service provider.

VTS Information Service: Existing VTS information services available in a particular VTS area, such as the provision of weather or oceanographic data, traffic, information on special restrictions, etc., may be made automatically available. Advanced standardized services based on the development of S-100 data structures [1] may be implemented and their availability announced via the Maritime Service Portfolio Registry of the Maritime Cloud. This will enable automatic recognition of the access point for such services. The chosen communication system may impose restrictions on the level of detail that can be contained in the VTS information service. Different versions (with different levels of detail) of the same information service may thus be implemented.

In the short term, mandatory reporting information might be encapsulated into Application Specific Messages, which can be transported via preferably cost-free digital communication systems such as AIS or other available communication system.

3.5   Options for Implementation of the Maritime Cloud

It is generally expected that registering actors for their participation in the Maritime Cloud will be a simple process, which may easily be integrated with existing work procedures, such as issuing call signs and Maritime Mobile Service Identities (MMSIs) for ships or shore stations, but including a more advanced digital certificate where needed. Once registered, each actor will be given access to maintain most parts of own contact information and decide whether access to it is public or restricted, such as the ship's e-mail address, a VTS centre's VHF working channel, or how to access local port information. The components included in Maritime Cloud Data Centres should be operated based on international standards for cyber security. There are several different options for implementing the data centres that host the core components of the Maritime Cloud, noting that these are not intended to include large-scale storage of all information, but only components that facilitate authenticated information exchange and automatic discovery of information services. The following paragraphs describe three scenarios and their associated advantages and disadvantages:

One International Data Centre: The simplest scenario would be one single company or organization operating a global data centre. Each flag State will have responsibility for the logical content of its own national part of the registries, and all maritime parties will be able to register through their National Competent Authority, enabling them to interact as authorized parties to the Maritime Cloud.

One International Organization and Three Regional Data Centres: In this scenario, one international organization governs three regional data centres divided evenly by time zones. These regional data centres should constantly synchronize public data on a peer-to-peer level, enabling functional transfer to another data centre, in case the connection to one data centre fails.

National Data Centres and an International Data Exchange: This scenario fully resembles the LRIT regime. Each flag State will either have its own data centre or join a regional data centre, and each data centre will exchange data through an international data exchange (this could be the LRIT International Data Exchange). Ships will connect through the data centre they are registered with.

4   Conclusion

E-Navigation is a broad concept that is aimed at enhancing navigation safety, security and the protection of the marine environment through the harmonised collection, integration, exchange, presentation and analysis of maritime information onboard and ashore by electronic means. It is envisioned that e-Navigation will be a 'living' concept that will evolve and adapt over a long time scale to support this objective. During this time information will change, technologies will change, political and commercial objectives will change, and tasks will change. However it is unlikely that the need for safe and efficient seaborne transport will change significantly.

It is also certain that the safe and efficient transport will continue to rely on good decisions being made on an increasingly constant and reliable basis. Some decisions may be made with increased dependence on technology, but at some level we will always rely on good human decisions being made and therefore every effort needs to be made to apply an understanding of the Human Element at all stages, of design, development, implementation and operation of e-Navigation.

The IMO as a specialized agency of the United Nations, which primary purpose is to develop and maintain a comprehensive regulatory framework for shipping and its remit includes safety, environmental concerns, legal matters, technical co-operation, maritime security and the efficiency of shipping and as the leading international body for maritime professionals will continue to use the resources of its members states to promote the effective application of the Maritime Cloud concept for e-Navigation and invites all maritime professionals to join in this critical effort.

References

1. IHO S-100. Universal Hydrographic Data Model. Edition 1.0.0. International Hydrographic Organization, Monaco (2010)
2. IMO FAL.5/Circ.40. Revised IMO Compendium on Facilitation and Electronic Business. International Maritime Organization, London (2013)
3. IMO, NAV 59/6. Development of an e-Navigation Strategy Implementation Plan, Report of the Correspondence Group on e-Navigation, submitted by Norway. IMO (2013)

4. IMO, NCSR 1/9. Report from the Correspondence Group on e-Navigation. Summited by Norway. International Maritime Organization, London (2014)
5. IMO, NCSR 1/INF.21. Development of an e-Navigation Strategy Implementation Plan. Overview of the Maritime Cloud Concept. Submitted by Denmark, France and the Republic of Korea. International Maritime Organization, London (2014)
6. Patraiko, D.: Introducing the e-Navigation Revolution. *Seaways*, The International Journal of the Nautical Institute (2007)
7. Patraiko, D., Wake, P., Weintrit, A.: e-Navigation and the Human Element. *TransNav*, the International Journal on Marine Navigation and Safety of Sea Transportation 4(1) (2010)
8. Tester K.: An e-Navigation Cultural Change. Leader from the December 2013-January 2014 Edition of Maritime IT & Electronics. IMarEST, http://www.imarest.org/MITE, (date of access:June 20, 2014)
9. Weintrit, A.: Prioritized Main Potential Solutions for the e-Navigation Concept. *TransNav*, the International Journal on Marine Navigation and Safety of Sea Transportation 7(1) (2013)

Polish Toll Collection System
as an Unexplored Data Source

Katarzyna Bołtowicz and Marek Chwal

Kapsch Telematic Services
ul. Poleczki 35A/1,
02-822 Warsaw, Poland
{Katarzyna.Boltowicz,Marek.Chwal}@kapsch.net

Abstract. In this article the authors shortly present major information on the PTCS (Polish Toll Collecting System) development, also known as viaTOLL, over the past three years. The article presents covering of road network divided into national roads, expressways and motorways, and, in parallel, the development of the distribution network. The authors also present some statistics and trends in the number of vehicles registered in the System.

The second part of the article presents the perspectives of the further PTCS development in terms of the road network coverage as well as the further development of the system functionalities in the context of the MLFF (Multi Lane Free Flow) plans and related changes in the Act on Public Roads, the Act on Toll Motorways and the National Road Fund that are currently being considered. The important message coming from the presented numbers, mentioned briefly in the Summary, is the system's unexplored possibilities.

Keywords: PTCS, viaTOLL, Electronic Toll Collecting System, ETC, MLFF.

1 Introduction

In July 2011, according to Act on Public Roads and Act on Toll Motorways and National Road Found, the Polish Toll Collection System began its operation at toll road sections indicated in the regulations. A tender for the construction and maintenance of the system was won by Kapsch Telematic Services sp. z o. o. The contract was concluded in November 2010, so the company had only eighth months for the construction and implementation of such a complex system.

The viaTOLL system is mandatory for all vehicles and combinations of vehicles with a maximum permissible weight exceeding 3.5 tons, as well as for buses, regardless of their maximum permissible weight. Users of toll liable vehicles are required to equip vehicles with electronic on board units. Since June 2012, the system also allows to make payments electronically for passenger cars (with a total permissible weight lower than 3.5 tons) on motorways managed by the General Directorate of National Roads and Motorways (GDDKiA), i.e. A2 motorway (Konin – Stryków section) and A4 motorway (Bielany Wrocławskie – Sośnica section).

J. Mikulski (Ed.): TST 2014, CCIS 471, pp. 91–99, 2014.
© Springer-Verlag Berlin Heidelberg 2014

Detailed information on the functioning of the viaTOLL system can be found at www.viatoll.pl. Persons interested in the viaTOLL system can also receive the required information by contacting the press office at: media@viatoll.pl.

The viaTOLL system is based on the DSRC (*Dedicated Short Range Communication*) microwave technology. Gantries situated over the road communicate during the passage with OBUs (*On Board Units*) installed in vehicles.

Fig. 1. OBUs used in PTCS for Heavy Vehicles and Light Vehicles [own study]

At the time of passage under a gantry in the system arises a transaction that contains information about the registered vehicle (its MPW, emission class, registration number) and the place and time of passage; on the basis the system precisely calculates the amount due for driven toll road segments indicated by the appropriate Regulation of the Council of Ministers concerning national roads or their sections, where the electronic toll is collected, as well as electronic toll rates, taking into account the appropriate tolls for various parameters of vehicles.

Some of the gantries are equipped with additional control devices, which verify the accuracy of the record for its compliance with the performed measurements. In this way, the system prevents frauds, and each violation is also recorded in the system and becomes the basis for initiating proceedings and the imposition of an administrative penalty. The diagram presented on Fig. 2. shows the areas of communication and metering of a vehicle at the time of its passage under a gantry equipped with components recording passage and control elements.

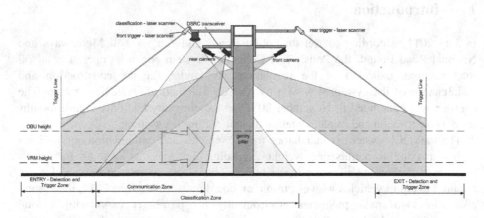

Fig. 2. Scheme of gantry areas with lasers and DSRC communication [own study]

The system used in Poland is a solution much more effective, efficient and equitable than the previously used vignette system. The system based on DSCR technology is also cheaper to maintain as compared to systems using GNSS satellite communication.

2   Development of PTCS in 2011-2014

The contract with Kapsch covers not only launch, but also the management and maintenance of the system until November 2018. Works on the project have been divided into stages; major milestones that have been already achieved are:

- the launch of the information campaign, including a hotline and a website, since mid-March 2011,
- the launch of the user registration process, since 2 May 2011,
- the full launch of the tolling system – electronic for heavy vehicles and manual for light vehicles – since 1 July 2011,
- the launch of the Electronic Toll Collection System for light vehicles since June 2012.

Additional assumptions included in the project are:

- preparation and implementation of the operational phase,
- adaptation of the system to the European interoperability directive – EETS,
- implementation of system extensions – covering new segments of the toll road network.

2.1   Road Network

At the launch of the system in July 2011, the system covered 1,560 km of roads including 582 km of motorways, 536 km of expressways and 442 km of national roads. Further extensions followed successively, according to the instructions by GDRNM, as the new roads were constructed. Currently, the Electronic Toll Collection System covers almost 3,000 km.

Table 1. Road network coverage extension [own study]

Valid from	07/02/2011	07/01/2012	12/01/2013	03/30/2013	10/31/2013	12/01/2013	09/01/2014	10/01/2014
Motorways	582 km	--	81 km	--	196 km	--	110 km	57 km
Expressways	536 km	13 km	54 km	105 km	134 km	122 km	86 km	--
National Roads	442 km	312 km	--	55 km	--	--	11 km	--
Gantries	458	576	616	666	711	731	753	758

The chart presented on Fig. 3. shows the growth of road coverage by the system in the years 2011-2014.

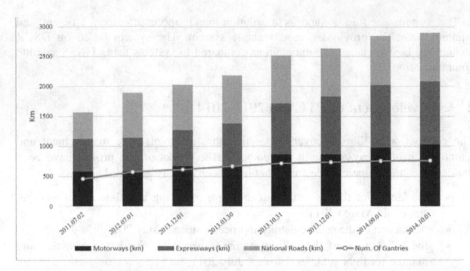

Fig. 3. Road network coverage extension [own study]

2.2 Distribution Network

With toll roads network coverage increase, the distribution network (primarily of direct distribution) also developed. At the beginning, the situation in this field, as in all other fields, was changing quite rapidly, flexibly and instantly responding to the current needs and demand in that area. With time, a process of cyclic (quarterly) verification and proper, the most optimal adjustment of the locations and amount of customer service facilities based on the results of performed analyzes, has been developed.

The distribution network now consists of 230 PoS (Point of Sales – Distribution Points located at gas stations of PKN Orlen, BP and Lotos, as well as Boarder Distribution Points and Contact Points located in each voivodeship).

Fleet card issuers is a separate indirect distribution channel. Currently, Kapsch co-operates with 11 companies in comparison to only 2 co-operating companies in the initial stage of the system.

2.3 Enforcement

A very important element of the system is the control area for preventing and detecting malpractices. Apart from enforcement (control) gantries generating evidential records, which in turn are verified by a dedicated team of the Manual Inspection of Violations (MIV), an additional protection component are Mobile Enforcement Units operated by the General Inspectorate of Road Transport (GITD), which serves as the control authority within the system. Currently, at the area of the entire country, 96 of such specialized units, equipped with devices allowing to communicate on route (without stopping vehicles) and in real time with *On Board Units*, and verify data in the system on the basis, are at the GITD's disposal.

Fig. 4. Mobile Enforcement Unit [own study]

2.4   Road Users

User registration process has begun as early as in May 2011, two months before the full launch of electronic toll collection. As a result, at the launch of the toll collection system, more than 300,000 vehicles were already registered in the system.

The number of OBUs delivered is growing steadily. Until January 2014, the system recorded more than 1,150,000 registrations of different vehicles.

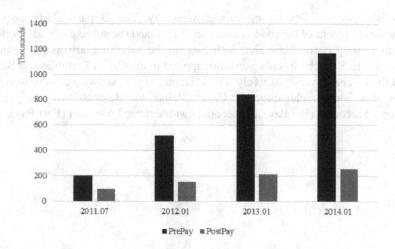

Fig. 5. PrePay/PostPay Registration – incremental [own study]

At the launch of the system, most of the aforementioned registered vehicles were of Polish origin. Currently, about 30% of the registration transactions relates to the foreign vehicles. These data indicate the size of the transit via Poland and can be further analyzed for the construction of a flow map as well as road network construction and maintenance planning.

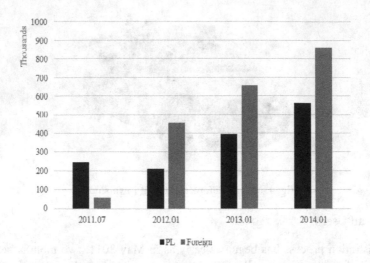

Fig. 6. PL/Foreign Registration – incremental [own study]

3   Comparison to Other National Toll Collecting Systems

The Polish system is developing very dynamically. This is particularly associated with the development of the road network in Poland and the subsequent addition of its segments to the system; compared with two similar solutions, also implemented on the basis of the Kapsch Group's portfolio, applied in the Czech Republic and Belarus, Poland distinguishes very positively. For example, Fig. 7. shows a comparison of the number of registered vehicles in the Czech, Polish and Belarussian system, divided into prepaid accounts (Pre Pay) and accounts with deferred payment (Post Pay).

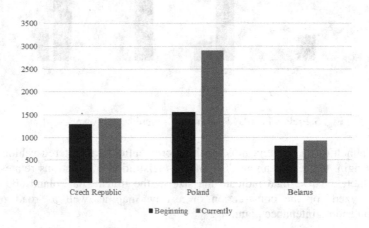

Fig. 7. Comparison of Czech/Polish/Belarussian toll systems – Accounts [own study]

Fig. 8. shows a relative comparison of the number of kilometers covered by the Czech, Polish and Belarussian electronic toll collection systems.

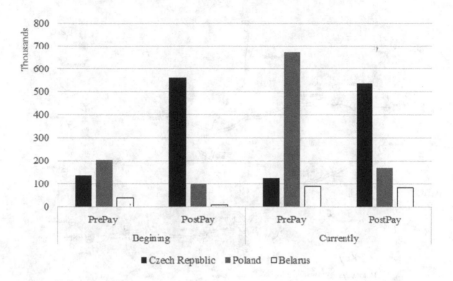

Fig. 8. Comparison of Czech/Polish/Belarussian toll systems – Kilometers [own study]

4   Prospects of Future Use

4.1   Road and Distribution Network Expansion

The PTCS system covers nearly 3,000 km[1] of roads throughout the country, including:

- more than 800 km of national roads,
- almost 1,100 km of expressways,
- almost 1,000 km of motorways.

In subsequent years, further extensions are planned, and according to the contract toll road network shall cover more than 7,000 km of national roads, expressways and motorways until 2018. Adequately to the development of the road network, the distribution network shall be also modified.

4.2   Multi Lane Free Flow

The PTCS system is built to allow quick transition from a manual toll collection on motorways to a fully electronic toll collection for all kinds of vehicles. Of course, such an adjustment would require a lot of effort, but the cost of such a modification would be significantly lower than that of building a separate system, and also the time

---

[1] Status on October 2014.

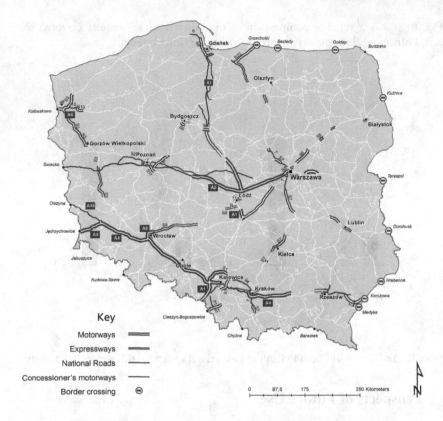

Fig. 9. Road network currently covered by PTCS [own study]

of its implementation would be much shorter, enabling faster launch of services including the collection of tolls. It should be noted that at present there are already many kilometers of motorways (A2, A1), which, due to the lack of an adequate system, are available free of charge. Lack of barriers and the need to stop at the entrances and exits of the motorways would maintain the capacity of these roads, additionally providing the drivers of vehicles with convenience and comfort. At the same time, the implementation of a modern and innovative solution would significantly reduce the cost of maintenance.

An additional advantage of such an approach is collecting and the ability to use much more detailed information about the passages, trends, directions of movement of vehicles of different classes and categories, which is virtually impossible in the classic, manual toll collection systems.

However, replacement of the traditional, manual toll collection system requires changes in Polish law. There are currently works performed on amendments to the Act on Public Roads and Act on Toll Motorways and the National Road Fund.

4.3   Other Usage

The PTCS system is a powerful database that can serve as a valuable and reliable source of information for many state authorities, scientific institutions, services (e.g.

police, courts), as well as other systems such as the National Traffic Management System. The collected data could be used for numerous and diverse analyzes on the use of Polish roads, travelling directions, loads. Such information could facilitate the planning of infrastructure development and maintenance of the good state of roads, increasing the comfort of road users by providing dynamic information about the situation on the road. There is certainly much more possibilities of using this information. These data could also be used for analysis and a more efficient use of the funds of the National Road Fund.

5   Conclusion[2]

The viaTOLL system, being in operation for over three years, is perfectly consistent with the objectives of fair and equitable toll collection. The expenditure incurred on the implementation of this solution paid back in just a year and a half, and now the system generates much more revenue to the NRF than the previous vignette solution did. Poland gains from this solution additional funds for the development of road infrastructure, which in combination with the EU funds allows rapid and visible improvement of the condition of Polish roads. At the same time, it is very important that this system is much more equitable, calculating tolls based on the actually travelled road segments, taking into account specific characteristics of the vehicles, which affect the consumption of these roads and the environmental impact.

At the same time, valuable and extensive data collected since 2011 are used at the moment to a very negligible extent. When starting the process of analyzing and utilizing the full capabilities of this system, one could obtain relevant information and knowledge, which in turn could be used to improve the comfort and safety of Polish roads, as well as the optimal planning of the expansion of the entire relevant infrastructure and exploration of the system's brand new, innovative applications.

References

1. Act on Public Roads - Journal of Laws 2007, nr 19, section 115, as amended
2. Act on Toll Motorways and National Road Found - Journal of Laws 2004, nr 256 section 2571, as amended
3. Official Polish Toll Collection System, http://www.viatoll.pl/en/ (date of access: July 09, 2014)
4. Official Czech Toll Collection System, http://www.mytocz.eu/en/ (date of access: July 09, 2014)
5. Official Belarus Toll Collection System, https://www.beltoll.by/en/ (date of access: July 09, 2014)
6. Krzak, J.: Electronic toll in European road transport, Bereau of Research. BAS Studies 4(32), 125–144 (2012)

---

[2] Content, images and information included in this article are the authors own elaboration based on data from the PTCS and Kapsch internal materials.

Concept of Smart Cities and Economic Model of Electric Buses Implementation

Ryszard Janecki[1] and Grzegorz Karoń[2]

[1] University of Economics in Katowice,
1 Maja 50, 40-287 Katowice, Poland
et@ae.katowice.pl
[2] Silesian University of Technology,
Krasińskiego 8, 40-019 Katowice, Poland
grzegorz.karon@polsl.pl

Abstract. The article presents selected definitions of the smart cities in the context of smart mobility and smart environment. Then presents the basic algorithms of the economic model for electric buses implementation in the Smart Cities. This models are implemented in model of evaluation for the optimization of battery charging in electric-powered buses.

Keywords: smart cities, economic model, electric buses.

1 Introduction to the Smart Cities

In the literature, there is no clear definition of intelligent sustainable city (Smart City). Among the many ideas for specific issues in general, can be considered the definition, that the Smart City is a territory whose attributes are high learning ability and innovation, creativity, allocation of many R&D institutions, higher education, IT infrastructure and technology communication and a high level of management efficiency [1]. In Europe, the concept of Smart Cities focuses on broad environmental issues, including on the one hand primarily aim to reduce CO_2 emissions and on the other hand, the objective is the efficient use of energy in each functional area of the city. All projects should be undertaken with the aim to improve the quality of life of residents [2]. In Poland the intelligent city is characterized by investments in social capital, transport, communication infrastructure, fuel and sustainable economic development and quality of life. A key determinant the achievement of these characteristics is cost-effective use of natural limited resources [3].

The idea of Smart Cities is currently being implemented and does not yet have a fully functioning system in the world. Leading cities are in Asia and the U.S., including Singapore, Malta, Kochi, Dubai, Dubuque and San Francisco. In Europe, leaders are the cities of Luxembourg (Luxembourg), Aarhus, Aalborg and Odense (Denmark) and Turku (Finland). Initiatives in this regard, the European Union supports allocating since 2013. for the concept of smart cities more than 360 million euros.

Smart City concept includes six basic elements – see Fig. 1 – among them were marked two, eg. Smart Mobility and Smart Environment. This elements of the Smart

J. Mikulski (Ed.): TST 2014, CCIS 471, pp. 100–109, 2014.
© Springer-Verlag Berlin Heidelberg 2014

City are directly related to urban smart transport with public transport (transit), which uses vehicles environmentally friendly including buses with electric drive. The question of the effectiveness of electric vehicles (buses) implementation was raised in the project "Models and Methods for the Evaluation and the Optimal Application of Battery Charging and Switching Technologies for Electric Busses" [4] and economic model has been developed [5]. Objectives, elements and evaluation criteria used in this model are presented as algorithms in the next chapter of the present article.

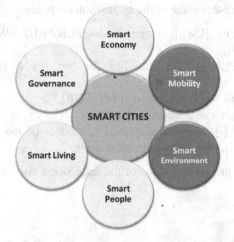

Fig. 1. Smart City concept. Source: own study based on [2].

2   Economic Model of Electric Buses in Smart Cities

Fundamental component of the economic model for buses with electric drive implementation is model of total costs of ownership for one bus. This component is a sum of following costs [7]:

- present value of the acquisition costs of bus,
- present value of the operating costs,
- present value of the infrastructure costs,
- present value of the external costs,
- present value of the proceeds of liquidation.

Basic algorithms for these five components of the economic model are presented in the next subsections. All formulas, constants, variables, and their explanation can be found on the following figures.

2.1   Acquisition Costs – Algorithm of Model

The present value of the acquisition costs for one bus consists of:

- nominal acquisition costs of bus,
- acquisition costs taking into account subsidies,

- self-financed acquisition costs,
- external acquisition costs,
- annual annuity acquisition costs,
- discounted annual annuity acquisition,
- discounted costs of the spare battery,
- self-financed acquisition costs of the spare battery,
- present value of the acquisition costs per passenger.

Input data for the present value of the acquisition costs are:

- battery capacity [kWh], battery costs [PLN, EUR/kWh], lifetime of the battery [years],
- bus costs [PLN, EUR], subsidies for bus [PLN, EUR], bus capacity [passengers],
- costs for double-layer capacitors [PLN, EUR],
- external finance rate acquisition [-],
- credit period [-], loan interest rate [-], number of interest rate [-], market interest rate [-], repayment term acquisition.

Implementation of the present value of the acquisition costs for one bus is shown as algorithm in Fig. 2.

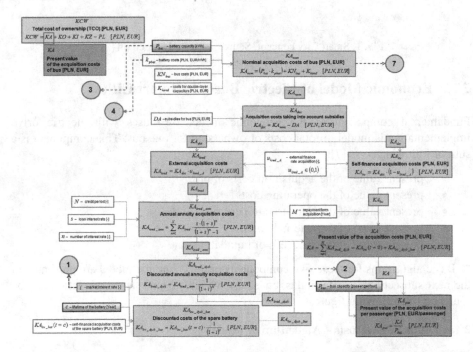

Fig. 2. Model of the present value of the acquisition costs. Source: own study based on [5].

2.2   Operating Costs – Algorithm of Model

The total annual operating costs for one bus consists of:

- annual energy costs,
- annual tire costs,
- annual maintenance costs,
- annual salary,
- annual insurance costs,
- annual costs for the daily supply of the buses..

Input data for the total annual operating costs are:

- annual operational use [km/year],
- average annual operational use [km/year],
- energy consumption[kWh/km]/[l/km],
- cost rate energy [euro/kWh]/[euro/l],
- tax relief [euro/l],
- cost rate of AdBlue [euro/l],
- consumption of AdBlue [l/km],
- tire cost rate [euro/km],
- scheduled speed [km/h]
- factor for additional equipment,
- extra costs of additional bus equipment,
- number of buses with additional equipment,
- total number of buses,
- staff index [man-year/vehicle/year],
- cost rate workshop staff [euro/man-year],
- factor to take the scheduled speed into account,
- scheduled speed [km/h],
- factor to take the bus age and bus type into account,
- factor to take the vehicle age into account,
- share of maintenance costs independent of the operational use,
- cost rate for the bus driver [EUR/year],
- costs for further education concerning operation, maintenance and repair of electric buses [EUR/year],
- market interest rate [-],
- annual operational use [km/year],
- cost rate of the daily supply [euro/km],
- bus capacity [passenger/bus],
- useful life of bus [years].

Implementation of the total annual operating costs for one bus is shown as algorithm in Fig. 3.

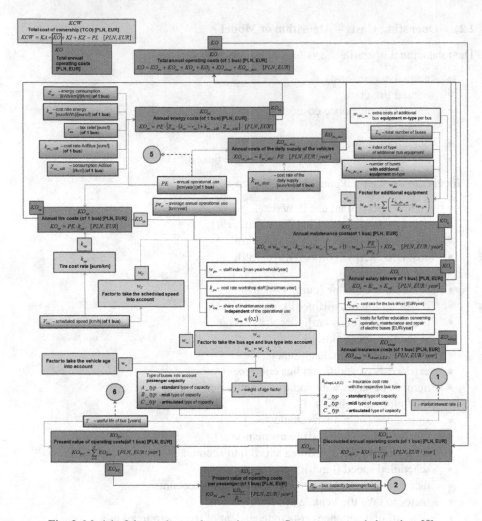

Fig. 3. Model of the total annual operating costs. Source: own study based on [5].

2.3   Infrastructure Costs – Algorithm of Model

The present value of infrastructure costs consists of:

- costs of battery swapping,
- costs of inductive charging,
- costs of conductive charging (plug-in),
- infrastructure costs taking into account subsidies,
- nominal infrastructure costs,
- annual annuity infrastructure costs,
- discounted annual annuity infrastructure costs
- discounted annual infrastructure maintenance costs,
- self-financed infrastructure costs.

Implementation of the present value of infrastructure costs for one bus is shown as algorithm in Fig. 4.

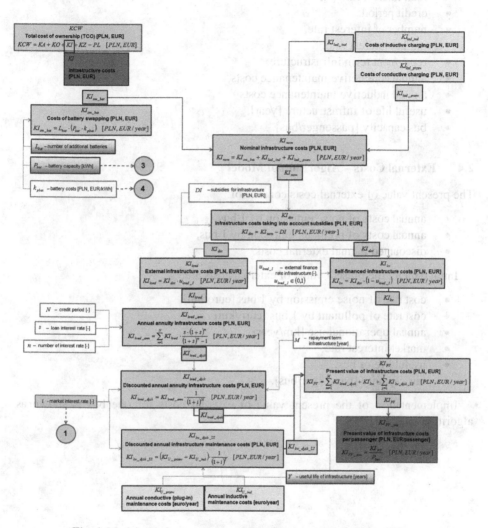

Fig. 4. Model of infrastructure costs. Source: own study based on [5].

Input data for the present value of infrastructure costs are:

- number of additional batteries for swapping,
- battery capacity [kWh],

- costs per unit of battery capacity [euro/kWh],
- infrastructure costs taking into account subsidies,
- subsidies for infrastructure,
- external finance rate infrastructure [-],
- loan interest rate [-],
- credit period,
- number of interest rate,
- market interest rate,
- repayment term infrastructure,
- annual conductive maintenance costs,
- annual inductive maintenance costs
- useful life of infrastructure [year],
- bus capacity [passenger/bus].

2.4   External Costs – Algorithm of Model

The present value of external costs consists of:

- annual costs of noise emission by 1 bus,
- annual costs of pollutant emission by 1 bus,
- discounted annual external costs.

Input data for the present value of external costs are:

- cost rate of noise emission by 1 bus [euro/km],
- cost rate of pollutant by 1 bus [euro/km]
- annual operational use [km/year],
- market interest rate,
- useful life of bus,
- bus capacity [passenger/bus].

Implementation of the present value of external costs for one bus is shown as algorithm in Fig. 5.

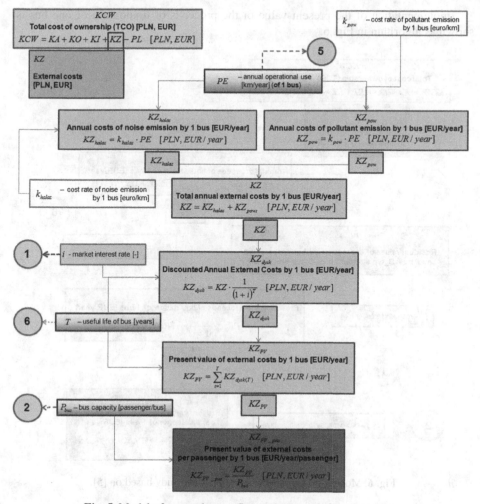

Fig. 5. Model of external costs. Source: own study based on [5].

2.5   Proceeds of Liquidation – Algorithm of Model

The present value of the proceeds of liquidation consists of:

- nominal acquisition costs,
- nominal proceeds of liquidation,

Input data for the present value of external costs are:

- residual value of bus,
- market interest rate [-],
- useful life of bus [years],
- bus capacity [passenger/bus].

Implementation of the present value of the proceeds of liquidation of one bus is shown as algorithm in Fig. 6.

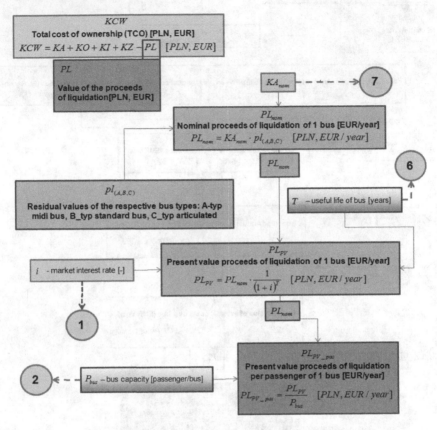

Fig. 6. Model of external costs. Source: own study based on [5].

3   Conclusion

Implementation of electric buses in the Smart Cities must take into account the economic aspect of such a solution. Especially due to the much higher current costs of electric buses in the text compared to traditional bus-powered. In addition, it should be taken into account the higher costs related to a special charging infrastructure necessary for such buses – especially in the case when the battery capacity is not sufficient for a daily bus service without charge.

Therefore, economic aspects have to be preceded by an analysis of energy consumption of the battery depending on the load of the bus due to profile of elevation of the route, passengers weight and power consumption by on-board systems (lighting and air conditioning). On the basis of this analysis it is possible to identifying appropriate routes and then estimate the number of electric buses as a part of buses fleet to service of urban transport networks [4], [5].

Therefore, the main problem of the electric buses implementation in the Smart Cities is the selection of optimal routes for electric buses, the choice of charging strategy (inductive, conductive, in the depot, on the route) and optimal location of charging points [4-6]. These issues require the use of appropriate tools for transportation systems modelling [7] and appropriate Public Transportation Management services, eg Transit Fleet Management, Transit Fixed-Route Operations, Demand Response Transit Operations, Multi-modal Coordination, Transit Signal Priority [8-10].

Acknowledgement. The present research has been financed from the means of the National Centre for Research and Development as a part of the international project within the scope of ERA-NET Electromobility+ Programme 'The Models and Evaluation Methods for the Optimization of Battery Charging in Electric-Powered Buses'.

References

1. Komninos, N.: Intelligent Cities: Innovation, Knowledge Systems and Digital Spaces, pp. 1–2. Spoon Press, London (2002)
2. Stawasz, D., Sikora-Fernandez, D., Turała, M.: Koncepcja Smart City jako wyznacznik podejmowania decyzji związanych z funkcjonowaniem i rozwojem miasta, pp. 98, Zeszyty Naukowe Uniwersytetu Szczecińskiego nr 721 Studia Informatica nr 29 (2012)
3. Więcławowicz-Bilska, E.: Miasto przyszłości – tendencje, koncepcje, realizacje, Architektura zeszyt 1, rok 109, p. 326, Wydawnictwo Politechniki Krakowskiej, Kraków (2012)
4. CACTUS. Models and Methods for the Evaluation and the Optimal Application of Battery Charging and Switching Technologies for Electric Busses, IFAK Magdeburg-Fraunhofer IML Stuttgart, Silesian University of Technology Katowice, Magdeburg-Stuttgart-Katowice 2012-2015
5. Janecki, R., Karoń, G., Sierpiński, G.: Economical Model (WP2-WP3) in: CACTUS. Models and Methods for the Evaluation and the Optimal Application of Battery Charging and Switching Technologies for Electric Busses, IFAK Magdeburg-Fraunhofer IML Stuttgart, Silesian University of Technology Katowice, Magdeburg-Stuttgart-Katowice 2012-2015
6. Janecki, R., et al.: The technical and operational aspects of the introduction of electric-powered buses to the public. In: Janecki, R., Krawiec, S., Sierpiński, G. (eds.) Contemporary Transportation Systems. Selected Theoretical and Practical Problems. The Co-modality of Transportation, pp. 163–186. Wyd. Politechniki Śląskiej, Gliwice (2013)
7. Karoń, G., Mikulski, J.: Transportation Systems Modelling as Planning, Organisation and Management for Solutions Created with ITS. In: Mikulski, J. (ed.) TST 2011. CCIS, vol. 239, pp. 277–290. Springer, Heidelberg (2011)
8. Karoń, G., Mikulski, J.: Problems of ITS Architecture Development and ITS Implementation in Upper-Silesian Conurbation in Poland. In: Mikulski, J. (ed.) TST 2012. CCIS, vol. 329, pp. 183–198. Springer, Heidelberg (2012)
9. Karoń, G., Mikulski, J.: Forecasts for Technical Variants of ITS Projects – Example of Upper-Silesian Conurbation. In: Mikulski, J. (ed.) TST 2013. CCIS, vol. 395, pp. 67–74. Springer, Heidelberg (2013)
10. Kalasova, A., Krchova, Z.: Telematics applications and their influence on the human factor. Transport Problems 8(2), 89–94 (2013)

Relationship between Vehicle Stream
in the Circular Roadway of a One-Lane Roundabout
and Traffic Volume on the Roundabout at Peak Hour

Elżbieta Macioszek

Silesian University of Technology
Krasińskiego 8, 40-019 Katowice, Poland
Elzbieta.Macioszek@polsl.pl

Abstract. One-lane roundabouts are popular mainly due to high traffic capacity and the opportunities for ensuring a high level of road traffic safety to the users. Furthermore, they have been very often used as an effective means of reducing the traffic. This paper presents the analysis of relationships of a one-lane roundabout on the main factors that determine its value, such as total traffic volume that unloads the intersection at a particular external diameter of the roundabout. The effect of the study is development of a nomogram of traffic capacity for one-lane roundabouts.

Keywords: one-lane roundabouts, roundabouts capacity, road traffic engineering.

1 Introduction

One of the basic characteristics which determine the usefulness of an intersection under specific road and traffic conditions is its traffic capacity. According to the definition adopted in Poland [23], the actual traffic capacity of the roundabout is considered as a sum of traffic intensities at the inlets to the roundabout that occur if, with the even increase in intensities at all inlets (the constant directional structure and proportions between inlets), the traffic capacity of one of the inlets will be exceeded. This definition shows that, on the one hand, traffic capacity should be considered as a random variable which is affected by a number of various random factors, which include in particular geometrical characteristics of the intersection, properties of the traffic streams at the inlets as well as psychophysiological characteristics of drivers. On the other hand, the awareness of the effect of the number of factors with random nature causes that the physical phenomenon has a character much similar to deterministic.

Based on the previous studies carried out by the author [7-16, 25], concerning roundabout traffic capacity, the paper analyses the relationships between traffic capacity and main factors that determine its value i.e. total traffic volume that in the intersection at a specific external diameter of the roundabout. The main determinant of traffic capacity in a roundabout is traffic capacity of its circular roadway.

J. Mikulski (Ed.): TST 2014, CCIS 471, pp. 110–119, 2014.

2   One-Lane Roundabout Capacity – A Literature Study

The behaviour of the vehicle streams, both in the country (among others: [5], [6], [17-19], [21], [22], [24]) and abroad (among others: [2], [3], [20]) and the problems of traffic capacity has been a focus of numerous scientific and research studies. The review of the related literature in this field revealed that traffic capacity of one-lane roundabouts:

- according to a study by W. Brilon, B. Stuwe, R. Bondzio (Germany) [3], ranges from 1,500-2,500 (2,800) E·h^{-1}. If total traffic volume of the vehicles from all the inlets does not exceed these values, there is no need for evaluation of traffic capacity of the roundabout. Higher values in the above ranges can be achieved at a substantial proportion of the dextral relation,
- according to W. Brilon (Germany) [2], for mini-roundabouts, this value is 20,000 P·24h^{-1}, and, in the case of small roundabouts, it is 25,000 P·24h^{-1},
- according to another German study [20], traffic capacity is 1,600 P·h^{-1} (15,000-25,000 P·24h^{-1}),
- according to R. Akcelik (Australia) [1], it reaches   2,570-2,620 P·h^{-1}. Furthermore, the first value is achieved at the directional structure of: L=0%, S=100%, R=0%, whereas in the second value, these proportions are: L=20%, S=60%, R=20% (where: L- to the left, S – to the straight, R – to the right),
- according to R. Camus et al. (Italy) [4], one-lane four-inlet roundabouts with external diameter of D_z =30.0 m reaches traffic capacity of 2,810 - 4,015 Ph^{-1}.

3   Relationship between Vehicle Stream in the Circular Roadway of a One-Lane Roundabout and Traffic Volume on the Roundabout at Peak Hour

Based on the results of empirical studies, the relationships were analyzed between the vehicle flow moving on the circular roadways with different values of the external diameters and total traffic volume on the intersection at peak hour (see Fig. 1 to Fig. 7). The values of capacities was submitted in E/h because of facilitate the ability to perform comparisons of traffic flows on different one-lane roundabouts with different loads and traffic flows.

The functions determined differ for individual cases of one-lane roundabouts with different values of external diameters. The common feature of the functions obtained is their form: polynomial of degree 2.

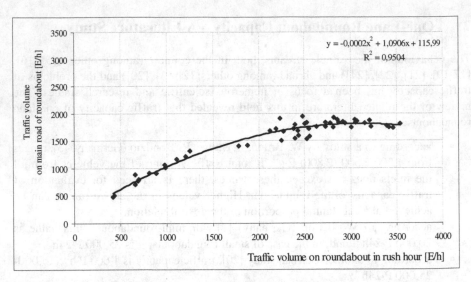

Fig. 1. Traffic volume on main road of roundabout about $D_z = 24,00$ m as a function of total traffic volume on roundabout in rush hour [own study]

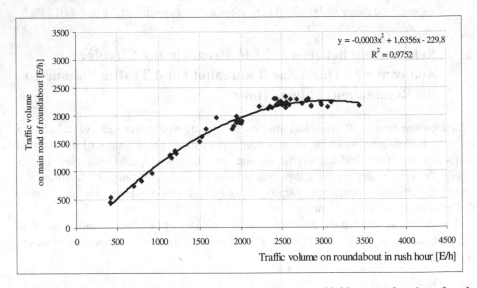

Fig. 2. Traffic volume on main road of roundabout about $D_z = 30,00$ m as a function of total traffic volume on roundabout in rush hour [own study]

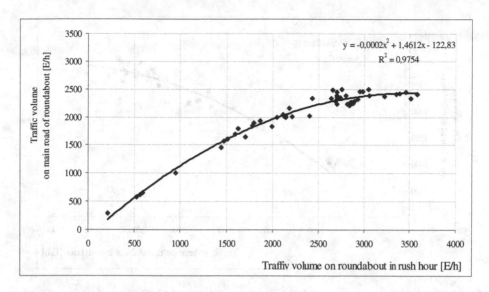

Fig. 3. Traffic volume on main road of roundabout about $D_z = 32,00$ m as a function of total traffic volume on roundabout in rush hour [own study]

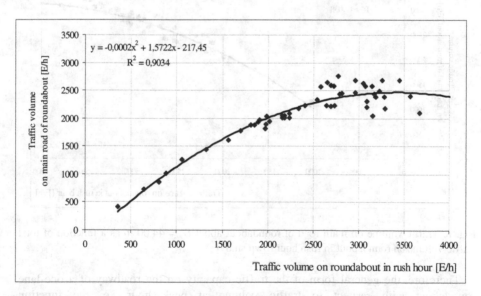

Fig. 4. Traffic volume on main road of roundabout about $D_z = 34,00$ m as a function of total traffic volume on roundabout in rush hour [own study]

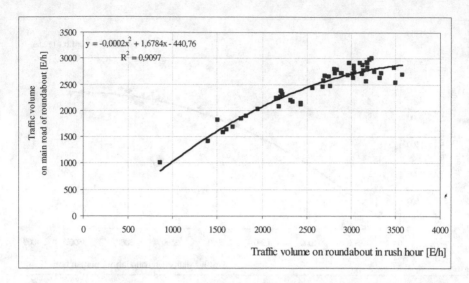

Fig. 5. Traffic volume on main road of roundabout about $D_z = 43,00$ m as a function of total traffic volume on roundabout in rush hour [own study]

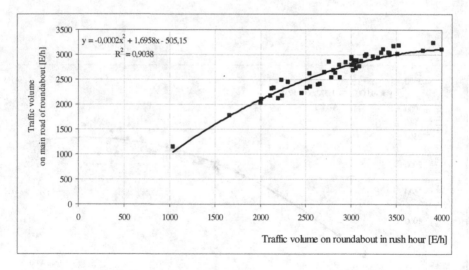

Fig. 6. Traffic volume on main road of roundabout about $D_z = 44,00$ m as a function of total traffic volume on roundabout in rush hour [own study]

Therefore, the general form of the traffic capacity on the roadway of a one-lane roundabout with respect to traffic volume at peak hour i.e. the function $Q_{jr} = f(Q_{szcz\_sk})$ can be rewritten using a square function as [7]:

$$Q_{jr} = A_1 \cdot Q_{szcz\_sk}^2 + A_2 \cdot Q_{szcz\_sk} + A_3 \ [E \cdot h^{-1}], \tag{1}$$

where:

Q_{jr} - traffic volume on main road of roundabout [E·h^{-1}],

A_1, A_2, A_3 - equation coefficients,

Q_{szcz_sk} - traffic volume on roundabout in rush hour [E·h^{-1}].

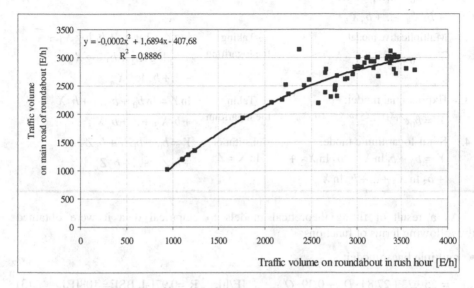

Fig. 7. Traffic volume on main road of roundabout about $D_z = 45,00$ m as a function of total traffic volume on roundabout in rush hour [own study]

It should be noted that the maximum of this function determines maximum value of vehicle traffic capacity that can be present on the roadway of a one-lane roundabout at specific geometry features, that is, it represents conditions of traffic capacity. Therefore, in each case, the highest values of traffic capacities in the roundabout can be evaluated using the following relationship [7]:

$$C_{jr} \cong Q_{jr\_max}\left(Q_{szcz\_sk}, Q_{jr}\right) = \left(-\frac{A_2}{2 \cdot A_1}, \quad -\frac{A_2^2 - 4 \cdot A_1 \cdot A_3}{4 \cdot A_1}\right) \quad [E \cdot h^{-1}], \qquad (2)$$

where: all designation as above.

The fact that the maximum traffic capacities of the roadways of one-lane roundabouts differ, depending on the geometrical characteristics of the object studied, demonstrates that the geometrical features of the intersection (including the external diameter) have the effect on the value of maximum traffic capacity on the roadway of the roundabout. Thus, the results obtained might represent the basis for development of nomogram of traffic capacity for one-lane roundabouts at specific values of traffic capacities at the intersection at peak time. In order to develop a nomogram of traffic capacity for one-lane roundabouts, the analysis used theoretical models presented in Table 1.

Table 1. Forms of theoretical models included in analysis. Source: own study based on [26].

L. p.	The form of model before transformation	Method of transformation	The form of model after transformation
1.	Multiple linear model: $Y = b_0 + b_1 X_1 + b_2 X_2 + b_3 X_3 + ... + b_n X_n$	-	-
2.	Multiplicative model: $Y = b_0 \cdot X_1^{b_1} \cdot X_2^{b_2} \cdot X_3^{b_3} \cdot ... \cdot X_n^{bn}$	Taking the logarithm	$\log Y = \log b_0 + b_1 \log X_1 + b_2 \log X_2 + b_3 \log X_3 + ... + b_n \log X_n$
3.	Exponential model: $Y = b_0 e^{b_1 X_1 + b_2 X_2 + b_3 X_3 + ... + b_n X_n}$	Taking the logarithm	$\ln Y = \ln b_0 + b_1 X_1 + b_2 X_2 + b_3 X_3 + ... + b_n X_n$
4.	Semi-logarithmic model: $Y = b_0 + b_1 \ln X_1 + b_2 \ln X_2 + b_3 \ln X_3 + ... + b_n \ln X_n$	Substitution: $\ln X = Z$	$Y = b_0 + b_1 Z_1 + b_2 Z_2 + b_3 Z_3 + ... + b_n Z_n$

As a result of fitting theoretical models to empirical data it were obtained the following forms of functions:

- multiple linear model:

$$C_{jr} = 259{,}73 + 27{,}84 \cdot D_z + 0{,}39 \cdot Q_{szcz\_sk} \text{ [E/h]},\quad R^2=0{,}97[\text{-}], \text{ BSE}= 108[\text{E}], \tag{3}$$

- multiplicative model:

$$C_{jr} = 12{,}19 \cdot D_z^{0{,}48} \cdot Q_{szcz\_sk}^{0{,}44} \quad \text{[E/h]}, R^2=0{,}97[\text{-}], \text{BSE}=1[\text{E}], \tag{4}$$

- exponential model:

$$C_{jr} = 6{,}86 \cdot e^{0{,}01 \cdot D_z + 0{,}0002 \cdot Q_{szcz\_sk}} \text{ [E/h]}, \quad R^2=0{,}95[\text{-}], \text{BSE}=1[\text{E}], \tag{5}$$

- semi-logarithmic model:

$$C_{jr} = -9755{,}21 + 1226{,}21 \cdot \ln(D_z) + 988{,}13 \cdot \ln(Q_{szcz\_sk}) \text{ [E/h]}, \tag{6}$$
$$R^2=0{,}98[\text{-}], \text{BSE}=84 \text{ [E]},$$

Based on the quality measures for adjustment of the models to the empirical data, it can be concluded that the best adjustment can be found for the semi-logarithmic (at determination coefficient of $R^2=0.98[\text{-}]$ and standard estimation error BSE=84 [E] - equation 6). Based on a semi-logarithmic model, the study developed the ranges in he nomogram for one-lane roundabouts (Fig. 8).

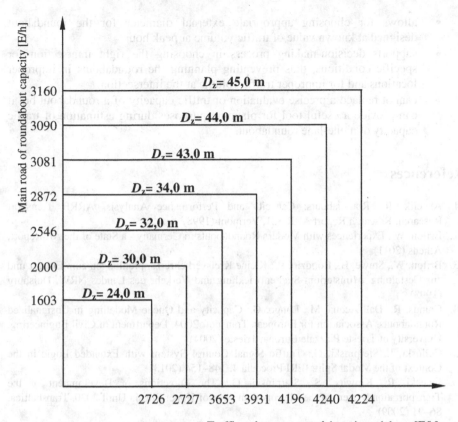

Fig. 8. The nomogram specifying capacity of one lane roundabouts [own study]

The use the nomogram of traffic capacity for one-lane roundabouts presented in the study offers opportunities for quick determination of the values of traffic capacity for an intersection for specific traffic volume at peak hour. This type of charts can be useful in the process of geometrical design of intersections at specific traffic conditions.

4   Conclusion

The simplicity of the structure of a one-lane roundabout and its values in the field of high traffic capacity and high level of road traffic safety caused that these solutions have been often used in Polish cities. Apart from the build-up area, they also meet the expectations of both designers and users. The nomogram of traffic capacity developed and presented in the paper for one-lane roundabouts:

- allows for quick determination of the values of traffic capacity at the intersection for specific value of traffic volume at peak hour,

- allows for choosing appropriate external diameter for the roundabout designed at known value of traffic volume at peak hour,
- supports decision-making process in choosing the right intersection for specific conditions, thus preventing planning the roundabouts in improper locations and for improper traffic volume at the intersection,
- cannot replace a precise evaluation of traffic capacity of a roundabout but it can provide a useful tool for planning purposes during estimation of traffic capacity of a one-lane roundabout.

References

1. Akcelik, R.: Roundabouts: Capacity and Performance Analysis. ARRB Transport Research, Research Report ARR 321, Vermont (1998)
2. Brilon, W.: Experiences with Modern Roundabouts in Germany - a State of the Art Report, Athens (2011)
3. Brilon, W., Stuwe, B., Bondzio, R.: Kleine Kreisverkehre-Empfehlungen zum Einsatz und zur Gestaltung. Ministerium Stadtentwicklung und Verkehr des Landes NRW, Duisburg (1993)
4. Camus, R., Dall'Acqua, M., Longo, G.: Capacity and Queue Modelling in Unsignalized Roundabouts. Association for European Transport 2004, Department of Civil Engineering, University of Trieste Piazzale Europa, Trieste (2004)
5. Celiński, I., Sierpiński, G.: Traffic Signal Control System with Extended Logic in the Context of the Modal Split. IERI Procedia 4, 148–154 (2013)
6. Janecki, R., Krawiec, S., Sierpiński, G.: The Directions of Development of the Transportation System of the Metropolitan Area of Upper Silesia Until 2030. Transbaltica, 86–91 (2009)
7. Macioszek, E.: Modele Przepustowości Wlotów Skrzyżowań Typu Rondo w Warunkach Wzorcowych (Models of Traffic Capacity in Roundabout Inlets in Ideal Conditions). Open Access Library 3(21), 1–260 (2013)
8. Macioszek, E.: Analysis of the Effect of Congestion in the Lanes at the Inlet to the Two-Lane Roundabout on Traffic Capacity of the Inlet. In: Mikulski, J. (ed.) TST 2013. CCIS, vol. 395, pp. 97–104. Springer, Heidelberg (2013)
9. Macioszek, E.: Geometrical Determinants of Car Equivalents for Heavy Vehicles Crossing Circular Intersections. In: Mikulski, J. (ed.) TST 2012. CCIS, vol. 329, pp. 221–228. Springer, Heidelberg (2012)
10. Macioszek, E.: The Influence of Motorcycling and Cycling on Small One-Lane Roundabouts Capacity. In: Mikulski, J. (ed.) TST 2011. CCIS, vol. 239, pp. 291–298. Springer, Heidelberg (2011)
11. Macioszek, E., Sierpiński, G., Czapkowski, L.: Methods of Modeling the Bicycle Traffic Flows on the Roundabouts. In: Mikulski, J. (ed.) TST 2010. CCIS, vol. 104, pp. 115–124. Springer, Heidelberg (2010)
12. Macioszek, E., Sierpiński, G., Czapkowski, L.: Problems and Issues with Running the Cycle Traffic through the Roundabouts. In: Mikulski, J. (ed.) TST 2010. CCIS, vol. 104, pp. 107–114. Springer, Heidelberg (2010)

13. Macioszek, E.: Safe Road Traffic on Roundabouts as an Element Assisting Efficient Road Transportation System Development in the Upper Silesia Region. In: Janecki, R., Krawiec, S., Sierpiński, G. (eds.) Contemporary Transportation Systems. Selected Theoretical and Practical Problems. the Transportation as the Factor of the Socio-Economic Development of the Regions. Monograph, vol. 386, pp. 85–95. Silesian University of Technology, Gliwice (2012)
14. Macioszek, E.: Road Traffic Safety as an Element Creating Mobility Culture in Cities. In: Janecki, R., Sierpiński, G. (eds.) Contemporary Transportation Systems. Selected Theoretical and Practical Problems. New mobility Culture. Monograph, vol. 324, pp. 61–71. ilesian University of Technology, Gliwice (2011)
15. Macioszek, E.: The Passenger Car Equivalent Factor for Heavy Vehicles on Roundabouts. In: Janecki, R., Sierpiński, G. (eds.) Contemporary Transportation Systems. Selected Theoretical and Practical Problems. The Development of Transportation Systems. Monograph, vol. 256, pp. 127–137. Silesian University of Technology, Gliwice (2010)
16. Macioszek, E.: Model Ruchu na Małych Rondach dla Potrzeb Obliczania Przepustowości (The Traffic Model for Small Roundabouts Capacity Calculation). Rozprawa doktorska. Instytut Inżynierii Lądowej i Wodnej Politechniki Wrocławskiej. Raport serii PRE nr 15/2006, Wrocław (2007)
17. Macioszek, E.: Wpływ Wybranych Cech Geometrycznych na Wartość Odstępu Czasu Pomiędzy Pojazdami Wjeżdżającymi z Kolejki na Wlotach Małych Rond. Transport Miejski i Regionalny 9, 18–23 (2008)
18. Macioszek, E., Woch, J.: The Follow-up Time Issue on Small Roundabouts. Transport Problems. International Scientific Journal 3, 25–31 (2008)
19. Macioszek, E.: Graniczny Odstęp Czasu Jako Jeden z Parametrów Procesu Decyzyjnego w Obsłudze Pojazdów z Wlotów Rond. Transport Miejski i Regionalny 2, 8–16 (2009)
20. Mauro, R.: Calculation of Roundabouts, Capacity, Waiting Phenomena and Reliability. Springer, Heidelberg (2010)
21. Małecki, K.: Programowy Symulator do Badania Zasad Ruchu Drogowego na Skrzyżowaniu o Ruchu Okrężnym. Logistyka 3 (2012)
22. Małecki, K., Wątróbki, J.: Przepustowość skrzyżowań o ruchu okrężnym jako element logistyki miejskiej. Logistyka 5, 9–13 (2010)
23. Metoda Obliczania Przepustowości Rond. GDDKiA, Warszawa (2004)
24. Sierpiński, G.: Revision of the Modal Split of Traffic Model. In: Mikulski, J. (ed.) TST 2013. CCIS, vol. 395, pp. 338–345. Springer, Heidelberg (2013)
25. Szczuraszek, T., Macioszek, E.: Proportion of Vehicles Moving Freely Depending on Traffic Volume and Proportion of Trucks and Buses. The Baltic Journal of Road and Bridge Engineering 8(2), 133–141 (2013)
26. Zeliaś, A., Pawelek, B., Wanat, S.: Metody statystyczne. Zadania i sprawdziany. PWE, Warszawa (2002)

Automatic Control Systems
and Control of Vibrations in Vehicles Car

Rafał Burdzik, Łukasz Konieczny, and Błażej Adamczyk

Silesian University of Technology,
Gliwice, Poland
{Rafal.Burdzik,Lukasz.Konieczny,Blazej.Adamczyk}@polsl.pl

Abstract. Growing customer requirements for comfort of vehicles more often become refer to vibrations that affect the people in transport. At the same time each car put into service must has the appropriate parameters traction to the road surface responsible for the safety. Due to the nature of the vibration transmitted to the vehicle body vibration requirements are of the often contradictory. Therefore, an intense research on modern control systems, active vibration damping system parameters are require. This paper presents the advantages and disadvantages associated with the suspension systems of vehicles of conventional and active and semiactiv based on the elements of a controlled characteristics of both elastic elements and damping. It was suggested the possibilities of advanced signal processing methods application developed in vibration research.

Keywords: automatic control system, active and semiactive suspension system.

1 Introduction

Vibration propagate and influence people via the vehicle structure, i.e. the frame or the body. Studying vibration phenomena in automotive vehicles should primarily pertain to their effects on men and the chosen structural elements of a vehicle [1]. In the scope of the impact on structural elements, one should perceive vibrations in terms of destructive factors, which can be affected on in the technical states considered reliability states of a motor vehicle [2]. Mechanical vibrations occurring in a working environment may be classified as general vibrations, i.e. those affecting the human organism via lower extremities, the pelvis and the back. The second category comprises local vibrations affecting the human organism through upper limbs. Vibrations are also a very ample source of information on the technical condition, and hence they are commonly used in diagnostic systems. The human exposure to vibrations is depended on time, energy and dynamics of the transfer vibration.

The compromise between comfort and safety of the vehicle driving is very difficult to achieve [3-4]. For the driving safety it is extremely important to provide constant contact of vehicle wheels to the road surface. It determines the high damping coefficient. For the comfort of the passengers it is important to minimize the vibration perception. It can be achieved by the gradual and smooth vibration absorbing. The driver

J. Mikulski (Ed.): TST 2014, CCIS 471, pp. 120–129, 2014.

and passengers exposure to whole-body vibration of the vehicle can affect from short-term body discomfort and inefficient performance to longterm physiological damage [5]. The vibrations of the vehicle body are main problem in ride comfort.

The vibration exposure of the car depends on road roughness, speed, engine and powertrain parameters. To provide the best vibration isolation for the passengers the damping properties of the suspension have to be changeable to the drive condition. At the present the numerous automotive companies offer adaptive shock absorbers or active suspensions. It contains many of mechatronics systems and elements which are perfect to adjust the damping parameters of the suspension to the drive condition [2].

For the proper analysis of vibration or acoustics signals, as the result of wave propagation, it is important to consider material properties and technologies and to use correct methods of signal processing [5-13].

Humans are exposed to whole-body vibration in many means of transport, such as: passenger cars, buses, trains, trams, ships, even airplanes. The whole-body vibration caused a subject discomfort, fatigue and physical pains and it can affect on driving safety. There are many models of vehicle dynamics but it is much harder to find complex model of human-vehicle system. The reason is the fact that it is difficult to accurately estimate the behaviour of the human body under vibration, because it is a complex active dynamic system. The paper [14] presents the vibration model with prediction of the characteristics of the three reactions (physical, physiological and psychological), of the human exposed to a vertical sinusoidal wave force. It was assumed that the characteristics of the vibration of the human body are explained by the three reactions when the human body is exposed to some vibration environments:

— physical reaction expressed by the transmissibility of the vibrations of each part of the human body to a standard part,
— physiological reaction manifested in terms of blood pressure, heart rate, etc.,
— psychological reaction as illustrated by manifestation of the different symptoms induced by vibration.

The paper [14] presents basic structure for a synthetic vibration model of human beings. It was assumed that there are some linear relations between the physical, physiological and psychological reactions, so that a multiple regression analysis could be applied to analyse these relations. In the synthetic vibration model, the physical reaction can be simulated by equations of motion formalized by using Lagrange's equation, and the physiological and psychological reactions can be predicted by multiple regression equations defined through the multiple regression analysis (Fig. 1). In the multiple regression equations, the physical reaction directly relates to explanatory variables to predict the physiological and psychological reaction.

Based on the synthetic vibration model it can be assumed that a two-dimensional model projected on the central plane, which is a midsagittal plane, of the human body would simulate the realistic vibration behaviour of the human body. The paper [14] presents two-dimensional vibration model consisting of masses, rigid links, springs and dampers with nine degrees of freedom. During the investigation described in [14] the human vibration model was installed on a concentrated frame of two-dimensional automobile vibration model [15] to simulate the vibration behaviour of a human body riding in an automobile (Fig. 2).

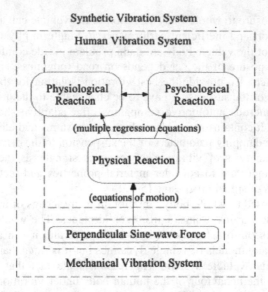

Fig. 1. A synthetic vibration model for human beings [14]

The paper [15] assumed prediction of unknown psychological and physiological reactions of a person riding the two-dimensional automobile vibrating at a given frequency, by using the multiple regression equation representing the relations between the psychological and physical reactions, and between the physiological and physical reactions.

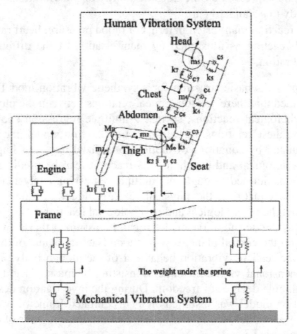

Fig. 2. A human vibration model riding in an automobile vibration model (right) [15]

2   Research on Vehicle Vibration

There are many publications about research on vibration in different kind of vehicles. The large possibilities of usage of vibration signals generate many conceptions and applications of systems based on vibration in cars. It is important to find proper vibration estimators due to destination of the system. It can be defined estimators based on amplitude, frequency or time-frequency representation of the vibration signal (Fig. 3). The previous publications presents applications of signal processing for determination of estimators of vehicle vibration signals [16-17].

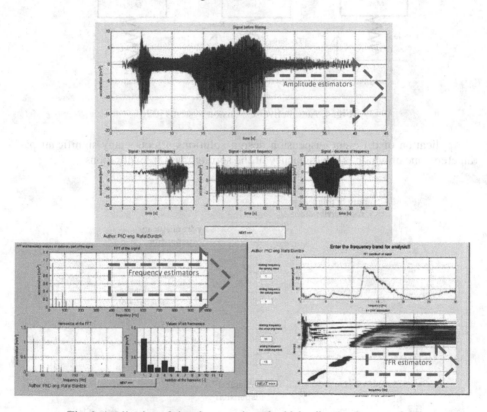

Fig. 3. Application of signal processing of vehicle vibration [own study]

3   Isolation of Vibration

In order to meet growing requirements, contemporary automotive suspension systems are highly complex mechatronic units. There are semi-active, active and adaptive suspension systems being developed and improved on an ongoing basis. Unlike passive suspension, all the aforementioned types enable adapting the suspension parameters to individual road conditions and driving styles [18-22]. Suspension control systems adjust the characteristics of elastic and damping components to match preset criteria, such as comfort or sport driving, for instance. In the most highly advanced active systems, those equipped with actuators, the said solutions require considerable power input of even up to 20 kW.

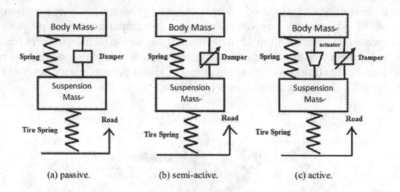

(a) passive.	(b) semi-active.	(c) active.

Fig. 4. Automotive suspension systems [22]

Application of different suspension design solutions affects many significant parameters, one of which is the frequency of the sprung mass free vibrations.

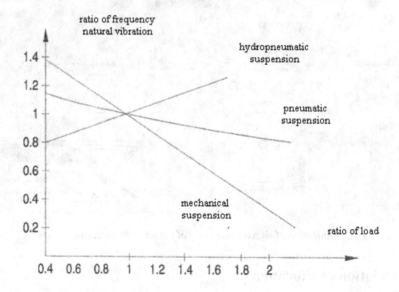

Fig. 5. Impact of the vehicle load variations on a change of the sprung mass free vibration frequency [23]

With regard to a classic example of passive mechanical suspension system, the frequency declines as the load rises. When considering pneumatic suspension (gas springs of constant gas volume), the frequency also decreases as the load increases, but not as much as in the previous case discussed. As for hydropneumatic suspension systems (gas spring of constant gas mass), frequency of the sprung mass free vibrations rises as the vehicle load does so. In order to exemplify the solutions applied in controlled suspension systems installed in automotive vehicles, adaptive pneumatic and hydropneumatic suspension types have been discussed.

4   Pneumatic Suspension Systems

On of such solutions is the pneumatic suspension which enables the static ground clearance value and its dynamic changes to be set independently (self-levelling depending on the suspension control algorithm). This solution has been applied in the following cars:

* Jaguar XJ featuring the Computer Active Technology Suspension (CATS),
* Volkswagen Phanteon featuring 4CL (4 Corner Luftfederung) and CDC (Continuous Damping Control) systems,
* Audi Allroad 4-Level.

Pneumatic suspension systems include multiple components, the most important of which are actuating units comprising the pneumatic system, i.e. the pressure air tank along with its equipment, the engine and actuators being pneumatic columns. The suspension control system operates via a number of sensors, such as the front and rear axle height sensors, wheel and body acceleration sensors, steering wheel turning sensor etc. An element which monitors the suspension system operation is a high performance control unit.

In adaptive pneumatic suspension systems, it is the principles of control that condition the way in which the suspension works (vehicle ground clearance setting). Values of adjustable ground clearance have been provided in the following table:

Table 1. Ground clearance values in adaptive pneumatic suspension systems [24]

Design solution	Clearance			
	Low [mm]	Normal [mm]	High 1 [mm]	High 2 [mm]
4-Level Audi Allroad	-25		+25	+41
4 CL VW Phaeton	-15	0	+25	-
Jaguar XJ	-15		-	-

The function of ground clearance adjustment while driving is often available in both the manual and the automatic mode. The control algorithm adjusts the ground clearance depending on the vehicle speed, and in each case, after a certain preset speed is exceeded the vehicle is automatically lowered. It causes the vehicle centre of gravity to move lower, thus improving its traction properties on higher speeds and reducing aerodynamic drag, which leads to reduced fuel consumption, at the same time. Fig. 6 illustrates sample principles according to which the pneumatic suspension is controlled in Audi Allroad.

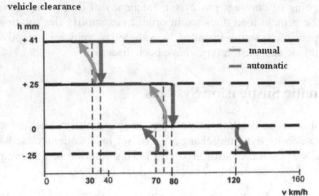

Fig. 6. Ground clearance control in Audi Allroad [24]

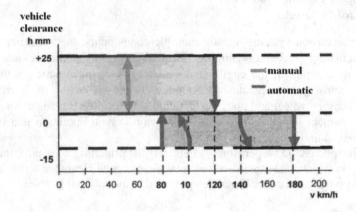

Fig. 7. Ground clearance control in WV Phaeton [24]

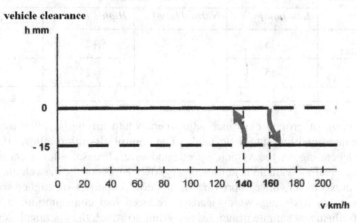

Fig. 8. Ground clearance control in Jaguar XJ [24]

Operation of an adaptive suspension system requires appropriate pressure values to be applied in the pneumatic system. A sample collation of values of this parameter for the suspension systems discussed has been provided in Table 2.

Table 2. Pressure and volume values applied in pneumatic suspension systems [24]

Design solution	Pneumatic system			Pressure vessel system	
	Operating pressure [bar]	Residual pressure [bar]	Maximum pressure [bar]	Volume [Litres]	Operating pressure [bar]
4-Level Audi Allroad	No data	3,5	13,5	6,5	16
4 CL VW Phaeton	No data	3,5	20	5	16
Jaguar XJ	15	3	17,5	4,5	9-15

5   Hydropneumatic Suspension Systems

Besides pneumatic suspension systems, there are also hydropneumatic systems where the functions of actuating units are performed by hydraulic cylinders. Unlike pneumatic suspension (based on springs of variable and controlled gas volume), the systems in question feature gas springs of constant gas mass.

Table 3. Ground clearance values in adaptive and smart hydropneumatic suspension systems [24]

Design solution	Clearance		
	Low [mm]	Normal [mm]	High [mm]
Citroen C5 Hydroactive 3	Front -10 Rear -6	0	+ 13
Citroen C6 Intelligent suspension: active suspension with electronically controlled springing and damping	The suspension control unit has two operating modes: "SkyHook" and "RoadHook". In specified conditions, this system can automatically lower the vehicle by around a dozen millimetres from 110 kph, thus optimising high-speed steering as well as fuel consumption.		

The solutions discussed are related to the adaptive properties (vehicle ground clearance changing) of an automotive suspension system. Such systems may additionally feature elements of controlled elasticity and damping characteristics, thus providing comprehensive smart suspension solutions (Citroen C6).

6   Conclusion

The perception of vibration is extremely important for evaluation of exposure to whole-body vibration in means of transport. Taken into consideration the impact of vibration on driving safety it is very important to prevent driver and occupants from vibration. The constant evolution in vibroacoustics methods and measurements equipments allow to design new damping and isolating system for vehicles.

The paper presents innovative solutions unconventional controlled suspension (pneumatic and hydropneumatic), increasing comfort and safety. Such solutions are often used in conjunction with damping control systems and allow you to adjust the suspension characteristics variables vibration excitation of the vehicle.

The paper, with group of previous papers of the authors, discusses novel approach to isolation of vibration in motor vehicles. The developed methods of signal processing with innovative systems of vibration damping allow to elaborate new integrated system for vehicle vibration management.

References

1. Maciejewski, M., Osmolski, W., Slaski, G.: Importance of Road Model in Simulation of Car Aerodynamics in a Wind-tunnel. In: Proceedings of 12th European Simulation Symposium, pp. 405–409 (2012)
2. Girtler, J., Ślęzak, M.: Four-state Stochastic Model of Changes in the Reliability States of a Motor Vehicle. Eksploatacja i Niezawodnosc – Maintenance and Reliability 15(2), 156–160 (2013)
3. Slaski, G.: A Concept of an Integrated Suspension Control Logic Architecture and its Testin. In: Proceedings of 5th International Industrial Simulation Conference, pp. 201–205 (2007)
4. Jurecki, R., Stańczyk, T.: The Test Methods and the Reaction Time of Drivers. Eksploatacja i Niezawodnosc - Maintenance and Reliability (3), 84–91 (2011)
5. Nader, M.: The Influence of Mechanical Vibrations on the Driver's Body. Journal of Biomechanics 27(6), 716 (1994)
6. Dąbrowski, D., Batko, W., Cioch, W.: Model of the Gears Based on Multibody System and its Validation by Application of Non-contact Methods. Acta Physica Polonica A 123(6), 1016–1019 (2013)
7. Cioch, W., Knapik, O., Leskow, J.: Finding a frequency signature for a cyclostationary signal with applications to wheel bearing diagnostics. Mechanical Systems and Signal Processing 38(1), Special Issue: SI 55–64 (2013)
8. Kłaczyński, M., Wszołek, T.: Artificial Intelligence and Learning Systems Methods in Supporting Long-Term Acoustic Climate Monitoring. Acta Physica Polonica A 123(6), 1024–1028 (2013)
9. Kłaczyński, M., Wszołek, T.: Detection and Classification of Selected Noise Sources in Long-Term Acoustic Climate Monitoring. Acta Physica Polonica A 121(1-A), A-179–A-182 (2012)
10. Dąbrowski, Z., Deuszkiewicz, P.: Nonlinear Dynamic Model of a Carbon-Epoxy Composite Structure. In: 20th International Congress On Sound & Vibration (2013)
11. Blacha, Ł., et al.: Application of the weakest link analysis to the area of fatigue design of steel welded joints. Engineering Failure Analysis 35 Special Issue: SI, 665–677 (2013)

12. Lisiecki, A.: Welding of Titanium Alloy by Disk Laser. In: Proc. of SPIE. Laser Technology 2012: Applications of Lasers, vol. 8703, p. 87030T (2013)
13. Węgrzyn, T., et al.: Control Over the Steel Welding Structure Parameters by Micro-Jet Cooling. Archives of Metallurgy And Materials 57(3), 679–684 (2012)
14. Kubo, M., et al.: An investigation into a synthetic vibration model for humans: An investigation into a mechanical vibration human model constructed according to the relations between the physical, psychological and physiological reactions of humans exposed to vibration. International Journal of Industrial Ergonomics 27, 219–232 (2001)
15. Nishiyama, S.: Development of simulation system on vehicle±occupant dynamic interaction. Transactions of the Japan Society of Mechanical Engineers Seriese-C 59 568, 1004–1012 (1993)
16. Burdzik, R.: Implementation of multidimensional identification of signal characteristics in the analysis of vibration properties of an automotive vehicle's floor panel. Eksploatacja i Niezawodnosc – Maintenance and Reliability Volume 16(3), 439–445 (2014)
17. Burdzik, R.: Identification of structure and directional distribution of vibration transferred to car-body from road roughness. Journal of Vibroengineering 16(1), 324–333 (2014)
18. Dixon, J.: The Shock Absorber Handbook, 2nd edn. Professional Engineering Publishing Ltd. (2007)
19. Balamurugan, L., Jancirani, J., Eltantawie, M.: Generalized Magnetorheological (MR) Damper Model and its Application in Semi-active Control of Vehicle Suspension System. International Journal of Automotive Technology 15(3), 419–427 (2014)
20. Snamina, J., Kowal, J., Orkisz, P.: Active Suspension Based on Low Dynamic Stiffness. Acta Physica Polonica A 123(6), 1118–1122 (2013)
21. Ho, C., Lang, Z.Q., Sapinski, B.: Vibration isolation using nonlinear damping implemented by a feedback-controlled MR damper. Smart Materials And Structures 22(10) Special Issue: SI, Article Number: 105010 (2013)
22. Seung-Bok, C., Yun-Hae, K., Prasad, Y.: Development of an Novel Adaptive Suspension System Based on Ball-Screw Mechanism. Applied Mechanics and Materials 477-478, 128 (2001)
23. Kowal, J.: Sterowanie drganiami. Gutenberg (1996)
24. Ł ęgiewicz, J.: Zawieszenia półaktywne, Auto Moto Serwis 1/2005, 29–32 (2005)
25. Karoń, G., Mikulski, J.: Transportation Systems Modelling as Planning, Organisation and Management for Solutions Created with ITS. In: Mikulski, J. (ed.) TST 2011. CCIS, vol. 239, pp. 277–290. Springer, Heidelberg (2011)
26. Mikulski, J.: Introduction of telematics for transport. In: Proceedings on 9th International Conference ELEKTRO 2012, Rajecke Teplice, IEEE Catalog Number CFP1248S-ART, May 21-22, pp. 336–340 (2012), http://ieexplore.ieee.org

Schema of Inference Processes
in a Preliminary Identification of Navigational Situation
in Maritime Transport

Anna Wójcik, Paweł Banaś, and Zbigniew Pietrzykowski

Maritime University of Szczecin,
Wały Chrobrego 1-2, 70-500 Szczecin, Poland
{a.wojcik,p.banas,z.pietrzykowski}@am.szczecin.pl

Abstract. Article presents a modified inference model for the automatic communication system at sea. After an expert examinations, the inference model based on mechanism used by navigators during decisions making has been developed. The results of expert examinations have been taken into account. The schema of actions during decision making in preliminary stage of navigational situations identification was presented on the example of collision situation at sea. The key values used in the assessment of navigational safety have been included. The examples of model application have been shown by making uses of the proposed schema.

Keywords: automatic communication, fuzzy sets, safety of navigation, e-navigation.

1 Introduction

System control and management is inherent in decision making and communication processes: internal and external. The communication process generally includes the transfer of information from sender to receiver and may concern acquisition, processing, transmission and sharing the information, including selective information acquisition. The mechanisms of cooperation and negotiation in the communication process are equally important. The communication process generally includes the transmission (exchange) of information between sender and receiver, perception of a message, understanding of message content by the receiver and interaction - cooperation or negotiation - between process participants. The context and feedback are important aspects of communication, especially in cooperation or negotiation. This is the reason that the mechanisms of cooperation and negotiation in the communication processes are so important.

While the systems of automatic exchange of information, including the selection of information have already been functioning for number of years, the solution of subject of cooperation and/or negotiation processes automation has been found only in certain areas of human activities and to a limited extent. An example is e-commerce, where the schemas of negotiation dialogues for sale/purchase of certain goods or groups of goods have been developed.

J. Mikulski (Ed.): TST 2014, CCIS 471, pp. 130–136, 2014.

Automation of communication processes, including cooperation and negotiation, gives a possibility to relieve the operator from above activities and prevents decision-making mistakes caused by, among others, lack of necessary information or misinterpretation. The information overload and inherent difficulty in reaching the needed information also creates the potential hazard. Among others due to the safety and efficiency of the processes or systems control and management, the increasing attention is being given to the listed issues. While IT and ICT technologies and existing telematic solutions create a technical and technological base to build systems, the implementation of automatic communication inference process still remains problematic. The same applies to communication processes in maritime transport.

2   The Inference Processes

Issues of inference process description in maritime transport have been presented, among others, in [1-3]. During the development of the model, according the way that the navigators act: first a brief look around and classification of potentially dangerous issues and then closer look at these which may need an action. Using such approach, the automatic inference process leading to the recognition of a navigational situation could be divided into two stages:

- preliminary recognition of conditions that may cause need of communication,
- detailed recognition of navigational situation and determination of requirements for communication.

These stages are presented on the figure below as "Preliminary inference" and "Navigational situation recognition". Both of them use navigational situation information (coming from shipboard systems – AIS, ARPA, etc.). All these data are available in an accurate form that does not require interpretation of imprecise terms.

Figure 1 illustrates a modified executive algorithm used in the process of automatic communication at sea. The following functional blocks are distinguished:

- **Preliminary Inference** – program block designed to initially determine the navigational situation as safe or potentially unsafe (requiring further analysis). The CPA and TCPA parameters are used in the calculations. It is also possible to use other parameters such as ship domain.
- **Navigational Situation Recognition** – program block designed to classify the current navigational situation (right of way or lack of it, necessity of performing the manoeuvre, etc.) and determine the need of communication.
- **Communication** – a block responsible for receiving and understanding the incoming message and generating outgoing. Its structure is presented on figure 2 and described later in this chapter.

The algorithm is based on a loop where set of basic conditions is checked (incoming call, end of algorithm) and preliminary inference is performed. The values of parameters CPA and TCPA used in initial recognition of navigational situation depend on set of individual factors such as:

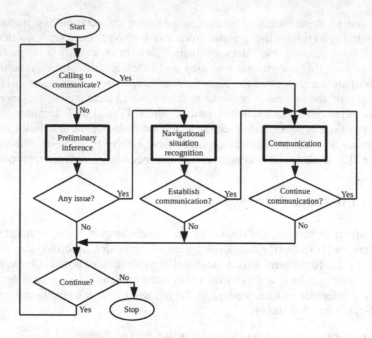

Fig. 1. Inference processes in an automatic maritime communication system [own study]

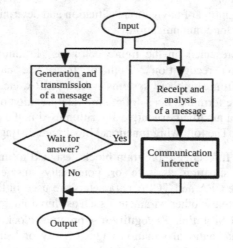

Fig. 2. Structure of "Communication" block [own study]

- ship's size,
- type of cruise,
- transported cargo,
- weather,
- geographical issues,
- local vessels traffic,
- navigator's individual preferences.

The mathematical mechanism of preliminary inference is presented in chapter 3.

If the "Preliminary inference" module will detect the possibility of too close passing, the "Navigational situation recognition" module is activated. The aim of it is to determine the type of hazard, its effects on the ship and to indicate the required action (ex. give the way, send warning to the other ship, etc.).

- **Communication Inference** – gives a basis to make a decision on further manner of communication. This module differs from the other in that is has a capability of analysing imprecise information [4]. After executed inference, new knowledge on a navigational situation is acquired.
- **Generation and Transmission of a Message** – given the inference outcome, this module prepares and sends a message to another ship or coast station.
- **Receipt and Analysis of a Message** – this module receives a message sent by another ship or coast station, then transforms it into a symbolic form, used in further stages of communication. The symbolic form will allow to further analyse a message by mathematical methods and tools (e.g. computing with words) [5].

As a result of principal inference, on the basis of a message received, the decision is made whether to continue communication or stop it. If it is to be continued, a control signal is sent to the message generation and transmission block, whose function has herein been described. This module utilizes the results of completed inference to generate a message of relevant content.

In the main loop, there is also checking whether there has been request of establishing contact, regardless of a navigational situation. Such case occurs when one navigator steering a ship calls another to establish contact, or his/her ship is called by another ship or a coast station.

3   Preliminary Inference

The first step in this model, is the preliminary inference. It is based on the analysis of the two parameters used in the assessment of safety of navigation: CPA and TCPA. In case of exceeding the limit values of both parameters (CPA_{Limit}, $TCPA_{Limit}$) for a meeting of vessels, actions are aimed at identifying navigational situation and ensuring the safety of navigation. The limit values of parameters are currently being put by the navigator to systems available on the ship. Navigator when determining these values take into account the weather conditions. In the case of the system limits for the situation of very good conditions at sea and very good visibility are pre-determined. For the specific situation sea conditions and visibility are taken into account for the determination of new parameters suggested to navigator.

In a situation of very good visibility the system having the input parameters CPA and TCPA makes classic reasoning based on the following implications:

$$\text{If } CPA < CPA_{Limit} \text{ and } TCPA < TCPA_{Limit} \text{ Then } risk \ of \ a \ collision \qquad (1)$$

In a situation of worsened conditions of visibility and sea conditions the limits are modified by the application of fuzzy set theory. Basic restrictions for these two parameters are subjected to fuzzyfication and presented in the form of fuzzy numbers using for example the triangular membership function:

$$\mu(x) = \begin{cases} 0 : x \le a \\ \dfrac{x-a}{b-a} : a \le x \le b \\ \dfrac{c-x}{c-b} : b \le x \le c \\ 1 : x \ge c \end{cases} \tag{2}$$

where the parameters a, b, c are real numbers.

Then there are various linguistic modifiers for the obtained fuzzy sets. Depending on the included conditions the modifiers might be operator of concentration (CON()), the operator pf expansion (dilution, DIL()) or contrast intensification operators (Int(), Blr()) described by the following formulas:

$$\mu_{CON(A)}(x) = Con(\mu_A(x)) = \mu_A(x)^2 \tag{3}$$

$$\mu_{DIL(A)}(x) = Dil(\mu_A(x)) = \sqrt{\mu_A(x)} \tag{4}$$

$$\mu_{INT(A)}(x) = Int(\mu_A(x)) = \begin{cases} 2(\mu_A(x))^2 : \mu_A(x) < 0.5 \\ 1 - 2(1 - \mu_A(x))^2 : \mu_A(x) \ge 0.5 \end{cases} \tag{5}$$

$$\mu_{BLR(A)}(x) = Blr(\mu_A(x)) = \begin{cases} 1 - 2(1 - \mu_A(x))^2 : \mu_A(x) < 0.5 \\ 2(\mu_A(x))^2 : \mu_A(x) \ge 0.5 \end{cases} \tag{6}$$

where $x \in X$ [6].

After an appropriate modification we received fuzzy numbers that are subjects of defuzzification process by applying the method of center of gravity and the method of half of the field. Applying the method of center of gravity the center is calculated from the figure underneath the curve plotted by the membership function and the axis OX. The value obtained with this method is as follows [7]:

$$\eta_S = \frac{\int_{x_{inf}}^{x_{sup}} \mu(x)x\,dx}{\int_{x_{inf}}^{x_{sup}} \mu(x)\,dx} \tag{7}$$

In the half field method the x_0 is calculated as a parameter for which the area under the curve defined by the membership function on the left side of x_0 is equal to the area under the curve on the right side of x_0 which is described by the following formula [7]:

$$\int_{x_{inf}}^{x_0} \mu(x)\,dx = \int_{x_0}^{x_{sup}} \mu(x)\,dx \tag{8}$$

Therefore we obtain a new values CPA_{Limit*} and $TCPA_{Limit*}$ suggested to navigator. On the basis and the inference methods we consider an implication of the form:

$$\text{If } CPA < CPA_{Limit*} \text{ and } TCPA < TCPA_{Limit*} \text{ Then } risk\ of\ a\ collision \qquad (9)$$

In the situation when the precedents of the implication are not satisfied the system generate the information *Safe situation*.

4   An Example of Scenarios

An example scenarios here presented shows how the model work. Let's consider four scenarios – one when there is no risk of collision ant three when potentially dangerous situation (risk of collision) appears:

- Detection of other ship, $CPA > CPA_{Limit}$ and $TCPA > TCPA_{Limit}$.
- Detection of other ship, $CPA < CPA_{Limit}$ and $TCPA < TCPA_{Limit}$, there is known the route of the other ship and it will turn to non-collision course in 5 minutes.
- Detection of other ship, $CPA < CPA_{Limit}$ and $TCPA < TCPA_{Limit}$.
- A change in the course of the ship and receding to a collision course was detected, $CPA < CPA_{Limit}$ and $TCPA < TCPA_{Limit}$.

The inference results and actions taken in above scenarios are shown in Table 1.

Table 1. Actions taken in examples of scenarios [own study]

Scenario nr.	Inference result	Taken actions
1.	Safe situation	No reaction.
2.	Risk of collision	1. Preliminary inference triggers Navigational situation recognition module. 2. Because of the distance and known route of other ship, take no action.
3.	Risk of collision	1. Preliminary inference triggers Navigational situation recognition module. 2. The situation was identified as crossing and own ship is a give-way ship. 3. The suggestion to change course to non-collision is displayed. 4. No communication required.
4.	Risk of collision	1. Preliminary inference triggers Navigational situation recognition module. 2. The situation was identified as dangerous. 3. The warning is displayed. 4. The warning message is send to the other ship.

5   Conclusion

Automation of communication processes gives a possibility to relieve the operator from activities related to the acquisition, processing, transmission and sharing of information necessary for system control and management processes.

The implementation of mechanisms of cooperation and negotiation, which are a part of the communication processes, requires further development of inference models.

References

1. Pietrzykowski Z., et al.: Reasoning Processes in Automatic Marine Communication System. Scientific Papers of Warsaw University of Technology, Warszawa, vol. XX (Transport) (2013) (in Polish)
2. Banaś, P., Wójcik, A., Pietrzykowski, Z.: Model of inference processes in the automatic maritime communication system. In: Mikulski, J. (ed.) TST 2013. Communications in Computer and Information Science, vol. 395, pp. 7–14. Springer, Heidelberg (2013)
3. Jazayeriy, H., et al.: A review on soft computing techniques in automated negotiation. Scientific Research and Essays 6(24), 5100–5106 (2011)
4. Pietrzykowski, Z., et al.: Information exchange automation in maritime communication. In: International Conference TransNav, Gdynia (2013)
5. Pietrzykowski, Z., Banaś, P., Wójcik, A.: Computing With Words in Communication Processes, Methods of Applied Computer Science, No 5/2011 (30), PAN Gdańsk Division, Szczecin, pp. 207–214 (2011)
6. Piegat, A.: Fuzzy modeling and control, pp. 40–46. EXIT, Warszawa (1999) (in Polish)
7. Bronsztejn, I.N., et al.: The modern compendium of mathematics, pp. 405–408. PWN, Warszawa (2009) (in Polish)

Evaluation of Unwanted Road Marking Crossing Detection Using Real-Traffic Data for Intelligent Transportation Systems

Emília Bubeníková, Mária Franeková, and Peter Holečko

University of Žilina,
Faculty of Electrical Engineering, Žilina, Slovak Republic
{emilia.bubenikova,maria.franekova,peter.holecko}@fel.uniza.sk

Abstract. The authors focus in the contribution on finding and testing effective digital image processing methods in line crossing detection systems. To verify experimental real-world results the authors used the Matlab 2013a and Digital Signal Processing Toolbox software tools. In the line detection block in the designed application the driving lane is searched using segmentation techniques suitable for line detection. The information on road position (driving lanes) has been acquired based on edge detection of guiding lines. For line detection, the proposed modifications of Hough transform and local processing methods have been used. During the testing process testing video-sequences were created with several parameters: traffic situations (day-drive, night-drive, drive on distinct road types, highway drive etc.), temporary traffic signs (presence of temporary traffic signs in form of orange lines, absence of temporary traffic signs). A change of light conditions has also been simulated during testing by adding an additional noise and by determining its effects on line detection.

Keywords: intelligent transportation system, LDWS system, image processing, Hough transform, edge detection, Sobel detector, SW realization.

1 Introduction

Currently, the development in ITS (*Intelligent Transportation Systems*) applications [1], [2], [3] is focused on support of driver services, whether because of security reasons, awareness or comfort. ITS applications are based on the use of information and telecommunications technology, and they use for its work algorithms of computer vision, namely image processing, and they have increasingly wider application in many industrial applications [4], [5]. After the initial research for this purpose, a high potential was discovered in the utilisation of Advanced Driver Assistance Systems (ADAS). For their operation, these systems utilise distinct types of sensors to gather data about vehicle and its environment and use modern methods for objects detection and recognition of threats, thereby assisting the driver while driving the vehicle [6]. The process of recognition, monitoring and interpretation of control is challenging. The quality of captured data using sensors is influenced by driving styles and conditions which can cover important information necessary for objects recognition and tracking [7]. Drivers drive their cars in distinct weather conditions (clear sunny

J. Mikulski (Ed.): TST 2014, CCIS 471, pp. 137–145, 2014.

weather, rain, snow, mist). However, processing of data has to be performed in real-time and the delay has to be below 30 milliseconds. Each step from data gathering to action execution requires significant abilities to process signal precisely and timely.

Within the contribution, the authors focused on a significant subset of ADAS, the Lane Departure Warning Systems (LDWS). These systems are located in the vehicle and based on computer vision technology they monitor the position of vehicle in the driving lane and warn the driver in case the vehicle departs or is going to depart beyond course. In case the vehicle drives from the safe zone into the warning zone, the system generates a warning for the driver. The LDWS does not intervene vehicle control and only warns the driver on possible lane departure [8]. Many LDWS were originally designed for truck drivers who are especially sensitive on exhaustion and sleepiness because of many hours lasting drives.

There are several different approaches that were gradually developed to detect lines, for example [9], [10], [11], in more detail in [13]. One set of approaches is the result of fundamental theoretically oriented research within research institutes. In parallel with these activities, an applied research performed by automotive companies is in progress by developing own systems. These systems are often company-labelled and because of competition reasons, many details of these solutions are not publically available.

The authors of the paper describe their own modified solution for road line detection based on Hough transform [12], which has been software-implemented together with other supporting programs eliminating the shortcomings of the original Hough transform.

The block scheme in Fig. 1 depicts particular problems that can influence the proper detection on horizontal traffic marking and its crossing. Grey coloured blocks were solved in the analysed SW implementation.

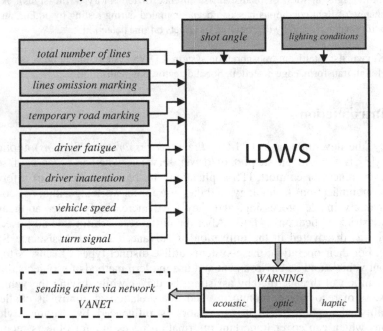

Fig. 1. Block scheme of effects on a correct detection of horizontal traffic marking [13]

2   Mathematical and Graphical Description of Proposed Solutions

A mathematical description of the modified algorithms based on Hough transformation used in SW implementation is based on the description of the line. As can be seen, the straight line is given by at least two points, for example $A=(X_1,X_2)$ a $B=(X_1',X_2')$. This means that any straight line passing through the point and must comply with the parametric equation of a line:

$$y = kx + q, \tag{1}$$

where k is the slope, and q is the shift in the y axis.

In Fig.2 is a position of a line plotted in the space of parameters k, q. Point A, B, C belong in the corresponding area of the three lines.

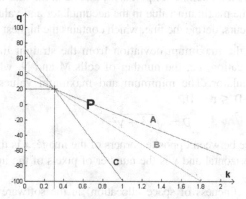

Fig. 2. Representation of line in space (k, q) [7]

Description line in the plane can be described also in polar coordinates:

$$x.\cos\theta + y.\sin\theta = r, \tag{2}$$

where r is the minimum distance from the line (at point X [x, y]) from the beginning of the coordinate system, Θ is the size of oriented angle from the positive x-axis to the half-line guided from the beginning of the coordinate system upright to the searched line. The use of normal form of line equation has the advantage that it is independent on the orientation of axes. In the processing of image information intended for the detection of lines, is the image of the one line in the matrix interpreted in terms of the ideal case (after thresholding) in the form of 0 and 1 in the Hough space (parameters (Θ, r)) as a sine waves, which intersect at one point .

Each point lying on a line is transformed into another sinusoid. All points lying on the same line created in Hough parametric space (accumulator) the amount of the sinusoid with one intersection P with parameters Θ and r that made up normal shape.

$$y = \frac{x.\cos\theta}{\sin\theta} + \frac{r}{\sin\theta} \tag{3}$$

Using the straight line equation of the normal form has the advantage of being independent of the orientation axes.

2.1   Description of Line Searching Algorithm

Input to the algorithm is an image brightness value 0 and 1. We are interested in points with brightness value logic 1. If we assume that the total number of such points K and line search algorithm (or line) is very simple and can be summarized in words:

1. We set the accumulator value to zero $A[\Theta_i, r_i] = 0$ for all values of Θ_i ,r_i , ...i.e. $i = 1,2, ..., M, j = 1,2,..., N$.
2. For each pixel in the image (x_k, y_k) $k =1,2,..., K$, whose brightness value is equal to 1 and each value Θ_i, $i = 1,2, ... M$ is calculated: $r_j = x_k cos\Theta_i + y_k sin\Theta_i$ and we increment the contents of accumulator $A[\Theta_i, r_j]$ at the position (Θ_i, r_j), i.e. $A[\Theta_i, r_j] = A[\Theta_i, r_j]+1$.
3. After processing all the image pixels, the value in the accumulator $A[\Theta_i, r_j]$ determines the total number of points n_{ij}, that lie in the line with parameters (Θ_i, r_j). We find the maximum value in the accumulator and values Θ_i, r_j, where the maximum occurs, define the line, which contains the highest number of points.

The accuracy, i.e. the maximum deviation from the straight line is given by the fineness of space allocation, i.e. the number of cells M and N, which determine the dimensions of accumulator. The minimum and maximum values are in the range $-90 \leq \Theta \leq 90$ and $-D \leq r \leq D$,

$$D = \sqrt{x^2 + y^2}. \tag{4}$$

where D is the distance between opposite corners of the image, x is the number of pixels of the image in the horizontal and y is the number of pixels of the image in the vertical direction.

Hough matrix size (fineness of space allocation) in the software implementation in Matlab tool is based on the parameters *val1* Hough function (*hough*), which determines the resolution for stepping values of variables Θ. This means that the minimum number of angles for resolution (*val1=1*) for which the hough matrix is calculated 180 = (90 - (-90)) and the largest number of angles for resolution *val1 = 0.1* is 1800.

For our purposes, we used the resolution of 1, as mentioned earlier, due to the reduction of computational complexity when working with matrices, because the size of the processed image has a significant impact on the size of the accumulator in the Hough transform.

3   Program Implementation and Results Obtained

The results of line crossing detection were gained using a designed program application in MatlabR2013a environment and Signal Processing Toolbox, in which the individual parts of the unwanted line crossing system were implemented (according to Fig. 1). Testing has been performed off-line for the acquired video files for different rides in *.avi format which were in advance recorded and stored on a PC hard drive. Initially, the acquired data were converted into the MJPG format [14] using a model designed in Simulink.

The software implementation went out from the international standard ISO 17361:2007 [15], which specifies system definition, classification, functions for human – machine interface and testing methods for unwanted lane departure warning systems.

LDWS considers situation safe, if the vehicle is moving around driving lane axis. This area is referred to as no warning zone or safe zone. The driving lane is delimited by horizontal traffic marking. The warning zone (WZ) is located around lane delimitation. In case the vehicle leaves the safe zone into the warning zone, the system issues a warning for driver.

The lane and vehicle trajectory are scanned using a camera. Then the system estimates from the video sequence the vehicle's position on road and lane width (LW). The line crossing detection in software implementation works on the principle of abscise intersection searching. For each frame the position of intersection of the nearest lines found to the left and right to the vehicle and the fictional vehicle area (blue colour) is compared (in Fig. 3 these intersections are marked by green vertical lines). From finding the intersections we calculate the position of vehicle's center, or two centers are calculated: Left Center of the Vehicle (CL) and Right Center of the Vehicle (CR), which are in Fig. 3 marked by two vertical blue lines. In case during line detection the information on horizontal road sign is lost, the system remembers last 10 values and the position of center is calculated based on them.

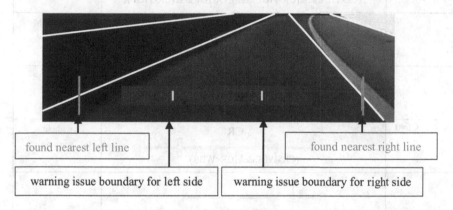

Fig. 3. Principle of line crossing detection used in SW implementation [13]

Based on the road geometry, the Warning Issue Boundary for Left Side (WBL) and the Warning Issue Boundary for Right Side (WBR) are determined from the recorded and defined data. Based on the position of Cl and CR of a fictive vehicle and based on position of warning issue boundaries, the software implementation determines a possible line crossing. In case the line is crossed, a warning for the driver is issued on the display in form of text „ALARM >>" or „<< ALARM" in the corresponding video sequence frame and the information „ALARM" is shown during the entire duration of lane deviation. An acoustic warning has also been tested, but this caused a slowdown of the detection process and the ending of acoustic warning was highly delayed because of the need to process the audio file.

Because during detection of horizontal road signs also situations occur, when information on line position is lost, the algorithm operates in two parts. In the first one, the position of both centers is compared (in case we have both lines determined) and in case when not both lines are found, only one of the vehicle's centers is compared with the position of warning zone boundaries. The functional principle of the algorithm is shown in Table 1.

3.1 Testing Stage and Comments on Results Obtained

After obtaining the complete algorithm for horizontal traffic marking finding using HT, the testing stage started. Based on the testing stage, we evaluated conclusions for recommendations for the most suitable setting of variable parameters of software implementation, with an objective to ensure successful detection of horizontal road signs and detection of its eventual crossing.

Table 1. Core of the designed line crossing detection algorithm

	WBL – warning issue boundary for left side WBR – warning issue boundary for right side CL – left center of the vehicle CR – right center of the vehicle	type of warning
CR=1, CL=1	WBL CL CR WBR (CL<HUL)&&(CR>HUL)&&(CL<HUP)&&(CR<HUP)	without warning
	(CL<HUL)&&(CR>HUL)OR(CL<HUL)&&(CR<HUL)	<< ALARM
	(SL<WBR)&&(SP>WBR) OR (SL>WBR)&&(CR>WBR)	ALARM >>
CR=1, CL=0	CR (CR>WBL)&&(CR<WBR)	without warning
	(CR<WBL)	<< ALARM
	(CR>WBR)	ALARM >>
CR=0, CL=1	CL (CL>WBL)&&(CL<WBR)	without warning
	(CL<WBL)	<< ALARM
	(CL>WBR)	ALARM >>
CR=1, CL=1	similar solution to the above	

During testing of SW application, the results were obtained by varying the following parameters:

- Setting of angle tolerance for lines joining (integer value degrees – range (1-6)).
- Setting the force ration of votes in (range 2/10-10/10).
- Setting of warning zone (range 5, 10, 20 pixels).

Table 2 shows only a fragment of tests on which the line crossing detection has been reliably captured by the software implementation for the given settings.

Table 2. Presentation of a part of results from the testing process in dependence on parameters set

			sensitivity setting of merging lines																				
			2		**3**						**4**						**5**						**6**	
	sample0009.avi simulation parameters	boundary warnings	numb. of warnin. - subjective	difference	frame number	frame number	frame number	numb. of warnin. - LDW	numb. of warnin. - subjective	difference	frame number	frame number	frame number	numb. of warnin. - LDW	numb. of warnin. - subjective	difference	frame number	frame number	frame number	numb. of warnin. - LDW	numb. of warnin. - subjective	difference	frame number	frame number
3	evaluated warning — timeliness of warning	20	3	0	49	214	416	3	3	0	49	164	403	3	3	0	49	164	403	3	3	0	49	164
	timeliness of warning	10	3	0	51	x	417	2	2	0	51	x	406	2	2	0	51	x	406	2	2	0	51	213
	timeliness of warning	5	3	0	52	x	417	2	2	0	52	x	417	2	2	0	52	x	410	2	2	0	52	x
4	danger. state- refer. frame				50	168	409				50	168	409				50	168	409				50	168
	evaluated warning — timeliness of warning	20	3	0	49	164	404	3	3	0	49	164	403	3	3	0	49	164	403	3	3	0	49	164
	timeliness of warning	10	2	0	51	165	416	3	3	0	51	164	406	3	3	0	51	165	406	3	3	0	51	213
	timeliness of warning	5	2	0	52	x	416	2	2	0	52	x	407	2	2	0	52	x	407	2	2	0	51	x
5	danger. state- refer. frame				50	168	409				50	168	409				50	168	409				50	168
	evaluated warning — timeliness of warning	20	3	0	49	164	404	3	3	0	49	164	403	3	3	0	49	164	403	3	3	0	49	164
	timeliness of warning	10	2	0	51	164	408	3	3	0	51	164	406	3	3	0	51	165	406	3	3	0	51	214
	timeliness of warning	5	2	0	52	x	410	2	2	0	52	x	407	2	2	0	51	x	409	2	2	0	52	x
6	danger. state- refer. frame				50	168	409			0	50	168	409				50	168	409				50	168
	evaluated warning — timeliness of warning	20	3	-1	49	163	407	3	3	0	48	162	403	3	3	0	49	162	403	3	3	0	49	164
	timeliness of warning	10	3	-1	51	163	410	3	3	0	51	163	406	3	3	0	51	165	406	3	3	0	51	x
	timeliness of warning	5	3	-1	52	x	411	2	2	0	52	x	408	2	3	-1	52	x	x		0		52	x
7	danger. state- refer. frame				50	168	409				50	168	409				50	168	409				50	168
	evaluated warning — timeliness of warning	20	3	-1	48	164	407	3	3	0	49	162	403	3	3	0	49	162	403	3	3	0	49	241
	timeliness of warning	10	3	-1	51	164	410	3	3	0	51	163	407	3	3	0	51	165	407	3	3	0	52	x
	timeliness of warning	5	3	-2	52	x	411	2	2	0	52	x	408	2	2	0	52	x	409	2	2	0	52	x
8	danger. state- refer. frame				50	168	409			0	50	168	409				50	168	409				50	168
	evaluated warning — timeliness of warning	20	3	-2	49	x	411	2	3	-1	49	163	406	3	3	0	49	164	406	3	3	0	49	215

(left vertical label: setting voting ratio (n out of 10))

3.2 Evaluation of Unwanted Horizontal Traffic Marking Crossing Using Real Drive Data

In program implementation it is possible to set several input parameters with different range. During testing several testing video files have been created with following parameters:

- traffic situations (daylight drive, night drive),
- drive on different types of traffic communications (drive on highway, drive on other traffic communications),
- drive style (not crossing line on a narrow road, crossing line on a narrow road, multiple line crossing),
- temporary traffic marking (presence of temporary traffic marking in form of orange lines, absence of temporary traffic marking).

The frame (0003.avi – Fig. 4) is capturing highway while crossing the line to the right. The detection of white traffic marking and its crossing with indication of this state is shown in computer screen. In addition to displaying a warning in form of the ALARM text which is shown the entire time the vehicle inheres in the warning zone, after the first zone crossing the monitor displays information on the direction of crossing. Crossing direction detection could provide driver a more precise warning signal (a tone from the or from the right speaker).

Fig. 4. Result of line crossing detection in direction to the right [13]

4   Conclusion

Based on the program designed and results obtained from testing we were able to prove usability of digital segmentation methods for processing of dynamic image information during detection of unwanted crossing of horizontal traffic marking.

During the process of testing and simulation several possible input variables occurred (lighting intensity, camera tilt angle) which are related to the problem solved. In order to investigate their effect, they would have to be incorporated into the current LDW system, which is even now of high degree of freedom. Testing of such system is time-consuming but can be performed in consequent work. The work can continue and physically solve the linkage of SW implementation with HW implementation and its testing in on-line mode, eventually send the output information on the issued warning to other vehicles via a VANET network [16], [17].

Acknowledgement. This work has been particularly supported by the Educational Grant Agency of the Slovak Republic (KEGA) Number: 024ŽU-4/2012: Modernization of technology and education methods orientated to area of cryptography for safety critical applications.

References

1. Mikulski, J.: Telematic Technologies in Transportation. In: Janecki, R., Sierpiński, G. (eds.) Contemporary Transportation Systems. Selected Theoretical and Practical Problems. New Culture of Mobility, pp. 131–143. Publishing House of the Silesian University of Technology, Monograph no. 324, Gliwice (2011)
2. Bubeníková, E., Franeková, M., Holečko, P.: Security increasing trends in intelligent transportation systems utilising modern image processing methods. In: Mikulski, J. (ed.) TST 2013. CCIS, vol. 395, pp. 353–360. Springer, Heidelberg (2013)
3. Pirník, R.: Application in transport telematics. ATP Journal Plus (2), 41–44 (2013) ISSN 1336-5010

4. Hargaš, L., Koniar, D., Štofan, S.: Advanced methodology for frequency description of biomechanical systems. In: Procedia Engineering, Modelling of Mechanical and Mechatronics Systems, vol. 48. Elsevier (2012)
5. Koniar, D., Hargaš, L., Štofan, S.: Segmentation of Motion Regions for Biomechanical Systems. In: Procedia Engineering, Modelling of Mechanical and Mechatronics Systems, vol. 48. Elsevier (2012)
6. Adas: making cars safer to drive in, http://www.eetimes.com/design/automotive-design/4004642/Adas-making-cars-safer-to-drive (date of access: July 09, 2014)
7. Hlaváč, V., Šonka, M.: Vision of computer. In: Czech, Grada, Praha (1992)
8. Bubeníková, E., Pirník, R., Holečko, P.: Optimization of video-data transmission in telematic system. Advances in Electrical and Electronic Engineering 11(2), 123–134 (2013)
9. Huh, K., et al.: Development of vision-based lane detection system considering configuration aspects. Optics and Lasers in Engineering, 43(11), 1193-113 (2005)
10. Kowsari, T., Beauchemin, S.S., Cho, J.: Real-time vehicle detection and tracking using stereo vision and multi-view adaboost. In: 2011 14th International IEEE Conference on Intelligent Transportation Systems (ITSC), pp. 1255–1260. IEEE (2011)
11. Sotelo, M.A., et al.: A color vision based lane tracking system for autonomous driving on umarked roads. Autonomous Robots 16(1), 95–116 (2004)
12. Bubeníková, E., Slotka, A., Muzikářová, L.: Utilization of image segmentation technique by the detection of road line. Slovak. Technológ Journal 4(2), 99–104 (2012)
13. Bubeníková, E.: Detection of lines in applications of control within intelligent transport. Dissertation work. In: Slovak, University of Žilina (2014)
14. Bubeníková, E., Franeková, M., Holečko, P.: Secure Solution of Collision Warning System Integration with Use of Vehicular Communications within Intelligent Transportation Systems. In: 12th IFAC/IEEE International konference on programmable Devices and Embedded Systems, VeľkéKarlovice, September 25-27 (2013)
15. ISO 17361:2007 Intelligent transport systems – Lane departure warning systems - Performance requirements and test procedures
16. Franeková, M., Lüley, P.: Security of Digital Signature Schemes for Car-to-Car Communications within Intelligent Transportation Systems. In: Mikulski, J. (ed.) TST 2013. CCIS, vol. 395, pp. 258–267. Springer, Heidelberg (2013)
17. Bubeníková, E., Franeková, M., Ďurech, J.: Security Solutions of Intelligent Transportation's Applications with using VANET Networks. In: 2014 15th International Carpathian Control Conference (ICCC), VeľkéKarlovice, pp. 424–429 (2014)
18. Mikulski, J. (ed.): TST 2011. CCIS, vol. 239. Springer, Heidelberg (2011)
19. Mikulski, J.: Introduction of telematics for transport. In: Proceedings on 9th International Conference ELEKTRO 2012, Rajecke Teplice, IEEE Catalog Number CFP1248S-ART, May 21-22, pp. 336–340 (2012), http://ieexplore.ieee.org

Choice of the Final Number of Satellite Navigation and Based Augmentation Systems in the Immediate and Not Too Distant Future

Jacek Januszewski

Gdynia Maritime University, al. Jana Pawla II 3
81–345 Gdynia, Poland
jacekjot@am.gdynia.pl

Abstract. Nowadays (June 2014) two satellite navigation systems (SNS), GPS and GLONASS, and four satellites based augmentation systems (SBAS), EGNOS, WAAS, MSAS, and GAGAN are fully operational, two next SNS, Galileo and BeiDou, and one SBAS, SDCM, are under construction. This paper gives the reply to some important questions as: these final numbers of the SNS and SBAS, four and five respectively, will be sufficient for all users in the whole world at any time or no; which user, why, where and when needs apart from GPS system the new SNS and next SBAS; which way the problem of compatibility and interoperability of all these systems will be solved; all these changes what it means for the users of different modes of transport.

Keywords: satellite navigation system, satellite based augmentation system, interoperability and compatibility of these systems.

1   Introduction

Nowadays information about user's position is obtained generally from specialized electronic positioning systems, in particular, at present functionally global satellite navigation systems (SNS) as the GPS and the GLONASS, and satellite based augmentation system (SBAS) as EGNOS, WAAS, MSAS and GAGAN (the last since February 14, 2014 formally offered to civil aviation users). Two next global SNS, Galileo in Europe and BeiDou (previous name Compass) in China and next SBAS, SDCM in Russia, are under construction. It means that by 2020 more than 120 satellites will be on the Earth's orbits and near 60 satellites at any moment and at any point on the Earth can be visible by the receiver's antenna simultaneously. SNS and SBAS are being developed and deployed by governments, international consortia and commercial interests. The generic name given to all these systems is Global Navigation Satellite Systems (GNSS). The most important parameters about all mentioned above four SNS and five SBAS are presented in the table 1 and 2, respectively. Two next regional SNS augmentation are under construction, IRNSS in India and QZSS in Japan [1-4].

J. Mikulski (Ed.): TST 2014, CCIS 471, pp. 146–155, 2014.
© Springer-Verlag Berlin Heidelberg 2014

Table 1. Parameters of Satellite Navigation Systems, May 15, 2014 [3], [4]

Parameter	System			
	GPS	GLONASS	Galileo	BeiDou
Operability	global FOC since 1995	global FOC since 2011	IOC – 2015/2016 FOC – 2020	Asia – 2012 global – 2020
Satellite identification	CDMA	FDMA – L1, L2 CDMA – L3	CDMA	CDMA
Number of satellites	32 in orbit 30 operational	29 in orbit 24 operational	4 MEO in orbit	14 in orbit 5 GEO, 5 IGSO, 4 MEO
Number of frequencies	2 (IIa, IIR, IIR–M) 3 (IIF)	2 (block M) 3 (block K1)	4	4
System time	GPST (GPS Time)	GLONASSST (GLONASS System Time)	GST (Galileo System Time)	BDT (BeiDou Time)
Datum	WGS 84	PZ 90.11	GTRF	China Geodetic System 2000
Integrity	no	No	yes (IMS service)	???
Accuracy 2D 95% [m]	$2 \div 4$	$2 \div 4$	few	10

2 Use of Satellite Navigation and Based Augmentation Systems

SNS and SBAS systems are used in different domains, among other things in every modes of transportation – land, marine and area. An uninterrupted information about the user's position is e.g. one of the most important elements of the safety of navigation in the sea transport in restricted and coastal areas, recommended by International Maritime Organization – IMO and in area transport, recommended by International Civil Aviation Organization – ICAO.

All systems at present functionally are under continuous development and modernization:

- the latest GPS satellites were successfully launched into orbit on February 21, 2014 (IIF–5) and on May 16, 2014 (IIF–6). The next IIF–7 will be launched in 2014. All 12 satellites in the GPS IIF series have completed production. The Air Force plans to launch the remaining IIF satellites by 2016 [3], [4].
- the latest GLONASS M satellite, designated No 54, was launched from the Russian Plesetsk Cosmodrome on March 23, 2014. It was the first of GLONASS satellite since three Russian navigation spacecrafts were lost in a Proton launch failure in July 2013. Next four satellites are scheduled for launch in 2014 (three in a single batch and one in single) in order to maintain GLONASS in its FOC [5].

Since December 31, 2013 the terrestrial geocentric coordinate system is for GLONASS PZ–90.11 (Parametry Zemli 1990), earlier it was PZ 90.02 [3].

- there will be three dual-Galileo satellites launches in 2014, in June, October and December [3].
- China will launch upgrated satellites and expand its at present regional BeiDou Navigation Satellite System (BDS) to global coverage by 2020 [6].
- Since February 2014 aircrafts equipped with SBAS receivers can use GAGAN signals in Indian airspace for en route navigation and non-precision approaches without vertical guidance. In the future GAGAN will provide augmentation service for GPS over not only India but also the Bay of Bengal, South East Asia and the Middle East expanding up to Africa [3], [4].
- for phase IV (planned for 2014–2028) WAAS shall begin to operate with Dual Frequency (GPS L1–GPS L5). Using two these signals all transport users, aviation and marine, in particular, can correct for ionospheric delay improving performance. That's why all existing SBAS systems will be upgrated in this time to broadcast new corrections for dual frequency users [7].

Table 2. Parameters of Satellite Based Augmentation Systems, May 15, 2014 [3], [4], [7]

Parameter	System				
	EGNOS	WAAS	MSA	GAGAN	SDCM
Operability	OS since 2009 IMS since 2011 EDAS since 2012	FOC since 2008	FOC since 2007	since 2014 for aviation	2014 ?
Aided system	GPS (GLONASS)	GPS	GPS	GPS	GPS (GLONASS)
Region	Europe North Africa	USA, Mexico, Canada	Japan	India	Russia
Number of satellites	4 (2 operational, 2 test signals)	3 operational	2 operational	2 (1 operatio-nal, 1 test)	2 (test signals)
Number of monitoring stations	39	38	6	15	21
Frequency	L1 GPS	L1 GPS (L5 GPS)	L1 GPS	L1 GPS	L3 GLO L1 GPS
Accuracy 2D 95% [m]	$1 \div 2$	3	2	few	few

On April 2, 2014 the GLONASS system has suffered a major problem, 11 hour downtime for the full constellation, due to an upload of bad ephemerides. Twelve days later, on April 14, eight GLONASS satellites were simultaneously set unhealthy for about half an hour, meaning that most GLONASS or multi-constellation receivers would have ignored those satellites in positioning computations. In addition, one other satellite in the fleet was out of commission undergoing maintenance. This might have left too few healthy satellites to compute GLONASS-only receiver positions in some locations. These both failures were caused by mathematical mistakes in software, in Russian space agency Roscosmos's view, the programmers who had designed the satellites' new software had made several mathematical mistakes [3].

In this situation each user of GNSS in transport can put two important questions:

- in the case of marine and area transportation how many GNSS receivers must be installed on the board of the ship or aircraft ?
- does he really need the next receiver of other GNSS, and if the response is yes, next question must be why, when and where ?

2.1   One or More GNSS Receivers on Board

The position's accuracy depends among other things on the number of satellites visible by receiver's antenna above masking elevation angle. Lower number of these satellites due to the natural or/and artificial obstacles decreases the accuracy of the position and sometimes can make impossible it's determination. This problem concerns all modes of transportation, e.g. in land transport in urban canyon, in marine transport the ship sailing along the height coast or in harbour entrance [8].

On each ship's bridge one GNSS stationary receiver is installed at least but on many ships there are two or even more GNSS receivers. Typical maritime applications consist in coupling GNSS receivers with dedicated sensors such as radar, ARPA, autopilot, echo-sounder, fish-finder, and so on.

At present (May 2014) the receivers used in transport are in the straight majority the units of GPS system only. In marine transport on the ships there are many DGPS receivers or GPS + SBAS or DGPS + SBAS models. Differential or satellite based augmentation cannot be considered as additional system because the functionality of both depends directly on GPS system and if for any reason this system is out of services or the number of GPS satellites visible by receiver's antenna is not sufficient the user's position cannot be determined.

As neither GPS system nor GLONASS system don't provide the information about integrity the DGPS and/or SBAS receivers are installed on many ships because this information can be obtained from terrestrial DGPS reference station about used GPS satellites only and from geostationary SBAS satellites about whole GPS system, respectively. That's why since few years the number of radiobeacons increases slowly but continuously (tab. 3). At present in the world there are near 290 operational radiobeacons. The information about the details of theirs services (8 parameters) and integrity monitoring can be found in the annual edited volume 2 of Admiralty List of Radio Signals (ALRS). The most of these radiobeacons (82%) provides integrity monitoring, both polish (Dziwnów and Rozewie) also [9].

2.2   The Choice of SNS and SBAS

Since 1995 year GPS system has dominate satellite navigation, especially in aviation applications. By contrast, the Russian GLONASS system cannot be used in western aviation because no approval guidelines exist for GLONASS equipment. In area transportation the Ground Based Augmentation System (GBAS) allows precision approaches to be performed using satellite navigation. Meanwhile from a technical perspective, GBAS can use either GPS or GLONASS system for differential corrections. Additional SNS at present under construction Galileo and BeiDou are not yet included within standardization documents, as these systems are not approved for aviation use themselves [10].

Table 3. Distribution in the world of the radiobeacons transmitting DGPS and DGLONASS corrections, information about details of services and integrity monitoring [9]

Year	Number of radiobeacons								
	Total	All details of services known	Integrity monitoring						
			Yes		No		No information		
			Num-ber	%	Num-ber	%	Num-ber	%	Num-ber	%
2013	283	224	79	232	82	11	3.9	40	14.1
2014	288	214	74	236	81.9	11	3.8	41	14.3

The number of GLONASS receivers in marine transport is still very small, these receivers usually are on the specialist ships, e.g. on the platform supply vessel Crest Mariner 2 is installed C–NAV 3050 DGNSS receiver which provides 66-channel tracking, including multi-constellation support for GPS, GLONASS and SBAS.

As the maximum number of the satellites is in the case of all SNS precisely determined and for many reasons cannot be greater in restricted area where the user's position cannot be determined because of too small number of visible satellites the solution is the possibility of the simultaneous use of next SNS. In this situation the user must choice the second SNS (at present GLONASS system only) and purchase the additional receiver, but which type of the receiver – dual SNS integrated or stand alone for this selected SNS only. The final decision depends on the pecuniary resources of the user and the price and parameters of these receivers. In author's view second stand-alone receiver will be better choice.

The first positioning with Galileo on December 4, 2012 and the first positioning with BeiDou in January 2013 will cover static and road tests of each constellation individually and together as a single positioning solution. Road tests in the United States and Europe will combine GPS/GLONASS/Galileo, while tests in the China region will combine GPS/Galileo/BeiDou [3].

Analysis of a GPS/Galileo receiver's test results confirm the advantages of GPS and Galileo constellation combination. The mean TTFF (Time To First Fix) is significantly lower when using Galileo satellites only (24.7 s), in the case of GPS satellites only it increases to 31.9 s. We can assume that TTFF for GPS and Galileo joint solution will be less more [11].

The using of two or more SNS, i.e. multiple constellations means: a faster first fix, added advantage of the authentication signal to guard against spoofing, greater resistance to multipath, especially in cities, improved indoor performance [4].

In the case of SBAS the problem of the choice of the right system does not exist because all these systems use the same frequency and signal (GPS L1) and additionally the coverage of each system is limited. In the straight majority at given moment and given point one geostationary satellite i.e. one SBAS can be used only, and it is sufficient.

Currently the coverage area of four operational mentioned above SBAS is limited to north hemisphere only, since there are no possibility to calculate corrections because of no sufficient number of monitoring stations in south hemisphere [3], [4]. That's why next monitoring stations will be installed in three SBAS:

- EGNOS, 7, in South Africa and Madagascar,
- WAAS, 13, in South and Middle America,
- MSAS, 9, in Australia, New Zealand and Indonesia.

3   Next SBAS and Regional Systems under Construction

The fifth SBAS, System for Differential Correction and Monitoring – SDCM, is under construction by Russia. This system will use a ground network of monitoring stations and Luch geostationary communication satellites to transmit correction and integrity data using the GPS L1 (1575.42 MHz) frequency. The main differentiator of SDCM with respect to all other SBAS is that it is conceived as an SBAS augmentation that would perform integrity monitoring of both GPS and GLONASS satellites, whereas the rest of current SBAS initiatives provide corrections and integrity just to GPS satellites [12]. Integrity monitoring system solves the issue of operating quality estimation of GLONASS and GPS systems. At present SDCM ground segment consists of 22 operational monitor stations – 18 in Russia, 3 in Antarctica and one in Brazil. At least next 40 stations are planned, 21 in Russia, the rest in the world but except Africa and USA. The spatial segment will consist of 3 GEO satellites, Luch–5A (107° E) and Luch–5B (016° W) are already in orbit transmitting test signal, the third Luch–5V (095° E) will be launched in 2014. The anticipated position accuracy is better than 0.5 m. A high accuracy service in conjunction with local ground station support may even provide a position accuracy between 0.02 and 0.5 m [3], [4].

Two next SBAS are under definition – Chinese SNAS (Satellite Navigation Augmentation System) and Korean K–SBAS.

In the future when SBAS systems will be dual frequency, the first WAAS satellites will transmit signal on L1 as well as L5 frequency, they will improve service world wide and drastically improve performance in the equatorial region.

As the access to both currently operational government-controlled SNS – GPS (USA) and GLONASS (Russia) – is not guaranteed in hostile situations India decided to develop autonomous regional SNS, IRNSS (Indian Regional Navigation Satellite

System) which would be under complete control of the Indian government. Spatial segment of this system will consist of seven satellites, 3 GEO (032.5° E, 083° E, 111.5° E) and two pairs of IGSO (Inclined GeoSynchronous Orbit) satellites with their nodes at 055° E and 111.5° E with an orbital inclination of 29°. The IRNSS will provide two types of services, the Standard Positioning Service (SPS) open for civilian use and the Restricted Service (RS), encrypted one, for authorised users. The signals will be carried on L5 (1176.45 MHz) and S band (2492.08 MHz). The applications of IRNSS will consist among other things terrestrial, aerial and marine navigation (transportation). In June 2014 two IGSO satellites were in orbit, IRNSS–1A since July 1, 2013 and IRNSS–1B since April 4, 2014 with node at 055°E. This system will be functional by the beginning of 2016 [3], [4].

Quasi Zenith Satellite System (QZSS), a Japanese regional satellite positioning system, will be composed of four IGSO satellites. These satellites operate in highly inclined (45°) elliptical orbits (HEO), semimajor axis (average) 42164 km, longitude of ascending node 146.3°E, argument of perigee 270°. Eccentricity (0.099) and inclination of the orbit are chosen in order to provide an elevation of more than 70° over the whole trajectory of the satellites when traveling over Japan. QZSS will provide three major services, complement GPS by broadcasting navigation signals compatible and interoperable with GPS, augmentation information to correct the GNSS signal for atmospheric effects, orbital and clock errors, broadcasting and communication service in order to enable, similar to the navigation objectives, communication in restricted area [4], [13].

The first QZSS satellite "Michibiki" is in orbit since September 11, 2010, the next three will be launched in 2016 and 2017. This satellite is the first in history to transmit L1C, new civil signal using PRN code 183, designed to be interoperable among GNSS. The QZSS L1C ranging codes and navigation messages are in accordance to the codes and messages envisioned for the GPS L1C signals. As a result of this constellation since 2018 three satellites will be visible at all times from locations in the Asia-Oceanic regions. In the future the number of satellites will be increased to seven therefore accurate position information will be possible even in urban areas and mountainous regions [3], [13].

4   Compatibility and Interoperability of the Systems

The announcements of many changes in the structure of GNSS, new frequencies and new signals, in particular, represent good news, but sometimes some not-such good news also for GNSS product designers, service providers, and finally users. For example, recent studies indicate that more than three GNSS systems operating in the same band can cause problems [14]. All these systems, all satellite signals and different services designed for the users must be compatible and open signals and services should also be interoperable to the maximum extent possible. Interoperability definition addresses signal in space, system time and geodetic reference frame considerations. These three parameters in all four SNS (table 1) are unfortunately different.

Table 4. Satellite navigation and satellite based augmentation systems, carrier frequencies, symbols, signals and services, today and in the future, $f_O = 10.23$ MHz, $f_B = 1.023$ MHz [3], [4]

Carrier frequency [MHz]	System, symbol, signals, services
1176.45 ($f_O \cdot 115$)	GPS – L5, signal C; GLONASS – L5, signal OCM; Galileo – E5a, signal 1 & 2, with service OS (DF,IA), SoL, CS (MC); QZSS – L5; IRNSS – L5; SBAS – L5 (in the future)
1202.025 ($f_B \cdot 1175$)	GLONASS – L3, signal OC & SC (both in the future)
1207.14 ($f_O \cdot 118$)	GLONASS – L3, signal OCM (in the future); Galileo – E5b, signal 3 & 4, service OS (IA), SoL, CS(MC); BeiDou – B2
1227.60 ($f_O \cdot 120$)	GPS – L2, signal C, M, P (service PPS); QZSS – L2, signal C
1242.9375 – 1247.75	GLONASS – L2, signal OF & SF
1248.06 ($f_B \cdot 1220$)	GLONASS – L2, signal OC & SC
1268.52 ($f_B \cdot 1240$)	BeiDou – B3
1278.75 ($f_O \cdot 125$)	Galileo – E6, signal 5 and service PRS, signal 6 & 7, service CS (VA, MC); QZSS – LEX
1542.50	SBAS based on Inmarsat (Omnistar, Starfire)
1561.098 ($f_B \cdot 1526$)	BeiDou – B1
1575.42 ($f_O \cdot 154$)	GPS – L1, signal C/A, M, P, service SPS: GLONASS – L1, signal OCM (in the future); Galileo – L1, signal 8 with service PRS, signal 9 & 10 with service OS (SF, DF, IA), SoL, CS (VA, MC); QZSS – L1, signal C/A, C, SAIF
1589.742 ($f_B \cdot 1554$)	BeiDou – B1–2
1600.995 ($f_B \cdot 1565$)	GLONASS – L1, signal OC & SC (in the future)
1598.0625 – 1604,25	GLONASS – L1, signal OF & SF
2492.08	IRNSS – signal in S band

CS – Commercial Service, DF – Dual Frequency, IA – Improved Accuracy, MC – Multi Carrier, OS – Open Service, PRS – Public Regulated Service, SF – Single Frequency, SoL – Safety of Life Service, VA – Value Added, O – open signal, S – obfuscated signal, F – FDMA, C– CDMA, M – interoperability CDMA signals, PPS – Precise Positioning Service, SPS – Standard Positioning Service

The carrier frequencies, symbols, signals and services of all SNS global as well as regional and SBAS are demonstrated in the table 4. We can say that:

- all five frequencies currently used or planned in three SNS, GPS, Galileo and BeiDou, and in all SBAS are based on the fundamental frequency $f_O = 10.23$ MHz, in the case of 1176.45 MHz, 1207.14 MHz, 1227.60 MHz, 1278.75 MHz and 1575.42 MHz, the factor $(\cdot f_O)$ is 115, 118, 120, 125 and 154, respectively,

- at least one frequency of each SNS is the same that in at least one other SNS.
- except B2 signal all three next BeiDou signals, B3, B1, B1–2, used in this system only, are based on the fundamental frequency f_B = 1.023 MHz, also all future GLONASS interoperability CDMA signals are based on this f_B.

GNSS positioning is based on the synchronization of emitting satellites to a common reference time. With at least 4 synchronized satellites, the user's receiver can calculate the four usual unknowns: the 3D position and the delay between receiver and system time. Therefore in order to combine measurements from different satellite systems like GPS and Galileo, the bias between the different system times shall be broadcast, or determined at the user level as additional unknowns. That's why Galileo satellites and future GPS satellites (block III) will transmit the time delay between both systems, which is called GGTO–Galileo to GPS Time Offset.

The time offset between the difference reference time SNS will be emitted in the navigation message of these systems. Various agreements already specify the time offsets and its provision to the user. The data concerning the offset of GST with respect to TAI and UTC will be included in the Galileo navigation message.

Although the international civil coordinate reference standard is the International Reference Frame (ITRF), each GNSS has its own reference frame, which depends on the control stations'coordinates hence guaranteeing independence among systems. The reference frame for GPS system is World Geodetic System 1984 (WGS84), its present version is almost identical with the latest version ITRF. The coordinates in GLONASS system are based on the parameter of the Earth 1990 (PZ–90) frame, since 2014 in version 90.11, also known as Parametry Zemli 1990 (PZ–90.11). This new system is already coordinated with the ITRF at the centimetre level. Galileo system will have its own reference frame GTRF (Galileo Terrestrial Reference Frame), while BeiDou system adopts the China Geodetic Coordinate System 2000 (CGCS2000). As currently all SBAS augment GPS system only, the reference frame for all these systems is WGS84 also. The QZSS geodetic coordinate system is known as the Japan satellite navigation Geodetic System (JGS). This coordinate system is defined as the approach to ITRF [3], [4], [13] .

Two SNS are said to be interoperable from a reference frame perspective if the difference between frames is below target accuracy. Three reference frames, WGS84, GTRF and ITRF, differ by only a few centimeters (i.e. this difference between WGS84 and GTRF is expected to be within 3 cm), so this is only an issue for high-precision users. Therefore we can say that the problem of compatibility of SNS and SBAS in the case of reference frame (datum) for transport users does not exist [3] [4].

5   Conclusion

- the operators of GPS and GLONASS have started modernization programs that will enable multi-frequency operations in the future; that's why, a large number of usable satellites and signals from multiple systems will soon be available
- four described in the paper SNS will be sufficient on condition that all these systems will be fully compatible and interoperable with regard to theirs three factors, carrier frequency, reference datum and system time, in particular

- only then several dozen additional monitor stations in south hemisphere of at present SBAS and next system SDCM will be operational, SBAS systems will cover all continents (except for Arctic and Antarctica) as well as all principal offshore tracks and will be sufficient for the straight majority of the users, all mode of transportation also
- as long as the global SNS will be in charge only of government institutions, at present GPS (U.S. Department of Defence) and GLONASS (Russian Aerospace Defence Forces), the regional systems as IRNSS in India and QZSS in Japan are and can be created in each part of the world
- the two April 2014 failures in GLONASS system show that some users must have the possibility to determine the position from more than one GNSS, in critical applications, in particular
- for all users one official reference frame (time and datum) of all SNS and SBAS would be very desirable, but actually this demand cannot be realized

References

1. Gleason, S., Gebre–Egziabher, D.: GNSS Applications and Methods. Artech House, Boston (2009)
2. Januszewski, J.: Systemy satelitarne GPS, Galileo i inne. PWN SA, Warszawa (2010)
3. http://www.gpsworld.com (date of access: May 15, 2014)
4. http://www.insidegnss.com (date of access: May 05, 2014)
5. http://www.spaceflightnow.com (date of access: May 15, 2014)
6. http://www.news.xinhuanet.com (date of access: May 14, 2014)
7. http://www.faa.gov (date of access: May 14, 2014)
8. Januszewski, J.: Geometry and Visibility of Satellite Navigation Systems in Restricted Area, Institute of Navigation, National Technical Meeting, San Diego (2005)
9. Admiralty List of Radio Signals. vol. 2, NP 282 The United Kingdom Hydrographic Office, Tauton (2013/2014)
10. Stanisak, M., et al.: Ground-Based Augmentation Combining Galileo with GPS and GLONASS. GPS World 25(4), 44–50 (2014)
11. Linty, N., et al.: A Mass-Market Galileo Receiver Its Algorithms and Performance. GPS World 25(4), 36–43 (2014)
12. http://www.navipedia.net (date of access: May 12, 2014)
13. http://www.qzs.jp (date of access: May 12, 2014)
14. Gibbons, G.: GNSS Interoperability Not So Easy. After All, InsideGNSS 6(1), 28–31 (2011)

Extension of the Tunnel Simulator
with the Traffic Flow Model

Igor Miklóšik and Juraj Spalek

University of Žilina,
Faculty of Electrical Engineering
010 26 Žilina, Slovakia
{igor.miklosik,juraj.spalek}@fel.uniza.sk

Abstract. The paper deals with macroscopic modeling of the traffic flow in the programmable logic controllerbased Tunnel Simulator. All relevant devices of the tunnel technological equipment are simulated by the software inside the programmable logic controller. Simulator offers many HMI/SCADA graphical screens to visualize the state of each subsystem of the technological equipment. Additional graphical screen has been created to add the traffic flow modeling functionality. Traffic flow model outputs (intensity, speed and density) are planned to be used as inputs for other models in the Tunnel Simulator e.g. Evacuation time estimation, Air flow speed modeling inside the tunnel tube.

Keywords: programmable logic controller, tunnel, simulation, macroscopic traffic flow model, visualization.

1 Introduction

Road tunnels are important part of traffic infrastructure since they shorten the paths in mountainous regions. Shorter travel times lead to higher economical effectiveness. A lot of technological equipment is necessary to provide the tunnel system safe in any circumstances. There are not many chances to simulate malfunctions of selected components in real 24 hour operation to see all consequences. Therefore Tunnel simulator (TuSim) has been developed to simulate the technological equipment of the tunnel.

1.1 Tunnel Simulator

TuSim is PLC based system running on the B&R Automation embedded PC (PLC) with UPS unit. Fig. 1 shows TuSim hardware from top to bottom: Master view LCD switch, B&R embedded PC, visualization server and UPS unit.

All devices of the tunnel technological subsystem equipment are simulated by the software inside the PLC[2]. Equipment of three tunnels is implemented: City tunnel (1 km), Motorway 2 tubes (1 km) and Motorway 1 tube tunnel (1 km).

J. Mikulski (Ed.): TST 2014, CCIS 471, pp. 156–165, 2014.

Fig. 1. TuSim hardware [own study]

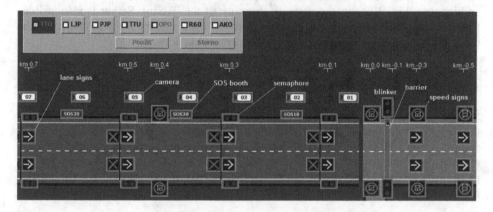

Fig. 2. Part of the traffic screen [1]

TuSim supports in addition to the simulation of the technological equipment also the control of the traffic sequences. Fig. 2 shows the part of the traffic screen with the status of the traffic sequence together with implemented devices of traffic control equipment. Each tunnel tube can operate in following traffic sequences: tunnel tube open (TTO), left lane closed (LJP), right lane closed (PJP), speed limit 60km/h (R60), accommodation (eye comfort) lighting failure (AKO), tunnel tube closed (TTU). Switching from one sequence to another follows the time requirements which allow all vehicles to adapt to the new conditions. Control of the tunnel reflexes is last important functionality implemented in the TuSim. Tunnel reflex is a reaction of the control system to relevant event in the tunnel like: complete or partial power failure, fire, traffic alarm or pre-alarm, lighting malfunction, SOS button, physical measurements alarm or pre-alarm[1].

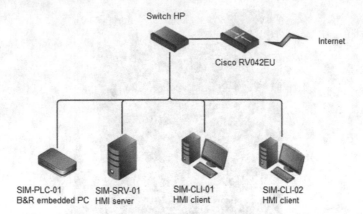

Fig. 3. TuSim network structure [3]

There are many graphical screens to visualize the state of each subsystem of the technological equipment – at least one for each subsystem. Handling of the screens and separate connections to the simulator is realized by visualization server and 2 client PCs with HMI/SCADA CIMPLICITY software which uses client/server architecture. Fig. 3 shows the network structure of the TuSim. Server is responsible for collection and distribution of the data from the PLC, clients allow to interact with the data distributed by the server and perform control actions.

2   Traffic Flow Model

Several models are necessary to be implemented to extend the TuSim functionality as the tool for evaluation of tunnel technological subsystems control and their impact on safety. Since traffic model affects other models eg. air flow simulation, persons evacuation, combustion products modeling - so it should be implemented before mentioned models.Motorway 2 tube tunnel model has been selected for the traffic model implementation.

2.1   Random Numbers

Simulated system is stochastic system when at least one variable describing the state of the system is random and is determined by random function. We need the source of random numbers for the simulation of such a system which generates the random inputs into the simulation model. Following functions are available in Visual Basic compatible (VBA) HMI/SCADA CIMPLICITY scripting language for generating pseudo random numbers [7]:

- Rnd () – generates pseudo random real number from interval (0,1)
- Random (a,b) – generates pseudo random integer number from interval <a,b>

Most of the computer systems use Linear congruential generator algorithm. The output of the algorithm is deterministic and after the input of the same initial value it generates same output numbers. So we call generated numbers pseudorandom numbers. The advantage is that the same testing inputs can be used if same circumstances of the experiment are desired. Otherwise system time value can be used as an initial value for the generator using Randomize() function from VBA.

2.2   Generation of Random Numbers According Specified Distribution

Distribution of continuous random variables is determined by probability density function f(t). It determines the probability that random variable takes the values in interval:

$$P(x \in< a, b >) = \int_a^b f(t)dt \tag{1}$$

Cumulative distribution function can be count from the density function:

$$F(t) = \int_{-\infty}^t f(\tau)d\tau \tag{2}$$

Value of the distribution function represents the probability that the random variable takes on a value less than or equal to t.

$$F(t) = P(x < t) \tag{3}$$

If distribution function takes in point x_z value $F(x_z) = z$ than we can mark inverse function:

$$F(x^{-1}) = x_z \tag{4}$$

If we have the generator of uniform distributed random numbers from interval (0,1) we can mark the generated values as u_i. Values of the random variable according the specified distribution function can be generated from the following equation [5]:

$$x_i = F^{-1}(u_i) \tag{5}$$

2.3   Generation of Random Numbers According the Exponential Distribution

Exponential distribution is used in traffic systems for modeling the arrival times of the vehicles into the system (tunnel). Probability density function of the exponential distribution is:

$$f(t) = \lambda. e^{-\lambda t} \ for \ t > 0$$
$$f(t) = 0 \ for \ t \leq 0 \tag{6}$$

Where $\lambda > 0$ characterizes the "load of the system", value $1/\lambda$ is expected average arrival time between the vehicles. Distribution function:

$$F(t) = \int_{-\infty}^{t} f(\tau)d\tau = \int_{0}^{t} \lambda.e^{-\lambda t}d\tau \ \ for \ t > 0$$

(7)

$$F(t) = 0 \ \ for \ t = 0$$

From the equation:

$$F(x_i) = 1 - e^{-\lambda x_i} = u_i$$

(8)

Inverse function can be derived:

$$x_i = -\frac{1}{\lambda}.\ln(1 - u_i)$$

(9)

Since u_i variable is uniform distributed on interval (0,1) expression $(1 - u_i)$ can be replaced by u_i[5]:

$$x_i = -\frac{1}{\lambda}.\ln(u_i)$$

(10)

Implementation in scripting language:

```
Function Exponen(lambda As double)As double
Exponen = -log(Rnd)/lambda
End Function
```

2.4   Generation of Random Numbers According the Poisson Distribution

If time of vehicles arrivals into the tunnel has exponential distribution, Poisson distribution is used for modeling the count of the vehicles over time interval. Count of the vehicles in the tunnel over time is determined:

$$g_k(t) = (t.\lambda)^k.\frac{1}{k!}.e^{-t.\lambda}$$

(11)

Where $g_k(t)$ determines the probability that exactly k vehicles arrive into the tunnel over t time interval. For t = 1:

$$g_k = \lambda^k.\frac{1}{k!}.e^{-\lambda}$$

(12)

Then:

$$t_1 + t_2 + t_3 + \cdots + t_k \leq 1 < t_1 + t_2 + \cdots + t_k + t_{k+1}$$

(13)

where t_i is time interval between the arrivals of i-1 and i-th vehicle and has exponential distribution. Intervals t_i can be count from the random numbers u_i from interval (0,1) according the equation (10):

$$-\frac{1}{\lambda} \cdot [\ln(u_1) + \cdots + \ln(u_k)] \leq 1 < -\frac{1}{\lambda} \cdot [\ln(u_1) + \cdots + \ln(u_{k+1})] \tag{14}$$

After the adjustment:

$$\prod_{i=1}^{k} u_i \geq e^{-\lambda} > \prod_{i=1}^{k+1} u_i \tag{15}$$

So count of the vehicles in the tunnel according the Poisson distribution can be generated by successive multiplication of random numbers u_i from interval $(0,1)$ using Rnd() function until the value of the compassion is lower than $e^{-\lambda}$. That's more preferable to calculate the sum of arrival times according exponential distribution [5].

Implementation in scripting language:

```
Function Poisson(Lambda As Double) As Integer
    Dim P As Double
    Dim Z As Double
    Dim K As Integer

    Z = exp(-Lambda)
    K = 0
    P = 1
    Do
        P = P * Rnd
        K = K + 1
    Loop While(P >= Z)
    Poisson = K-1
End Function
```

2.5   Macroscopic Models

Microscopic modeling describes the behavior of the drivers in individual vehicles, motion and interaction between these vehicles:car following, lane changing, gap acceptance. Macroscopic modeling looks at the traffic flow from a global perspective and assumes traffic flow as homogenous. It represents how one parameter of traffic flow changes with respect to another. Most important is the relation between speedand density. The first and most simple relation between speed-density is proposed by Greenshields. Green shields assumed a linear speed-density relationship to derive the model. Linearity is useful feature because simple linear regression can be used to fit the model parameters from the measured data. But in the field we can hardly find such a relationship between the speed and density. Therefore many other models came up. Some ofthem are: Greenberg's logarithmic model, Underwood's exponential model, Pipe's generalized model. Fig. 4 shows the equations for these models to be implemented in the TuSim. Nice graphical comparison how all mentioned models fit the measured data from the motorway can be found in [6].The above models are called single-regime models because they are one-equationmodels.

None of the single-regime models is able to fit precisely over the whole range. Therefore multi-regime models have been developed.Multiple equations are used, each equation for one part of the range. Macroscopic model is enough as a first step for TuSim traffic simulation and interaction with other models. The relationship between basic traffic flow parameters is as follows:

$$q = k.v \qquad (16)$$

Intensity (q): number of the vehicles in the time period (veh/h)
Density (k): number of the vehicles per unit of length (veh/km)
Speed (v): average speed of the vehicles (km/h)

Author	Model	Parameters
Greenshields	$v = v_f(1 - \frac{k}{k_j})$	v_f, k_j
Greenberg	$v = v_m \ln(\frac{k_j}{k})$	v_m, k_j
Underwood	$v = v_f e^{-\frac{k}{k_m}}$	v_f, k_m
Northwestern	$v = v_f e^{-\frac{1}{2}(\frac{k}{k_m})^2}$	v_f, k_m
Drew	$v = v_f[1 - (\frac{k}{k_j})^{n+\frac{1}{2}}]$	v_f, k_j, n
Pipes-Munjal	$v = v_f[1 - (\frac{k}{k_j})^n]$	v_f, k_j, n

Fig. 4. Single-regime models [6] v_f- free-flow speed, k_j - jam density, v_m - optimal speed, k_m - optimal density, n - exponent

Maximum speed from the speed signs is used as thefree flow speed input to the model. Let's assume that all drivers are disciplined and no additional value needs to be added to the free flowspeed - that's not the truth in the real operation according the measured data. Number of open lanes of each tunnel tube is used for multiplying the density in case that one lane is closed. Also maximum speed is automatically updated by the control system to 60km/h in this case for the other open lane.

Table 1. Traffic sequences and inputs to the model [own study]

Traffic sequence	v_f	Number of open lanes
Tunnel tube open	80km/h	2
Left or right lane closed	60km/h	1
Speed limit 60km/h	60km/h	2
Tunnel tube closed	0km/h	0

3   Models Implementation into the TuSim

Sending of the real measured data from the CSV file from Czech tunnel Mrazovka has been implemented first to simulate the real scenarios.Data have been obtained from video detection cameras in the west portal of the tunnel. Checkbox at the bottom of the screen on Fig. 5allows sending the random data from the traffic model or

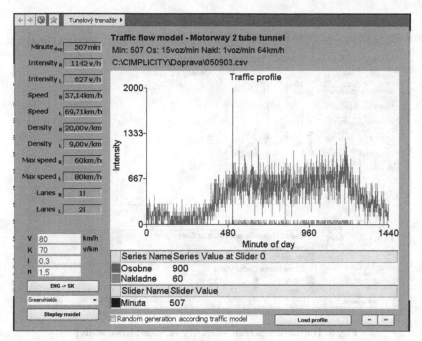

Fig. 5. Traffic flow screen – Traffic profile [own study]

sending the real data. Fig. 5 shows the real traffic profile for each minute of the dayof the tunnel operation. Total intensity has been counted from the intensity of vehicles (red line) and trucks (green line) measured from the CSV file. Of course user traffic profile can be created to be used with the traffic model. Slider moves according the time of the day to simulate the 24h scenario.Since placement of several graphs on the graphical screen is necessary to display all traffic flow characteristics, Frame container component has been used to spare the space on the screen. Switching between the graphs is realized by the two buttons in the bottom right corner of the screen on Fig. 5.XY plot control object has been used to display the data in form of graphs [8]. Following graphs have been implemented and placed in the Frame container component: Traffic profile, Density profile, Density vs. speed, Density vs. intensity and Intensity vs. speed. Last three mentioned graphs allow comparing the measured data (Series of the XY plot object - red circle markers on Fig. 6) with the model (Series of the XY plot object – blue line Fig. 6).As can be seen no congestions were present in the measured data – tested on several CSV files. The speed of the vehicles on the motorway was often higher than the speed limit and didn't decrease even if density increased.

Traffic model can be selected in the combobox in the bottom left corner and after specifying models parametersit can be displayed in the graph. Fig. 6 shows the screen Density vs. speed with Green shields model selected in the combobox. Sliders show the density for each tunnel tube. The recounted outputsare sent into the PLC for each tunnel tube according the selected model and their values can be seen on the left part of the screen. Index behind the description determines proper tunnel tube. Database logger from HMI/SCADA CIMPLICITY has been configured to see the results of 24h traffic datasending from the model (intensity, density and speed) into the TuSim.

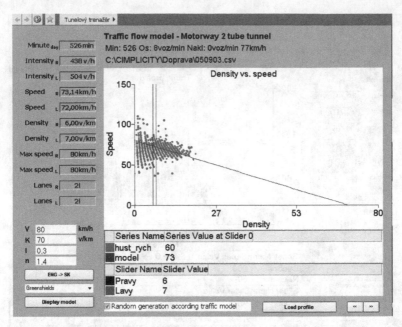

Fig. 6. Traffic flow screen – Density vs. speed [own study]

4   Conclusion

Several single-regime macroscopic models have been implemented into the graphical screen to extend the functionality of the TuSim -best fitting model can be easily selected. The output of the model is planned to be used as piston effect contributionfor air flow modeling and as an input for combustion products modeling in the tunnel tube. Also the number of persons in the cars should be considered for future evacuation time estimation.Separate traffic models for each tunnel tube should be implemented as the next step. Current state of the vehicles animation in the tunnel tube just displays the active traffic sequence, so also modification of thisanimation is expected.

Acknowledgment. This contribution/publication is the result of the project implementation: Centre of excellence for systems and services of intelligent transport, ITMS 26220120050 supported by the Research & Development Operational Program funded by the ERDF.

References

1. Kopásek, J.: SW for simulation of functionality of road tunnel technology equipment, Eltodo EG. User Manual, pp. 68–73 (2013)
2. Přibyl, P., Svitek, M.: Intelligent traffic systems, pp.480—482. BEN – technical literature (2011)

3. Tuček, V., Jankovský, V.: HW and SW environment for simulation of the road tunnels technological equipment functionality and operator's workplace for research of the operator's behavior under critical situations. Design document, p. 43, Eltodo EG (2013)
4. TP98: Technological equipment of the road tunnels, Design document, pp.40—42, Eltodo EG (2013)
5. Cenek, P., Klima, V., Janáček, J.: Optimization of traffic and telecommunication processes, pp. 264–275. VŠDS (1994)
6. Ni, D.: Lecture Notes in Traffic Flow Theory – A Unified Perspective, University of Massachusetts Amherst (1994)
7. GE Fanuc Automation: Cimplicity HMI, Basic Control Engine, Language reference Manual, GFK-1283G (2001)
8. GE Fanuc Automation: Cimplicity HMI Plant Edition, Trend and XY Chart, Operation Manual, GFK-1260H (2001)

Estimation of Travel Times
and Identification of Traffic Excesses on Roads

Jan Šilar, Tomáš Tichý, and Jan Přikryl

ELTODO a.s., Novodvorská 1010/14,
142 01 Prague 4, Czech Republic
{silarj,tichyt,prikrylj}@eltodo.cz

Abstract. We made an analysis on the selected road in Prague road network, by help of research project SATEL, which aimed to automated detection of traffic excesses (AID) and estimating travel times on urban road net. For data collection were intended two types of traffic detectors – static data from loops, videodetection etc. and data from floating cars. The project introduces a new method for obtaining traffic data, which includes estimated travel times through data fusion from floating cars and traffic road detectors from on-line traffic and calibration by historical data. The proposed model uses the real data from traffic detectors with floating cars and it was proved its strength and application for estimation traffic excesses and travel times on the road network as well.

Keywords: ITS, urban traffic control, FCD.

1 Introduction

Estimating travel times is becoming increasingly significant in contemporary transport. This is closely associated with the identification of traffic excesses which have a significant and negative influence on travel times. The timely discovery of traffic excesses (traffic accidents, congestion) and the provision of information to traffic participants may reduce their negative impacts. This means that drivers are informed of expected delays and they can therefore react in time and adequately. This article involves a description of the area of estimating travel times and the AID (Automatic Incident Detection) of traffic excesses. Part of the inner ring road of Prague ("Jižní spojka") was used to test the system. One of the reasons for this was the use of existing infrastructure for part of the measurement and estimation of travel times. A further reason was the fact that congestion frequently occurs there, unlike on the other considered roads, and as such it was possible to verify the identification of traffic excesses. Emphasis was placed on testing the proposed model, updating the historical models, calibrating the algorithm, displaying the outputs and modifying the GUI in such a way so that it is well arranged clear and comprehensible even for the layman. The hybrid model has been modified so that it is not necessary to acquire the further data from the floating cars on-line and the model is merely calibrated based on the historical traffic data from the floating cars and the on-line data for estimating traffic excesses is not necessary for the set-up model. The recalibration of

J. Mikulski (Ed.): TST 2014, CCIS 471, pp. 166–173, 2014.

the model is necessary in the case of any changes in the transport or organizational relations. The model only receives online data from strategic traffic detectors and it works with its own historical outputs. Model these outputs archives and this also provides the added value of online data as well as historical data from the floating cars. This also enabled the pilot project using real time data from the detectors and the floating cars to display its potency for discovering traffic excesses within the framework of the SATEL (2A-1TP1/023) project and experience we can use in the TAČR RODOS project (TE01020155).

2   The Proposed Location

The original plan to estimate the travel times on motorways and two-lane expressways came up against a problem involving the fact that the selected sections where traffic detectors were already located were not subject to regular congestion or that it was not possible to designate a critical monitoring section within the framework of the pilot project from a historical point of view. A section of the "Jižní spojka" in the urban area of Prague was therefore selected, because it is one of the roads with the highest traffic intensity in the Czech Republic (ca 100,000 – 120,000 vehicles/24 hours in the measured section).

A section of the "Jižní spojka" was chosen for the purposes of verifying the function of the hybrid system in real traffic. The road has three lanes in each direction in the given section. The entire section is 3.6 km long and the highest permitted speed in the given section is 80 km/h. The theoretical travel time is therefore approximately 2 min, 45 s. The section has speed cameras at the beginning and the end of the section. These cameras monitor the vehicles in each lane and read their license plate numbers. If the vehicle drives through the entire section and is caught on camera at both ends, the given vehicle's license plate is paired. The monitoring has shown that this occurred in the case of ca 40% of vehicles during the first years of measurement in this section. The pairing of the license plates did not occur in case that vehicles left the test section before its end or if they entered it behind the initial camera. The pairing of license plates gradually occurred for a greater percentage of vehicles due to a change in the transport relations and the composition of the traffic flow. As a result there was achieved the more precise calibration of the model. The availability of the values of the resulting speeds (and therefore also the travel times) means that a highly precise verification tool exists for verifying the travel time estimation methods in this section. Three first generation strategic TrafiCam detectors from the Traficon Company were placed within the section. Every camera monitored the carriageway surface in front of it where so called virtual loops were defined for each lane.

The location of the strategic detectors can be seen in Fig. 1. The strategic cameras and the IDs of the individual lanes are marked by the points and the captions designating the IDs of the individual virtual loops. The lowest number in the trio designates the left-hand lane and the highest number designates the right-hand lane. The monitored section evaluated the movement of vehicles in the direction from the centre to the east, i.e. in the direction from the "Barrandovský most" to "Štěrboholská spojka".

Fig. 1. The map of the area for the proposed model [7]

Fig. 2. Speed measurement in the section [7]

3   The Types of Data

The traffic data was acquired from several sources. The measured data was transferred to the ELTODO laboratory. The actual calculation and calibration of the hybrid model took place on a server in the MATLAB program. The outputs of the model were automatically sent to the *satel.eltodo.cz* web server where the calculated travel times were presented using simple animation. The server is administered from the internet using a special application. This model is a hybrid and at the same time it is also unique in that it processes data from several sources of traffic variables provided by:

- the strategic detectors,
- the speed measurement in the section,
- the floating cars,
- the vehicles for model calibration.

3.1   The Data from the Strategic Detectors

The strategic detectors measure the traffic intensity (vehicles per hour) and occupancy of the virtual loop (percentage) at five-minute intervals (the data is aggregated every five minutes). There were a total of 9 virtual loops located at three measuring sites (profiles). In the case of a detector outage, an occupancy value of 101% and an intensity of 0 vehicles/5min was recorded which meant that any such outages were readily apparent and easily noticeable. The date and time, the detector's ID, the traffic intensity and the occupancy were the important outputs from the strategic detectors.

3.2   The Data from the Speed Measurement in the Section

The already installed speed measurement system in the section was used for the evaluation using the speed measurement in the section. The cameras recognise the license plates of the passing vehicles. The individual cameras use a signal from GPS satellites for precise synchronisation. They are also equipped with infra-red reflectors or infra-red flashes to ensure their reliable functioning at night. The vehicle's license plate is scanned at the beginning and the end of the measured section. The precise time of the vehicle's passage is essential for the system's functioning. Given the fact that the detector position is known and unchanging, the speed in the section can be calculated according to the simple formula: $v=s/(t_1-t_2)$, where s is the known distance between the two cameras and t_1 and t_2 are the precise times when the vehicle passed through the first and second measured profiles. The date, time, speed and lane designation were also processed. Otherwise, the file also included information about the set speed limit and the tolerance above the given speed limit

3.3   GPS Data from Company Vehicles

The data from the company cars of Telefonica O2 Czech Republic, a.s. was provided by Secar Bohemia a.s. The company cars were equipped with a GPS/GPRS modem which receives a signal from the GPS satellites and sends information on the position of the vehicle to a server.

The data was provided from two locations; 0 – 35 km of the D1 motorway from Prague and the larger part of the "Jižní spojka" at a length in excess of 9.4 km. The depiction of the positions of all the records gives rise to a map of the part of "Jižní spojka". This part was not further researched in 2011 due to the failure to resolve the financial requirements of the aforementioned companies pertaining to the provision of the on-line data. The hybrid model further makes use of the measured historical data which is assigned a weight. The modification of the statistical weight of the data entering the hybrid model was taken into according during the updating of the database. This data was given priority designation for training the neural networks which had already been trained from previous years and the data from other sources was used for their calibration, for example the ELTODO floating car which was simultaneously used as a calibration and test vehicle. The test vehicle was equipped with a new unit which also had the option of making a video recording. The unit provided GPS coordinates, speed and altitude. This data entered the hybrid model off-line and the model could subsequently be visually checked thanks to the video recording.

4   Data Processing

As has been stated above, the data inputs to the hybrid model involved data from 3 types of detectors:

- Camea section detectors (the speed measurement in the section),
- the data from SECAR Bohemia floating cars (the immediate speed of the vehicles) and the ELTODO calibration car (GPS, the route, time and speed),
- the data from the strategic video detection detectors (the vehicle intensity, the occupancy in the detector's virtual loop).

The data output is an estimate of the travel time on the "Jižní spojka", on the basis of which it is possible to identify a traffic excess. The trained and calibrated neural networks which designate the travel time in the monitored section on the basis of the inputted traffic data constitute the heart of the model. The sets of data entering the neural networks must be pre-processed so that they can subsequently be merged with the hybrid model. The model of the estimated travel times based on decision trees is preserved in the hybrid model for the comparison and evaluation of the functionality of the proposed model. The creation of the final data matrix for training the neural networks especially requires the harmonisation of the time base and the aggregation and position of the data source. Five-minute sections are created for each selected day of the week and the averages of the individual values are entered into them. The five-minute time aggregation has been selected upon the basis of the time aggregation of the strategic detectors, because they are the main source of the on-line data. This leads to the creation of an input matrix for the neural networks for all the data inputs during the calculation.

4.1   The Selection of Suitable Data for Training the Hybrid System

The input data was not always simultaneously available from all the data sources. The data was not provided continuously from a legislative and political point of view. Therefore, the data set was used for the calibration of the hybrid model retroactively for the provided period with the allocation of the appropriate statistical weight of the data.

In the last year of the solution, there was added a module for filtering and modifying data in the case of the entry of inconsistent data into the model. This mainly involves data outages from the strategic detectors, inconsistent data matrices and cases involving faults in the detectors. Three protective methods were implemented against the possible disruption of the input data:

- a detector outage / a communication error – the missing data is additionally calculated from the historical model
- inconsistent data matrices – empty / incomplete lines are deleted and the matrix is recalculated with regard to the time aggregation
- upon the detection of malfunctioning / a missing function in the model, the model is automatically renewed at its previous position

5   The Architecture and Training of the Hybrid System Module

The architecture of the hybrid model combines two methods of evaluating the traffic data. In this sense, hybrid means the use of off-line and on-line traffic data from various sources which are merged.

5.1   The Decision Trees

The decision trees were created upon the basis of the training set in MATLAB. The input data from the traffic detectors on the lane occupancy and the measured speeds from the floating cars were introduced after the creation of the model from the training data. The input data was subsequently compared with the data measured by the Camea system. Fig. 3 contains an example of a created decision tree for a given day based on the training data set.

The model's output includes the section speeds for a group of vehicles which are subsequently recalculated for the travel time through the measured section. Optimisation criteria are calculated for the verifying data set.

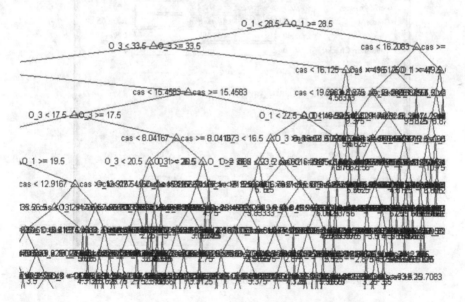

Fig. 3. An example of a decision tree [7]

5.2   The Neural Networks

The neural networks have been created by a function at MATLAB. This involves a feed-forward neural network with seven neurons in one hidden layer. The teaching takes place in a maximum of 100 stages. The same input and output data as for the decision tree is used for the teaching. Given the fact that the teaching is a random process, several neural networks are created, from which the neural network with the best result in the verifying data sample is subsequently selected.

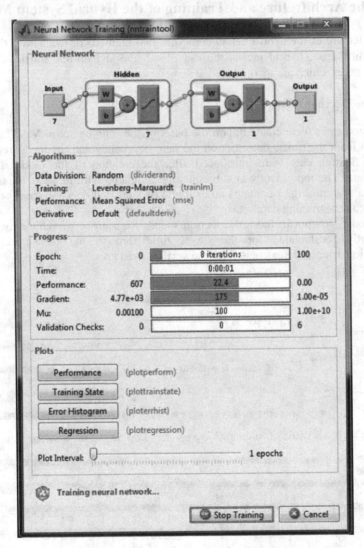

Fig. 4. An example of the use of the neural network [7]

6   Conclusion

A higher degree of accuracy in the hybrid model for estimating travel times with the lower penetration of floating cars has been achieved thanks to the added modules working with the historical data. The data from the strategic detectors has become the main data matrix and the other data from the floating cars is only used for calibration and it is only possible to use data from the strategic detectors for the estimation of traffic excesses once the neural networks or the decision trees have been trained. In 2011, it was shown that historical traffic data can also be used to train the hybrid model. The retroactive calibration on the basis of the historical data is conditional upon the traffic data from all the detectors used in the model being from the same period.

The pilot project within the framework of the SATEL project has been transferred to a real application which is able to work without an operator and to automatically provide information using the web presentation of the travel times on the monitored road ("Jižní spojka") merely upon the basis of strategic detectors. This fact has been confirmed thanks to the year-round monitoring and evaluation of the traffic on the ring road. The training of the hybrid model took place gradually and the model was also later calibrated. An important factor was the addition of a module to account for the case of damaged or missing data. The conclusion is that this system may be applied on general (any) roads with the use of minimal telematic equipment in the form of strategic detectors, provided data is also acquired (collected) from floating cars (on-line or off-line) which can then be paired with the data from the strategic detectors.

References

1. Přikryl, J., et al.: A comparison by Simulation of Different Approaches to the Urban Traffic Control. Archives of Transport System Telematic 5(4) (November 2012)
2. Coifman, B.: Estimating Travel Times and Vehicle Trajectories on Freeways Using Dual Loop Detectors. Ohio State University: Columbus (2008)
3. Wardrop, J.G.: Some Theoretical Aspects of Road Traffic Research. Proc. of the Institute of Civil Engineers 1-2, 325–378 (1952)
4. Liu, B., Zhang, T., Li, Q., Wang, L.: A Traffic Control Method Based on the Real Time Detector Delay. Communications – Scientific Letter of Zilina University 2 (2010)
5. Hai-Min, J., Yu-Long, P.: Neural Network Optimized by Generic Algorithm of Models for Real Time Forecast of Traffic Flow, Communications – Scientific Letter of Zilina University, 3 (2010)
6. Shen, L.: Freeway Travel Time Estimation and Prediction Using Dynamic Neural Networks, FIU Electronic Theses and Dissertations, Paper 17 (2008)
7. Škodáček, M., Smutný, M.: Satelitni lokalizace vozidel v dopravni telematice – SATEL [Vehicle Satellite Localization in Traffic Telematics], Projekt MPO #. 2A_1TP1/023, VZ 337-2011-1930-EEG, Prague (2011)

Influence of Road Conditions on the Stability of a Laden Vehicle Mathematical Model, Realising a Single Lane Change Maneuver

Jarosław Zalewski

Warsaw University of Technology,
Faculty of Administration and Social Sciences,
Pl. Politechniki 1, 00-661 Warsaw, Poland
j.zalewski@ans.pw.edu.pl

Abstract. An analysis of the impact of road conditions on the stochastic technical stability of a motor vehicle mathematical model was prepared, with additional, non-uniform load, and for the necessity to change lanes due to eg. bypassing obstacles or overtaking. The simulation was performed for adverse road conditions at randomly occurring surface unevenness.

Research was based on a motion simulation of a vehicle model at a speed of 100km/h, enabling analysis of the influence of both the mass – inertia parameters and the road surface conditions. Two cases were considered: the motion on a flat and icy and an uneven and icy road. Simulation of a mathematical model of a sports vehicle was prepared in an MSC Adams/Car environment. The considered model included non-linear characteristics of its flexible elements.

Presented results can also be used as one of the series of experiments proving the versatility of the discussed method, not only for the road vehicles.

Keywords: stability, motor vehicle load, single lane change.

1   Introduction

Stability examination of mathematical models of motor vehicles can not only reduce costs and logistics when comparing with road tests, but also facilitate the selection of the definition, according to which the motion of a model is examined, as well as analysis of the same maneuver in various traffic conditions.

Among the most popular stability definitions for the examination of motion of mathematical models, the most appropriate seem to be the definition of stochastic technical stability [1]. Its advantage is the ability to analyse the motion of a modeled system with occurrence of random disturbances (eg. deriving from an uneven road surface in case of examination of a moving vehicle, or track unevenness for the models of railway vehicles [2]), and the ability to compare the obtained results with the results (trajectories) for the real technical objects.

To examine the stability, a model of a sports two-seater, rear-engine motor vehicle was selected. The simulation of a single lane change was implemented for a flat and a

J. Mikulski (Ed.): TST 2014, CCIS 471, pp. 174–184, 2014.

randomly uneven road surface, both icy, in order to provide the extreme conditions at which it is easy for a vehicle to lose its stability.

2   Assumptions

The purpose of the simulation was to verify the effect of uneven load distribution in the vehicle body on the stochastic technical stability of a vehicle model, performing a specific maneuver in different road conditions. The single lane change maneuver in extreme conditions with a definite path was selected, while the simulation itself was accomplished using MSC Adams/Car component.

Figure 1 shows a physical model of the simulated sport vehicle having 90 degrees of freedom [5], consisting of several modules (sub-systems) with dynamic properties similar to the real ones. The presented model is a two-seater motor vehicle (Fig.1), thus the load is represented by the two masses (driver and passenger) as well as the luggage placed in the front. The location of the center of mass is defined in relation to a point called "origo" (Fig. 2), which represents the origin of the coordinate system attached with the road, but moving along with the vehicle. Other necessary coordinate systems were adopted in accordance with the assumptions in the work [8].

Suspension of the physical model in MSC Adams consists of transverse links and MacPherson strut with nonlinear dampers and springs. Power is transferred to the rear axle, the engine is also mounted on the back of the vehicle, behind the passenger compartment.

The following assumptions, both for the load of the vehicle and the course of the maneuver, were taken:

- vehicle body mass qeual to 995kg was increased by the mass of luggage (60kg), the driver (75kg) and the passenger (110kg), which is shown in Fig. 3 and 4;
- the initial speed of the car was 100km/h, the vehicle was moving at the fifth gear;
- the motion took place on a flat and icy road surface ($\mu = 0.3$), as well as on an icy surface with randomly occurring unevenness;

Fig. 1. The view of a tested vehicle model [7]

Fig. 2. Location of the „origo" point [7]

Assuming that the motor vehicle body can be represented as a collection of rectangulars or cuboids representing specific body element, description of the mathematical model of the vehicle was taken from [5-6], or in a more complex way – [8].

Using the static moments the coordinates of the center of mass in the analysed vehicle were determined, taking into account the location of the driver and the passenger, the masses m1 = 75kg and m2 = 110kg respectively, as well as the baggage mB = 60kg (Fig. 3). It was assumed that the location of the masses m1 and m2 lies in one plane.

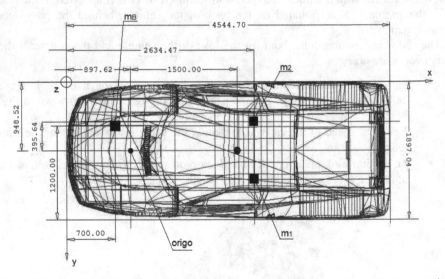

Fig. 3. Distribution of the aggravating masses in the body of a tested model, the overview [own study]

As a result of the calculations the following results were obtained:

- the coordinates of the center of mass of an unladen vehicle body relative to the "origo" point:

$$x_c = 1{,}5m, \quad y_c = 0, \quad z_c = 0{,}45m \, ;$$

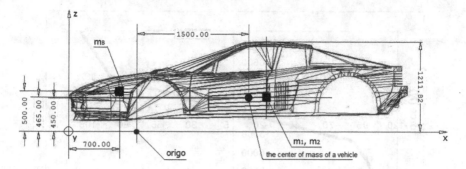

Fig. 4. Distribution of the aggravating masses in the body of a tested model, the side view [own study]

- the coordinates of the center of mass of a vehicle body laden with the driver, passenger and the baggage, relative to the "origo" point:

$$x_c = 1,472m, \quad y_c = 0,085m, \quad z_c = 0,454m.$$

Selected mass – inertia parameters of the sports vehicle model used in the simulation:

- unladen body mass: $m_n = 995kg$;
- the mass of the body laden with two passengers and the baggage: $m_o = 1240kg$;
- the mass of the unladen vehicle: $m_{pn} = 1528kg$;
- the mass of the vehicle laden with two passengers and the baggage: $m_{po} = 1773kg$;
- nominal coordinates of the vehicle center of mass relative to the front left corner: $x_c = 2,2m, \quad y_c = 0,948m, \quad z_c = 0,45m$;
- coordinates of the laden vehicle center of mass relative to the front left corner: $x_c = 2,172m, \quad y_c = 1,033m, \quad z_c = 0,454m$;
- nominal values of the moments of inertia and deviation relative to the center of mass of the unladen vehicle :

$$I_x = 299\,kg \cdot m^2, \quad I_y = 1260\,kg \cdot m^2, \quad I_z = 1437\,kg \cdot m^2$$

$$I_{xy} = 1,34kg \cdot m^2, \quad I_{xz} = -0,785kg \cdot m^2, \quad I_{yz} = -0,33kg \cdot m^2 \;;$$

- the moments of inertia and deviation in relation to the center of mass of the laden vehicle:

$$I_x = 303\,kg \cdot m^2, \quad I_y = 1281\,kg \cdot m^2, \quad I_z = 1463\,kg \cdot m^2$$

$$I_{xy} = -32,4kg \cdot m^2, \quad I_{xz} = -3,16kg \cdot m^2, \quad I_{yz} = 2,24kg \cdot m^2 \,.$$

The model used in the simulation has nonlinear elastic – damping elements. In Fig. 5 the characteristics of the spring deflection is shown, whereas in Fig. 6 –the damping force versus the velocity of the acting damper in a MacPherson strut column.

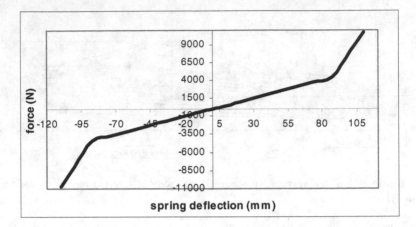

Fig. 5. The force as a function of the spring deflection in the suspension of the analysed model [own study]

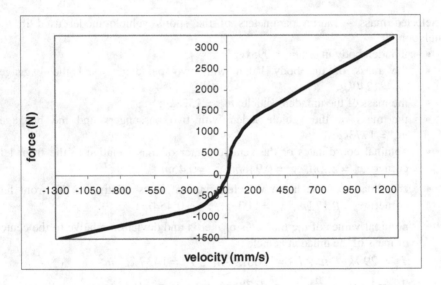

Fig. 6. The damping force as a function of velocity in the damper of the analysed vehicle suspension [own study]

Because of the random nature of road unevenness an FTIRE (flexible tire ring) model was used, insteaed of the nominal PAC89 tire model, as the only available in the Adams/Car database able to cooperate with such road surface [7].

The FTIRE model is made of deformable panels connected with spring elements and able to deform in the longitudinal, transverse and vertical direction. Other typical tire models do not have this feature, because their properties do not allow running the simulation on the uneven road surface profile, whose unevenness wavelength is shorter than the radius of the wheel [7].

3   Simulation Description

The simulation of the single lane change manuver was run for the following sets of vehicle and road configurations:

a) a vehicle laden with a driver, a passenger and a baggage, according to the assumptions, moving on a flat and icy (μ=0.3) road;

b) a vehicle laden with a driver, a passenger and a baggage moving on an icy road with randomly occurring unevenness.

Using the static moments the new coordinates of the center of mass in the analysed vehicle were calculated. As a result of these, the new values of the moments of inertia and deviation of the whole vehicle model were obtained.

The maneuver of a single lane change was realised on a road section, which was 480m long, at a constant speed of 100km/h. Random disturbances originating from the road surface are described in [8]. The described maneuver was carried out in the extreme road conditions (icy surface).

The aim of research for both road configurations was to verify the influence of the uneven mass distribution, as well as the difficult road conditions, on the stability of the analysed vehicle mathematical model. For the motion at random disturbances the additional extreme conditions were used, i.e. randomly occurring road unevenness.

4   Definition of the Stochastic Technical Stability

The definition of stochastic technical stability are based on the work [1].

Given a system of stochastic equations

$$\frac{dx}{dt} = f[x,t,\xi(t)] \tag{1}$$

where $x=(x_1,...,x_n)$ and $f(x,t,y)=(f_1,...f_n)$ are vectors, however $\xi(t)=(\xi_1,..., \xi_n)$, $t{\geq}0$ is a stochastic process describing randomly occurring disturbances. The function $f(x,t,y)$ is assumed to be determined for each $x, y \in E_n$ and $t{\geq}0$. It was also assumed that for the stochastic process $f(0,t,\xi(t))$ occurs

$$P\{\int_0^T |f(0,t,\xi(t))| dt < \infty\} = 1 \quad for\ each T > 0 \tag{2}$$

The existence of a stochastic process $f(X,t,\xi(t))$ satisfying the Lipschitz criterion in the interval [0, T] was also assumed

$$|f(x_2,t,\xi(t)) - f(x_1,t,\xi(t))| \leq \eta(t)|x_2 - x_1| \tag{3}$$

for another process $\eta(t)$, absolutely integrable in the given interval.

The result of the above assumptions is the existence of only one solution with the initial conditions $t=t_0$ and $x(t_0)=x_0$, which is an absolutely continuous stochastic process, with the probability 1 for $t{\geq}t_0$.

It was assumed that in the Euclidean space E_n exist two areas: ω – limited and open, as well as Ω – limited and closed, where $\omega \subset \Omega$. The existence of a positive number ε, where $0 < \varepsilon < 1$, and a stochastic process $X(t)$ specified for $t \geq t_0$ was also assumed.

The initial conditions of each solution were described as $t=t_0$, $x(t_0)=x_0$ and the solution itself as (t,t_0,x_0).

The definition of stochastic technical stability is:

if each of the solutions of equation (1), having its initial conditions in ω area, belongs to the Ω area with the probability $1-\varepsilon$, then the system (1) is stochastically technically stable towards ω, Ω and the process $\xi(t)$ with the probability $1-\varepsilon$ (Fig. 7).

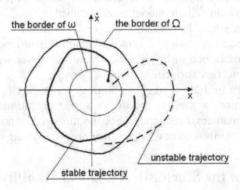

the border of ω the border of Ω

unstable trajectory

stable trajectory

Fig. 7. Graphic interpretation of the stochastic technical stability [3]

$$P\{(t,t_0,x_0) \in \Omega\} > 1-\varepsilon, \quad for \ \ \overline{x}_0 \in \omega \tag{4}$$

5   Results

As a result of the simulations two trajectories were obtained for each of the described traffic conditions – for the vehicle traveling on a road with a flat surface (thin curve), and for the vehicle on a road with an uneven surface (bold curve) (Fig. 8). For further analysis a part of both trajectories, corresponding with the interval from 160 to 480 meters, was used. This interval is marked as [x; x+dx], which is presented in Fig. 9. It was divided into sub-intervals with the step of $\Delta s=10m$. As a consequence, 32 sub-intervals were obtained.

As an Ω area, a set of state space E was adopted, containing a part of the trajectory associated with the [x; x+dx] interval. This set is therefore the width of the road, on which the motion for the selected stage of the maneuver has occurred. The area was divided into 10 classes [K1 ;K10], every 0.1m (Fig. 9). This range represents the part of the trajectory, where the model of the vehicle enters the adjacent lane, endeavouring to realise the linear motion.

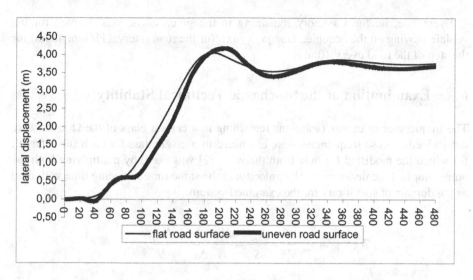

Fig. 8. Lateral displacement as a function of the road [own study]

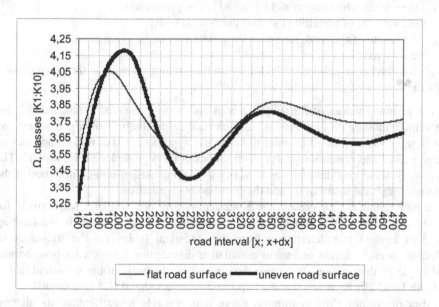

Fig. 9. The markings of both the road interval [x; x+dx] and the classes of the Ω area [own study]

The vehicle motion was subject to the greatest disruption in the given interval, because of the pursuit to straightforwardness in order to the stay on an occupied lane. On the axis of the lateral displacement (Fig. 9) the classes belonging to the set Ω (vertical lines) were marked, however on the road length axis – the sub-intervals of the interval [x ;x+dx]. Both markings created a grid composed of gray lines.

Event rate, ie. the trajectory remaining in the given class, was counted for the vehicle moving on the occupied lane [x; x+dx], for the road interval [160m, 480m] for the step of the road every 10m.

6   Examination of the Stochastic Technical Stability

The frequencies of events (solutions remaining in a certain class of the Ω area) were determined. Thsese frequencies were examined in a given class for each sub-interval, for which the modified formula from the work [2] was used, by multiplying both the numerator and the denominator by velocity, at the same time replacing time with road as the domain of specificity for the examined system.

$$W(K_j) = \frac{T_{Kj} \cdot V}{T \cdot V} = \frac{S_{Kj}}{S} = \frac{N_{Kj} \cdot \Delta s}{N \cdot \Delta s} = \frac{N_{Kj}}{N} \tag{5}$$

where:
- T_{Kj} - the time at which the model remained in the given class;
- T - the total time of travelling the road interval [s; s+ds];
- S_{Kj} - the length of the road, for which the model was in the given class;
- S - the total road length;
- N_{Kj} - the number of sub-intervals, for which the solution remains in the given class;
- N - the number of all sub-intervals.

The resulting values of the frequencies of events are presented in tab. 1 and 2, for the vehicle moving on the even and uneven road respectively. Kolmogorov-Smirnov test (λ test) was conducted in order to verify the hypothesis H0 of non-compliance of the staggered and continuous curve distributions at the significance level α=0.05. The purpose of these calculations was to verify the hypothesis of non-compliance of the obtained empirical distribution and the continuous distribution.

In both tables D_n, D_x present the Kolmogorov-Smirnov statistics respectively for the normal (Gaussian) and the Rayleigh distribution. Critical value is the limiting value of lambda test determined from the statistical tables for the frequency of solutions in each class. Continuous cumulative distribution function for both normal and Rayleigh distributions were also determined on the basis of the statistical tables. In table 1 and 2 H.R. means that the hypothesis is rejected and H.A. – accepted.

After determining the continuous curve it is possible to extrapolate to adjacent intervals, especially higher ones, which is important especially for the maximum displacements. As a result, it allows to determine the probability of the trajectory remaining not only in the considered range of random variables, but also in the subsequent intervals.

Table 1. Verification of the hypothesis of non-compliance of distributions for the [x ;x+dx] interval on the basis of the lambda test for the flat road surface

class	N_{Kj}	W(Kj)	critical value	stepped curve F(Kj)	cumulative distribution function (normal distribution) F(u)	D_n	lambda test (α = 0,05)	cumulative distribution function (Rayleigh distribution) F(x)	D_x	lambda test (α = 0,05)
1	0	0	-	0	0	0	-	0	0	-
2	0	0	-	0	0	0	-	0	0	-
3	4	0,125	0,624	0,125	0	0,125	H.R.	0,046	0,079	H.R.
4	4	0,125	0,624	0,250	0	0,25	H.R.	0,173	0,077	H.R.
5	6	0,188	0,519	0,438	0	0,438	H.R.	0,44	0,003	H.R.
6	11	0,344	0,391	0,781	0,715	0,066	H.R.	0,843	0,062	H.R.
7	4	0,125	0,624	0,906	0,810	0,096	H.R.	0,917	0,011	H.R.
8	2	0,063	0,842	0,969	0,848	0,121	H.R.	0,942	0,027	H.R.
9	1	0,031	0,975	1	0,866	0,134	H.R.	0,952	0,048	H.R.
10	0	0	-	1	0,866	0,134	-	0,952	0,048	-

Table 2. Verification of the hypothesis of non-compliance of distributions for the [x; x+dx] interval on the basis of the lambda test for the uneven road surface

class	N_{Kj}	W(Kj)	critical value	stepped curve F(Kj)	cumulative distribution function (normal distribution) F(u)	D_n	lambda test (α = 0,05)	cumulative distribution function (Rayleigh distribution) F(x)	D_x	lambda test (α = 0,05)
1	1	0,031	0,975	0,031	0	0,031	H.R.	0,004	0,027	H.R.
2	3	0,094	0,707	0,125	0	0,125	H.R.	0,061	0,064	H.R.
3	2	0,063	0,841	0,188	0	0,188	H.R.	0,131	0,057	H.R.
4	8	0,250	0,454	0,438	0	0,438	H.R.	0,535	0,098	H.R.
5	7	0,219	0,483	0,656	0,563	0,093	H.R.	0,821	0,165	H.R.
6	6	0,188	0,519	0,844	0,754	0,090	H.R.	0,942	0,098	H.R.
7	1	0,031	0,975	0,875	0,779	0,096	H.R.	0,953	0,078	H.R.
8	1	0,031	0,975	0,906	0,805	0,101	H.R.	0,962	0,056	H.R.
9	1	0,031	0,975	0,938	0,828	0,110	H.R.	0,970	0,033	H.R.
10	2	0,063	0,841	1	0,870	0,130	H.R.	0,982	0,018	H.R.

7   Conclusion

The maximum amplitude values of the trajectories for the vehicle with disturbances of the center of mass are, in accordance with the accepted principles, near the boundary of stability, for which the road width of 5m was adopted. It has to be taken into account that the trajectories show the motion of a representative point of the whole system, i.e. the center of mass. If the width of the vehicle (about 1.8m) is also considered, then the wheels on the outside of the occupied lane, for the largest amplitudes, are outside the road, however during its efforts to perform the straightline motion the vehicle remained at the boundary of stability.

In both compared tables in the specific classes there are differences between the rates of the event frequencies obtained for both disturbed and undisturbed motion. This is particularly evident for the interval between 180 and 320m of the road. The largest differences exist for the classes:

- 4 (0.125 for the motion on the smooth surface and 0.25 on the uneven one);
- 5 (0.188 for the motion on the smooth surface and 0.219 on the uneven one);
- 6 (0.344 for the motion on the smooth surface and 0.188 on the uneven one);
- 7 (0.125 for the motion on the smooth surface and 0.031 on the uneven one);

The maximum amplitude of the trajectory of the moving vehicle on the smooth surface for the class no. 10 is 0, while on the uneven surface it is 0.063.

From the presented considerations it can be concluded that the condition of the surface, especially with adverse road conditions (ice) affects the movement of a vehicle with a non-uniform load, especially at higher speeds and abrupt maneuvers.

From the analysis of the trajectories as a whole it can also be observed that the worse the certain road surface conditions, the more difficult the return of the vehicle to the steady state of motion.

References

1. Bogusz, W.: Stateczność techniczna. PWN, Warszawa (1972)
2. Kisilowski, J., Kardas-Cinal, E.: On a Certain Method of Examining Stability of Mathematical Models of railway Vehicles with Disturbances Occurring in Real Objects, VSD Suplement. In: Proceedings of 13th IAVSD Symposium held in Chengdu, Sichuan, P. R. China, vol. 23 (1993)
3. Kisilowski, J., Zalewski, J.: On a certain possibility of practical application of stochastic technical stability. Eksploatacja i niezawodność, Maintenance and Reliability 1(37) (2008)
4. Kisilowski, J., Zalewski, J.: Certain results of examination of technical stochastic stability of a car after accident repair. Zeszyty Naukowe Instytutu Pojazdów 5(81) (2010)
5. Nabagło, T.: Synteza układu sterowania semiaktywnego zawieszenia samochodu z elementami magnetoreologicznymi, Rozprawa doktorska. Politechnika Krakowska, Kraków (2006)
6. Luke, N.: Reinforcement learning of dynamic collaborative driving, Doctoral thesis, Waterloo, Ontario, Canada (2008)
7. Using Adams Guide, MSC Software Corporation
8. Zalewski, J.: Modelowanie wpływu zaburzeń geometrii nadwozia na stateczność ruchu pojazdu samochodowego, Rozprawa doktorska, Politechnika Warszawska (2011)

Telematics of Supply Chain –
Areas, Opportunities, Challenges

Andrzej Bujak[1], Anna Orzeł[1], and Ryszard K. Miler[2]

[1] Wrocław School of Banking, Institute of Logistics,
Fabryczna 29-31, 53-609 Wrocław, Poland
andrzej.bujak@interia.pl,
anna.orzel@wsb.wroclaw.pl
[2] Gdańsk School of Banking, Faculty of Finance and Management,
Dolna Brama 8, 80-821 Gdańsk, Poland
rmiler@poczta.onet.pl

Abstract. The knowledge of the latest concepts and solutions dealing with a multitude of areas including telematic solutions and their correct implementation to support actions in progress, becomes one of the essential elements of gaining success in current market conditions. Telematic solutions make it possible not only to automate and shorten processes and logistic activities, but also affect their safety and enable greater flexibility and reliability in the supply chain. They also constitute a feature that allows to reduce the negative impact of transport on the environment. The use of telematics solutions within the supply chain should be considered as a process of dissemination of technological innovation, the result of which should be a clear improvement of the functioning of many processes within the chain, especially the increase in the level of transport services. Therefore, the research and analysis from this area related to the implementation in logistics practice, should be considered as a priority now.

Keywords: telematics, telematics of supply chain, technological innovation, safety, flexibility and reliability in the supply chain.

1 Introduction

Modern logistics is perceived globally and, similarly to science, is constantly expanding its borders to effectively adapt to global trends and strategies. Permanently increasing complexity of processes and logistics activities resulting from the global expansion, as well as various circumstances generated in heterogeneous parts of the world, makes it necessary to not only constantly improve them, but also prepare new, often innovative, solutions or concepts. Modern logistics has to generate such capabilities, which will allow to effectively implement the tasks placed before it in current and prospective conditions, and this, in particular, refers to the functioning of supply chains. A key factor affecting the future logistic solutions in the area of organisation and operation of a modern and prospective supply chain will be the implementation of technical solutions from a variety of areas including telematics.

J. Mikulski (Ed.): TST 2014, CCIS 471, pp. 185–195, 2014.
© Springer-Verlag Berlin Heidelberg 2014

The knowledge of the latest and future telematic concepts and solutions and their correct implementation to support actions in progress, becomes one of the essential elements of gaining success in current market conditions. The introduction of telematic solutions makes it possible not only to automate and shorten processes and logistic activities, but also affects their safety and enables greater flexibility and reliability of the activities within supply chain. Additionally, it is a feature that allows to reduce the negative impact of transport on the environment. Therefore, the ability to properly use even wider range of opportunities which are generated by modern telematics and its solutions for conducted logistic activities, becomes one of the fundamental issues.

The article partly presents the results of studies conducted by the Institute of Logistics at Wrocław School of Banking. The pace of modern transformations, which is primarily the result of the technological revolution, generates the need for constant identifying the key changes that will occur in the near future. This refers, in particular, to logistics, which nowadays is subject to especially rapid change. These changes concern not only technology, strategy but first of all relevant training of personnel – their mobility, skills and ability for creative and experienced thinking and the ability for developing new solutions and paradigms in logistics, which meet the needs of the market and customers. Therefore, the Institute of Logistics at Wrocław School of Banking, which is responsible for educating more than 2.5 thousand students studying logistics, carries out empirical research programme, the aim of which is to indicate the directions of the development of logistics and the dynamics of the anticipated changes in particularly important areas, which, among others, include: new concepts (strategies) for accomplishing logistic tasks, new technologies used in logistics, innovativeness as well as safety and risk in logistics. In addition to the indicated aim connected with a pragmatic adaptation of training programmes for logistics personnel to market requirements and customers expectations, an important objective is also an indication of changes in the area of logistics system of Lower Silesia and its functioning, which in combination with the first objective will increase the level of attractiveness and competitiveness of the region. The already existing and emerging (newly created) logistics companies, mainly from the region of Lower Silesia, will benefit from the project. These will include such commercial entities like: investors, forwarding companies, transport companies, logistics operators, as well as public and research organisations.

The indicated targets, which have been broken down in more detail, as well as the desire to obtain the most reliable results of conducted research led to the adoption of appropriate methods of research. In general, the study was conducted in accordance with the Delphi method, which belongs to heuristic methods of forecasting. It uses the knowledge of experts and their assumptions concerning the future emergence of solutions to problems, assuming that the predictions made by a group of people are characterized by greater accuracy than estimates of individuals. The study was conducted in two stages using a survey techniques. The main research tool was a questionnaire consisting of a few to several questions. Also the expert in-depth interviews with specialists from the industry, based on a screenplay of the conversation were performed. The tools also included a scenario method, which was used to study the changes that may occur in the implementation of the logistics processes in a given time horizon. The scenarios presented have shown a string of events starting from the initial situation through a logical sequence of events leading to possible future taking into account the tendencies and trends currently dominating and the foreseeable future.

2   Modern Supply Chain

One of the key challenges facing the modern logistics are issues related to the management and operation of a modern supply chain. A supply chain can be defined as "a network of organizations engaged, through the relationships with suppliers and customers, in a variety of processes and activities that make up the value in the form of products and services provided to final consumers" [1]. In defining the concept of "supply chain" there is a consensus among many theorists on how to present this term [2-5]. A slightly different situation occurs when specifying the basis for supply chain management. It was already noticed in [6], where, it is stated that: "*while a consensus can be seen in the definition of the supply chain, there is a lack of harmony in the definitions of activities and types of relationships that are within the range of supply chain management*". This lack of consistency in this area stems from the fact that the authors of the considerations choose different perspectives and approaches to this problem [7-10].

The latest trends and concepts of functioning of SCM relate to the possibility of building a comprehensive management of all the links and processes in it. It is not possible to manage something which cannot be seen - this is the primary issue. There are numerous logistic processes implemented by individual links in the supply chain. The scale of this problem is, for instance is illustrated in [2] where it is refers to the process of evolution of logistics leading to modern supply chain management (SCM) (Fig. 1) [2].

Contemporary development and creation of supply chains, which are increasingly global in nature, results from changes in the following circumstances: economic, financial, organizational, international legal, technical and technological. Changes to these conditions, which have been undergoing more or less dynamically, led to a gradual transformation of the traditional model of functioning of the economy into a very dynamic network of links and dependencies.

A contemporary modern supply chain is characterized by many features, but the essential ones include:

- capacity for rapid reaction, ability to meet rapidly changing demand;
- flexibility and ability to adapt to the optimum: cost-level of service;
- ability to make optimal use of the resources of the company;
- ability to use all of the available information.

Today, in the era of integration and internationalisation as well as rapid and dynamic changes, a lot of attention is paid to the search for new forms, ways and concepts of operation of supply chain, which would meet current and future requirements, especially in the area of meeting customer's expectations, thereby creating a competitive advantage. It is difficult to identify and describe all concepts in this area, however, two of them have a crucial meaning:

- transfer of competitive struggle to the entire supply chain;
- increase in transparency of the supply chain.

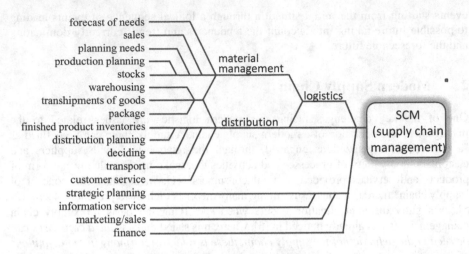

Fig. 1. Evolution of logistics [2]

The technical and technological revolution, which we have been witnessing since the turn of the centuries, changed the way of collaborating of suppliers and customers, as well as other traditional links of supply chains. To be on time with the booming market, today's companies must seek opportunities to build a competitive advantage outside their organizations. Individual effort often turns out to be insufficient to fully meet customer expectations. To be able to meet them companies are forced to carry out joint activities together with their trading partners.

"Transparency in the supply chain" - the main objective of the solutions for transparency in the supply chain solutions is to improve the organizational capacity of the operators to connect logistics and transport functions, and through the use of global standards to increase productivity. The increase in transparency in the supply chain is an element which can lead to a reduction in costs and result in improved performance. In addition, it is necessary to recognize changes in the approach to the issue of product knowledge among today's customers. Consumers, public authorities and businesses are demanding detailed information on systems and sources of supply, and are directly interested in issues such as the quality of the particular activities and processes, safety, ethics and the impact of a business on the environment. There are more and more tools which ensure the transparency of supply chains. These include product labels and Internet databases available to customers as well as Web cams, which show in real time what happens in the suppliers' plants throughout the whole supply chain, at any stage of the flows. Thus, the following questions occur more frequently: where are my goods, what is happening to them, how are they transported, where do they come from. Today's companies must know the answers to these questions, give chances to a potential customer to track their goods (consignment). The lack of such opportunities brings on the consequence of leaving (the loss of) customers.

A crucial element as well as a determinant of modern supply chains is their improvement by applying the methods of lean logistics and the use of the latest solutions from the IT area, especially ERP software (Enterprise Requirements Planning), systems allowing for appropriate and efficient planning and using the resources of the company. The combination of this concept and the use of modern tools gives a chance to better deal with many contemporary problems, e.g. the problem of uncertainty, which is one of the conditions of operation of supply chains in the market economy.

A lot of analyses and searching for new and better (innovative) solutions also apply to the issue of raising the efficiency of supply chain management. In this context, most often "automatization of transaction" and "stabilizing operating conditions" are pointed out as more effective solutions. Elimination and simplification of transactions shall be treated as a way to improve supply chain management.

Nowadays, the development of technologies and the competitive struggle have led to a situation where consumers have a choice of many technologically advanced goods, whose quality is comparable, or the difference of which is increasingly difficult to notice. In this situation, gaining a competitive advantage and its maintenance is becoming more and more dependent on the efficiency of the entire supply chain rather than the product itself. Key success factors in the supply chain become, apart from its organization (range), speed and flexibility to respond to changing market situation, including issues related to safety and effective response to possible risks of logistics tasks.

3   Telematic Solutions in Supply Chain

A supply chain should be characterized by an ongoing process of improvements. Therefore, managing the supply chain, being the coordinator of this chain, becomes a very important task. Today, there is an increase in customer requirements in terms of duration of delivery services, their flexibility, availability and reliability. The expectations and the requirements of customers grow and, on the other hand, a need occurs to reduce costs and limit the amount of capital tie-up. Currently, it is very important for consumers that products and services are tailored to their individual needs. Consumers are becoming more and more impatient. How to meet these expectations in the context of supply chain? The required speed of response and need to ensure high level of safety as well as the possibility to efficiently respond to potential dangers in the supply chain, generates the need to use all the modern technical and technological solutions and latest concepts for functioning of logistics, including solutions from the area of telematics.

The broadest area of use of telematic solutions in the supply chain is, of course, transport, which combines the individual links. In this case, telematics, or rather telematics of transport, will refer to the movement of people and goods (the cargo), using the appropriate means of transport and technical solutions - organizational, which through integrating IT and telecommunication solutions allow for proper management and control of movement in transport systems to improve efficiency and safety of operation of these systems and positively affect the environment.

The objective of telematics is to support, supervise, control and manage the processes in transport and link these systems within all transport tasks carried out in the supply chain. The priority element for the implementation of these tasks in telematic systems are functions of operating of information, which primarily relate to the collecting, processing and distributing of data essential for making the right decision. Such processes are both processes implemented in the manner determined in advance (for example, automatic control of movement) or processes arising from the ad hoc situations (decisions of the operators, dispatchers, independent users of infrastructure such as drivers or pedestrians, etc., supported by updated information) [11]

Today, the ability to ensure fluent and efficient transport of people and goods, transport prepared for the implementation of tasks in conditions of interference, is an essential requirement. The way to guarantee such possibilities is the introduction and extensive use of telematic solutions in the supply chain. The delay in implementation or the lack of such solutions will affect the level of competitiveness and will generate the unsustainable use of logistic infrastructure.

The validity of presented arguments were confirmed by a study conducted in years 2012-2013 by the Institute of Logistics at Wrocław School of Banking in Wrocław, which related to the areas, opportunities and needs of use of telematic solutions in implementation of logistic tasks among the 47 logistics companies of Lower Silesia. The results of this study indicated not only the perception of this type of solutions as needed and innovative but primarily as a cost effective way of obtaining better results in supporting the management of transport services within the supply chain. The respondents in these studies have indicated such essential elements as:

- increase of efficiency of transport management in real time;
- comprehensive fleet management;
- improving the quality and reliability of services;
- increase in the level of safety of implementation of logistic processes and activities;
- ability to track (to obtain information about the status of) transported goods;
- more efficient use of infrastructure, particularly capacity of roads;
- obtaining and using information about weather conditions, accidents and other incidents in order to change and modify routes;
- time-saving transport;
- implementation of electronic payment and charging fees
- reduce pollution caused by transport;
- reduction of road accidents victims.

The analysis of the obtained research results also indicated the need for large compatibility of various considerations and telematic applications, which can be used by the various participants in implementing the tasks within the supply chain. The use of different devices and applications within this concept, such as mobile networks and the Internet, radio communications systems, geographical databases, road databases, satellite navigation systems, traffic monitoring devices (sensors, detectors, cameras, radars), weather monitoring devices, data transmission devices to users of transport systems (e.g. variable message boards) and other, requires the creation of a common concept (platforms), which will allow for their rational and joined use.

It is well justified for solving this problem, which was confirmed by respondents, to use "ITS Architecture", described in the literature of the subject [12]. This architecture can be created for the needs at the national, regional or municipal level or can relate to specific sectors or services. It should ensure that the implemented ITS system will [12]:

- be scheduled in a logical manner;
- be effectively integrated with other systems;
- meet performance requirements;
- behave in the desired manner;
- be easy to manage;
- be easy to maintain;
- be simple in expansion of an existing system;
- meet the expectations of users.

Adopted considerations within this platform should give the opportunity to:

- manage traffic;
- give support for the management of public transport;
- manage demand;
- provide information for passengers;
- manage vehicle fleet;
- manage incidents and support emergency services;
- implement electronic payments and charging fees;
- introduce advanced technology inside the vehicles.

The aim of this platform is to organize the conditions to increase the efficiency and flexibility of the activities within the supply chain, especially in the area of transport, increase the security and transport tasks, taking into account the concept of sustainable development. In addition, the objective is to permit an initial cost-benefit analysis identifying the sources of likely profits and costs. It is also to provide the possibility of risk analysis, test potential problems, for example, the reliability of technology, the uncertainty of the sources and the size of revenue and potential problems and risks. Gaining such opportunities can significantly improve planning, managing and operating the supply chain.

Currently, there is no uniform concept of the use of telematic solutions in the implementation of logistic tasks in the supply chain. These tasks are very diverse in nature and concern both the processes of planning and organizing as well as forwarding tasks, storage area, transport and many other activities undertaken under modern logistics, and especially TSL systems. In all of these areas, particularly in their development, the opportunities of using modern telematic systems can be seen. It can be assumed that more and more demands from supply chains, shorter time frames, expectations related to the optimization of production and cutting costs will result in further fast implementation of many new solutions from this area. It also seems to be justified to set an argument that the pace of the development of new applications and telematic solutions and their implementation will be constantly growing, causing further automatization of many processes within the supply chain.

To indicate the possible developments of these systems it is worth looking into the results of the above mentioned study concerning the analyzed issues. In the second part, the respondents had to indicate the areas of application of telematic solutions and the directions of their development. Below are the four most commonly mentioned solutions.

The solution most frequently indicated (93.75%) were the applications to support the management of fleet vehicles and control vehicles in motion. The essential elements of those applications have been identified:

- systems of planning and "matching" vehicles, cargo and drivers;
- generating a list of drivers on the route, along with full contact details;
- a quick preview of the current location and indicating the status of the vehicle (movement, stop);
- planning and optimization of routes and the ability to preview the area of activity of the vehicle on the basis of archival records.
- recording the trace of the journey of the car using GPS techniques;
- full report from the route together with the status (deliverability and receipts);
- providing "offices in the cabin" for vehicle owners/drivers;
- automatic reporting.

Respondents also indicate different telematic applications available for drivers and freight forwarders by making it easier to carry out the transport process, increase the efficiency of operations and identify opportunities and solutions associated with the use of different means of transport. The analysis of their applications also indicates the following additional features:

- optimum selecting routes for carriage of goods dangerous and harmful to the environment;
- using oversized vehicles and planning their routes;
- monitoring security-related processes, with saving relevant data in order to present them at the request of the road Inspection or other authorized bodies;
- location and tracking of vehicles, containers and cargo along the entire length of their routes, with physical monitoring of their condition;
- automatization of documentation distribution accompanying the vehicles and loads.

A solution also often indicated (87.5%) was: Management of events in the supply chain. The basis for action taken in this application is confronting the data from the actual situation with assumed plans. This is the effect of constant comparing between what "should" and what "is" in the course of the transport of the goods. Due to the use of telematic solutions it is possible to obtain fully automatic information about critical incidents during the entire transport process.

A lot of attention (83.33 %) was also paid to the concepts of use of mobile devices connected to the IT network within telematic solutions. According to the respondents their use will allow for:

- obtaining real-time information about the status and the place of the goods being transported (consignments);
- immediate transfer of the status of the consignment;
- transfer in real time and in digital form (reports, pictures, video) information on any incidents associated with the movement of goods in the supply chain
- instant sending of digital confirmation of receipt relating to the release and receipt of digital goods between the various links of the supply chain;

- scanning and sending the receipts and deliveries of supplies;
- for changes in the archiving of documents - digital data sending (receipts, photos, reports);

81.25% of respondents paid their attention to the application designed to monitor traffic and to assist drivers on motorways and other non-urban roads. Excessive traffic congestion is a problem both in cities and beyond them, and the indicated applications allow for:

- the dosage of entry in order to secure the entry of vehicles on the motorway or ring road;
- providing information about traffic through variable content boards or onboard devices;
- speed control on crowded motorways in order to improve the flow of vehicles (avoiding the "spring effect");
- collision detection, which is able to automatically send the information to the traffic management centers and provide immediate warning to drivers;
- the use of Intelligent Speed Adaptation (ISA) Systems to ensure continuous compliance with speed limits as well as to dynamically change these restrictions depending on weather conditions, traffic and road conditions.

The implementation of such measures, however, demands that the on-board ITS systems are able to communicate and receive information from roadside devices regardless of location. Therefore, an important element will be interoperability of both overall system (supervision of road) as well as systems and equipment mounted in vehicles.

It is understood that the intelligent transport is cooperating of three settings: intelligent way, intelligent vehicle, or a vehicle equipped with devices maintaining the continued, in particular, wireless exchange of information with the devices that are installed along the transport routes and intelligent management centers.

The reflections and the very results of the study not only confirmed the need and rationale for the implementation of telematic solutions within the supply chain. Their use not only allows for greater flexibility and transparency in the supply chain, optimization and acceleration as well as minimizing the cost of many processes and procedures but also provides [12]:

- free market for services and equipment due to the existence of standard interfaces between components, which enables the use of economies of scale in supply, production and distribution, and, as a result, reduces the cost of products and services;
- ensures consistency of information provided to end users;
- encourages to invest in applications and telematic solutions;
- provides interoperability of elements, even if they are produced by different manufacturers, which is especially beneficial for small and medium-sized businesses;
- provides an adequate level of technological independence and easy implementation of new technology.

4   Conclusion

Nowadays, the market is devoid of many barriers, continuously raises the level of competition, pointing to the need to implement more and more efficient logistic processes. The essential challenges facing logistics are: reconfiguring, integrating and optimizing the supply chains within the global logistics network. Effective management of the supply chain requires not only to view all processes and links of the chain, but also automate many processes. Efficient and flexible supply chain management also requires a lot of data, which must be obtained in real time. The realization of expectations which are generated in relation to contemporary and future supply chain continues to grow, and the requirements grow while the costs and turnaround time for logistics activities is expected to decrease. A solution that will allow, or to a large extent, facilitate the fulfillment of these requirements, is telematics and the pragmatic solutions related to it.

Therefore, the knowledge of the latest telematic concepts and solutions and their correct implementation to support actions in progress, becomes one of the essential elements of gaining success in current market conditions.

The conducted study proved the argument: the introduction of telematic solutions makes it possible not only to automate and shorten processes and logistic activities, but also affects their safety and enables greater flexibility and reliability of the activities within supply chain. The effect of their implementation is a clear improvement of the functioning of many processes within the chain, especially the increase in the level of quality and speed of implementation of transport services. Additionally, it is a feature that allows to reduce the negative impact of transport on the environment.

Additionally, the study also allows to claim that the ability to properly use even wider range of opportunities which are generated by modern telematics and its solutions for conducted logistic activities, becomes one of the fundamental issues. The use of telematic solutions within the supply chain should be considered as a process of dissemination of technological innovation. The research and analysis from this area related to the implementation in logistics practice, should be considered as one of today's priorities .

References

1. Christopher, M.: Logistics and supply chain management: Strategies for reducing costs and improving service. Financial Times. Prentice Hall, London (1998)
2. Ballou, R.H.: Business Logistics/Supply Chain Management. Pearson Prentice Hall, New York (2004)
3. Chopra, S., Meindl, P.: Supply Chain Management. Strategy, Planning & Operations. Pearson Prentice Hall, New York (2007)
4. Ross, D.F.: The Intimate Supply Chain. CRC Press, London (2008)
5. Mangan, J., Lalwani, C., Butcher, T.: Global Logistics and Supply Chain Management. John Wiley & Sons Ltd. (2008)
6. Koulikoff-Souviron, M., Harrison, A.: A model of perspectives on supply chain management. LERC, Cardiff (2000)

7. Mentzer, J.T., Myers, M.B., Stank, T.P.: Handbook of Global Supply Chain Management, University of Tennessee-Knoxville. SAGE Publications Inc. (2007)
8. Mentzer, J.T.: Fundamentals of Supply Chain Management. Twelve Drivers of Competitive Advantage. SAGE Publications, Inc. (2004)
9. Blanchard, B.S.: Logistics engineering and management, 6th edn. Pearson Prentice Hall, New York (2004)
10. Stevens, G.C.: Integration of the Supply Chain. International Journal of Physical Distribution & Logistics Management 19(8) (1989)
11. Wydro, K., et al.: Analiza stanu i potrzeb prac rozwojowych w zakresie telematyki transportu w Polsce. Instytut Łączności, Prace Zespołu Międzyzakładowego. Warszawa (2002)
12. http://www.frame-online.net/ (date of access: January 20, 2014)
13. Mikulski, J. (ed.): TST 2011. CCIS, vol. 239. Springer, Heidelberg (2011)
14. Mikulski, J. (ed.): Transport Systems Telematics, TST2010. CCIS, vol. 104. Springer, Heidelberg (2010)
15. Mikulski, J.: Introduction of telematics for transport. In: Proceedings on 9th International Conference ELEKTRO 2012, Rajecke Teplice, IEEE Catalog Number CFP1248S-ART, , May 21-22, pp. 336–340 (2012), http://ieexplore.ieee.org

Computer Simulation Studies
of Capacity of the Railway Line

Sławomir Jasiński

KONTRON East Europe
03-821 Warszawa, Żupnicza 17, Poland
slawomir.jasinski@kontron.pl

Abstract. The author presented the structure and capabilities of SYM_POC simulation software designed for modelling traffic flows of trains on railway lines. He presented the results of simulations carried out for the Polish Railways State selected railway line with regard to different methods of the railway traffic control (fixed block interval rule, moving block interval rule) and various traffic flows. The presented method of computer modeling of train traffic flows using the SYM_POC software confirms the effectiveness of the method in planning and estimating the capacity of railway lines

Keywords: computer modelling capacity, rail traffic, stochastic modelling.

1   Introduction

The changing market of transport services requires an optimisation of railway traffic control and an adjustment of operational railway line parameters to the changing needs. Increase in the number of travels and railway operators make is necessary to guarantee, among others, that the railway line will be adequate for new conditions and disturbances in train traffic will be limited and the time needed unloading queues will be reduced. However, this process however an accurate assessment of needs concerning parameters of the railway line. The line capacity parameter is inseparably linked to technical appliances, i.e. railway traffic control devices, which need to be installed on the railway line in order to achieve the required parameters.

This paper presents one of the tools for simulation studies of railway line capacity, which enables you to optimize modernization processes of railway lines, in particular to estimate and verify potential effects of the introduced line alterations, e.g. optimization of block spacing during the reconstruction of the automatic block system on rail routes, or to introduce time spacing control in accordance with the principle of a moving block section.

The paper presents examples of results of simulation studies carried out using the SYM_POC software on a selected, real railway line section.

2   Simulation Studies of Railway Line Capacity

The simulation studies were carried out with SYM_POC software, written in the Borland Pascal programming language (version 2006 in the WINDOWS system

J. Mikulski (Ed.): TST 2014, CCIS 471, pp. 196–204, 2014.

environment), in a application which supports the visualization of Rapid Application Design processes in accordance with the PN-EN 50 128:2007 standard. The SYM_POC programme is a configurable (i.e. supporting individual parameterization) simulation tool which facilitates calculating railway line capacity for various conditions and traffic control principles. Functionally, the programme consists of two modules (components):

- the train editor module – SYM_POC_Edytor_Pociagow,
- the actual simulation module – SYM_POC.

The role of the train editor module is to describe and define train types, and then use them as input data for the description of traffic flows in order to run a simulation with the actual simulation module. It is noteworthy that in order to build (put together) a train, the programme uses a database describing actual parameters of individual vehicles and cars in the train concerned (mass, wheel-base, maximum speed, …). Figure 1 shows the train editor dialogue window in SYM_POC and user interface during the definition of a passenger train with an EP-09 locomotive and car types 110AB and 111A.

As you can see in Figure 1, using the dialogue window, you can define any actual train composition. A train is put together by selecting an appropriate locomotive and cars from the assigned database with their specific characteristics. After selecting the name of locomotive or car, we receive the basic characteristics of the selected element, i.e. information about its weight, length, maximum speed. An important advantage of the editor lies in the possibility to define the train's running parameters in the "dynamika pociągu" ("train dynamics") tab, where we can define the train's traction characteristics: acceleration, braking and coasting with 5 km/h accuracy, and acceleration or retardation $a = 0.01\frac{m}{s^2}$.

Another important functionality is the possibility for the designer to determine a design speed for the designed train $V_{designed}$ which is lower than the maximum speed of the designed train resulting from the technical parameters of actual locomotives and cars ($V_{designed} < V_{max}$). After the train is defined, it is stored on the hard drive under a name visible in the box "nazwa" ("name") with extension *.conf. (e.g. #EAP-09.conf).

Files describing train compositions are stored in a directory called Lista_Pociągów (List of Trains) and can be updated anytime.

Apart from preparing train type data for the proper preparation of simulation parameters, the text file editor is used to prepare a configuration file based on which the simulation module of SYM_POC will work. The file includes descriptions of routes (linking route components by defining successors and predecessors for every route component), description of single components, e.g. track section, switch with parameters defining each element (length, construction-related speed limit). In addition, the configuration file includes a description of the train traffic flow.

The role of the actual simulation module is to carry out simulations based on previously defined configuration files describing train types, infrastructure and the train traffic flow structure that needs to be simulated. After triggering the simulation process, we are given access to the user interface of the SYM_POC software, which allows you to set parameters for relevant conditions of the simulation without the need to change configuration files. It is a very user friendly programming tool that makes changing simulation parameters easy.

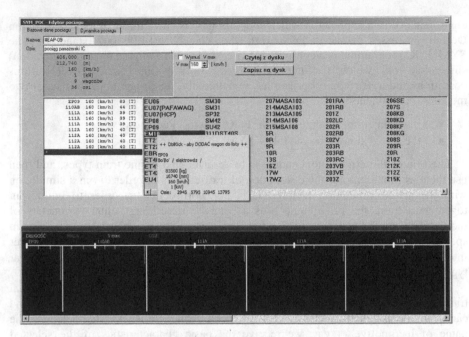

Fig. 1. Dialogue window of the train editor [software windows]

The simulation programme window is divided into several fixed areas, in which you can set parameters for the simulation process, e.g. by setting such important simulation parameters as simulation time, traffic flow coefficient or number of technical breaks in which the train traffic is interrupted (trains are not dispatched). An important functionality lies the possibility to manually set the initial parameter for the pseudo-random number generator because the initial number is randomly generated for every consecutive simulation and for this reason also the order of train composition is different for individual simulations. Entering the initial number makes it possible to achieve identical work of the pseudo-random number generator, and identical order of the random train selection, which is very important when we want to obtain full comparability of simulation conditions. In addition, in this area there are navigations buttons that make it possible to trigger the simulation process in various modes (continuous simulation, stepwise simulation), turn graphic presentation of simulation results on and off, or stop the simulation process at any time. During the simulation, immediate and final simulation results are presented in text and graphic form. The graphic presentation window dynamically presents the movement of a train (accelerating and braking curves for train front and back). Graphic presentation of the course of simulation facilitates ongoing control and evaluation of the quality of simulation as well as its verification because during the simulation we are able to observe the sequence of randomly selected train types, we see train lengths, minimum recorded distance to the preceding train, current braking distance, etc.

In general, the simulation process consists in a random selection of a train from a pool of trains (uniform distribution) defined for this simulation. Then, after checking the fulfilment of conditions with regard to time spacing regulations (is it possible to dispatch the train), the train is dispatched. Trains on the route are moved and tracked in the simulation programme until they leave the route. Train types are generated using the standard in-built pseudo-random number generator in the Borland Pascal programming language. It is a generator with uniform distribution (because in order to design data for the simulation, we define the share of individual train types in the traffic flow, and the order of trains reporting for service is random. Train order conditions are controlled based on information about occupation of individual block intervals.

Simulation results are recorded in separate text files, which include information about the adopted simulation parameters and its course (time, type of train that was randomly selected, order of trains, time of travel, etc.).

Simulation studies using the SYM_POC software were carried out on a section of the international E-65 corridor, Central Rail Line (Centralna Magistrala Kolejowa) between Psary and Góra Włodowska. The line has the following technical and operational characteristics:

- along the entire section, the line is equipped with a typical relay-based, bi-directional, 4-aspect automatic block signalling system (ABS) (Eac type block), which means that according to the fixed block interval principle and national signalling regulations, the train driver receives information about three consecutive block intervals in front of him at most – S2 signal (green continuous light means that at least three block intervals behind the signal are "free"),
- mixed traffic (passenger and freight flows) runs on the line with maximum speeds permitted in Poland (passenger trains $V_{max}=160$ $^{km}/_h$, freight trains $V_{max}=120^{km}/_h$),
- the passenger traffic on the selected section, just like on the entire line 4(with the exception of Włoszczowa North), runs without stopping,

Based on the timetable, due to the maximum speed parameter V_{max}, we selected the following representative train types (defined below), which travelled in 2013 on the analysed railway line section:

$V_{max} = 160^{km}\backslash_h$, EuroCity, InterCity, (35% fast trains excluded),
$V_{max} = 140^{km}\backslash_h$, national express, (30%),
$V_{max} = 120^{km}\backslash_h$, (interregional through trains, freight (non-bulk) trains) (10%),
$V_{max} = 70^{km}\backslash_h$, freight trains (break-bulk) – (25%),

The daily traffic flow structure (shares are given in brackets for every train types) was adopted for the purposes of the simulation based on the actual, current traffic flow on the analysed railway line section (within the range from $V_{max}=70^{km}\backslash_h$ to $V_{max}=160^{km}\backslash_h$). For the purposes of the simulation, the following train compositions were defined in the train editor:

- passenger train $V=160^{km}/_h$ – locomotive EP-09, train weight 400T, train length 205m, number of cars – 7, normal braking distance – 1600m,
- passenger train $V=140^{km}/_h$ – locomotive EP-08, train weight 400T, train length 205m, number of cars – 7, normal braking distance – 1250m.

- freight train $V=120^{km}/_h$ – locomotive EBR-189, train weight 1000T, train length 600m, number of cars – 30, normal braking distance – 900m.
- freight train $V=70^{km}/_h$ – locomotive ET-22, train weight 3200T, train length 600m, number of cars – 30, normal braking distance – 900m.

As a result of simulation studies (Figure 2 – simulation window), we obtained results for the line capacity coefficient N in the following range :

$$N \in \langle 416 - 440 \rangle \left[\frac{train}{day} \right] \tag{1}$$

for 10 consecutive simulation processes.

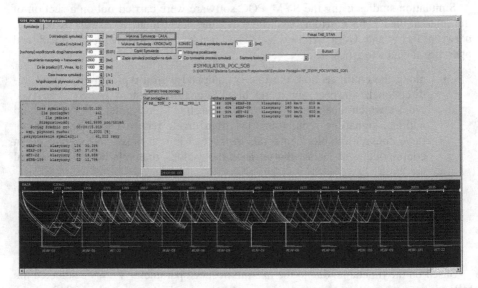

Fig. 2. Simulation window [software windows]

Results obtained in the simulation studies were verified with classic analytical methods for estimating railway line capacity [1], [4], [7] using for this purpose the basic traffic engineering equations.

$$N_{max} = (1 - \varphi) * \frac{1440}{T} \tag{2}$$

where:

N_{max} – theoretical maximum route capacity,

1440   – number of minutes in a day

T   – section blocking time (period of the traffic diagram)

φ – traffic flow coefficient (within the range 0.2 – 0.3)

As a result of the analysis, it was determined that for track no. 1 between Psary and Góra Włodowska, the critical section is OKr=5952m (the longest section with three consecutive block intervals, in the analysed section these would be intervals no.: 1881, 1897, 1917). The analytically determined theoretical coefficients of railway line capacity for mixed traffic amounted to N_{max}=500.87[train/day] for the maximum capacity (not taking into account the traffic flow structure) and Nr=397.52[train/day] for reduced capacity (taking into account the traffic flow structure) respectively.

Results obtained in simulation studies differ from the capacity parameter obtained analytically (the simulation studies showed a higher capacity of the line than theoretical calculations for this line section), however they are within the statistical error range because in the simulation process the order of trains was random and a train was dispatched as soon as the time spacing condition was fulfilled. Due to the random character of simulation, the results of individual simulations differed strongly because in the simulation studies the order of randomly selected trains mattered (e.g. if a freight train went first, the speed of consecutive trans was reduced). Whereas in analytical calculations the worst case condition is adopted, e.g. the train with the worst traffic characteristics.

Therefore, the analytical calculations confirmed proper operation of the simulation software.

3   Probability Estimation of Events That Disturb Train Traffic

An additional functionality of the SYM_POC software makes it possible to estimate the time necessary to dissolve a queue of trains which formed as a result of an unexpected stop of trains on track.

First, using stochastic methods (also used to determine the probability of certain events in the case of other control systems) [2-4] based on homogenous, ergodic and stationary Markov processes, the author proved that for the analysed railway line in the current operating conditions there is a certain probability of an event in which a train would stop on the route due to a failure of the traffic control system.

The author used the general time spacing control model for travelling trains presented in Figure 3.

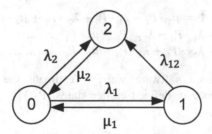

Fig. 3. Model of a traffic control system based on automatic block signalling. Source: own study based on [4].

State 0 – correct operation – the train is moving in accordance with the permission to travel it received,

State 1 – receipt of information about the further travel mode,

State 2 – train stops due to failure of the signalling system, driver's mistake or safety response of the automatic train stopping device / automatic warning system.

By solving the Fokker – Planck system of equations (3) for the model presented in Figure 4, we obtained cut-off probabilities of being in individual states (4). For the purposes of estimating disturbances in train traffic, particularly interesting is the limit probability of state P2.

The differential equations describing the transitions between states of the system are corresponding to [3], [7] to assumed Markov model the Fokker-Planc (Kolmogorov) equations are derived:

$$\begin{cases} \dfrac{dP_0(t)}{dt} = -\lambda_1 \cdot P_0(t) + \mu_1 \cdot P_1(t) - \lambda_2 \cdot P_0(t) + \mu_2 \cdot P_2(t) \\ \dfrac{dP_1(t)}{dt} = \lambda_1 \cdot P_0(t) - \lambda_{12} \cdot P_1(t) - \mu_1 \cdot P_1(t) \\ \dfrac{dP_2(t)}{dt} = \lambda_{12} \cdot P_1(t) - \mu_2 \cdot P_2(t) + \lambda_2 \cdot P_0(t) \\ \qquad\quad P_0(t) + P_1(t) + P_2(t) = 1 \end{cases} \tag{3}$$

where:

P_0, P_1, P_2 – probabilities of being in a specific state 0, 1,2,

λ_1 –   advice intensity – the train has approached the signal,

λ_{12} –   intensity of events consisting in wrong reaction of the driver or failure of the signalling system,

λ_2 –   intensity of events in which the train receives the RadioStop signal, spontaneous brake application (without driver's intervention) until the train stops completely,

μ_1 –   service ratio – transfer of information about further travel mode to the driver,

μ_2 – service ratio – return to the travel mode after a stop..

The linear equations (3) after Laplace transform have a form (4) .

$$\begin{cases} s \cdot P_0 - 1 = \mu_1 \cdot P_1 - \lambda_1 \cdot P_0 - \lambda_2 \cdot P_0 + \mu_2 \cdot P_2 \\ s \cdot P_1 = \lambda_1 \cdot P_0 - \lambda_{12} \cdot P_1 - \mu_1 \cdot P_1 \dots \dots \dots \dots \dots \dots \\ s \cdot P_2 = \lambda_{12} \cdot P_1 + \lambda_2 \cdot P_0 - \mu_2 \cdot P_2 \dots \dots \dots \dots \dots \dots \end{cases} \tag{4}$$

Using the Mathematica software we can estimate the boundary values of probabilities of occurrence in defined earlier states. $P_i(t)\big|_{t\to\infty}$. The solution is as follows (5):

$$P_0 = P_0(t)\,|_{t\to\infty} = \frac{\mu_2 \cdot (\lambda_{12} + \mu_1)}{(\lambda_{12} + \mu_1) \cdot (\lambda_2 + \mu_2) + \lambda_1 \cdot (\lambda_{12} + \mu_2)}$$

$$P_1 = P_1(t)\,|_{t\to\infty} = \frac{\lambda_1 \cdot \mu_2}{(\lambda_{12} + \mu_1) \cdot (\lambda_2 + \mu_2) + \lambda_1 \cdot (\lambda_{12} + \mu_2)} \tag{5}$$

$$P_2 = P_2(t)\,|_{t\to\infty} = \frac{\lambda_1 \cdot \lambda_{12} + \lambda_2 \cdot (\lambda_{12} + \mu_1)}{(\lambda_{12} + \mu_1) \cdot (\lambda_2 + \mu_2) + \lambda_1 \cdot (\lambda_{12} + \mu_2)}$$

Assuming that for a 1300 m long block interval and speed V=160$^{km}/_h$ advice is given every 29.25 s., and the time necessary for interpreting the signal and confirming receipt of the advice is 15s., and assuming that the failure ratio leading to train stop is at the level of $10^{-2}h^{-1}$, we obtained the probability of train traffic disturbance on the way at the level of P2 = 4.997*10^{-4}.

Table 1. Simulation results for FIFO queues [own study]

Structure of the served queue, order according to randomly selected train types	Time T needed to dispatch five consecutive trains [s]	
[FIFO queue]	T_{SOB}	T_{ROB}
EAP-08 EAP-08 EAP-09 EAP-09 EAP-09	563	220
EAP-08 EAP-08 EAP-08 EAP-08 ET-22	827	279
EAP-08 EAP-08 EAP-08 EBR-189 EAP-09	604	316
EAP-08 ET-22 EAP-08 EAP-08 EAP-09	632	269
EAP-08 ET-22 EAP-08 EAP-08 EBR-189	607	270
ET-22 EAP-08 EBR-189 ET-22 EAP-09	678	276
ET-22 EBR-189 EBR-189 EAP-09 ET-22	759	307
EAP-09 EAP-09 ET-22 ET-22 ET-22	911	400
EBR-189 ET-22 ET-22 EAP-08 EAP-08	775	314
EAP-09 EAP-08 ET-22 EAP-09 EAP-09	651	248

Because the train disturbance probability does not equal zero, using the SYM_POC software, the author estimated the time necessary to dissolve of a randomly generated queue of trains on the way in accordance with the principles of FIFO queues.

Table 1 presents an example of a summary list of times necessary to dispatch a queue of trains. The analysis was carried out for train queues randomly selected in a simulation served in a traditional way using automatic block signals (fixed block interval/SOB) and for train queues which are identical in terms of structure and order of random selection but served based on the moving block interval rule (ROB).

4   Conclusion

Thanks to configuration of input data describing the traffic flow structure and data describing infrastructure of the line for which the simulations are carried out, simulation studies carried out using the SYM_POC software provide a realistic reflection of operating conditions on the railway line concerned. Obtained simulation results, both in terms of the railway line capacity parameter and optimising queue dissolution time, make it possible to confirm, both theoretically and in simulations, that the operating conditions of the line change as a result of line modernisation or additional railway traffic control equipment.

References

1. Gajda, B.: Technika ruchu kolejowego cz. 2 Technologia ruchu kolejowego. WKiŁ Warszawa (1978)
2. Iosifescu, M.: Skończone procesy Markowa i ich zastosowania, 1st edn. Wydawnictwo Naukowe PWN, Warszawa (1988)
3. Lewiński, A., Bester, L.: Additional warning system for cross level. In: Mikulski, J. (ed.) TST 2010. CCIS, vol. 104, pp. 226–231. Springer, Heidelberg (2010)
4. Lewiński, A., Toruń, A.: The changeable block distance system analysis. In: Mikulski, J. (ed.) TST 2010. CCIS, vol. 104, pp. 67–74. Springer, Heidelberg (2010)
5. Toruń, A., Bester, L., Siergiejczyk, M.: Szacowanie funkcjonalności i bezpieczeństwa systemów sterowania ruchem kolejowym. Prace Naukowe Politechniki Warszawskiej, Transport z. 96. Konferencja Naukowa TRANSPORT XXI WIEKU 2013, Ryn (2013)
6. Toruń, A., Lewiński, A.: Efficiency analysis of train monitoring system applying the changeable block distance method. In: Mikulski, J. (ed.) TST 2013. CCIS, vol. 395, pp. 178–187. Springer, Heidelberg (2013)
7. Toruń, A.: The method of train positioning in railway control process. Ph D. dissertation, University of Technology and Humanities in Radom (December 2013)
8. UIC CODE 406 – "Capacity" UIC, Editions Techniques Ferroviaires, Paris (2004)

Influence of Operator on Safety of the Signalling System during Emergency Operation

Peter Nagy, Karol Rástočný, and Juraj Ždánsky

University of Žilina, Faculty of Electrical Engineering,
Univerzitná 1, 01026 Žilina, Slovakia
{peter.nagy,karol.rastocny,juraj.zdansky}@fel.uniza.sk

Abstract. A signalling system is a technological instrument for railway transport process controlling and its role is to replace or check human (operator of the signalling system) in applying the safety critical operations related to railway traffic control. The aim of such replacement or checking is contribution to safety of the railway transport so that the signalling system eliminates errors of operator. Because of continuous character of operation control of the railway transport process, there is a need to ensure control of the railway transport in the case of partial or total failure of the signalling system. An objective assessment of the operator´s influence on railway transport safety (especially in the case of not availability of one or more safety functions) is possible only on the quantitative model base. Creation of such model requires not only knowledge of the signalling system technical design, but the specific data about it what safety critical commands are used by operator and the frequency of their using by the operator too.

Keywords: safety, operator, emergency operation, signalling system.

1 Introduction

A possible cause of the danger resulted from the operation of railway signalling system can be the operator`s error in the performance of safety-relevant activities related to the controlling of the trains movement. In general, we can assume a different participation of the operator on the performance of the control functions [1]:

- Neither – the control system is fully operational and supervises safety-relevant commands issued by the operator to the full extent;
- Partial:
  - the control system is operational, but its technical design doesn´t support supervision of all safety-relevant commands issued by the operator;
  - the system is partially operational; the operator executes some safety-relevant operations without following checking by the control system;
  - Complete – the system is non-functional; the operator performs all safety-relevant operations through commands for emergency operation without following checking by the control (signalling) system.

J. Mikulski (Ed.): TST 2014, CCIS 471, pp. 205–214, 2014.
© Springer-Verlag Berlin Heidelberg 2014

A safety level of control during the execution of emergency commands depends on observing of the organisational measures by the operator of the signalling system. Checking of the safety-relevant conditions for train movement is reduced to the administrative form in this case and full weight of the safety stay on the signalling system operator. The operator is required either alone or in co-operation with other staff participated in the transport process control to check and ensure fulfilment of administrative conditions for safe train movement. The administrative measures usually require visual inspection of state of all controlled and checked elements in the track by the operator. In case of correct function of controlled technology states visualisation on video display units is allowed to derive some checks from indications provided by the signalling system – for example vacancy of the track section, switch point position and so on. This requires ensuring adequate safety of the displaying.

At the correct operation of the signalling system the operator is checked by the signalling system in applying the safety risk operations. In case of partial or total failure of the signalling system operator is under psychical pressure because he assumes responsibility for the safety and besides he must to continue control of the transport process. In case of accumulation of stress factors such a longer duration of the signalling system functionality limitation, a complicated traffic situation, operator`s fatigue and other factors, there may be a conditions where the operator makes a mistake – he will use an emergency command without authorization. For example: he will mistakenly apply a command for emergency operation to the wrong element in the track; he will mistakenly will apply the administrative check which conditions an execution of the emergency operation on another element in the track; he will not check all administrative measures, which condition the emergency command execution or he will make another mistake. Long-term use of certain emergency commands in situations when it is impossible fully use of the traffic-safety algorithms of signalling systems to ensure the safety control of the transport process (for example, when reconstructing or modernize stations) leads to routine work and it often has the effect of omission or negligence of some required administrative tasks and it can lead to accident again.

In such circumstances there is a danger that the operator of the signalling system use command for emergency operation in a situation, when the appropriate safety function is functional and the signalling system rightly rules out execution of the command because conditions for command execution are not fulfilled. The operator mistakenly supposes that disabling of the command execution is caused by prolonged lockout or long-term failure of the signalling system. Or the operator gets the feeling that the degradation of the signalling system continues and based on this he decides to use command for emergency operation, although there are no reasons for the emergency operation. Application of the command for emergency operation in such situation again can lead to such state of controlled transport process which is a precondition of an accident.

2   Causes of the Operator Failure

It is necessary to identify the causes of human errors to be possible assess the reliability of the human factor. According to [2] human error includes all events that do not lead to the achievement of the planed results at planed sequence of mental or physical activities, and these errors cannot be affected by the action of random effects.

An error occurs when a goal or desired result is not achieved, and it is manifested as deviation from the requested state.

Human errors can be divided into two basic groups:

- omission errors – errors arising from inattention and manifested as non-performance (omission) of specified activity in result of oblivion, unrecognition of the signal, ...;
- execution errors (comission) – errors manifested by performance of the wrong operation, wrong execution of the operation, execution of more operations in the wrong order, too early or too late, insufficient or too strong execution of the operation or operation execution in the wrong direction.

According to [14] the most important causes of human errors are:

- errors caused by momentary inattention – the goal of the operator is correct, but it is not properly implemented;
- errors due to incorrect intent – errors are caused by the lack of training of the operator;
- errors caused by lack of physical or mental capacity of the operator;
- errors caused by lack of motivation;
- management errors – worker is incorrect guided, poorly or improperly trained.

3   Reliability of the Operator

To determine the reliability of the operator is a difficult and complex task. A man in the same situation does not behave the same; the same operation can perform in various ways without compromising the safety of the controlled system. Therefore, the estimation of the reliability of the human is complex.

The reliability of a man is described by analogous parameters as the reliability of technical systems – human error probability (HEP), or the probability of successful execution of operations (human success probability – the HSP). The human error probability is defined as the ratio:

$$HEP = \frac{n}{N},$$ (1)

$$HSP = 1 - HEP$$ (2)

where: *HEP* is human error probability, *HSP* is human success probability, n is the number of monitored incorrect operations and N is total number of operator acts.

The incidence of human error is in ([2-3]) considered as a analog random quantity with a log-normal distribution.

Different methods are used in the world to estimate the probability of human error for each service activities. Among the most commonly used methods of probabilistic estimation of human reliability include the following methods [4]:

- THERP (Technique for Human Error Rate Prediction) – a method of prediction of human errors intensity describes in details monitored human activity, through the use of appropriately selected probability estimates of

HEP evaluates partial activities related to task, identifies the influencing factors of the human reliability – performance shaping factors (PSF). The method on the basis of created diagnostic model allows time assessment of the human probability and gives detailed overview of the vulnerabilities and possible malfunctions of the system.

- SLIM (Success Likelihood Index Method) – a method for estimation of human reliability depending on the performance shaping factors allows the quantification with possibilities of choice of analysed unit according to progress of the assessed task. The method determines the influencing factors and their importance, PSF factors evaluates using the conversion index and transforms them into probabilistic scale of at least two reference HEP estimates.
- HRC (Human Cognitive Reliability) – a method enables assessment of interfering influences that affect human thinking. The method enables the quantification of probabilistic estimates of HEP, allows the creation of standardized time curves of the HEP for different levels of the human behaviour based on skills, rules, knowledge and thought processes.
- ESAT (Experten System zur Aufgaben – Taxonomie) – expert system, which allows the quantification of any task with respect to the influencing factors of PSF in the form of reliability scale. The functional relationship between the reliability scale and the PSF is based partially on expert estimates and partly on the measurement of labour efficiency.
- SHARP (Systematic Human Action Reliability Procedure) – a procedure for determining of the probability of operator behaviours. The method determines the intervals of human error probability for basic patterns of operator behaviour, whereby determines interval and the fundamental value of the probability.

According the literature [5-7] the probability of human error depends on the operator behaviour mode. In the analysis there are 3 base modes of behaviour considered:

- Skill-based behaviour mode – this mode means that the operator responds to known stimulus instinctively. Acceptance of this behaviour mode depends on the level of experience and skill of the operator. Because the operator is accustomed to the situation, he does not use the complicated thought processes. Behaviour based on experiences is typical for solution of routine operations.
- Rule-based behaviour mode – this behaviour mode means that the operator must perform each activity sequential in accordance with the established operating procedure. The procedure can be defined by written, oral or just thought forms.
- Knowledge-based behaviour mode – this behaviour mode is used in case that the operational situation is unknown for the operator and the operator has not met with that situation. In such case, the operator must recognize the state of the process and make a decision depending on his own experience and knowledge. If the states of the process are ambiguous or conflicting and there is no available pre-defined procedure to resolve the situation, the operator usually tries to resolve the situation on the basis of his experience.

There is no clear boundary between these behaviour modes and the operator usually combines individual behaviours on the basis of the following factors [7]:

- level of the training;
- level of experiences:
  - experiences with the tasks of the same type;
  - experiences with known tasks;
  - the time interval between two successive operations.
- knowledge of the operational situation;
- the working procedures availability;
- the size of the time pressure – the ratio between the time available to deal with the situation and the time necessary to resolve the situation.

On the basis of different levels of the above mentioned factors we can determine the probabilities of the operator error for individual behaviours.

Table 1. HEP probability for different modes of operator behaviour [7]

Behaviour mode	The base HEP value	Interval of values of the HEP
Skill-based	5.10^{-4}	$(5.10^{-5}, 5.10^{-3})$
Rule-based	5.10^{-3}	$(5.10^{-4}, 5.10^{-2})$
Knowledge-based	7.10^{-2}	$(5.10^{-3}, 1)$

The following influencing factors of the human reliability influence the overall error rate of the operator in process controlling:

- the quality of available operating procedures;
- the number of simultaneous control tasks;
- time of obligations fulfilment (day, night);
- the quality of the human-machine interface (HMI);
- the state and progress tendency of critical parameters of the controlled process;
- the external environment;
- co-operation and communication between operators;
- organizational factors and safety culture in the company.

Listed influencing factors have a different effect on individual operator behaviours. For the overall assessment of the operator error probability it is necessary to take into account the different weight of mentioned influencing factors.

4   The Accident Analysis in the   SR Railway Network

One of the documents needed to determine the impact of the human factor on the safety of the railway transport process is the analysis of accidents on the railway network of Railways of Slovak republic (ŽSR). During processing of this analysis were used the data from information system of the ŽSR EVINEHOD, which contains records of all safety incidents resulting in the ŽSR network since 2003. In the information system EVINEHOD together with the registered events there is also recorded the category of the event cause, employee category which event caused. In case of participation of several culprits there is also registered a proportion of event cause. Database contains record of the place of registered incident (track section and railway station), branch which includes registered event culprit and the resulting damage [8].

4.1   Accidents Caused by Faulty Operation

Table 2 contains a summary of incidents in the ŽSR network in the period of years 2003 to 2012 years and to compare the numbers of incidents that were caused by the mistakes of the operator. Figure 1 shows the percentage of incidents caused by signalling systems operators on the total number of incidents.

Table 2. Number of accidents in the ŽSR network caused by operator error [10]

	2003	2004	2005	2006	2007	2008	2009	2010	2011	2012
Total number of incidents in ŽSR	905	514	604	626	613	624	499	891	694	740
Number of events caused by operator	28	33	36	52	43	50	25	32	17	31

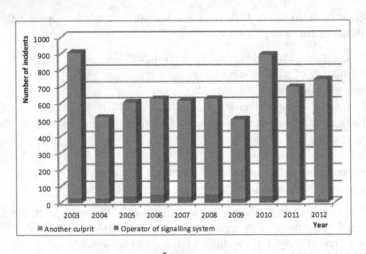

Fig. 1. Number of incidents in the ŽSR network in the period 2003 – 2012 [10]

From Table 2 and the chart in Fig. 1 results that errors of operators participated in total number of incidents in each year of reference period are in the percentage share of 2.45 % to 8.31 % per year. There was an average 671 incidents per year during the reporting period. The average number of incidents caused by the operator's error was 34.7 events for the period and its share of the average number of incidents was 5.71 %.

To determine how the incorrect operation of signalling system which caused incidents participated workers categories attended in direct control of railroad traffic there was made next data analysis focused on the treatment of the causes of incidents from point of view of operators. For further analysis were selected only incidents caused by workers on position station dispatcher, signalman, supervisor of switches, operator of crossing gates and operator of track block or train announcing point. There were recorded 347 such incidents in the period from 2003 to 2012. Workers directly participated on operational control traffic have caused an average 4.36 % of these events. The remaining 95.64 % of incidents were caused by another culprits (for example drivers of motor vehicles, train drivers, etc.).

From more detailed analyses resulted [10] that in the observed 10-year period became a total 39 accidents directly caused by wrong or illegal operation of signalling system.

4.2   Frequency of Use of Emergency Operations

In order to create a model, which allows determining the probability of an incident caused by fault operation of the signalling system, it is necessary to determine the frequency of the signalling system operations and a share of the signalling system emergency operations to all operations of the signalling system. It is very difficult to acquire such information. Conventional signalling systems based on fixed control logic do not record any standard use of control elements and record only limited range of emergency operations. There is no central registration of use emergency control elements in ŽSR network. The use of emergency control elements is recorded and analysed only in case of accident. The only possibility to get an overview of the frequency of signalling system commands and of proportion of emergency operations is to use electronic event recorder which is a standard part of electronic signalling systems built in network of ŽSR.

There were analysed data from the electronic recorders of interlocking systems applied in track section Nové Mesto nad Váhom – Rača. Analysed set of records contained records of registered special operations related to railway transport controlling in time period from 19th October 2009 18:24 to 19th October 2011 09:07. Total number of operations when trains movement was determined on the basis of time table of analysed track section in analysed time period. Table 3 shows a part of results of the data analysis.

The data related to emergency operation were for more detail analysed in [10], depending on:

- what activity related to train movement or shunting was made as a result of this command using;
- with which element in the track (signal, switch point …) or with which device the order related.

Just to illustrate, in the reference period the command "NUL" (reset of the axle counter) was used 4760 times and the command "PN" (calling-on signal) was used 2301 times.

Table 3. Number of signalling system operations in period from 19.10.2009 to 19.10.2011 [10]

	Number of standard operations in trains movement controlling		Number of emergency operation		Total number of operations	
	Total	Average per day	Total	Average per day	Total	Average per day
Brestovany	160 144	219.98	1 500	2.06	161 644	222.04
Cífer	199 490	274.02	3 547	4.87	203 037	278.90
Horná Streda	153 259	210.52	855	1.17	154 114	211.70
Leopoldov	315 733	433.70	68 077	93.51	383 810	527.21
Pezinok	188 554	259.00	6 465	8.88	195 019	267.88
Piešťany	159 829	219.55	5 254	7.22	165 083	226.76
Svätý Jur	188 554	259.00	4 611	6.33	193 165	265.34
Šenkvice	195 124	268.03	314	0.43	195 438	268.46
Trnava	331 784	455.75	49 635	68.18	381 419	523.93
Veľké Kostoľany	153 259	210.52	2 007	2.76	155 266	213.28
Total	**2 045 730**	**2 810.07**	**142 265**	**195.42**	**2 187 995**	**3 005.49**

5   Use of Obtained Information

There must be ensured that the operator can control the process in the case of partial or full malfunction of the signalling system in the case of control of process with continuous operation. In such case the operator must replace the safety functions of the control system which are not available (they are non-functional) and therefore he must take responsibility for process controlling. The operator on the basis of information of the state of railroad process issues the safety relevant orders, which control the elements in the track. Depending on the technical design of the signalling system and the scope of its malfunction can control elements in the rail yard either directly (single-stage controlling) or indirectly (multi-stage controlling via the logic of signalling system).

The single-stage controlling during emergency operation is typical for traditional signalling systems (mechanical, electromechanical, relay systems). In this case the safety of railway transport depends on:

- the credibility of information of the state of the railway transport process and of the state of elements in the track which signalling system gives to operator;
- technical safety of connection between operating element and controlled element in the track – usually each control element correspond to one controlled element;
- operator error rate.

The multi-stage control during emergency operation is typical for electronic signalling systems. For electronic signalling system is characteristic that their logic is designed on the basis of the multichannel architecture, but displaying of traffic information and control (HMI) is designed on the basis of single-channel architecture with minimal safety integrity level (SIL 0). During fault-free operation of the signalling system the potential error commands (can be caused by operator error or by failure of the HMI) are supressed by the safe logic of the signalling system. In case of the partial malfunction of the signalling system or in case that logic of the signalling system does not have all information needed for safe control of the transport process, the operator must take the responsibility for the traffic safety. There is used multi-stage controlling to minimize influence of the operator error rate and to eliminate the influence of technical solution of the HMI failure to transport safety.

The safety of the railway traffic at multi-stage control is ensured through so-called procedural safety. In this case the change of the track element state will take place only after multiple performing service procedures. Chronology of procedures, their way of implementation and related data are evaluated by the logic of the signalling system. Sufficiency of these procedural acts is currently assessed subjectively. The aim is to create a model which allows an objective safety evaluation process of the railway transport control. Such model can be created on the basis of a thorough knowledge of the signalling system technical design and the definition of "standard" operator's error rate and the frequency of critical commands for the control of the railway transport process [9].

6 Conclusion

When assessing the safety of railway signalling systems it is needed a comprehensive approach. It means that in the safety assessment must be taken into account not only the impact of a technical failure of the signalling system but also influence of the operator's error on the safety. It means especially errors of the operator when he uses the emergency commands. Given that is necessary to consider the signalling system as a system with high requesting (respectively with continuous operation), the existence of the emergency operation is necessary and also required by the network operators. More detailed information about issues related to the evaluation of the emergency operation of the signalling system is described in [10].

Acknowledgement. This paper was written with the support of VEGA. the scientific grant agency. Grant No. VEGA-1/0388/12 "Quantitative Safety Integrity Level Evaluation of Control Systems in Railway Application".

References

1. Rástočný, K., Ždánsky, J., Nagy, P.: Some specific activities at the railway signalling system development. In: Mikulski, J. (ed.) TST 2012. CCIS, vol. 329, pp. 349–355. Springer, Heidelberg (2012)
2. Reason. J.: Human error: models and management. Western Journal of Medicine, http://www.ncbi.nlm.nih.gov/pmc/articles/PMC1070929/ (date of access: October 11, 2013)
3. Gertman. D. I., Blackman. H. S.: Human Reliability & Safety Analysis. Data Handbook. John Wiley & Sons. Inc. (1993)

4. Sträter, O.: Investigations on the Influence of Situational Conditions on Human Reliability in Technical Systems. In: Proceedings of the 13th Triennial Congress of the International Ergonomics Association, Tampere (1997)
5. Chandler, F., Presley, A., Mongan, P.: NASA Human Error Analysis, http://www.hq.nasa.gov/office/codeq/rm/docs/hra.pdf (date of access: November 16, 2013)
6. Clemens. P.L.: Human Factors and Operator Errors, http://www.ceet.niu.edu/depts/tech/asse/tech482/ humanfactors.pdf (date of access: November 16, 2013)
7. Zhiqiang, S., Hongwei, X., Xiujian, S., Fengqiang, L.: Engineering approach for human error probability quantification. Journal of Systems Engineering and Electronics 20(5), 1144–1152 (2009), http://ieeexplore.ieee.org/xpl/login.jsp?tp=& arnumber=6074557&url=http%3A%2F%2Fieeexplore.ieee.org%2Fxpls %2Fabs_all.jsp%3Farnumber%3D6074557 (date of access: November 21, 2013)
8. Z 17 Predpis ŽSR: Nehody a mimoriadne udalosti (2007), http://www.zsr.sk/buxus/docs/legislativa/Predpisy/D_17 (date of access: June 03, 2013)
9. Nagy, P., Rástočný, K.: Analysis of the Operator´s Error Influence on the Safety of the Controlled Process. In: ELEKTRO 2014 10th International Conference, Rajecké Teplice. Proceedings, Catalogue number: CFP1448S-CDR (2014)
10. Nagy, P.: Emergency operation of external elements of railway signalling systems. Doctor's dissertation work. Faculty of Electrical Engineering. University of Žilina (2014)
11. Gorczyca, P., Mikulski, J., Białoń, A.: Wireless Local Networks to Record the Railway Traffic Control Equipment Data. Advances Electrical and Electronic Engineering, Žilina 5(1/2), 128–131 (2006)

Telematic Support of Baggage Security Control at the Airport

Jacek Skorupski[1] and Piotr Uchroński[1,2]

[1] Warsaw University of Technology, Faculty of Transport
jsk@wt.pw.edu.pl
[2] Upper Silesian Aviation Group
puchronski@gtl.com.pl

Abstract. A key element of baggage security control at the airport is a human - the security screener. He/she performs some of the tasks remotely, and is supported by the telematic system, making the x-ray baggage screening. The aim of this paper was to analyze the dependence of the number of errors on the experience and the frequency of virtual threat images projection (TIP). The study was based on measurements under real conditions at the Katowice-Pyrzowice International Airport. In the framework of this research two basic types of errors made by security screeners were identified. The results show that the number of errors is dependent from both the experience and the frequency of stimulus, represented by TIP images. As a result, it was possible to determine the boundary level of experience that entitles security screener to independent work. Also the recommended frequency of threat images projections was determined.

Keywords: telematic support, security control, baggage screening, airport, system operator's errors, air transport safety and security.

1 Introduction

Special procedures and devices that lead to a high level of safety and security are used in present air transport in two main areas. In the first one (safety) unintentional operational errors are considered. They consist in non-compliance to procedures, technical failures, making the wrong decisions and many more [9]. In the second area (security) acts of unlawful interference i.e. intentional acts of hooliganism and even terrorism are being analyzed [6,7].

In this paper, we focus on the second of these areas, in particular the issue of baggage security control at the airport. This is an extremely important issue, because people who plan actions against the security of air transport, very often tend to put onboard the aircraft objects (cold steel, explosives, corrosives, etc.) that can help them in hijacking the aircraft or carrying out a terrorist attack [2]. Such attempts are usually made by trying to hide these items in hand baggage or in hold baggage.

Considering the traffic volume on the average airport, the issue of passengers and staff security, and the time needed to control all the baggage, one can easily conclude

J. Mikulski (Ed.): TST 2014, CCIS 471, pp. 215–224, 2014.

that security screeners' work must be supported by a specialized telematic system [20]. It consists of an x-ray devices and software responsible for:

- generating high-quality image of baggage content [4],
- automatic image recognition of threats [19],
- delivering the image to a security screener, located at some distance from the control point,
- checking the screeners' work by: displaying TIP (Threat Image Projection) images, registering the remote detection of an image of prohibited object, detection performance analysis, archiving results [18].

The whole security check point (SCP) can be regarded as a complex socio-technical telematic system, supporting the maintenance of a high level of aviation security. A technical standard of the x-ray equipment used, control process organisation option and the technical condition of the equipment are some of the important factors that determine the level of safety and security [14]. However, the main factor is the quality of security screeners' work [13].

Analysis of the errors committed by the screeners, their causes and possibilities of their elimination [3] is the main research problem this study. Results are based on measurements made in 2014 at the Katowice-Pyrzowice Airport. Answers to the following questions that the existing literature does not answer were sought:

1. What experience of screener is needed to let him/her to work independently at the security check point, with the maximum possible level of security?
2. What is the dependence of the frequency of errors on the frequency of displaying TIP images? On this basis the best frequency of TIP's was sought.

The paper is structured as follows. Section 1 provides an introduction and formulation of the research problem. Section 2 presents the TIP system as a tool for telematic support of security screeners' work and at the same time for its assessment. Section 3 presents an analysis of the human factor as one of the key elements of the baggage security control at the airport. Special attention was paid to the types of errors and their possible causes. Section 4 contains the main part of the paper - analysis of the dependence of the number of errors from experience, expressed by working time and number of checked bags. Quantitative relation between the number of errors committed and TIP frequency was analysed, as well as possible actions that will minimize the number of errors. Chapter 5 provides a summary and conclusions.

2   TIP as a Telematic Support System for Security Screeners

The idea of TIP system is to project a virtual prohibited item on the image of the piece of baggage being screened. A database of images of items prohibited for air transport, that is included in TIP software, contains different images, depending on whether we are dealing with a hand baggage or a hold baggage. In the latter case, all kinds of explosives and pyrotechnics are prohibited. The catalogue of prohibited items is much broader in case of hand baggage. It includes also objects with sharp ends and liquids. Colloquially, we simply call these images TIP-s, and in the situation when the system displays an image from the database we can say that a TIP is displayed.

The operator's task is to detect the virtual object in the image and confirm this fact by pressing the button on the x-ray device. This increases the screeners' awareness, as they are forced to search for prohibited items in the baggage image more often than is the case when the TIP system is not used. If the response is correct, the system confirms that the screener has detected the TIP and records his/her reaction time. In case of no reaction, the system informs about an error and records this fact for further analysis. Such data is the basis for the research presented in Chapter 4.

The TIP system fulfils two important functions. On the one hand, it allows checking alertness, perceptiveness and knowledge of the screener. Depending on the number of mistakes, one can work out an opinion on the effectiveness of the employee. On the other hand, the system forces the screener to pay more attention to his/her work, thereby raising the level of safety of air travel. This kind of stimulation is beneficial for the effectiveness of the control. The issue of the impact of the frequency of these stimuli on screeners' work is the subject of analysis in Chapter 4.

3   Human as a Part of Baggage Security Control at the Airport

Technical solutions used for automatic image recognition of threats, made a great progress in the last decade. However, fully automated solutions do not apply so far. Around 30% of hold baggage and 100% of hand baggage is controlled with the participation of human - manually or remotely using x-ray devices.

3.1   Effectiveness of the Remote Control of the Baggage

The effectiveness of baggage control process performed remotely by the screener is affected by numerous factors. They can be divided into two main groups. The first one is related to the class of x-ray device used and was analysed in [15]. The second group is related to the human - the security screener and can include:

- an overall assessment of the screener's potential, depending on his/her experience, level of training and the overall attitude to his/her duties: restrictive or lenient,
- number of errors committed during baggage control,
- organizational factors, characterizing the degree of screener's involvement throughout the whole baggage security control process.

In this paper we deal with factors from the second group and in particular with the issue of screeners' errors.

3.2   Causes of System Operator's Errors

There are several groups of causes contributing to the errors made by the operator of a telematic system, an example of which is considered in this paper. These include:

- baggage characteristics: the complexity of the evaluated image, orientation of a prohibited object in relation to the screener and the degree of overlap between the different images adjacent to the forbidden item [12],
- technical factors : the type and condition of the telematic support equipment that generate and transmit x-ray images [8],
- environmental factors : workplace organisation, lighting, temperature,
- individual short-term factors: nervousness, lack of sleep, weariness (resulting from the monotony of work and lack of incentives), fatigue (due to the length of the work, work at night or due to an excess of stimuli) [17],
- individual long-term factors: level of training, experience, security culture [16].

3.3   Types of Screeners' Errors

Within the research measurements were carried out at Katowice-Pyrzowice International Airport from January to April 2014. Types and frequency of the errors were specified. We have established that screeners make the following types of errors:

- They do not point (notice) the virtual prohibited item located in the image of the scanned baggage. We called it the type A error. It is a very worrying situation. Because if the screener did not notice the image of the virtual prohibited item it can be assumed with the same probability that they will not notice a real prohibited item. A large number of such mistakes would mean that the whole security system of the airport is of poor quality. This is because the main purpose of the baggage security control, i.e. detecting the prohibited item, is not fulfilled.
- They point as dangerous the bags which in fact contain neither a virtual, nor a real prohibited item. We called it type B errors. This situation can be interpreted in two ways. We can assume that the operator had (due to the analysis of the image displayed on the screen of the x-ray scanner) reasonable concern and suspicion as to the content of baggage so he/she showed alertness, which undoubtedly is a positive feature. However, it is also possible that in order to get a good rating, he/she marked automatically, and without a thorough analysis of the image, many scanned baggage as suspicious.

From the security point of view, the most important are the type A errors. The essence of the security control carried out by an operator with the use of x-ray scanners is the ability to recognise the images of the prohibited items. The number of type A errors is the measure of this ability. In turn, type B errors can disorganize the screeners' work, resulting in the need for very frequent manual control of the baggage. This reduces the throughput of such a system, but more important is that a large number of false alarms weakens the screener's vigilance.

4   The Dependence of Errors on the Experience and Frequency of Stimulus

The theoretical knowledge that screeners acquire during training in civil aviation security establishes certain frameworks and patterns which they will use when performing their duties. However, just like in any other occupation that requires employees to operate equipment, assess the situation, relate facts to one another or make decisions, one cannot become theoretically prepared for all possible situations that can occur in real life. This is particularly true of non-standard situations or emergencies [1], [10], [13]. Such situations require solving unusual decision-making problems and being able to assess possible options for action in a factual, substantive and calm way as well as in the context of the current legal and organisational regulations or infrastructural limitations. An employee acquires these skills over time while working at a security screening checkpoint, thus gaining experience [5].

It is very difficult to assess experience of a security screener, i.e. the extent to which he/she is able to work independently or even supervise and train new employees. This is because it is a subjective matter and, additionally, an employee's performance depends on his/her personality as well as his/her ability to work in a group; therefore, it is hard to carry out an unambiguous assessment in this area [11].

4.1   Measurements of Errors Made by Security Screeners

The effectiveness of security screeners in detecting prohibited items was measured during the period from March 2013 to February 2014. The statistics of errors that had been recorded by baggage screening equipment with the TIP system were used for this purpose. Measurements were made of the number of TIP images which were not recognised by a security screener (type A error) and the number of identifications of a prohibited item that was not really there (type B error).

As a measure of type A errors we assumed the ratio of the number of unrecognized TIP-s to the total number of displayed TIP-s. As a measure of type B errors we assumed ratio of the number of false positives (the number of luggage mistakenly identified as containing prohibited items) for all checked baggage.

4.2   Analysis of the Number of Errors Depending on Experience

To find the relation between the number of errors and experience, measurements were carried out for three employees who had just begun working as security screeners. The results of the measurements are presented in Table 1, whereas their graphical representation is shown in Figure 1.

The measurement results clearly show that the number of errors (both type A and type B errors) committed by inexperienced security screeners during their first months of work is very large. The number of both types of errors decreases over time as the employees gain experience. It can be noticed that the error rate decreases to a level that is acceptable according to the regulations after about five months and it can be said that the rate stabilises after about eight months.

Table 1. Measurements of errors made by security screeners with respect to the number of months of work experience [own study]

Month	Number of TIPs	Number of bags	Number of type A errors	Percentage of type A errors	Number of type B errors	Percentage of type B errors
1	61	3185	38	62.30%	66	2.07%
2	261	10625	104	39.85%	172	1.62%
3	199	8577	50	25.13%	340	3.96%
4	218	9058	52	23.85%	217	2.40%
5	186	8271	39	20.97%	90	1.09%
6	242	10158	45	18.60%	101	0.99%
7	193	8060	47	24.35%	80	0.99%
8	195	8507	28	14.36%	99	1.16%
9	174	7198	30	17.24%	67	0.93%
10	188	8184	29	15.43%	61	0.75%
11	127	7809	23	18.11%	61	0.78%
12	85	6131	20	23.53%	28	0.46%

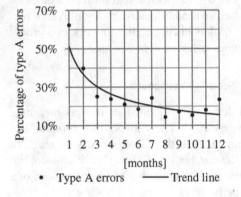 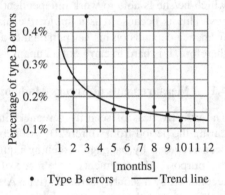

Fig. 1. The relation between type A and type B errors and one's work experience [own study]

4.3   Optimisation of the Training Process

A very important factor in the analysis of the training process is the number of errors, related to the cumulative number of screened bags, which parameterizes the training process. To examine this factor and to determine the appropriate moment at which an employee can be considered experienced enough for standalone baggage screening, moving averages were used for type A errors, using the following model.

Designations:

n - the number of the month,
N - the total number of months,
$x_t(n)$ - the number of TIP-s displayed during the n th month,
$x_b(n)$ - the number of bags screened during the n-th month,
$x_{eA}(n)$ - the number of type A errors committed during the n-th month,
$y_{eA}(n)$ - the percentage of type A errors committed during the n-th month,

$y_b(n)$ - the cumulative number of bags screened during n months,
k - the number of periods considered in moving averages.

Moving average characterising the rate of the screener's errors can be determined from the following formula

$$y_{eA}(n) = \frac{\sum_{i=\max(1,n-k+1)}^{n} x_{eA}(i)}{\sum_{i=\max(1,n-k+1)}^{n} x_t(i)} \qquad (1)$$

In turn, the indicator characterising the experience can be described as follows

$$y_b(n) = \sum_{i=1}^{n} x_b(i) \qquad (2)$$

The graph of the rate of errors y_{eA} related to the cumulative number of baggages y_b averaged for one screener is shown in Figure 2.

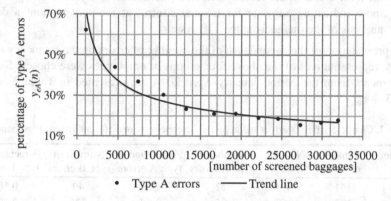

Fig. 2. Dependence of the rate of errors on the number of screened baggage [own study]

Empirically determined relation shown in Figure 2 specifies the moment after which the security screener may be allowed to work independently. Assuming a boundary error rate $y_{eA} = 0.2$, one can see that the screener has the appropriate skills after controlling about 22,000 bags. In turn, the maximum error rate allowed by the regulations $y_{eA} = 0.25$ is obtained after controlling about 13,000 bags. The study shows that the recommended number of controlled bags before the screener is allowed to work standalone should be set to 20 thousand.

4.4   Relation between the Screener's Errors and TIP Frequency

The frequency of the stimulus, defined as the TIP appearance in the x-ray image, has been listed in Section 3 as one of the causes of errors. In order to find the proper frequency of TIPs an experiment involving 93 security screeners from Katowice-Pyrzowice International Airport was conducted. Results averaged for all employees together, show no statistical relation between the frequency of errors and the TIP frequency. However, closer analysis of the results of measurements allows for the identification of four groups of screeners:

1. Those who commit few type A errors and few type B errors. These persons have an ideal profile for the security screener position.
2. Persons of a precautionary nature. They commit few errors of type A and a lot of type B errors. These screeners are carrying out a rational principle: 'better express doubts and proceed with manual baggage check than over-look the forbidden item'.
3. Persons restrained in identifying suspicious baggage. They commit a lot of type A and few of type B errors. Doing so may result from both a psycho-logical determinants but also from difficulties in the perception of images of prohibited items.
4. Those who commit a lot of type A and type B errors. This type of person is the least useful in the security screener position. Employees in this group are those indicating baggage for manual control at random, without a deeper analysis of the image from the TIP system.

For the presentation of the dependence of the number of errors on the frequency of the stimulus, representatives of the above four groups of employees were chosen. Sample measurements from the period January-April 2014 are presented in Table 2 and in Figure 3.

Table 2. Characteristics of errors made by the screeners from different groups [own study]

Screener type	Number of TIPs	Number of bags	Number of type A errors	Percentage of type A errors	Number of type B errors	Percentage of type B errors
Group 1	161	9739	12	7.5	49	0.50
Group 2	172	10678	26	15.1	235	2.20
Group 3	185	11187	72	38.9	75	0.67
Group 4	257	16943	68	26.5	554	3.27

The graphs in Figure 3 show the results for the usable range of TIP frequencies, i.e. from 1% to 3%. Some interesting regularities can be observed:

1. Screeners committing a small number of type A errors (group 1 and 2) are characterized by an increase in the number of errors with increasing TIP fre-quency. For those who commit a large number of type A errors (group 3 and 4), this relation is reversed: the higher the TIP frequency the lower the num-ber of errors.
2. Screeners committing a small number of type B errors (group 1 and 3) are characterized by an increase in the frequency of errors with increasing TIP frequency. Similarly, screeners with a high number of type B errors (group 2 and 4), record its' decrease with increasing TIP frequency.

Psychological analysis of the reasons of such screeners' behaviour goes beyond the scope of this work. The conclusion of this analysis is that in the general case neither very low nor very high TIP frequency is appropriate. Most preferred is the intermediate TIP frequency, about 2%. Only when we know to which of the four identified groups the screener belongs, we can select individual TIP frequency to him/her.

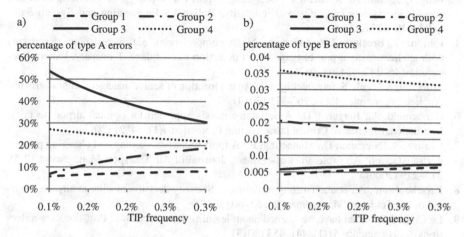

Fig. 3. Relation between the screener's errors and TIP frequency a) - type A errors, b) - type B errors [own study]

5   Conclusion

The paper presents an analysis of the dependence of the number and types of errors made by the security screeners on their experience and the frequency of the stimulus, represented by an image of a prohibited object. The basic material for analysis were measurements of errors committed by the screeners. They were recorded in real conditions, using the telematic support of Threat Image Projection (TIP) system.

One of the results of the research is finding the relation between the screeners' experience and the number of errors they commit. This allowed for an indication of the boundary number of 20,000 controlled bags, which may entitle the employee to work independently with screened image analysis.

The second result was to determine the relation between the TIP frequency and the number of type A and type B errors. This dependence on a general level does not exist. However, the identification of four groups of screeners, characterized respectively by low and high number of errors of type A and B, allows observing some interesting relations. This makes it possible to say that neither very low nor very high TIP frequency is appropriate in the general case. However, with the knowledge how effective the screener's work is (i.e. to which of the four groups he/she belongs) it is possible to select TIP frequency best for him/her.

References

1. Bazargan, M., Guzhva, V.S.: Impact of gender, age and experience of pilots on general aviation accidents. Accident Analysis & Prevention 43(3), 962–970 (2011)

2. Butler, V., Poole, R.W.: Rethinking Checked Baggage Screening, Policy Study 297, Reason Public Policy Institute (2002)
3. Feng, Q., Sahin, H., Kapur, K.C.: Designing airport checked-baggage-screening strategies considering system capability and reliability. Reliability Engineering and System Safety 94, 618–627 (2009)
4. Flitton, G., Breckon, T.P., Megherbi, N.: A comparison of 3D interest point descriptors with application to airport baggage object detection in complex CT imagery. Pattern Recognition 46, 2420–2436 (2013)
5. Fruhen, L.S., et al.: Safety intelligence: An exploration of senior managers' characteristics. Applied Ergonomics 45(4), 967–975 (2014)
6. Gerstenfeld, A., Berger, P.D.: A decision-analysis approach for optimal airport security. International Journal of Critical Infrastructure Protection 4(1), 14–21 (2011)
7. Gkritza, K., Niemeier, D., Mannering, F.: Airport security screening and changing passenger satisfaction: An exploratory assessment. Journal of Air Transport Management 12(5), 213–219 (2006)
8. Kirschenbaum, A., et al.: Trusting technology: Security decision making at airports. Journal of Air Transport Management 25, 57–60 (2012)
9. Le Coze, J.C.: What have we learned about learning from accidents? Post-disasters reflections. Safety Science 51(1), 441–453 (2013)
10. Malakis, S., Kontogiannis, T., Kirwan, B.: Managing emergencies and abnormal situations in air traffic control (part I): Taskwork strategies. Applied Ergonomics 41(4), 620–627 (2010)
11. Malakis, S., Kontogiannis, T., Kirwan, B.: Managing emergencies and abnormal situations in air traffic control (part II): Teamwork strategies. Applied Ergonomics 41(4), 628–635 (2010)
12. Michel, S., Mendes, M., Schwaninger, A.: Can the difficulty level reached in computer-based training predict the results in x-ray image interpretation tasks? In: 2010 International IEEE Carnahan Conference on Security Technology, pp. 146–155 (2010)
13. Schwaninger, A., Hardmeier, D., Hofer, F.: Measuring visual abilities and visual knowledge of aviation security screeners. In: 38th Annual IEEE International Carnahan Conference Security Technology, pp. 258–264 (2004)
14. Skorupski, J., Uchroński, P.: Rozmyty model oceny urządzeń systemu kontroli bagażu w porcie lotniczym. In: Skorupski, J. (ed.) Współczesne problemy inżynierii ruchu lotniczego—modele i metody, Oficyna Wydawnicza Politechniki Warszawskiej, Warszawa, pp. 113–130 (2014)
15. Skorupski, J., Uchroński, P.: A fuzzy system for evaluation of baggage screening devices at an airport, European Safety and Reliability Conference, Wrocław (in press, 2014)
16. Stroeve, S.H., Sharpanskykh, A., Kirwan, B.: Agent-based organizational modelling for analysis of safety culture at an air navigation service provider. Reliability Engineering and System Safety 96(5), 515–533 (2011)
17. Wang, T., Chuang, L.: Psychological and physiological fatigue variation and fatigue factors in aircraft line maintenance crews. International Journal of Industrial Ergonomics 44(1), 107–113 (2014)
18. Wales, A., Halbherr, T., Schwaninger, A.: Using speed measure to predict performance in x-ray luggage screening tasks. In: 43rd Annual Carnahan Conference on Security Technology, pp. 212–215 (2009)
19. Wells, K., Bradley, D.A.: A review of X-ray explosives detection techniques for checked baggage. Applied Radiation and Isotopes 70, 1729–1746 (2012)
20. Wetter, O.E.: Imaging in airport security: Past, present, future, and the link to forensic and clinical radiology. Journal of Forensic Radiology and Imaging 1(4), 152–160 (2013)

Application of Bayes Classifier and Entropy of Vibration Signals to Diagnose Damage of Head Gasket in Internal Combustion Engine of a Car

Piotr Czech and Jerzy Mikulski

Silesian University of Technology
Krasinskiego 8, 40-019 Katowice, Poland
{piotr.czech,jerzy.mikulski}@polsl.pl

Abstract. Currently applied diagnostic systems of technical condition use more and more advanced methods of gathering and processing input data. Many scientific research centres all over the world deal with problems connected with this topic. Up till now no such unified set of guidelines has been constructed which would allow for construction of properly functioning diagnostic system no matter which object is chosen. That is why there is a constant need to test the possibilities of application of existing methods and their modification to match given diagnostic cases. In this article the results of tests conducted with the use of Bayes classifier for diagnostic purposes are presented. The purpose of the tests was diagnosis of technical condition of head gasket in internal combustion engine of a car. The source of information about technical condition was the vibration signal measured in various measurement points. In order to describe the character of changes occurring in vibration signal the measurement in form of entropy was marked for decomposed signal with the use of discrete wavelet transform (DWT).

Keywords: internal combustion engines, diagnostics, Bayesian classifier, pattern recognising.

1 Introduction

At present there is a common need of automatic recognition of standards. One of the areas where the need exists is the diagnostics of technical condition of objects [9, 20]. Unfortunately up till now no such universal method has been created which would enable the recognition of a type of standard which could be used in all possible cases [2, 4-7, 12, 19, 20]. As it was presented in [10], the lack of universal solutions is not the result of imperfections of the methods applied so far. According to the author it is a result of complexity of signals which are sources of information.

Identification of standards is based on scientific notions connected with information theory, mathematical analysis and statistics [1-4], [8-10], [12], [14],

J. Mikulski (Ed.): TST 2014, CCIS 471, pp. 225–232, 2014.
© Springer-Verlag Berlin Heidelberg 2014

[16-17], [19-20]. One of the methods of identification of standards is classification. In short it can be described as [8]:

- determination of features of a standard,
- construction of a classifier of features,
- assigning the features of a model to a given class.

Many different suggestions can be found in literature which use static classifiers, minimum-distance classifiers, neural classifiers and other types. At the same time for each type of classifiers there are also many varieties [1-4], [8-10], [12], [14], [16-17], [19-20].

It should not be forgotten, however, that the correctness of functioning for each automatic conclusion system is based on quality of applied model. Quality here is understood as big amount of diagnostic information and at the same time lack of information pollution. That is why some activities are performed to eliminate the influence of unnecessary factors to simplify the structure of the model. It must be conducted with the smallest possible diagnostic information loss included in the model. Systems of automatic conclusion manage with decision making far better if they use simplified models. However, the unskilled initial processing of diagnostic signal may lead to irreversible loss of such information.

In conducted tests an attempt was made to use Bayes classifier in a task to diagnose the technical condition of car internal combustion engine. Vibration signals generated during the work of the test object were used as source of information about technical condition. In constructing diagnostic models the entropy of decomposed signals was applied with the use of discrete wavelet transform (DWT).

2   The Basis of Functioning of Bayes Classifier

In systems of technical diagnostics, among classification methods which are possible to be applied, there are statistic methods. In conducted tests the possibility of application for one such method was checked – namely Bayes classifier [1], [8], [10], [14]. The functioning of Bayes classifier is based on Bayes theorem.

According to probability theory:

$$P(Y/X) = \frac{P(Y \cap X)}{P(X)} \tag{1}$$

$$P(X/Y) = \frac{P(Y \cap X)}{P(Y)} \tag{2}$$

where:

$P(Y/X)$ – there is the probability of occurrence of Y event on condition of occurrence of X event,

$P(X/Y)$ – there is the probability of occurrence of X event on condition of occurrence of Y event,

$P(Y \cap X)$ – there is the probability of coincident occurrence of events Y and X,

$P(X)$ – there is the probability of occurrence of X event,

$P(Y)$ – there is the probability of occurrence of Y event.

In transformation of (1) and (2) we get:

$$P(Y \cap X) = P(Y/X) \cdot P(X) \tag{3}$$

$$P(Y \cap X) = P(X/Y) \cdot P(Y) \tag{4}$$

Therefore:

$$P(Y/X) = \frac{P(X/Y) \cdot P(Y)}{P(X)} \tag{5}$$

Formula (5) is called Bayes rule.

At the same time the total probability equals:

$$P(X) = P(X/Y_1) \cdot P(Y_1) + P(X/Y_2) \cdot P(Y_2) + \cdots + P(X/Y_n) \cdot P(Y_n) \tag{6}$$

With the assumption that Y is a representation of given class and X is the set of attributes determining a given class, depending on the number of classes and attributes the Bayes rule can be written as [14]:

- for one class and one attribute:

$$P(Y/X) = \frac{P(X/Y) \cdot P(Y)}{P(X/Y) \cdot P(Y) + P(X/\bar{Y}) \cdot P(\bar{Y})} \tag{7}$$

where:

$P(\bar{Y})$ – probability of occurrence of event contrary to Y,

- for N classes and one attribute the probability of K class:

$$P(Y_K/X) = \frac{P(X/Y_K) \cdot P(Y_K)}{\sum_{i=1}^{N} P(X/Y_i) \cdot P(Y_i)} \tag{8}$$

- for N classes and M attributes the probability of K class:

$$P(Y_K/(X_1, X_2, \cdots, X_M)) = \frac{P((X_1, X_2, \cdots, X_M)/Y_K) \cdot P(Y_K)}{\sum_{i=1}^{N} P((X_1, X_2, \cdots, X_M)/Y_i) \cdot P(Y_i)} \tag{9}$$

If the independence of attributes is assumed, the formula (9) can be written as:

$$P(Y_K/(X_1, X_2, \cdots, X_M)) = \frac{P(X_1/Y_K) \cdot P(X_2/Y_K) \cdot \cdots \cdot P(X_M/Y_K) \cdot P(Y_K)}{\sum_{i=1}^{N} (P(X_1/Y_i) \cdot P(X_2/Y_i) \cdot \cdots \cdot P(X_M/Y_i) \cdot P(Y_i))} \tag{10}$$

The biggest value of probability of given class occurrence means the adhesion of input data, described with agreed attributes X, as one that belongs to a given class.

3   Description and Results of Experiment

The research object was an internal combustion engine of a car powered by petrol with engine capacity of 1.6 dm3.

The aim of tests was an attempt to determine damage of engine head gasket on the basis of vibration signals generated by the engine.

In conducted experiment the engine acceleration signals were registered in the following areas: area of exhaust valve and suction valve of 1st cylinder, area of the exhaust valve of 4th cylinder and area of gear transmission. Measurements were conducted in engine test bench for a car moving at various speeds. Registration of signals was conducted for gears 3, 4 and 5 with rotation speeds of engine which equalled: 2000 rpm, 3000 rpm and 4000 rpm.

A multi-channel recording device by National Instruments company was used to record the vibration signals. The recorder enabled to simultaneous sampling with frequency of 50 kHz. Vibration acceleration converters types ICP by PCB Piezotronics company were used for measurements. The steering of data acquisition system was conducted with the use of application written in LabView environment. The process of vibration signals recording was conducted for properly working engine and for one with damaged engine head gasket. The damage of the gasket was based on bridge interrupt between 1st and 2nd cylinder.

Example of recorded vibration signals are shown in Fig. 1.

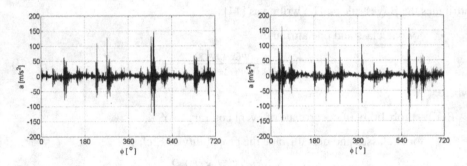

Fig. 1. Vibration signal of engine without damage (a) and with damaged engine head gasket (b) [own study]

In order to use diagnostic information included in vibration signal it should be first correctly processed. In conducted tests it was decided to apply discrete wavelet transform (DWT) [9], [20]. It can be defined as:

$$DWT = \int_{-\infty}^{+\infty} \psi(t) \cdot x(t)dt \qquad (11)$$

where:

$x(t)$ – analysed signal,
$\psi(t)$ – base function.

As a result of application of DWT analysis the multi-level signal $x(t)$ decomposition is achieved into high-frequency components $d_j(t)$ and low-frequency components $a_j(t)$:

$$x(t) = a_J(t) + \sum_{j=1}^{J} d_j(t) \qquad (12)$$

To describe the changes occurring in decomposed vibration signal into approximation signal and details signal the entropy measurement was used in the form of:

$$E_{sh} = -\sum x^2(t) \cdot \log(x^2(t)) \qquad (13)$$

In the process of model construction it had to be determined on how many levels the reference signal would be decomposed and what base wavelet would be applied. In conducted experiment the suitability of 52 base wavelets and 10 decomposition levels were checked. The wavelets from families: haar, daubechies, biorthogonal, coiflets, symlets, reverse biorthogonal and discrete Meyer were used.

Depending on the number of decomposition levels the size of model changed in the range from 2 – for one decomposition level to 11 for 10 decomposition levels. The influence of size of applied model on diagnostic classification result was checked.

Created models served to build Bayes classifiers for 10 options of model size and each option was checked for 52 base wavelets.

It was aimed, during the experiment, to classify the measured vibration signal into one of two classes which matched the engine in good working condition and the one with damaged engine head gasket.

According to assumptions assumed during tests, in equation (10) the number of attributes equals from 2 to 11 (X_1,X_2 or X_1,X_2,X_3 or … or $X_1,X_2,X_3,…,X_{11}$), whereas the number of classes equals 2 (either Y_1 or Y_2).

In teaching process 200 examples were used, a 100 for each identified class. The same number of cases was assumed for testing process. It gave a total number of 400 various examples for process of teaching and testing.

Example data distribution applied in process of teaching and testing is shown in Figure 2.

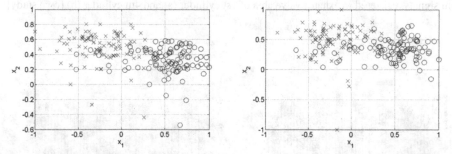

Fig. 2. Data distribution applied in the process of teaching (a) and testing (b) [own study]

During the experiment the functioning of classifiers which used models coming from vibration signals recorded in determined places was tested (4 places of measurement: exhaust valve of 1st cylinder, suction valve of 1st cylinder, exhaust valve of 4th cylinder and gear transmission) for engine working on given gear (3 gears) and with determined speed (3 different speeds).

The influence of wavelet choice depending on the area of vibration signal registration is shown in Fig. 3 and 4.

Figures show the distribution of the number of cases for which, with the use of given base wavelet, the classifiers were characterised with the minimum error value (no matter which gear was chosen – 3 gears, rotation speed of engine – 3 speeds and the size of model – 10 options). The best base wavelet would be characterised with number of cases equal to 90. In the experiment, however, such situation did not occur.

In the analysis of presented results it can be pointed out that independently from the chosen place of registration of vibration signal the best wavelet applied in the process of model construction is discrete Meyer wavelet.

Presented figures also show that the best measurement place among the ones tested in the experiments was the area of exhaust valve of 1st cylinder. It can result from the fact that measurement in this case was conducted in the place closest to the place of simulated damage.

Figure 5 presents example influence of model size (chosen number of decomposition levels) on classification result.

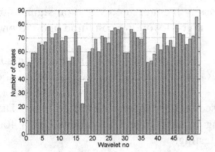 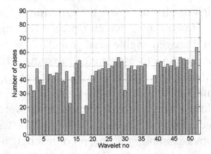

Fig. 3. The influence of wavelet choice on the correctness of classification for models achieved from signals registered in exhaust valve area of 1st cylinder (a) and 4th cylinder (b) [own study]

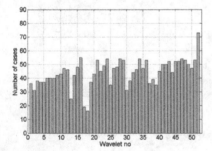 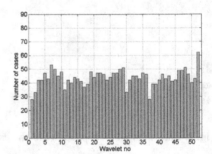

Fig. 4. Influence of wavelet choice on the correctness of classification for models achieved from signals registered in area of suction valve of 1st cylinder (a) and gear transmission (b) [own study]

In case of Bayes classifiers which were characterised with bigger error it can be observed that the bigger the size of the model (chosen number of decomposition levels) the smaller the testing error. For classifiers options with small testing error values it cannot be unambiguously determined how the size of model affects the achieved result.

Experiments which were conducted here allowed for confirmation of the usefulness of Bayes classifier in diagnostics process of the technical condition of engine head gasket in internal combustion engine of a car. The results of the experiments were classifiers working without errors or almost without errors.

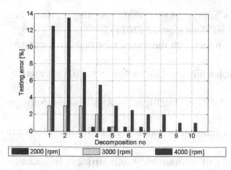 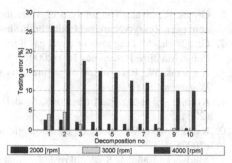

Fig. 5. The influence of the choice of the number of decomposition levels on classification results for model achieved from signals registered around the suction valve of 1 cylinder (a) and gear transmission (b) [own study]

4   Conclusion

Every year the number of cars moving on the roads of the world significantly increases. At the same time there is a tendency that the users have bigger and bigger requirements towards the cars when it comes to their reliability, safety and ecology. All over the world many scientific research centres conduct works to meet those requirements [2-7], [11-13], [15], [18-20]. Development of technology allowed for application in vehicles more and more advanced systems which monitor the technical condition of each of the elements as well as all systems. Modern diagnostic systems use a number of different methods to gain and process information to get the most correct diagnosis [1-10], [12], [14-20].

This article presents an attempt to use vibration signal to diagnose the technical condition of engine head gasket in internal combustion engine in a car. The use of Bayes classifier was suggested here which was taught on data based on entropy of signals achieved in decomposition with the use of discrete wavelet transform. Achieved results confirm the possibility to use the suggested method for diagnostic purposes.

References

1. Christensen, R., et al.: Bayesian ideas and data analysis: an introduction for scientists and statisticians. CRC Science (2010)
2. Czech, P., Madej, H.: Application of spectrum and spectrum histograms of vibration engine body for setting up the clearance model of the piston-cylinder assembly for RBF neural classifier. EksploatacjaiNiezawodność - Maintenance And Reliability 4 (2011)
3. Dąbrowski, D., Cioch, W.: Neural classifiers of vibroacoustic signals in implementation on programmable devices (FPGA) – Comparison. ActaPhysicaPolonica, 119(6-A) (2011)
4. Dybała, J., Zimroz, R.: Rolling bearing diagnosing method based on Empirical Mode Decomposition of machine vibration signal. Applied Acoustics 77 (2014)
5. Figlus, T.: Diagnosing the engine valve clearance, on the basis of the energy changes of the vibratory signal. Maintenance Problems 1 (2009)

6. Grega, R., et al.: The analyse of vibrations after changing shaft coupling in drive belt conveyer. ZeszytyNaukowePolitechnikiŚląskiej. Transport 72 (2011)
7. Grządziela, A.: Diagnosis of naval gas turbine rotors with the use of vibroacousticpapmeters. Polish Maritime Researches 7(3) (2000)
8. Kasprzak, W.: Recognition of pictures and voice signals. OficynaPolitechnikiWarszawskiej, Warszawa (2009)
9. Korbicz, J., et al.: Fault diagnosis, Models, Artificial Intelligence, Applications. Springer (2004)
10. Kwiatkowski, W.: Methods of automatic recognition of models. BEL Studio, Warszawa (2007)
11. Medvecká-Beňová, S., Vojtková, J.: Analysis of asymmetric tooth stiffness in eccentric elliptical gearing. Technolog 5(4) (2013)
12. Mikulski, J. (ed.): TST 2013. CCIS, vol. 395. Springer, Heidelberg (2013)
13. Mikulski, J.: Introduction of telematics for transport. In: Proceedings on 9th International Conference ELEKTRO 2012, Rajecke Teplice, IEEE Catalog Number CFP1248S-ART, May 21-22, pp. 336–340 (2012), http://ieexplore.ieee.org
14. Osowski, S.: Methods and tools for data exploration. Wydawnictwobtc, Legionowo (2013)
15. Puškár, M., Bigoš, P., Puškárová, P.: Accurate measurements of output characteristics and detonations of motorbike high-speed racing engine and their optimization at actual atmospheric conditions and combusted mixture composition. Measurement 45 (2012)
16. Tadeusiewicz, R., Chaki, R., Chaki, N.: Exploring Neural Networks with C#. CRC Press, Taylor & Francis Group, Boca Raton (2014)
17. Tadeusiewicz, R., et al. (eds.): Neural Networks in Biomedical Engineering. Biomedical Engineering. Basics and Applications. Exit, Warsaw (2013)
18. Urbanský, M., Homišin, J., Krajňák, J.: Analysis of the causes of gaseous medium pressure changes in compression space of pneumatic coupling. Transactions of the Universities of Košice, 2 (2011)
19. Zuber, N., Bajrić, R., Šostakov, R.: Gearbox faults identification using vibration signal analysis and artificial intelligence methods. EksploatacjaiNiezawodnosc - Maintenance and Reliability 16(1) (2014)
20. Żółtowski, B., Cempel, C.: Machine diagnostics engineering. ITE, Radom (2004)

Conditions of Telematics Service
for Purposes of the Army

Andrzej Bujak[1] and Marek Witkowski[2]

[1] Wrocław School of Banking, Institute of Logistics,
Fabryczna 29-31, 53-609 Wrocław, Poland
andrzej.bujak@interia.pl
[2] Military Academy of Land Forces in Wrocław, Institute of Command,
Czajkowskiego 109, 51-150 Wroclaw, Poland
m.witkowski@wso.wroc.pl

Abstract. The paper presents modern transport systems telematics solutions that can be adapted to the needs of the military. The requirements that must be met in order to increase the possibility of the use of transport telematics in military logistics. It highlights the role of wired and wireless telecommunications in data transmission systems telematics. In the publication, a special attention was paid to the safety and reliability of transport systems telematics in military applications, with particular emphasis on emergencies.

Keywords: transport systems telematics, ICT (teleinformation) infrastructure, data security.

1   Introduction

The use of telematics is noticeable in different areas of life and human activity. Professional telematics solutions help remote monitoring and supervision of transport services and security services, related to the control equipment and installations using telecommunications networks [1]. Telematics, after meeting certain requirements - can also perform supervisory tasks, remote diagnostics of certain objects and transport services for military purposes. This is mainly done with dedicated modules which transmit information using wired links, but mostly – is based on radio links. These are generally based on the link mobile network GSM (Global System for Mobile Communications) and satellite systems GPS (Global Positioning System). Modern and pervasive ICT infrastructure in a larger part contributed to the development of telematics in logistic applications. With the wireless data transmission – telematics devices can collect and transmit information from objects at any distance. An additional advantage of the described technology is relatively low cost of purchasing the telematics equipment and speed of implementation and expansion of the system. Telematics, which is largely based on monitoring, making measurements and transferring them to the management centers - has been applied in various modes of transport, industry, medicine and supervisory services in everyday human activity. Telematic systems can also successfully be used for military purposes. For example, remote surveillance, airports, polygons,

J. Mikulski (Ed.): TST 2014, CCIS 471, pp. 233–241, 2014.

databases, warehouses and areas in which you can deploy monitoring equipment movement or entry into the zone to be protected [2]. The use of telematics services can improve the functioning of military logistics. This is especially important in organizing military transport, where modern telematics systems - can be beneficial for providing mobility equipment and people in crisis situations. These systems can also be used to track the movement of vehicles which are subject to special protection when they transport materials such as hazardous substances, explosives, weapons, ammunition or sensitive documents. Using modern technology, which undoubtedly is telematics, one can also control many other systems and devices that equip the army (Fig. 1.). However, due to the specificity of the tasks that concern the army - the systems should be properly secured and prepared to work not only in daily activities, but also in emergencies and war. In the following part of the publication, the authors focused on the presentation of the possibilities of using telematics systems and services in the army, in particular on the principles of protection and reliability.

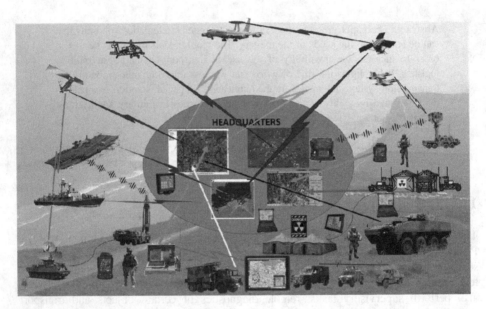

Fig. 1. The possibility of the use of telematics services in the military [own study]

2   Telematics Services

Connection devices and telematics services systems exchange information contributed to the development of telematics services. The use of modern technology in different areas of life and human activity improves the possibilities for remote monitoring of different types of services and devices. This also applies to possible improvements to transport services using innovative telematics solutions. There are more and more telematics systems that are working to improve transport services, freight forwarding and logistics. Almost each system is characterized by modern devices and specialized software that read and monitor the performance of telematics, and then transfer them to the specified control centers. Modern telematics systems provide access to the vehicle parameters, provide view of the current traffic situation and suggest optimal connection to the goal.

With the offered services, one can also control the basic parameters of the vehicle, as well as have access to other information, depending on the selected option and matched to the user needs of the system. For example, the user of the telematics system can receive permanent or periodic access to detailed information about the monitored vehicle, such as:

- observing the exact position of the vehicle while driving and when parked;
- when to start and stop the engine;
- controlling the driving time of the vehicle driver;
- generating a message to the driver about exceeding the allowed speed on the stretch of road;
- showing sections and indicating the value exceeding the speed limit by vehicle driver;
- number of kilometers;
- overseeing fuel consumption and its cost;
- overseeing fuel consumption, depending on the driving speed;
- temperature in the engine compartment;
- sending messages about the failure of monitored components of the vehicle;
- reporting unauthorized start of the engine;
- checking other declared parameters.

The above services provide constant supervision of vehicles, cargo and observance of traffic rules by drivers, and thus can increase safety and the level of transport services. Access to different telematic services may be directly carried on the device installed in the vehicle or be sent to the declared members. Sending information to the control center is possible using a variety of transmission media, but mostly this is done via a radio link communication technologies (GPS, GSM). This kind of solutions can streamline transport processes related to the transport of people and goods. The implementation of telematics systems allows for efficient management of transport processes, forwarding, and allows monitoring of the vehicle and cargo. The use of intelligent telematics systems [3] for the military can help increase the efficiency and safety of transport. In addition, well prepared and acting in crisis situations telematics transport systems ensure, in the event of need, the ability to move quickly troops and military equipment in the new area of operations. For example, through the use of technology in transport telematics the army will be able to determine the optimum road directions to that objective. This is particularly important in the case of a crisis in a given area, where the time to reach the designated location may be crucial. Using telematics devices, one can also locate obstacles or other difficulties along the route of military columns and through constant monitoring - direct vehicles with soldiers and equipment transported on backup roads.

3   Public Teleinformation Infrastructure Use in Telematics

Wired and wireless telecommunication devices, as well as communications and information technology, which are used to transfer information more often are defined as a common concept - teleinformation infrastructure. This infrastructure is largely being built by public operators, but increasingly also relies on private companies. Among the presented infrastructure, telecommunication components should also be distinguished, which have been prepared and are used only for the specified recipients. For this type of public includes, among others, units responsible for the security of the country, including the armed forces. Within the framework of the so prepared departmental infrastructure, there are mostly services which are associated with the provision of secure flow of information.

Within the framework of a public telecommunication network and a dedicated infrastructure for the security and defense of the state, there are two types of communication networks:

- wire;
- wireless.

The first group are wired networks, which are based on stationary infrastructure, and were built from different types of cables (e.g. copper or optical) and peripheral devices (such as: telephone, amplifier devices, switches, routers). Built teletransmission tracks provide the connection cable line in the telecommunications nodes that come along with additional devices which make stationary telecommunications infrastructure.

A big disadvantage of the use of wire communications telematics services is that these wire tracts can be offered only in those areas where that infrastructure is installed. In addition, such solutions must take into account the fact that the infrastructure is built stationary, in the event of technical failure or natural disaster can be damaged or destroyed.

The second group of networks is wireless connection, which mainly includes: a system for mobile communications and satellite communications system. Mobile communications is a service well known and used to transmit voice messages and data. Similarly, the satellite communication services which, through a system spread in Earth orbit satellites also provides transmission of information. A big disadvantage of this type of communication is that the use of satellite telephony services is associated with significant costs. The costs are generated not only due to the purchase of mobile satellite communications, but also due to the high license fees and royalties associated with the time of the talks and the transmitted data.

At present, to transfer telemetric information one can use commonly available mobile phone and high speed packet data transmission, provided by GSM operators. The big advantage of this type of service is that you are charged for actually sent bytes of information, and not for the connection time.

Increasingly, the needs of telematics systems are also used for Internet connections. This is done by combining global connections (within the WAN) and local calls (within the LAN).

The Internet can be accessed via the following wireless links:

- mobile services WAP (Wireless Application Protocol), GPRS (General Packet Radio Service), UMTS (Universal Mobile Telecommunications System), EDGE (Enhanced Data Rates for Global Evolution), HSCSD (High Speed Circuit Switched Data), HSDPA (High-Speed Downlink Packet Access);

- cellular modem - connected directly to the computer PCMCIA (Personal Computer Memory Card International Association) or USB (Universal Serial Bus);
- a radio access LMDS (Local Multipoint Distribution Service);
- public Internet access point PIAP (Public Internet Access Point) using radio links;
- wireless communication standard Wi-Fi (Wireless Fidelity), Bluetooth, HomeRF, IrDA (InfraredData Association), WiMAX (Worldwide Interoperability for Microwave Access);
- satellite links - need to install the expansion card and satellite dish.

In summary, the use of telematics services using wireless networks allows for rapid development and general accessibility of this technology. This also results from the fact that the cost of purchasing telematics devices and their operation are relatively low. Such factors contribute to the widespread use of this technology in various branches of human activity.

4   Military Teleinformation Infrastructure

For military purposes and to ensure its operation in all conditions, independent military infrastructure is built. This infrastructure is based on stationary and field elements of communication. Similarly to the public network it consists of wired and wireless components. The difference is that the military networks can work independently, without plugging them to the network of civilians operators. The separation of infrastructure of public operators is a way to restrict access to the resources to people who, accidentally or intentionally, seek to disrupt the telematics systems in military applications.

Stationary infrastructure in the army is based on local communications nodes and (regional) data communication support elements. Their equipment includes telecommunications equipment, which is capable of handling connections, mostly wired, for the military. One of the basic tasks is to implement the above-mentioned components to secure the ICT systems of all individuals and institutions of the military units in their area of responsibility.

The infrastructure of the military field consists of communications nodes that perform tasks on behalf of the authorities of command. The subunits, which are responsible for the development, exploitation, winding and displacement, are equipped with mobile (autonomous) communications and information equipment. This equipment includes both construction devices for building wired network and equipment for the implementation of services using wireless links. Similarly to public telecommunication networks, also the military wired and wireless networks use equipment, means of radio communication and connecting lines that allow the circulation of information.

The group of military wireless links are [4]:

- satellite;
- the radio relay;
- radio.

Similarly, like in the civilian communications, satellite connection needs the right phone (or satellite terminal) and telecommunications satellite.

Radio relay communication uses trunk nodes that lie in the area of military action. The trunk nodes can be separated from each other even at a distance of tens of kilometers (30-50 km), the most common links are called: mesh system, which allows for direct connections and cross between radio relay. Such a structure has very positive influence on the "vitality" of the system, as in the case of destruction of individual trunk node - the system is still working, creating, in a fully automatic way, a call bypass (substitute). Bit rate links created using radio relay equipment achieve up to 34 Mb/s.

Military radios, due to the power of transmitters and reach can be divided into four groups:

- low-power radio stations (up to 100 Watts);
- medium-power radio stations (over 100 watts);
- short-wave radio stations (VHF – Very High Frequency) – a range from a few to tens of kilometers;
- radios short (HF – High Frequency) – with a maximum range exceeding several hundred kilometers.

Radio stations were primarily used for voice communications (phonic) and for exchanging data in digital radio channels. Speed rate is not as high as with a radio relay units, but it is enough to send short text messages or alarm messages.

The big advantage of military communications is the possibility to link the military elements of the network to the public network operators. Thanks to the compatibility of connecting devices with the civilian-military they can work together and connect to an extensive telecommunications network.

5   Telecommunications Infrastructure Requirements for Purposes of Military Telematics

Public teleinformation infrastructure, because of its public character, is exposed to disruption or destruction. This situation can be caused both by natural disasters, technical failures, or deliberate actions of persons or organizations that will work to the detriment of a country or group of countries.

For this purpose, to avoid or at least reduce the negative impact of these factors on IT infrastructure - communications tracts and replacement devices must be prepared. If loss of communications will just be the interference of telematic support systems, the effects of such interference should not cause serious losses. However, this can contribute to the reduction in the quality of services provided and the lack of the expected information from the telematics infrastructure. Unfortunately, if such interference will concern telematics systems directly related to security and state of defense, then the consequences of the lack of this information may be very serious. Due to the fact that the accidental or intentional immobilization of network for the flow of information in telematics services is highly probable, therefore in the military one can not be limited to transfer the data only by public infrastructure. Wired and wireless infrastructure, which is used for the purpose of telematic services in the army - should have a high resistance for the interference and overpowering, especially in a dangerous situation. If a constant information flow between the telematics elements is not provided, it will result in a lack of data flow. The lack of such data could contribute to inadequate decision and, consequently, to the loss of lives of soldiers and equipment damage. Therefore, the use of communication devices is needed in the way that will provide telematics information flow in all conditions, especially in crisis situations. The services and telematics systems, which are used for military purposes, should be characterized (Fig. 2.) by:

- high reliability and readiness to act;
- high level of resistance to intrusion and placing unauthorized changes;
- resistance to interference;
- ability to secure transmission of information;
- ability to maintain the continuity of the flow of information;
- ability to provide lossless service transmitted data;
- ability to preferential handling special users;
- the possibility for flexible reconfiguration of the system.

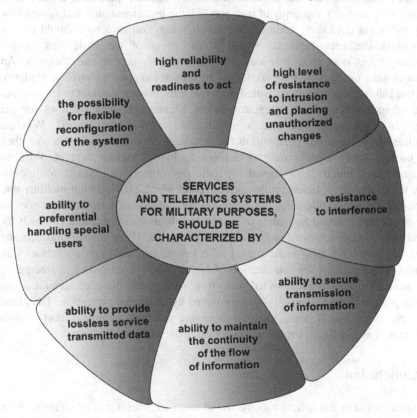

Fig. 2. The features of telematics systems and services that are used for military purposes [own study]

The features presented above that characterize the telecommunications systems used for military purposes must comply with these and many other requirements. For this reason, military components, in addition to telecommunications services provided by civilian contractors, are obliged to have their own independent network and data exchange devices. For example, telecommunications systems, which are to be processed classified information, should be accredited IT security services of the country. In addition, the networks and communication systems used in the military require certain security which can prevent or at least make it difficult to access their resources in an unauthorized way.

The fulfilment of this kind of requirements in relation to communications systems, can effectively restrict unauthorized access to areas of the devices and the information that was classified as secret. This also applies to the exchange of information between telematics systems that may contain sensitive information (classified), and, in accordance with the provisions must be adequately protected and transmitted via specified links. The fulfillment of these conditions will help impove the protection of telematics information and reduce the possibility of making modifications to the data, including the parameters of the monitoring equipment, measuring and warning.

Stationary teleinformation infrastructure, used for military purposes, should have opportunities for remote monitoring of transport [5], the instrumentation and systems for warning and alarm detection. Additionally, the stationary infrastructure should have a wired network elements duplicate, which in the event of the basic link failure, automatically takes over their role and provides the data sent to the recipient. An important element of the fixed network should be able to integrate its wireless platform, which would allow for a smooth transition from one transmission medium to another. An example of such solutions are integrators-WAN IP network, which allows for the exchange of data, either through a wired link or wireless (radio). Wireless communications become big competition for stationary communications because they can be used in every area of military activity, including logistic support. Wireless infrastructure only minimally is based on stationary objects (e.g. masts for mobile phones), the remainder is based on the moving parts which provide high mobility and large area coverage. Additionally, the condition for the use of telematics services in military applications should be stationary telecommunications infrastructure, which for increased safety could be located in special protection areas. These areas include, among others: the areas which belong to the army, police, fire stations and other institutions with daily shifts. In the case of the introduction of higher states of readiness or emergency such areas shall be subject to enhanced protection. As a result, the telecommunications equipment placed in their area will also be covered by additional protection. Therefore, even in crisis situations it could be used to ensure the flow of information to state security, as well as to monitor threats and alerts using the telematics systems.

6   Conclusion

The problem raised in this article was the use of telematics services and equipment for the army. The objective was to present the complexity of the requirements that must be met to the maximum extent possible to ensure the smooth functioning of the military telematics systems in all conditions. This is especially important when used for the purpose of military communications equipment and information technology will affect the reliability of telematics services. This also applies to transport telematics systems that can monitor vehicles transporting hazardous materials. Based on the information received from telematics devices, working in favor of the army, a decision may be taken to send, in the area of tasks, additional forces and resources to provide support and protection activities. Telematic systems for military applications can contribute to better maneuverability of troops and increase the level of logistical support during the preparation and conduct of military operations. Modern telematics infrastructure, working for the army, may provide information to the authorities of the command that will be used to take decisions, adequate to the situation. Properly prepared communications networks and computer science should ensure uninterrupted service of telematics systems, which are used for military purposes. They ensure the proper functioning of increased confidence in their reliability and the possibility of use in daily activities. It will also contribute to the search for innovative solutions to wider use of telematics services in the army.

To sum up, the authors of the article are hoping that telematics systems will find wide use in modern army and will be used on larger scale, and that the telematics information, transmitted via telecommunication networks can ensure increased combat readiness of troops and contribute to raising the level of security. Therefore, it is essential that the telematics services introduced to the army were reliable and based on data communication networks, which will operate in all conditions.

References

1. Mikulski, J.: Advances in Transport Systems Telematics 2, Chair of Automatic Control in Transport, Faculty of Transport, Silesian University of Technology, Katowice (2007)
2. Klein, L.A.: Sensor Technologies and date requirements if ITS. Artech Hause, ITS Library (2001)
3. Adamski, A.: Intelligent Transport Systems. Institutional Scientific and Technical Publishing AGH, Kraków (2003)
4. http://www.sceno.edu.pl/konferencja/6_19.pdf (date of access: March 20, 2014)
5. Freight Exchange, http://www.freight-exchange.co.uk/ (date of access: January 15, 2014)
6. Mikulski, J. (ed.): TST 2011. CCIS, vol. 239. Springer, Heidelberg (2011)
7. Mikulski, J. (ed.): TST 2010. CCIS, vol. 104. Springer, Heidelberg (2010)
8. Mikulski, J.: Introduction of telematics for transport. In: Proceedings on 9th International Conference ELEKTRO 2012, Rajecke Teplice, IEEE Catalog Number CFP1248S-ART, May 21-22, pp. 336–340 (2012), http://ieexplore.ieee.org

Problems of Systems Engineering for ITS in Large Agglomeration – Upper-Silesian Agglomeration in Poland

Grzegorz Karoń[1] and Jerzy Mikulski[2]

[1] Silesian University of Technology,
Krasińskiego 8, 40-019 Katowice, Poland
grzegorz.karon@polsl.pl
[2] University of Economics,
1maja 47, 40-287 Katowice, Poland
jerzy.mikulski@ue.katowice.pl

Abstract. Systems engineering and list of good practices has been presented in the context of ITS systems for Upper-Silesian Agglomeration. Selected results of surveys which confirm a complexity of the problems of ITS development in Silesian Region have been presented too. The differences in SWOT analysis for urban transport and variation of ITS level implementations including National Traffic Management System have been mentioned as examples.

Keywords: ITS systems, intelligent transport systems, Upper-Silesian Agglomeration, systems engineering.

1 Introduction

In some municipalities of Silesia Region and Upper-Silesian Agglomeration applications of ITS and telematics technologies are already being deployed in the road transport sector. However, such deployment remains fragmented and uncoordinated and cannot provide geographical continuity of ITS services throughout the agglomeration, region and at its external borders. The development of specific solutions ITS must take into account the diversity of their application needs arising from factors like functional, spatial and organizational [6]. On the one hand, local authorities and engineers looking for the biggest functional scope of ITS and on the other hand, they should take into account local needs of the cities, towns and urban agglomerations.

Identification of needs differentiation of transport investment has been the subject of research by questionnaire survey among 120 of 167 local municipality authorities in Silesia Region [1], [7], [8]. A particular aspect of the research was evaluation (SWOT method – identification of strengths, weaknesses, opportunities and threats) of development factors of public transport. There was evaluated 23 predefined factors such as location of municipality in region, structure of the settlement, commercial building, science and education, health centers and health care, centers of culture, art, entertainment, sport and recreation, transport infrastructure, structure of public

J. Mikulski (Ed.): TST 2014, CCIS 471, pp. 242–251, 2014.

transport network, integration and priority for public transport (see Fig 1), and many others [7]. Furthermore there was assessment of current state and investment plans related to ITS systems with regards to the delimitation of the area into municipalities, cities, agglomerations, subregions, Silesian Region and country. Based on results of this survey in Silesian Region there is variation and lack of consistency of spatial conditions for the functioning and development of public transport and implementation of ITS solutions (see fig.1). In addition, ITS development processes may be dependent on the method of financing model with co-financing from the EU funds, e.g. increasing the use of territorial potentials through integrated interventions targeted at selected areas. This model is called the Integrated Territorial Investments (abbreviation in Poland: ZIT) and assumes: first, the common planning of strategic objectives and secondly the choice of activities and projects to fulfill the objectives consistent with strategic area of intervention. Such strategy has been prepared also for Central Subregion where Upper-Silesian Agglomeration is situated [8]. This is very important in engineering systems in order to identify and solve the problem, i.e. development and implementation of an appropriate ITS systems.

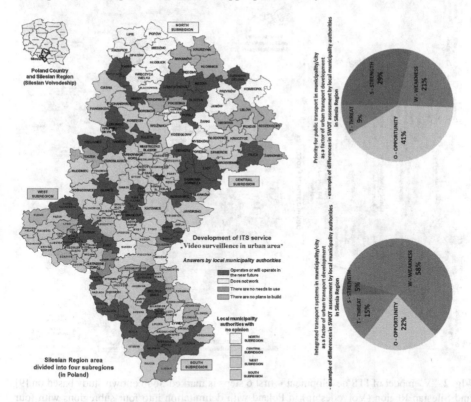

Fig. 1. Selected results of preliminary surveys among local municipality authorities in Silesia Region: left map – assessment of development of ITS systems "Video surveillance in urban area" in the SWOT analysis; right charts – SWOT assessment of urban transport development for strategic factors "Priority for public transport" and "Integrated transport systems". Source: own study based on [7].

2   Systems Engineering in ITS Development for Upper-Silesian Agglomeration

The early steps in the "V" model of ITS development (Fig. 2) support planning and budgeting since they are intended to identify risks, benefits, and costs to determine if the ITS project is a good investment. These steps define the project scope and determine the feasibility and acceptability of the Project [9].

The 1st step "**Determinants of Intelligent Transportation Systems**" (Fig. 2) defines lists of project stakeholders and roles and responsibilities, list of inventory elements included in or affected by the project, list of requirements the proposed systems must meet, list of interfaces and the information to be exchanged or shared by the systems and feedback to the regional ITS architecture that covers the geographic area where agglomeration architecture will be implemented.

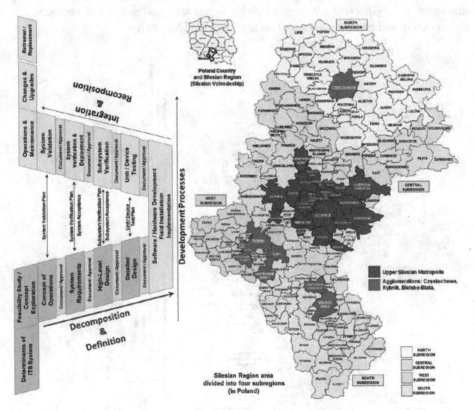

Fig. 2. "V" model of ITS development – first 6 steps is marked Source: own study based on [9] and Silesian Region (Voivodeship) in Poland with delimitation into four subregions with four agglomerations: Upper-Silesian Metropolis, Częstochowa, Rybnik and Bielsko-Biała

For Upper Silesian Agglomeration the such a regional ITS architecture is National Traffic Management System (abbreviation KSZR) of General Directorate for National

Roads and Motorways (abbreviation GDDKiA) [4] (Fig. 3). The overal objectives of National Traffic Management System (KSZR) are raising the level of road traffic safety, time loss reduction and other values added, such as e.g. optimization of road maintenance management, reduction of burdens to the natural environment, increase in the travelling comfort. Basic benefits of KSZR are: minimization of the number and effects of traffic incidents by transferring warnings, redirecting traffic, more effective rescue operations, improved traffic flow, improved efficiency of road maintenance, better quality of freight transport handling (providing information on available parking spaces), provision of current and forecast information on traffic conditions regarding the national road system.

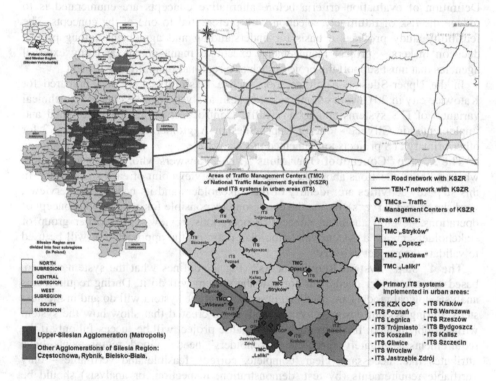

Fig. 3. Silesian Region with agglomerations and road network that will be controlled by National Traffic Management System (KSZR) of General Directorate for National Roads and Motorways (GDDKiA), TMCs of KSZR areas and primary ITS systems in urban areas in Poland; Source: own study based on [4],[1]

Given the functional complexity, technological advancement, extensive implementation area, and on account of financial and organizational reasons it was decided to divide KSZR implementation into stages and therefore KSZR was divided into four major projects: "KSZR on TEN-T", "KSZR and OP I&E II", "KSZR as an element of road construction", "KSZR in other projects". All this projects covering geographic area of Upper-Silesian Agglomeration and especially "KSZR and OP I&E II" project will be implemented mainly in relation to national roads related to the area of Warsaw agglomeration and Upper-Silesian conurbation. Additionally Local Traffic Control Center for Silesia Region (one of four) will be in **Laliki city** – see Fig 3.

The **2nd step "Feasibility Study / Conception Exploration"** (Fig. 2) defines feasibility study that identifies alternative concepts and makes the business case for the project and the selected concept. The alternative concepts should be defined in clear, technology-independent terms that all affected organizations will understand. One alternative should always be "do nothing", which provides a basis for comparison with the other alternatives. The alternatives should be high-level concepts to avoid idication of specific products or vendors. The concepts are compared relative to measures that assess the relative benefits, costs, and risks of each alternative. Definition of evaluation criteria before alternative concepts are enumerated is to reduce the risk of intuitively selection with preferential to one of the concepts. The feasibility study provides a basis for understanding and agreement among project decision makers – project management, executive management, and any external agencies that must support the project, such as a regional planning department.

In the Upper-Silesian Agglomeration such a feasibility study was prepared for Katowice city in 2011 with complex cost-benefit analysis for five concepts (technical variants) of ITS systems and urban Traffic Control Center has been designed and implemented in Gliwice – one of Upper-Silesian Agglomeration city (see Fig. 3 for other primary ITS projects implemented in Poland).

The **3rd step "Concept of Operations"** (Fig. 2) answers who, what, where, when, why, and how questions about the project from the viewpoint of each stakeholder. In this step key activities are: identify of the stakeholders and its needs (by interviews, workshops, and surveys), define the core group responsible for creating the concept of operations, develop an initial concept of operations, review with broader group of stakeholders, create a system validation plan defining the approach that will be used to validate the project delivery.

The **4th step "System Requirements"** (Fig. 2) defines what the system will do, based on stakeholder needs, but not how the system will do it. During requirements analysis, logical models are used that describe what the system will do and in the next steps, during system design, physical models are created that show how the system will be implemented. It is important rule because project will be successful only if the requirements adequately represent stakeholders' needs. Good requirements have attributes like: necessary, clear, complete, correct, feasible and verifiable – only verifiable requirements (by test, demonstration, inspection, or analysis) should be included in documentation of project. The system requirements specification should fully specify the system to be developed.

The **5th and 6th steps "High-Level Design"** and **"Detailed Design"** (Fig. 2) high-level are stage where development proces focus on the solution. This steps link the system requirements with system implementation that will be performed in the next step. High-level Design step defines a framework for all project components such as: computer systems (hardware and software), a communications network, distributed devices, facilities, and people – it is architectural design. Main four steps of high-level design are:

- identification of components that will be purchased, reused, or developed from scratch,

- partial decomposition of ITS system into subsystems and components,
- development and evaluation of high-level design alternatives (consisting of subsystems and components) – it can have a significant impact on the performance, reliability, and life-cycle costs of the overal ITS system,
- analyzing and allocating of requirements – the relationships between the required system functions are analyzed in detail and detailed functional requirements and associated performance requirements are allocated to the system components – there are many software tools that support requirements analysis and architectural design,
- documentation of the interfaces and identifying of the ITS standards – specifications should be developed for internal interfaces (i.e., interfaces between project components) and for external interfaces (i.e., interfaces between the current project and external systems such as regional ITS) including nature of the data, formats, ranges of values, and periodicity of the information exchanged,
- parallel creation of integration plan, subsystem verification plans, and subsystem acceptance plans.

Mentioned steps lead to description of ITS system into four views:

- physical view of the system components and their relationships,
- functional view of the system's behavior,
- technical view of interfaces, including the standards to be used by ITS system,
- informational view of information that will be managed by the ITS system.

Complete specification of the software, hardware and communications components is developed in the Detailed Design step. Each component is defined in terms of its functionality and performance, with particular focus on its interfaces to external systems and other components. In this step specifications are described in enough detail that the software team can write the individual software module and hardware components can be fabricated or purchased. For larger projects, such as ITS for Upper-Sielsian Agglomeration, coordination meetings should be held to ensure that concurrent design activities are coordinated to mitigate future integration risks. Furthermore a broader stakeholder meeting should be held after completion of the detailed design step to review and approve the design before the implementation team begins to build the solution.

3   Good Practices of ITS Development

The confirmation of the systems engineering principles, outlined in the previous chapter, are the conclusions of the evaluation of some projects that are already implemented in Poland. Synthetic presentation of the problems that occur during the implementation of ITS projects has been presented by the Centre for EU Transport Projects (CEUTP) [2]. List of selected good practices cover the following aspects related to the implementation of feasibility studies for ITS projects. Full recommendations for beneficiaries are in [1].

Identification of Needs – Good Practices

1) Proper preparation of the project for implementation with reliable identification of the problem, a description and analysis of various solutions. An important element in the preparation of the project is carried out feasibility study (in the early stage). Feasibility study should include realistic and reliably diagnosed investment needs of the beneficiary.

2) Taking into account needs assessment for the implementation of ITS projects in strategic documents for regions, agglomerations and cities. Strategic documents should clearly define the objectives (e.g. improving traffic safety, improving traffic smoothness) and tools (e.g. the implementation of ITS projects) designed to serve their implementation.

3) Ensure appropriate coordination of the implementation of various infrastructure projects at cities of agglomeration level (e.g. roads, sewage, water, etc.). With this process, from the planning stage of individual investments can be pre-identify potential spatial conflicts, e.g. realization of investments in a particular place at the same time, the investment planning sequence: first the underground infrastructure, then ITS hardware installation and resurfacing the road and.

4) Exchange of information and good practice about projects by the various local authorities and establishing cooperation investors (creating partnership agreements) can a good way to approach the implementation of the ITS project. Coordination of activities in the implementation of the ITS project will better fit the needs of urban transport in agglomeration. Potential beneficiaries who are planning ITS projects should cooperate with more experienced beneficiaries. Additionally given the innovative nature of the ITS a site visits of implemented projects can be useful.

5) Ensuring the use of the output data from implemented systems – data should be available. In agreements with contractors for the implementation of ITS beneficiaries should stipulate that the output data of the system can be shared, so output data can be easily managed by the beneficiaries (investor), including shared with third parties without any special conditions. An important is also managing with choice of the data format generated by the system, so that it can be used for analysis of software owned by the beneficiary.

6) Risk of starting the project before agreement of co-financing from UE funds. It is worth mentioning that possibly the lack of grant funding could result in a delay in the implementation of the investment or reduce the scope (and thus the results achieved).

Terms of Reference and Contractor Selection – Good Practices

7) Appropriate design of the Terms of Reference (access criteria and evaluation criteria) – appropriate formulation of the requirements in the tender documents in such areas as required experience and qualifications, can reduce the risk of unreliable contractor choice. The use of criteria other than price, such as methodology, allows the selection of the contractor characterized by

better understanding the needs of the project. An example of methodological criteria are:

- understanding of the subject (e.g. define the objectives and expected results of the project, identify and describe the main products of the project, explanation of the risks),
- management strategy (e.g. description of the concept of project organization, correctly assignment of roles to tasks, identification and description of the principles of cooperation, communication, reporting and escalation of issues, risk management),
- schedule of activities (taking into account objectives, requirements and constraints of the project, presenting a graphical and summary schedule, division into organizational and technical stages, taking into account the ability to parallelize the work and ensure the reserves of time, indicating dependencies, milestones and critical path),
- quality control (definition and description of the progress monitoring rules, criteria for verifying and testing the quality of products),

8) Do not use in the tender documentation (Terms of Reference) entries restricting fair competition and resulting in unequal treatment of potential contractors. Beneficiary should objectively determine the criteria for selecting the contractor who will be able to carry out the contract. Formulation of the condition of experience in projects co-financed from a specific source, such as EU funds, is an example of bad practice.

9) Paying particular attention to the content of the Terms of Reference in terms of trademarks, names of manufacturers, technical standards during the description of equivalent solutions. When the beneficiary indicates the possibility of equivalent solutions it is necessary to formulate precise parameters of equivalence of solutions in the Terms of Reference.

10) Determining the real implementation schedules of tasks. Throughout the project, it is necessary to plan accurate at the time of the individual tasks to be implemented. Some contractors and CEUTP pointed to the unreality of schedules constructed by the beneficiaries.

11) A thorough verification of the prepared project documentation (during the announcement of tendering procedures and during the acceptance of works). Without this process, at the stage of inspections conducted by CEUTP, weaknesses in the tender documentation the beneficiaries are trying to explain as "writing mistake".

12) Allowing collectively the conditions of participation for all members of the consortium during the procedure of contractor selection. Forcing the compliance with condition of experience by all the consortium members is too restrictive for entities submitting a shared offer with respect to contractors acting individually. This provision violates the principle of equal treatment and fair competition. In addition, the requirement to fulfill the condition experience by all the consortium members is contrary to the goal of creating a project consortia. Furthermore, beneficiaries improperly did not allow subcontracting because restrictions on subcontracting must be based on the Terms of Reference and can only "due to the nature of the order." However

Beneficiaries should note that as a rule subcontracting should always be possible and should comply with the principles of equal treatment of tenderers.

Project Organization – Good Practices

13) Appropriate selection the organizational structure, the persons responsible for carrying out the project and method of conducting the project. A good flows of information conducive to the project: it is possible to precise assessment of the investment and take appropriate corrective action when there are deviations. The beneficiary should not give the whole operating project in the hands of the contract engineer. The beneficiary should conduct regular supervision of the work performed by the contract engineer and the general contractor. An important of project management is the involvement of a minimum one person from the structure of the human resources of the investor in the project implementation process (a full-time employee, or a person employed on contract work exclusively for the project).

14) Supporting contractors (designers) in obtaining required arrangements and opinions. Prolonged reconciliation process documentation can be a big difficulty during the development of the ITS project. This issue was particularly emphasized by contractors ITS.

15) The use of all available sources of information relevant to the project. It is important that the beneficiary was aware that the conditions of the project change over time. Therefore, the beneficiaries should alone show interest and use relevant sources of information, such as websites relevant institutions, legal opinions, the audit findings and newsletters, such as CEUTP.

16) Ensuring adequate social acceptance of the project (information and promotion). For example in the news on the investor/beneficiary website (and the entities responsible for the implementation of the project) should be available information about any planned difficulties caused by installation of ITS (e.g. lane closure, changes in traffic lights to action, etc.). Other activities include the organization of open days and educational activities, during which citizens can see the stages of system implementation.

4   Conclusion

According to a study [1],[7] in Poland are the following main barriers to the implementation of ITS: insufficient knowledge of the potential beneficiaries and public users about functionalities offered by ITS systems and the different types of this systems, still small experience in the implementation of such projects in Poland (only 14 projects implemented in years 2007-2013 – in EU Infrastructure and Environment Programme – Measure 8.3. Development of Intelligent Transport Systems), the lack of architecture of ITS deployment (all projects are "insular").

The application of systems engineering [9] is recommended for Upper-Silesian Agglomeration at every stage of the ITS development proceedings, both at stages characterized in chapter 2 (steps of decomposition and definition processes) as well as in the implementation and operation (steps of integration and recomposition processes) – see fig. 2. Logical and physical architectures for necessary services is recommended to prepare using the tools of E-FRAME [3]. It is also necessary to prepare a feasibility study with cost-benefit analysis for alternative concepts using a transportation systems modellig [5]. A good example of this approach is the KSZR project which is available on the dedicated website of General Directorate for National Roads and Motorways [4]

References

1. Assessment of Key Issues in Projects in the Field of ITS in the Framework of – Measure 8.3. Development of Intelligent Transport Systems. Polish Ministry of Infrastructure and Development (2012), http://www.ewaluacja.gov.pl (date of access: June 14, 2014)
2. Centre for EU Transport Projects (CEUTP), http://www.cupt.gov.pl/ (date of access: June 14, 2014)
3. European Intelligent Transport System (ITS) Framework Architecture (E-FRAME), http://www.frame-online.net/ (date of access: June 14, 2014)
4. Feasibility study of National Traffic Management System, Kraków, General Directorate for National Roads and Motorways (GDDKiA) (2012), http://www.kszr.gddkia.gov.pl/ (date of access: June 14, 2014)
5. Karoń, G., Mikulski, J.: Transportation Systems Modelling as Planning, Organisation and Management for Solutions Created with ITS. In: Mikulski, J. (ed.) TST 2011. CCIS, vol. 239, pp. 277–290. Springer, Heidelberg (2011)
6. Karoń, G., Mikulski, J.: Problems of ITS Architecture Development and ITS Implementation in Upper-Silesian Conurbation in Poland. In: Mikulski, J. (ed.) TST 2012. CCIS, vol. 329, pp. 183–198. Springer, Heidelberg (2012)
7. Karoń, G., Sobota, A., et al.: Analysis of the existing transport systems in the Upper-Silesian Agglomerationon the basis of quantitative and qualitative surveys. Silesian Cluster of Urban Transport – Centre of Transport Development, Katowice (2014)
8. Tomanek, R., et al.: Strategy of Development for Central Subregion of Silesia in the years 2014-2020 with a perspective for 2030 with particular emphasis on the development of urban transport, together with the Programme of Action for Integrated Territorial Investments (ZIT), The Research and Expertise Centre University of Economics in Katowice (2013)
9. Systems Engineering for Intelligent Transportation Systems. U.S. Department of Transportation. FHWA-HOP-07-069 (January 2007)

Impact Electric Component of the Electromagnetic Field on Electronic Security and Steering Systems in Personal Rapid Transit

Jacek Paś[1] and Włodzimierz Choromański[2]

[1] Warsaw Military University of Technology,
00-908 Warsaw, Poland
JPas@wat.edu.pl
[2] Warsaw University of Technology,
00-662 Warsaw, Poland
wch@wt.pw.edu.pl

Abstract. Transport safety systems and electronic security system Personal Rapid Transit (PRT) steering systems constitute a spatially formed set of elements that operate together in order to achieve the assumed level of security at a railway station or during the performance of transportation operations. Occurring intended or unintended electromagnetic interferences in the process of exploitation electronic systems may cause the occurrence of catastrophic damages or can be the reason of a reduction of the work quality of these systems. Small frequency range electromagnetic interference (up to 100 kHz) that occurs in an extensive "railway" area should be considered separately, i.e. the electric and magnetic components of this field should be distinguished. Because of measurements and legal regulations concerning the impact of this interference on elements, devices and electronic systems. Any disruption of the primary functions of the steering system can be the cause of the occurrence of human life and health hazards. The present article discusses the impact of electromagnetic interference: the electric component of the field on the process of the operation of the PRT steering and security system.

Keywords: Small frequency, electromagnetic interference, security system.

1 Introduction

Personal Rapid Transit (PRT) is a zero-emission public transport system of an individual nature. The system provides a "door to door" transport: without any intermediate stops and with an adaptation to the disabled people [1-2]. When implementing the project, the following assumptions were accepted:

- ensuring the maximum safety for passengers [8], [12];
- ensuring the maximum reliability of the operation of the PRT system;
- a limitation of energy consumption (a minimum of energy consumption);

J. Mikulski (Ed.): TST 2014, CCIS 471, pp. 252–262, 2014.

- ergonomics (an adaptation to disabled people), no impact of the PRT system on the surrounding environment (no emission of pollutants by the transport system: e.g. of carbon dioxide, noise, mechanical vibrations including the generation of an unintended distorting electromagnetic field [6], [8-9].

The fulfilment of these assumptions (particularly the first two points above) is dependent on PRT steering and security system(s). Electromagnetic interference generated intentionally (e.g. systems of communication, radio and TV stations etc.) and unintentionally (a side effect of the processing of electric signals in PRT systems and in the surrounding electric infrastructure: e.g. power lines, transformer stations) have an impact on steering and security systems which realize specific operating tasks, cf. Fig. 1 [7], [11].

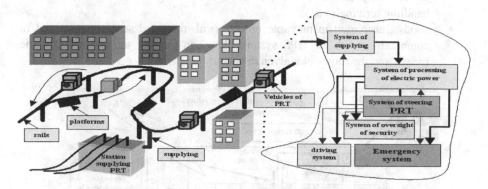

Fig. 1. Infrastructure of PRT system: connections of the steering system [6,8,12]

2   Impact of Electromagnetic Interference on PRT Steering and Security Systems

In the 20th century, as a result of human activity, artificial factors that form the electro-climate were introduced. There occurred serious changes to the electromagnetic environment of the Earth as a result of the formation of innumerable sources of radiation. The development of electrical engineering and electronics has caused an introduction of innumerable artificial sources of non-ionizing electromagnetic radiation, ones which emit fields in a very wide frequency range. Miniaturization, a limited consumption of electric energy and a great reliability of operation is required from modern electronic devices that are used in the steering systems of rail traffic, electronic security systems and PRT steering systems. The consequence of the introduction of these limitations is that the level of the signals of useful devices can be comparable with the level of interference generated by e.g. stationery and movable sources of interference (e.g. base, radio and television stations, medium and high voltage lines, transformer stations, commonly used electric devices, traction vehicles etc.). Therefore, a continuous evaluation of the conditions of the electromagnetic environment is of such a great importance in relation to the introduction of new devices and systems whose nominal power is large, e.g. an alteration of the power of a transformer station, the use of driving engines with a greater power in traction vehicles, an increase of the power of the transmitters in mobile telephony station [1-2], [6], [9]. The problem of electromagnetic interference occurred in the early period of the development of radio broadcasting. Electronic security systems are those systems whose purpose is to detect hazards that occur in the transportation process (in relation both to stationary and movable objects: PRT vehicles). These systems are increasingly frequently used in the transportation process, where they ensure safety to [10-11]:

- people (e.g. surveillance systems installed in the permanent objects of airports, railway stations, ports etc.);
- goods transported in permanent objects (e.g. logistic bases, land and sea handling terminals etc.);
- goods transported in movable objects (rail, road and sea transport; and in combination with the GPS system, they can monitor the condition of the freight and the routes of a given means of transport).

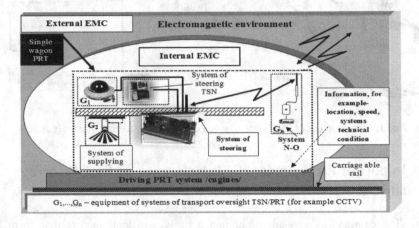

Fig. 2. Internal and external electromagnetic compatibility [own study]

Transport system are operated in diversified climatic conditions and in various electromagnetic environments that surround them, which can be the cause of the occurrence of interference. The correct functioning of the security and steering system is dependent from the following:

- the reliability of the individual elements the system is composed of;
- the internal reliability structure of the security and steering system;
- the accepted strategies of the operation of the system;
- those electromagnetic interference that have an impact on the process of the operation of the system, cf. Fig. 2.

Security and steering systems that are installed in an extensive railway area are exposed to the impact of electromagnetic interference, whose sources are both movable objects (traction vehicles) and the whole electric and electronic infrastructure of the railway area: the traction power supply, electro energetic transformer stations, rail traffic steering systems and telecommunication systems. A high level of interference can be the cause of the occurrence of disturbances to the operation of digital systems, micro-processor systems that security and steering systems are composed of (e.g. a burglary and assault signaling system, a fire signaling system, a CCTV system, an access control system) [1], [4-5], [12]. There occurs interference with various frequencies and amplitudes in a railway area. The electric traction and transformer stations generate interference in small frequency ranges, while impulse devices that are used as start-up devices in traction vehicles generate interference with very wide frequency ranges. The issue of the resistance to interference of security and steering systems and thereby ensuring the safety of the rail traffic is of a special significance in relation to the introduction by operators of electric locomotives of a great power, e.g. locomotives with the power above 6 MW into the traffic [6], [12]. The problem of electromagnetic interference occurred in the early period of the development of radio broadcasting; cf. Fig. 3. At present, both electronic analogue and digital devices are used in the railway area. They themselves generate unintended electromagnetic fields during their work, and they are exposed to external fields that are generated by other devices. There occurred a wide interest in the unfavorable impact of electromagnetic fields in different frequency ranges on the human organism and the work of electronic devices at the moment of the introduction of the EU Directive concerning electromagnetic compatibility. The determination of permissible conditions in relation to the impact of external electromagnetic fields on the operation of electronic devices and equipment that include electronic circuits was defined as the electromagnetic compatibility [6-7], [12].

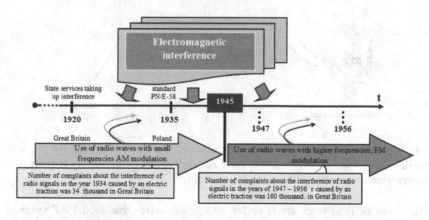

Fig. 3. Electromagnetic interference in a railway area [1,6,12]

In order to assess the quantity of electromagnetic interference that occurs in a railway area, the parameters of the following circuits need to be determined:

- circuits with large value currents (traction substations, overhead cables, return system, traction vehicles, electroenergetic supply network);

- circuits with current of small values, i.e.: rail traffic steering systems, systems of wired, radio and broadcast communication, PRT security and steering systems.

The existing electromagnetic interference in the railway area has an impact on the PRT security and steering system with the aid of couplings [7]:

- radiated couplings (frequency range from 30 MHz: the quantity of interference being proportional to the electromagnetic field parameters, i.e. the intensity E of the electric field and the intensity H of the magnetic field);
- conducted couplings: that are proportional to the value of the current I[A], interfering voltage U [V];
- induction couplings (the amplitude of interference being proportional to the rate of the change of current in time);
- capacity couplings (the amplitude of interference being proportional to the rate of the change of voltage in time).

The rail traction of the PRT system is supplied by a high voltage power line: 110 or 220 kV. Around the power energy wires, there occur electromagnetic fields, which have an impact on the systems and also on the animate matter; cf. fig. 4 a). The distribution of the lines of the electric field generated by the power lines that supply the PRT system is presented in Fig. 4b).

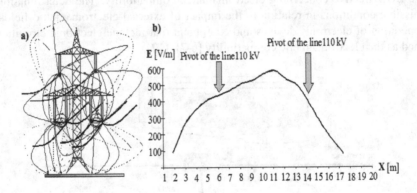

Fig. 4. a) distribution of the lines of the forces of the electric field around the wires of the power line that powers devices in an extensive railway area, b) field intensity E under two 110 kV power wires that supply PRT systems [own study]

The value of field intensity E under two power wires that feed PRT systems is presented in Fig. 5b. LCD or CRT computer monitors are used to supervise and display the states of the operation processes of PRT security and steering systems [12-13]. Monitors generate unintended electric and magnetic fields in a wide frequency range. Fig. 5 presents omni-directional characteristics of the radiation of the CRT monitor for various distances of the measurement and the standards of protection against this radiation: MPR and TCO 95 [6], [11], [12].

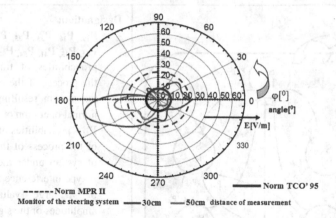

Fig. 5. Field intensity E generated by a CRT monitor CRT (the computer monitor being placed in point 0, the centre of the screen directed at 0^0 angle) [own study]

3   Impact of Interference – The Electric Field Component on the PRT Security and Steering Systems

If the electric and magnetic fields change in time, there occurs a phenomenon of the mutual induction of these fields, and the areas of mutual inductions move in space and create an electromagnetic wave. Electric charges constitute the source of the electric field. Each electric charge produces electric field in space which acts on the another charge with the aid of the Lorentz's force. The following regularities can be distinguished based on the Maxwell's equations: a variable magnetic field produces a rotational electric field (the Faraday's law) and an electric field that is variable in time, and flowing electric charges produce a rotational magnetic field (the Ampere's law). The abovementioned equations are supplemented with the so-called material equations, which mutually bind the primary physical quantities that describe the electromagnetic field. In a railway area, there are electric and electronic devices which generate an unintended electromagnetic field. The rail environment is one of the most difficult environments regarding the provision of electromagnetic compatibility [3], [6], [12].

Electronic systems: steering and security systems installed in a railway area work in a diversified electromagnetic environment. In the range of small frequencies, there occur fairly serious deformations of the electromagnetic environment in this area. Security and steering systems consist of highly reliable devices (e.g. the use of initial ageing, redundancy or a technique damage toleration), R(t) → 1; therefore, we can accept that:

$$\lambda(t) = \frac{\partial F(t)}{\partial t} = \frac{\partial F(t)}{\partial X} \cdot \frac{\partial X}{\partial t} \qquad (1)$$

where: X – the margin of the strength of the elements the security and steering systems are composed of; X – strength: to interference X_Z; mechanical X_M; electric X_E and heat X_C interference [7].

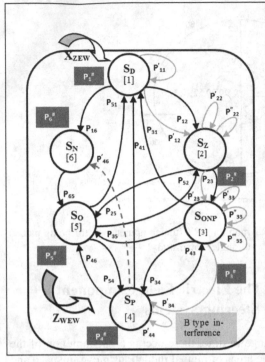

Designation:

- P_{12}, P_{16}, P_{23}, P_{25}, P_{34}, P_{31}, P_{35}, P_{43}, P_{45}, P_{41}, P_{54}, P_{52}, P_{51}, P_{65} – probabilities of transitions of the process of the operation of the system resulting from the normal operation of the system;

- P_{46} – probabilities of transitions of the process of the operation of system under the impact of A type interference for the case of a large value of the amplitudes of the signal;

- P'_{11}, P'_{12}, P'_{22}, P''_{22}, P'_{23}, P'_{33}, P''_{33}, P'''_{33}, P'_{34}, P'_{44} – probabilities of transitions of the process of the operation of the system under the impact of B type interference for the case of a small value of the amplitudes of interference

Fig. 6. Model of the impact of interference on the PRT security Denotations in Figs. ⟶ impact of interference with large amplitude values; ----▶ impact of interference with small amplitude values; S_D – state of diagnosing; S_Z – state of usability; S_{ONP} – state of waiting for work; S_P – state of work; S_O – state of servicing; S_N – state of incapacity [own study].

Security and steering systems include a great number of elements with different degrees of the margin of strength to electromagnetic, mechanical, electric and heat interference. These strengths change under the impact of various forcing factors: climatic and environmental ones (e.g. level of electromagnetic interference is subject to change under the impact of interference from those external and internal sources that exist in a railway area). Therefore, the margin X of the strength of the security and steering system can be written as:

$$X = \sum_{i=1}^{k} X_i \qquad (2)$$

where: X_i – the margin of strength for the individual elements and systems that security and steering systems are composed of (e.g. detectors, transistors, resistors, coils etc.).

Taking into consideration the abovementioned margins of strength, the intensity of damage to the security and steering system can be defined as:

$$\lambda(t) = \frac{\partial F(t)}{\partial X_Z} \cdot \sum_{1}^{k_Z} \frac{\partial X_Z}{\partial t} + \frac{\partial F(t)}{\partial X_m} \cdot \sum_{1}^{k_m} \frac{\partial X_m}{\partial t} + \frac{\partial F(t)}{\partial X_E} \cdot \sum_{1}^{k_E} \frac{\partial X_E}{\partial t} + \frac{\partial F(t)}{\partial X_C} \cdot \sum_{1}^{k_C} \frac{\partial X_C}{\partial t} \qquad (3)$$

The electromagnetic field which exerts an impact on steering and security systems in the range of small frequencies from 0 Hz to 100 kHz should be considered separately for each electric and magnetic components which form this field. The mechanism of the impact of the individual components that form an electromagnetic field on those electronic elements and devices which form the steering and security system is different. In the range of small frequencies, we separately define the individual components of the electromagnetic field by making measurements which define the field intensity E and the magnetic field intensity H (or interchangeably the induction B) of the magnetic field. The electric field is very well attenuated in the range of small frequencies by all the housings of elements and electronic devices: both metal and plastic ones (and also by structural partitions) [6], [11], [12]. Therefore, when defining the rate of the changes to the margin of the strength and the unreliability of an element under the impact of the interference of an electromagnetic field, the impact of the electric component X_E and of the magnetic component of the field X_B should be considered separately; cf. dependence 4.

$$\frac{\partial X(t)_{ZE}}{\partial t} = \frac{\partial X(t)_E}{\partial t}; \qquad \frac{\partial X(t)_{ZB}}{\partial t} = \frac{\partial X(t)_B}{\partial t} \qquad (4)$$

4 Electric Field and the Safety States of the Operation Process of Steering and Security Systems used in PRT

A simulation of the behavior for security and steering systems was conducted for interference that is produced in an extensive railway area: from the value of the electromagnetic field that exists in a usable room, through the values of the field generated at a train platform, to an atmospheric discharge (the range of changes to the γ value: cf. Fig. 7). For the abovementioned γ values, the indexes were determined: $R_0(t)$, $Q_{ZB1}(t)$ and $Q_B(t)$ of the safety of the operation of security and steering systems; cf. Fig. 8. When analyzing Fig. 7 and 8, one can find that for the small values of the indexes γ of interference, the system practically maintains a constant value of the $R_0(t_b)_Z$ parameter: the security and steering system is insensitive to interference with small amplitudes ($\approx \gamma = 10 \cdot 10^{-6}$). If a security and steering system is installed in the buildings of a railway station, the screening impact is to be taken into account of the lightning protection installation with various dimensions of the lightning protection installation eye. The dimensions of the lightning protection installation eye exert an influence on the course of the complete serviceability function $R_0(t_b)_Z$ – (Fig. 7). A reduction of the lightning protection installation eye (20x20 m by 5x5 m) results in security and steering systems being less sensitive to interference (the index of the level of safety Γ being $\gamma = 100 \cdot 10^{-6}$). The level of the safety Γ of the work of security and steering systems depends on the location of their installation: an open area (a train platform), a closed area (buildings located in a vast railway area) [1], [11]. The values of the individual probabilities of the system remaining in states depend from the properties of the interfering electromagnetic field (the vector of the magnetic or electric field).

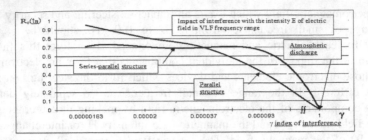

Fig. 7. Change to the value of the probability of the complete serviceability of security and steering systems $R_0(t_b)$ under the impact of interference [own study]

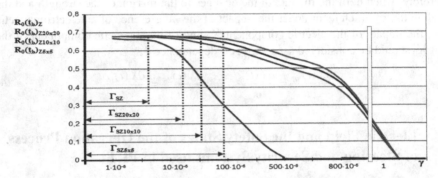

Fig. 8. Course of the probability of security and steering systems with a series-parallel structure remaining in the complete serviceability state $R_0(t_b)_Z$ in the function of the index γ of interference. Notes to Fig. 8: ($R_0(t_b)_Z$ – complete serviceability state, system installed at a train platform; $R_0(t_b)_{Z20X20},...,R_0(t_b)_{Z5X5}$ – system installed in the rooms of a railway station that possesses a lightning protection installation with various eye dimensions [own study].

5   Conclusion

Security and steering systems installed in railway facilities are exposed to the impact of electromagnetic interference with a wide spectrum of frequencies. This article presents the impact of interference from a low frequency range: up to 100kHz on security and steering systems with various reliability structures. Based on the analyzes conducted, the following conclusions and observations can be formulated in the present study:

- the interference that security and steering systems in a railway area are exposed to causes an increase of the intensity of damage in relation to all systems regardless of their reliability structures;
- a supervision system with a series structure is most susceptible to the impact of interference (the smallest value of the expected life);
- concerning the impact of interference, security and steering systems installed at railway platforms are characterized by the smallest value of the expected life as there is no phenomenon of the attenuation of electromagnetic interference [1], [12];

- security and steering systems installed in usable rooms located at a railway station are less sensitive to the impact of interference owing to the screening effect of the lightning protection grid;
- the value of the expected life of security and steering systems installed in railway station buildings depends from the dimensions of the eye of the lightning protection installation;
- the values of the individual probabilities of security and steering systems to remain in states depend from the properties of the interfering electromagnetic field (the vector of the magnetic or electric field) [1], [7], [12];
- there is a smaller influence on the probabilities of the system to remain in the abovementioned states of the intensity E of the electric field in the VLF frequency range (for this electromagnetic field component, the values of $R_0(t)$, $Q_{ZB1}(t)$ and $Q_B(t)$ probabilities reach the maximum values for the different indexes γ of interference);
- for small values of interference indexes $\gamma = 10 \cdot 10^{-6}$ that have an impact on security and steering systems, the function of the probability of the systems to remain in the complete serviceability state remains on a constant level;
- the value of the permissible level of the resistance of security and steering systems to interference can be determined with the aid of the interference index γ;
- the determined value of the permissible interference level can be defined as the resistance of security and steering systems to the impact of electromagnetic interference;
- the resistance of security and steering systems depends from the properties of the electromagnetic field that interferes with the operation of the system: whether the nature of the said field is predominantly magnetic (E/H < 337 [Ω]) or electric (E/H > 337 [Ω]) [7], [12];
- the safety level Γ of the operation of security and steering systems is a function that depends from the following:
  - the properties of the electromagnetic field: E and H field components;
  - those components of the systems that have the properties of screening the electromagnetic interference;
  - the location of the elements of the systems: an open area or a closed area of a railway facility: an attenuation of interference by structural partitions.

Acknowledgment. The present paper was prepared under the 'ECO MOBILITY" Research Project WND no.: POIG.01.03.01-14-154/09 that is implemented under the Innovative Economy Operating Program. This program is co-financed from the European Fund of Regional Development.

References

1. Paś, J., Duer, S.: Determination of the impact indicators of electromagnetic interferences on computer information systems. Neural Computing & Applications 23(7-8), Special Issue: SI 2143–2157 (2013) ISSN: 0941-0643, Published: DEC
2. Duer, S., et al.: Designing of an effective structure of system for the maintenance of a technical object with the using information from an artificial neural network. Neural Computing and Applications 23(3-4), 913–925 (2013)
3. Siergiejczyk, M., Paś, J., Rosiński, A.: Application of closed circuit television for highway telematics. In: Mikulski, J. (ed.) TST 2012. CCIS, vol. 329, pp. 159–165. Springer, Heidelberg (2012)
4. Kasprzyk, Z.: Delivering payment services through manual toll collection system. In: Mikulski, J. (ed.) TST 2012. CCIS, vol. 329, pp. 60–68. Springer, Heidelberg (2012)
5. Rosiński, A.: Design of the electronic protection systems with utilization of the method of analysis of reliability structures. In: Nineteenth International Conference On Systems Engineering (ICSEng 2008), Las Vegas, USA (2008)
6. Choromański, W., Dyduch, J., Paś, J.: Minimizing the Impact of Electromagnetic Interference Affecting the Steering System of Personal Rapid Transit in the Context of the Competitiveness of the Supply Chain. Archives Of Transport, Polish Academy of Sciences Index 201 901, Warsaw 23(2) (2011)
7. Charoy, A.: Interference in electronic equipment. WNT, Warsaw (1999)
8. Choromański, W., Kowara, J.: PRT - modeling and dynamic simulation of track and vehicle. In: 13th International Conference, Sharing vision from People Movers to Fully Automated Urban Mass Transit, Paris (2011)
9. Dabrowski, T., et al.: The method of threshold-comparative diagnosing insensitive on disturbances of diagnostic signals. Przeglad Elektrotechniczny - Electrical Review 88(11A) (2012)
10. Lubkowski, P., Laskowski, D.: The end-to-end rate adaptation application for real-time video monitoring. In: Zamojski, W., Mazurkiewicz, J., Sugier, J., Walkowiak, T., Kacprzyk, J. (eds.) New Results in Dependability & Comput. Syst. AISC, vol. 224, pp. 295–305. Springer, Heidelberg (2013)
11. Siergiejczyk, M., Rosiński, A.: Reliability analysis of power supply systems for devices used in transport telematic systems. In: Mikulski, J. (ed.) TST 2011. CCIS, vol. 239, pp. 314–319. Springer, Heidelberg (2011)
12. Dyduch, J., Pas, J., Rosinski, A.: The basic of the exploitation of transport electronic systems. Technical University of Radom, Radom (2011)

Energy Intensity and Greenhouse Gases Production of the Road and Rail Cargo Transport Using a Software to Simulate the Energy Consumption of a Train

Tomáš Skrúcaný and Jozef Gnap

University of Žilina,
Faculty of Operation and Economics of Transport and Communications,
Univerzitná 1, 01026 Žilina, Slovakia
{Tomas.Skrucany,Jozef.Gnap}@fpedas.uniza.sk

Abstract. The paper describes the energy consumption and GHG production comparison of two transport kinds – road and rail. The calculations are done according to the legislation in force – standard EN 16 258:2012 Methodology for calculation and declaration of energy consumption and GHG emissions of transport services (freight and passengers). The results have high informative value because they take into account energy consumption and emissions from primary and secondary consideration – life cycle analyses and the result is a summary of consumption and emissions of transport the cargo, handling and support activities. By the energy and emissions calculation was considering with normative values from the standard. It is the first part of the life cycle. The second part – secondary consumption and emissions were calculated according to the standard fuel consumption of specific road vehicles. The electric energy consumption of a train was simulated through the software Train Dynamic.

Keywords: energy consumption, emissions, road transport, rail transport, software simulation, EN standard.

1   Introduction

The current economic situation is directly dependent on transport. Without the possibility to transport goods, or without providing transport services to the population could not be implemented further follow-up activities leading to the creation of value products and services that satisfy society and the individual.

During the transportation process energy entering transforms in to the movement of vehicles which provide the required transfer of goods and people in the area. Therefore, the transport depends on the supply of energy. Today transportation is largely dependent on oil, as the vast majority of vehicles are driven engines combusting petroleum products - hydrocarbon fuels. In particular, the transport by road, air and water. Most rail vehicles are now powered by electric traction motors, so the rate of dependence on oil is lower than previous modes. But the fact is that in most countries the electricity is produced

J. Mikulski (Ed.): TST 2014, CCIS 471, pp. 263–272, 2014.

through petroleum products or coal. All of these are non-renewable natural resources and their stocks have steadily declined.

Given the above, it is an effort to streamline the transport of energy dependence, as suggested by the legislative measures such as the White Book on a European level or different policies and programs at national state level.

Energy intensity of modes of transport to the greatest extent represents the energy consumption of vehicles. Comparison of consumption and consumption of handling and support activities are more devoted to this study.

2   Standard EN 16258: 2012 and Its Using in Calculations

This European Standard specifies general methodology for calculation and declaration of energy consumption and greenhouse gas emissions (GHG) in connection with any services (cargo, passengers or both). Specifies general principles, definitions, system boundaries, methods of calculation, allocation rules (allocation, assignment) and recommendations on information to support standardized, accurate, reliable and verifiable declarations regarding energy consumption and greenhouse gas emissions associated with any the freight service . It also contains examples of the use of these principles.

The calculation for one given transport service must be performed using the following three main steps [1]:

Step 1: Identification of the various sections of the service;

Step 2: Calculation of energy consumption and greenhouse gas emissions for each section;

Step 3: Sum the results for each section.

The standard does not consider only the secondary emissions produced and energy consumed during combustion of the fuel (energy conversion from fuel to mechanical energy), as well as primary, incurred in the extraction, production and distribution.

e_w well-to-wheels energetic factor for defined fuel;
g_w well-to-wheels emissions factor for defined fuel;
e_t tank-to-wheels energetic factor for defined fuel;
g_t tank-to-wheels emissions factor for defined fuel;

Well-to-wheels is "well on wheels", that are also covered primary, and secondary emissions and consumption. Somewhere mentioned this factor also called LCA (life-cycle-analysis).

Tank-to-Wheels factor is thinking only of secondary emission and consumption.

This Standard specifies general methodology for calculation and declared value for the energetic factor and factor in greenhouse gas emissions must be selected in accordance with Annex A. [1]

Emission gases are composed of several individual components (gas). Each having different chemical and physical properties, so otherwise participates in environmental degradation. In order to compare emissions from different activities, fuels, vehicles, where emissions have different track must designate one representative unit used in the comparison. This is the CO_2 equivalent, which is a measure of the impact of specific emissions and likens it to the impact of CO_2. The label is CO_2e (equivalent).

3   Energy Consumption

1.   Energy and emission factor ($e_{w,}$ g_w) reflects a partial loss of production and distribution of power energy in the chain:
     Energy mixture used in the manufacture of electric energy,
2.   the efficiency of power. various energy sources,
3.   transfer efficiency (distribution) el. supply to the final consumer.

From this fact implies the fact that the effectiveness (efficacy) el. energy is directly related to power production technology. energy, the composition and proportions of individual resources and the effectiveness of its distribution.

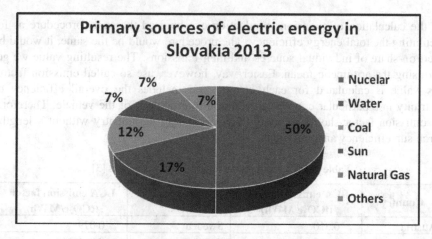

Fig. 1. Shares of the resources in the production of electricity [2]

Energy efficiency in electricity production can be calculated as a weighted arithmetic mean of primary resources and efficiency in power. various energy sources. Weight values represent the proportions of the various sources. Efficiency values were chosen on the basis of national regulation in Slovakia, which prescribes their height (Fig. 1).

Energy produced gets to consumers through the transmission system. This process has taken place without losses and efficiency of power transmission network in Slovakia was last year at about 93 % [3].

Recent losses in the transmission of power produced energy in locomotive wheels are custom transmission losses from conduction through the collector and control system locomotive. The efficiency of this process is approximately 90%. So overall energy efficiency supplied power for rail transport in Slovakia:

$$\eta_{CE} = \eta_V \cdot \eta_P \cdot \eta_{DP} = \left(\sum (\eta_{Zi} \cdot p_{Zi}) / p_Z \right) \cdot \eta_P \cdot \eta_{DP} \qquad (1)$$

where:

η_{CE}	overall energy efficiency [-]
η_V	efficiency of power. energy [-]
η_P	power transfer efficiency [-]
η_{DP}	efficiency of vehicle system [-]
η_{Zi}	effectiveness of a particular primary source [-]
p_{Zi}	share of a given resource in the production of electric power [-]
p_Z	sum of partial fractions of the individual sources [-]

The value of overall energy efficiency is 0.34. Regard to the value calculated on the basis of statistical data, but when compared with that in Germany, for example, this value is the same.

4   Production of Emissions and Electric Energy

For the calculation of emissions production can be used the same procedure as for calculating the total energy efficiency. The procedure would be the same, it would be based on share of individual sources and their emissions. The resulting value we get also using the arithmetic mean. Easier way, however, use so-called emission factor. This value is calculated for each country and includes the overall efficiency of electricity in a particular country, in addition to efficiency of the vehicle. Therefore, this emission factor should be used when comparing the country without a lengthy search sub efficiency and emissions.

Table 1. LCA emission factors of EU-27 countries [3]

Country	LCA emission factor (tCO_2e/MWh)	Country	LCA emission factor (tCO_2e/MWh)
Austria	0.310	Sweden	0.079
Belgium	0.402	Bulgaria	0.906
Germany	0.706	Cyprus	1.019
Denmark	0.760	Czech Republic	0.802
Spain	0.639	Estonia	1.593
Finland	0.418	Hungary	0.678
France	0.146	Lithuania	0.174
UK	0.658	Latvia	0.563
Greece	1.167	Poland	1.185
Ireland	0.870	Romania	1.084
Italy	0.708	Slovenia	0.602
Netherlands	0.716	Slovakia	0.353
Portugal	0.750	**EU-27 average value**	**0.578**

For Slovakia this value represents 0.353 tCO2e/MW, which is 90.81 gCO2e/MJ.

5   Calculation of Energy Consumption and Emission Production

To calculate the energy consumption of the train has been used software Railway dynamics. One based on predefined and selected values calculates the power consumption of the train on the defined route. The software works with maps and elevation profile rail routes in Slovakia. Based on these defaults and selected (type locomotive, train weight, train length, axle load, number and location of stop) calculates power consumption of kWh.

The 5 train stops envisaged during transporting. That is the average value of operating on the defined route and the distance. The output data consumption was calculated for further calculations and comparisons.

Calculated energy is the mechanical work needed to move the train. After transformed it into units of MJ, it can be subsequently converted to total consumed energy by an overall energy efficiency of equation (1).

$$E_{CE} = (E_{VD} \cdot 3{,}6) \cdot \eta_{CE} \qquad [MJ] \qquad (2)$$

where:

E_{CE} total energy consumed electric traction [MJ]
E_{VD} mechanical energy consumed by the movement of the train (train dynamics software result) [kWh]

We used emission factor LCA to calculate the amount of emissions produced [Tab. 1]. The resulting energy consumed train [MJ] is computed by dividing mechanical work and efficiency of the vehicle.

$$G_{CE} = [(E_{VD} / \eta_{DP}) \cdot 1000] \cdot f_{LCA} \quad [tCO2e]$$

$$(3)$$

$$G_{CE} = [(E_{VD} / \eta_{DP}) \cdot 3{,}6] \cdot f_{LCA}^{g} \quad [gCO2e]$$

where:

G_{CE} the total amount of emissions produced electric traction
f_{LCA} emission factor fot electric energy in Slovakia [tCO2e/MWh]
f_{LCA}^{g} emission factor for electric energy in Slovakia [gCO2e/MJ]

When calculating the energy consumption of road transport was considered with consumption of 28 l/100km fuel at long distances. On shorter distance this value rises because the vehicle consumes more energy to start-up and the standby operating mode. The constant speed is kept a short time or not at all. Increased fuel consumption values were chosen for the start and end of freight for combined transport (35 and 40 l/100km). The selected values represent the average figures for the type of vehicle and traffic.

Handling of bulk materials is carried out wheeled front loader. It is equipped with a bucket of 5 m3 volume. With this device the loader is able to load up to 6.5 tons of materia. When loading articulated vehicles, the average time of a single turnover (cycle) is 40 seconds. When operating wagons takes one cycle 120 seconds. This is due to a longer period of driving the loader from the place of storage material to coaches about the length of the train. Wheel loader with such equipment has an average hourly fuel consumption of 17 l. Cycles for a given fuel consumption reaches 0.3 l/t (road transport) and 0.9 l/t (rail transport).

To calculate the total energy consumption, the amount of consumed fuel should be multiplied by energy factor for that fuel from Appendix A of the standard.

$$E_{CPV} = [(S_{km} \cdot L) / 100] \cdot e_W \quad [MJ] \quad\quad (4)$$

where:

E_{CPV} total energy consumed by vehicles [MJ]
S_{km} vehicle fuel consumption [l/100km]
L   driven distance [km]
e_W energetic factor „wtw" for defined fuel [MJ/l]

$$E_{CPN} = (S_t \cdot Q) \cdot e_W \quad [MJ] \quad\quad (5)$$

where:

E_{CPN} total energy consumed by loader [MJ]
S_t loader fuel consumption [l/t]
Q   loaded mass of cargo [t]

To calculate the total energy consumption, the consumed amount of fuel should be multiplied by an emission factor for that fuel from Appendix A of the standard.

$$G_{CPV} = [(S_{km} \cdot L) / 100] \cdot g_W \quad [gCO_2e] \quad\quad (6)$$

where:

G_{CPV} the total amount of emissions produced by vehicles [gCO$_2$e]
g_W emission factor for defined fuel [tCO2e/MWh]

$$G_{CPN} = (S_t \cdot Q) \cdot g_W \quad [gCO_2e] \quad\quad (7)$$

Each route consists of several operations (loading, unloading, transport), because the expression of energy consumption and emissions for the transport, we added up all the values of the partial activities.

$$E_C = \sum E_{CEi} + \sum E_{CPVi} + \sum E_{CPNi} \quad [MJ] \quad\quad (8)$$

$$G_C = \sum G_{CEi} + \sum G_{CPVi} + \sum G_{CPNi} \quad [gCO_2e] \quad\quad (9)$$

For the calculations I chose the basic units of MJ and gCO$_2$ because a declared value in the standard. However, for better comparison and expression, it is able to expressed individual amounts in other units, for example GJ, KJ, tCO$_2$, kgCO$_2$e or a combination thereof, in the case of proportional expressing quantities (see the evaluation).

6   Model Study

In this case study we consider the transport across almost the entire Slovak. The route connects the eastern and western metropolis and thus Kosice and Bratislava.

Both routes also for road- and for rail transport will be kept after the junction of the north direction Bratislava, Trnava, Žilina, Poprad, Kosice.

Train tracks used directly led by the mentioned cities. Road vehicles used on roads maintained in parallel with the railway and giving priority to highways and expressways.

Railway stations cities are located 449 km by road, by rail 445 km. To this must be added the distance from the station to the place of loading and unloading a railway siding for transport modeling using direct rail transport (4 km and 20 km) and the direct road transport and their combination to this distance adds more (7 km and 25 km). We will consider two different sites with different distances – 2 model places and freights.

Landing locations were selected as model points. They are in peripheral industrial towns in the first case and in nearby villages in the second case. They are located in industrial zones where is the possibility of using rail siding. For this reason, in order to model the freight from Bratislava to Košice only with the using of direct rail, or direct road, or a combination thereof (combined transport).

Loading is carried out described front loader. That operates in cycles. Cycle length is mainly dependent on the distance of the vehicle from the place of taking goods with spoon. Goods are stored in the form of pouring heaps from which were taken and loaded onto vehicles.

Unloading of goods is realized by tilting and spillage of cargo space vehicle at the landing location. Consumption of energy spent on this action is included in the average energy consumption of vehicles.

6.1   Cargo and Vehicles

Vehicles are transporting bulk materials. Specifically, the compost plant. This product can be stored and transported in open air. Bulk density of compost is 1200 - 1400 $kg.m^{-3}$. It also depends on the humidity of the substrate. We consider the mean value of 1300 $kg.m^{-3}$. Given the technical parameters of wagons and railway line will be considered the transport limiting quantities for one train. It seems per one transport 1482 t of cargo (one train equates to 55 articulated vehicles – semitrailer sets).

Road vehicles are artuclutaed semitrailer sets with dump body maden of aluminium. Their less wieght is 13 t, the payload 27 t and the body capacity 24 m^3. Considering to the maximal weight limit (40 t) it is possible to load only 20,8 m^3 of cargo (87 % of capacity).

The train is composed of 30 Faccs wagons and locomotives Skoda E69 and E 479. The locomotives are using according to the track elevation (needed higher pulling power). This train is 430 m long and its gross weight is 2428 t. The payload represents 1482 t.

Front loader is equipped with a volume of 5 m^3 bucket. With this device the loader is able to load up to 6.5 tons of material buckets.

7   Evaluation

Fig. 2. describes the values of energy consumption of each transport ways. The left columns are in an absolute expression of GJ. But a higher comparative value have the right columns expressed by kJ/tkm. This units consider (driven distance and cargo weight).

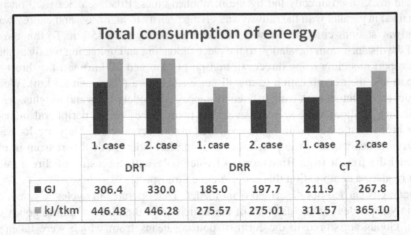

Fig. 2. Total consumption of energy. Overall summary of energy consumed during the transport. DRT (direct road transport), DRR (direct rail transport), CT (combined transport). [own study]

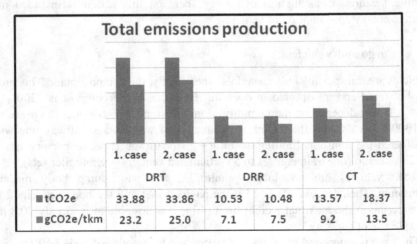

Fig. 3. Total emissions production. Overall summary of emissions produced during the transport. DRT (direct road transport), DRR (direct rail transport), CT (combined transport). [own study]

There is the same evaluation in this figure described above, as in the previous one (Fig. 2).

This two previous figures show the differences between the energy consumption and the GHG production according to the transport way. The direct road transport represents the largest consumption and production. The best values reaches the rail transport. But this is only a model case. In praxis it is very difficult to use only this one transport way, because it is not the way door-to-door and often it is a necessary to use a support action – the road transport. And then it is connected with another handling with cargo. For the real case it is better to compare only two ways – direct road transport and the combined transport. From two cases of CT we chose the 2nd because of higher probability in praxis (the driven distance by road transport is longer).

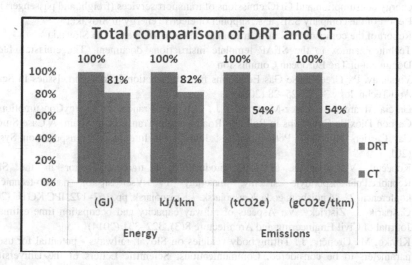

Fig. 4. Total comparison of DRT and CT. Overall summary of emissions produced during the transport. DRT (direct road transport), DRR (direct rail transport), CT (combined transport) [own study]

The total comparison of two the most used transport ways shows the more eco-friendly way. It is the combined transport. Despite the overloading the cargo and using both transport ways reaches CT lower energy consumption and emissions production. It seems approximately 19% less of energy and 46% of GHG. The huge difference of GHG is caused by no secondary emissions of the rail transport. This difference decreases with increasing driven distance of road transport.

Also this comparison done only of this one model case, so we do not consider driving the vehicle empty returns, the coefficient of vehicle drives utilization. In the global point of view, with this taken into account when rail shall reach higher values of empty rides, the results came out in favor of road transport. It is determined mainly more possibilities to utilize the road vehicle on the reverse route than the railway.

8   Conclusion

This paper deals with problematic of energy consumption and GHG production of chosen transport duties. The comparison is done, which take in account LCA or well-to-wheels factor. The study compare two ways to transport bulk cargo between two points in Slovakia. The road transport and the rail transport, also their combination. The evaluation gives results with high informative and comparative value. The simulation of energy consumption was done for chosen road and rail in Slovakia, but some average values can be used on European level.

References

1. European standard EN 16 258:2012. Methodology for calculation and declaration of energy consumption and GHG emissions of transport services (freight and passengers)
2. Report of the company SSE, a. s., supplier of electric energy in Slovakia
3. Report of the company SPS, a. s., transmission network operator in Slovakia
4. Technical annex to the SEAP template instructions document: The emission factors. Document of The European Commission
5. Vaishnav, P.: Greenhouse Gas Emissions from International Transport. Issues In Science And Technology 30(2), 25–28 (2014)
6. Garcia-Alvarez, A., Perez-Martinez, P.J., Gonzalez-Franco, I.: EnergyConsumption and Carbon Dioxide Emissions in Rail and Road Freight Transport in Spain: A Case Study of Car Carriers and Bulk Petrochemicals. Journal Of Intelligent Transportation Systems (2013)
7. Konečný, V.: Analysis of CO2 production of transport sector in the Slovak Republic.Politransportnyje sistemy: materialy IV Vserossijskoj naučno-techničeskoj konferencii, 22-24 nojabria, goda, Krasnojarsk. – Krasnojarsk, pp. 167–172, IPC KGTU (2006)
8. Gašparík, J., Zistrický, V.: Aspects of railway capacity and occupation time estimation. Journal of Civil Engineering and Architecture 8(3), 322–331 (2014)
9. Klinko, M., Grenčík, J.: Tilting body vehicles on Slovak railways - potential for use and parameters to be considered. Communications: Scientific Letters of the University of Žilina 10(3), 45–49 (2008)
10. Höger, M., Roch, M., Barcinák, P.: Simulator of power substation operation. Energyspectrum [electronic issue] 9(1), 1–6 (2014)

Identification of Information Systems Application in Road Transport Companies in Silesia Region

Sebastian Kot, Bogdan Marczyk, and Beata Ślusarczyk

Czestochowa University of Technology, Faculty Management,
42-201 Częstochowa, Poland
sebacat@zim.pcz.czest.pl

Abstract. Rapid analysis and transport's information transfer are extremely important in order to achieve the efficient transport system, which main task is to fulfil users' needs and requirements. Therefore, telematics called also intelligent transport system is gaining popularity and is still expanding its field of activity. The aim of the article is to identify the information systems applied in road transport companies in Silesian Region. The authors also draw their attention to the effects and benefits of using information technology in transport companies, functions and tools used in road transport activities and identify elements which are essential in the implementation of rapid and efficient transport.

Keywords: road transport, transport telematics, information technology.

1 Introduction

Means of transport along with indispensable technical devices constitute the basic component of the logistic infrastructure. They have the direct influence on the time of transferring goods, the quality and the productivity of transport and manipulative processes, but at the same time they guard against the loss of functionality. Moreover, means of transport indeed influence the realization of the production cycle. Available technologies, which serve for observation, supervising and managing transport processes are become more and more common through transport systems. They play an important role in supply chains, in which the greatest abilities of developing the economy and creating profits exist [1]. Intelligent transport systems enable the growth of productivity and safety of transport, through the exploitation of high-tech IT solutions [2-3]. Specifying - connecting information systems allows for the implementation of streamlining, test and organizational actions in transport. These connections create the multi structure of transport, consisting of the road infrastructure; of road users, cars and the organization and movement control system. *The application of ITS allows to streamline the information exchange between drivers, carriers and logistic centres"* [4].

In order to achieve the efficient transport system a rapid analysis and transport's information transfer is required. It results from the fact that during transporting goods a few factors are changing themselves in a constant way, e.g. conditioning of the traffic, customers' orders etc. The main task of the transport system is the fulfillment

J. Mikulski (Ed.): TST 2014, CCIS 471, pp. 273–283, 2014.

of users' needs and requirements, mainly of shipping companies in the area of accessibility of information, which are required for achieving deliberate objectives. Tasks of information concern limiting uncertainty of surroundings, the level of the risk taken, as well as the evaluation of chances and threats accompanying the company on the market [5]. Above all, information must be current and full, because they influence the quality of decisions made and the time of the response. Apart from that, obtained information should be readily available, what justify creating and using telematics systems. Which are cheap in the maintenance and give full and accurate details about current situations on roads. Telematics transport systems represents a new approach to solving transportation problems[6], enabling transport entities to make fast and precise decisions, those should be backed up with modern technologies.

Transport's information systems concern essential elements in terms of the realization of fast and efficient transport, i.e. the navigation system, communications, traffic control, cargo tracking, condition control of vehicles essential for the activity of transport and shipping companies. They also allow to prepare and to use databases, which support the area of the management. In the result of using the information technology, the following benefits can be achieved by the transport company [7]:

- improvement of financial results;
- growth of the productivity of the transport;
- improvement of the coordination in the communication and the transport in the global scale;
- limitation of the negative impact on the environment;
- optimization of the transport of cargo;
- improvement of the quality of transport;
- obtaining information about the current localization of vehicles and cargoes in the traffic;
- possibility of remote monitoring of conditions of transporting goods and the condition of the vehicle.

Moreover, in the macroeconomic scale these systems cause i.a. [8]:

- growth of the economic productivity;
- increase in the road safety;
- limiting the negative environmental impact;
- balancing the cooperation in the transport industry;
- greater possibility of the accumulation and using transport data.

Applications of systems and information tools are important also for the safety of vehicles, because they allow to control costs, to improve the profitability and to diversify products and services [5]. The condition of the proper implementation and using the application is the rational planning of supplies in the road transport. Such a plan fulfills customer's requirements; the lack of the correct planning causes the majority of failures of the implementation. However, before the schedule of routes is created, one should obtain answers to a few questions, what will cause avoiding generation of higher costs, associated with possible damage or delays.

2   Identification of the Applied Information Technology in Road Transport Companies – Case Study

The purpose of this research was an identification of applied information technologies in transport companies in terms of planning haulage activity.

The research was conducted via e-mail in the first quarter of 2013. The questionnaire was dispatched to randomly selected private sector road transport companies of the Silesia province. The analysis included micro, small, average and large enterprises (recognized on the basis of the number of employed workers), carrying out earning and economic transport with using delivery vans with laden weight above 3.5 tones. The sample put through the examination consist of 51 companies. Depending on their size, small and medium-sized companies constituted the greatest contribution (altogether 43 companies). Two large enterprises employing more than 250 workers and six micro companies took part in the examination.

Functions of information systems suggested in the questionnaire were indicated based on the information technology universally used in transport abroad. Evaluations of benefits resulting from functioning of systems, i.e. streamlining transport activity of goods, was made on the basis of systems' functions and tasks, which are directly connected with the implementation of shipments and which are being exploited also in transport companies.

Due to the fact that the technical interoperability between functions is the same as the interoperability between transport companies, it is possible to exploit individual functions in different information systems, what provides the flexibility of the information exchange among companies applying these systems. Therefore, in order to assess relations between different systems, they were classified according to the area of activity of the transport of goods, which they are supporting.

The most important area, which needs to be considered in the implementation of shipments is the assistance of the driver. In this area needs of drivers, concerning planning and completion of transport operations, safety etc., are important. In this area the main goal of functioning of IT system is streamlining the road to the destination, the safety assurance of the driver, as well as minimizing other road threats associated with driver's objectives.

The support for administrative actions, including staff management, training etc., is also essential. Moreover, managing of the mobile staff peculiar to the transport industry is much more demanding than of employees acting "on the spot". The area of administrative support includes planning, mapping up documentation, supervision, tracking shipments, solving out legal an salary issues. The majority of actions of the system in this are regard the service of orders and play an important role in the implementation of transport's operating activities.

In the transport company, which has at least a few vehicles, efficient vehicles management with the support of owned information system, is significant. Information concerning the condition of vehicles and their location constitutes the main data source for transport companies. Appropriate fleet management can be the essential factor of the competitiveness on the market. It has also an affect on the level of generated income and costs. Thanks to the correctly managed fleet of vehicles, the company is increasing the level of customer service and can gain distinct financial benefits. An important aspect is the management of transport operations, which directly concern considered operations and are taking place in the transport of goods from one place to another. This sort of actions embrace locating and collecting appropriate packages, assigning packages to vehicles, reducing empty runs etc.

Table 1. Functions and devices used in the road transport's activity

Services/devices	Use area
Road tolls	traffic management
eCall (Pan-European emergency-call system)	driver's support, transport's operations management, traffic management
Navigation	driver's support, fleet management
Product mass index	driver's support, traffic management
Automatic speed adaptation	driver's support, traffic management
Accidents reporting	driver's support, transport's operations management, traffic management
Automatic driver's daily log	driver's support, administrative activities support
Monitoring of employees	administrative activities support
Transport resources optimization	administrative activities support, fleet management
Remote monitoring	fleet management
Goods identification	transport's operations management
Tracking real time	fleet management, transport's operations management
Goods monitoring	transport's operations management
Traffic informations	traffic management
Pointing direction	traffic management, fleet management
Burglar alarm	driver's support, fleet management, transport's operations management
Geofencing	fleet management, transport's operations management
Shipping orders service	administrative activities support, transport's operations management
Speed limit (traffic signs)	traffic management
Driver's working hours planning	administrative activities support

Source: own study based on [9]

Different kind of system's services, which aim is to streamline the flow of goods, are included in the area of traffic management. The strong emphasis is being put on the road safety, as well as on the mobility. This issue is important enough, because the efficient flow has an influence on the rest of the flow's participants. So, crucial functions support making the decision about planning routes out.

Data processed by information system with the help of different kind of transportation tools, are applied for monitoring the transport before, during and after executing the order by different transport's participants. Table 1. shows chosen devices and services, streamlining the transport activity, which deliver to information system the necessary data, which are the base of decision-making processes in the company.

In the international scale, information systems applied in transport, contain specific functions, being based on specific transportation devices and participating in the implementation of transport services. It is possible to characterize these systems with specifications of services directed for performing various tasks, in accordance with users' needs. Each of systems listed in Table 46 is characterized by more than one function, which are repeatable in many systems simultaneously.

Information systems applied in transport were described through 38 functions (Table 2.). They include the following areas: traffic management, public management, transport, electronic payments, crisis management, advanced safety of the vehicle, information management and roads maintenance.

Table 2. Functions of information systems applied in transport

Abbreviated form	IT system features
as	Accident sensing e.g. using sensors for detecting the occurrence of accidents
asg	Alarm signaling in vehicle for use during the occurrence of an event e.g. accidents
at	Automatic triggering for initiating events in vehicle e.g. over speeding, theft
btb	Back office-to-back office communication e.g. using Internet
cv	Camera vision (observation) for collecting video data in or out of vehicle environment
lrc	Long range two way communication to and from vehicle
da	Data anonymity for sensitive data that require advanced encryption into and from vehicle
db	Data broadcast for sending data to multiple vehicles with receivers/antennas
ds	Data storage for saving data within a certain time period in a vehicle
du	Data updates for downloading data into a vehicle from a database
dt	Event timer in in the vehicle e.g. OBU (for discharging tolls in electronic systems of toll collecting)
dd	Driver data logging for collecting data about driver such as id, health etc.
fcd	Floating car data collection e.g. using road side equipment
gp	Global positioning for determining the position of a vehicle internally
gds	Goods damage sensing for determining unusual changes to goods data
gd	Goods data logging for collecting and storing goods data

Table 2. (Continued).

Abbreviated form	IT system features
hs	Human sensing for detecting the presence of a person e.g. in accidents
ids	Identification of infrastructure changes e.g. infrastructure malfunctions
ind	Infrastructure data logging for collecting and storing infrastructure data
lp	Local positioning for location determination with respect to a reference point
mp	Map positioning and updates for calculating and updating map position
m	Monitoring for frequent report of changes on the road
no	Network optimization for determining the best possible route in the network
obu	On-board unit processing of vehicle data
odd	Origin-destination data information of the work of the vehicle
rm	Ramp metering for regulating traffic flow in given road segments
rc	Route congestion information for determining the average HGV density on route segment
di	Driver information display, e.g. LCD display
ed	Emission data logging for collecting emission data, e.g. CO_2 in a region/vehicle
src	Short range communication for transmitting small amount of data, e.g. DSRC between the vehicle and road side
sd	Signal delay information for pre-empting traffic light signals
tfc	Tidal flow control and traffic priority assignment for associating priority to given vehicles
ts	Time stamping for logging the time an event of interest occurred
wf	Weather forecasting information e.g. from weather station
vds	Vehicle damage sensing for detecting unusual changes to vehicle conditions
vd	Vehicle data logging e.g. vehicle number, category etc.
vs	Vehicle speed information collection e.g. using odometer
vc	Voice communication for transmitting audio signals

Source: own study based on [9]

On the base of mentioned above functions 33 IT systems were characterized, which streamline transport activity of examined companies [9]:

- Accident Warning Information (AWI) – informs drivers of accidents on roads in the real time, warns about the possibility of an accident depending on the style of the ride, of weather conditions etc., warns problems and proposes alternative solutions concerning the redirection to other route;

- Advanced Driver Logs (ADL) – is aimed at the accurate registration of the time of individual tasks of drivers, collects data about the driver, i.e. working hours, overtime, sick leave, vacation, additions etc., gathers information needed for the service for the driver, e.g. the tuning of the armchair, an inspection of the level of alcohol, keeping up with the driver's activity on the route, department's staff and lorries' drivers management;
- Driver Planning (DP) - improves the productivity of shipments by planning, which includes successive factors: the time of the day, route, vehicle, goods etc., collects and fulfills preferences for the driver, i.e.: the time of the day, route, season, what is important at planning the work of a few drivers out, determines expected workloads for the driver, collects details about transport orders, develops the work schedule for the driver;
- Dynamic Traffic Information (DTI) –ensures the accessibility of information in the real time about traffic and contributes itself to removal expenses, connected with delays for example in the result of traffic hold-ups;
- eCall – the Pan-European emergency-call system, which lets to reduce the duration of the location of the accident and saving their victims, facilitates intervention associated with the accident, e.g. through alarms, which can be started by hand by the driver;
- Emission Testing and Mitigation (ETM) – it serves the measurement and supporting the politics of the sustainable development, informs road users of consequences of the negative impact on the environment and thereby supports decisions, concerning reducing the emission of gases and other factors tied together with the road traffic, collects details about production from the vehicle along with determining possible damages, resulting from current production in real time;
- En-Route Information Driver (EDI) – provides information about the route of the loading or the unloading of goods, enables the communication with the back, determines based on the route such data as: traffic congestion, traffic conditions, weather conditions, traffic control;
- Estimated Time of Arrival (ETA) - serves monitoring the current situation and the evaluation of the departure time in place;
- Freight Mobility (FM) - transmitting current details about cargo between drivers, dispatchers, owners of goods etc.;
- Geofencing(GEO) – is a critical element of IT and communications system of transport companies, serves for the inspection of the location of the vehicle, provides information about the access to an area or to the infrastructure, dispatchers and owners of goods; enables non-impact control of the public sphere by accumulation, processing and sending information in the real time, determining the possible unauthorized access and potential consequences of action;
- Goods Identification (GI) - streamlines the transportation of goods (loading/unloading etc.) with the help of non-impact identification, provides up-to-date information about the state of goods for owners of goods, gates controllers, inspectors and emergency units, streamlines the identification

of goods for the purpose of the physical manoeuvreetc. by gates or loading-unloading stations, collects data based on documentation about goods e.g. of bills of ladingand of sensors of the goods data collection;

- Information About Infrastructure Repair and Maintenance (IRM) – is provides current information about infrastructure condition;
- Information about the transport of heavy loads (XXL);
- Information on Truck Parking (ITP)–providing information about car parks' location in the real time;
- Intelligent Speed Adaptation (ISA) – ensures up-to-date information about the current speed limit on the road;
- Navigation via a network of routes with the help of information on the map (NAV) which has the task to reduce delays;
- On-board Monitoring Driver (ODM) – tracking information concerning drivers in the real time;
- On-board Safety and Security Monitoring (OSM) –allows the driver for permanently monitoring the vehicle and his contents without manual monitoring;
- Pay as You Drive (PYD) - delivery of information associated with vehicles' insurance, collecting information for insurance companies, drivers and environmental inspectors, managing the history of transports i.e. parameters of the vehicle, speed, location of the delivery, time, productions etc., in the purpose of precise determining the amount of insurance premiums;
- Real Time Track & Trace (RTT) - provides such information as speed, location and status of goods in the real time;
- Remote Declaration (RED) – enables sending freelance agreements via e-mail, provides information for the owner of goods to places of loading, unloading and to vehicles about the whereabouts in order to reduce the time by goods gates, the meaning of this information depends on the origin and the aim of the delivery of goods and of the type of goods and information connected with it;
- Remote Monitoring (RM)- provides information about the diagnostics of the vehicle and their preventive conservation – to workshops, driversand dispatchers, information is being collected on the base of archived historical and current details about the technical condition of the vehicle;
- Road Hindrance Warning (RHW) – road information in the real time and advice to avoid traffic hold-ups;
- Road User Charging (RUC) - collection of fees connected with using of road infrastructure depending on place, time, type of the road and the vehicle;
- Route Guidance (RG) – information essential for specific places;
- Sensitive Goods Monitoring (SGM) - transmission of information about sensitive goods, e.g. perishable food products, medicines and other goods classified as dangerous, for transport's managers and the government control units;
- Staff Monitoring (SM) - gathering information referring to the health of staff;
- Theft Alarm and Recovery (TAR) – informs the owner of goods, entities managing the transport of goods etc. about the temporary actual location and about the condition of stolen goods;

- Transport Order Handling (TOH) – informs owners of goods, transport's managers, drivers etc. about ordering in the real time;
- Transport Resource Optimization (TRO) - the optimization of general stores, i.e. road infrastructure, vehicles' load capacities etc., information delivery to units managing the infrastructure about the way of the exploitation of it i.e.: roads, vehicles, bridges, tunnels, information are being collected on the base of data connected with the infrastructure capacity, with the schedule of exploitation etc.;
- Vehicle Follow-up (VF)- collecting and analysis of the data associated with the productivity - for example empty runs, fuel consumption etc., and then handing this over to all sorts of interested groups e.g. fleets owners;
- Weight Indication (WI) - making available in the real time information about the weight of vehicles and restrictions connected with it, the system hands over restrictions of the road infrastructure and the weight of the vehicle to drivers and control units, this information is based on data connected with restrictions of the infrastructure, so as the maximum height, total weight of the vehicle and other.

In order to identify individual information systems in companies researched, the research questionnaire was used. Through obtained replies it was possible to determine, what functions researched companies made use of.

Results showed, that entities applied 29 of 38 proposed functions of the system, which are possible to be assigned to 21 described information systems in the transport.

DTI and RHW systems, which are concentrated on the delivery of current information about the situation on the road to drivers, have the largest amount of functions. The large amount of exploited functions causes simultaneously, that they have the greatest potential of reducing costs generated while using the system and therefore of operating costs. There is a high plausibility of copying the function as a result of applying more than one system. Out of distinguished systems the least functions have ADL and IRM systems, which task is to register the work of drivers and vehicles.

The number of recommendations for individual functions was described in Fig. 1.

Based on the graph it is possible to notice that the most often indicated function was signed with symbol:

- lp, for local positioning for location determination with respect to a reference point;
- di, for driver information display, e.g. LCD display;
- gp, for global positioning for determining the position of a vehicle internally as information generated in the firm's main office.

The least applied functions in researched companies are voice communication for transmitting audio signals (vc), time stamping for logging the time an event of interest occurred(ts),weather forecasting information e.g. from weather station (wf).

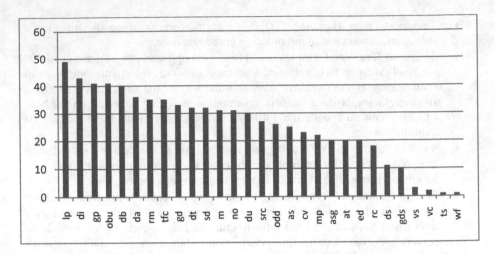

Fig. 1. The number of IT functions used transport management in researched companies [own study]

3   Conclusion

On the basis of an analysis of given functions of information systems according to companies' size, it is possible to point that:

- micro companies use the lowest number of functions of systems which most often concern supporting basic shipping activities, which are: downloading data from the vehicle to the database, determining geographical location of the vehicle, evaluating of the speed of the vehicle and the verbal communication between the driver and the base of the company, in their activity micro entities usually use up to 6 functions observed in ADL and IRM systems;

- amongst small-sized companies the number of used functions is rising, since these entities apart from functions used by micro companies, also apply the data transfer between the vehicle and the base of the company or between other vehicles, the monitoring and tracking the relocation of goods, showing information needed for drivers in the vehicle, determining the date of the appearance of the event, e.g. deliveries of goods, in their activity small-sized companies use up to 11 functions observed in DP, ETM, EDI, OSM, RUC and SM systems;

- medium-sized enterprises use similar functions as smaller companies. Moreover, the detection of accidents was being signed, e.g. with special sensors - clock of the event in the vehicle, concerning e.g. paying tolls in electronic systems of the collection of road tolls, sensor of the priority flow and the inspection of the vehicle connected with data of the vehicle. Altogether, in their activity medium-sized companies use up to 15 functions,

corresponding to AWI, ISA, PYD, NAV, RTT, RED, RM, RG, SGM, IRM, TOH and WI systems;
- large companies usually have at their disposal all functions of systems i.e.: DTI and RHW systems.

Systems identified on the base on the questionnaire, used in researched companies accomplish a lot of tasks associated with the main activity of the road transport correspondent to tracking, positioning of vehicles and goods and sending the relevant information to and from the driver. Above presented identification of information systems application in road transport companies allows for future researches on the information systems application effectiveness analysis as well as construction of model choice for choosing the suitable set of it systems for usage in particular road transport firm.

References

1. Grabara, J.: Sustainable Logistics Management. EdituraUniversitatii "Lucian Blaga"din Sibiu, Sibiu (2013)
2. Szołtysek, J., Jaroszyński, J.: Telematyka transportowa w sterowaniu przepływami ładunków na terenie miasta. GospodarkaMateriałowa i Logistyka 4, 11–12 (2009)
3. Ślusarczyk, B.: Transport Importance in Global Trade. Advanced Logistics Systems 4, 186–192 (2010)
4. Kożlak, A.: Innowacyjność w podaży usług, jako czynnik konkurencyjności przedsiębiorstw sektora TSL. In: KonferencjaEurotrans, Warsaw (2008)
5. Korczak, J.: Logistyka. Systemy, modelowanie, informatyzacja. BEL Studio, Warsaw (2010)
6. Mikulski, J.: Using Telematics in Transport. In: Mikulski, J. (ed.) TST 2011. CCIS, vol. 239, pp. 175–182. Springer, Heidelberg (2011)
7. Bartczak, K.: Korzyści zastosowania telematyki w transporcie, Materiały konferencyjne: Telematykaw transporcie, Uniwersytet Szczeciński, Szczecin (2003)
8. Laurie, A.: Telematics. the New Auto Insurance, http://www.towerswatson.com/assets/pdf/4125/1101-Telematics-FIN.pdf (date of access: June 14, 2014)
9. Mbiydzenyuy, G.: Assessment of Telematic Systems for Road Freight Transport. Blekinge Institute of Technology, Sweden (2010)
10. Mikulski, J.: Introduction of telematics for transport. In: Proceedings on 9th International Conference ELEKTRO 2012, Rajecke Teplice, IEEE Catalog Number CFP1248S-ART, May 21-22, pp. 336–340 (2012), http://ieexplore.ieee.org

Multiple-Objective Simulated Annealing Optimization Approach for Vehicle Management in Personal Rapid Transit Systems

Olfa Chebbi[1] and Jouhaina Chaouachi[2]

[1] Institut Supérieur de Gestion de Tunis
Université de Tunis
41, Rue de la Liberté - Bouchoucha - 2000 Bardo, Tunisie
[2] Institut des Hautes Etudes Commerciales de Carthage
Université de Carthage
IHEC Carthage Présidence-2016 Tunis, Tunisie
{olfaa.chebbi,siala.jouhaina}@gmail.com

Abstract. This paper presents a multi-objective simulated annealing (MOSA) algorithm for the static problem of routing electric vehicles with limited battery capacity in a Personal Rapid Transit (PRT) system. The problem studied in this work aims to minimize both the total energy consumption and the number of vehicles used. Our algorithm uses a strategy of Pareto-dominant-based fitness to accept new solutions. The performance and computational costs of MOSA are studied on a set of randomly generated instances. Algorithm is found to be effective for the multi-objective version of the PRT problem.

Keywords: Personal Rapid Transit, Routing, Multiobjectif programming, Simulated Annealing.

1 Introduction

Since the 1970s, automated guided vehicles (AGVs) have been employed in many industrial and urban areas. AGVs are considered suitable for providing high-quality public transportation within cities, such as part of a Personal Rapid Transit (PRT) system. PRT is a public transportation tool that aims to:

- Provide an on-demand responsive transit service.
- Provide a taxi-like transportation service for individuals or small groups of up to six passengers.

PRT driverless vehicles run on a segregated guideway in order to provide direct trips between origin and destination stations. This is made possible by the fact that stations are located off the main guideway. Offline stations ensure PRT vehicles that are not stopping at a specified station can proceed directly to their destination. Therefore, the transit service offered by PRT is quick and does not suffer from congestion on the guideways or at stations. Compared with traditional public transportation tools, PRT systems provide

J. Mikulski (Ed.): TST 2014, CCIS 471, pp. 284–293, 2014.
© Springer-Verlag Berlin Heidelberg 2014

an efficient, green, clean, and sustainable transit solution. The first commercial implementation of a PRT system was at Heathrow airport in London (UK) in 2010. This transports people between the business car park and Heathrow's Terminal 5. PRT has also been implemented in Masdar city in Abu Dhabi (UAE). Masdar aims to be the first car-free and carbon-neutral city. Hence, PRT was chosen as the only transportation tool in the city. There are also projects to implement PRT in Suncheon, South Korea, and at Amritsar in Punjab, India. Several optimization problems related to PRT have been studied in the literature. These include the empty vehicle allocation problem [1], network design problem [2], station design [1], minimization of the fleet size [3], minimization waiting time of passenger [4-7] minimization of energy consumption [8], [9]. In this paper, we focus on the multi-objective static problem of energy consumption minimization, under the constraint that PRT vehicles can only charge their batteries in the depot. For this purpose, different trips on the PRT system will be represented by a network in which nodes correspond to PRT trips, and each arc will have an associated cost representing a specified amount of energy. Based on this problem representation, we present a multi-objective simulated annealing (MOSA) algorithm that minimizes both the energy consumption and the total number of PRT vehicles used

2   Problem Definition

In this section, we define the static PRT problem under consideration. This problem definition is based on [8]. Through several steps, this problem is transformed into an asymmetric distance-constrained vehicle routing problem, i.e., a vehicle routing problem without the time window restriction imposed by passenger demands. First, consider the PRT system proposed in Section 1. Suppose we have a list of passengers, and an unlimited number of vehicles, initially located in the depot, with battery capacity B. Each trip is characterized by the following:

- OT: Departure Time
- AT: Arrival Time
- OS: Departure Station
- AS: Arrival Station

In order to satisfy all passenger requests while considering the battery capacity of the vehicles, we must formally define our PRT problem. Let $G=\{V,E\}$ be a directed graph. $V = V_{i=0}^{n}$ is the list of vertices, where v_0 denotes the depot. Each vertex v_i, $i \in [1,n]$, has an associated passenger trip. An edge in G between nodes i and j denotes that a vehicle could serve trip j after finishing serving trip i. This is made possible by verifying the time at which trip i finishes, in addition to the time needed to travel from the arrival station of trip i to the departure station of trip j. The cost of traversing an arc (v_i, v_j), where $(i,j) \neq 0$, corresponds to the cost of moving from the arrival station of trip i to the departure station of trip j plus the cost of trip j itself. To this set of edges, we add an arc from node v_0 to each node v_i, where $i \neq 0$, and the cost of this arc is simply the cost of moving from the depot to the departure station plus the energy needed to finish trip i. Finally, we add a set of edges $(i,0)$, where $i \neq 0$. The cost of these edges is the cost of moving from initial station i to the depot. From this problem definition, we can see that our problem is an asymmetric distance-constrained vehicle routing problem (ADCVRP). The distance constraint is imposed by the battery capacity in this case. Our problem is NP-hard, and is asymmetric because the distance from node i to node j is different to the distance from node j to node i.

3   Multi-Objective Simulated Annealing Algorithm

Simulated annealing is an iterative stochastic computational technique that finds non-optimal solutions to combinatorial problems. The simulated annealing method is inspired by the process of annealing metals in order to get the lowest free energy state [6]. In fact, when a metal is cooled slowly, it tends to reach a solid state using the minimum energy possible. This overall process is used and mimicked by the simulated annealing search algorithm to solve optimization and combinatorial problems. The main feature of this algorithm is its ability to accept solutions that could be worse than the actual solution in order to escape from local minima, and therefore locate and reach the global optimal solution. The simulated annealing algorithm accepts worse solutions following the Boltzmann probability [10]:

$$Probability(P) = exp(-\Delta E / K_B T). \tag{1}$$

where ΔE is the difference between the fitness values of the current solution and the candidate solution, T is a control parameter that refers to a temperature that regulates the search process, and K_B is the Boltzmann constant. In general, at the start of the simulated annealing algorithm, any move within the search space is acceptable. This helps the algorithm to discover the search space in a more extensive way. The control parameter T is then decreased, making the algorithm more selective in accepting new solutions. This is done iteratively until we reach a state where only moves that improve the best solution are accepted. In the literature, there exist different simulated annealing algorithms that are able to tackle multi-objective problems, such as SMOSA [11], UMOSA [12], Pareto simulated annealing [13], [14] (which modified the procedure of [15]), and WMOSA [16]. In this paper, we develop a specific modified MOSA algorithm that finds at least a Pareto solution. In fact, our MOSA applies the concept of Pareto optimality to find the best compromise between the number of vehicles used and the total energy consumption in the PRT system. Details of our MOSA are presented in Algorithms 1 and 2.

Algorithm 1 Multi-objective Simulated Annealing Algorithm
_____

```
1: Initialize population()
2: for all Individuals in the population do
3:     Choose randomly a SA improvement procedure with a
given neighborhood operator
4:     Apply the choosing procedure on the individual
5: end for
6: Assign rank()
7: compute metrics evaluation()
```

Algorithm 2 SA improvement Procedure(Neighborhood Operator)

```
 1:  r=0
 2:  X_best=Ø
 3:  while (R ≤ MT)AND(T_r ≥ 0) do
 4:     n=0
 5:     while n ≤ EL do
 6:        X_new=NeighborhoodOperator(X_n)
 7: if(Energy(X_new)<Energy(X_best))AND(Vehicle(X_new)<Vehicle(X_best))
then
 8:           X_best= X_new
 9:           X_n= X_new
10:        else
11:           y=RAND(0,1)
```

$$12: \quad \Delta = \sqrt{(Energy(X_{new}) - Energy(X_{best}))^2 + (Vehicle(X_{new}) - Vehicle(X_{best}))^2}$$

```
13:           Z = e^{-Δ/T}
14:           if (y<Z) then
15:              n=n+1
16:              X_n= X_new
17:           end if
18:        end if
19:     end while
20:     r=r+1
21:     T_r=T_{r-1}- αT_{r-1}
22: end while
```

In order to ensure MOSA converges to the Pareto optimal set, the algorithm should maintain a sufficiently diverse population of solutions. As the basic simulated annealing algorithm is a single search method, our MOSA will first create a random set of initial solutions. Then we add to this initial population two permutation that will results from solving these two linear program :

$$x_{ij} = \begin{cases} 1 & \text{if node } j \text{ is visited after node } i \\ 0 & \text{Otherwise} \end{cases}$$

$$PRT : Min \sum_{(i,j) \in E} c_{ij} x_{ij}$$

$$\sum_{j \in \delta^+(i)} x_{ij} = 1 \forall i \in V^*$$

$$\sum_{j \in \delta^-(i)} x_{ji} = 1 \forall i \in V^*$$

$$x_{ij} \in \{0,1\} \forall \ (i,j) \in E$$

$$x_{ij} = \begin{cases} 1 & \text{if node j is visited after node i} \\ 0 & \text{Otherwise} \end{cases}$$

$$PRT : Min \sum_{(i) \in E} x_{0i}$$

$$\sum_{j \in \delta^+(i)} x_{ij} = 1 \forall i \in V^*$$

$$\sum_{j \in \delta^-(i)} x_{ji} = 1 \forall i \in V^*$$

$$x_{ij} \in \{0,1\} \forall \ (i,j) \in E$$

These two linear program that minimize the energy consumption or the number of used vehicles contribute to accelerate the convergence rate of our algorithm as the solution generated contains promising roads that could enhance the overall quality of our algorithm.

Then apply a specific simulated annealing procedure to each of them. In our algorithm, the solution will be represented as a simple permutation of trips (see Figure 1). Thus, the initial solution generator will simply have to pick a random permutation of the available trips. As mentioned earlier, MOSA must maintain a set of diverse solutions. This diversity will be produced by the different neighborhood procedure, whereby each solution will use a different neighborhood operator or a mix of them to maintain diversity in the population. The different neighborhood operators used are: Exchange Mutation, Displacement Mutation, Inversion Mutation, Insertion Mutation, and Displacement-Inversion Mutation [17]. Finally, we should mention that we tested different transition rules in our MOSA, as the classic metropolis rule could not be applied directly to the multi-objective version of the simulated annealing algorithm. The suggested transition criterion from a given solution $X_{current}$ to a new solution X_{new} is given by the following formula:

$$Z = \frac{e^{-\sqrt{(Energy(X_{new})-Energy(X_{current}))^2 + (Vehicle(X_{new})-Vehicle(X_{current}))^2}}}{T} \tag{2}$$

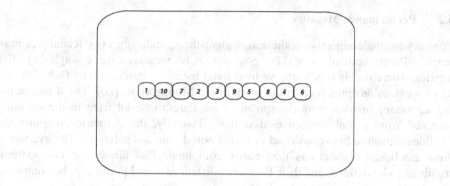

Fig. 1. Permutation [18]

4   Computational Results

In this section, we present the computational results from our MOSA algorithm. The tests in this paper were performed on a PC with an Intel(R) Core (TM) i3 CPU M 380 2.53 GHz processor and 3 GB RAM (Windows 7 64-bit).

4.1   Testing Instances

To test the validity of the ideas presented in this paper, we developed a random PRT instances generator. This generates a random matrix of the cost of moving between each pair of stations. Then, we used the Floyd–Warshall algorithm to compute the shortest path between any two stations, and generated a list of PRT passenger transit requests. The transit requests were generated based on the assumptions shown in Table 1.

Table 1. Experimental assumptions [own study]

Number of stations	12
Cost of arcs	Generated randomly between 1 and 15
Departure station	Generated randomly between 1 and 12
Arrival stations	Generated randomly between 1 and 12
Departure time	Generated randomly between 1 and 3600
Arrival time	Sum of departure time and trip duration
Battery capacity	40 min
Max-wait	1000 s

The network was assumed to have 12 stations and one depot. The battery capacity of each vehicle was assumed to enable the vehicle to run for 40 min. We also added a restriction to our graph construction so as not to allow a vehicle to wait in a station for more than 1000 s.

4.2 Performance Measure

Contrary to single-objective optimization algorithms, multi-objective techniques must reach a Pareto optimal front. This goal cannot be measured using single-objective metrics. Therefore, in this work, we used the Δ measure, introduced by Deb [19], and its two extensions presented in the work of Jin-Myung et al. [20]. The Δ metric has the advantage of measuring the spread of the Pareto optimal front in the solutions obtained from a multi-objective algorithm. Basically, the Δ metric computes the Euclidean distance between the set of sorted non-dominated solutions. The average of these Euclidean distances is then easily computed. This allows the two extreme solutions to be defined, and their Euclidean distances d_f and d_l can also be computed. The Δ metric is then computed as follows:

$$\Delta = \frac{d_f + d_l + \sum_{i=1}^{N-1} |d_i - \overline{d}|}{d_f + d_l + (N-1)\overline{d}}. \tag{3}$$

More details about the Δ metric are given in [19]. Table 2 lists the average value of these three metrics. It can be seen from Table 3 that MOSA was not very successful in finding a diverse and large Pareto optimal front. We then sought to determine whether the MOSA algorithm found more than one solution in its Pareto approximation front.

Table 2. Average of metric values [own study]

Size	d_f	d_l	Δ
10	0.918	0.918	1
15	0.54	0.54	1
20	3.423	3.709	0.98
25	12.549	12.549	1
30	10.309	10.309	1
35	18.212	12.52	0.96
40	20.817	20.817	1
45	46.312	36.425	0.96
50	23.809	19.049	0.98
55	14.402	14.402	1
60	23.604	23.604	1
65	24.102	24.102	1
70	13	13	1
75	0	0	1
80	0	0	1
85	0	0	1
90	1.301	31.301	1
95	0	0	1
100	18.7	18.7	1
Average	13.78936842	12.73394737	0.993684211

Table 3. Size of the MOSA Pareto front for each instance size [own study]

Size	One solution	Two solutions	Three solutions
10	6	4	0
15	8	2	0
20	4	5	1
25	3	7	0
30	6	4	0
35	5	3	2
40	5	5	0
45	2	6	2
50	6	3	1
55	8	2	0
60	7	3	0
65	8	2	0
70	9	1	0
75	10	0	0
80	10	0	0
85	10	0	0
90	8	2	0
95	10	0	0
100	9	1	0

Table 4. Comparison between GAP energy consumption and GAP vehicle results [own study]

Size	GAP energy	GAP vehicle
10	0.00	13.33
15	0.58	3.33
20	2.45	18.67
25	3.05	14.76
30	4.76	21.52
35	4.49	22.34
40	2.84	30.96
45	4.85	26.69
50	3.99	25.91
55	3.49	19.01
60	4.31	26.48
65	3.89	30.17
70	5.68	31.45
75	4.27	27.89
80	5.43	33.16
85	6.29	34.02
90	4.06	25.19
95	4.12	29.28
100	6.73	25.86
Average	3.96	24.21

Note that there are many PRT instances without conflicting objectives (one solution in the Pareto front), but we can also see the presence of different instances with multiple solutions in the Pareto front. In total, 56 out of 190 instances were found to have conflicting objectives. These results suggest that the two objectives of minimizing the number of vehicles and total energy consumption are positively correlated in many instances.

We compared the performance of our MOSA algorithm with the results from a single-objective algorithm. For this, we used the mathematical formulation of Kara [21] for an ADCVRP, and adapted it to our context in order to minimize the energy consumption and the number of vehicles. Table 4 presents the average GAP metric of these results for the energy consumption and number of vehicles used. GAP is calculated as follows:

$$GAPenergy = (\frac{(SOL_{energy} - LB_{energy})}{LB_{energy}}) \times 100 \tag{4}$$

where LB_{energy} is calculated from the linear relaxation of Kara's formulation [21].

$$GAPvehicle = (\frac{(SOL_{vehicle} - LB_{vehicle})}{LB_{vehicle}}) \times 100 \tag{5}$$

where $LB_{vehicle}$ is calculated from the adaptation of the linear relaxation of Kara's formulation.

MOSA finds a solution with equal energy for 31 instances, and an equal number of vehicles for 22 instances. This confirms the good performance of MOSA, and the correlation of the two objectives for different instances.

5   Conclusion

In this paper, we prepared a MOSA algorithm for a PRT routing problem. The static problem aimed to minimize the empty movement of vehicles and the total number of electric PRT pods used. To overcome the problem faced by many heuristic methods of finding only local optima within the search space, our algorithm used different neighborhood operators to guarantee a minimum degree of diversity in the search for a global optimal solution. Contrary to traditional simulated annealing algorithms, our approach used a population of solutions in its quest to find the Pareto optimal front. Computational results showed that our algorithm gives promising results. As an extension to this work, we could include more global search operators to enhance the results of our algorithm. It would be interesting to study different versions of this problem, such as the PRT problem with limited parking places in the stations, or the provision of superchargers in the stations to allow PRT vehicles to recharge their batteries outside the depot.

References

1. Won, J.M., Choe, H., Karray, F.: Optimal design of personal rapid transit. In: Intelligent Transportation Systems Conference (2006)
2. Won, J.M., et al.: Guideway network design of personalrapid transit system: A multiobjective genetic algorithm approach. In: 2006Ieee Congress on Evolutionary Computation, vol. 1-6 (2006)

3. Li, J., Chen, et al.: Optimizing the _eet sizeof a personal rapid transit system: A case study in port of rotterdam. In: 2010 13th International IEEE Conference on Intelligent Transportation Systems (ITSC) (2010)
4. Lees-Miller, et al.: Theoretical maximum capacityas benchmark for empty vehicle redistribution in personal rapid transit. TransportationResearch Record: Journal of the Transportation Research Board 2146(1) (2010)
5. Lees-Miller, J.D., Wilson, R.E.: Sampling for personal rapid transit empty vehicleredistribution (2011)
6. Lees-Miller, J.D.: Minimising average passenger waiting time in personal rapidtransit systems. Annals of Operations Research (2013)
7. Daszczuk, W.B.: Empty vehicles management as a method for reducing passengerwaiting time in personal rapid transit networks. IET Intelligent Transport Systems (2014)
8. Mrad, M., Hidri, L.: Optimal consumed electric energy for a personal rapid transition transportation system (2014)
9. Mrad, M., et al.: Synchronous routing for personalrapid transit pods (2014)
10. Kirkpatrick, S., Gelatt Jr., D., Vecchi, M.P.: Optimization by simmulated annealing. Science 220(4598) (1983)
11. Suppapitnarm, A., Parks, G.: Simulated annealing: an alternative approach totrue multiobjective optimization. In: Proceedings of the Genetic and EvolutionaryComputation Conference (GECCO 1999). Morgan Kaufmann Publishers (1999)
12. Ulungu, E., Teghem, J., Ost, C.: Efficiency of interactive multi-objective simulated annealing through a case study. Journal of the Operational Research Society 49(10) (1998)
13. Czyzak, P., Hapke, M., Jaszkiewicz, A.: Application of the pareto-simulated annealing to the multiple criteria shortest path problem. Technical Report. Politechnika Poznanska Instytut Informatyki, Poland (1994)
14. Czyzak, P., Jaszkiewicz, A.: Pareto simulated annealing-a metaheuristic techniquefor multiple-objective combinatorial optimization. Journal of Multi-CriteriaDecision Analysis 7(1) (1998)
15. Ulungu, E., et al.: Mosa method: a tool forsolving multiobjective combinatorial optimization problems. Journal of Multi-Criteria Decision Analysis 8(4) (1999)
16. Suman, B.: Simulated annealing-based multiobjective algorithms and their applicationfor system reliability. Engineering Optimization 35(4) (2003)
17. Ahuja, R.K., et al.: A survey of very large-scaleneighborhood search techniques. Discrete Applied Mathematics 123(1-3) (2002)
18. Prins, C.: A simple and effective evolutionary algorithm for the vehicle routing problem. Computers & Operations Research 31(12), 1985–2002 (2004)
19. Deb, K., et al.: A fast and elitist multiobjectivegenetic algorithm: Nsga-ii. IEEE Transactions on Evolutionary Computation 6(2) (2002)
20. Won, J.M., et al.: Guideway network design of personalrapid transit system: A multiobjective genetic algorithm approach. In: IEEE Congress on EvolutionaryComputation, CEC 2006. IEEE (2006)
21. Kara, I.: Two indexed polonomyal size formulationsfor vehicle routing problems. Technical Report. BaskentUniversity, Ankara/Turkey (2008)

Exchange of Navigational Information between VTS and RIS for Inland Shipping User Needs

Witold Kazimierski[1] and Natalia Wawrzyniak[2]

[1] Marine Technology Ltd.,
Klonowica Str. 47/5, 71-248 Szczecin, Poland
w.kazimierski@marinetechnology.pl
[2] Maritime University of Szczecin,
Waly Chrobrego 1-2, 70-500 Szczecin, Poland
n.wawrzyniak@am.szczecin.pl

Abstract. The paper presents a concept of data exchange between Vessel Traffic Services and River Information Services using Inter VTS Exchange format. The motivation is given presenting the problem of lack of communication between both parties sometimes sharing same or neighboring area of interest or administration. Further, internal data exchange processes in both systems are described. Based on undertaken research a common model of exchange is proposed using an approach to enhance IVEF with additional features available in RIS. Main changes assume improvement of data model and expanding of interaction model. Data cross-coherence map is presented and new service parameters are proposed.

Keywords: vessel traffic monitoring, VTS, RIS, information exchange.

1 Introduction

Vessels traffic monitoring is a key problem for safety of navigation in restricted waters. This issue is getting even more important for ports situated further inland, by the river, like Hamburg or Szczecin, where dual sea-river navigation is growing rapidly. Systems that are responsible for traffic control and management on marine waters are called VTS (Vessel Traffic Services). On inland waters RIS (River Information Services) systems exist, which provide necessary information to support navigation. Although functional requirements of both systems differ, their main goal is to provide wildly understood shipping information for waterways users.

According to IALA (International Association of Lighthouse Authorities) VTS should provide information about traffic on fairway [1]. With the development of e-Navigation concept by IMO a need for exchange information between various VTS as part of e-Navigation shore services appeared [2]. The response for this is IVEF (Inter VTS Exchange format) created and developed under IALA supervision.

River Information Services are a package of solutions for the needs of inland shipping, which has been worked upon for a dozen years by representatives of most European countries. Main goal of RIS is to provide varied information about fairway, traffic

J. Mikulski (Ed.): TST 2014, CCIS 471, pp. 294–303, 2014.

situation or transport logistics to all RIS users. For providing these services, four main technologies are defined, namely electronic navigational charts presented on Inland ECDIS, Vessel tracking and tracing (VTT), electronic reporting international (ERI) and notices to skippers (NtS). RIS concept assumes also extensive exchange of information between RIS centres as well as with external parties.

Usually the border between inland and sea waters as well as areas of responsibility of RIS and VTS are well defined; however it is very often that inland ships continue their voyage up to sea harbour. It seems reasonable for these two often neighbouring systems to exchange navigational information (including traffic data but not exclusively) automatically between each other to enhance safety and efficiency of shipping.

The main goal of our research was to examine the thematic coherence of both systems applicable standards, which are developed by separate independent organisations. In this paper we indicate the services for data exchange given in IVEF format and RIS system, which could provide a data-exchange platform. Created logic cross-coherence map of navigational information in both systems was used to later propose a data model for exchange between RIS services and VTS information in IVEF format. Analysis of functionality of both systems led to proposal of interaction model in exchange platform.

2   Exchange of Navigational Information

Exchange of navigational information has always been essential for shipping safety. Some restricted areas lie within interest of more than one VTS (marine) or RIS (inland) centre and both systems have developed ways to share crucial information for its users with other system nodes of their own kind. Development of SOA/XML technology allowed easy exchange of data by providing services and information to interested parties. Both VTS and RIS handle this matter differently, but because of common goal in ensuring safe and efficient navigation their basic approach is similar.

2.1   International Data Exchange in RIS

Main purpose of RIS system is to increase safety and efficiency of inland navigation by providing as much relevant information to its relevant stakeholders as possible [3]. The weight of responsibility in right usage of the data is to stay with its user. Such approach put emphasis on distributing information rather than managing navigational traffic and has been reflected in systems architecture.

Most of all, data can be exchanged between different national and international RIS centers across Europe and its users. Moreover the information can be also provided to different, external systems (eg. governmental) by SOAP interfaces and from/to other external users for which proper access rights had been predefined. Generally the RIS data is divided into 5 main categories traffic information, cargo and voyage information, vessel hull information, emergency information and other notifications (NtS data). First category covers all essencial stattic and dynamic traffic information coming from AIS and radar sensors managed by a RIS center with the suitable data fusion, if available [4]. The quality of data provided by tracking system depends on the sensor distribution in RIS area [5], [6]. Cargo and voyage information is provided by ship's owners and carried by the system in XML format of ERI reports containing data about carried goods, destination and voyage plan. Both first data categories are related with vessels hull information, which is provided by authorities in a form of minimum set of vessels certification data, handled in the European Minimum Hull Data Base (MHDB). Emergency data consist of class, severness, involved vessels, location etc. and is provided by RIS center operator together with Notices to Skippers, which distribute information on fairway traffic, water levels, weather information and ice messages. Notices can be displayed on ENC, which itself is a source of important information about area, especcially about its bathymetry [7], [8].

Data Exchange systems in RIS is based fully on XML technology. Schemas for all data in the system are developed by RIS Expert Groups and approved by European Comission. Service Oriented Architecture (SOA) allows to connect different RIS subsytems and external systems as services providing specified functionality. Services are described by WSDL and carried using SOAP protocol. To ensure data-exchange functionality a number of interfaces must be created:

- to the RIS infrastructure in order to have access to the relevant data,
- for the national users in order to enable them to interact with the system,
- to foreign data exchange systems in order to ensure international exchange of RIS data.

The exchange of data between users proceeds based either on triggering events or on request/response flow. System pushes data to national and international systems and stakeholders based on predefined trigger events. It also receives notifications of relevant RIS data from foreign systems and forward it to the related national systems and stakeholders. It also enables its users to request relevant RIS data by defining specific search criteria and respond to the request accordingly.

The SOAP protocol provides ways of contacting the servers with predefined XML structures which describe the functions provided by the web applications to its users. When receiving such SOAP calls the web application will execute the matching function using the necessary parameters included in the XML structure.

For users authorisation RIS system uses Role-based Access Control (RBAC) due to a great number of stakeholders in data exchange processes. RBAC allow a very flexible authorization layer defining roles and permissions for each roles, which are tuneable until the level of data fields. Each user has assigned role and when loging into webservice his role determines the functionality and data he has access to.

The main advantage of data exchange concept in RIS is its openness to other systems with widely used SOAP interface and easy data transport over TCP/IP protocol.

2.2　　Inter VTS Exchange Format

IVEF has been developed by an expert group consisting of industrial members of IALA. It is defined as a gateway service specialised in VTS data exchange, which interfaces to other e-Navigation systems and to external systems of 'third parties'. E-navigation is a wide concept covering a lot of systems (e.g. decision support systems, described in [9]). According to IALA Recommendation there is only one basic IVEF Service, which is Vessel Traffic Image Data Exchange Service [10]. It delivers traffic situation data, according to a specific service profile. The service is a part of e-Navigation Client/Server-based architecture. The service is defined with suitable data model and an interaction model. Additionally, if needed security model may define login/logout procedure for filtering and access rights management.

Data Model of the IVEF service is intended to be a part of a concept called IALA Universal Maritime Data Model (UMDM). UMDM is flexible and extendable f - new entities can be added to the model. IALA invites the Maritime and Inland Waterways Communities to consider using and contributing to the IALA Universal Maritime Data Model [11]. In general three types of data can be exchanged via IVEF, namely vessel data, track data and voyage-related data. All these data combined represent actual traffic image. Vessel information is used to identify and classify ships. It is obtained from several sources, mainly from AIS and local VTS database. Track data can be considered as a core information about vessel's movement. These are dynamic characteristics of the ship's movement. Track data is the result of multisensory fusion of various sensors, including AIS, VTS radar sensors and other tracking methods. Problem of data fusion from various sensor, which is here crucial is fully presented in [12, 13]. It has to be remembered that quality of these data may be various depending on the sensor, tracking algorithm and integrating method used. More information about modern tracking methods with the use of artificial intelligence can be found in [14, 15, 16]. They have been verified and confirmed both in shore stations and in ship stations [17, 18]. Voyage-related information is used to classify ships according to its cargo, draught, destination and route. The voyage information comes from manual input on-board or ashore as well as from automatic reporting systems like PHICS in polish waters (for electronic exchange of IMO FAL forms). It includes destination and origin ports, type of cargo, passenger information, etc.

Interaction model of IVEF service included in [10] presents the dynamics of the interaction of individual components. IVEF service interfaces are in fact point-to-point connections between two e-Navigation gateways. One acts as an information source and the other as the information sink. Both gateways are connected with secured linked usually based on TCP/IP protocol for data transport, TLS or SSL for encryption and ZLIB for compression [19].

The IVEF interface is a service based protocol using client-server architecture. Data exchange is thus not pre-defined, but negotiated between parties, while connection is established. The client initiates the service by authenticating. After the client is logged on, server starts outputting the traffic image according to service specification. However client has the possibility to send request to change active service parameters or to terminate service. Service parameters are:

- filters defining which object should be sent – area based filter, object properties based filter;
- data selection, defining which information should be send – track information, vessel information, voyage information;

- transmission category, defining when the data should be sent - single occurrence (pull service); periodic with specified update rate (push service); A-periodic, synchronous with the received track update (push service); on change, updates are sent as data elements change.

Basic IVEF service includes three major components: service status, object data and session management. Service status component sends information and receives heartbeat messages, confirming if service is alive. Object data component is responsible for sending requested data according to negotiated service parameters and session management component covers authentication issues as well as service parameters negotiation process. IVEF is well-described service to provide traffic image data exchange between different VTS as well as with external services. One of these could be RIS, which although is not a part of e-Navigation concept, performs a lot of functions covered by this idea.

3   Concept of Data Exchange between VTS and RIS

While analysing both systems it can be noticed that RIS implements much wider concept in which VTS is only one of the services which might be provided. Looking at the scope of data exchange services it is apparent that RIS range is wider. More data is exchanged and the services themselves cover more functionalities. Therefore data exchange concept presented here is in fact a proposal of expanding IVEF format to meet some of RIS data exchange requirements.

The research focused on Data Model and Interaction Model, leaving other parts of service model (like security model) for further consideration. Gap analysis has been performed resulting in logic map of navigational information in both systems. Based on this common platform IVEF interaction model is presented. In general three core activities were examined:

- implementing new data in IVEF data model
- implementing new filters dedicated for RIS in IVEF interaction model
- implementing new transmission category in IVEF interaction model.

3.1   Data Model for VTS-RIS Exchange

Looking at data exchanged in both systems many common fields can be found. These are mainly static and dynamic vessels characteristics as well as some voyage related data. The common source for this information is in both cases Automatic Identification System (AIS). However, it has to be noted that AIS format has been widely expanded in Inland AIS specification comparing to its maritime version. Additional data fields have been added and certain values have been changed. On the other there are usually independent sensors to obtain dynamic information in VTS systems, e.g. radar with suitable tracking algorithms, which are very rarely implemented in RIS. Also so called hull data usually come not only from AIS but also from inner or external hull databases as well. In RIS this would be wide concept of European Hull

DataBase (EHDB) and in case of VTS it would be GISIS (Global Integrated Shipping Information System) by IMO. Voyage-related information are also available in both systems, but in different forms. In RIS these are standardized ERI messages and in VTS these are usually IMO FAL forms send to port of destination. It can be thus said that first group of data to be exchanged between VTS and RIS is Vessel Traffic Image data, which in some form exists in both systems, it has to be however mapped and connected.

The other group would be the data which are exchanged only in RIS like meteorological data, hydrological information and traffic management information. These are not included at all in IVEF, however they can be considered as important and worth of being exchanged.

In Table 1 general matching map of information to be exchanged in RIS/VTS data exchange platform is presented.

Table 1. General matching map for VTS and IVEF data models [own study]

RIS	sensors/services	IVEF								
		Vessel Data			Track Data			Voyage Data		
		AIS	VTS DataBase	International DB	AIS	VTS own sensors	External sensors	IMO FAL forms	VTS operator	AIS
Static Ship Information	Inland AIS	1								
	VTT Database		1							
	EHDB			1						
Dynamic Ship Information	Inland AIS				1	-	-			
Voyage Related Information	Inland AIS									1
	ERI							2		
	RIS Operator (if any)								2	
Traffic Management Information	Inland AIS		x			x			x	
Fairway Information	NtS		x			x			x	
Weather Information	NtS		x			x			x	
Water level Information	NtS		x			x			x	
Ice Information	NtS		x			x			x	
Calamity Information	NtS		x			x			x	

1 – matching possible, minor amendments to data definition needed; 2 - matching possible, major amendments to data definition needed; "-" – matching not possible, no suitable service available in RIS; "x" – matching not possible, no suitable service available in IVEF, introducing new data definition to IVEF needed.

It can be seen in the table that most of data requires only minor amendments in data definition. The easiest situation is matching dynamic ship's data. These are in RIS directly given by InlandAIS. In case of VTS this is usually a fusion of various sensors, however they can be considered as always complimentary. In Inland AIS there is additional information about blue sign carried by vessel and quality of speed, course and heading. These information are not important from VTS point of view so they can be in fact omitted.

Similar situation with AIS is also in case of static ships data, where Inland AIS includes a few extensions like inland identification number, decimetre accuracy of size and loaded/unloaded information. There is a lack of IMO number, which is not used for inland ships. All of these can be omitted as they are not important from exchange point of view. One field which really has to be mapped in details is type of ship and cargo which has different values in AIS and can be supplemented with type of vessel and convoy which is additional field in Inland AIS. Cargo information can be however obtained in voyage related data from other services like ERI in inland shipping and IMO FAL forms in marine waters. In any case detailed matching of cargo and vessel type field should be done.

Summing up it can be said that matching map for traffic image information is relatively easy. It is proposed that for the needs of RIS/VTS exchange, data model is reduced only to necessary data. Two fields that required detailed mapping are type of vessel, and cargo information. The last one however is the most important as it is crucial to exchange cargo information especially about dangerous goods on board.

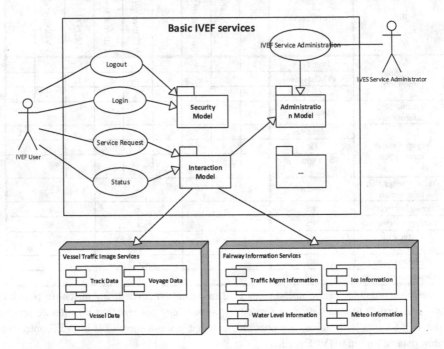

Fig. 1. Enhanced IVEF Service Primary Use Case. Source: own study based on [10]

There is also a large group of data not exchanged in IVEF, but exchanged in RIS. Some of them are in fact not needed in VTS, but it should be considered to enhance exchange data model with traffic management information like traffic obstacles or changes in vessels movement and with selected notices to skippers, including meteorological warnings and ice warnings. To cover these requirements it is proposed to enhance IVEF services with Fairway Information Services, containing fairway data as presented in Fig.1.

3.2   Interaction Model for VTS-RIS Data Exchange

In general interaction model for both systems looks very similar. Both systems are client-server architecture, both of them are based on machine to machine interface and both of them provide push and pull services. Information flow always includes steps presented in Fig. 2. Main differences between these services are within service request. It seems reasonable to enhance IVEF interaction model with additional filtering possibilities. Currently only category and area filters are available. The proposal is to include trigger events concept in interaction model. It should be possible to define events, which would initiate data transmission process. Such an event could be crossing of defined line going upstream or entering RIS area. Technically client application or server application should periodically check if trigger requirement is fulfilled and if so initiate the service. Additionally a few filters dedicated for VTS/RIS should be defined, like vessels with destination within VTS or RIS area, vessels carrying dangerous cargo, etc.

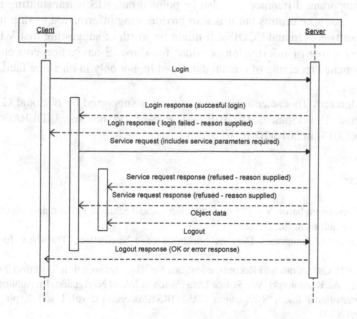

Fig. 2. Steps of information flow in proposed interaction model [own study]

4   Conclusion

The paper discussed a problem of lack of common data exchange format between VTS and RIS. Both systems include data exchange and each of the system has its own service definition. However the concept of data exchange is very similar and it is possible to create a common exchange platform with some modifications of existing standards.

It has been noticed that data exchange concept is wider in RIS based on SOA architecture that provides services designed for reuse, thus most of the proposed changes is addressed to IVEF models. Proposed changes can be summarized as follows:

- IVEF data model should be enhanced with additional services, including hydro meteorological information and traffic management information
- only data needed to be exchanged should be included in the new data model
- dedicated interface for mapping of particular fields in data model should be created
- IVEF interaction model should be enhanced with the possibility of defining trigger events for initiating of service
- dedicated filters for VTS/IVEF exchange should be defined in both interaction models.

One more important difference can also be pointed out. RIS is transmitting information not only to shore centres but it is also broadcasting information to ship user having proper software (Inland ECDIS). It might be worth of suggesting that VTS could also perform a role of information provider for ships. E-navigation concept should include automated receiving of crucial data on-ship, not only in on-shore facilities.

Acknowledgment. This scientific research work is supported by National Centre for Research and Development (NCBiR) of Poland (grant No. LIDER/039/693/L-4/12/NCBR/2013) in 2013-2016.

References

1. IALA Recommendation V – 128 on Operational and Technical Performance Requirements for. VTS Equipment Ed. 2.0 (2005)
2. Bergmann, M.: Integrated Data as backbone of e-Navigation. TransNav Journal 7(3) (2013)
3. PIANC RIS Guidelines and Recommendations for River Information Systems (2011)
4. Stateczny, A., Kazimierski, W.: Sensor Data Fusion in Inland Navigation. In: Rohling, H. (ed.) 14th International Radar Symposium (IRS). IRS Proceedings, vol. 1 and 2, pp. 264–269. Dresden (2013)
5. Lubczonek, J.: Application of Modified Method of Viewshed Analysis in Radar Sensor Network Planning on Inland Waterways. In: Kulpa, K. (ed.) 13th International Radar Symposium (IRS), Warsaw. International Radar Symposium Proceedings, pp. 269–274 (2012)

6. Lubczonek, J.,, S.: Aspects of spatial planning of radar sensor network for inland waterways surveillance. In: 6th European Radar Conference (EURAD 2009), Rome. European Radar Conference-EuRAD, pp. 501–504 (2009)
7. Weintrit, A.: Presentation of safety contours on electronic navigational charts. In: 11th International Congress of the International Maritime Association of the Mediterranean (IMAM 2005). Maritime Transportation and Exploitation of Ocean and Coastal Resources, Lisbon, vols 1 and 2: vol. 1: Vessels For Maritime Transportation – vol. 2: Exploitation of Ocean and Coastal Resources, pp. 1659–1666 (2005)
8. Wawrzyniak, N., Hyla, T.: Managing Depth Information Uncertainty in Inland Mobile Navigation Systems. In: Kryszkiewicz, M., Cornelis, C., Ciucci, D., Medina-Moreno, J., Motoda, H., Raś, Z.W. (eds.) RSEISP 2014. LNCS (LNAI), vol. 8537, pp. 343–350. Springer, Heidelberg (2014)
9. Pietrzykowski, Z., Borkowski, P., Wołejsza, P.: Marine integrated navigational decision support system. In: Mikulski, J. (ed.) TST 2012. CCIS, vol. 329, pp. 284–292. Springer, Heidelberg (2012)
10. IALA Recommendation V-145 on the Inter-VTS Exchange Format (IVEF) Service, Edition 1.0 (2011)
11. Weintrit, A.: The Concept of a Universal Maritime Data Model (UMDM) Essential for E-Navigation. Journal of KONES Powertrain and Transport 17(2) (2010)
12. Kazimierski, W.: Problems of Data Fusion of Tracking Radar, and AIS for the Needs of Integrated Navigation Systems at Sea. In: Rohling, H. (ed.) 14th International Radar Symposium (IRS). IRS Proceedings, vol. 1 and 2, pp. 270–275. Dresden (2013)
13. Borkowski, P.: Data fusion in a navigational decision support system on a sea-going vessel. Polish Maritime Research 19(4), 78–85 (2012)
14. Stateczny, A., Kazimierski, W.: A comparison of the target tracking in marine navigational radars by means of GRNN filter and numerical filter. In: 2008 IEEE Radar Conference, Rome. IEEE Radar Conference, vol. 1-4, pp. 1994–1997 (2008)
15. Kazimierski, W., Stateczny, A.: Optimization of multiple model neural tracking filter for marine targets. In: Kulpa, K. (ed.) 13th International Radar Symposium (IRS), Warsaw. IRS Proceedings, pp. 543–548 (2012)
16. Stateczny, A., Kazimierski, W.: Determining Manoeuvre Detection Threshold of GRNN Filter in the Process of Tracking in Marine Navigational Radars. In: Kawalec, A., Kaniewski, P. (eds.) Proceedings of IRS, Wrocław, pp. 242–245 (2008)
17. Kazimierski, W., Lubczonek, J.: Verification of marine multiple model neural tracking filter for the needs of shore radar stations. In: Kulpa, K. (ed.) 13th International Radar Symposium (IRS), Warsaw. IRS Proceedings, pp. 554–559 (2012)
18. Kazimierski, W., Zaniewicz, G., Stateczny, A.: Verification of multiple model neural tracking filter with ship's radar. In: Kulpa, K. (ed.) 13th International Radar Symposium (IRS), Warsaw. IRS Proceedings, pp. 549–553 (2012)
19. IALA Recommendation e-NAV-140 on The e-Navigation Architecture - the initial Shore-based Perspective, Edition 1.0 (2009)

Safe Ship Trajectory Determination in the ENC Environment

Zbigniew Pietrzykowski, Janusz Magaj, and Marcin Mąka

Maritime University of Szczecin,
70-500 Szczecin, Poland
{z.pietrzykowski,j.magaj,m.maka}am.szczecin.pl

Abstract. The paper presents the problem of determining a safe ship trajectory in real conditions with the use of information comprised in electronic navigational charts (ENC). Ship trajectory optimisation is one of essential functionalities of decision support systems which are part of intelligent transport systems. An ENC data transformation method herein presented is aimed to reduce the time of creating the numerical terrain model for an optimization problem. Trapezoidal meshes are proposed for this purpose. Water area parameters as well as moving targets are considered. The three dimensional ship domain is used as a safety criterion. The implementation of the presented method is discussed.

Keywords: optimization, ship trajectory, trapezoidal mesh, ship domain.

1   Introduction

The rapid development of IT and ICT technologies enables the implementation of increasingly complex methods and computational algorithms, carried out to extend currently available functions of the navigation systems on board ships and in land-based centres. This includes, among others, ship movement prediction, navigational situation solution, i.e. safe ship route determination, as well as the deciding on individual ship manoeuvres.

The diversity of users' needs regarding the scope and form of presented information has led to the development of existing as well as new navigation systems. These include automatic radar plotting aid (ARPA), electronic navigation chart display and information system (ECDIS), automatic identification system (AIS), pilot navigation systems (PNS), docking systems (DS), dynamic positioning systems (DP), systems used on drilling and production platforms, vessel traffic services (VTS) and other specialized systems. The development of such systems tends to transform navigation information systems into decision support systems.

The determination of ship trajectory is one of important issues regarding the safety and efficiency of maritime transport. This issue applies to voyage planning, execution and monitoring. These are i.e. voyage planning based on the decision of the charterer or ship owner and captain, weather routing recommendations, assurance of prompt

J. Mikulski (Ed.): TST 2014, CCIS 471, pp. 304–312, 2014.

ship operations by services responsible for organization and supervision of vessel traffic as well as ship movement control (sea voyage) according to ship owner's guidelines and, at the same time, observation of the principles of safe navigation, regulations in force and instructions of VTS operators. The determined route must satisfy the conditions of acceptability and rationality. It aims to enable the safe ship operation taking into account the economic aspects, resulting from the ongoing task.

A navigational chart is an important information source for performing the above mentioned tasks. Currently used electronic navigational charts (vector charts) allow to use information about features such as land, navigational danger, or depth to plan a safe ship route and monitor the voyage. These features are described with points which determine lines and areas. A large number of data describing objects can result in extended computation time, and thus delayed determination of a safe ship trajectory. This is especially important in systems at the operational level (safe ship conduct), working in an online mode. The task in such case can be formulated as follows: select and integrate data on a specific area around the ship allowing their use in an online mode in the process of safe ship trajectory determination. This task can be done in different ways. The task completion speed and efficiency are the assessment criteria of the developed algorithms.

2   Safe Ship Trajectory Determination Problem

An optimal route choice involves the determination of a own ship's course, speed and/or trajectory assuring safe passing of encountered objects [10]. The most common objective is to minimize the loss of way, time or fuel consumption. Basic limitations are safe passing distances to other objects. Furthermore, navigators should take into account international collision regulations [4] as well as principles of good sea practice, e.g. substantial course alterations or manoeuvres performed early enough. The problem can be presented as a static optimization problem: linear or non-linear programming.

In case of static optimization (linear programming) the problem assumes the form

$$\min \mathbf{c}^T \mathbf{x}. \tag{1}$$

with constraints:

$$\mathbf{A}\mathbf{x} \leq \mathbf{b}$$

$$\mathbf{x} \geq \mathbf{0} \tag{2}$$

where:

$\mathbf{x} \in R$ – variables vector,
$\mathbf{c} \in R$ – vector of objective function coefficients,
$\mathbf{A} \in R$ – constraint coefficient matrix,
$\mathbf{b} \in R$ – vector of right-hand side constraints,

The consideration of additional criteria, such as distance to be covered or fuel consumption, can lead to the formulation of multi-criteria optimization task.

The movement control of a sea-going ship, a multidimensional non-linear dynamic object, requires that multiple decisions be made. These decisions are of dynamic nature and consist in the selection of settings (rudder, propulsion) for safe manoeuvre performance. This type of problem is solved by methods of dynamic optimization.

For ship trajectory optimization we use the dynamic programming, one of the standard methods of dynamic optimization in problems of multistage decision making and control. Optimal ship control in terms of pre-set control quality indicator can be determined by using the Bellman's principle of optimality [1]. For instance, to solve the problem of optimal trajectory determination we will specify return points and courses on the designated waypoints or rudder or/and propulsion settings in selected moments of time.

The basic issue of the method is the amount of computations, growing exponentially with the number of control stages.

The optimization problem is to find such control function $\hat{\mathbf{u}}(t)$ defining the optimal trajectory $\hat{\mathbf{x}}(t)$ that the quality functional J will assume a minimum value:

$$J(\hat{\mathbf{x}}(t), \hat{\mathbf{u}}(t), t) = \min_{\mathbf{u}(t) \in \mathbf{U}_0, \, \mathbf{x}(t) \in \mathbf{X}_0} \int_{t_0}^{t_k} f_0(\mathbf{x}(t), \mathbf{u}(t), t) dt \tag{3}$$

where:

f_0 – function of instantaneous losses,

$u(t) \in U_0$ – set of allowable controls,

$x(t) \in X_0$ – maximum trajectory space.

In a discrete approach, for a given n-dimensional space of states $\mathbf{X} = \{x_1, \dots x_n\}$ and m-dimensional space of controls $\mathbf{U} = \{u_1, \dots u_m\}$, state transitions in subsequent k stages of control ($k=0, 1, \dots, K$) are represented by this function:

$$f : \mathbf{X} \times \mathbf{U} \to \mathbf{X} \tag{4}$$

$$\begin{cases} \mathbf{x}_1 = f(\mathbf{x}_0, \mathbf{u}_0) \\ \mathbf{x}_2 = f(\mathbf{x}_1, \mathbf{u}_1) = f(f(\mathbf{x}_0, \mathbf{u}_0), \mathbf{u}_1) \\ \dots\dots\dots\dots\dots\dots\dots\dots\dots\dots\dots \\ \mathbf{x}_k = f(\mathbf{x}_{k-1}, \mathbf{u}_{N-1}) = f(f(\dots(f(\mathbf{x}_0, \mathbf{u}_0), \mathbf{u}_1)\dots, \mathbf{u}_{k-2})\mathbf{u}_{k-1}) \end{cases} \tag{5}$$

The control strategy, determining the optimal trajectory, consists of a series of controls:

$$\hat{u} = (\hat{u}_{t_o}, \hat{u}_{t_1}, \dots, \hat{u}_{t_{k-1}}) \tag{6}$$

The loss of distance, paradoxically understood here as extra distance the ship has to cover, is often used as a quality control indicator of (optimality criterion), which at a constant ship's speed leads to the time optimal control. As a safety criterion the collision risk area, defined by the closest point of approach, ship domain or ship fuzzy domain [11], [13], [15] is used. Consideration of constraints on state and control variables (i.e. safety criterion, collision regulations) is implemented by checking whether the variables do not exceed the allowable trajectory space or set of allowable controls and the rejection of nodes in which such excess has been detected.

In real decision-making problems more than one criterion should be taken into the consideration. The optimization problem takes the form of multi criteria optimization and can be simplified due to prioritization and weight determination of each individual criterion. Additional difficulties are created by variables disturbing the movement process and the need to consider them.

Implemented optimization algorithms for determining the safe ship trajectory motion can be used in navigational decision support systems on board a sea-going ship [12], [14]. It is possible to automate the ship control process in the mentioned systems, for example by connecting such system with the implemented control algorithm, for instance, an autopilot, steering gear, main engine and screw propeller [2], [3].

3 ENC Data Representation in an Optimization Problem

An electronic navigational chart (ENC), made in a vector format, geometrically is an ordered set of elements on a plane: points, lines and polygons (Fig. 1) which represent objects of the chart. The elements are described by their coordinates and object attributes. The chart presented on the display consists of a number of elementary cells (charts), in particular of selected cell elements. The selection of displayed elements depends on the chart scale and configuration settings (day, night, choice of display elements: Base, Standard, others). As chart data are stored in files, the user may read the information he needs and utilize in a navigational decision support system N [9].

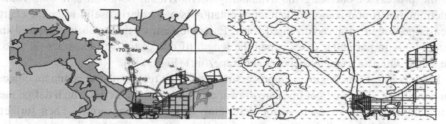

Fig. 1. Electronic navigational chart and its vector representation [9]

The navigational analysis uses mainly such details as:

- shorelines,
- depths (isobaths),
- area temporarily or permanently prohibited for shipping,
- traffic separation schemes,
- dangerous objects and areas prohibited for navigation (wrecks etc.).

A large number of objects and corresponding data cause difficulties in their prompt use. One method used in algorithms for determining trajectories of vessel movement is the use of a regular grid. Consideration of restrictions, i.e. navigational dangers or obstructions, leads to a rejection of prohibited nodes in the grid. This necessitates verification of the availability of all the nodes in the grid and consists in an iterative check if a node is in the prohibited area. Relatively long checking time is also caused by the fact that areas identified as prohibited are not ordered. The solution can be that for an analysis only a relevant chart fragment is chosen, in which prohibited areas are identified and ordered (Fig. 2).

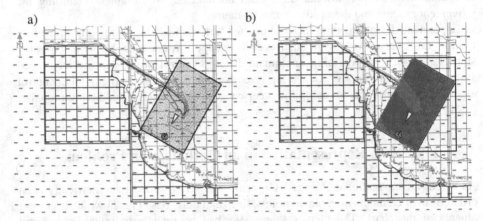

Fig. 2. A regular grid of nodes for route determination in a navigational situation: a) before node availability check; b) after node availability check [own study]

One of the selection methods is changing to the description of prohibited areas using a trapezoidal mesh [8], [16], which allows to organize the listed areas and speed up the process of checking the availability of individual nodes in safe ship route determination (optimization). Such representation is particularly useful when the chart area is presented in a vector-based form. Each element of the mesh is trapezoid in shape. Only in particular cases, when the length of one of the vertical sides is zero, the shape will be a triangle (degenerated trapezoid) (Fig. 3) [8].

Mesh construction begins with processing a selected rectangular area and an object contained in it. Two vertical lines are drawn, originating in the nodes which define the start and end point of each vector describing the object concerned. Then further objects are added, and the generated mesh is locally modified to incorporate the subsequent added object.

Obtaining information on the location of points contained within the analysed area and on the properties of the mesh containing these points consists in the identification of a mesh element which contains the examined point (its coordinates). Because all mesh elements are stored in an array ordered by the coordinates λ, searching consists in the identification of those elements whose coordinates λ of the left-hand and right-hand vertical segments are respectively greater and smaller than λ-coordinate of the examined point. Then coordinates φ of the analysed point and marked out elements are checked in order to determine the element that contains the point. Knowing the element index, the details of a particular area can be read out [6], [7].

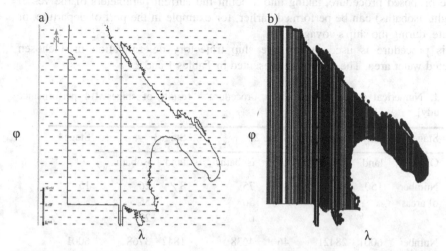

Fig. 3. Trapezoidal mesh construction: a) original water area model; b) water area model represented by a trapezoidal mesh [own study]

4 Ship Trajectory Determination

The process of safe ship trajectory determination can be described by the following steps:

1. identify chart fragment boundaries which define an area around the ship for the safe ship trajectory optimization problem,
2. define ordinary mesh nodes for an optimization problem
3. verify the availability of mesh nodes (permitted/prohibited) regarding ENC objects
4. safe ship trajectory determination based on the chosen optimization method.

In order to reduce the time of numerical model determination for an optimization problem (step 3), a procedure is worked out where the trapezoidal mesh method is one of the essential tools. The procedure includes the following stages:

1. uploading object data from an ENC,
2. data selection (land, isobaths, navigational dangers etc.)
3. object integration in each chart layer,
4. integration of objects in all chart layers,
5. trapezoidal mesh determination,
6. checking the availability of mesh nodes.

It is possible to create in advance a numerical model based on the trapezoidal mesh for the planned ship voyage. This speeds up the model preparation for the selected chart fragment described with the regular grid for optimization problems (steps 1 and 2) and verification of availability of grid nodes (step 3).

The proposed procedure, taking into account the current parameters of the vessel (draught/ isobaths) can be performed earlier, for example in the port of departure, or en route, during the ship's voyage.

This procedure is used in the safe ship trajectory determination in a chosen restricted water area. The results are presented in Tables 1 and 2.

Table 1. Numerical model determination procedure - results of stages 1-4 performance [own study]

Stages	Stage 1		Stage 2		Stage3		Stage4
Objects	land	isobaths	land	isobaths	land	isobaths	
Number of areas	150	366	2048	75 56 63	8	26 55 23	15
Number of points	6001	28421	46	4638 5606 5899	1842	3768 5027 4635	6001

Table 2. Numerical model determination procedure - results of stage 5 performance [own study]

Number of nodes		909
Number of lines		910
Number of trapezoids	total	2409
	permitted	1361
	prohibited	1048
Execution time	total	1022 ms
	load, selection and sorting	36 ms
	mesh generation	813 ms
	determination of prohibited trapezoids	173 ms

The test was carried out to compare performance time of grid node availability check (stage 6, without the use of trapezoidal mesh) and mesh nodes availability check with the use of trapezoidal mesh (stages 5 and 6).

The use of proposed trapezoidal mesh allowed to reduce nodes availability check time (step 3 in the safe ship trajectory determination process) by half.

The above described procedure of creating a numerical model of the water area was used for ship trajectory optimization. The moving objects – ships – were taken into consideration.

The authors have simulated a ship encounter situation according to a prepared scenario (Figure 4). To determine a safe trajectory of ship movement we have used Dijkstra algorithm [5], [10], [15].

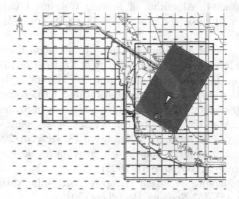

Fig. 4. Safe ship trajectory for a chosen navigational situation [own study]

5   Conclusion

This paper presents the problem of ship safe trajectory determination in real conditions with the use of ENC data.

In the described procedure of creating a water area numerical model for the purpose of trajectory optimization, we have used a trapezoidal mesh. This allows to reduce significantly the nodes availability check time in solving a ship trajectory optimization problem.

We have simulated a ship encounter situation, according to a prepared scenario, to verify the ship trajectory optimization method. In the simulation the water area parameters retrieved from an ENC are taken into account.

The proposed procedure of creating a water area numerical model using a trapezoidal mesh can be implemented in a navigational decision support system for solving ship trajectory optimization problems.

References

1. Bellman, R.E., Zadeh, L.A.: Decision making in a fuzzy environment. Management Science (17) (1970)
2. Borkowski, P.: Ship course stabilization by feedback linearization with adaptive object model. Polish Maritime Research 21(1(81)) (2014)
3. Borkowski, P., Zwierzewicz, Z.: Ship course-keeping algorithm based on knowledge base. Intelligent Automation and Soft Computing 17(2) (2011)

4. COLREGs, Convention on the international regulations for preventing collisions at sea, International Maritime Organization (1972)
5. Deo, N.: The Theory of Graphs and its Application in Technology and Computer Science. PWN Warszawa (1980)
6. Dramski, M., Mąka, M.: Selected shortest path in the graph algorithms with a use of trapezoidal grid in navigation in restricted area. In: Mikulski, J. (ed.) TST 2012. CCIS, vol. 329, pp. 3–7. Springer, Heidelberg (2012)
7. Dramski, M., Mąka, M.: Algorithm of Solving Collision Problem of Two Objects in Restricted Area. In: Mikulski, J. (ed.) TST 2013. CCIS, vol. 395, pp. 251–257. Springer, Heidelberg (2013)
8. Mąka, M.: The recurrent algorithm for area discretization using the trapezoidal mesh method. Scientific Journals Maritime University of Szczecin 29(101), 134–139 (2012)
9. Mąka, M., Magaj, J.: Data extraction from an electronic S-57 standard chart for navigational decision systems. VII Międzynarodowa Konferencja Naukowo-Techniczna Explo-Ship 2012 (Scientific Journals Maritime University of Szczecin) 30(102) (2012)
10. Pietrzykowski, Z.: Modeling of decision processes in sea-going ship movement control, Maritime University of Szczecin, Series Study No 43, Szczecin (2004)
11. Pietrzykowski, Z.: Ship's fuzzy domain – a criterion for navigational safety in narrow fairways. The Journal of Navigation 61 (2008)
12. Pietrzykowski, Z.: Maritime Intelligent Transport Systems. In: Mikulski, J. (ed.) TST 2010. CCIS, vol. 104, pp. 455–462. Springer, Heidelberg (2010)
13. Pietrzykowski, Z., Magaj, J., Wołejsza, P., Chomski, J.: Fuzzy logic in the navigational decision support process onboard a sea-going vessel. In: Rutkowski, L., Scherer, R., Tadeusiewicz, R., Zadeh, L.A., Zurada, J.M. (eds.) ICAISC 2010, Part I. LNCS, vol. 6113, pp. 185–193. Springer, Heidelberg (2010)
14. Pietrzykowski, Z., Borkowski, P., Wołejsza, P.: Marine integrated navigational decision support system. In: Mikulski, J. (ed.) TST 2012. CCIS, vol. 329, pp. 284–292. Springer, Heidelberg (2012)
15. Pietrzykowski, Z., Magaj, J.: The problem of route determination in ship movement in a restricted area. Annual of Navigation, nr 19/2012/part 2, Gdynia, pp. 53–69 (2012)
16. Van Kreveld M., et al.: Computational geometry – algorithms and applications. Warsaw WNT (2007) (in Polish)

Adaptive Method of Raster Images Compression and Examples of Its Applications in the Transport Telematic Systems

Marcin Sokół, Małgorzata Gajewska and Sławomir Gajewski

Gdansk University of Technology
Faculty of Electronics, Telecommunications and Informatics
G. Narutowicza 11/12, PL-80-233 Gdansk, Poland
{marcin.sokol,malgorzata.gajewska,
slawomir.gajewski}@eti.pg.gda.pl

Abstract. The paper presents a concept and exemplary application of an adaptive method of compression of raster images which may be applied, i.a. in ITS systems. The described method allows to improve the efficiency of systems belonging to ITS category, which require transmission of large volumes of image data through telecommunications networks. The concept of the adaptive method of compression of raster images described in the paper uses a compressor with a variable compressor ratio and is based on the dependence of the degree of compression of each transmitted digital image on the transmission conditions (defined by the average data transmission rate) and the number of digital images queuing in the buffer to be processed and transmitted.

Keywords: compression, JPEG, transmission, TST.

1 Introduction

In recent years, systems of intelligent video monitoring dedicated to different branches of the transport sector (especially public transport) have been developing in a very dynamic way. Discussing the subject of generally understood transport and safety, it is impossible to overlook their close connection to *Intelligent Transport Systems* - ITS, which have been developing effectively in recent years. Systems of video monitoring are used, e.g. for sourcing, transmitting and storing video streams and static images related to some objects and phenomena occurring in a given geographical area [1-2]. Video monitoring is becoming more and more often a key element of integrated surveillance systems and public safety systems. It is now often found on the premises of many companies, sports facilities, shopping centres, and places of high level car and pedestrian traffic [2].

Growing expectations of users and administrators of ITS systems (using more or less advanced subsystems of video monitoring) when it comes to the quality of the delivered visual material, are followed with more and more restrictive requirements concerning the data transmission services, offered by different types of telecommunications networks [1-3]. For obvious reasons, a vast majority of these type of systems uses public

J. Mikulski (Ed.): TST 2014, CCIS 471, pp. 313–320, 2014.

telecommunications networks for transmitting data, and especially public systems of cellular radio communication. The main problem occurring when using this type of network in ITS systems is lack of guarantee for the quality of services, mainly when it comes to the transmission rate and delays [2-4]. Problems with access to radio signal or limited capacity of mobile networks in many areas, sensitivity to all kind of abuse, and the characteristics of the network itself, make their use in subsystems of video monitoring, where the amount of data sent is often large, quite problematic [1].

The concept of adaptive method of compression of raster images has been developed in the Department of Radiocommunication Systems and Networks of Gdansk University of Technology. The method was first used in the System of Radio Monitoring and Data Acquisition from Photo Radar Devices (RSMAD[1]) [4]. The discussed method has been practically implemented also in other systems related to RSMAD, and connected with, e.g. detection of traffic violation in the place of its occurrence. During the research it turned out that because of a large amount of visual data (connected with a great number of registered traffic incidents) obtained by this type of systems, as well as problems resulting from the specifics of the mobile network itself, their application in some areas may pose some technical problems connected, e.g. with efficient transmission of video signal in real-time.

2   Concept of Adaptive Method of Visual Data Compression

Most ITS systems which use subsystems of intelligent video monitoring are characterised by openness to various techniques and technologies of radio or / and wire data transmission. In the case of distributed video monitoring, visual data is transferred mainly through radio communication networks in which because of variability of radio channel characteristics and parameters and time-varying network load factor, average transmission time of pictures coming from video cameras / digital cameras (transmitted to acquisition centres) is highly variable over time. The proposed method uses a completely innovative approach to data processing and data compression before transmission over telecommunications network (Fig. 1). The innovation of the proposed method consists in creating a dependency between the degree of compression of each image processed in the system and the transmission parameters of the telecomnunications link and the number of images queuing to be processed and transmitted. In other words, in the discussed method the information about the average transmission rate and the number of files queuing in the buffer has an immediate effect on the choice of the degree of compression and the efficiency of transmission (Fig. 1). The compression factor is determined dynamically, according to clearly and strictly defined rules implemented in the data compression module (Table 1).

The idea behind the transmission module using the adaptive method of compression (Fig. 1) consists in the fact that the registered and archived raster images saved as digital images are firstly read by a special read-out module. The information from the

---

[1] The scope of features offered by RSMAD system is similar to the one now offered by the Automatic Traffic Surveillance System used by the Main Inspectorate of Road Transport (to find out more about RSMAD go to papers [2], [3], [4], [7]).

module is next transferred independently in the form of digital signal into compression and analysis modules. The read-out module has the following functions [5]:

- reads out all images stored in a digital form,
- precisely calculates the number of pictures queuing for transmission,
- transfers information by means of digital signal into the analysis module,
- transfers registered digital images into an adaptive compressor.

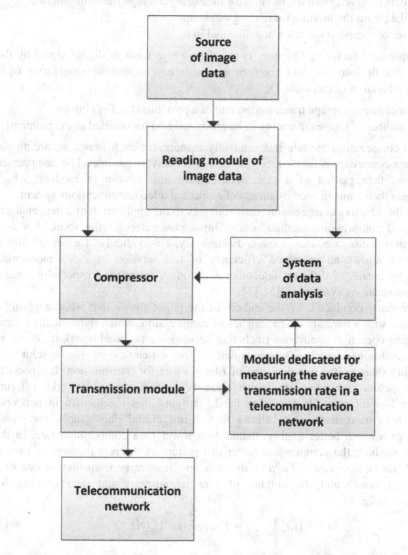

Fig. 1. Demonstrative block diagram of the transmission module using the adaptive compression method [own study]

The module measuring average transmission rate in a telecommunication network, on the other hand, determines the average number of elementary signals (bits) in a time unit. The information from this module is then transferred in a form of digital signal into an analysis module, which processes all the data received from cooperating modules in real-time. It also determines the compression ratio for each processed in the system *i*- image, based on [5], [7]:

- data received from the module for measuring average transmission rate,
- data from the module for reading out images,
- set of compression rules implemented in it.

The compression factor of *i*-picture, is transferred in a form of digital signal by the analysis module into the data compression module. The compression factor of *i*-image, is a function of (formula 1):

- measured, average transmission rate of a previous (i.e. *i−1*) image,
- number of images queueing to be processed and transmitted at the moment.

Then the compression module independently compresses each image according the the picture compression factor received from the analysis module. The compressed images are then passed to do the data transmission system (a modem) which implements their transmission by means of a selected telecommunications system.

Using the adaptive compression method thanks to the application of a data analysis module and compression module, whose input parameters in the form of a data compression ratio are determined dynamically, individually for each digital photograph, allows an increased efficiency of transmission in video monitoring systems, by means of different telecommunications systems, and especially a radio telecommunications system [1], [5], [7].

The research conducted by the authors of the paper shows that when applying a compressor with a variable characteristics of compression, which dynamically adapts to changing operation conditions (including network-traffic conditions), it allows, in certain conditions, to significantly improve the efficiency of the system and measurably shortens the queuing time of files waiting for transmission. It especially refers to solutions when data transmission is performed by networks offering relatively low bit rate. On the other hand, applying this mechanism in networks offering high transmission rate allows to transmit digital photographs and video material of a much better quality, thanks to a lower data compression rate. In the proposed method, the compression factor of *i*-picture in discrete moment of time t_n (PCF, *Picture Compression Factor*), depends on the average transmission rate of a file *i-1* (previous) and the number of files including visual data queuing for transmission (fig. 1).

$$PCF\left(i,t_n\right)\big|_{i=0,1,\ldots} = f\left(avgT\left(i-1\right),Q\left(t_n\right)\right) \tag{1}$$

where:

PCF - picture compression factor
avgT - average transmission rate
Q - queue length

Table 1. A set of some exemplary rules for determining PCF factor by an analysis module in a system for digital photographs transmission

Number of pictures waiting in the queue ($Q(t_n)$ [pictures]):	Traffic rate ($avgT(i-1)$ [kbps]):	compression factor:	
		Target picture quality (x_m):	Target picture resolution (y_n):
$0 \leq Q(t_n) \leq 50$	$avgT(i-1) \leq 50$	75	1600x1062
	$50 < avgT(i-1) \leq 75$	75	2573x1828
	$75 < avgT(i-1) \leq 150$	75	2573x1828
	$150 < avgT(i-1) \leq 300$	90	2573x1828
	$avgT(i-1) > 300$	90	2573x1828
$50 < Q(t_n) \leq 100$	$avgT(i-1) \leq 50$	75	1600x1062
	$50 < avgT(i-1) \leq 75$	75	1600x1062
	$75 < avgT(i-1) \leq 150$	90	1600x1062
	$150 < avgT(i-1) \leq 300$	90	1600x1062
	$avgT(i-1) > 300$	90	2573x1828
$100 < Q(t_n) \leq 500$	$avgT(i-1) \leq 50$	75	1600x1062
	$50 < avgT(i-1) \leq 75$	75	1600x1062
	$75 < avgT(i-1) \leq 150$	75	1600x1062
	$150 < avgT(i-1) \leq 300$	90	1600x1062
	$avgT(i-1) > 300$	90	2573x1828
$500 < Q(t_n) \leq 1000$	$avgT(i-1) \leq 50$	50	1024x680
	$50 < avgT(i-1) \leq 75$	75	1024x680
	$75 < avgT(i-1) \leq 150$	75	1600x1062
	$150 < avgT(i-1) \leq 300$	90	1600x1062
	$avgT(i-1) > 300$	90	2573x1828
$Q(t_n) < 1000$	$avgT(i-1) \leq 50$	50	1024x680
	$50 < avgT(i-1) \leq 75$	75	1024x680
	$75 < avgT(i-1) \leq 150$	75	1600x1062
	$150 < avgT(i-1) \leq 300$	90	1600x1062
	$avgT(i-1) > 300$	90	2573x1828

The PCF factor has been defined as a 2 element vector:

$$PCF(i,t_n) = \begin{bmatrix} x_m(i,t_n) \\ y_n(i,t_n) \end{bmatrix} \text{ for } x_m \in \mathbf{X}, y_n \in \mathbf{Y} \quad (2)$$

where:

$$\mathbf{X} = \begin{bmatrix} x_0 \\ x_1 \\ (...) \\ x_m \end{bmatrix} \quad \mathbf{Y} = \begin{bmatrix} y_0 \\ y_1 \\ (...) \\ y_n \end{bmatrix}$$

According to the formula (2) the compression factor of i-picture consists of a couple of digits. The first of them is the target picture quality, the second is its target resolution. The way to select the date compression factor depends on a particular implementation, the specifics of the ITS system, assumed quality scale and applied picture compression method. Vector $\mathbf{X}$ consists of m elements, where each of the elements describes target quality of the digital photograph. Each of the elements of the matrix $\mathbf{X}$ should satisfy the condition: $x_0 < x_1 < (...) < x_m$. Vector $\mathbf{Y}$ consists of n elements, where each of the elements describes a target resolution of the picture. E.g. y_0=640x480 pixels, y_1= 800x600 pixels, etc. It is recommended that the content of the matrix $\mathbf{X}$ and $\mathbf{Y}$ is selected experimentally depending on the specifics of a given application [5].

3   Adaptive Compression Algorithm Used in the RSMAD System

Tab. 1 shows an exemplary selection of compression factors used in RSMAD system. Digital photographs acquired from photo radars usually include only smooth colour gradation, thanks to which even the highest degree of compression makes it possible to preserve an acceptable quality of pictures, which has been confirmed by practical observations in the real operating conditions of the system.

Tab. 1 shows the quality scale suggested for JPEG format by IJP *(Independent JPEG Group)*. According to the IJG recommendations, the quality of picture is described by a number between 0 and 100, where 0 describes the lowest quality (the highest degree of decompression), 100 the highest (the lowest degree of decompression). In the algorithm of visual data processing, implemented in the communication module of RSMAD system, which uses dynamic compression of picture, the matrices $\mathbf{X}$ and $\mathbf{Y}$ are as follows:

$$\mathbf{X} = \begin{bmatrix} 50 \\ 75 \\ 90 \end{bmatrix} \quad \mathbf{Y} = \begin{bmatrix} 1024x680 \\ 1600x1062 \\ 2753x1828 \end{bmatrix} [pixels] \tag{3}$$

The compression in RSMAD system, which was the first to use the proposed method, because of finding application in photo radars, is based on JPEG standard, MJPEG version. After some slight adjustments of the application, it is possible to apply more modern compression standards, such as: JPEG-2000 or H.264-intra and thus significantly broaden the range of applications of the method described in this paper.

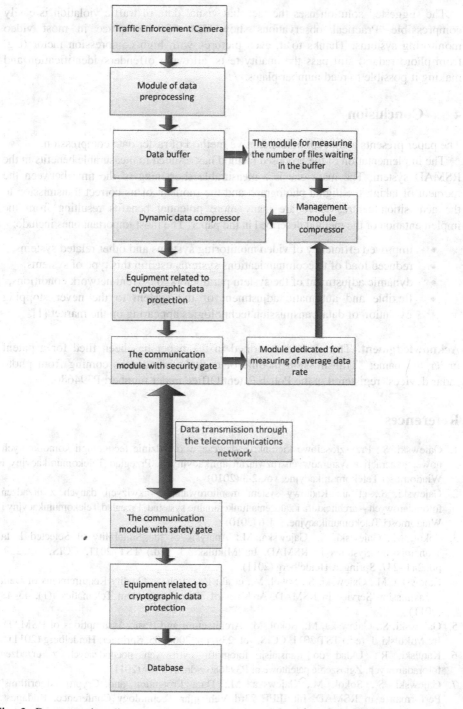

Fig. 2. Demonstrative diagram of a transmission module using the adaptive compression method [own study]

The suggested solution uses the fact that visual data of traffic violation is easily compressible. Practical observations show that this has place in most video monitoring systems. Thanks to it, even pictures with high compression factor (e.g. from photo radars) still pass the quality tests, allowing offenders' identification and making it possible to read number plates.

4   Conclusion

The paper presents a concept of an adaptive method of raster data compression.

The implementation of the proposed method has resulted in measurable benefits in the RSMAD system. The main one is a measurable shortening of the time between the moment of taking the digital photograph and the moment of its correct transmission to the acquisition centre. There are many more potential benefits resulting from the implementation of the method described in the paper. The most important ones include:

- improved efficiency of video monitoring systems and other related systems,
- reduced load of telecommunications systems used in this type of systems,
- dynamic adjustment of the system parameters to current network conditions,
- flexible and automatic adjustment of the system to the never stopping evolution of data transmission technologies appearing on the market [1].

Acknowledgment. The method described in the paper has been filed for a patent under the name: "Transmission module of digital photographs coming from photo radar devices" registered in the Polish Patent Office under number: P394686.

References

1. Gajewski, S.: Przyszłościowe kierunki badawcze w dziedzinie technologii komórkowych nowej generacji i systemowych rozwiązań aplikacyjnych, Przegląd Telekomunikacyjny i Wiadomości Telekomunikacyjne, vol. 2-3 (2010)
2. Gajewski, S., et al.: Radiowy system monitorowania i akwizycji danych z urządzeń fotoradarowych – architektura i założenia funkcjonalne systemu, Przegląd Telekomunikacyjny i Wiadomości Telekomunikacyjne, vol. 6 (2010)
3. Sokol, M., Gajewski, S., Gajewski, M.: Analysis of the Suitability of Selected Data Transmission Systems in RSMAD. In: Mikulski, J. (ed.) TST 2011. CCIS, vol. 239, pp. 241–247. Springer, Heidelberg (2011)
4. Gajewska, M., Gajewski, S., Sokol, M., et al.: Research on Quality Requirements of Data Transmission Service in RSMAD. Archives of Transport System Telematics 4(1), 43–48 (2011)
5. Gajewski, S., Gajewska, M., Sokol, M.: Architecture and Basic Assumptions of RSMAD. In: Mikulski, J. (ed.) TST 2011. CCIS, vol. 239, pp. 200–205. Springer, Heidelberg (2011)
6. Katulski, R.: Układ do transmisji fotografii cyfrowych pochodzących z urządzeń fotoradarowych. Zgłoszenie patentowe nr P394686 z dn. 27.04, r (2011)
7. Gajewski, S., Sokol, M., Gajewska, M.: Data Protection and Crypto Algorithms' Performance in RSMAD. In: IEEE 73rd Vehicular Technology Conference, Budapest, Hungary (2011)

Algorithm Determining the Setting Force at Point Machines

Jakub Młyńczak

Silesian University of Technology, Faculty of Transport
Krasińskiego 8, 40-019 Katowice, Poland
jakub.mlynczak@polsl.pl

Abstract. This paper is an attempt to develop a precise algorithm determining the value of the setting force. This is extremely essential for telematic and diagnostic measuring systems. What makes the task difficult is that no method, which determines the value of the setting force, has been defined so far. Although it is understandable what kind of force it is, there are some misunderstanding and doubt as to its definition and the determination of its value. As manufacturers of point machines define the same concept differently as well, the task is not easier. Frequently, instead of the setting force, slipping of the switch coupling is mentioned.

Keywords: point machine, setting force, methodology.

1 Introduction

A point machine is a very important element of railway traffic control equipment. It directly influences the safety of passengers and cargo being transported. Operation of the machine with railway points is the most significant element of the traffic control process. The diagnostics of the point machine and its operation with the points are very important as well. Unfortunately, diagnostics and analyses of the condition of the point machine/points system are not investigated sufficiently. It may seem that technology development should improve diagnostics and analyses of equipment condition. This is not true in reality. Firstly, there is no precise definition of forces occurring in the point machine/points system. Secondly, there are no clear guidelines relating to the interpretation of measurement results.

2 Point Machine Inspection

The diagnostics of railway traffic control equipment consist of [1]:

- gathering information on railway traffic control equipment based on visual inspections, tests, functional tests, and parameter measurements without having the assemblies of such equipment dismantled;
- learning about the operating environment;
- comparing the gathered information with the required parameters or permissible conditions.

J. Mikulski (Ed.): TST 2014, CCIS 471, pp. 321–330, 2014.
© Springer-Verlag Berlin Heidelberg 2014

By complying with the above requirements, the diagnostics can be deemed as performed.

The aim of diagnostics is to obtain information necessary to make diagnoses based on the current degree of wear and identified operating environment of railway traffic control equipment to be able to draw conclusions relating to [1]:

— necessary repair measures;
— technical conditions for continuing equipment operation;
— recommended maintenance and service.

Serving as railway traffic equipment, point machines are subject to periodic diagnostics. Such an inspection must be performed at intervals defined in the operation and maintenance documentation. If such operation and maintenance documentation does not specify inspection intervals or they are longer than one year, the inspection must be performed within cycles as required by the Ie-7 (E-14) Instruction.

3   Setting Force

The setting force is the maximum force exerted by the switch slide of the machine to move the points, the derail or swing nose crossing [3].

Measurements of the setting force must be taken during an official technical inspection of railroad points.

In order to measure the setting force of the machine, a measurement shank of the measuring instrument should be inserted in the place, where the pin couples the slide of the machine with the switch rod. By disabling or cranking the machine when the blade is disabled, it results in generating a force between the slide and the switch rod, the value of which is indicated by the measuring instrument. For single-type machines, switching can be performed electrically or by cranking. For multi-machine systems, the measurement of the setting force should be taken simultaneously at all point machines when switched electrically. The measurement of setting forces should be performed in a manner, which can ensure that bending of switch blades is avoided. This means that the switch blade should be disabled in accordance with the following principles [2]:

— for points with a machine equipped with an internal facing point lock, a blocking element should be inserted between the switch blade and the saver at the height of the switch rod of the point machine;
— for points with one facing point lock and mechanical coupling of the facing point locks, a blocking element should be inserted between the switch blade and the saver at the height of the first lock;
— for the points switched by means of several point machines, blocking elements of an adequate thickness should be inserted at the same time at the height of switch rods of all point machines operated at the points; this method also applies to the measurement of setting forces of machines switching the swing nose crossing of a frog.

To present a practical interpretation of the setting force, it can be said that the setting force is the value of the force generated by the point machine that occurs at the switch slide of the point machine when the points are switched. Its maximum value occurs when the overload coupling slips; this refers to the force value of coupling slipping.

It can be observed that the setting force for the point machine implemented at points is equal to the switching resistance. For diagnostic purposes, it is essential to measure the maximum setting force, i.e. the force when slipping of the overload (switch) coupling occurs. Therefore, in some countries, a concept of the slip force of the coupling has been introduced in addition to the setting force. For most point machines, manufacturers have assumed that the switching resistance of the points should not exceed 80 % of the (maximum) setting force.

For diagnostic purposes, the following assumptions should be made:

1. The measurement of the switching resistance is the same as the setting force measurement if slipping of the overload coupling does not occur. Thus, diagnostics should use the concept of *a switching resistance measurement*.
2. The measurement of the setting force with forced slipping of the coupling (coupling slip force) should be referred to as *a setting force measurement*.

If the measurement is taken using an instrument capable of recording the measured curve, some parameters are explicit. By measuring the switching resistance and recording it, unambiguous records of parameters are obtained. The maximum force measured is recognised as reliable.

When interpreting measurement results, the major problem is presented by the interpretation of the value of the setting force. In electronic devices, the setting force is often mistakenly equated with the maximum value of the force measured.

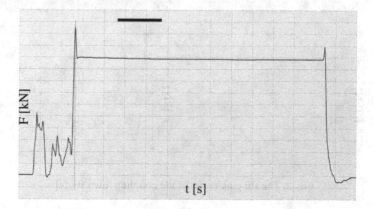

Fig. 1. Example characteristic curves of setting force [own study]

For the measurement results presented in Fig. 1, an obvious increase in the force value at the beginning of coupling slip is noticeable. It is a mistake to assume that the values are the setting force. In the examples shown, the determination of the setting force seems relatively simple. The setting force is the value marked by a bold section (a varied length of the marking is associated with the curve scale being adapted to the duration of the recorded measurement). This approach complies with the requirements of the German railway [4] - the setting force is equal to the mean value of one-second time period, occurring one second after the occurrence of slipping of the overload coupling.

Obviously, the moment, at which slipping of the coupling occurs, must be determined as well.

Why the German approach is correct:

It must be admitted that it is the only approach in Europe providing an unambiguous definition of the setting force value. It must be taken into account that the measuring technician equipped with analogue instruments used to determine the force value based on their subjective opinion. For instruments providing registration, some interpretation was possible when the entire curve of the measured force was examined. A clear definition narrows the need of interpretation.

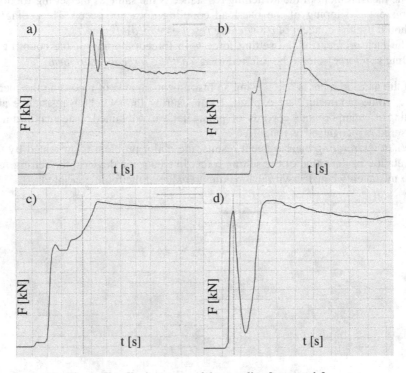

Fig. 2. The slipping curve of the coupling [own study]

Fig. 2 presents four different curves of the force recorded when the switch coupling slips. If the German definition of setting force is accepted, there is a problem with detecting the coupling slip. Such a detection is required to determine the value of the setting force unambiguously. For the cases presented in Fig. 1, there is no doubt; slipping of the overload coupling is accompanied with a rapid increase of the force being measured. As for the examples presented in Fig. 2, the problem is not unambiguous. It can be stated that a precise definition of the force is obtained. However, the definition of coupling slip must be made more precise. The curves in a), b), and d) are similar in their nature; the coupling experienced slipping twice. The second slipping was continuous. The case in 2c) allows noticing that slipping is not a rapid force change (in a short time), but it begins to increase up to the maximum value after the first stage of slipping. Further in this paper, an attempt is made to automate the procedure of detecting slipping of the overload coupling at the point machine and translate it into an algorithm. Unfortunately, this problem is complicated because precise algorithms are not suitable for the application in instrumentation due to insufficient computation power. It is not allowable to have such instrumentation compute in a manner different from the PC diagnostic software.

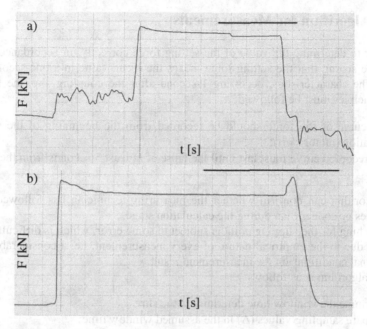

Fig. 3. A curve showing a too short duration of slipping [own study]

Another problem is that the measuring technician does not ensure that the motor operates under slipping for a sufficient amount of time. This problem, however, has been solved in a simple way:

1. provisions in relevant documentation have been made, stating that the coupling slip during measurements should last at least 3 seconds;
2. if the measurement time is not sufficient, the instrumentation must report a measurement error to the measuring technician.

Therefore, it may be assumed that the measuring technician can do their best to ensure a proper measurement. Fig. 3 presents two cases, in which the coupling slip was not maintained for a sufficient amount of time. In such cases, there is no possibility of determining the value of the setting force in accordance with the principle already mentioned.

It is frequent to find a divergence between the concept of the setting force and coupling slip force. As an example, according to [5], the slip force of the coupling can be greater than the setting force, defined by the manufacturer of the point machine, by 50 %. As the provision is not accepted and verified unambiguously, a dangerous situation may result. It is known that the setting force measured during a technical inspection of the point machine is the force occurring during the coupling slip. Nevertheless, there is no ground for accepting the requirement stating that the force can be 50 % greater than the force determined as setting force; here, this is the maximum switching resistance, which the machine can overcome.

4   Algorithm for Measurements

In order to determine the value of the setting force correctly, in accordance with the principle stating that the setting force means the mean value in a one-second period within the characteristics, occurring 1 second after the coupling slip, the following two principles must be followed:

— The curve of the force should be recorded from the beginning of the switching operation (motor start);
— The recorded curve must last until the lapse of at least 3 seconds from the coupling slip.

The algorithm can confirm whether the measuring technician has followed the two principles no sooner than during the calculation stage.

Searching for the slipping point is subject to some error, which is difficult to be estimated due to the empirical nature of every measurement, i.e. a considerable impact of external conditions on the measurement result.

The algorithm is as follows:

1. determine the window time determining the slip;
2. compare sampling values (Δ) in the assumed window time;
3. determine the maximum Δ for the samples collected;
4. define the sample with the maximum value at the interval with the maximum Δ as the slipping point;
5. check whether the samples occurring after the slipping point last for more than 2 seconds;
6. check whether the samples occurring 1 second after the slip are characterised by a dispersion smaller than the known threshold;
7. compute a mean value within the one-second period of the characteristics, occurring 1 second after the slip of the coupling.

Items 1 and 6 can be defined permanently or selected as required.

The algorithm is advantageous due to the simplicity of calculations. In telematic measuring-diagnostic equipment, this feature is particularly significant. Such equipment is often designed using rather basic processor assemblies with a small amount of RAM memory.

Designations used in the block diagram (Fig. 5) are as follows:

WT – window time; ΔF – difference of force value; TmaxF – occurrence of the maximum force in the selected window time WT; $\Delta 1$ – force oscillation in the time analysed; Δ NOM. – maximum force oscillation in the time analysed; PP – slipping point of the coupling; SF – setting force; mean F (t=1s) – mean value of the force within 1 second.

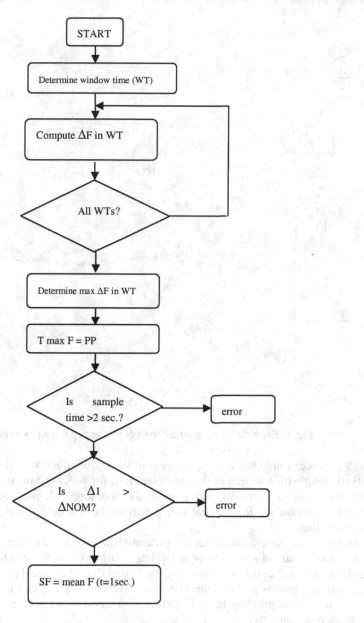

Fig. 4. A block diagram of the algorithm determining the setting force [own study].

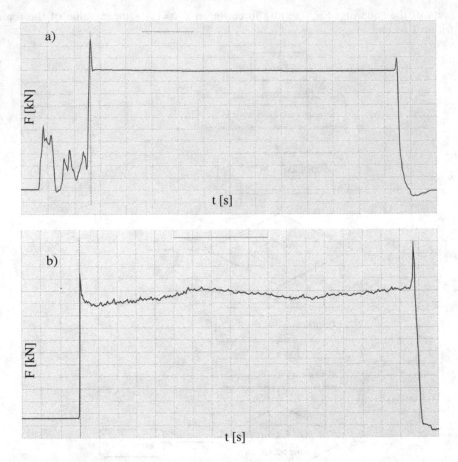

Fig. 5. Example characteristic curves of the setting force [own study]

Fig. 5 shows example characteristic curves of the setting force with the slipping point marked along with a section of the characteristics, for which the mean value of setting force was computed. The slipping point of the coupling is defined by the developed algorithm, marked by the vertical line, whereas the setting force is marked by the horizontal line.

As far as the measurement results presented in Fig. 5 are concerned, a clear increase in the value of setting force at the beginning (a) or at the end (b) of the coupling slip is noticeable. It is a mistake to assume that the values are the setting force.

Experience proves that the interpretation of results is a difficult task. If it is difficult to describe a problem in words, there is a question of how it can be done by means of programming.

In order to avoid doubts during the interpretation, people taking measurements must be required to follow standard procedures.

If the value of the setting force exceeds the range imposed by regulations, it must be added that the analysis should be carried out only if measured values (excluding the peak in Fig. 5a and 5b) are within the tolerance limit as imposed by a given regulation and documentation. Here, many applied devices encounter a problem. Such devices cannot plot the graph of the value being measured, or they provide the user only with the maximum and minimum values, whereas graphic representation is barely legible. Therefore, it is reasonable to force the application of the method for determining the setting force by the instrument so as to limit the possibility of making a mistake during the measurements and interpretation to a minimum.

The analysis detecting the slip of the coupling has been carried out for several hundred curves. In 96 % of the cases, slipping detection has been successful. As the window time increases (100, 500, 750, and 1000 ms), the moment when slipping is detected starts shifting. The situation results from no unambiguous point, at which the characteristic breaks out. Obviously, the setting force has been calculated correctly in both cases.

Therefore, for avoidance of any interpretation-related problems, it has been assumed that the window time should be at the level of 500 ms. More than 500 curves have been tested in the course of algorithm development. Correctness of the accepted algorithm has been confirmed by the analysis. Nevertheless, once the algorithm is implemented in the measuring instrument, it still must be tested carefully.

5   Conclusion

The issues presented in this paper are a continuation of works aimed at optimum algorithms for finding the proper values of forces occurring in the point machine/points system. It seems appropriate to put forward a unified procedure of force value determination in the point motor/points system. Divergence of methodologies and definitions is a source of problems and misunderstandings at the interface of manufacturer – user – research entity. In addition, it is possible that the instrumentation manufacturer participating in the chain may want to implement algorithms detecting and determining values according to the definition. An example of implemented algorithms may be found in one piece of the equipment applied in railway. This is the first device in the world, which indicates the value of setting force, not the minimum or maximum values. The value of setting force is computed directly after a field measurement and is presented at once. Other manufacturers calculate the value of the setting force (or indicate the range in which it can be found) not earlier than after carrying out a PC computer analysis. The applied algorithms considerably speed up diagnostics and allow a wider implementation in telematic monitoring and diagnostic systems of point machines.

References

1. Instruction Ie7 (E14) – Technical diagnostic and periodic inspection instruction of rail traffic control devices, Warsaw (2005)
2. Instruction Ie12 (E24) – Instruction for maintenance, inspection and current repairs of rail traffic control devices, Warsaw (2005)
3. Dokumentacja techniczno – ruchowa nr DTR-2006/EBISwitch 700, Bombardier, Katowice (2006)

4. Technische Mitteilung - als Handlungsanweisung gemäß Konzernrichtlinie 138.0202 - zum sicherungstechnischen Regelwerk (Stell- und Überwachungssystem), TM 2007 – 040 I.NVT (F), 09.03.2007, DB Netz AG (2007)
5. Elektryczne napędy zwrotnicowe, Dokument normatywny nr 86/98, CNTK, Warszawa (2000)
6. Standardy techniczne - szczegółowe warunki techniczne dla modernizacji lub budowy linii kolejowych do prędkości Vmax ≤ 200 km/h (dla taboru konwencjonalnego) / 250 km/h (dla taboru z wychylnym pudłem) Tom VI Sygnalizacja, sterowanie i kierowanie ruchem, wersja 1.1, PKP PLK, Warszawa (2009)
7. Burdzik, R., Konieczny, Ł., Figlus, T.: Concept of On-Board Comfort Vibration Monitoring System for Vehicles. In: Mikulski, J. (ed.) TST 2013. CCIS, vol. 395, pp. 418–425. Springer, Heidelberg (2013)
8. Gorczyca, P., Mikulski, J., Białoń, A.: Wireless Local Networks to Record the Railway Traffic Control Equipment Data. Advances Electrical and Electronic Engineering, Žilina 5(1/2), 128–131 (2006)
9. Surma, S., Mikulski, J.: Koncepcja utrzymania i eksploatacji zintegrowanych systemów sterowania o podwyższonym poziomie niezawodności. Prace naukowe Transport z. 95 Inteligentne Systemy Transportowe i Sterowanie Ruchem w Transporcie, Oficyna Wydawnicza Politechniki Warszawskiej, Warszawa (2013)

Smart City Concept – The Citizens' Perspective

Anna Dewalska–Opitek

Silesian School of Management,
40-952 Katowice, Poland
a.dewalska-opitek@swsz.katowice.pl

Abstract. One of the biggest challenges for the European Union is to transform European cities into intelligent, sustainable places of living in the social, economic and environmental context, called "smart cities". The smart city concept is a natural result of the evolution of cities – from knowledge-based cities, through digital cities (cyber-cities), intelligent cities, up to the most complex model – a city based on IC technologies used to increase the interactivity and efficiency of the urban infrastructure and its components. There are six modules creating the basics of functioning and ranking of smart cities concept, i.e.: smart economy, smart mobility, smart environment, smart people, smart living and smart governance. The implementation of the smart city concept in Poland is the subject matter of the paper. It also presents the citizens' approach towards the most important modules of smart cities (with the stress put on smart mobility) and perspectives for its development in future.

Keywords: smart city, smart mobility.

1   Introduction

Highly progressive urbanization is a characteristic feature of the modern world. The urban population of the world accounts now for 53% of the whole population and, according to forecasts of the World Bank, it will be increasing [8]. The reasons for this situation can be traced, among others, in the growing migration to urban areas and transformation of rural areas into peripheral urban districts. Municipal authorities face, therefore, major challenges to offset many adverse effects, such as pollution, noise and congestion, and ensure sustainable development of the city as well as improve the quality of life of residents.

Consequently, it becomes necessary to organize urban space in which it is possible to implement processes to prevent negative phenomena, optimize the use of resources of the city through a network of cyber connections using equally advanced technologies and social capital. Hence there are formed smart and sustainable living environments with social, economic and environmental point of view, called "smart cities".

The scope of the implementation of the concept in Poland is the subject to a closer identification in this paper. The theoretical considerations have been subjected to empirical verification through direct research conducted by a diagnostic survey. The subject of the study was the opinion of the citizens of the Silesian Voivodship on

J. Mikulski (Ed.): TST 2014, CCIS 471, pp. 331–340, 2014.

the most important dimensions of the smart city concept and the prospects for their implementation.

2   The Smart City Concept

The smart city concept is a natural consequence of the evolution of the urban centres from cities as scientific centres, through digital, intelligent, eco cities, to the currently most advanced form - a city that uses information and communication technologies in order to increase interactivity and efficiency of urban infrastructure and its constituent components, and to raise awareness of residents [9].

Knowledge-based cities focus primarily on education, the development of intellectual capital, permanent learning, creativity, and maintaining a high level of innovation. In turn, communication and information technologies found there are the factors in the development of digital cities. Intelligent cities are cities that implement knowledge-based economy. Eco-cities, by contrast, use renewable energy sources and focus their efforts on protecting the environment and its resources. In fact, the "smart" city must combine all these elements. It should also meet certain economic criteria, in particular, have a high level of profitability and ability to compete with other cities in the global knowledge-based economy. Fulfilling these criteria and maintaining a high level of performance requires, first of all, continuous learning, appropriate innovation culture, collaboration and partnerships between local authorities and various user groups of the city. It also becomes necessary to attract and retain high-class professionals and entrepreneurs [2].

The literature points to six elements of the smart cities concept, namely [5]:

- economy (*smart economy*) - cities should have a high productivity, innovation climate and labour market flexibility,
- people (*smart people*) – the initiators of change in cities should be their inhabitants, who, with appropriate technical support, are able to prevent excessive energy consumption, pollution, and strive to improve the quality of life,
- intelligent management (*smart governance*) - development in this aspect requires an appropriate system of city management, developing procedures that require cooperation of local authorities and other users of the city and the use of modern technology in the city functioning,
- transport and communication (*smart mobility*) – thanks to ITC sector, the city is a giant network of high-speed links connecting all the resources of the city,
- environment (*smart environment*) – an intelligent city optimizes energy consumption, among other things, through the use of renewable energy sources, takes action to reduce the emission of pollutants into the environment, and its resource management is based on the principle of sustainable development,
- quality of life (*smart living*) – an intelligent city provides its inhabitants with a friendly environment, in particular by providing broad access to public services, technical and social infrastructure, a high level of security and thanks to an appropriate cultural and entertainment offer as well as care for the environment and green areas.

These elements of a smart city are presented in Figure 1.

SMART ECONOMY
(Competitiveness)

- Innovative spirit
- Entrepreneurship
- Economic image & trademarks
- Productivity
- Flexibility of labour market
- International embeddedness
- Ability to transform

SMART PEOPLE
(Social and Human Capital)

- Level of qualification
- Affinity to lifelong learning
- Social and ethnic plurality
- Flexibility
- Creativity
- Cosmopolitanism/ Open-mindedness
- Participation in public life

SMART GOVERNANCE
(Participation)

- Participation in decision-making
- Public and social services
- Transparent governance
- Political strategies & perspectives

SMART MOBILITY
(Transport and ICT)

- Local accessibility
- (Inter-)national accessibility
- Availability of ICT-infrastructure
- Sustainable, innovative and safe transport systems

SMART ENVIRONMENT
(Natural resources)

- Attractivity of natural conditions
- Pollution
- Environmental protection
- Sustainable resource management

SMART LIVING
(Quality of life)

- Cultural facilities
- Health conditions
- Individual safety
- Housing quality
- Education facilities
- Touristic attractivity
- Social cohesion

Fig. 1. Elements constituting the smart city concept [4]

Therefore, cities can be defined as "smart" when they have human and social capital, traditional and modern transport-communication infrastructure (public transport and communication technologies respectively), their development is consistent with the theory of sustainable development, and participatory governance ensures better quality of life.

There are many world rankings positioning cities in a category of a smart city. It may be noted that these are big cities, metropolises, where both the range of challenges and the opportunities are impressive. According to *the Cities in Motion Index 2014* of the top 20 cities ten are European, six American, three Asian and one Oceanian. Switzerland is the country with the best results overall, with three of its cities ranked in the top 10. A detailed list of smart cities has been presented in Table 2.

Table 1. The top 10 world's smart cities according to *the City in Motion Index 2014* [6]

No.	Index	City/ Country
1	100	Tokyo/ Japan
2	84.3	London/ Great Britain
3	81.2	New York/ USA
4	78.9	Zurich/ Switzerland
5	78.1	Paris/ France
6	75.6	Geneva/ Switzerland
7	70.9	Basel/ Switzerland
8	68.7	Osaka/ Japan
9	68.2	Seoul/ South Korea
10	68	Oslo/ Norway

According to Forbes, the most advanced smart cities in the world are: Singapore, Hong Kong, Curitiba (Brazil), Monterrey (Mexico), Amsterdam (the Netherlands), Seattle (the USA), Houston (the USA), Charleston (the USA), Huntsville (the USA) and Calgary (Canada). The ranking is apparently dominated by American cities.

However, according to *the Innovation Cities Top 100* 2012, the title of Top 10 smart cities deserve: Vienna (Austria) Toronto (Canada), Paris (France), New York (The USA), London (Great Britain), Tokyo (Japan), Berlin (Germany), Copenhagen (Denmark), Honk Kong, Barcelona (Spain).

A separate category is build up by the ranking of medium-sized cities. The number of solutions to smart cities and the extent of implementation of the concept does not allow them to compete with global metropolises. The most advanced European medium-sized smart cities are shown in Table 2.

Polish cities are also in the ranking. They are: Rzeszow, Bialystok, Bydgoszcz, Szczecin and Kielce, occupying respectively 48, 53, 57, 62 and 64th position. The causes of this state of affairs may be sought in the fact that the smart city concept is generally unknown and the costs of its implementation are expected to be high. Such an approach should be considered improper. Expenditure incurred as an investment in the development of smart cities bear fruit not only in the form of lower costs of urban resource consumption, but also in qualitative changes in the form of improving the living conditions of residents, enhancing the image of the place, thereby attracting residents and investors and, consequently, improving the competitiveness of the city.

Table 2. Smart cities – Ranking of European medium-sized cities [1]

No.	City/ Country
1	Luxembourg/ Luxembourg
2	Aarhus/ Denmark
3	Turku/ Finland
4	Aalborg/ Denmark
5	Odense/ Denmark
6	Tampere/ Finland
7	Oulu/ Finland
8	Eidnhoven/ the Netherlands
9	Linz/ Austria
10	Salzbourg/ Austria

3   Smart Mobility

Urban mobility and transport is vital for the functioning of smart cities. Urban mobility means local, national and international accessibility of the smart city, availability of ICT infrastructure as well as innovative and safe transport system. The current emergence of systemic solution in transport is one part of moving towards sustainable mobility. Not only does it enable proper development of a city, but also helps to overcome difficulties notably visible in urbanized, densely inhibited areas, like traffic jams, polluting emissions, noise congestion, separation of living spaces and others.

The idea of smart mobility is introduced in Figure 2.

The user level of the smart mobility should be integrated with transportation services, information collection, management and control as well as transportation company coordination as shown in Figure 3.

In order to maintain or increase the level of mobility for citizens and goods, the current infrastructure should be used more efficiently. One key approach to do this is to encourage multimodality by creating or developing multimodal trip chains always using the optimal vehicle. In this way the route from origin to destination may be constructed in a seamless manner. It requires a technological support - like a smartphone and web applications facilitating the processes of booking, ticketing, and organization of city logistics.

For improving the traffic flow of passenger and freight vehicles, the intelligent transport systems and services (ITS) are implemented. They enable exchanging data between vehicles and roadside units and aim at raising the efficiency, transport safety and reducing congestion.

Technological solutions are also needed in terms of integration of smart grids, battery range and alternative vehicle drive concepts, such as hydrogen fuel cells. Data provision and exchange among the different stakeholders is the key issue for diffusion of new approaches [3].

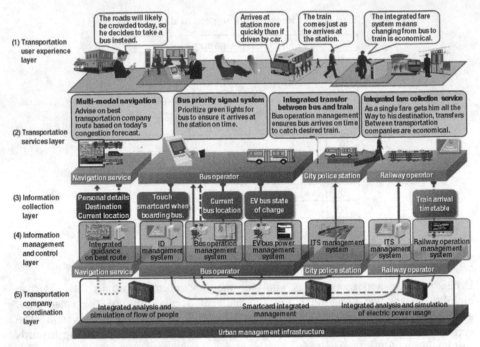

Fig. 2. Urban mobility as a systemic solution [7]

4   The Smart City Concept in the Citizens' Opinions – Empirical Approach

In the light of the presented theoretical considerations, cognitively interesting are the results of empirical research conducted by a diagnostic survey, a questionnaire technique, using a standardized research tool in the form of a questionnaire.

The aim of the study was to get to know respondents' opinions on the smart city concept and the prospects for its implementation in Poland. The survey subjects were urban residents of the Silesian Voivodship. The survey was conducted on a representative sample of 322 respondents. They were mainly people aged 35 - 54, having a secondary and higher education, being active labour force. Detailed sample characteristics are presented in Table 3.

It has been assumed that the maximum fraction estimation error in the binomial distribution should not exceed 5.5% at a confidence level of 0.95.

The spatial scope of the study is the Silesian Voivodship and the time range is from May to June 2014.

The subjects were asked whether they know the smart city concept. From the answers of the subjects it can be indicated that this concept is not particularly popular among the respondents. Only a third of respondents (33%) declared knowledge of the smart city. They were mainly people in employment with higher education (Figure 3).

Table 3. Respondents' characteristics [own study]

Categories	Total sample (%)	Categories	Total sample (%)
1. Sex:		3. Professional activity:	
• female	53	• working	52
• male	46	• not working	48
2. Age:		4. Education:	
• 18 – 24 years	11	• elementary	6
• 25 – 34 years	24	• vocational	17
• 35 – 44 years	27	• secondary	43
• 45 – 54 years	26	• higher	34
• 55 – 64 years	8		
• 65 and more	4		

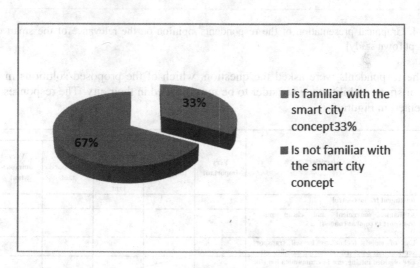

Fig. 3. Graphic representation of respondents' opinion on knowledge of the smart city concept [own study]

The respondents were asked to indicate which elements of the smart city concept would be the most important from the point of view of quality of life in the city. In the opinion of the respondents definitely the most important element responsible for the quality of life is the smart living. Business management (smart economy) is ranked second, and the third - transport and communication i.e. smart mobility. According to the every fifth surveyed inhabitant of the Silesian Voivodship all elements of smart city are equally important. The dependence is illustrated in Figure 4.

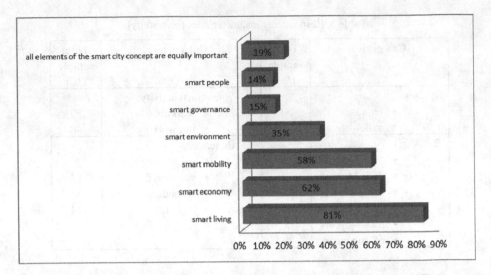

Fig. 4. Graphical presentation of the respondents' opinion on the relevance of the smart city concept [own study]

The respondents were asked the question, which of the proposed solutions in the area of smart mobility they consider to be most needed in their city. The responses are presented in Figure 5.

	Categories	Evaluation				
		Very important	Rather important	Neither important nor unimportant	Rather unimportant	Very unimportant
1	Intelligent traffic control					
2	Available, convenient and cheap public transport to combat congestion					
3	Use of mobile technology to sell transport services (e.g. e-tickets, carsharing mobility, etc.)					
4	Use of video intelligence in communication (for security purposes, marketing, information, etc.)					
5	Adapting public transport for disabled people					
6	Environmentally friendly means of transport					
7	Maintaining the quality of transport infrastructure					
8	Reducing the negative impact of transport on the environment					
9	Reducing the negative impact of transport on the quality of life in the city.					

Fig. 5. Semantic profile of respondents' opinion [own study]

As the most useful solutions in their cities respondents indicated accessible, convenient and cheap means of public transport, the use of mobile technology to sell transport services and reduce the negative impact of transport on the quality of life in the city. In contrast, the relatively smallest factor of importance was, in the respondents' opinion, the use of video intelligence in communication - the weighted average of responses allowed for qualifying this solution as "neither important nor unimportant."

The respondents were asked whether they would like to have their city smart, and the vast majority (96% of respondents) believed that they would. Only 4% had no opinion on the subject. When they were asked to indicate what are the prospects for their city to become a smart city in the next decade, the respondents expressed certain pessimism - every seventh surveyed person declared that they see such a possibility and more than half, as much as 65%, claimed that their city is not able to become smart in the next 10 years; every fifth person had no opinion on the subject.

5   Conclusion

The smart city concept is now a concept of a modern city, well organized, accessible, intelligent and, above all, friendly towards people. World rankings indicate that not only large metropolis may be smart, as more and more medium-sized urban centres successfully implement this concept. The ranking of the European medium-sized smart cities also listed 4 Polish cities, although all of them are outside the Silesian Voivodship.

According to information obtained in the course of direct examination conducted among the citizens of the Silesian Voivodship, the smart city concept is not well known to the respondents. This means, therefore, the need to improve the level of knowledge on the subject matter and, above all, to realize the benefits of implementing a smart city. The key elements of smart city for the inhabitants would be: improvement of the quality of life (smart living), proper management of urban space (smart economy) and efficient public transport and communication (smart mobility). When asked if they would like to have their city smart, the surveyed residents declared that they would, but they did not think that such a change would take place in the next 10 years.

The analysis of the collected empirical material allows for pointing at the existence of information gap in this respect. Of course, the study was regional in nature, and the results may not be generalized. It would be cognitively interesting to make a comparison of knowledge on the smart city concept in other Polish regions, especially among the residents of those cities that were considered smart. This indicates, therefore, the direction of future research on the smart city concept in Poland.

References

1. European smart cities, http://www.smart-cities.eu/ranking.html (date of access: May 16, 2014)
2. Murray, A., Minevich, M., Abdoullaev, A.: Being smart about smart cities. Searcher, vol. 19, special section, p. 20 (2011)
3. Neuschmid, J., Johnsson, A.: Mobility and Transport, http://eu-smartcities.eu/mobility_transport (date of access: May 18, 2014)

4. Smart cities – Ranking of European medium-sized cities, Centre of Regional Science, Vienna UT, p.12 (2007)
5. Stawasz, D., Sikora-Fernandez, D., Turała, M.: Koncepcja smart city jako wyznacznik podejmowania decyzji związanych z funkcjonowaniem i rozwojem miasta. Zeszyty Naukowe Uniwersytetu Szczecińskiego. Studia Informatica 29, 100 (2012)
6. Top 10 smart cities, http://www.businessinsider.com/iese-smartest-cities-in-motion-index-2014 (date of access: May 20, 2014)
7. Smart City Commuting Scenario Pursued by Hitachi, http://www.hitachi.com/products/smartcity/smart-infrastructure/mobility/solution.html (date of access: May 16, 2014)
8. Urban development 2012, The World Bank, http://data.worldbank.org (date of access: May 17, 2014)
9. Wdowiarz-Bilska, M.: Od miasta naukowego do smart city. Czasopismo Techniczne Architektura Wydawnictwo Politechniki Krakowskiej 1, 306–307 (2012)
10. Karoń, G., Mikulski, J.: Transportation Systems Modelling as Planning, Organisation and Management for Solutions Created with ITS. In: Mikulski, J. (ed.) TST 2011. CCIS, vol. 239, pp. 277–290. Springer, Heidelberg (2011)
11. Mikulski, J. (ed.): TST 2010. CCIS, vol. 104. Springer, Heidelberg (2010)
12. Mikulski, J.: Introduction of telematics for transport. In: Proceedings on 9th International Conference ELEKTRO 2012, Rajecke Teplice, IEEE Catalog Number CFP1248S-ART, May 21-22, pp. 336–340 (2012), http://ieexplore.ieee.org
13. Mikulski, J.: The possibility of using telematics in urban transportation. In: Mikulski, J. (ed.) TST 2011. CCIS, vol. 239, pp. 54–69. Springer, Heidelberg (2011)

Areas of Using Telematic Tools in the High Speed Rail Integration Process in Europe

Barbara Kos and Anna Urbanek

University of Economics in Katowice
1 maja 47, 40-287 Katowice, Poland
{bkos,anna.urbanek}@ue.katowice.pl

Abstract. High speed rails services are the most dynamically developing branch of collective transport in Europe. The development of the already existing high speed rail network and the integration of the national systems so that they create strong trans-European network is one of the priorities for European Union transport policy. The realization of this goal depends on implementing modern telematics tools which play dominating role not only in the process of technical harmonization of the trans-European high speed rail network, but also in the process of services integration, thus the integration of the seat booking and ticket sale systems, or the passenger information system. In the article there have been presented the examples of telematics tools used in the integration process of high speed rail in Europe; there have also been presented the directions for telematics development in this segment of passenger transport.

Keywords: transport integration, high speed rails, telematics, trans-European high speed network, interoperability.

1 Introduction

Passenger transport integration is most commonly defined as the organizational process through which the elements of passenger transport system (the network and the infrastructure, tariffs and tickets, information and marketing etc.) of various transport branches and of transport providers cooperate better and more effectively, the result of which is the increase of the collective transport services joined with the elements of individual travels [1].

European Union policy supports the integration of the national high speed rail to one trans-European network. It is one of the means used to reach the most important aims of the Community, to which there belong providing social, economic and territorial integrity as well as supporting the development of the internal European market.

The area of high speed rail transport is the place to use many technological innovations, as well as new solutions within the organization. Building trans-European high speed rail network is significantly conditioned with the use of telematic tools.

J. Mikulski (Ed.): TST 2014, CCIS 471, pp. 341–349, 2014.
© Springer-Verlag Berlin Heidelberg 2014

They play the key role not only in the technical infrastructure integration process, but also allow the providers to cooperate and to integrate the services offered.

2   The Development of the Trans-European High Speed Rail Network

Building the trans-European high speed rail network started on 1980s at the same time in two countries: in Italy and in France. In those countries there appeared first lines for high speed rail. Since that time high speed rail have been dynamically developing in Europe, linking more and more countries (Table 1). In 2008, 25 years after the first line was built, European high speed line was almost 6 thousand kilometers long and connected the biggest European agglomerations, from London, through greatest French cities including Paris, Lyon, then Brussels, Amsterdam and German system with the city of Cologne and Frankfurt.

Table 1. The length of high speed rail lines (km) in particular European cities in the chosen years (for 1st July 2013) [2-3]

Country/ year	Austria	Belgium	Germany	Spain	France	Italy	Holland	UK	Switzerland	Europe	Increase dynamics 1981=100
1981	-	-	-	-	301	150		-	-	**451**	100
1983	-	-	-	-	417	150		-	-	**567**	125,7
1988	-	-	90	-	419	224	-	-	-	**733**	162,5
1993	-	-	199	471	831	248	-	-	-	**1 749**	387,8
1998	-	72	636	471	1 281	248	-	-	-	**2 708**	600,4
2003	-	137	875	1 069	1 540	248	-	74	-	**3 943**	874,3
2008	-	137	1 285	1 599	1 872	744	-	113	35	**5 785**	1282,7
2013	93	209	1 334	2 515	2 036	923	120	113	35	**7 378**	1635,9

Until 2010, the country that has dominated in Europe as far as the length of the high speed lines is concerned was France; currently Spain owns the longest network and it is developing it very dynamically. From over 2500 European lines designed for high speed rail that are currently being built, around 51% is Spanish.

From the moment high speed rail was initiated, the demand of such type of travel is constantly rising. In the countries using high speed systems, the performance made with this type of trains was increased from 0,7 billion passenger- kilometer in 1981 [4] to over 106 billion in 2011 [2]. Within 21 years those performance increased six times and the leaders in this area are France and Germany. Over half of European high speed rail market are the routes in France, where TGV trains are extremely popular. High speed rail transport is also the most dynamically developing passenger transport segment. High speed rail transport market was increasing within 1981-2011 over twice as fast as the air transport market.

Forecasts concerning mobility show that until 2050 it will increase over four times when compared to the level from 2000 [5]. In Europe, particularly great increase is predicted in the high speed passenger transport, meaning air transport and high speed rail transport. However, one should take into consideration the fact that the time of a travel is influenced not only by the given means of transport, but also by the level of system integration that allows for minimizing the time "wasted" by a passenger, needed to gain information, to change the vehicle or to buy a ticket. Therefore ensuring the proper mobility level of the Union members and the transport integration are the basis for common European transport policy and the fundamental condition for internal EU market development.

3   High Speed Rail Integration as One of the Major Priorities of European Union Transport Policy

Transport integration, especially rail transport integration, including high speed rail, has been many times the main topic of White and Green Papers published by European Commission. In the White Paper from 1992, *The Future Development of the Common Transport Policy: A Global Approach to the Construction of a Community Framework for Sustainable Mobility* transport integration was shown as the main factor for collective transport popularity increase in Europe [6]. National rail systems integration into common trans-European network is the main topic of White Paper published in 1996: *A Strategy for Revitalizing the Community's Railways.* Moreover, one of the priorities presented in this document was initiating research and development works on rail sector in Europe. Within the Fourth EU Framework Program there was created a special group entitles *Trains and Railway Systems of the Future,* the goal of which was to support research works concerning the new organization methods and cooperation of rail companies and new technologies in the area of high speed rail, urban transport, traffic management, rail freight transport and rail rolling stock [7].

European rail systems integration and the high speed train development are also the priorities for the White Paper from 2001: *European Transport Policy for 2010: Time to Decide.* In the chapter concerning fast passenger networks it was claimed that the EU widening and therefore increasing the distance among the key points in the border regions of the Community requires creating the network of fast passenger transport. Such network is to consist mainly of high speed rail and the modernized lines, as well as such systems and connections, thanks to which the widely understood integration of two transport branches services is possible: of air and rail [8]. The revision of the White Paper from 2001, performed in 2006, maintained the main goals of transport policy set then, underlining the need to support sustainable mobility need, thus limiting the negative influence of transport on the environment, limiting the passenger transport congestion, more effective use of transport resources through supporting the intermodality and the need to support innovations in the transport sector [9].

In 2011 European Commission published another White Paper *Roadmap to a Single European Transport Area – towards a* competitive and resource efficient transport system. It is a new, very ambitious development strategy of transport in the Community until 2050, again prioritizing the development of trans-European high speed rail system. The central part of the White Paper is the EU inhabitants mobility, especially important for the internal market development and for the life quality and following those, the networks integration that will allow the passengers to choose better means of transport. Interchanges among various transport branches (airports, railway stations, bus stations etc.) should become "the multimodal connecting platforms for passengers" [10]. To the main targets of EU transport policy within the area of passenger high speed rail transport one should include [10]:

- finishing the high speed rail network building until 2050 and tripling the length of currently working high speed rail network until 2030, maintaining at the same time the density of the network in all Member States,
- until 2030 creating general multimodal base TEN-T network, and until 2050 reaching high quality and capacity of this network together with appropriate IT services development,
- until 2050 majority of medium- length travels in Europe should be made by rail transport,
- until 2050 connecting all major airports with the rail network, preferably with high speed rail and undertaking the actions stimulating the cooperation among high speed rail providers, the airports and the air transport providers.

Of the crucial importance in the high speed rail integration process are the modern tools connecting IT and ICT technologies. In EU documents, apart from the technical aspect of infrastructure harmonization, one ought to pay attention to the fact that multimodal journey should be made easier thanks to IT information systems and electronic booking and payment systems.

4   The Role of the Telematic Tools in the High Speed Rail Integration Process in Europe

High speed rail integration may be perceived from two perspectives:

- technical, meaning technical rail infrastructure harmonization in the whole Europe,
- organizational, e.g. within timetables coordination, tariff- tickets, marketing or information integrations.

Technical infrastructure integration is understood as following interoperability, which concerns standardized and compatible infrastructure, technology, all devices and equipment including technical parameters of the means of transport. Interoperability means full technical and operational unification (institutional, legal, financial, physical, cultural and political) in order to increase the efficiency of the provided services [11].

Rail networks interoperability is one of the priorities for European Union, regulated in 2008/57/WE Directive of the European Parliament and of the Council of 17 June 2008 on the interoperability of the rail system within the Community [12]. Due to the lack of compatibility among national rail networks in European Union it was decided to create detailed technical interoperability requirements for specific rail system elements. TSI, Technical Specifications for Interoperability include basic technical and exploitation requirements for the following sub-systems [13]:

- infrastructure (rail lines),
- energy (electrical power supply for the vehicles),
- rail traffic management,
- rolling stock,
- traffic (staff qualification, organization),
- telematic applications (passenger information systems, booking and payment systems).

In the technical harmonization process of trans-European high speed rail network, creating and implementing the standardized system for rail traffic management, meaning ERTMS – European Railway Traffic Management System [14], was of great importance. In Europe there exists over 20 systems for signaling and controlling the train speed and 6 different navigation systems, which greatly limits fluent rail traffic among EU countries and makes cross-border traffic trains be equipped with several system: so called multi-system trains [15]. An example to such may be high speed trains of Thalys PBKA that run among Paris, Brussels, Amsterdam and Cologne and own 8 various signalization systems which influences their defectiveness and the building and maintenance costs [16].

Implementing ERTMS is obligatory in case of high speed rail, as it allows for traffic management with speed higher than 200 km/h when the current system of a train driver reading the signals from line devices is of no use. ERTMS enables passing information e.g. concerning allowed speed directly to the driver's cab (so called cab signalization). The system consists of two sub-systems: ETCS, European Train Control System and GSM-R, Global System for Mobil Communication-Rail. Their functioning is based on devices enabling passing information from devices installed on rail lines to the driver's cab and provide voice contact with traffic dispatchers as well as digital data transmission.

From the European countries experience, ERTMS greatly increase safety level and its implementation offers additional profits connected with bigger traffic fluency, train reliability and punctuality [17]. ERTMS is an example of technological innovation which is the result of common work of rail companies and industry, supervised by European Union. The standards implemented thanks to this systems gave European Union the leading position in rail traffic management systems area.

Telematic applications for passenger transport of trans-European high speed rail system, defined in TSI, include mainly as follows [19]:

- the systems offering information to passengers before and during the journey,
- systems for booking seats and paying for services,

- managing luggage,
- selling tickets in ticket counters, ticket vending machines, via mobile, Internet or other generally available IT technologies, also directly in trains,
- managing communications among trains and with other means of transport.

Technical specification for interoperability for this sub-system (TAP-TSI) mostly include compatibility of the systems of rail providers, infrastructure managers and the service sellers in European Union, together with mutual data exchange which in result is to increase the services integration. The works on implementing TAP-TSI are realized by the team consisting of Directorate - General for Mobility and Transport (DG MOVE), The European Railway Agency (ERA) and the international rail organizations representatives, including The Community of European Railways and Infrastructure Companies CER, The European Travel Agents' and Tour Operator Associations ECTAA, The International Union of Railways UIC, The European Technology and Travel Services Association (ETTSA), and The Association of the European Rail Industry (UNIFE) [20]. The implementation process was divided into three steps: preparing detailed IT specifications, managing and general plan, then working on data exchange system and its implementation as the last stage. According to the settings of one of the last master-plan projects for telematic applications in passenger transport, total TAP-TSI is to be implemented until 2021 the latest [21].

In the high speed rail sector the first activities for integrating the international transport offer using telematic tools were made in 2007 together with creating international strategic alliance Railteam. The alliance consists of seven high speed rail operators: German lines DB AG, French SNCF, Belgian SNCB, Dutch NS Hispeed, national Autrian ÖBB, Swiss SBB and Eurostar International Ltd. Alliance partners are transport providers Thalys International and TGV Lyria. The main goal of the Railteam alliance is to perform actions for increasing competitiveness and attractiveness of rail when compared to other means of transport, mainly through high standard of the journey and passenger service, facilitating buying tickets and booking seats and better information [22-23].

On their website, Railteam offers the search engine, thanks to which a passenger may plan their journey with high speed rail and with traditional national and regional trains (within the network belonging to the team). Moreover, the alliance offers also the service called Railteam Mobile, thanks to which a passenger, having installed the application on their mobile, has access to timetables of majority of European rail providers, a map of main Railteam railway stations, and to the dynamic, current information concerning delays, modifications, cancelled services or changes made in the train composition. The application is installed on the mobiles equipped with GPS (Global Positioning System) and with the proper operational system which also enables planning the journey based on data coming from GPS [24].

Unfortunately, Railteam has not so far managed to realize one of their most goals: to implement the integrated booking and buying seats system. Works over such system, called Railteam Broker, were run from 2007 to 2009. Previously, the system was to cost 30 million euro. However, the project realization was terminated after it turned out that with so big level of differences and complication of the selling systems used by particular providers, the cost of such system would be much greater [25].

Therefore, currently Railteam website each time links a passenger who wants to buy a ticket to the website of the chosen transport provider- an alliance member.

Booking and payment system integration turned out to be possible among air transport and high speed rail basing on the contracts code – share type. Those are the business agreements to code together the flights/ runs according to the modified IATA (International Air Transport) methodology and common seat selling in a contract partner means of transport [26].

In such case rail connection is treated by the air transport provider as the flight extension. Railway stations included in such service have the status of the airport code and are visible in the flight booking system. Such integration level among high speed rail provider and air transport providers requires integrating IT booking systems. Those are so called GDS, Global Distribution Systems, used worldwide, among others, by airlines, hotels or touristic operators. Among the most popular and most noted GDS in the world there are Amadeus and Sabre [27].

In Europe there function only few such agreements. One may enumerate the following [28]:

- tgvair, code-share agreement among SNCF and over 10 airlines, such as Cathay Pacific, AirFrance and Qatar Airways [29],
- AIRail, the agreement among Lufthansa, DB AG and the international airport Fraport International in Frankfurt [30].

In case of German AIRail service, common tickets for flight and for high speed rail may be bought not only via Internet website, but also through the Lufthansa Call Center or a special application for a mobile.

Another example of sale integration among two branches of fast passenger transport may be the project of the international high speed rail operator, Eurostar International Ltd. In 2008 they finished the GDS3, project, which allows to see Eurostar services in the same way as in case if flight providers in the flight booking system [31]. Rail services are sold separately or in connection with flights. GDS3 is designed for touristic agencies and touristic operators, it enables booking via several systems, among which there are Amadeus, Sabre, Galileo/Apollo, Elgar, and Worldspan [32].

5 Conclusion

The integration process in high speed rail sector is stimulated by greater economic integration of European Union member countries, both in technical aspects, meaning infrastructure development, and in organizational aspects, understood as the drive to integrate the services. In order to integrate national systems into trans-European network, there were created legal frameworks, defined in directive concerning interoperability of rail system in Europe. To provide rail infrastructure compatibility and the highest safety at the international level, technical and construction parameters, used in the process of building new lines and producing new rolling stock, were unified. They were described in technical specifications for interoperability defined for particular sub-systems: infrastructure, traffic, energy, rolling stock, rail traffic management and telematic applications supporting the process of passenger information and service selling. Implementing the European Railway Traffic Management System, which is to change over 20 various systems for signaling and controlling vehicles speed that exist in Europe is one of the main tasks realized in order to provide interoperability of the high speed network.

Moreover, among the biggest challenges within national high speed systems integration for the next several years there is mainly implementing the Europe-integrated booking and selling system for rail tickets. It is the chance for the development of integration with other branches of passenger transport and therefore, the chance the increase the attractiveness and competitiveness of the collective transport in Europe.

References

1. Integration and Regulatory Structures in Public Transport. Final Report. Project Leader NEA Transport Research and Training, Study commissioned by European Commission DG TREN, pp.5–7. Rijswijk (2003)
2. EU transport in figures. Statistical Pocketbook 2013, European Commission, pp. 1–82. European Union (2013), http://ec.europa.eu (date of access: May 05, 2014)
3. High speed lines in the World, pp. 1–4. UIC High Speed Department (2013), http://www.uic.org (date of access: May 05, 2014)
4. Igliński, I.: Europejskie koleje dużych prędkości – czynniki sukcesu, teraźniejszość i przyszłość. Transport i Komunikacja 4, 62–65 (2006)
5. Transport Outlook 2011: Meeting the Needs of 9 Billion People, pp. 2–11. International Transport Forum/OECD, ITF (2011)
6. The future development of the common transport policy. A global approach to the construction of a Community framework for sustainable mobility, COM (92) 494 final, 2.12.1992, pp. 5–68. Archive of European Integration (AEI) University of Pittsburgh, http://aei.pitt.edu (date of access: May 05, 2014)
7. White Paper. A strategy for revitalising the Community's Railways, COM (96) 421 final, pp. 3–29. European Commission (1996)
8. White Paper. European transport policy for 2010: time to decide, COM (2001) 370, pp. 5–51. European Commission (2001)
9. Communication from the Commission to the Council and the European Parliament: Keep Europe moving - Sustainable mobility for our continent - Mid-term review of the European Commission's 2001 Transport White Paper, COM (2006) 314, pp. 7–24. European Commission (2006)
10. White paper. Roadmap to a Single European Transport Area - Towards a competitive and resource efficient transport system, COM (2011) 144, pp. 6–12. European Commission (2011)
11. Janic, M., Reggiani, A.: Integrated transport systems in the European Union: an overview of some recent developments. Transport Reviews 4 21, 469–497 (2001)
12. Directive 2008/57/EC of the European Parliament and of the Council of 17 June 2008 on the interoperability of the rail system within the Community (Recast), pp. 1–45. Official Journal of the European Union, L 191, (2008)
13. Pawlik, M.: Interoperacyjność kolei skonsolidowana i uzupełniona dyrektywą 2008/57/WE. Technika Transportu Szynowego 10, 66–67 (2008)

14. Urbanek, A.: Europejski System Zarządzania Ruchem Kolejowym (ERTMS) – stan obecny i perspektywy rozwoju. In: Załoga, E., Liberadzki, B. (eds.) Innowacje w transporcie. Korzyści dla użytkownika, Ekonomiczne Problemy Usług nr 59, Zeszyty Naukowe Uniwersytetu Szczecińskiego nr 603, pp. 241–251. Szczecin (2010)
15. Nowy standard sygnalizacji dla pociągów europejskich, In: Aktualności. Technika Transportu Szynowego 5, pp. 8–9 (2006)
16. Rabsztyn, M.: System ERTMS na linii Rzym – Neapol. Technika Transportu Szynowego 6, 55–56 (2006)
17. Białoń, A., Gradowski, P.: System zarządzania ruchem kolejowym (ERTMS). Telekomunikacja i sterowanie ruchem 1 1, 2–3 (2007)
18. Thompson, L.: A Vision for Railways in 2050. International Transport Forum 2010, Transport and Innovation: Unleashing the Potential, Forum Papers 4, pp. 16–29. OECD/ITF (2010)
19. Commission Regulation (EU) No 454/2011of 5 May 2011 on the technical specification for interoperability relating to the subsystem 'telematics applications for passenger services' of the trans-European rail system, p. 11. Official Journal of the European Union L 123, (2011)
20. TAP-TSI UIC, http://tap-tsi.uic.org/Partners.html (date of access: May 05, 2014)
21. TAP TSI Telematics Applications for Passenger Services. Technical Specifications for Interoperability. Project: TAP Phase Two Transition. 1.0-To TAP Steering Committee, 28 April 2013, Version 1.0, p. 7. http://tap-tsi.uic.org (date of access: May 05, 2014)
22. Urbanek, A.: Alians Railteam jako przykład kooperacji w zakresie międzynarodowych przewozów high speed. In: B. Kos (ed.) Współczesna gospodarka – wyzwania i oczekiwania, pp. 177–185. Prace Naukowe Uniwersytetu Ekonomicznego w Katowicach, Katowice (2011)
23. Röder, J.: Railteam – eine starke Alianz für Europa. Eisenbahntechnische Rundschau 3, 128–129 (2008)
24. Railteam Alliance, http://www.railteam.eu (date of access: May 05, 2014)
25. Barrow, K.: Harmonised fares systems are ticket to success. International Railway Journal 56 (2011)
26. Holloway, S.: Straight and Level, 3rd edn. Ashgate Publishing, England (2008)
27. Shaw, S.: Airline Marketing and Management, 7th edn. Ashgate Publishing, England (2012)
28. Chambaretto, P., Decker, C.: Air – rail intermodal agreements: Balancing the competition and environmental effects. Journal of Air Transport Management 23, 37–38 (2012)
29. TGV air pour vos voyages internationaux, partez depuis la province avec TGV, Documentation TGV AIR, SNCF (2013), http://agence.voyages-sncf.com (date of access: May 05, 2014)
30. Rail & Fly: Unsere Partner – Reiseveranstalter Our Partner Tour Operator, http://www.bahn.com (date of access: May 05, 2014)
31. Interconnect. InterconnecTion Between Short- and Long-Distance Transport Networks, Interconnect deliverable D3.1, An analysis of potential solutions for improving interconnectivity of passenger networks, pp. 1–151. Transport Research Institute, Edinburgh (2011)
32. Eurostar International Ltd. Website, http://www.eurostar4agents.com (date of access: May 05, 2014)

Comparative Analysis of the Roughness
of Asphalt and Concrete Surface

Jakub Polasik and Konrad J. Waluś

Poznan University of Technology,
60-965 Poznan, Poland
polasik@interia.eu, konrad.walus@put.poznan.pl

Abstract. The paper presents a comparative analysis of the measurement results of the roughness for two types of road surfaces. The tests were performed using the British pendulum on the airport auxiliary roads of the Aero Club Piła. The tests were done for concrete and bituminous pavement. The measurements were conducted at four measuring points of the cross section of the road and the roughness was measured six times at each point. The measurements were repeated at every 30m for the longitudinal section of the road with the length of 120m. This situation allowed us to elaborate our own roughness maps of the investigated road surfaces in a form of 3D charts. The authors have assessed the state of the road surface contamination before and after the measurements. During the tests the authors have also conducted the environmental investigations in order to determine the parameters of the road surface and the environment. The roughness investigations are particularly important during safety determination of the road traffic. The parameters of the road surface have a direct impact on the behaviour of the vehicle, its acceleration, braking, steerability and motion stability. These parameters are defined by the interaction between the tyre and the ground.

Keywords: Roughness maps, The British Pendulum, Antislip properties, Concrete pavement, Asphalt pavement.

1   Introduction

The road transport is the most common way for relocation of passengers and goods. The development of motorization was the reason of the general availability of this type of transport. The road transport is used on the roads with a different state and type of the pavement [6], [7], [8]. The road vehicles have to satisfy the conditions which are defined by legal requirements[21], [22]. To permit the vehicle to driving on the highways, the vehicle has to be periodically inspected and has to be equipped with the tyres which have the defined geometrical features. Some other regulations determine the geometrical and antislip features which have to be satisfied by the road surfaces. In Poland, the Ministry of Infrastructure and Transport defines the guidelines for the adhesion coefficient of the road surfaces (Tab. 1-4).

J. Mikulski (Ed.): TST 2014, CCIS 471, pp. 350–358, 2014.

Table 1. Classification of the road surfaces in respect of the antislip properties [1,2,3]

Class of adhesion according to ASRS	Limit values of the authoritative adhesion coefficient	Class of the road surface
A	≥ 0,52	good
B	0,37 ÷ 0,51	satisfactory
C	0,30 ÷ 0,36	unsatisfactory
D	≤ 0,29	poor

Table 2. The parameters of the authoritative coefficient of friction which are required after two months of putting the road into service [1,2,3]

Road class	Pavement element	Authoritative coefficient of friction for the velocity of the locked car wheel			
		30km/h	60km/h	90km/h	120km/h
1	2	3	4	5	6
A	Basic, additional and emergency traffic lanes	0,52	0,46	0,42	0,37
	Acceleration, deceleration and connecting lanes	0,52	0,48	0,44	---
A S,GP,G	Traffic lane, additional lanes, hard shoulder	0,48	0,39	0,32	0,30

Table 3. Classification criteria for basic and additional traffic lanes of the motorway surface [1,2,3]

Macrostructure depth [mm]	Authoritative coefficient of friction [-]				
	0 - 0,15	0,16 - 0,22	0,23 - 0,30	0,31 – 0,38	>0,38
< 0,60	C	C	C	B	B
0,60 – 0,80	C	C	B	B	A
0,81 – 1,00	C	C	B	A	A
> 1,00	C	B	A	A	A

Table 4. Classification criteria for acceleration, deceleration and connecting lanes of the motorway surface[1,2,3]

Macrostructure depth [mm]	Authoritative coefficient of friction [-]				
	0 - 0,15	0,16 - 0,22	0,23 - 0,30	0,31 – 0,38	>0,38
< 0,60	C	C	C	B	B
0,60 – 0,90	C	C	B	B	A
0,91 – 1,20	C	C	B	A	A
> 1,20	C	B	A	A	A

The test results of the road surface parameters are published in the periodic reports of the Assessment System of Road Surfaces (ASRS) which are published on a web site of the General Head Office of Domestic Roads and Motorways[15]. The aim of these tests is the determination of the roughness indicator, road surface texture and adhesion coefficient. The above mentioned parameters of the road surface can be determined by the following methods:

- method of calibrated sand (measurement of pavement texture),
- rotary measuring instrument CT-Meter (measurement of pavement texture)[4], [19],
- method of negative replica (measurement of pavement texture) [9,10],
- dynamometer trailer STR-3 and SRT-4 (measurement of adhesion coefficient)[11,12],
- British pendulum (roughness rate of pavement)[23],
- mobile roughness tester T2GO.

The paper presents the results of the experimental investigations on determination of the roughness rate for bituminous and concrete road surfaces with the application of the British pendulum.

2   The Methodology and Points of Measurement

The measurements with the use of the British pendulum BSRT (British Portable Skid Resistance Tester) allow to represent the motion conditions of a vehicle wheel which is moving with the velocity of 50-60km/h. The investigations of the roughness rate are preceded by levelling the measuring device with the application of adjusting screws. The pendulum should move in accordance with the vehicle movement on the investigated measuring length. The calibration consists in setting the length of the slide of the certified rubber pad by the vertical adjustment of the distance between the slider and road surface. Next step is wetting the road surface and lock release of the pendulum arm. During the return path the pendulum arm must be stopped. After one measurement the roughness value can be read on the pendulum scale [23].

Fig. 1. View of the British pendulum [own study]

Two types of road surfaces, i.e. bituminous and concrete one, have been chosen to compare the roughness values. The tests were performed on the auxiliary roads of the airport in Piła. The first road was a concrete road which is placed along the forest. The measurements were done for equal intervals, i.e. 5m, and connections of reinforced slabs were omitted. (Fig. 2).

The second road was a bituminous road which was used as an access road to hangars and taxing road (Fig. 3).

Fig. 2. View of the investigated concrete pavement (left photo) and its structure (right photo) [own study]

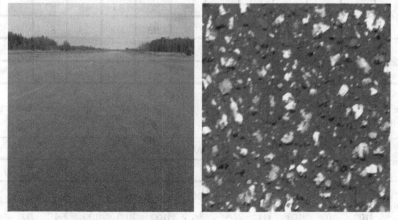

Fig. 3. View of the investigated bituminous pavement (left photo) and its structure (right photo) [own study]

3   The Measurement Results

The experimental investigations on determination of the roughness rate of the road surface were performed for two spots at the airport in Piła. The first measurement was done on the concrete pavement which was characterised by a lack of longitudinal inclination. The second measurement was done for the asphalt road which was used for ground handling and was used as an access road to hangars. The longitudinal inclination of this road was equal to 0°. For both cases the measurements were conducted on a test section of the road for equal intervals, i.e. 30m, and at four measuring points across the road. The results of the conducted experimental investigations are presented in Tables 5 and 6.

Table 5. The measurement results of the roughness rate for the concrete pavement from 24 November 2013 [own study]

Distance	Measurements											
	I			II			III			IV		
0m	73,4	73,4	73	73	74	72	69	70	69	70	69	69
	74	74	74	74	74	72	70	69	68	69	69	69
30m	74	74	74	71	73	72	73	74	74	86	86	87
	72	73	73	71	73	73	74	74	74	86	86	86
60m	85	86	80	80	81	80	80	85	85	85	85	85
	80	84	83	81	80	80	85	85	85	85	85	85
90m	85	81	82	78	77	78	83	84	84	66	85	85
	83	82	83	78	78	76	82	84	84	85	85	85
120m	83	80	80	85	84	85	80	87	83	87	88	88
	83	83	83	85	85	84	83	80	83	88	88	86
150m	80	80	80	78	78	78	81	82	82	81	84	84
	80	80	80	78	78	77	81	83	83	83	84	83

Table 6. The measurement results of the roughness rate for the bituminous pavement from 24 November 2013 [own study]

Distance	Measurements											
	I			II			III			IV		
0m	94	103	100	90	96	96	96	100	100	92	96	96
	100	103	103	94	95	96	100	100	100	94	97	98
30m	90	92	90	95	100	100	102	95	100	95	101	100
	90	94	92	100	100	100	102	98	100	98	103	100
60m	95	102	100	100	100	100	94	105	102	93	90	94
	100	101	100	100	100	100	100	105	105	94	92	94
90m	97	102	107	105	96	105	103	100	104	98	100	100
	97	105	106	105	104	105	104	104	78	102	100	98
120m	95	96	96	95	96	100	100	102	101	102	102	102
	95	96	96	97	96	96	100	102	100	103	103	101

4 Analysis of the Measurement Results

All measurements were performed for similar environmental conditions. The investigated road surface was dry and clean, and ambient temperature was equal to +4,0°C (concrete pavement) and +5,1°C (asphalt pavement). Graphical image of the pavement roughness is presented in Figures 4 and 5.

Concrete pavement is characterised by uniform results and curve profile for the particular measurements across the road (Fig. 4). The initial measuring point was placed in a small distance form intersection of access and auxiliary roads. So, we can conclude that the area of intensive using is characterised by a lower porosity and low roughness rate of the pavement. Concrete pavement is characterised by small fluctuations of the obtained results. This fact indicates the uniform wear of the road surface.

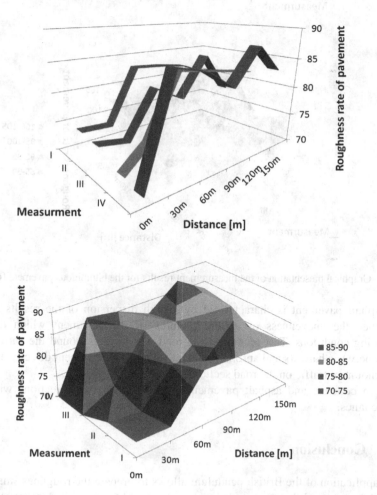

Fig. 4. Graphical presentation of the measurement results for the concrete pavement [own study]

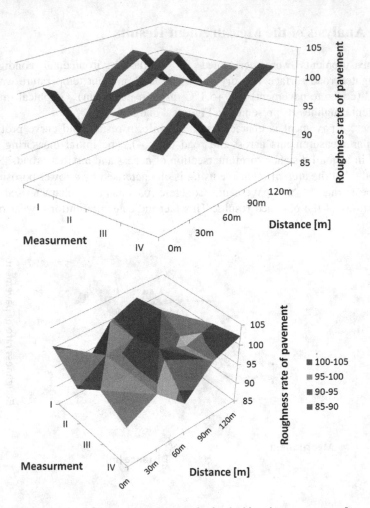

Fig. 5. Graphical presentation of the measurement results for the bituminous pavement [own study]

Asphalt pavement is characterised by a high dispersion of the results. This fact indicates the unevenness of texture features of the pavement which depend on operating conditions. Test section of the road was located around the various access roads between hangars and apron. The local wear of the pavement directly depends on the amount of traffic on the road section.

Both concrete and asphalt pavements were used in two directions without any traffic lanes.

5   Conclusion

The application of the British pendulum allows to prepare the roughness maps for the selected areas, and the characteristics (Figures 4 and 5) give us an information on the local changes of the antislip properties. Comparison of the values of the roughness rate for the concrete and asphalt pavements shows that the concrete pavement is more uniform, but it is characterised by the lower roughness rates. The asphalt pavement is characterised by higher fluctuations of the roughness rate with the simultaneous increase of the value of this rate. The value of the roughness parameter shows the advantage of the asphalt pavements over the concrete pavements. One should remember that the concrete pavement has a higher load capacity and does not deform plastically irrespective of temperature and load.

References

1. Ocena wpływu typu i technologii wykonania nawierzchni drogowej na hałaśliwość ruchu drogowego i jego uciążliwość dla środowiska, Instytut Badawczy Dróg i Mostów, Zakład Technologii Nawierzchni, Pracownia Technologii Nawierzchni, Temat WS-05, Sprawozdanie końcowe, Warszawa (2005)
2. Rozporządzenie Ministra Transportu i Gospodarki Morskiej z dnia 2 marca 1999 r. w sprawie warunków technicznych, jakim powinny odpowiadać drogi publiczne i ich usytuowanie
3. Rozporządzenie Ministra Infrastruktury z dnia 16 stycznia 2002 r. w sprawie przepisów techniczno-budowlanych dotyczących autostrad płatnych
4. DF-Tester and CT-Meter, Tics Ltd., Transportation Infrastructure Consultation Services Ltd. Dynamic Friction Tester, http://www.appliedpavement.com/techResources_equipLoanProg_dftester.html, (date of access: February 19, 2014)
5. DF-Tester Dynamic Friction Tester, http://www.epc.com.hk/uploadfiles/DF%20Tester.pdf, (date of access: February 19, 2014)
6. Dudziak, M., Kędziora, K., Warszczyński, J.: Szorstkość suchej nawierzchni bitumicznej a efektywność intensywnego hamowania samochodu osobowego. Zeszyty Naukowe PP 60, 41–48 (2006)
7. Grajek, M.: Współczynnik przyczepności koła ogumionego do jezdni w funkcji prędkości i poślizgu. Praca Inżynierska WMRiT, p. 85. Poznań (2007)
8. Heller, S.: Pavement management system on the strategic and operative level. In: Proceedings of The 3rd European Pavement & Asset Management Conference, Portugal (2008)
9. Kędziora, K.: Parametryzacja cech geometrycznych nawierzchni drogowych w aspekcie efektywności hamowania samochodu osobowego. Rozprawa doktorska, Poznań (2006)
10. Kędziora, K., Waluś, J.K.: Makrotekstura nawierzchni a bezpieczeństwo ruchu pojazdu. Warszawa (2003)
11. Mechowski, T.: Pomiar współczynnika tarcia nawierzchni dróg krajowych. Zeszyty naukowe instytutu pojazdów, Warszawa (2009)
12. Pokorski, J., Reński, A., Sar, H.: SRT-4 Nowa generacja zestawu pomiarowego do badania przyczepności nawierzchni drogowych i opon samochodowych. Zeszyty Naukowe Instytutu Pojazdów 2(74) (2009)
13. Pokorski, J., Szwabik, B.: Doświadczalne i obliczeniowe charakterystyki przyczepności opon samochodowych i nawierzchni drogowych. Zeszyty Naukowe Instytutu Pojazdów 3 (42), Politechnika Warszawska (2001)
14. Pokorski, J., Szwabik, B.: Dynamiczne charakterystyki przyczepności nawierzchni drogowych i opon samochodowych. Czasopismo Techniczne 6M/1998. Wydawnictwo Politechniki Krakowskiej (1995)

15. Radzikowski, M., Forys, G.: Raport o stanie technicznym nawierzchni sieci dróg krajowych na koniec 2007. Generalna Dyrekcja Dróg Krajowych i Autostrad, Warszawa (2008)
16. Rozporządzenie Ministra Infrastruktury z dnia 16.1.2002r w sprawie przepisów techniczno – budowlanych dotyczących autostrad płatnych. Dziennik Ustaw nr 12, poz. 116
17. Rozporządzenie Ministra Transportu i Gospodarki Morskiej z dnia 2 marca 1999r w sprawie warunków technicznych jakimi powinny odpowiadać drogi publiczne i ich usytuowanie. Dziennik Ustaw nr 43, poz. 430
18. Sołowczuk, A.: Ocena stanu dróg i ich wartosci użytkowych. Autostrady, nr 10 (2008)
19. Standard Test Method for Measuring Paved Surface Frictional Properties Using the Dynamic Friction Tester, ASTM E1911 – 09ae1
20. Staniek, M.: Metody oceny stanu sieci nawierzchni drogowych. Zeszyty Naukowe Politechniki Śląskiej, Transport Z.72 (2011)
21. Sudyka, J., Mechowski, T., Harasim, P.: Nowoczesne metody oceny stanu nawierzchni w utrzymaniu sieci drogowej. IV Miedzynarodowa Konferencja "Nowoczesne technologie w budownictwie drogowym", Poznan (2009)
22. Sybylski, D., et al.: Ocena stanu nawierzchni dróg. Autostrady, nr 7 (2007)
23. Wahadło angielskie do pomiaru tarcia (wahadłowy wskaźnik szorstkości PTV) – Instrukcja obsługi

Hierarchical Hydrographic Data Fusion for Precise Port Electronic Navigational Chart Production

Andrzej Stateczny[1] and Izabela Bodus-Olkowska[2]

[1] Marine Technology Ltd., Szczecin, Poland
a.stateczny@marinetechnology.pl
[2] Maritime University, Szczecin, Poland
i.olkowska@am.szczecin.pl

Abstract. One of crucial problems in the process of precise Port Electronic Navigational Chart (Port ENC) production is the seabed objects charting. General knowledge about the underwater objects is very important for the improvement in navigational safety, especially important in harbour areas. The article presents the concept of hierarchical hydrographic data fusion from different hydrographical sources for seabed object`s detection. Simultaneous processing of 3D seabed model obtained by measuring the water depths, sonar mosaicked images (illustrating the seabed characteristic) and the magnetic anomalies map could be remarkably helpful for discrimination of ferrous features, establishing their highly precise positions and to determine their placing characteristics. An attempt to integrate all the above is expected to provide a significant enhancement of the interpretation of the whole context of the seabed situation. The image obtained from hydrographic data will be much more helpful than considering all acquired information separately as individual data sets. This approach is believed to be of great importance for Port ENC production process.

Keywords: hydrography, data fusion, electronic navigational chart.

1 Introduction

The purpose of this paper is to present the possibilities of fusion data obtained from various hydrographic sensors and to use them for the production of ENC. The authors objective was to present the concept of hierarchical hydrographic data fusion, especially useful for a delivery of fused data for precise Port ENC production. To achieve this goal it is very important to use as accurate data as possible. Some aspects of bathymetric data processing for the ENC production and data reduction were presented in [1,2].

Modern approach to a precise chart production not only needs to be more and more accurate but also more and more complex as well. It should also include hydrographic information about objects hidden under the see bottom. The well-known approach to detect objects lying on the seabed or buried underneath it is to identify magnetic anomalies. Magnetometers are commonly used in marine environment to collect geodata about bottom objects like sunken vessels, unexploded ferrous ordnance and mines,

J. Mikulski (Ed.): TST 2014, CCIS 471, pp. 359–368, 2014.

cables, pipelines and much more, also about underwater archaeological sites. Aspects of magnetometer applications are described in [3,4].

The magnetometer most widely used for marine survey is a proton passive magnetometer. A complex version of this magnetometer is a gradiometer, constructed by using at least two magnetometer`s heads. Using more than two magnetometers allows to obtain much more precise data, taken as the difference between single magnetometer sensors. Another advantage of the gradiometer is that it can detect the location of the target by a comparison of both sensors positions.

Several geometrical configurations of gradiometers (planar or vertical) are possible to use. Some aspects of gathering data by a gradiometer were presented in [5]. A configuration with at least three sensors has a possibility to additionally assess the burial depth of an object. The idea which seems exceedingly interesting is to implement a gradiometer sensor to an Autonomous Underwater Vehicle (AUV) for objects detection close to the seafloor [6].

A very modern and perspective approach to spatial data processing is to use artificial intelligence (AI) methods, especially artificial neural networks (ANN) [7]. Some of them were used to analyse magnetometer [8], gradiometr and also radar spatial data for the marine environment [9, 10, 11, 12] with the idea of ANN implementation [13, 14, 15]. The General Regression Neural Networks (GRNN) application was an especially interesting solution [16, 17, 18, 19].

Various accurate methods of Digital Terrain Model (DTM) construction [20, 21, 22, 23, 24] may be applied in building 3D bathymetric bottom models [25, 26] which could be used during the data fusion process [27, 28, 29].

Often, magnetic data is acquired to crosscheck it with side scan sonar data [30, 31]. Data from one source is complement to other sources in the process of data mining [32, 33, 34].

The proposed data fusion process is divided into two parts: a local data fusion and a global data fusion. The first one assumes a multi-sensor fusion takes place in hydrographic systems: main hydrographic data with reference to navigational data, such as the position, course and data from motion unit sensors. The second includes fusion of final processed hydrographic product, such as bathymetry, sonar mosaicked image and magnetic anomalies distribution map.

The article consists of three sections. Section 2 contains description of a background of a hydrographic data fusion and a commonly used fusion. Section 3 illustrates the concept of multi-sensor hydrographic data fusion in order to obtain more informed interpretation about the subsurface view. The paper ends with conclusions and overview of future work.

The data fusion of different sources like bathymetric data, sonar image and magnetometer survey is a perfect solution for a system where very precise information is required.

2 Background of Research

The data fusion is a widely ranging subject that is extensively applied to many various research areas such as image processing, and intelligence systems [35, 36, 37]. Generally, the data fusion can be divided into three main categories: a multi-sensor fusion, an image fusion and an information fusion [38]. In the hydrographic data fusion we deal with data gained from different hydrographic sensors. In such case the concept of multi-sensor fusion is presented. A pixel and a feature fusion is the next step. The last one is the information fusion which affects the decision-making process. The data fusion from different sources like bathymetry, sonar mosaicked imagery and marine magnetometer survey is an excellent idea for systems where very high precision information is required.

2.1   Hydrographic Data Characteristic

The main issue in hydrographic data fusion lies mainly in characteristics diversity of data gathered by different hydrographic sensors. Proposing the concept of hydrographic data fusion, the authors make use of the data obtained from a high resolution side scan sonar, a bathymetric swath system and a marine magnetometer.

Side scan sonar (further SSS) waterfall views, merged into one mosaicked imagery, illustrate the seafloor bottom characteristic and provide detection of potential surface obstructions. A side scan sonar system consists of a recording device, an underwater sensor – towfish. Transmitted acoustic waves interact with the seafloor and most of their energy is reflected. The returning echoes are transmitted up the tow cable to the recorder, which processes these signals, calculates their proper position converting into the right value pixel by pixel, and then visualizes these echoes on the monitor screen [39]. The inaccuracy in positioning of the towfish is a major issue during the side scan data collecting. The position is calculated from the layback value and offsets the towpoint from the positioning system antenna. For the purpose of object detection and its precise identification, fusion with bathymetric data is commonly used. In the concept of presented hydrographic data fusion, mosaicked imagery is used for further processing flow.

Data collected by bathymetric sensors - multibeam systems (further MBES), provides very precise full seafloor search depth values. The final processed product contains depth areas, points of depths and contours. To provide precise measurements several issues must be taken into consideration. Firstly, the echosounder must be calibrated. During the measurements, a surveyor continuously needs to control the sound speed values. Also, the beam patterns, ping length`s and the whole water area characteristic need to be accounted. The processing procedure is time-consuming. Major benefit of this data is a fact that in such bathymetric system a full seafloor search is obtained with high resolution and very precise positioning at the same time.

Marine magnetometer data illustrates the magnetic anomalies distribution map, which provides detection of a potential submerged or buried ferrous-feature. For successful magnetic anomalies measurements, the surveyor should determine the smallest volume of the ferrous-feature expected to detect. This needs to be also related to the magnetic field intensity that can be reliably detected. Generally, it is 5nT value [39]. Also, several distortions of the signal due to vessel`s hull and towing cable or interference with other high-frequency navigational equipment, need to be taken into account. The magnetometer transducer is towed overboard on the cable, which determines inaccuracy in positioning of the towfish – the same as in SSS measurements. The results are graphs with the magnetic field changes distribution. To improve interpretation, a common practice is to use the magnetic anomalies chart as a texture of magnetic anomalies contour map to bathymetric grid or as a magnetic anomalies 3D plot to sonar mosaicked imagery. For the concept of data fusion, the authors take into further consideration the magnetic anomalies 3D plot.

All of the mentioned hydrographic measurements methods are used to collect the data representing information about the seabed situation required in production of precise electronic navigational chart: depths values, surface obstructions and buried features.

All of these data vary in the processed hydrographic final product. It means that the sonar mosaic imagery, the digital depth model, and the magnetic anomalies distribution 3D plot cannot be easily combined.

2.2   Existent Hydrographic Data Fusion

For the purpose of this section, the authors surveyed the literature on commonly used hydrographic data fusion. Firstly, let us discuss fusion of high resolution side-scan sonar mosaic imagery and bathymetric data (Fig. 1). This kind of integration is commonly used as an aid to more informed interpretation of subsurface view context. A big benefit is completion of another one, e.g. an improved slant-range correction of a side-scan image or removal of topographic effects from sonar back-scatter intensities [40]. Also, it provides full identification of potential surface obstructions: detection, precise positioning and full measurements: depth clearance above the highest point, high above the surface and its dimensions. A high resolution side-scan sonar mosaic and magnetic anomalies distribution data (Fig. 2) is the next type of hydrographic data fusion. This helps to comprehend the context of the seabed situation, especially if there is a need to detect a seabed cable, pipeline or another potential submerged ferrous-object. This data integration is realized in computer software as an image matching result. In general it illustrates seafloor and subsurface geological conditions – by sonar mosaicked imagery – as a background of visualization and magnetic anomalies contour map or 3D plot of ferrous-magnetic objects. The second one is used as a texture layer. In fact, it visualizes the subsurface situation which consists of two different separated data sets. The last type of hydrographic data fusion is an integration of bathymetry and magnetic anomalies distribution map (fig. 3). The knowledge of depth values in the research area is used as a source of information about the laying characteristic and depth situation above and in the vicinity of a ferrous-magnetic object. This fusion type is realized in standard software dedicated to visualization of the data.

The concept of the authors` research work is to integrate all mentioned above hydrographic data into one data set. This approach is assumed to ensure significant enhancement of the interpretation of the whole context of the seabed situation. It will also provide a number of benefits to the user of Port ENC. The major one is a more informed interpretation about the depth clearance and the surface or subsurface potential obstruction. Also, it supports decision making, while safe navigation in harbour areas is guaranteed.

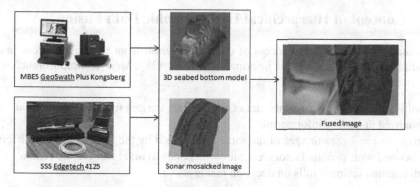

Fig. 1. Image integration: 3D seabed model with side scan sonar image [own studies]

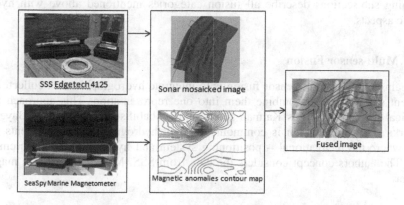

Fig. 2. Image integration: side scan sonar image and magnetic anomalies contour map [own studies]

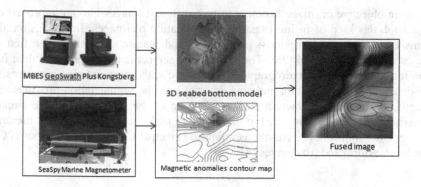

Fig. 3. Image integration: 3D seabed model and magnetic anomalies contour map [own studies]

3   Concept of Hierarchical Hydrographic Data Fusion

The data fusion means any process of data aggregation from multiple sources into a single composite with a higher information quality [38]. Most common branches of data fusion are [35, 38]:

- multi-sensor fusion – fuses the data from various sensors to integrate them into one enhanced in quality information;
- image fusion – uses images of the same area gained by the same sensor, at different times and with various factors, etc.; it corresponds to pixel and feature fusion;
- information fusion – falls on decision making.

Figure 4 illustrates author`s concept of hierarchical hydrographic data fusion. The following sub-sections describe all fusion categories mentioned above with hydrographic aspects.

3.1   Multi-sensor Fusion

The main goal of a multi-sensor fusion is to integrate hydrographic data collected by different sensors and to combine them into one representation. This approach uses statistical methods, such as Kalman filters and probabilistic techniques – Bayesian networks [38]. Such fusion is commonly used in hydrographic measurements systems, where the navigational – positioning system and hydrographic measurements meet. The authors concept considers the data from SSS, MBES and marine magnetometer.

3.2   Image Fusion

The main objective of image fusion is to fuse different images into an improved one. In general, this kind of fusion uses the multiplication of images. Image fusion algorithms consist of two categories: pixel based and feature extraction. The first one merges data pixel-by-pixel [38]. The second one segments the images and then fuses them into one. From the hydrographic point of view, the segmentation presumes feature detection, edge detection and area description. The segmentation provides, also, potential obstructions extraction with completion of the whole subsurface situation context. The algorithms proposed in literature are multi-resolution analysis, hierarchical image decomposition, pyramid techniques, Principal Component Analysis (PCA), wavelet transform and fuzzy rules [41, 42].

3.3   Information Fusion

The information fusion is a multi-level process of combining various data collected from different sources to create the fused information. Moreover, in this stage it is assumed to combine processed outputs of each source to create a new more informing interpretation [43]. The information fusion has two major aims: to support decision making and to improve understanding of the whole context about the area. From the hydrographic point of view, it is crucial, especially during conducting navigation in caution areas such as harbours. The knowledge about: depth and possibility to establish safety areas, dimensions of subsurface potential obstructions and buried pipelines or cables localization seems to be crucial for safe harbour manoeuvres.

The following figure 4 illustrates the concept of hierarchical hydrographic data fusion.

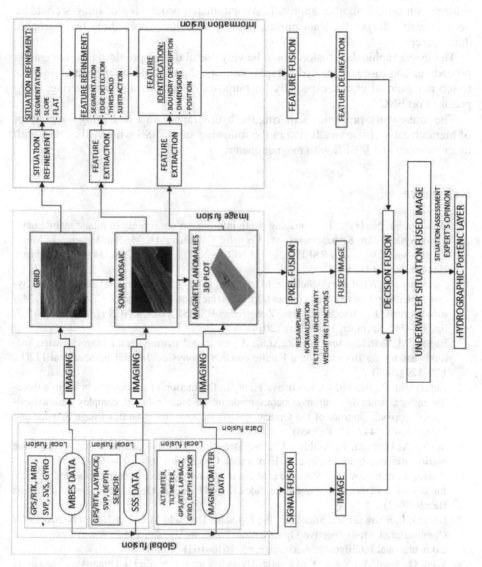

Fig. 4. Concept of hierarchical hydrographic data fusion [own studies]

4   Conclusions

The main intention of this paper was to present the concept of hierarchical hydrographic data fusion. It was achieved by surveying the literature on data fusion methods and handled by presenting schematic diagrams relevant to the nature of hydrographic data. A common analysis of spatial data from different hydrographical tools for data mining is presented. Marine magnetic, bathymetric and sonar data analysis fused together give a hydrographer a chance to obtain much more information than in another approach. An automated processing of images could be very effective during the data mining process with the whole three hydrographic data sources.

The hydrographic data fusion would be very useful during providing the navigation procedure. The fused, from hydrographic sensors, data should be presented on electronic navigational charts, especially for purposes of conducting maneuvering, using precise Port ENC.

The future work presumes acquiring the hydrographic data and using the concept of hierarchical multi-sensor fusion in the following steps: SSS with MBES, SSS with magnetometer and MBES with magnetometer.

References

1. Wawrzyniak, N., Hyla, T.: Managing depth information uncertainty in inland mobile navigation systems. In: Kryszkiewicz, M., Cornelis, C., Ciucci, D., Medina-Moreno, J., Motoda, H., Raś, Z.W. (eds.) RSEISP 2014. LNCS (LNAI), vol. 8537, pp. 343–350. Springer, Heidelberg (2014)
2. Stateczny, A., Wlodarczyk-Sielicka, M.: Self-organizing artificial neural networks into hydrographic big data reduction process. In: Kryszkiewicz, M., Cornelis, C., Ciucci, D., Medina-Moreno, J., Motoda, H., Raś, Z.W. (eds.) RSEISP 2014. LNCS (LNAI), vol. 8537, pp. 335–342. Springer, Heidelberg (2014)
3. Engels, M., Barckhausen, U., Gee, J.S.: A new towed marine vector magnetometer: methods and results from a Central Pacific cruise. Geophysical Journal International 172(1), 115–129 (2008)
4. Berczynski, P., Bliokh, K., Kravtsov, Y., et al.: Diffraction of a Gaussian beam in a three-dimensional smoothly inhomogeneous medium: an eikonal-based complex geometrical-optics approach. Journal of the Optical Society of America A-Optics Image Science and Vision 23(6), 1442–1451 (2006)
5. Salem, A., Hamada, T., Asahina, J., et al.: Detection of unexploded ordnance (UXO) using marine magnetic gradiometer data. Exploration Geophysics 36(1), 97–103 (2005)
6. Araya, A., Kanazawa, T., Shinohara, M., et al.: Gravity gradiometer implemented in AUV for detection of seafloor massive sulfides. In: MTS/IEEE Oceans Conference, Virginia Beach (2012)
7. Balicki, J., Kitowski, Z., Stateczny, A.: Extended Hopfield Model of Neural Networks for Combinatorial Multiobjective Optimization Problems. In: 2th IEEE World Congress on Computational Intelligence, Anchorage, pp. 1646–1651 (1998)
8. Wen, Q., Shao, Y., Yang, Y.: Genetic Algorithm for Calibrating a Three-Axis Measuring System. Journal of Aerospace Engineering 25(3), 431–435 (2012)

9. Lubczonek, J.: Application of Modified Method of Viewshed Analysis in Radar Sensor Network Planning on Inland Waterways. In: Kulpa, K. (ed.) 13th International Radar Symposium (IRS), Warsaw. International Radar Symposium Proceedings, pp. 269–274 (2012)
10. Lubczonek, J., Stateczny, A.: Aspects of spatial planning of radar sensor network for inland waterways surveillance. In: 6th European Radar Conference (EURAD 2009), Rome. European Radar Conference-EuRAD, pp. 501–504 (2009)
11. Lubczonek, J.: Application of GIS Techniques in VTS Radar Stations Planning. In: Kawalec, A., Kaniewski, P. (eds.) 2008 International Radar Symposium, Wroclaw, pp. 277–280 (2008)
12. Stateczny, A., Lubczonek, J.: Radar Sensors Implementation in River Information Services in Poland. In: 15th International Radar Symposium (IRS), Gdansk. International Radar Symposium Proceedings, pp. 199–203 (2014)
13. Kazimierski, W., Lubczonek, J.: Verification of marine multiple model neural tracking filter for the needs of shore radar stations. In: Kulpa, K. (ed.) 13th International Radar Symposium (IRS), Warsaw. International Radar Symposium Proceedings, pp. 554–559 (2012)
14. Kazimierski, W., Stateczny, A.: Optimization of multiple model neural tracking filter for marine targets. In: Kulpa, K. (ed.) 13th International Radar Symposium (IRS), Warsaw. International Radar Symposium Proceedings, pp. 543–548 (2012)
15. Kazimierski, W., Zaniewicz, G., Stateczny, A.: Verification of multiple model neural tracking filter with ship's radar. In: Kulpa, K. (ed.) 13th International Radar Symposium (IRS), Warsaw. International Radar Symposium Proceedings, pp. 549–553 (2012)
16. Stateczny, A., Kazimierski, W.: A comparison of the target tracking in marine navigational radars by means of GRNN filter and numerical filter. In: 2008 IEEE Radar Conference, Rome. IEEE Radar Conference, vol. 1-4, pp. 1994–1997 (2008)
17. Stateczny, A., Kazimierski, W.: Determining Manoeuvre Detection Threshold of GRNN Filter in the Process of Tracking in Marine Navigational Radars. In: Kawalec, A., Kaniewski, P. (eds.) 2008 Proceedings International Radar Symposium, Wroclaw, pp. 242–245 (2008)
18. Stateczny, A., Kazimierski, W.: Selection of GRNN network parameters for the needs of state vector estimation of manoeuvring target in ARPA devices. In: Romaniuk, R.S. (ed.) Photonics Applications in Astronomy, Communications, Industry, and High-Energy Physics Experiments IV, Wilga. Proceedings of the Society of Photo-Optical Instrumentation Engineers (SPIE), vol. 6159, pp. F1591-F1591 (2006)
19. Stateczny, A.: Neural manoeuvre detection of the tracked target in ARPA systems. In: Katebi, R. (ed.) Control Applications in Marine Systems 2001 (CAMS 2001), Glasgow. IFAC Proceedings Series, pp. 209–214 (2002)
20. Lubczonek, J., Stateczny, A.: Concept of neural model of the sea bottom surface. In: Rutkowski, L., Kacprzyk, J. (eds.) Neural Networks and Soft Computing, Zakopane. Advances in Soft Computing, pp. 861–866 (2003)
21. Lubczonek, J.: Hybrid neural model of the sea bottom surface. In: Rutkowski, L., Siekmann, J.H., Tadeusiewicz, R., Zadeh, L.A. (eds.) ICAISC 2004. LNCS (LNAI), vol. 3070, pp. 1154–1160. Springer, Heidelberg (2004)
22. Stateczny, A.: Artificial neural networks for comparative navigation. In: Rutkowski, L., Siekmann, J.H., Tadeusiewicz, R., Zadeh, L.A. (eds.) ICAISC 2004. LNCS (LNAI), vol. 3070, pp. 1187–1192. Springer, Heidelberg (2004)
23. Stateczny, A.: Methods of comparative plotting of the ship's position. In: Brebbia, C., Sciutto, G. (eds.) Maritime Engineering & Ports III, Rhodes. Water Studies Series, vol. 12, pp. 61–68 (2002)
24. Stateczny, A.: The neural method of sea bottom shape modelling for the spatial maritime information system. In: Brebbia, C., Olivella, J. (eds.) Maritime Engineering and Ports II, Barcelona. Water Studies Series, vol. 9, pp. 251–259 (2000)

25. Maleika, W.: The influence of track configuration and multibeam echosounder parameters on the accuracy of seabed DTMs obtained in shallow water. Earth Science Informatics 6(2), 47–69 (2013)
26. Maleika, W.: Development of a Method for the Estimation of Multibeam Echosounder Measurement Accuracy. Przeglad Elektrotechniczny 88(10B), 205–208 (2012)
27. Kazimierski, W., Stateczny, A.: Fusion of Data from AIS and Tracking Radar for the Needs of ECDIS. IEEE Aerospace and Electronic Systems Magazine (in press, 2014)
28. Borkowski, P.: Data fusion in a navigational decision support system on a sea-going vessel. Polish Maritime Research 19(4), 78–85 (2012)
29. Kazimierski, W.: Problems of Data Fusion of Tracking Radar and AIS for the Needs of Integrated Navigation Systems at Sea. In: Rohling, H. (ed.) 14th International Radar Symposium (IRS), Dresden. International Radar Symposium Proceedings, vol. 1 and 2, pp. 270–275 (2013)
30. Sonnenburg, E., Boyce, J.: Data-fused digital bathymetry and side-scan sonar as a base for archaeological inventory of submerged landscapes in the Rideau Canal, Ontario, Canada. Geoarchaeology-An International Journal 23(5), 654–674 (2008)
31. Kazimierski, W., Zaniewicz, G.: Analysis of the possibility of using radar tracking method based on GRNN for processing sonar spatial data. In: Kryszkiewicz, M., Cornelis, C., Ciucci, D., Medina-Moreno, J., Motoda, H., Raś, Z.W. (eds.) RSEISP 2014. LNCS, vol. 8537, pp. 319–326. Springer, Heidelberg (2014)
32. Maj, K., Stepien, G.: The method of the calculating of frequency characteristics of image gaining and processing systems. In: Progress in Electromagnetics Research Symposium (PIERS 2008), Cambridge. Progress in Electromagnetics Research Symposium, pp. 125–129 (2008)
33. Przyborski, M.: Possible determinism and the real world data. Physica A-Statistical Mechanics and its Applications 309(3-4), 297–303 (2002)
34. Przyborski, M., Pyrchla, J.: Reliability of the navigational data. In: Klopotek, M.A., Wierzchon, S.T., Trojanowski, K. (eds.) International Intelligent Information Systems/Intelligent Information Processing and Web Mining Conference (IIS: IIPWM 2003), Zakopane. Advances in Soft Computing, pp. 541–545 (2003)
35. Khaleghi, B., Khamis, A., Karray, F.O., Razavi, S.N.: Multisensor data fusion: a review of the state-of-the-art. Information Fusion 14(1), 28–44 (2013)
36. Stateczny, A., Kazimierski, W.: Sensor Data Fusion in Inland Navigation. In: Rohling, H. (ed.) 14th International Radar Symposium (IRS), Dresden. International Radar Symposium Proceedings, vol. 1 and 2 (2013)
37. Rudas, I.J., Pap, E., Fodor, J.: Information aggregation in intelligent systems: an application oriented approach. Knowledge-Based Systems 38, 3–13 (2013)
38. Ribeiro, R., Falcao, A., Mora, A., Fonseca, J.M.: FIF: A fuzzy information fusion algorithm based on multi-criteria decision making. Knowledge-Based Systems 58, 23–32 (2014)
39. IHO C-13, Manual on Hydrography, 1st Ed., Monaco (2005, Corr. to February 2011)
40. Le Bas, T.P., Mason, D.C.: Automatic Registration of TOBI Side-Scan Sonar and Multi-Beam Bathymetry Images for Improved Data Fusion. Marine Geophysical Researches 19, 163–176 (1997)
41. Hsu, S.S., Gau, P.P., Wu, I.I., Jeng, J.J.: Region-based image fusion with artificial neural network. World Academy of Science, Engineering and Technology 29, 156–159 (2009)
42. Dong, J., Zhuang, D., Huang, Y., Fu, J.: Advances in multi-sensor data fusion: algorithms and applications. Sensors 9, 7771–7784 (2009)
43. Torra, V., Narukawa, Y.: Modeling Decisions: Information Fusion and Aggregation Operators. Springer (2007)

Network Model of the Shortest Path Selection in Transport

Mariusz Dramski, Marcin Mąka, and Waldemar Uchacz

Maritime University of Szczecin, Wały Chrobrego 1-2
70-500 Szczecin, Poland
{m.dramski,m.maka,w.uchacz}@am.szczecin.pl

Abstract. The network models are often used to solve transport problems. In this paper authors propose such application in the field of finding optimal path in transport. Furthermore, a comparison with other known methods is described. This paper touches only the theoretical aspect of transport problems, but the results can be successfully applied to real transport systems.

Keywords: network model, optimization, shortest path, restricted area, Dijkstra algorithm, graph's theory.

1   Introduction

Transport is probably the most important sector of the world's economy. The ensuring of uninterrupted supply chain is necessary for existence and development. All the shipments should reach the destination points safely and on time. This fact is indeed obvious, but requires a lot of work to find a solution. In addition, there is a need to take into account economic factors too.

The most often used approach to solve the shortest path problem in transport is to create a graph of all possible paths in a given area and bring the job to the optimal search path algorithms like Dijkstra [2] , A* [1] etc. This approach is described in literature very well e.g. in [3], [6] or [8]. In some cases researchers propose alternative methods based on artificial intelligence [4], which can be applied when the classical ones fail.

In this paper authors propose the other kind of solution - the network model of the shortest path selection in transport systems. The content is divided into three sections:

- the methodology for discretization of the area,
- finding an optimal path,
- conclusions and summary.

All the results are discussed and a summary is done.

2   Discretization of the Area

The aim of the construction of the numerical representation of the area in the form of a grid (triangles, trapezoids etc.) is the localization of the map points and the relations

J. Mikulski (Ed.): TST 2014, CCIS 471, pp. 369–375, 2014.

between them. In the case of grid the problem focuses only on determining the number of the element which contains the investigated point or the edge between two neighbouring elements.

In this paper a trapezoid grid was used [5-7]. This representation is especially useful when the map is given in a vector form. It allows the discretization of the area with the use of a recurrent algorithm which uses, during the construction process, the existing points – beginnings and ends of vectors defining the objects. The use of existing points results in a very short execution time of the algorithm [5]. Besides, there is a possibility of the local modifications of the grid, so it can be applied in dynamic situations too.

During the creation of the grid a neighbourhood between elements is determined. Four optional are taken into account (Fig. 1):

- upper left,
- upper right,
- lower left,
- lower right.

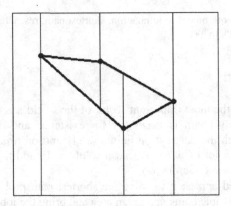

Fig. 1. The trapezoid grid creation process [7]

When the trapezoid grid is created, the prohibited areas are determined. These areas represent coastlines, obstacles, wrecks etc. They also can be eliminated in further stages of processing which results in faster calculations. This solution simplifies the representation of the transport network in a given area and it is applied in the problem described below.

3   The Network Model

The network models are often used in the optimization of transport networks. In this paper we consider an area given in Fig. 2. The grid can be described as an oriented graph where the edges represent the corresponding distances on the map. Let's assume that:

Q – the total number of edges in the network,

A_k^+ - the set of edges coming out from node k,

A_k^- - the set of edges coming into node k,

d_{ij} – Euclidean distance between node i and j,

c_{ij} – weight coefficient representing traffic hindrances,

n – the destination point,

0 – the departure point,

x_{ij} - binary variable where:

$$x_{ij} = \begin{cases} 1 - & arch\ (i,j)\ is\ chosen\ as\ path\ element \\ 0 - & else \end{cases} \tag{1}$$

So, the optimization model is:

$$FC = min \sum_{i \in A^+} \sum_{j \in A^-} c_{ij}\, d_{ij} x_{ij} \tag{2}$$

Limitations:

$$\sum_{i \in A_k^+} x_{ki} - \sum_{j \in A_k^-} x_{kj} = 0 \tag{3}$$

$$\sum_{i \in A_0^+} x_{0i} = 1 \tag{4}$$

$$\sum_{i \in A_0^-} x_{ni} = 1 \tag{5}$$

where: $(i,j) \in Q,\ \ x_{ij} \in \{0,1\},\ \ d_{ij} \geq 0,\ \ c_{ij} \geq 0$

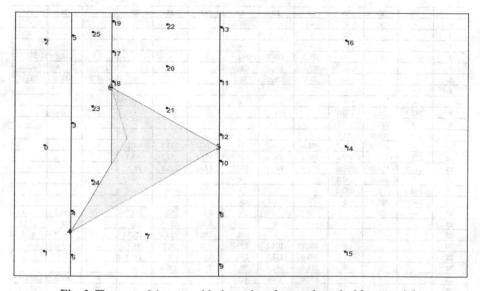

Fig. 2. The map of the area with the nodes of network marked [own study]

The target function allows finding the shortest path between the nodes (0,n). The edges have also the coefficients cij, which represent other conditions and limitations such as: weather forecasts, traffic level etc. Equation (3) is the limitation for each node which allows to choose a single edge coming into node k and one edge coming out from this node. Limitations (4) and (5) are formulated for the start and destination nodes respectively.

Table 1. Distances between the nodes of the network illustrated in Fig. 1. – part 1

	0	1	2	3	4	5	6	7	8	9	10	11	12	13
0	0	240	240	71	156	255	254	-	-	-	-	-	-	-
1	240,0	0	480,0	295,2	104,3	492,7	50,3	-	-	-	-	-	-	-
2	240,0	480,0	0	195,4	391,3	50,5	491,5	-	-	-	-	-	-	-
3	71,1	295,2	195,4	0	-	-	-	-	-	-	-	-	-	-
4	156,2	104,3	391,3	-	0	-	-	-	-	-	-	-	-	-
5	255,0	492,7	50,5	-	-	0	-	-	-	-	-	-	-	-
6	253,9	50,3	491,5	-	-	-	0	139,1	278,3	261,9	337,8	-	-	-
7	-	-	-	-	-	-	139,1	0	139,1	148,0	211,4	-	-	-
8	-	-	-	-	-	-	278,3	139,1	0	-	-	-	-	-
9	-	-	-	-	-	-	261,9	148,0	-	0	-	-	-	-
10	-	-	-	-	-	-	337,8	211,4	-	-	0	-	-	-
11	-	-	-	-	-	-	-	-	-	-	-	0	-	-
12	-	-	-	-	-	-	-	-	-	-	-	-	0	-
13	-	-	-	-	-	-	-	-	-	-	-	-	-	0
14	-	-	-	-	-	-	-	-	267,7	348,7	222,7	264,9	221,5	347,9
15	-	-	-	-	-	-	-	-	236,8	222,1	301,0	445,6	344,8	555,0
16	-	-	-	-	-	-	-	-	450,0	555,9	351,8	238,7	307,3	222,0
17	-	-	-	178,3	369,6	79,5	-	-	-	-	-	201,5	268,0	197,8
18	-	-	-	118,7	302,7	126,0	-	-	-	-	-	190,0	225,0	226,6
19	-	-	-	242,5	436,9	78,2	-	-	-	-	-	233,3	319,9	190,5
20	-	-	-	-	-	-	-	-	-	-	-	100,7	182,2	129,8
21	-	-	-	-	-	-	-	-	-	-	-	113,3	112,5	206,8
22	-	-	-	-	-	-	-	-	-	-	-	160,0	268,1	95,2
23	-	-	-	52,3	240,2	164,7	-	-	-	-	-	-	-	-
24	-	-	-	134,8	77,7	331,2	-	-	-	-	-	-	-	-
25	-	-	-	209,9	407,6	36,3	-	-	-	-	-	-	-	-

Table 2. Distances between the nodes of the network illustrated in Fig. 1. – part 2

	14	15	16	17	18	19	20	21	22	23	24	25
0	-	-	-	-	-	-	-	-	-	-	-	-
1	-	-	-	-	-	-	-	-	-	-	-	-
2	-	-	-	-	-	-	-	-	-	-	-	-
3	-	-	-	178,3	118,7	242,5	-	-	-	52,3	134,8	209,9
4	-	-	-	369,6	302,7	436,9	-	-	-	240,2	77,7	407,6
5	-	-	-	79,5	126,0	78,2	-	-	-	164,7	331,2	36,3
6	-	-	-	-	-	-	-	-	-	-	-	-
7	-	-	-	-	-	-	-	-	-	-	-	-
8	267,7	236,8	450,0	-	-	-	-	-	-	-	-	-
9	348,7	222,1	555,9	-	-	-	-	-	-	-	-	-
10	222,7	301,0	351,8	-	-	-	-	-	-	-	-	-
11	264,9	445,6	238,7	201,5	190,0	233,3	100,7	113,3	160,0	-	-	-
12	221,5	344,8	307,3	268,0	225,0	319,9	182,2	112,5	268,1	-	-	-
13	347,9	555,0	222,0	197,8	226,6	190,5	129,8	206,8	95,2	-	-	-
14	0	240,0	240,0	-	-	-	-	-	-	-	-	-
15	240,0	0	480,0	-	-	-	-	-	-	-	-	-
16	240,0	480,0	0	-	-	-	-	-	-	-	-	-
17	-	-	-	0	-	-	100,7	160,0	113,3	130,0	295,7	56,1
18	-	-	-	-	0	-	101,2	112,5	161,1	66,9	228,0	117,3
19	-	-	-	-	-	0	139,3	218,8	95,2	196,7	363,7	43,4
20	-	-	-	100,7	101,2	139,3	0	95,2	95,2	-	-	-
21	-	-	-	160,0	112,5	218,8	95,2	0	190,4	-	-	-
22	-	-	-	113,3	161,1	95,2	95,2	190,4	0	-	-	-
23	-	-	-	130,0	66,9	196,7	-	-	-	0	168,5	168,5
24	-	-	-	295,7	228,0	363,7	-	-	-	168,5	0	337,0
25	-	-	-	56,1	117,3	43,4	-	-	-	168,5	337,0	0

The headers (vertical and horizontal) of the tables above represent the numbers of the nodes. The data structure is symmetric and the darkened cells represent the orientation of the edge in the graph. As we can see, both tables can be treated also as an adjacent matrix of the graph. The values in the cells are the Euclidean distances between the points on the map.

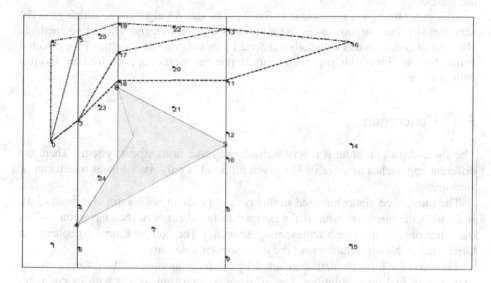

Fig. 3. The result of calculations [own study]

4   The Experiment

The experiment can be divided into three steps:

- Discretization of the area in the form of a trapezoid grid (point 2 of this paper),
- Creating the network model,
- Shortest path search using the network model.

The aim of the experiment was of course to find an optimal path between the start and destination nodes. Nodes 0 and 16 were chosen. Modifying coefficients cij (application of other criteria), different paths were obtained. The results are illustrated in Fig. 3 and in Table 3.

Table 3. The result of calculations for different coefficients

No.	$C_{0,3}$	$C_{0,5}$	$C_{3,18}$	other c_{ij}	Path	FC
1	1	1	1	1	0-3-18-11-16	618,4
2	1	1	2	1	0-3-17-13-16	669,1
3	3	1	1	1	0-5-19-13-16	745,7
4	4	2	1	1	0-2-5-19-13-16	781,1

As it can be seen in Fig. 3. and in the table above, the modification of cij coefficients causes changes in the final result. This is justified because these coefficients are simply the weights of the edges of the graph. Modifying them we change the distances between the corresponding nodes. So the method proposed in this paper gives a possibility to apply other conditions or criteria, not only the Euclidean distance between the nodes.

This experiment was repeated also for Dijkstra and A* algorithms, which gave the same results, but without using the additional cij coefficients. These two methods allow us of course to add some other criteria by modifying the weights of the oriented graph, but the aim of this paper was only to present another approach to the shortest path problem.

5   Conclusion

The shortest path problem is a very well-known issue in transport systems. There are different approaches to solve it. The given proposal is only one of ideas which can be very useful.

The most often algorithm used in this type of problem is Dijkstra algorithm [2-4]. It answers the question: what is the optimal distance between the start point and all the other ones in the graph representing an area ? The computational complexity at $O(n2)$ makes this algorithm one of the most popular solutions.

The need for fast calculations, caused by the huge amount of data, forced the researchers to find other solutions. One of them is algorithm A* [1] with its computational complexity equal to $O(n)$ which makes this approach one of the fastest [3]. The only disadvantage of the A* method in comparison with the Dijkstra algorithm is that in this case there is a need to know the exact geometric position of the destination point. If the destination point coordinates are changed during the voyage, it makes necessary to process the algorithm once again.

The proposed method is able to find an optimal path as well as other well-known algorithms. In further considerations it is necessary to take into account also the computational complexity, which can be significant in some situations, especially if we want to apply it to real decision support systems in transport. The additional advantage of this approach is that it can be applied in other domains of transport, not only in maritime transport.

Besides, in real life the conditions of environment change dynamically, so it leads to the obvious conclusion, that it is necessary to focus on such situations in further researches. Anyway, the proposed method is an excellent introduction to solving the problem of optimal path in the field of transport systems.

Of course, this form of the method described in this paper cannot be applied in a decision support system directly. The paths found are optimal, but also they should be reliable. It is a well-known fact, that there is a need to take into account the dynamics of the moving object. This characteristics is different for ships, cars, trucks etc. Otherwise in real situations in maritime traffic a lot of moving objects are present in the area at the same moment (especially in restricted areas). This is an obvious fact which comes from the development of the global economy.

References

1. Dechter, R., Pearl, J.: Generalized best-search strategies and the optimality of A*. Journal of the ACM 32(3), 505–536 (1985)
2. Dijkstra, E.W.: A note on two problems in connexion with graphs. Numerische Mathematik 1, 269–271 (1959)
3. Dramski, M.: Shortest path problem in static navigation situations. Metody Informatyki Stosowanej 5 (2011)
4. Dramski, M.: A comparison between Dijkstra and SACO algorithms in navigation. In: Explo-Ship Conference (2012)
5. Dramski, M., Mąka, M.: Selected shortest path in the graph algorithms with a use of trapezoidal grid in navigation in restricted area. Archives of Transport System Telematics 5, 3–7 (2012)
6. Dramski, M., Mąka, M.: Algorithm of solving collision problem of two objects in restricted area. In: Mikulski, J. (ed.) TST 2013. CCIS, vol. 395, pp. 251–257. Springer, Heidelberg (2013)
7. Mąka, M.: The recurrent algorithm for area discretization using the trapezoidal mesh method. Zeszyty Naukowe AM w Szczecinie 29(101), 134–139 (2012)
8. Wilson, R.J.: Wprowadzenie do teorii grafów. PWN, Warszawa (2000)

Integrated E-ticketing System – Possibilities of Introduction in EU

Joanna Kos-Łabędowicz

University of Economics,
1 Maja 47, 40-287 Katowice, Poland
jkos@ue.katowice.pl

Abstract. Development of information and communication technologies changes the manner in which many industries and services operate. Those changes are concerning public transport as well. One of the ways public transport can be improved is the introduction of integrated e-ticketing. The point of integrated e-ticketing is combining various modes of transport with use of a single ticket. In principle, the integrated e-ticketing simplifies switching between various modes of transport, making public transport easier to use and thus more attractive to potential users. For more than a decade, integrated e-ticketing system has been one of the goals of EU transport policy; nonetheless, its current application remains limited. Author attempts, based on analysis of existing integrated e-ticketing systems, to show potential dangers and costs connected to introduction of such solutions, along with possible gains for all parties involved – both the travellers and organizations that provide the services.

Keywords: keywords integrated e-ticketing, EU transport policy, e-ticket.

1 Introduction

Information and communication technologies change the way in which industries and services work. This includes public services, among them – public transport system. The development influences the way the travellers look up the information about travel routes and plan their travels; it allows for better organisation of transport flows as well. One application of information and communication technology developments in improvement of public transport is the introduction of integrated e-ticketing. Integrated e-ticketing is essentially a tool that combines various modes of transport – for example buses, trams, car-sharing and bike-sharing – into a single-ticket system. The integrated e-ticketing makes switching between means of transportation easier, simplifying the public transport for an average passenger; this in turn makes it more attractive to passengers. Integrated e-ticketing system became one of the goals of EU transport policy more than a decade ago. In 2011, a goal of integrating various systems in framework for a European multimodal transport information, management and payment system before 2020 was stated as part of 10 goals of transport policy [1]. The CIVITAS (Cleaner and better transport in cities) initiative, co-financed by EU,

J. Mikulski (Ed.): TST 2014, CCIS 471, pp. 376–385, 2014.
© Springer-Verlag Berlin Heidelberg 2014

includes introduction of integrated e-ticket systems in cities as well [2-3]. In spite of that, application of the initiative is not widespread: many European cities (many of those cities are capitals) operate their own integrated e-ticket systems, yet the systems to date are not very numerous and are incompatible with each other. This paper is based on analysis of existing integrated e-ticketing systems; the goal of the author is to demonstrate potential dangers and costs that are integral to introduction of such solutions, along with presenting gains that might be achieved for passengers and providers both.

2   Integrated E-ticket Services

E-ticket is a form of electronic trade, providing new distribution channel for various tickets, for instance: public transportation, long-distance travel by train or airplane, or access tickets to cultural institutions like cinemas, museums or exhibitions [4]. E-ticket systems must contain elements providing security and ensuring privacy. Depending on the specific application of the e-ticket, those requirements may vary significantly. In case of plane e-tickets, security and counterfeit protection is crucial, whilst in other cases client's anonymity is far more important [5]. The point of integrated e-ticketing is combining various modes of transport with use of a single ticket. In principle, the integrated e-ticketing simplifies switching between various modes of transport, making public transport easier to use and thus more attractive to potential users.

E-ticket systems commonly use one of two technical solutions: smart cards or mobile ticketing. In case of smart cards, two types can be singled-out, based on the way they communicate with other devices: contact-based smart cards that require direct contact with reading sensor, and contactless smart cards, read by passing them in proximity to the sensor [6]. In case of mobile ticketing, the role of the ticket is played by cell phone, smart phone, tablet or personal digital assistant (PDA). There are three basic implementations of mobile ticketing: premium SMS based transactional payments, optical character recognition (OCR), and contactless (Near Field Communication – NFC or Radio Frequency Identifier – RFID) [7].

Application of electronic tickets allows for introduction of quality change in applying fare charges, making charging options that were previously infeasible for technical reasons practical. Examples of tools made possible by e-ticket are: fare capping, frequency-based discounts, mileage service, sales channels incentives, time-of-day proving, minus ride system [8].

In many EU cities e-tickets have been introduced in public transportation systems, yet integrated, inter-operatible and multimodal e-ticket systems remain characteristic to large cities (mainly capitals). Author presents short descriptions of chosen integrated e-ticket systems operating on in EU countries.

Oyster card is a e-ticket system for public transportation in city of London, United Kingdom. The system encompasses the following means of transportation: London Bus, London Underground, London Overground, Docklands Light Railway (DLR), Tramlink, London River Services (in limited manner) and National Rail (except the fast trains). The scheme was put in motion in 2003, after completing a test run, as private-public partnership of Transport for London and Department for Transport, and transportation operators: EDS, Cubic Transportation and TranSys consortium (ICL and WS Atkins) [9]. Standard Oyster card has size and shape similar to standard credit card and is blue. Card can store single tickets, period tickets and travel permits added before entering a mean of transport. Card can be charged directly from an account, thorough the Internet or in an ATM [10]. Tourists and business visitors may purchase an Oyster Visitor Card, which works in similar way [11]. Oyster Visitor card provides only means to use public transportation – tourists that wish to purchase e-ticket allowing access to tourist attractions have to use London Pass [12].

TfL (Transport for London), according to goals set by Mayor of London, works towards improving transport quality, reduce pollution in order to curb influence on climate, and increase safety and security of the passengers [13]. In some means of transportation (mainly buses), it is possible to use contactless ticket. TfL plans on improving Oyster card to make all passengers benefit from access to many of the same feature as contactless payment cards [14].

Another example of integrated e-ticket system is „I amsterdam City Card", a system introduced in Amsterdam and enveloping neighbouring Haarlem, Zaanse Schans, Volendam/Marken and Enkhuizen. „I amsterdam" card works for a given time (24, 48 or 72 hours) since first use and allows for use of public transportation (municipal trams, busses and metro trains) controlled by GVB (Gemeentelijke VervoerBedrijf) – city Transport Company [15]. „I amsterdam" card includes free admissions to museums, discounts and seasonal promotions for other tourist attractions [16]; in some cases, discounts are available for the entire year for which it was issued, not only for the time it is valid as a ticket. "I amsterdam" card is compatible with Nederland OV-chipkaart e-ticket system operated by Trans Link Systems (TLS). TLS was founded in 2001 by five largest transport operators of Netherlands: main rail company Nederlandse Spoorwegen (NS), bus operator Conexxion and municipal transport operators of three largest cities: abovementioned GVB (Amsterdam), Haagsche Tramweg Maatschappij (HTM, Hague) and Rotterdamse Elektrosche Tram (RET, Rotterdam). TLS was created in order to design and implement OV-chipkaart system [17]. OV-chipkaart is as large as typical debit card and contains contactless RFID chip that can be used as electronic wallet and contain public transport module that stores information about travels and traveler (e.g. Date of birth). There are three types of OV-chipkaart: personal, P-card, that contains passenger personal data and permits the travel only to its named owner; anonymous, A-card, allowing the travel to any person that owns it, but only one at a time; business, available since 2012 and issued by companies in cooperation with TLS that manufacture their own OV-chipkaart with additional services included [18].

Both "I amsterdam City Card" and London Pass are part of group that consist of 41 e-ticket systems in European cities; the city cards that form the systems allow for use of selected means of public transportation and free admission or discounts to tourist attractions, all in framework of EuropeanCityCards initiative coordinated by European Cities Marketing [19].

Atlas Public Transport Ticketing System (a complete solution developed by French company Xerox) [20] was implemented in 2009 in Riga by municipal transport company Rīgas satiksme. The system was based on BOT agreement (Build, Operate and Transfer) between Rīgas satiksme and Rigas Karte (joint-venture with Xerox) [21]. System encompasses public transportation: buses, trolleybuses and trams. The system does not include private means of mass transport in Riga. The system uses several kinds of ticket: blue plastic cards (both personal and anonymous), valid for five years; temporary cardboard yellow cards, valid for duration of the ticket; and Riga resident's card and pupil's e-card [22]. Plastic cards provide an e-wallet service, allowing for charging the card with e-money and its later use; currently only service that uses this component is parking lot system operated by Rīgas satiksme, but future extension of the system is planned [23].

Table 1 presents comparisons of described integrated e-ticket systems implemented in European capitals.

Table 1. Comparison between described integrated e-ticket systems [own study]

Item	Oyster	I amsterdam city card	Rigas Karte
Funding	Public-private	Public-private (OV-chipkaart)	BOT agreement, public-private
Started	2003	2013	2009
Technology	MIFARE	RFID	NFC
Payment system	Prepaid public transport smart card	Prepaid public transport smart card with touristic features	Prepaid public transport smart card
Includes public transportation	yes	yes	yes
Includes tourist attractions	no	yes	no
Integrated with countrywide system	no	yes	no

It is worth mentioning that integrated e-ticket systems vary significantly: they have different scope of services (some are based only on public transportation, while others encompass tourist attractions) and different degree of integration with national e-ticket systems. Nonetheless, in all cases the initial project was started by public administration with cooperation with transport operators. Detailed description of parties that are part of the implementation of e-ticket system follows in next section.

3   Stakeholders and Parties Involved

Implementation of integrated e-ticket system is a complicated process (not only on the technical side [24]) that requires involvement of numerous participators. All participators must decide on two crucial aspects of the e-ticketing system. First decision concerns entire technical side of the enterprise: choosing used hardware, software and data management system. Equally important aspects of the system are the legal and economic choices: division of labour (tasks and responsibilities), division of revenue, ways of promoting the system and many others. The process described above (technical, legal and economic aspects) may seem simple, but this is an erroneous impression: every city or region that wishes to introduce integrated e-ticket system will have different set of actors and significantly different circumstances that have to be considered.

Analysis of the previously presented examples, along with further research of integrated e-ticket systems show what kind of parties are involved in introduction of an integrated e-ticket system. In virtually all cases, the simplest system requires three kinds of actors: government and other administrative authorities, public transport operators and authorities, and users (both existing and potential). Those are three fundamental groups, necessary for proper operation of the system; each of them fulfils a different role, bears different costs and expects different benefits [25]. Roles, costs and benefits of those three groups of stakeholders are shown in Table 2 [26].

In more complex e-ticket systems other stakeholders can appear; their presence is dependent on complexity of the system, degree in which it is integrated with its external environment and provided additional services. In previously mentioned e-ticket systems, examples of such components could be: ability to charge the card directly from a bank account (financial intermediary), option to use card as an e-wallet (another example of financial intermediary), ability to use the card to receive tourist information or discount for admission to tourist attractions (tourist sector). In case when e-ticket is implemented on a mobile device (mobile phone, tablet, etc.), telecommunication operators are also included. Roles, costs and benefits of stakeholders mentioned are shown in table 3 [26].

Table 2. Possible role, costs and benefits for usual stakeholders of integrated e-ticketing systems

Role	Costs	Benefits
Governments and other administrative authorities		
Provide strategic leadership (e.g. provide incentives, encourage use of standards); support the roll-out (e.g. through additional funding); engage in the integration of existing schemes and coordination of stakeholders.	Costs for financing (pilot) projects; subsidies for installation. Cost for setting up a platform for the stakeholders to push initiatives forward. In case of general project (regional or national) risk of falling to fulfill specific/local needs.	Economic effects: increased expertise in ICT which can be applied to other sectors; better economic conditions for companies so that they locate or expand their businesses in that area; provides identity to the community; potential to implement nation-wide technical specifications. Environmental effects: increase in public transport usage; reductions in traffic congestion.

Table 2. (*continued*)

Role	Costs	Benefits
Public transport operators and authorities		
Offer a well-established market segment (either existing users or additional passengers who will be attracted through the new medium); information about tariffs and prices.	Capital costs: e.g., for buying or upgrading equipment and infrastructure. Operating costs: maintenance and replacement. Additional costs: e.g., for training staff to use and handle new technology or campaigns to inform users about new technology, cost for resolving passengers disputes (especially in the first year of operation). Costs for outsourcing clearinghouse functions for the fare and data collection system, for marketing and distribution.	Reduced administrative costs through automation of manual processes: fewer cashiers needed, reduced fare-processing time, better passenger throughput in high-demand areas. Reduction of fraud resulting from cash handling and fare evasion. Better price differentiation, e.g. flexible fare structure depending on the mode and time of the day. Better transport statistics for planning purposes and thus for a better exploitation of the network capacities. Multi-application potential for a better integration with other services. Safety improvements and better working conditions for operators. Reputation as a modern enterprise.
Existing and potential end-users		
Purchase the products they require based on their preferences and willingness to become involved.	Burden of using new fare medium; time needed to learn handling of the new medium. Costs for purchasing the card. Need to divulge personal information. Loosing e-ticket posses more risks (both financial, and potential for leak of sensitive information).	Improved convenience: no (exact) tariff knowledge needed (if automatic price calculation is available), no need to take card out of the wallet (if contactless); online top-up usually possible; no need to have cash. Time savings due to faster fare processing. Cost savings due to loyalty programs and individually targeted services (if existing). Improved availability of real-time service information (especially when mobile phones are used.

Table 3. Possible role, costs and benefits for additional stakeholders of integrated e-ticketing systems

Role	Costs	Benefits
Tourism sector		
European cities – as a main touristic destinations and major centres of entertainment activities – offer a well-established market segment.	Capital costs: e.g., for buying or upgrading equipment and infrastructure. Operating costs: maintenance and replacement. Additional costs: e.g., for training staff to use and handle new technology or campaigns to inform users about new technology. Costs for outsourcing clearinghouse functions for the fare and data collection system, for marketing and distribution.	Ticketing offers a well-established market segment and thus a strong potential for additional transactions. Reduced administrative costs through automation of manual processes: fewer cashiers needed, better visitors throughput in high-demand areas. Reduction of fraud resulting from cash handling and fee evasion. Better price differentiation, e.g. flexible fee structure depending on the visitors characteristics and time of the visit. Better visitors statistics for events' planning purposes.
Intermediaries: financial service providers		
Develop interoperable application software; access to technical assistance and expertise; issuing contactless cards and promoting them to end-users.	Implementation costs: issuing contactless cards; promoting services to end-users and public transport authorities.	Ticketing offers a well-established market segment and thus a strong potential for additional transactions. Pushing forward the general acceptance of e-payment; replacing small-cash transactions and thus reducing cash handling costs.
Intermediaries: telecommunications operators		
Provide access to customers' mobile devices; development of NCF applications for these devices.	Implementation costs: building NFC chip into mobile devices, possibly promotion campaigns to motivate customers to use NFC. Costs for development and management of NFC applications for ticketing.	Ticketing offers a well-established market segment and thus a strong potential for additional GSM/ UMTS transactions. Additional services generated by NFC technology might attract and retain customers.

In order to summarise, it should be pointed out that every stakeholder in an integrated e-ticket system has a different role to play; same goes for incurred costs and expected benefits. Effective and successful implementation of an integrated e-ticket system requires involvement of all interested parties and cooperation between institutions responsible for supply side of the undertaking. The initial costs are also very high (cost of necessary hardware and software, adaptation of existing system without causing disruption, etc.), while revenues are delayed – this is the main reason governments and other administrative authorities are leading forces of such projects. Nonetheless, there are several cases of initiatives that came from different sources – transport operators themselves – without support from public administration [24]. In case of users of the e-ticket systems (both actual and potential) it might seem that they benefit the most (convenience, speed, cost reduction) [27], but there are issues that have to be taken into account – for instance, education of potentially excluded groups (both digitally and socially excluded – which is most noticeable among elderly people and ethnic minorities), change of habits, and access to passengers' travel history (on one hand, such data provide traffic information and simplify planning for operators, on the other, they cause breach of privacy and can be used to profile a person) [25].

4   Conclusion

Integrated e-ticket systems are one of priorities of EU transportation policy. Numerous initiatives are undertaken as parts of this policy in order to promote and popularise e-ticket systems (CIVITAS, or actions of Science and Technology Options Assessment – STOA, a European Parliamentary Research Service). Another initiative – Smart Ticket Alliance (STA), housed in Brussels and using UITP (L'Union internationale des transports publics – International Association of Public Transport) as secretariat and contact point, begins its operations on 17.06.2014, after its charter has been officially approved. STA is a successor of EU project of Interoperable Fare Management (IFM) that is supposed to work towards interoperability in public transportation on three levels: Local Schemes (travel within a city or a region), National Schemes (within a state or country) and International Schemes (especially in case of cross-boarder travel between countries). The founding members are: ITSO (United Kingdom), VDV eTicket Service (Germany), Calypso Networks Association, AFIMB (France) and UITP Advancing Public Transport. STA is to be a platform for cooperation and coordination of actions with ultimate goal of reaching interoperability of ticket systems in public transportation [28]. Official cooperation in organisation and acceptation of its charter allows other smart ticketing schemes to join STA and its Working Groups [29]. In spite of that progress, considering the sheer number of existing integrated e-ticket systems and differences between them (in applied technology, offered transport options and other services), the success of the plan to complete the goals before 2020 is far from certain. Planned extension of STA role to act as a platform integrating existing systems, along with creation of general standards gives some hope in that regard, but it is too early to judge the effect of planned actions.

References

1. White paper on transport. Roadmap to a Single European Transport Area –Towards a competitive and resource-effective transport system, Directorate-General for Mobility and Transport, European Commission, p. 9, Luxemburg (2011)
2. Cleaner and better transport in cities, CIVITAS 2020, http://www.civitas.eu/ (date of access: May 22, 2014)
3. Innovative ticketing systems for public transport, Policy Advice Notes, CIVITAS (2010), http://www.civitas.eu/sites/default/files/Results%20and%20Pu blications/CIVITAS_II_Policy_Advice_Notes_10_Ticketing.pdf (date of access: May 22, 2014)
4. Haneberg, D.: Electronic ticketing: risks in e-commerce applications. In: Walfens, P., Walther-Klaus, E. (eds.) Digital Excellence, University Meets Economy, pp. 55–66. Springer, Heidelberg (2008)
5. Mut-Puigserver, et al.: A Survey of Electronic Ticketing Applied to Transport (2012), http://www.academia.edu/6150844/A_Survey_of_Electronic_Ticke ting_Applied_to_Transport (date of access: May 24, 2014)
6. Smart Card FAQ, Smart Card Alliance, http://www.smartcardalliance.org/ pages/smart-cards-faq#what-is-a-smart-card (date of access: May 24, 2014)
7. Mobile Ticket to Ride, Whitepaper extract from: Mobile Ticketing Applications & Markets, Transport, Sport & Entertainment 2009-2014, Juniper Research (2010), http://www.juniperresearch.com/reports/mobile_ticketing_appl ications_and_markets (date of access: May 24, 2014)
8. Mezghani, M.: Study on electronic ticketing in public transport, Final Report, European Metropolitan Transport Authorities (EMTA), pp. 30–31, (2008), http://www.emta.com/IMG/pdf/EMTA-Ticketing.pdf (date of access: May 24, 2014)
9. Oyster Factsheet, Transport for London, London (2012), http://www.tfl.gov.uk/ cdn/static/cms/documents/oyster-factsheet.pdf (date of access: May 02, 2014)
10. What is Oyster?, Transport for London, http://www.tfl.gov.uk/fares-and-payments/oyster/what-is-oyster?intcmp=1685 (date of access: May 25, 2014)
11. Visitor Oyster card, Transport for London, http://www.tfl.gov.uk/travel-information/visiting-london/visitor-oyster-card (date of access: May 25, 2014)
12. The London Pass, The leisure Pass Group Ltd., http://www.londonpass.com/ index.php?aid=27&gclid=CIaf06_i2r4CFXLJtAodongAJg#.U4w065qKC Uk (date of access: May 25, 2014)
13. Annual Report and Statement of Accounts 2012/2013, Mayor of London, Transport for London, London (2013), http://www.tfl.gov.uk/cdn/static/cms/documents/annual-report-and-statement-of-accounts-2013.pdf (date of access: May 25, 2014)
14. Business Plan 2013 Transport for London's plans into next decade, Mayor of London, Transport for London London (2013), http://www.tfl.gov.uk/cdn/static/cms/documents/tfl-business-plan-december-2013.pdf (date of access: May 25, 2014)

15. How to use you City Card, I amsterdam, http://www.iamsterdam.com/en-GB/experience/deals/i-amsterdam-city-card/using-your-card (date of access: May 25, 2014)

16. I amsterdam City Card offers, I amsterdam (2014), http://www.iamsterdam.com/en-GB/experience/deals/i-amsterdam-city-card/i-amsterdam-city-card-offers (date of access: May 25, 2014)

17. Twelve years of TLS, Trans Link Systems, https://www.translink.nl/en-GB/Over-ons/Geschiedenis (date of access: May 25, 2014)

18. What is OV-chipkaart?, Trans Link Systems, https://www.translink.nl/en-GB/OV-chipkaart/Wat-is-de-OV-chipkaart (date of access: May 25, 2014)

19. EuropeanCityCards, Your Passport to Europe – See More and Pay Less, European Cities Marketing, http://www.europeancitycards.com/default.asp (date of access: May 26, 2014)

20. Atlas® Ticketing Solution. The futeru is already on board, Xerox, http://www.acs-inc.com/public-transport/central-mgmt-systems/br-altas-public-transport-ticketing-system.pdf (date of access: May 27, 2014)

21. Atlas public transport ticketing system in Riga, Policy Learning in information technologies for public transport enhancement, POLITE, INTERREG IVC, http://www.polite-project.eu/images/good_practices/payment_systems/atlas_public_transport_ticketing_system_in_riga.pdf (date of access: May 27, 2014)

22. Types of e-ticket, Rīgas satiksme, https://www.rigassatiksme.lv/en/tickets-and-e-ticket/types-of-e-tickets/ (date of access: May 27, 2014)

23. E-wallet, Rīgas satiksme, https://www.rigassatiksme.lv/en/services/e-wallet/ (date of access: May 27, 2014)

24. Vasconellos, S.C., Freire da Costa, F.: Electronic Ticketing System: Implementation Process. In: Hensher D.,A. (ed.): Thredbo 10 Reforms in Public Transport. Research in Transportation Economics, No. 22, ed., Sydney (2008)

25. Smart Ticketing, Guidelines for ITS deployment in urban areas, Urban ITS Expert Group (2012), http://ec.europa.eu/transport/themes/its/road/action_plan/doc/2013-urban-its-expert_group-guidelines-on-smart-ticketing.pdf (date of access: May 30, 2014)

26. Integrated urban e-ticketing for public transport and touristic sites, Science and Technology Options Assessment, European Parliamentary Research Service, (2014), http://www.europarl.europa.eu/RegData/etudes/etudes/join/2014/513551/IPOL-JOIN_ET(2014)513551_EN.pdf (date of access: May 30, 2014)

27. Lubieniecka - Kocoń, K., Kos, B., Kosobucki, Ł., Urbanek, A.: Modern tools of passenger public transport integration. In: Mikulski, J. (ed.) TST 2013. CCIS, vol. 395, pp. 81–88. Springer, Heidelberg (2013)

28. Smart Ticketing Alliance, http://www.smart-ticketing.org/ (date of access: May 30, 2014)

29. Newsletter e-TSAP, e-Ticketing Schemes Association in Public transport (2014), http://www.e-tsap.net/newsletter/2014-e5.htm (date of access: May 30, 2014)

Mobile Highway Telematics System on D1 Highway in the Czech Republic

Pavel Přibyl[1], Ondřej Přibyl[1], and Tomáš Apeltauer[2]

[1] Faculty of Transportation Sciences Czech Technical University,
110 00 Praha, Czech Republic
{pribyl,pribylo}@fd.cvut.cz
[2] University of Technology, Faculty of Civil Engineering
602 00 Brno, Czech Republic
apeltauer.t@fce.vutbr.cz

Abstract. Highway management systems belong to modern methods enhancing capacity and increasing safety on highways, while using strategies such as variable speed limits, ramp metering, information about alternative routes or danger on road and others. Typically, they use static infrastructure, i.e. fixed sensors and gantries with variable message signs, which are not very effective in case of constructions.

In this paper, a mobile telematics system (mRLTC) aiming on enhancing the common static highway management system in work zones is presented. Its objective is to inform drivers about the traffic situation ahead and warn them in case of traffic instability. This is essential primarily to increase the safety on roads and secondly also the driver's comfort. The system, its major components and the different modes of operation are presented as well. In order to be able to place the system into operation under real world conditions, an evaluation within microsimulation environment has been performed for an existing work zone on the major Czech highway, D1. In this way, the algorithms and settings of the system can be optimized and its performance and effect on traffic can be determined for different traffic scenarios without any disruption to traffic. The simulation process and its results are discussed within this paper as well.

Keywords: dynamic control, highway, ITS, simulation model.

1 Introduction

The highway D1 connecting two large cities in the Czech Republic, Prague and Brno, has been in operation for more than 30 years. The first sections were built in the sixties are the poor quality of the road surface clearly demonstrates this. Additionally, there is currently no adequate alternative route. For these reasons, the Ministry of Transport decided to modernize this highway. The project should ensure continuous operation of the highway and takes place between the years 2014 and 2018.

The basic objective of this modernization is to change the width of the highway from the original 26.5 meters to 28 meters. This increases the safety on the highway and better access for emergency vehicles. In addition, the adjustment of cross slopes,

J. Mikulski (Ed.): TST 2014, CCIS 471, pp. 386–395, 2014.

repairing drains, laying of fibre optic cables and other changes towards to the overall modernization will be performed. The construction works are divided into 21 sections. At most times, there will be 2+2 lines in operation and only rarely it will be readjusted to 2+1 lines. The latter case will be in operation only for maximal days, and only in cases such as laying bridges and other demanding operations requiring occupation of clearance profile highway. The Fig. 1 shows an example of laying the final surface on one half of the road profile (but still in the 2+2 lines operations).

Fig. 1. An example of a work zone on the highway D1, together with the organization of traffic [12]

The construction work will take place in several sections simultaneously. At present, the driver traveling from Prague to Brno (distance of 200 km) has to pass through a section with traffic restrictions five times. The speed in the work zones is reduced in order to change the character of driving through the narrow traffic lanes.

Currently, the national standards prescribe using of static traffic signs for work zones. The existing regulations even do not require using of traffic sensors to monitor a quality of traffic in the construction areas. Such approach causes well known problems mostly due to the fact that the upstream traffic flow is not regulated. Drivers entering the work zones are not informed about current traffic situation and cannot adjust their driving style. It is demonstrated by research [1], that facing unexpected situations especially those leading to sudden drop of speed result in more accidents and their severity is higher.

Since the mentioned project concerns the most heavily used highway in the Czech Republic and it will spread for at least 5 years, a solution minimizing the social, economic and environmental impact is looked for. For this reason, the work zones will be equipped with a mobile telematics system.

This article describes the basic concept of such telematics system and the arguments for its necessity during such large projects. The real data from the highway D1 are used and together with a microsimulation provide evidence for its usability and necessity.

2   Concept for Designing a Traffic Telematics System

Traffic telematics is a field where the collection, processing and subsequent interpretation of measured data can bring relatively high added value. This is also the main aim of design of Mobile Road Line Traffic Control (mRLTC) System described within this paper. Its basic principle is based on the national ITS architecture developed by a team of experts chaired by the Faculty of Transportation Sciences at the Czech Technical University [2]. This follows the principles from the European project KAREN [3], and FRAME [4]. The French ITS architecture ACTIF (The ITS Framework Architecture for France) [5] is another useful source covering this topic.

The architecture is strongly based on the user needs (UN) formulated by potential users of the telematics system (actors). Based on the UN, the system requirements are collected and these are the source for definition of particular system functions and relations between them, as well as the proposed the physical architecture, Fig. 2.

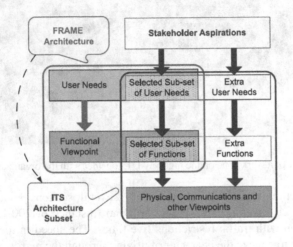

Fig. 2. Process for designing a traffic telematics system [13]

The following issues are a subset of user needs defined for the proposed mRLTC system:

- mRLTC shall monitor and predict traffic status upstream and inside the area with construction works in the time horizon of at least 20 minutes
- mRLTC shall assess automatically all extraordinary traffic situations and transmit information about them to the appropriate organizations;
- mRLTC shall harmonize traffic flow upstream of a traffic restriction to enhance throughput of this section
- mRLTC shall minimize occurrence and impact of traffic accidents
- mRLTC shall integrate data and information from all possible sources.

Based on the user needs, a *System concept document* was prepared, which in a simple manner summarizes the objectives of the system, proposed solution as well as definition of all system constraints and the role of particular stakeholders. Such concept shall not exceed fifty pages and must use a language and terminology which is clearly defined or commonly used within the stakeholder community.

The *System concept* was elaborated by Faculty of Transportation Sciences Czech Technical University in Prague [6] and subsequently approved by all participants in the process, inclusive most importantly the customer, i.e. the Ministry of transport. All the steps needed to design a traffic telematics system and the resulting deliverables are provided and discussed in the methodological guidelines [7].

3   Management of Traffic Flow Upstream the Area of Construction Works

Contrary to the static signs applied to work zones, the mRTLC system aims primarily at harmonization of traffic steam by changing different pictograms at the variable message signs VMS. The harmonization is achieved through limiting the maximal allowed speed upstream to the work zone. It has been demonstrated that speed harmonization has a direct effect not only on the safety, but also on the capacity of the highway [8], [9]. The safety can be further enhanced by informing the drivers dynamically about dangerous situation (such as congestion, or bad wetter) ahead.

The above assumptions are also encouraged by the usage of active traffic signs in the form of LED. It is known that these signs are accepted by drivers much better than static traffic signs as was confirmed by case studies in Germany, where mRLTC is getting more attention in the last time [10].

The mRLTC system described in this paper consists of the following modules:

- two videodetectors which measure traffic flow, speed and ratio of lorries before the work zone
- five Bluetooth detectors measuring travel time;
- two fully equipped graphical boards displaying written text and traffic signs; and
- three pairs of VMS displaying speed limits.

The performance of any telematics system is strongly dependent on the quality of the available data and its interpretation in the form of relevant traffic model. The two videodetectors located upstream the work zone measure basic traffic parameters in each line. This information determines the level of service for incoming traffic flow. Application of Bluetooth detectors in traffic is relatively new. These detectors identify unique ID number of each device using this technology in the target area. This can be a mobile phone, hands-free kit, or other. As our practical experiments on D1 shown, the level of penetration of cars with some Bluetooth technology is about 8-15 %. This is sufficient for reliable travel time estimation.

The position of the detectors is determined by a simulation model. The first one is placed on a location with a small probability of queue occurrence. Knowing the ID and the passing time, the travel time between particular detector positions is calculated.

In addition to the harmonization of traffic flow by speed restrictions, the drivers are additionally informed about the traffic situation on road. In order to do this effectively, prediction of the traffic situation is performed.

A prediction in the time horizon of up to 30 minutes is displayed on the mobile information tables (part of mRLTC system), Fig. 3. The information is available always before the last exit upstream of the work zone and allows drivers to select an alternative route if necessarily.

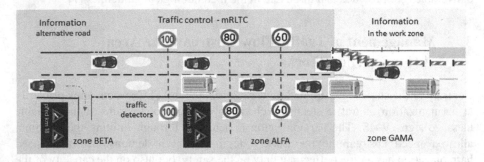

Fig. 3. The three zones for complex traffic management [own study]

The middle term prediction with time horizon of 1 or 2 hours is displayed on the fixed information tables (gantries which are part of the existing highway management system) prior to the work zone. This gives the drivers the option to use a better alternative road and not to enter the problem area.

Last but not least, a long term prediction based on historical models (time horizon 6 to 12 hours) is used to inform the drivers on a web site about the expected traffic situation. In this way the drivers can change the time or route of the trip and the overall travel demand can be affected.

The system works fully automaticaly in the frame of predefined and simulated scenarios. In the case of some extraordinary situation which is not implemented in the control system it is possible to manage each actor (VMS, information board) separately by operator or police.

The incoming traffic is managed through the existing VMS displaying the sign B20 "Maximum speed" and B22 "No overtaking for trucks". The efficiency of the traffic signs can be increased by using additional information or warning traffic signs displayed at second information board placed more close to the area of a construction works. In terms of traffic management it is possible to recognize three zones, as depicted in Fig. 4:

1. ALFA: the traffic flow is controlled most effectively in this zone, using VMS and information boards. Traffic flow is harmonized by speed reduction. It induces a number and consequences of accidents.
2. BETA: is the section before the last free exit. At a sufficient distance before this exit, an information board shows the travel time and appropriate warning signs in terms on accident or queue downstream of the board.

3. GAMA: is the section with construction works. There are narrower traffic lines and drivers should be well concentrated on driving. The fixed traffic signs highlight the necessity to preserve safe distance.

3.1   The Work Zone Model Validation

For the evaluation of the active traffic management, a microscopic simulation model Aimsun [11] was used. The internal parameters of the model have been calibrated by floating car fleet. The data was obtained from 385 floating vehicles, which corresponds to a 3.6% of traffic penetration. The part of this data set was used for calibration and the second part for verification of microsimulation model.

The measured traffic intensity at the entrance to the road segment about 7 km long was the input for microsimulation model. An estimated travel time at the output of this section was the output from model.

Figure 8 depicts a comparison between the travel time obtained from floating cars and the travel time estimated as the output of the model. At first sight it is obvious that the simulation model estimates the travel time very well.

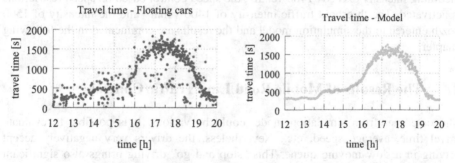

Fig. 4. The travel time as was obtained by floating car fleet (left) and estimated travel time by simulation model (right) [own study]

3.2   Scenarios of Active Traffic Management

According to Czech standards (and majority of national standards other countries), the speed is restricted by static traffic signs about 500 m before a working zone. In contrast to this "static control" the range of traffic management of mRLTC which has been tested by simulation model is significantly enhanced. The length of section under control is 5 kilometers, Fig. 5. The traffic parameters, as traffic intensity, speed and vehicles classes are measured even 7 kilometers upstream of working zone.

The incoming simulated traffic flow was managed by variable speed limit signs placed on the profile 5 (speed limit 100 $km.h^{-1}$), 4 (speed limit 80 $km.h^{-1}$) and 3 (speed limit 60 $km.h^{-1}$). The different scenarios and different input parameters were tested in the frame of searching the most appropriate strategy of traffic management by the simulation model. The positive impact of traffic control will be demonstrated by the model where intensity is input variable. The intensity measured at a greater distance before work zone proved to be more appropriate input parameter to the simulation model than measured queue length. This phenomenon is possible to explain by the fact that a creation of a queue is only consequence of increased intensity far before bottleneck.

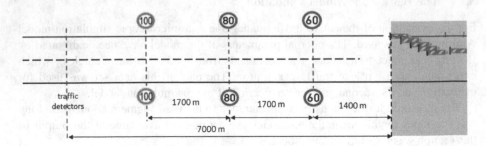

Fig. 5. The scheme of mRLTC [own study]

The incoming traffic intensity is measured 7 km before the bottleneck. If the incoming intensity exceeds 1400 veh.h^{-1}, the speed control based on speed restrictions is activated. The threshold traffic intensity of 1400 veh.h^{-1} and the intensity of 1500 voz/h entered to the simulation model and the results are commented in the following chapter.

4   The Results of Mobile Road Line Traffic Control

The outcomes from simulation model could be various. It is possible to evaluate travel time, average speed, etc.. Nevertheless, the drivers very negatively accept driving in a slow moving queue. This "stop and go" driving brings also significant increase in the number of accidents. This was the reason to evaluate the different strategies of traffic management by the parameter "number of vehicles in the traffic jam". In short, it can be called a "congestion indicator" CI [veh.ΔT^{-1}].

The CI is determined by the simulation model on the basis of instantaneous vehicles speeds within the entire network. If a vehicle's speed drops below 1 m.s^{-1} (3,6 km.h^{-1}) during the monitored simulation time interval (in our case 1 minute), the value of the parameter is increased. The vehicle is considered to be in the traffic jam. The simulation model enables to monitor each car individually through the set of virtual detectors dispersed around the whole road section.

Fig. 6 shows results of simulation for two average values of traffic intensity. The average value 1400 veh.h^{-1} is on the left hand side of figure. The dispersion σ is 200 veh.h^{-1}. The cars are generated randomly according Gaussian distribution. Similarly, it is for the average value 1500 veh.h^{-1} (right side of figure), σ =200 veh.h^{-1} and Gaussian distribution is used.

The simulation time was six hours in both cases. The results in Fig. 6 - left demonstrate, that the mRLTC system significantly reduces CI factor (number of vehicles in the traffic jam). The average number of the cars driving in the congestion is about eight if mRLTC is in operation and speed is restricted through three profiles with traffic signs (var. 1). The number of cars affected by congestion approaches average value about 20, if there is not any traffic control (var. 0).

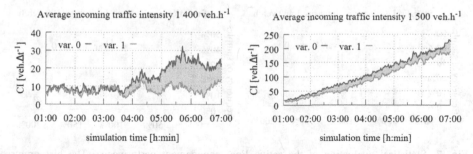

Fig. 6. Comparison of the controlled situation (var. 1) with no control (var. 0) for the incoming average traffic flow a) 1400 veh.h^{-1} and b) 1500 veh.h^{-1} measured 7 km prior to the working zone [own study]

If the incoming traffic flow is still growing the possibility of a reduction of moving queues is limited and the number of slowly moving cars is increasing according time of simulation as demonstrated in Fig. 6 - right. The slope of both curves is similar. However, also this results show that it is advantageous to manage the speed by mRLTC. The difference between var. 0 (without control) and var. 1 (mRLTC) is twenty cars in average.

To demonstrate the performance of the system from other perspective, the following figure depicts a histogram comparing the case of active management and without it. The relative number

$$\varphi = \frac{(Nr\ slow\ cars)_{var1}}{(Nr\ slow\ cars)_{var0}} \cdot 100 \tag{1}$$

for 3600 samples was calculated. Percentage number of samples is depicted on y-axes. The lower value φ takes, the more successful is the traffic control. In other words, the number of vehicles moving in a jam is significantly lower if mRLTC is active.

Statistical evaluation for the average traffic intensity 1400 veh.h^{-1} (Fig. 7 - left) shows that the number of slow cars for mRLTC is frequently in the range between 30-60% in comparison to the slow cars without any control. There are also cases that the performance of mRLTC is worst. These situations express the columns of histogram to the right of the red line depicting the 100%. The level of 100% means that the number of vehicles moving in the traffic jam are the same in the case of active management and without it. Nevertheless, the frequency of these occurrences is very low compared to the positive impact of mRLTC – the columns to the left of the red line.

Statistical evaluation for average traffic intensity 1500 veh.h^{-1} (Fig. 7 - right) looks rather different than the previous case and it confirms the results from Fig. 6b. The mRTC is better within all samples, but the range of φ is limited between 60-90%. In other words, active control decreases the number of slow moving cars by 10 to 40 percent.

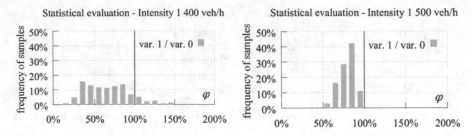

Fig. 7. Statistical evaluation of the active line management performance. The histograms express the frequency of the parameter φ. The average traffic intensity 1400 veh.h^{-1} (left) and 1400 veh.h^{-1}(right) [own study].

In the frame of our research a few of the hypothesis of the traffic control ahead of working zones have been tested. Different input variables entered into the simulation model. The results confirmed our preliminary premise about the measurable benefits of active traffic management. The largest efficiency of traffic management is achieved if the input parameter is incoming traffic intensity measured at large distance before the work zone. The method is able to efficiently reduce the number of slow-moving vehicles by progressive reducing the speed of vehicles approaching to the bottleneck by variable message signs. The slower jam propagation brings secondary the lower number of accidents.

The results of the simulation model of the active traffic control in work zones are prepared for implementation in the real control.

5   Conclusion

The paper introduced the Mobile Road Line Traffic Control (mRLTC) system, which is designed for the management of work zones during the reconstruction works on the main highway in the Czech Republic, D1.

The principles of systematic design of the mRLTC are presented in the first part of this paper. The basis is ITS architecture and definition of a user needs with respect to all actors. System concept document summarizes in a simple manner the objectives of system design. Additionally, the advantages of using short, middle as well as long term prediction was discussed and tits advantages presented.

The major contribution of this paper is in evaluation the impacts of the mRLTC. The stated benefits of such subsystem are in harmonizing of the traffic flow and thus increasing the throughput the road, as well as improvements with respect to traffic safety. This latter benefit was already demonstrated by international research as well as real-world projects.

In this paper, the improvements aiming on driver's comfort are presented. This is caused not only through better information on road, but mainly due to lower formation of queues and slowly moving cars. The control system model was calibrated by the real data measured on D1. This allowed us for example to place the particular system components in a way optimising the effects of the control system.

The results clearly prove usability of the mRLTC system. The throughput increased and the number of slow moving vehicles decreased significantly when the dynamic control was activated. Together with the fact, that the drivers feel better informed and through this fact are tending to drive more carefully and considerate, a major improvement to the overall comfort is achieved by this solution.

Over the next months, the real implementation of such telematics system is expected on the highway D1. The highway administration already started a tender for traffic telematics system on the construction works. This will allow evaluation of the proposed system in the real-world conditions and confirm the simulation results presented here.

References

1. Hellinga, B., Allaby, P.: The Potential for variable Speed Control to Improve Safety on Urban Freeways. In: Transportation Association of Canada Annual Conference, Saskatoon, Saskatchewan (2007)
2. Svítek M., et al: ITS v podmínkách dopravně telekomunikačního prostředí ČR, report 802/210/108, Faculty of Transportation Sciences CTU, Praha, p. 65 (2005), http://www.lt.fd.cvut.cz/its/rok_2005/dokumenty/technicka_zprava_its_2005.pdf (date of access: June 10, 2014)
3. KAREN, http://cordis.europa.eu/telematics (data of access: May 27, 2014)
4. FRAME architecture, http://www.transport-research.info/upload (data of access: May 27, 2014)
5. ACTIF architecture, http://www.its-actif.org (data of access: May 27, 2014)
6. Dopravní telematika při modernizaci D1 - Konceptuální projekt, (Traffic telematics in modernizing D1 – System concept), p. 72. Faculty of Transportation Sciences CTU, Praha, (2012)
7. Projektování dopravně-telematických aplikací; Metodický pokyn (Design of transport telematics systems; Methodological Guidelines), p. 130. ŘSD, Praha, (2010)
8. Cho, H., Kim, Y.: Analysis of Traffic Flow with Variable Speed Limit on Highways. Department of Transportation Engineering, University of Seoul, Seoul, Korea (2011)
9. Papageorgiou, M., Kosmatopoulos, E.: Papamichail. I.: Effects of Variable Speed Limits on Motorway Traffic Flow Transportation Research Record: Journal of the Transportation Research Board, No. 2047, pp. 37–48, Transportation Research Board of the National Academies, Washington, D.C (2008)
10. Kirschfink, H., Poschman, M.: Bauen unter Betrieb – Stau unter Kontrolle. Strassenverkehrstechnik 5, 327–334 (2014)
11. Barceló, J., Casas, J.: Dynamic network simulation with AIMSUN. In: Kitamura, R., Kuwahara, M. (eds.) Simulation Approaches in Transportation Analysis. Operations Research/Computer Science Interfaces Series, vol. 31, pp. 57–98. Springer US (2005)
12. http://www.rsd.cz (date of access: June 10, 2014)
13. http://www.transport-research.info (date of access: June 10, 2014)

Evaluation of the Drivers' Distraction Caused by Dashboard MMI Interface

Marek Sumiła

Warsaw University of Technology,
00-662 Warsaw, Poland
sumila@wt.pw.edu.pl

Abstract. The article attempts to the aspect of driver distraction caused by the embedded the MMI interface. At the beginning the concept of drivers' distraction and related works were submitted. Next were presented same of nowadays dashboards examples. Emphasized that even in a class of small passenger cars MMI interface are standard. In the following part was presented a method for evaluating the impact of the built-in LCD panel on the driver's distraction. The method is static and is based on the measurement of the luminance level of the background environment and MMI. The results and their evaluation is a summary of the work.

Keywords: driver's distraction, MMI interface, luminance level.

1   Introduction

Nowadays, it can be observed the steady increase in traffic complexity and information density requires elaborate concepts to provide the driver in a comfortable way with the necessary information [8]. These expectations arising from the development of advanced ITS systems are the challenge for automotive designers to map the classic circular shape gages and buttons on the versatile liquid crystal displays. The information content of a pointer instrument is almost immediately conceived, its mechanic nature allows the representation of value through appropriate material choice. On the other hand, dot matrix liquid crystal displays are flexible to display almost all kinds of text, graphics, and symbols, but turn out to be less attractive areas when switched off. As a result, manufacturers are increasingly willing to use in the cockpits of cars of this type of screens. Such solutions are also an important part of marketing. The appearance of touch screens in vehicles is due to the huge popularity of navigation systems and smartphones. Acceptance of operating these last has become the main reason for the warm reception of these devices in vehicles. Is confirmed by the results of research conducted by the author and presented in [6].

On the other hand, such devices can cause driver distraction while driving. Distraction of the driver may be caused by the information provided at the wrong time with the wrong frequency, wrong priority, wrong way of presence or the wrong

J. Mikulski (Ed.): TST 2014, CCIS 471, pp. 396–403, 2014.

number. This is particularly important when the vehicle is equipped with a wide variety of information systems. These are so-called IVIS systems. In general, IVISs (*In-Vehicle Information Systems*) include navigation systems, entertainment systems such as music/video players and satellite broadcasting receivers, and various car management systems. The later in the article will be taken up the problem of driver distraction during night driving caused by on-board telematics. In particular, the LCD touch screens. The first part will be presented dashboards of several currently manufactured cars. The second part presents results of measurements of the luminance of the LCD display mounted as standard in a car Chevrolet Orlando.

2   Methods for the Assessment of Drivers' Distraction

Paying attention to operating the vehicle or watching the traffic is very important and being distracted from this is directly relevant to traffic safety. In the definition given by the AAA Foundation for Traffic Safety the distraction was defined as "when a driver is delayed in the recognition of information needed to safely accomplish the driving task because some event, activity, object, or person within or outside the vehicle compelled or tended to induce the driver's shifting attention away from the driving task." [7]. Distraction leads to a reduced amount of attention on either task, the initially or primary and the new or secondary [11]. If the performed tasks rely on the same resource, they can interfere with each other and affect the performance. As driving a car is visually demanding, the visual interface of a built-in LCD panel competes for the same resource associated with visual perception and can therefore cause distraction from the primary (driving) task [12].

Distraction caused by a flashing alert on the screen, although momentary, divert the attention from the task at hand. Distraction from the driving the car, can reduce driver safety by degrading the vehicle control and object or event detection [9]. As has been shown in [4] and [13] the complexity of the competing tasks plays a key role. Physical and cognitive distraction significantly impair the driver's visual search patterns, reaction times, decision-making processes and the ability to maintain speed or lateral position on the road. The perceived complexity of tasks depends amongst other things on age, emotional state and driving experience.

In respect to what has been written so far the current trend of promoting the LCD panels in the cockpits of cars can adversely affect the drivers and cause their distraction or even more it can be dangerous.

There are many research methods to assess the driver while driving. These can be divided into two categories, with the participation of the driver and without his participation. The first may include the experimental methods to assess e.g. the NASA TLX test or QUIS test. The second category includes experiments in which the driver's task is limited to driving the car. In contrast, the measurement is making by the devices installed in the cabin of the car, and their analysis is carried out after the experiment.

Indicated for the first category test NASA TLX [5] is a multi-dimensional rating procedure that derives an overall workload score based on a weighted average of ratings on six subscales: mental demand, physical demand, temporal demand, performance, effort level and frustration level. Mentioned the QUIS test [10] was designed to assess the users' subjective satisfaction with specific aspects of the human–computer interface. With our questionnaire we intended to measure the overall system satisfaction (the reaction to the software used in the experiment).

Both of these tests rely on subjective assessment expressed by the driver, and therefore do not allow for an assessment of when and what attracts the attention of the driver.

Methods belonging to the second category are more efficient, because rely on the analysis of driver behavior while driving. This analysis is based on measuring the driver's reaction time to the event occurred or now increasingly appreciated analysis of the driver's concentration on the basis of eye movement. Devices for studies of this type usually use the camera placed in glasses that wears the driver for the time the experiment. Examples of these devices and their operation can be found on the manufacturers [1-2].

3   Case Study

Looking at the current offer car manufacturers we can say that all of they offer advanced telematics technologies in their vehicles. This concerns almost all offer currently manufactured vehicles.

3.1   Modern Dashboards in Cars

As an example in this section three models of different sizes and brands of cars will be presented. These examples come from the current offer car manufacturers. As the first example the interior of a small French car Renault Clio will be presented.

Fig. 1. Interior of Renault Clio and MMI interface [14]

In terms of innovative new Renault Clio has one of two multimedia systems: MEDIA NAV Renault R-Link. Renault R-Link is a multimedia tablet with a touch screen 7", TomTom navigation system, audio system with surround sound 3D Sound by Arkamys, Bluetooth, USB and jack and access to information about the car and services on line.

As an example of a larger family car is Skoda Octavia. This is a automotive brand particularly appreciated by Polish drivers. In this year's edition of the Octavia beyond the built-in media has advanced telematics systems. These include Lane Assistant, Intelligent Light Assistant, Front assistant, Adaptive Cruise Assistant Crew Protect Assistant, Driver Activity Assistant. The LCD panel in the cockpit is the most important part of that informs about the status of these systems, driver assistance.

Fig. 2. Interior of Skoda Octavia [15]

As a last example, introduction of innovative telematic solutions in the car Chevrolet Orlando was selected. The vehicle spite of its dimensions is relatively cheap. For this reason it is popular both as a private car and as a vehicle for small businesses. Chevrolet MyLink is a high-tech infotainment system is standard on the Orlando. The MMI display panel is a 7" color touch-screen. The screen displays information such as telematics and multimedia. The device has a built-in speech recognition system allowing users to issue voice commands by the driver. This allows you to speak short commands to make and receive hands-free phone calls, control key features of the infotainment system and to tell the optional embedded Navigation system where you want to go.

Fig. 3. Cockpit of Chevrolet Orlando and MMI interface [16]

4   Research Method

To research carried out by the author was used an alternative tool to assess the distraction effect. It was used the camera LMK Mobile Advanced [3]. The LMK is imaging photometer that allows analysis of luminance ranges objects for verifying existing standards and design projects to be made with regard to full illumination, glare, ergonomics and well-being.

Concept study closely relates to cover up statements regarding that distraction due to the performed tasks rely on the same resource i.e. focusing of visual attention. The cause of driver distraction can be an unexpected change the content displayed on the LCD panel especially connected with an audio alert and more over the driver can focusing his sight on the screen when the level of luminance is much more higher then outside the vehicle. Of course, the luminance of the LCD panel will have a greater impact on the distraction during a night driving. Change the field of view shown in Figure 4.

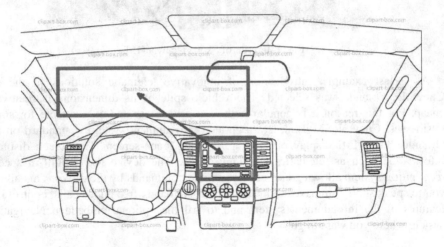

Fig. 4. Change the field of view in the cabin of the vehicle [own study]

To investigate was chosen a Chevrolet Orlando. The interior of the vehicle was shown in Figure 3. During the measurements the telematics device were turned off. MMI display the image, you cannot turn off (manufacturer's logo). The main areas of research are the LCD panel and the view of the observation field outside the vehicle. The study was performed at night at 23:30 in typical urban night scenery. Measurement location was shown in Figure 5.

During the experiment, were made seven of measurements luminance level inside the vehicle. Among them was selected one of the most representative. Further investigations were carried out using the LMK-2000 software. At the beginning areas of the highest luminance were marked. They were the LCD panel (1), an exterior view (2), the small panel between the gauges (3) and rearview mirror (4). Selected areas shown in Figure 6.

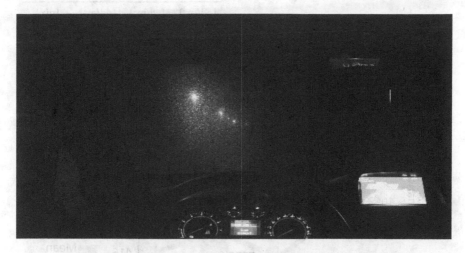

Fig. 5. View of the interior of the vehicle during the tests [own study]

Fig. 6. Selected regions of analysis [own study]

The results of measurement of luminance are shown in Table 1.

The first result of the study is the high level of luminance of LCD displays. Their brightness goes much beyond the legal limit. The level of luminance of LCD's (1) and (2) are similar and is about 13-15 lm/m^2. External view of the brightest point is located about 14 lm/m^2. More important is the analysis of the average level luminance.

Table 1. The results of measurement of luminance

No.	Source	Region	Min [cd/m²]	Max [cd/m²]	Mean [cd/m²]	Area [pix]
1	Luminance image	LCD panel	0,07	14,93	8,25	54620
2	Luminance image	Exterior view	0,00	13,65	0,78	691300
3	Luminance image	Small display	0,05	12,60	4,63	11120
4	Luminance image	Rearview mirror	0,00	6,26	1,42	8493

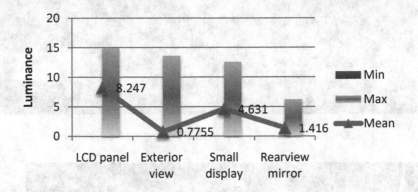

Fig. 7. Graphical presentation of results [own study]

High and constant brightness the LCD panel (1) has over eight times the mean value than the exterior view. It will cause cut the driver's sight after dusk. High brightness of this piece of the cockpit's equipment will also reduce the visibility of unlit objects on the road. This is confirmed by the analysis of the transverse image at the level of the eye and the LCD panel. When an external light source will disappear, the driver's gaze will be catches by the bright LCD panel.

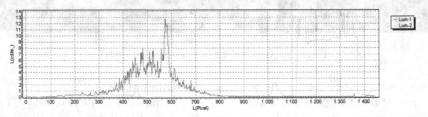

Fig. 8. Analysis of the luminance level on two levels: Lum-1 - an exterior view and Lum-2 - a LCD panel [own study]

5   Conclusion

The paper focuses on the aspect of driver distraction caused by the embedded the MMI interface. This is especially important in a situation where almost every new car comes standard with such equipment. According to desire for modernity does not go hand in hand with safety. The research at random selected car confirms this opinion. Research the luminance level of the LCD panel and the background should be treated as a static method. This study, together with the study of effects of dynamic impact on drivers can be used to aggregate assessment.

References

1. http://www.neurodevice.pl/pl/produkty/eyetracking-smi (date of access: May 2, 2014)
2. http://www.tobii.com (date of access: May 2, 2014)
3. http://www.technoteam.de/product_overview/lmk/products/lmk_m obile_advanced/index_eng.html (date of access: May 2, 2014)
4. McKnight, J., McKnight, A.S.: The Effect of Cellular Phone Use Upon Driver Attention. National Public Services Research Institute (1991), http://www.aaafoundation.org /resources/index.cfm?button=cellphone
5. NASA TLX, http://www.nrl.navy.mil/aic/ide/NASATLX.php
6. Siergiejczyk, M., Paś, J., Rosiński, A.: Application of closed circuit television for highway telematics. In: Mikulski, J. (ed.) TST 2012. CCIS, vol. 329, pp. 159–165. Springer, Heidelberg (2012)
7. Stutts, J.C., Reinfurt, D.W., Staplin, L., Rodgman, E.A.: The role of driver distraction in traffic crashes (2001), http://www.aaafoundation.org/projects/index. cfm?button=distraction
8. Sumiła, M.: Impact of Telematics-enabled devices on driver behaviour. Archives of Transport System Telematics 6(1), 48–51 (2013)
9. Tijerina, L.: Issues in the evaluation of driver distraction associated with in-vehicle information and telecommunications systems (2000), http://www-nrd.nhtsa.dot.gov/departments/nrd-13/ driver-distraction/PDF/3.PDF
10. QUIS test, http://www.lap.umd.edu/quis/publications/ newspaper1.html
11. Vollrath, M., Trotzke, I.: In-vehicle communication and driving: an attempt to overcome their interferences. Center for Traffic Sciences, IZVW, University of Wuerzburg. Germany (2000), http://www-nrd.nhtsa.dot.gov/departments/nrd-13/driver- distraction/PDF/33.PDF
12. Wierwille, W., Tijerina, L.: Vision in vehicles VI. In: Gale, A., Brown, I., Haslegrave, C., Taylor, S. (eds.) Modelling the Relationship Between Driver In-Vehicle Visual Demands and Accident Occurrence, pp. 233–244. Elsevier, USA (1998)
13. Young, K.L., Regan, M.A., Hammer, M.: Driver Distraction: A Review of the Literature, Victoria. Monash University Accident Research Centre, Australia (2003)
14. http://www.renault.pl/samochody-nowe/samochody- osobowe/clio/clio-IV-grandtour/intuicyjne-multimedia.jsp (date of access: May 2, 2014)
15. http://www.skoda-auto.pl/modele/octavia-combi/pages/ przestrzen.aspx#SliderModuleWebPart (date of access: April 14, 2014)
16. https://www.chevrolet.pl/samochody/orlando/ (date of access: May 4, 2014)

Crane Payload Position Measurement Vision-Based System Dedicated for Anti-sway Solutions

Paweł Hyla and Janusz Szpytko

AGH University of Science and Technology,
A. Mickiewicza Av. 30, 30-059 Krakow, Poland
{hyla,szpytko}@agh.edu.pl

Abstract. Handling operation efficiency in cargo transportation realized by the cranes mainly depends on counteractions against undesirable phenomena's such as payload swing, crane bridge deflections in vertical plane and many others. Although experienced crane operators are an experts in suppressing an excessive payload sway, there is a strong need to develop robust anti-sway systems supporting their work. In this paper authors propose a kind of an absolute payload position measurement system with the use of an image sensor for sway detection. The proposed technique is based on kind of template matching method with the use of a smartcam as a reliable vision sensor. In the described system, vision sensor measures displacement of the markers attached to the cranes hook. On the markers shifts base measure from equilibrium position and actual crane rope length, the payload swing can be estimated. All experiments and tests presented in this paper were conducted on the scaled physical model of overhead travelling crane with hosting capability of 150 kg.

Keywords: sway sensor, image analysis, overhead travelling crane, smart camera.

1   Introduction

In industrial practice the process of moving loads with the crane help were burdened with various types of issues [1]. One of the crucial problem constitute induce the free payload swinging effect [2] under dynamic forces impact. The oscillation frequency of crane payloads is the main and most important issue in the cranes proper exploitation, especially in anti-sway control system [3]. Although, experienced crane operators can control crane in such a way to minimize or even prevent against the sway payload adverse effects. However, there is a strong need to develop robust anti-sway systems supporting crane operator work independently, freeing completely formation of this unwanted effect from human factor influence [4].

On the second hand, automation level of the contemporaneous material handling devices involves a need of improving the crane control system solutions oriented into reducing or even eliminating the unwanted sway effect [5] by applying soft computing method like a fuzzy logic [6-8], genetic algorithm [9], neural networks [10-11] as well as their hybrids [12-13] into anti-sway control algorithms to obtain

J. Mikulski (Ed.): TST 2014, CCIS 471, pp. 404–413, 2014.
© Springer-Verlag Berlin Heidelberg 2014

stabilized cargo trajectory effect, which enable high precision payload positioning with simultaneous cargo safety assurance.

In the scientific literature the anti-sway effect was achieved through using a close-loop and an open-loop control systems. Main advantage of the open-loop control systems contains possibility of eliminating the feedback of the swinging angle of a payload although the close-loop control system can ensure the robustness against disturbances and many others parameters variations. Unfortunately the close-loop control systems need a sway sensor for reliable sway measurement of a payload suspended on a wire, what constitutes the main disadvantage [14], regardless of the used control algorithms or similar applications.

The presented solution vision-based non-contact sway sensor based on payload position measurement technique was dedicated for use in overhead travelling crane (OTC) as a sway feedback in close-loop anti-sway system types.

2   Crane Payload Position Measurement Vision-Based System Architecture

Software for image analysis action of the presented payload position measurement vision-based sway system was developed by using template matching algorithm. As the hardware part of the system was chosen smart camera [15-17] as a device linked video stream gathering possibilities with simultaneous image analysis action. The camera was suspended under crane trolley in perpendicular position (Fig. 1), additionally the plate with four markers was mounted on the crane hook in such a way that markers were always in the smartcam field of view (Fig. 2).

Fig. 1. The smart camera suspended under the crane's trolley in perpendicular position [own study]   **Fig. 2.** The hook block with the plate with markers [own study]

Having regard the described vision-based sway sensor architecture, to achieve the possibility of measure the rope sway their actual length was needed, so this was achieved generally through the incremental encoder sensor fixed to the rope drum rotation centre line. However, the scaled physical model of overhead travelling crane with hosting capability 150 kg is equipped in five incremental encoders with wide variety of applications what was presented in the Figure 3. The detailed technical specifications of used incremental rotary encoders were shown in the Tab.1.

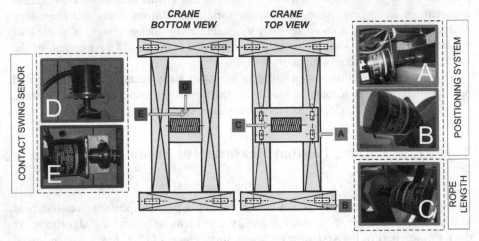

Fig. 3. Location and function of incremental encoders mounted on the scaled crane model [own study]

Table 1. Rotary encoders types mounted on the overhead travelling crane

Measurand	Encoder type	Sensor resolution	Measurement precision
Bridge position (B)	Rotary encoder A/B phase	400 [imp./rot.]	7.85×10^{-4} [m]
Trolley position (A)	Rotary encoder A/B phase	200 [imp./rot.]	3.14×10^{-4} [m]
Payload altitude (C)	Rotary encoder A/B phase	100 [imp./rot.]	4.19×10^{-4} [m]
Contact sway sensor (D) (x direction)	Rotary encoder A/B phase	2000 [imp./rot.]	1.57×10^{-3} [rad]
Contact sway sensor (E) (y direction)	Rotary encoder A/B phase	400 [imp./rot.]	7.85×10^{-3} [rad]

2.1   The Methodology of the Non-contact Vision-Based Sway Measurement

In the presented solution the non-contact vision-based payload displacement measure system was used as an indirect method of measure the payload swing. The basic limitation of the presented method depends on indispensable restrictive conditions which should be adopted. The principle of sway estimating in the single step was shown in Figure 4.

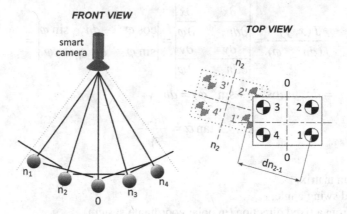

Fig. 4. The payload position measurement vision-based system – rope sway methodology extraction scheme [own study]

There is a necessity to assume that in a given period of time the rope length is constant and the payload swings are relatively small. For such restrictive conditions the displacement of the payload isn't realized as an arc, whose radius constitute the actual rope length, but it is directly realized through straight line. The analysis of the geometry configuration of the presented measurement system shows that the rope length and payload movement are the hypotenuse of the right-angled triangle. In this consideration the payload movement was calculated on the average displacement of at least minimum two markers found in the analyses images, while actual rope length was measured with rotary encoder help (Tab. 1). The detailed diagram taking into account both front and top plane was presented in the Figure 5.

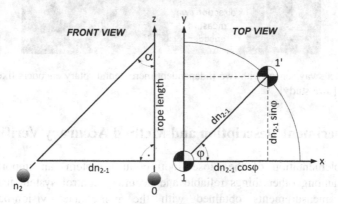

Fig. 5. The geometry of the payload sway measurement system shown in front and top view [own study]

On the geometrical relationships base illustrated in Figure 5 it may be formulated the following mathematical equations:

$$\frac{J(x, y)}{J(dn_{2-1}, \varphi)} = \begin{vmatrix} \dfrac{\partial x}{\partial dn_{2-1}} & \dfrac{\partial x}{\partial \varphi} \\ \dfrac{\partial y}{\partial dn_{2-1}} & \dfrac{\partial y}{\partial \varphi} \end{vmatrix} = \begin{vmatrix} \cos\varphi & -dn_{2-1}\sin\varphi \\ \sin\varphi & dn_{2-1}\cos\varphi \end{vmatrix} = \qquad (1)$$

$$= dn_{2-1}(\cos^2\varphi + \sin^2\varphi) = dn_{2-1}$$

$$\tan\alpha = \frac{dn_{2-1}}{r_l}. \qquad (2)$$

where:

J – Jacobian matrix,

α – payload swing angle,

φ – angle from a fixed direction (in polar coordinate system),

r_l – rope length.

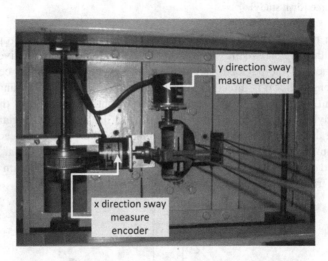

Fig. 6. Contact sway sensor with two independent incremental rotary encoders fixed under the crane trolley [own study]

3   Experiment Description and Method Accuracy Verification

In the implementation of the closed-loop control system, an important factor constitutes among other things reliable and accuracy control system feedback. To verify the measurements obtained with the non-contact vision-based sway measurement sensor was used high sensitive contact sway sensor. The used sensor was compiled with two independent rotary encoders (a detailed description of the encoders type was presented in the Table 1) with additional equipment. Each encoders were fixed with the leveler formed as a "L" letter shape. In the lower part of the leveler was made the longitudinal groove for the crane rope. The formed groove shape allows rope movement in the vertical and horizontal direction during the scaled crane model normal work.

3.1   The Non-contact Vision-Based Sway Measurement – An Experiment

In the experiment carried out on the scaled model of the overhead travelling crane the 10 kg payload mass was suspended at the three different heights: 0.87 m, 1.37 m and 1.87 m. More details about payload altitude location during an experiment were presented in figure 7. In the figure 8 there were presented a three unprocessed snapshots taken by the smart camera when the payload was at different altitudes.

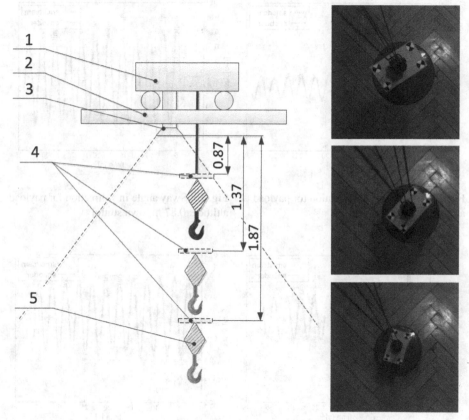

Fig. 7. Payload altitude location during an experiment: 1 - crane trolley, 2 - crane rails, 3 - smartcam, 4 - markers altitude, 5 - hook block [own study]

Fig. 8. The view of the hook block with markers. (from the top adequacy: 0.87 m, 1.37 m and 1.87 m) -[own study]

The sway in x and y direction was obtained with the encoders sway sensor and non-contact vision system. For distinction and better obtained data visualization, the sway run received from the vision system was marked as a dot line. The gathered data were synchronized in time domain and superimposed on each other. The obtained results were combined in pairs. Each presented graph contains two run. The first one is related with the sway angle received form vision sensor and the second one shows the sway run form contact sway sensor. Additionally in the same row there were shown two diagrams concerning the sway both in x and y direction registered on the same latitude. The final results and all measurements were presented in the figures 9-15.

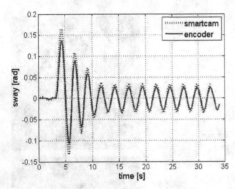

Fig. 9. Sway angle in x direction for payload altitude: 0.87 m [own study]

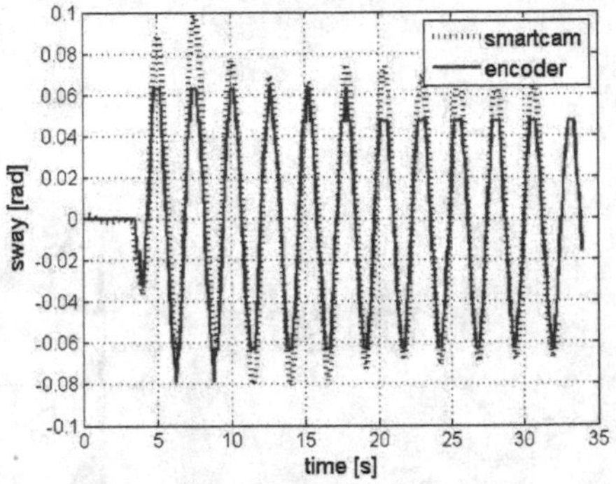

Fig. 10. Sway angle in y direction for payload altitude: 0.87 m [own study]

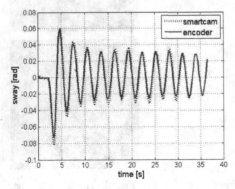

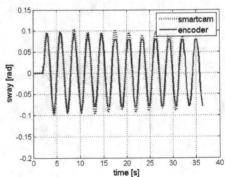

Fig. 11. Sway angle in x direction for payload altitude: 1.37 m [own study]

Fig. 12. Sway angle in y direction for payload altitude: 1.37 m [own study]

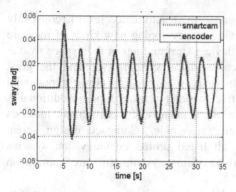
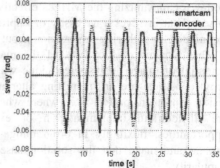

Fig. 13. Sway angle in x direction for payload altitude: 1.87 m [own study]

Fig. 14. Sway angle in y direction for payload altitude: 1.87 m [own study]

3.2   Summary

Analysis of the carried experiments can be concluded that the measurement of the payload position base sway extractions are not only possible but also they constitute an alternative for other sway sensor types, including mainly the existing contact methods. Main advantage of the presented solution constitute their architecture, because only the one smartcam was used to measure the payload sway both in x and y direction. However, it is should be noted that presented application has some inconveniences. First of all, during normal crane operation, the payload suspension altitude is continuously changing, therefore the perspective of obtained photos changes too. This phenomenon can be observed especially in the set of images presented in figure 8. When the distance between camera lens and markers fixed to the crane hook grows, the diameter of visible markers are smaller. It makes difficult a reliable image analysis. Additionally, the distance between camera lens and four markers set has an influence into measurement error. In figure 10 it can be observed the largest difference (on the level of 0.02 radians) between the sway measurement realized with the contact sway sensor and the vision-based. This can be explained by the small distance between the camera and the markers set. In the presented measure system distance from camera lens has an influence into visible markers displacement. Small distance generates marginal markers shifts. Therefore the greater distance between camera and hook with the markers should generate more precisely measurement.

4   Conclusion

Effective material handling is the most important element in all technological processes. Without efficiency, a final product cannot be turned into economic profit. Although, the direct cost of contemporary MHD's aided system cannot be measured. The main factor attributing to material handling costs are connected with idle time.

Today for maximizing the MHD's effectiveness, their automation level is constantly raised. That involves a necessity of improving or developing new kinds of measure techniques for gathering information about devices surroundings or their space work.

The dynamic development of the machine vision systems type and the great potential of image analysis technique with regard to computing power exponential grow constitute are an interesting alternative to other sensors types. Additionally, vision sensor are perfect everywhere where the standards of measurement methods are difficult in implementation or even impossible. Compact design, great opportunities, flexibility in programing - all listed profits enable vision systems expand and make that the solution based on vision systems still are gaining on popularity.

In the paper it was presented a method solving the problem concerning an issue to use one standalone camera as a sway sensor both into x and y directions. The problem was solved through the using machine vision system as a payload top view position measurement system. The sway angle estimation was achieved through indirect calculation.

However, there have already existed applications in which it is used a vision system as a sway sensor to obtain the sway angle in two direction, but their basic disadvantage constitutes architecture and necessity of use at last minimum two smartcams, what significantly increase difficulty in the reliable image analysis technique. Especially in relation to these type of applications, presented in this paper solution seems to be an interesting solution. The obtained results are very promising and provide for further method development as well as other tests connected with adaptation and implementation of presented solution for the larger and more responsible devices than scaled model of the overhead travelling crane.

Acknowledgment. The research project is financed from the Polish Science budget in the year 2014.

References

1. Szpytko, J.: Exploitation testing approaches for large dimensional rails devices. In: Proc. of the 9th IEEE International Conference on Methods and Models in Automation and Robotics MMAR, Poland, pp. 763–768 (2004)
2. Szpytko, J.: Integrated decision making supporting the exploitation and control of transport devices. UWND AGH, Kraków (2004)
3. Ziyad, N.M.: Effect of hoisting cable elasticity on anti-sway controllers of quay-side container cranes. Nonlinear Dyn. 58, 129–140 (2009)
4. Szpytko, J., Wozniak, D.A.: To keep operational potential of transport device e-based on reliability indicators. In: European Safety and Reliability Conference ESREL, Stavanger, Norway, pp. 2377–2384 (2007)
5. Sawodny, O., Neupert, J., Arnold, E.: Actual Trends in Crane Automation – Directions for the Future. FME Transactions 37(4), 167–174 (2009)

6. Smoczek, J.: Evolutionary optimization of interval mathematics-based design of TSK fuzzy controller for anti-sway crane control. International Journal of Applied Mathematics and Computer Science 23(4), 749–759 (2013)
7. Smoczek, J.: Interval arithmetic-based fuzzy discrete-time crane control scheme design. Bulletin of the Polish Academy of Sciences - Technical Sciences 61(4), 863–870 (2013)
8. Smoczek, J.: Fuzzy crane control with sensorless payload deflection feedback for vibration reduction. Mechanical Systems and Signal Processing 46(1), 70–81 (2014)
9. Saeidi, H., Naraghi, M., Abolghasem, A.R.: A neural network self tuner based on input shapers behavior for anti sway system of gantry cranes. Journal of Vibration and Control 19(13), 1936–1949 (2012)
10. Akira, A.: Anti-sway control for overhead cranes using neural networks. International Jouranla of Innovative Computing, Information and Control 7(7(B)), 4251–4262 (2011)
11. Mendez, J.A.: An application of a neural self controller to an overhead crane. Neural Computing and Applications 8, 143–150 (1999)
12. Smoczek, J., Szpytko, J.: Evolutionary algorithm-based design of a fuzzy TBF predictive model and TSK fuzzy anti-sway crane control system. Engineering Applications of Artificial Intelligence 28, 190–200 (2014)
13. Nakazono, K.: Ohnisihi,t K., Kinjot, H.: Load swing suppression in jib crane systems using a genetic algorithm-trained neuro-controller. In: Proceedings of International Conference on Mechatronics, Kumamoto Japan, pp. 1–4 (2007)
14. Hyla, P., Szpytko, J.: Vision method for rope angle swing measurement for overhead travelling cranes – validation approach. In: Mikulski, J. (ed.) TST 2013. CCIS, vol. 395, pp. 370–377. Springer, Heidelberg (2013)
15. Wang, L., Xi, J. (eds.): Smart devices and machines for advanced manufacturing. Springer, London (2008)
16. Yu, S., Real, F.D.: Smart Cameras: Fundamentals and classification. In.: Belbachir, A.N. (ed.) Smart Cameras. Springer (2010)
17. Hornberg, A. (ed.): Handbook of machine vision. Wiley-Vch Verlag, Darmstadt (2006)

Microscopic Simulation of Optimal Use of Communication Network

Simona Kubíková, Alica Kalašová, and Ľubomír Černický

University of Žilina,
Faculty of Operation and Economics of Transport and Communications,
Univerzitná 1, 01026 Žilina, Slovakia
{Alica.Kalasova,Lubomir.Cernicky,
Simona.Kubikova}@fpedas.uniza.sk

Abstract. The development of transportation in Slovakia has an increasing character as in the other developed countries, and the negative impacts of transport are still rising. To handle this situation, the Slovak cities should have to solve their transport situations with more often use of ITS elements. One of the possibilities of optimal communication network use in the city is the management of traffic flow on the route, or its reroute from congested stretches to existing alternative routes of transport network. This use is suitable, if the likelihood of overloading is high, and the lateral routes have a sufficient reserve. High proportion of transport which is possible to reroute is a condition for success of this system. In our article we build a cost- benefit based model to compare two variants. The first variant includes a current state and in the second one designed changes will be incorporated. We use this model to solve the problems on communication network in the city of Žilina. As a modelling tool we use software Aimsun which allows a microscopic simulation. AIMSUN (Advanced Interactive Microscopic Simulator for Urban and Non-Urban Networks) is a software tool which is able to reproduce real traffic conditions on any network. It means that we can also use it to predict behaviour of network with implementation of vehicle guidance systems.

Keywords: Model, Traffic light, rerouting.

1 Introduction

Problem of traffic control in urban agglomeration is very old theme. Despite of the fact that a lot of work has been done and many partial successes have been achieved, this problem still stays relevant and very important. This is caused mainly by still increasing demandingness of traffic control in urban agglomerations which is derived from increasing motorization, but also from range of urban agglomerations, population density, expansion of shopping centres, industrial activities, and from development of tourism. Significant problem is also little respect for important factors such as impact on the environment, changes in the social structure of the population and living standards growth. All these factors lead to generally applicable knowledge

J. Mikulski (Ed.): TST 2014, CCIS 471, pp. 414–423, 2014.

that conventional methods of traffic control in urban agglomerations are insufficient for current requirements and there is a need to use new approaches. The solution is based on using of telematics applications and can be achieved only by sustained and long-term effort to gradually build up a sufficiently sophisticated system that allows analysis of current traffic situation and then optimise traffic control on the communication network. Telematics applications allow optimising traffic flow and also solving traffic flow within the city. Because of still growing traffic there is a necessary to look for appropriate methods that are applicable in practice. These methods include simulation tools that are useful during communication designing, but also during designing of own control algorithms.

2   Characteristic of the Analysed Area

Analysed Street is the main radial road from Žilina city centre, which connect Vlčince housing estate, University of Žilina and leads traffic to municipalities Rosina and Višňové. Along the street there are located several shopping centres, gas stations, urban indoor swimming pool, gym, companies, mixed-use buildings, health centre, police station, university facilities and dormitories. The length of the street is approximately 2.6 km and several bus and trolley-bus lines pass through the parts of this street. It is distributor road of the urban roads category B1 [1].

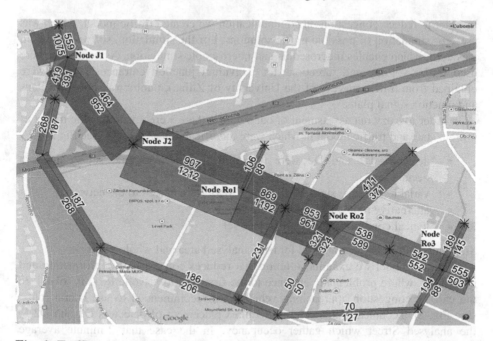

Fig. 1. Traffic volume of analysed area during traffic peak (15:00 – 16:00) [veh/h] and position of junction nodes [own study]

The Street starts at the junction of the streets – Vojtecha Spanyola – Vysokoškolákov – Tajovského (Node J1 – see Fig. 1). At its beginning there is grade-separated interchange with the through road I/18 (Mostná and Nemocničná streets) (Node J2). From this road a large amount of vehicles are coming to this street. Further the street crosses the street Obchodná (Roundabout – Node Ro2) and Matica Slovenská (not included in Fig. 1), which are the main roads for transport service of the biggest Žilina housing estate – Vlčince. The street also crosses the streets Veľký diel (connection between housing estates Solinky and Vlčince) and Univerzitná Street (Node Ro3), which services area of University of Žilina and ends at the junction of the streets – Vysokoškolákov – Rosinská (not included in Fig. 1). In the Fig. 1 you can find traffic volume during traffic peak of analysed area and location of above mentioned junctions. As you can see in this figure, traffic volume at the communication is high, and mainly during traffic peak left turns at all these junctions are problematic [5]. Another problem is high density of traffic and queues before roundabouts (Node Ro1, Ro2, and Ro3), mainly recurring congestion before first roundabout (Node Ro1) in the direction from city centre. The congestions usually run to junction Spanyola – Vysokoškolákov – Tajovského (Node J1) and also to the through road I/18 (from the street Mostná).

3   Model Creation

In order to reduce congestion on communication we created traffic model, which was used for simulation of possible traffic solutions. For the simulation, software Aimsun was used, which enables macroscopic and microscopic simulation. As input data were used traffic volume and directions for individual junction entrances (which were obtained from traffic surveys of the University of Žilina), public transport line plans and junction signal plans.

In order to carry out assessment of our solution there were created traffic model of present state and traffic model in which were modifications as follows (see Fig.2):

- detectors D1 and D2 were placed to the network and set to measure occupancy
- variable message signs VMS1 and VMS2 were placed to the network
- alternative routes R1 and R2 were set
- logical conditions of rerouting were set

Simulation outputs were gathered for both analysed area and whole network.

In traffic model we examine solution that reduces congestion by information and navigating, where problematic entrance to the first junction (Node Ro1) is solved. In the case of congestion approaching vehicles are recommended to use lateral route. (see Fig. 2). Technically this solution requires placement of detectors D1 and D2 to the analysed Street which gather occupancy. In the case that 2-minute average occupancy of detector D1 or detector D2 is over 80%, drivers via variable message signs VMS1 and VMS2 are recommended to use lateral route R1 and R2. Our assumption is that lateral route R1 will be accepted by 30% of drivers and lateral route R2 will be accepted by 30% of those drivers, whose journey leads on sections S1 and S2. This rerouting lasts until the 2-minute average occupancy of both detectors is below 50%.

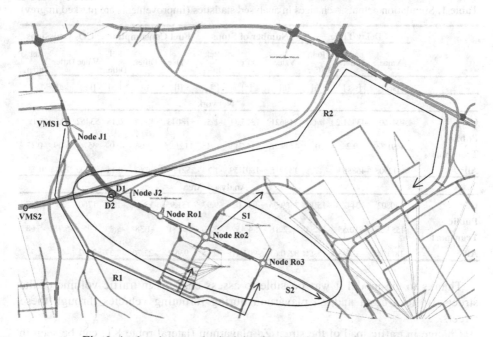

Fig. 2. Analysed area and principle of analysed solution [own study]

Our estimation of economic demandingness of this solution is: building and acquisition costs = 21,000 €, and operating and maintenance costs = 2,000 € a year. Estimation of economic demandingness was based only on costs of technology and earthworks.

From rerouting of vehicles to the lateral routes we estimated less traffic at the problematic entrance to the first roundabout. This should lead to smoothen car passage, and also to reduction in number of stops, fuel consumption, and produced emissions. Table 1 shows, that our solution in the area of analysed Street could reduce delay time by about 15.14%, number of stops by about nearly 10%, fuel consumption by about 2.37% and emissions produced by 1.74%. Similarly it is possible to see that statistics for public transport in the analysed area could be better as well.

Looking at the whole traffic network statistics you can see that our solution could bring reduction in delay time by about 1.05%, and reduction in number of stops by about 1.34%, but fuel consumption would rise by about 0.14% and emission produced by about 0.23%. It is possible to assume that this phenomenon is caused just by rerouting of vehicles. In the case of rerouting of the vehicles fewer vehicles will pass through the analysed Street. These results in decrease in delay time, number of stops, and in fuel consumption and emission produced, but these rerouted vehicles will travel more kilometres during their journey to the destination. Therefore total delay time could be lower, but fuel consumed and emission produced could be higher compared to the situation without rerouting.

Table 1. Simulation outputs – changes in analysed statistics (improvements are marked in grey)

	Delay Time			Number of Stops			Fuel Consumption			CO$_2$ Emissions		
	Value	Differ.	Rel. Differ.	Value	Differ.	Rel. Differ.	Value	Differ.	Rel. Differ.	Value	Differ	Rel. Differ.
	[sec]	[sec]	[%]	[#]	[#]	[%]	[l]	[l]	[%]	[kg]	[kg]	[%]
						Network						
Car	4041602	-43451.2	- 1.06	118621	-1815.31	-1.51	18043	32.28	0.18	53462	102	0.19
Public Transport	4691.38	0.2	0	4799.28	-16.71	-0.35	1121.26	-1.06	-0.09	3578	-6.09	-0.17
All	4413908	-46886.9	- 1.05	132915	-1801.59	-1.34	25212.98	34.62	0.14	87006	200	0.23
						Analysed Area						
Car	170802	-30442.3	-15.13	7689.96	-848.02	-9.93	751.95	-13.13	-1.74	1760	-26	-1.47
Public Transport	1553.26	-210.55	-11.94	122.81	-4.45	-3.50	24.81	-1.38	-5.29	96	-5.78	-5.68
All	181102	-32443.1	-15.14	8270.61	-903.41	-9.85	936.2	-22.70	-2.37	2362	-42	-1.74

Thanks to the model it was possible to assess changes in traffic volume of the streets Bôrická cesta and Za plavárňou during rerouting vehicles through these streets.

Change in traffic load of the street Za plavárňou (lateral route R1) can be seen in figure 3 on the left. According to traffic model, during simulation time (4 hours) traffic would be rerouted only at the end of traffic peak. Traffic peak for this area is between 15:00 and 16:00 and total number of such rerouted vehicles would be equal 26. At the same time rerouting to lateral route R2 would be running. Resulting from logical condition of rerouting and input data, 24 vehicles would be rerouted to the lateral route R2. Since traffic volume at lateral route R2 is much higher, increase of volume of 24 vehicles is difficult to see. (Fig. 3 on right)

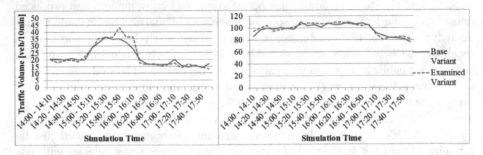

Fig. 3. Changes in traffic volume of the streets: on the left: Za plavárňou (lateral route R1), on the right: Nemocničná (lateral route R2) [own study]

4   Cost – Benefit Based Model

In previous part there was assessed traffic solution with the help of traffic model. Assessment was based on changes in traffic characteristics. Our examined solution could result in traffic improvements in analysed area, but also this solution is expensive. In order to assess whether the benefits of the traffic solution are higher than the cost of this solution, the cost-benefit based model was created (see Fig. 4). This model is based on cost – benefit analysis [2-3] and the heart of the model can be used for assessment of effectiveness of investment in ITS. It is designed in the way that allows comparing costs (costs savings) in money (€).

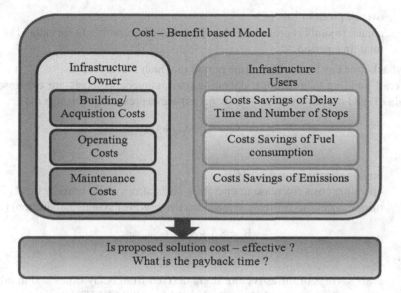

Fig. 4. Principle of cost – benefit based model [own study]

Cost – benefit based model is designed for comparing two variants the first of which is usually base (present) state and the second variant includes proposed changes. The heart is comparison of costs savings (of particular users in the case of introduction of new equipment) and costs for building, operating and maintenance (see formula 1).

$$P/L_i = B_i - C_i. \tag{1}$$

where:

P/L_i profit or loss for the period i [€]
B_i costs savings (Benefits) for the period i [€]
C_i sum of costs for the period i [€]
i   period of system operation (year, month) [1,2,3...n]

According to formula (1) profit or loss per time period is calculated. But here is need to be aware of uneven distribution of costs over time, the highest costs (building/acquisition) are expected only once during the first period and during other periods there are expected only operating and maintenance costs. On the other hand, costs savings (benefits) are expected equal during the whole period of operation. Therefore, in order to assess the effectiveness of the proposed solution, long-term development of individual costs (costs savings) should be monitored. Then overall benefits (profit) or loss is calculated as the sum of P/L for the whole period (formula 2).

$$P/L = \sum_{i=1}^{n} P/L_i \qquad (2)$$

where:

P/L   overall profit or loss [€]
P/L_i   annual (monthly) profit or loss [€] calculated according to formula (1)
n   total time period

Payback time can be set as the time period in which P/L equals 0.

Overall building (acquisition), operating and maintenance costs are expressed by formula (3) and overall costs savings (benefits) are expressed by formula (4)

$$C_i = C_b + C_o + C_m \qquad (3)$$

where:

C_B building/acquisition costs [€]
C_O operating costs (increase in operating costs after system introduction) [€]
C_m maintenance costs (increase in maintenance costs after system introduction) [€]

$$B_i = S_{PI} + S_{Fuel} + S_{Emission} \qquad (4)$$

where:

S_{PI} costs savings of infrastructure users derived from delay times and number of stops or Performance Index (PI) derived from TRANSYT [€]
S_{Fuel} Fuel costs savings derived from fuel consumption change [€]
$S_{Emission}$ Emission cost savings derived from Emission change [€]

Costs savings of infrastructure users derived from delay time and number of stops are calculated as Performance index which is known from TRANSYT. Traffic input data for cost-benefit based model are achieved from Aimsun simulation outputs[6].

4.1   Simplifications

Due to demandingness on input data and demandingness of traffic model in Aimsun our cost – benefit based model considers following simplifications:

- Price of fuel does not change with time, price of petrol = 1,477 €/litre, price of diesel = 1.39 €/litre (average price of fuel in the Slovak Republic in 2013).
- Considered are only CO2 emissions, the price of which does not change with time, price of CO_2 Emissions = 4,19 €/t.

- Costs savings are only during traffic peak, during traffic saddle there are no costs savings.
- Daily costs savings are estimated two times higher than costs savings during simulation (during day there are usually 2 traffic peaks – morning and afternoon). [4]
- Weekly cost savings are estimated 5 times higher than daily costs savings.
- Annual costs savings are estimated 52 times higher than weekly costs savings.
- Operating costs are only cost for electricity, while considered price for electricity is 0.11 €/kWh, consumption of controller 80 Watts,
- Maintenance costs = 1800 €/year.
- W for calculation PI = 6.84 €/ pcu-hour of delay, K = 1.37 €/100 pcu-stops, w = 1 and k = 1.

Table 2. Payback time of analysed solution [own study] (N – negative costs savings, L – cost savings are lower than costs)

| | | Reduction in Costs | | | | |
		Operating	PI	Fuel Consumption	Emissions	Sum
Analysed Area	All	N	0.51	1.25	L	0.359
	Public Transport	N	33.92	63.20	L	19.45
Whole Network	All	N	0.334	N	N	0.562
	Public Transport	N	L	L	L	L

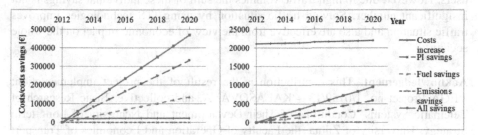

Fig. 5. Costs/costs reduction for the analysed area according to Cost benefits based model. On the left all vehicles, on the right public transport vehicles [own study]

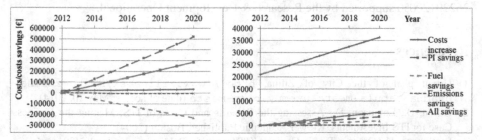

Fig. 6. Costs/costs reduction for the whole network according to Cost benefits based model. On the left all vehicles, on the right public transport vehicles [own study]

4.2   Assessment According to Cost-Benefit Based Model

As you can see in figure 5 and Figure 6 and also in Table 2, economic return (payback time) according to cost – benefits based model is very short. For the whole network payback time is 0.562 years and for the analysed area (Vysokoškolákov) it is 0.359 years. Here is important to realize, that this payback time is derived mainly from reduction in costs for delay time and number of stops (PI). If we consider whole network, reduction in cost on fuel an emission for the reaches negative values, only if we consider only analysed area, reduction in costs on fuel and emission reaches positive values. Our solution of traffic situation has also positive impact on operation of public transport vehicles. Thanks to lower delay time these vehicles also reaches reduction in costs, but this reduction is lower than maintenance and operating costs. You can see quantifying of these costs reduction in figure 5 and figure 6 on the right.

5   Conclusion

Traffic model in Aimsun confirms improvements in traffic in analysed area after implementation examined solution; moreover, results according cost-benefit based model point at economic return of this solutions. But this economic return should be understood from the point of view of whole society, not from the point of view of individual user. For example, when we reduce delay time by 10% and fuel consumption by 3%, one user delay time savings could be 4 sec and fuel savings are in dimensions of millilitres. This savings are probably unnoticeable by individual users. However, due to high traffic volumes the sum of these individual savings is not insignificant number. Solving traffic situation by using ITS technologies improves traffic situation and also are effective from the view of economic impact on the whole society.

Acknowledgement. This contribution is the result of the project implementation: VEGA Project no. 1/0159/13 – KALAŠOVÁ, A. and collective: Basic Research of Telematic Systems, Conditions of Their Development and Necessity of Long-term Strategy. University of Žilina, the Faculty of Operation and Economics of Transport and Communications, 2013-2015.

Centre of Excellence for Systems and Services of Intelligent Transport II., ITMS 26220120050 supported by the Research & Development Operational.

References

1. Urban plan of the City of Žilina, http://www.zilina.sk/mesto-zilina-uradna-tabula-mesta-uzemny-plan-mesta (date of access: May 20, 2014)
2. Gillen, D., Levinson, D.: Assessing the Benefits and Costs of ITS, Making the Business Case for ITS Investments. Kluwer Academic Publisher, Boston (2004)
3. Prothmann, H.: Organic Traffic Control. KIT Scientific Publishing, Karlsruhe (2011)

4. Faith, P., Paľo, P.: Road and Urban Communications. University of Žilina, Žilina (2013) (in Slovak)
5. Gogola, M.: The Microscopic Modelling of Traffic on Chosen Part of Commercial Area in the City of Žilina. In: Perner´s Contact 41–46 (2012), http://pernerscontacts.upce.cz/25_2011/Gogola.pdf (June 07, 2013)
6. Sekulová, J., Nedeliak, I.: Utilization of GAP model in providing of services in the railway freight transport. In: Perner´s Contacts, Number 4, vol. VIII, pp. 67–75 (December 2013)
7. Mikulski, J. (ed.): TST 2011. CCIS, vol. 239. Springer, Heidelberg (2011)
8. Gnap J.: Modelovanie dopravného a prepravného procesu v cestnej a nákladnej doprave, EDIS vydavateľstvo ŽU (2013) ISBN 978-80-554-0744-9

Evaluating the Efficiency of Road Traffic Management System in Chorzow

Artur Ryguła[1], Andrzej Maczyński[1], and Paweł Piwowarczyk[2]

[1] University of Bielsko-Biala,
43-309 Bielsko-Biała, Poland
{arygula,amaczynski}@ath.eu
[2] APM Konior Piwowarczyk Konior,
43-309 Bielsko-Biała, Poland
pawel.piwowarczyk@apm.pl

Abstract. In the article the effectiveness of the traffic management system, on the diametral highway in Chorzow was described. The presented analysis has a multi-criteria character taking into account the efficiency of the recording units, detection of hazardous road conditions and assessment of the impact of variable message on the particular traffic streams. The subject of the analysis were the systems of weather information, vehicle identification, speed section control and variable message sings. An important part of the work was also an empirical attempt to estimate the dependency between selected traffic flows parameter and the road conditions.

Keywords: ITS efficiency, traffic stream analysis, road traffic safety.

1   Introduction

Traffic management system in Chorzów came into operation in October 2013. The systems works on the voivodeship road no. 902 (diametral highway). The road is a dual carriageway with at least 3 lanes in each direction. The section, which has been equipped with an intelligent transport system, is 2,4 kilometers long. The primary element of the system are variable message signs, weather protection, automatic number plate recognition and video monitoring subsystems (Figure 1).

Variable message signs subsystem consists of four VMS (Figure 2). At the beginning of the section, at each direction, are mounted the type A sings, which have two text lines and the limited part area to display the road signs. At a distance of about 500 meters from the type A sing, the type B VMS are installed. Type B signs have only two text lines on which the text information from the type A sign is repeated.

Automatic number plate recognition (ANPR) cameras subsystem is composed of four cameras mounted on the overpasses near the type A variable message signs. Cameras are able to detect the vehicles at the beginning and end of the section at each direction. Cameras cover only two internal lanes (high speed). Using GPS synchronization and

J. Mikulski (Ed.): TST 2014, CCIS 471, pp. 424–433, 2014.
© Springer-Verlag Berlin Heidelberg 2014

knowing the distance between the units, system allows the assessment of the average vehicle speed.

Fig. 1. The VMS signs and the weather stations in Chorzów [own study]

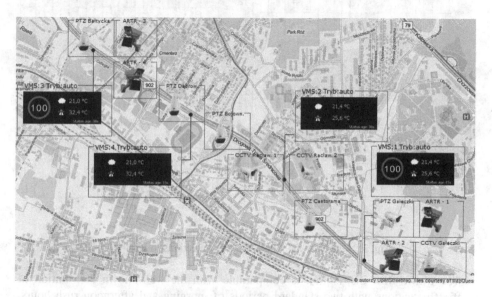

Fig. 2. ITS devices in Chorzów (voivodeship road no. 902) [own study]

The weather subsystem consists of two independent weather stations measuring the basic road pavement parameters (surface temperature, road conditions, water film height, freezing temperature) and atmospheric conditions (air temperature, humidity, dew point temperature, precipitation intensity and type, wind speed and direction).

Video monitoring subsystem uses five pan-tile-zoom cameras and three fixed devices cameras.

Presented in next chapters systems analysis took into account data form September till June 2014.

2   The Efficiency Assessment of System Units

The first analyzed system was the automatic number plate recognition module. The evaluation of the ANPR camera effectiveness was done with the use of the detected traffic flow distribution. The analysis take into account only the working days of the week. The distribution of values with a median (redline) are shown in Figure 3.

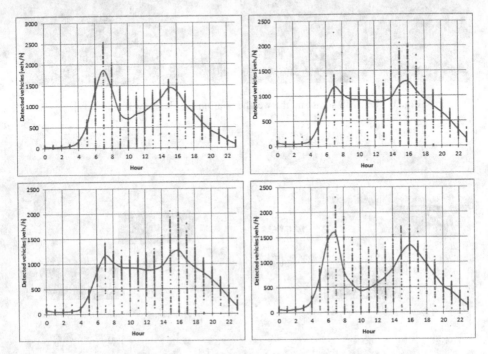

Fig. 3. Number of the APNR camera detections [own study]

The traffic flow distribution is comparable with the well-known distribution of traffic fluctuations with two standard periods of morning and afternoon rush hours. The differences in the number of detection at camera 1 and 4 , especially visible from 7 a.m. to 4 p.m., is most likely resulting from the fact that some of the vehicle are exiting/entering the highway on interchanges located at the section. The variability of the data has been determined using the standard deviation of the detection numbers (Figure 4).

The obtained results show a clearly visible increase in the variability of the vehicles detections numbers for the camera 1 and 4 in the morning rush hours. For camera 2 and 4 the peak appears in the afternoon hours. The value increase is most likely related to the camera position and the sun light which is illuminating the camera lens.

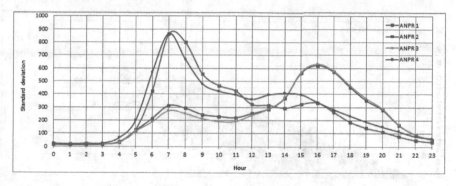

Fig. 4. Standard deviation of vehicle detections [own study]

Another important issue is the influence of precipitation intensity on the vehicle detection rate. This relationship was determined using the following equation:

$$v_{i,r} = (1 - \frac{\sum_1^{n_i}(q_{i,r} - Q_{i,r})}{n_{i,r}}) * 100\% \qquad (1)$$

where:

$Q_{i,r}$ – the median of traffic intensity for i-th hours and r-th precipitation intensity class

$q_{i,r}$ – traffic intensity for i-th hour and r-th precipitation intensity class

$n_{i,r}$ – number of i-th hours with r-th precipitation intensity class

Table 1. The influence of precipitation intensity to vehicle detection rate [own study]

Rain	ANPR 1	ANPR 2	ANPR 3	ANPR 4
Light (0÷0,2 mm/h)	28%	30%	31%	50%
Medium (0÷6,35 mm/h)	25%	28%	29%	50%
High (>6,35 mm/h)	36%	62%	62%	92%

The analysis of the data presented in table 1 indicates about thirty percent decrease in the number of detection for low and medium rain intensity. Precipitation above 6,35 mm/h reduces the average detection efficiency to the level below 40%.

The next stage of evaluating the ANPR subsystem efficiency system was an assessment of the number of vehicle which was detected at the beginning and end of the section and for which the section speed can be calculated.

The results shown in Figure 5 indicate that the average speed estimation can be achieved only for around 20% of vehicles. This low rate level is related to the fact that the camera are only detecting vehicles on the two inner lanes (high speed lanes) and the some of the vehicles exit the section at the intersection between the measuring points.

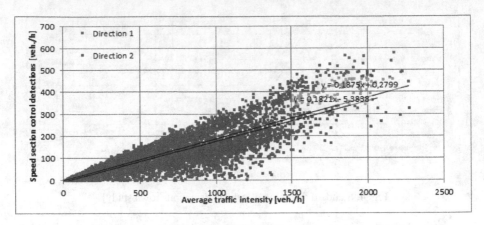

Fig. 5. Number of speed section control detections [own study]

In the case of a weather subsystem verification was made on the basis of a comparative analysis of the number of alarms registered by two independent weather stations. The analysis take into account the slippery state, hard rime and strong wind alarms (Figure 6).

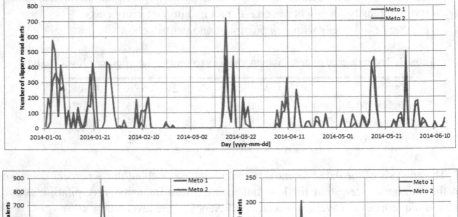

Fig. 6. Number of alerts for slipper road/hard rime/strong wind [own study]

Analysis of the data presented in Figure 6 show the apparent relationship of the particular states, which is was described using the correlation coefficients (Table 2).

Table 2. The correlation coefficient [own study]

Slippery road alerts	Hard rime alerts	Strong wind alerts
0,81	0,51	0,64

Final stage of the analysis was the efficiency determination of the variable message sign system. As a measure of efficiency used the indicator of the response amount for an executive and status commands (Figure 7).

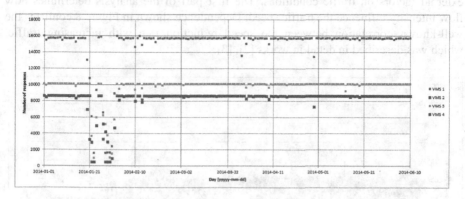

Fig. 7. Variable Message Sing availability – number of responses per day [own study]

Difference in the number of responses for each VMS depends on the number of drivers/logical fields on the signs. Observing the response variability (Figure 7) the high stability of the proposed indicator can be seen. The exception occurs at the end of January / beginning of February, in time when the parameterization of the system was made. In addition, according to the analysis presented in the work [1], the estimation of the availability factor was calculated:

$$Availability = \frac{t_u}{t_u + t_d} \cdot 100\% \qquad (2)$$

where:

t_u - VMS total uptime

t_d - VMS total downtime

Assuming that the request is carried out in one-minute intervals the values shown in table 3 were computed.

Table 3. VMS availability factor [own study]

Factor	VMS 1	VMS 2	VMS 3	VMS 4
Availability (concerning parameterization period)	95%	95%	95%	95%
Availability (without parameterization period)	99,7%	99,6%	99,6%	99,6%

The results indicate the high reliability of VMS devices. Statistically, the unavailability of the unit during the day was summarily four minutes, which could essentially result from the busy time states (in case of processing previous orders) or VMS internal testing processes.

3   The Impact of Weather Conditions on Road Traffic

The presented multimodal management system allows to analyze the impact of external factors on traffic conditions. The first part of the analysis determines how flow intensity influence the traffic speed. Dependence shown in Figure 8 confirms the well-known correlation between the speed reduction rate with increasing traffic, which was described in detail in works [2], [3].

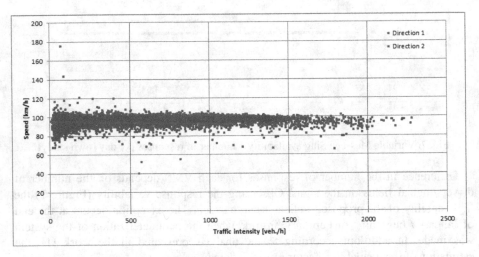

Fig. 8. Speed in the function of traffic intensity [own study]

As part of the work, referring to the methodology presented in [4], the speed of free flow as a weighted mean was calculated. As the weights used traffic intensity values. Results were determined for the speed range from 80 km/h to 120 km/h. The values were determined separately for the winter time (December-February) and spring time (April-June).

Table 4. Free flow speed

Free flow speed	Direction 1	Direction 2
Winter time	96,5 km/h	94,9 km/h
Spring time	98,5 km/h	98,2 km/h

The results shown in Table 4 indicate the differences in speed of almost three percent for the winter and spring.

The next stage of the analysis was the precipitation intensity impact on the average speed. Dependence presented in table 5 indicates a negligible effect of light rainfall on average speed. Precipitation in the range 0,2 to 6,3 mm/h reduced the speed by about 5%, while above 6,3 mm/h and more by even 7%. These results confirm the dependence described in work [4].

Table 5. Rain influence on traffic speed (spring time) [own study]

Rain	Direction 1	Direction 2
Light (0÷0,2 mm/h)	96,5 km/h	96,8 km/h
Medium (0,2÷6,35 mm/h)	91,2 km/h	94,6 km/h
High (>6,35 mm/h)	89,2 km/h	93,5 km/h

As an another criterion of the weather impact analysis took into account the effect snowfall on driving speed reducement. The work [4] indicates that light precipitation reduces the speed by 4% and approximately 20% for the heavy snowfall. For data analysed in work the values ranged from 6% to 9% (Table 3). In analysed period the heavy snow precipitation did not appear.

Table 6. Snow influence on traffic speed (winter time) [own study]

Snow	Direction 1	Direction 2
Light (0÷0,4 mm/h)	88,6 km/h	87,1 km/h
Medium (0,4÷12,7 mm/h)	88,1 km/h	90,1 km/h

The final stage of analysis was the determination of the average driving speed to the air temperature. The results (Table 7) indicate almost linear dependency of particular values.

Table 7. Temperature influence on traffic speed [own study]

Temperature	Direction 1	Direction 2	Temperature	Direction 1	Direction 2
-10 °C <	88,1 km/h	87,7 km/h	10 °C ÷ 20 °C	98,6 km/h	97,9 km/h
-10 °C ÷ 0 °C	90,5 km/h	90,3 km/h	> 20 °C	99,5 km/h	98,7 km/h
0°C÷ 10 °C	95,9 km/h	95,3 km/h			

4   Effectiveness of the VMS Content on the Drivers Beahoviours

The final stage of the work was an attempt to determine the drivers response to traffic information displayed on VMS. The first case refers to the situation when the permissible speed changes. The 70 km/h speed limit sign was displayed right after the 100 km/h limit and has been replaced with 100 km/h limit. The 70 km/h limit duration was nearly 30 minutes (Figure 9).

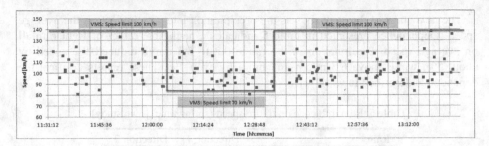

Fig. 9. Vehicle speed (speed limit 70 km/h) [own study]

Analysis of speed distribution histogram and cumulative distribution graph (Figure 10) shows a lack of the speed reducement by the drivers. In the figure 10, at the state of the 70 km/h, can only be notice the lack of speed recording over 130 km/h. It is worth recalling that speed was only registered for internal lanes (high speed).

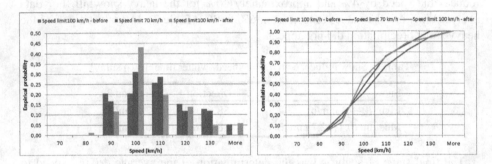

Fig. 10. Speed histogram / distribution function [own study]

The next stage of the analysis was the assessment of driver reaction for the strong, side wind sign (Figure 11).

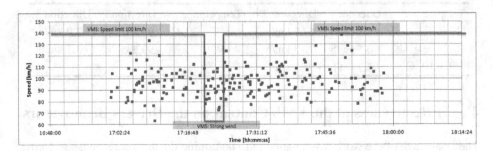

Fig. 11. Vehicle speed (strong wind) [own study]

Histogram and distribution of the speed values indicates that in this case the driver reduces the speed, especially for the range above 110 km/h. In the Figure 12 an increase of vehicles moving with speeds up to 80 km/h is clearly visible.

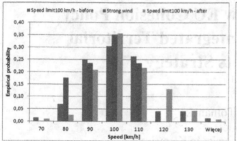 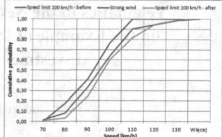

Fig. 12. Speed histogram / distribution function [own study]

5   Conclusion

The analysis presented in the paper confirmed the usefulness of the ITS solutions as well as units for current traffic management and as a tool for the multicriteria offline analysis. The carried out preliminary studies, taking into account the data form automated license plate recognitions and weather systems, confirmed the impact of the current atmospheric situation on (road) traffic.

The influence analysis of the variable message sign information on the drivers beahoviours, pointed to the need for further, extensive studies on the effectiveness of the impact of display content on traffic users. The further studies should concern the registration on all road lanes using additionally speed recording devices.

References

1. Mitas, A.W., et al.: Wybrane problemy utrzymania systemów telematyki drogowej na przykładzie znaków o zmiennej treści (VMS) oraz ważenia w ruchu (WIM). In: Siergiejczyk M. (eds.) Problemy utrzymania systemów technicznych. WPW, Warszawa (2014)
2. Gaca, S., Suchorzewski, W., Tracz, M.: Traffic engineering.Theory and practice. WKŁ Warszawa (2008) (in Polish)
3. HCM2000, Highway Capacity Manual 2000 by Transportation Research Board (2000)
4. Agarwal, M., Maze, T.H., Souleyrette, R.: Impact of Weather on Urban Freeway Traffic Flow Characteristics and Facility Capacity. Iowa State Univesity (2005)

Telematics in the New EU Cohesion Policy on the Example of Integrated Territorial Investments Strategy

Robert Tomanek

University of Economics in Katowice,
40-287 Katowice, 1 Maja 50 str., Poland
tomanek@ue.katowice.pl

Abstract. The new instruments of the European Cohesion Policy , which are Integrated Territorial Investments (ITI), first as a field of intervention, define sustainable transport. ITI does not replace other tools and operational programs, financing at 4.5 % of the funds may, however, in the case of individual agglomerations increase the integration leading to metropolisation of these areas , including the integration of transport. In particular- the Upper Silesian agglomeration along with the entire subregion in which it is located. The purpose of this article is to show the role of an ITI in balancing the development of transport by supporting the integration processes of transport in metropolitan areas and an indication of the example of the Upper Silesian agglomeration advantages and disadvantages of extension support area to the area of the central subregion. The article presents the experience of the preparation of one of the first ITI strategies in Poland for a subregion of the central province of Silesia.

Keywords: public transport, transport integrations, telematics in public transport.

1   Introduction

Priorities of the strategy "Europe 2020" (smart growth, sustainable and inclusive growth) means the need for change, but also the development opportunities for the European transport system. An important novelty of the European Cohesion Policy is a territorial dimension, which indicates a preference for integrated solutions in urban areas, especially urban and functional areas [1]. EU Common Strategic Framework (CSF) of 11 thematic objectives recognize the promotion of sustainable transport, and in several other purposes are also the problems of development and balancing of transport and mobility. The new instrument EPS, which are Integrated Territorial Investments (ITI) as a key intervention determines the direction of sustainable transport. ITI (does not replace other tools and operational programs), financing at 4.5% of the funds may, however, in the case of agglomeration increase the integration leading to metropolisation of these areas, including the integration of transport. In contrast to other metropolitan areas in Poland, in the Silesian Province ITI are related not only to the immediate vicinity of agglomeration, but to sub-regions. In particular, ITI for the Upper Silesian agglomeration will largely be used to finance transport

J. Mikulski (Ed.): TST 2014, CCIS 471, pp. 434–440, 2014.

integration, particularly with the use of telematics. Thus, this new instrument of EU Cohesion Policy will be an important tool for integration of transport with the use of telematics systems. The basis of this article is one of the first in Poland ITI strategy, prepared at the University of Economics in Katowice as work Research and implementation based on the analysis of sources and primary research conducted by a workshop with representatives of local government units [9].

2   Development and Integration of Transport within the European Cohesion Policy for 2014-2020

Transport and transport policy have played and will play a key role in the development of the common market and social development of the European Union. Over the years, changing conditions and the direction of transport development-currently particularly exposed to integration and sustainable development [12]. Despite the existence of the principle of subsidiarity, more often and more strongly the emphasis is on the development of urban transport - integrated and low-carbon.

European Cohesion Policy for the 2014-2020 period defined regulations adopted on the basis of the strategy "Europe 2020" approved by the European Council of 17.06.2010. Even the title of the Strategy ("Strategy for smart, sustainable and inclusive growth") defines its priorities, and also indicates the importance of telematics solutions [3]. From the viewpoint of transport development a second priority is particularly important: sustainable development understood as "promoting a more resource efficient, greener and more competitive." The development is to take place through the implementation of:

- the flagship initiative 'Europe Resource Efficient", where it draws attention to the development of intelligent, low-emission and intermodal transport and logistics decarbonisation,
- the flagship initiative "An industrial policy for the globalization era", where declares that "the transport and logistics networks" will improve the availability of the Union industry to the EU market and international markets.

References to the development of transport can be traced also in the other flagship "Europe 2020". The accomplishment of European Cohesion Policy in relation to the Polish occurred at the level of the Partnership Agreement, which sets out specific directions and rules for intervention in 2014-2020 with the three EU policies in Poland - Cohesion Policy, Common Agricultural Policy, the Common Fisheries Policy. The agreement was adopted by the Council of Ministers of 8 January 2014 [5]. Partnership Agreement in two thematic objectives WRS directly related to transportation:

- thematic objective 4: To support the transition to a low carbon economy in all sectors,
- thematic objective 7: Promoting sustainable transport and removing bottlenecks in key network infrastructures.

Implementing the Partnership Agreement consistent with the thematic objective called "Reduce the emissivity of the economy", is assumed as one of the priorities of the "reduction of emissions from transport in urban areas" through projects aimed at increasing the importance of collective urban transport use transportation needs using solutions that integrate investment and transport, including telematics (ITS). Here, too, there is a reference to the role played in this respect by the integrated Territorial Investments. Total cash (the allocation) into the thematic 4 in Poland, is Eur 8.1 billion (or 10.5% total aid granted to Poland in the financial perspective) [5].

Objective Subject 7 in the area of transport will be implemented by the specific objective of the Partnership Agreement, called "Improving the quality and functioning of the transport system and offer an increase in the transport accessibility of the country in the European and national level". The documents, which define the strategy in this regard are: "Transport Development Strategy until 2020" - as a synthetic document integrating all modes of transport, and the supplementary document is a "Master Plan for railway transport in Poland until 2030", which contains the concept of supra-regional transport development strategy station [11]. While the action on transport within the thematic 4 will be implemented with strong involvement of regional measures, it is already the case for the thematic 7 in terms of funds from the national level. The implementation of the thematic 7 provides approximately 24.1 billion euros or more than 30% of the total. It should be stressed that the allocation in this area in the new financial perspective is lower than in the previous [5].

Implementation of the objectives 4 and 7 will be associated with the need to manage infrastructure investments, but undoubtedly successful projects undertaken increasingly will depend on maximizing the efficiency potential of infrastructure and transport systems operator resources, and it depends on organizational solutions. Therefore, implementation of systems telematics takes priority [4].

3   The Importance of Integrated Territorial Investments in the Development of Public Transport

The role of Integrated Territorial Investment (ITI) listed in the Partnership Agreement [5] is defined in the Ordinance already cited the European Parliament and of the Council (EU) No 1303/2013 of 17.12.2013. In particular, in the Article 36 of that Ordinance it is noted that-applying the integrated approach of ITI between different EU funds is required. ITI is also encouraged in the Common Strategic Framework, as shown in the Annex to this Regulation. The Regulation does not define in detail the principles of the implementation of the ITI [7].

The Partnership Agreement states here in particular that integrated actions for sustainable urban development will be supported in accordance with Art. 7 of the Regulation of the European Parliament and Council Regulation (EC) 1301/2013 of 17.12.2013 [6]. It is obligatorily indicated that ITI "provincial" have to be implemented in the provincial cities and related indicated functional areas. According to the designated 17 areas of obligatory implementation of the ITI (in Kujawsko-Pomorskie Bydgoszcz and Torun form one area, while in the Lubuskie there are two areas. The total of national funds allocated for mandatory ITI is 2.4 billion (the minimum value that can even be increased) - at the level of the Partnership Agreement. At the same time that agreement stated that these funds should be increased by means of the Regional Operational Programme (ROP). The Provinces can run ITI also on the functional areas of cities of regional and sub-regional levels [13]. The condition for implementing ITI is creating a group of the communes of the support region (counties can also be included in this group) An important element of the strategy ITI are the areas of potential support [6]:

- the development of a sustainable, efficient transportation connecting the city and its functional area,
- restoring the socio-economic functions of degraded urban functional area,
- improvement of the natural environment in the functional area of the city,
- promote energy efficiency and the promotion of low-carbon strategies,
- strengthening the development of symbolic functions that build the international character and importance of urban-regional functional area and to improve the access and quality of public services across the functional area.

As far as the presented areas of support are concerned, it is clear that the issue of the development of sustainable urban transport is one of the essential elements of the strategy of the ITI. At the same time in terms of cities, ITI are strategic projects (mainly due to their complexity). Detailed rules for the implementation of the ITI document defines "The Principles of implementation of the Integrated Territorial Investments in Poland" [13]. The document reaffirms the principles set out in the Partnership Agreement, however, it also strengthens the relationship between the thematic objectives 4 and 7 evidenced by the record of the directions of intervention: "the development of a sustainable, efficient transport between the city and its functional area - implementation of environment-friendly and low-carbon strategy of the organization of the public transport are common to the entire functional area (eg, implementation of projects concerning the introduction of integrated travel cards, facilities for multimodal travel and mobility of employees (including the construction of the "park and ride" centers, interchanges, bicycle parking), implementation innovative transport information systems and traffic management, reduction and calming traffic in city centers, construction of bicycle paths for communication purposes (commuting), infrastructure development to promote green transport) (thematic objectives 4 and 7). "Clearly the importance of potential directions deployment of telematics in urban transport - spurred particularly characteristic of the mass-transport system [2], [4], public transport is a massive, hundreds of thousands of passengers and vehicles as many favors computerization.

4   ITI for the Upper Silesian Agglomeration

The Silesian province provides the greatest means of co-financing from the national ITI - 484 million euros which is almost twice as much for the provinces of Malopolska and Lodz [5]. Then there are the measures of the Regional Operational

Programme. The concept of the implementation of the ITI in the voivodship is based on the allocation of funds to the sub-regions and their associated centers of agglomeration. In particular ITI financed from the national level has been assigned the central subregion (mainly from Katowice). This is an expansion area in relation to the "Rules ...". The same sub-region has great economic importance. It is worth at this point to provide some basic data [9]:

- 5577 sq km (45% of the area Province), 81 units of local government (including the 8 counties and 14 cities-counties),
- around 2.8 million inhabitants (60% of the region),
- about 280 thousand traders (61% of the region, 7% of the country),
- 8.5% of the GDP of the country, over 11% of production sold.

The allocation provided for ITI for the sub-region of the central province of Silesia is the highest in Poland. Including the ROPs - ERDF provided 693.1 million, and the ESF almost 100 million Euro, which gives the amount of support in the-region of 793 million Euro. The predominant activity is the "low-carbon urban transport", which accounts for 50.2% of the funds. Under these conditions, it becomes understandable why the coordinator of ITI for the preparation of the strategy of the central sub-region has become the organizer of urban transport which is the Communications Municipal Association GOP (KZK GOP). KZK GOP to the creation of the Union of ITI under the guidelines of the Ministry of Regional Development conducted this work (now working longer Association of Municipalities and Districts of the Central Subregion, whose headquarters is located in Gliwice, the association has 81 local government units - municipalities and counties) [8-9].

The ITI Strategy prepared for the sub-region of the central activities in the field of urban transport occupy a special place. Several hundred projects submitted in the framework of the ITI for the central sub-region has been grouped into 18 strategic bundles with 6 of them directly affected by urban transport. It is clear that the emphasis is on the integration of mass transport inside the system as well as external relations. This is reflected in the proposed projects, which play a key role in the centers, interchanges and telematics solutions (bundle 12: The development of intelligent transport systems). In the framework of projects already submitted the beam projects should be mentioned [9]:

- the development of a traffic control system in Gliwice and the creation of such a system in Tychy,
- develop a system of electronic card (ŚKUP - Silesian Public Services Card) of Tychy,
- dynamic passenger information systems in Ornontowice, Tychy and in the rural district of Pszczyna.

Strengthening the activities of the ITI will probably be targeting the "Strategy for the development of the transport system Silesian province", which was adopted in April 2014 and also to promote smart solutions - including traffic management system in the Upper Silesian agglomeration, which was considered one of the key projects (up to implementation by 2020) [10].

5   Conclusion

The new instrument of the European Cohesion Policy, which are integrated territorial investment will lead to the implementation of this policy on the territorial dimension in the big cities and their surroundings. The pursuit of sustainable development in a natural way is part of the ITI in action for an integrated, collective transport. This objective will be based increasingly on implementing telematics solutions, including in particular:

* the dynamic transport information systems,
* electronic and virtual payment,
* traffic control systems communication.

The importance of telematics in improving the effectiveness and efficiency of the transport system is already widely recognized. The telematics systems are accepted in the Silesian Province strategic documents not only as a necessary element of transport systems, but also as an alternative to capital-intensive and time-consuming infrastructure investments.

Implementation of the Strategy will be a challenge to ITI - hundreds of projects and management will require great organizational effort to establish the Association of the and individual local government units. The effect of ITI on metropolitanisation and integration of collective urban transport will be an interesting research problem of theoretical and practical importance.

References

1. Drobniak, A.: Projekty strategiczne w mieście poprzemysłowym. UE Katowice, Katowice (2012)
2. Dydkowski, G., Urbanek, A.: Directions and Benefits of Using Traffic Modelling Software in the Urban Public Transport. In: Mikulski, J. (ed.) TST 2013. CCIS, vol. 395, pp. 23–31. Springer, Heidelberg (2013)
3. Europe 2020. A strategy for smart, sustainable and inclusive growth, COM (2010) 2020. Brussels (March 3, 2010)
4. Mikulski, J.: Using Telematics In Transport. In: Mikulski, J. (ed.) TST 2010. CCIS, vol. 104, pp. 175–182. Springer, Heidelberg (2010)
5. Programowanie perspektywy finansowej na lata 2014-2020. Umowa Partnerstwa. Ministerstwo Infrastruktury i Rozwoju, Warszawa (January 8, 2014),
   http://www.mir.gov.pl/fundusze/Fundusze_Europejskie_2014_2020/
   Programowanie_2014_2020/Umowa_partnerstwa/Documents/UPRM.pdf
   (date of access: June 20, 2014)
6. Regulation (EU) No 1301/2013 of the European Parliament and of the Council of 17 December 2013 on the European Regional Development Fund and on specific provisions concerning the Investment for growth and jobs goal and repealing Regulation (EC) No 1080/2006

7. Regulation (EU) No 1303/2013 of the European Parliament and of the Council of 17 December 2013 laying down common provisions on the European Regional Development Fund, the European Social Fund, the Cohesion Fund, the European Agricultural Fund for Rural Development and the European Maritime and Fisheries Fund and laying down general provisions on the European Regional Development Fund, the European Social Fund, the Cohesion Fund and the European Maritime and Fisheries Fund and repealing Council Regulation (EC) No 1083/2006

8. Statut Związku Gmin i Powiatów Subregionu Centralnego Województwa Śląskiego, https://gliwice.eu/sites/default/files/imce/statut_tekst_jed nolity.pdf (date of access: June 20, 2014)

9. Strategia rozwoju Subregionu Centralnego Województwa Śląskiego na lata 2014-2020 z perspektywą do 2030 r., ze szczególnym uwzględnieniem zagadnień rozwoju transportu miejskiego, wraz z programem działań dla zintegrowanych inwestycji terytorialnych (ZIT). Praca zbiorowa pod red. R. Tomanka. Centrum Badań i Ekspertyz Uniwersytetu Ekonomicznego w Katowicach, Katowice (2013)

10. Strategii rozwoju systemu transportu województwa śląskiego, Katowice, kwiecień (2014)

11. Strategia rozwoju transportu do 2020 roku z perspektywą do 2030 roku. Ministerstwo Transportu, Budownictwa i Gospodarki Morskiej, Warszawa (January 21, 2013), http://www.mir.gov.pl/Transport/Zrownowazony_transport/SRT/ Strony/start.aspx (date of access: June 20, 2014)

12. Załoga, E.: Trendy w transporcie lądowym Unii Europejskiej. Uniwersytet Szczeciński, Szczecin (2013)

13. Zasady realizacji Zintegrowanych Inwestycji Terytorialnych w Polsce. Ministerstwo Rozwoju Regionalnego, Warszawa lipiec (2013), http://www.mir.gov.pl/rozwoj_regionalny/Polityka_regionalna/ rozwoj_miast/Documents/ZIT_na_WWW_26_07_2013.pdf (date of access: June 20, 2014)

14. Mikulski, J.: Introduction of telematics for transport. In: Proceedings on 9th International Conference ELEKTRO 2012, 21-22 May, Rajecke Teplice, IEEE Catalog Number CFP1248S-ART, pp. 336–340 (2012), http://ieexplore.ieee.org

Automated Bias-Correction for Accurate FCD Processing Systems

Günter Kuhns and Rüdiger Ebendt

German Aerospace Center,
12489 Berlin, Germany
{Guenter.Kuhns,Ruediger.Ebendt}@dlr.de

Abstract. Within the European research project SimpleFleet, a fleet management system for small and medium enterprises has been developed. GPS traces are collected from equipped vehicles and fed into an FCD processing system to generate traffic data. To estimate the quality of derived traffic data and determine the systematic bias of a FCD processing system a previous method called "self-evaluation" was applied for specific times of day and roads with similar characteristics. With the assumption that the relative bias is the same for corresponding traffic situations, it can be transferred and used to correct results of further computations. Notice that this opens up a convenient road for automated online corrections based on really large amounts of data, rather than on small data sets from costly measurement campaigns.

Keywords: Floating Car Data (FCD), Correction of Bias, Quality of Traffic Data.

1   Introduction

Real-time traffic information is one of the most important data for operative traffic management as well as for traffic-related applications. In the European research project SimpleFleet with the main application areas geomarketing and fleet management systems for small and medium enterprises, the cost efficient access to these data with coverage of a whole road network were important requirements. Since conventional sources did not meet these requirements and equipped logistic fleets can also be used as sensors to generate further traffic data, FCD was chosen as source for this information. While other systems store information that allows identification of individual drivers, FCD only requires the re-identification of a vehicle during one trip and allows collection of traffic data while respecting the privacy of its users.

During the last years the Institute of Transportation Systems at the German Aerospace Center (DLR-TS) has developed algorithms and technologies to exploit GPS data from probe vehicles ("floating cars"). Especially taxi fleets have been used in several applications as probe vehicles realizing implementations for different cities in Europe and Asia. Current work is mostly focused on the handling of new sources

J. Mikulski (Ed.): TST 2014, CCIS 471, pp. 441–449, 2014.

for traffic data with similar characteristics (e.g. smartphones with GPS sensors), creating new fields of FCD applications, assessing and improving the quality of generated FCD. For a number of different reasons, FCD processing systems can be prone to systematic bias, e.g. because of the need to decompose the travel time between two subsequent reporting positions to several links [5], and because of GPS measurement errors, due to clouding or multi path signals.

In many investigations to assess the quality of FCD, measurement campaigns were conducted, using vehicles which are equipped with higher quality GPS systems [1],[2],[3]. While these campaigns yield reliable results that can be evaluated and compared to FCD results easily, they are quite costly and usually only cover short times or small areas.

2   Self-evaluation Approach

The self-evaluation approach presented here relies on the basic assumption that the observed actual travel times for individual vehicle trajectories can be used as a ground truth for the mean link travel times computed by a FCD system.

If this assumption holds, then, for a particular observation period, the absolute systematic bias can be computed as the difference of two mean values, namely the mean actual trajectory travel time and the mean travel time on these trajectories computed by the FCD system (see [4]). More precisely, the first mean value is that of m observed actual travel times o_i for $i = 1, ..., m$ for individual vehicle trajectories (denoted $\bar{o}$), and the second mean value is that of the travel times c_i, $i = 1, ..., m$, computed by the FCD system along the same trajectories at the time of observation (denoted $\bar{c}$). The travel times c_i for $i = 1, ..., m$ are computed by summing up the mean link travel times computed by the FCD system at the respective periods of travel on a trajectory, for all links constituting the respective individual trajectories.

It is of note that, in the scope of self-evaluation, the mean link travel times are computed without use of the link travel times observed for the vehicle which generated the respective trajectory. In other words, yet it is computed as usual as the arithmetic mean of the travel times of all individual vehicles observed on that link during the respective period, but the link travel time of the vehicle which drove the ground truth trajectory is excluded from this arithmetic mean. This is done in order to avoid any circular reasoning, which would be introduced by comparing an observation, namely the actual trajectory travel time, with a computed value (partly) based on exactly this observation.

The relative systematic bias then of course is the ratio of the absolute systematic bias and the mean observed actual trajectory travel time, given as percentage $\frac{\bar{c}-\bar{o}}{\bar{o}} * 100\%$. Also notice that the original method as described in [4] yields only one global value for the overall systematic bias of the FCD system per observation period (e.g., one hour), and that only one data source (i.e., one vehicle fleet) is considered.

2.1   A First Extension of the Approach: Analysis with Additional Separation Criteria

A practical implementation can use a digital road map. In such a map, links of the road network are usually tagged with constructional attributes like e.g. speed limits. A first extension of the self-evaluation approach makes use of this fact to obtain a more fine-granular distinction of the data used for determining systematic bias.

Already this first extension (like the final approach presented in this paper) is also based on the following basic assumption: it is assumed that on all links with identical constructional attributes, there are similar traffic conditions for corresponding periods. Moreover, one assumes that similar relative systematic biases are in effect on links with identical constructional attributes in corresponding periods. Then, no further distinction needs to be made between such links, and, for every set of corresponding periods, the same relative systematic bias can be assumed and later applied for correction.

In a first extension of the existing algorithm, five hierarchical street categories from 0 (highways and other similar major roads) to 4 (minor roads) used by the provider (Navteq/HERE) of the digital map to tag street segments, were used as separation criterion. For each category $j = 0, ..., 4$ the sums $\bar{o}_j$ and $\bar{c}_j$ are generated separately as $\bar{o}_j = \sum_{i=1}^{m} o_{ji}$ and $\bar{c}_j = \sum_{i=1}^{m} c_{ji}$ with o_{ji}.being the ith observed travel time on a road segment of category j (and analogously for c_{ji}). The relative systematic bias is determined for each category j separately as $\frac{\bar{c}_j - \bar{o}_j}{\bar{o}_j} \cdot 100\%$.

2.2   Results of the First Extension of the Approach

For this analysis, the extended self-evaluation approach as described in Section 2.1 was applied on FCD for Berlin from October to December 2012 to assess the quality of the traffic data. The data pool consists of ten Wednesdays within this period, none of them being a public holiday in Germany.

Since the used algorithm also includes historic speeds as input for the computation of FCD results, similar to the observations in [4], significant changes in the systematic bias have been observed, which correspond to the change of traffic states in the course of a day (see Fig. 1).

For all categories the systematic error follows the typical daily course of speeds, where free flow at night and breakdowns during the rush hours in the morning and late afternoon can be observed. But only for category 0 between the morning and afternoon rush hours the same level of systematic error as for free flow intervals is reached again. All other categories have completely different systematic errors in the course of the whole day, and when comparing the free flow intervals during the night. Also for category 4, in contrast to other categories, travel times are greatly overestimated in comparison to trajectory travel times.

Potential reasons for differences in these results are category-specific traffic capacities or demands, but also category-specific speed limits which could have an influence if used as initial values for historic speeds. Since the adaption of traveling speed for a vehicle to the given speed limits often occurs at the transition between street categories as well as delay times due to right of way for roads of higher categories, the travel time decomposition is even more complicated for these cases and could also lead to systematic errors in the distribution of travel times between street categories (cf. [5]).

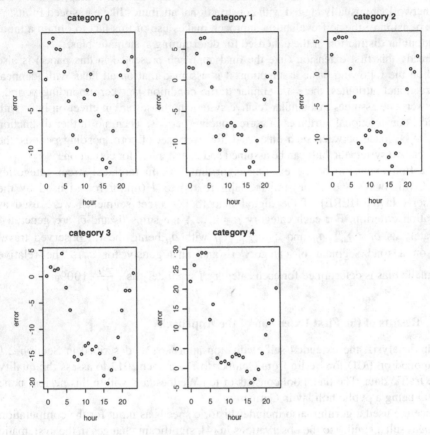

Fig. 1. Systematic errors per street category and hour of day [own study]

3   Bias-Correction and Results

This section gives the final approach to automated bias correction as a second extension of the original self-evaluation approach in [4].

The aim is an area-wide correction of the systematic bias on every link of the road map. It must be expected that the systematic error of the mean link travel times derived from the FCD system varies from one location (that is, from one section of road) to another. Due to the typically rather low penetration rates for PVD and the resulting lack of sufficient amounts of tracking data, it will often not be possible to do this separately for every individual link and for every period of interest. In other words, an area-wide bias correction would require an unrealistic amount of reference data covering all road sections.

For this reason, we propose a slightly different approach: with the assumption that the *relative* bias is fixed, i.e. *the same* for *corresponding traffic situations*, it can be transferred and used to correct the results of further computations.

More precisely: let $\hat{v}$ denote the "true" reference value for travel time on a link. Given that $\mu_i \neq 0$ for all of n data sources $i = 1, \dots, n$ where $\hat{v}$ is the "true" expected value for data source i during a particular time of day and on a particular road segment, we assume that $p_i := \frac{\hat{v}}{\mu_i}$ for all $i = 1, \dots, n$ is (more or less) constant for all considered roads. Then, each data source has a *fixed relative error* regarding its expectation $\mu_i = \mathbb{E}(X_i)$, where X_i is the random variable for data source i. Notice that in contrast to the method of [4], this new approach aims at bias correction of n data sources (e.g., FCD from n vehicle fleets), which are now considered instead of only one. Therefore, the computation of systematic biases is done for each of the n data sources separately.

The idea then is to estimate p_i from a number of m reference measurements (i.e. $p_i^{(j)}$ where $j = 1, \cdots, m$) and to apply the sample mean $\bar{p}_i := \frac{1}{m}\sum_{j=1}^{m} p_i^{(j)}$ with $i = 1, \cdots, n$ again denoting the n data sources, as a correction factor for area-wide online bias correction. For a practical implementation, and with the introductory remarks, this can only be done using the same relative systematic error for corresponding traffic situations.

Given that p_i is a fixed number (i.e. $\bar{p}_i = p_i = \frac{\hat{v}}{\mu_i}$ for all $i = 1, \cdots, n$) by assumption, we formally obtain

$$\mathbb{E}(p_i X_i) = \frac{\hat{v}}{\mu_i}\mathbb{E}(X_i) = \hat{v}. \tag{1}$$

Hence, $Y_i := \bar{p}_i X_i$ is an *unbiased* random measurement of the true value $\hat{v}$. Next, we need to state in more detail

- how to estimate the sample means $\bar{p}_i$
- what precisely is meant by "corresponding traffic situations".

Regarding the first point: analogously to the previous method of self-evaluation, for $i = 1, \cdots, n$, percentage systematic biases are calculated as $\frac{\bar{c}-\bar{o}}{\bar{o}} \cdot 100\%$ (cf. Section 2). Moreover, whereas the previous method was used for the diagnosis of the (global) systematic bias only, the present approach also aims at correcting any systematic bias in the data. For this purpose, correction factors $\bar{p}_i = \frac{\bar{o}_i}{\bar{c}_i}$ for every data source $i = 1, \cdots, n$ are calculated alongside the systematic biases. To see that the $\bar{p}_i$ with $i = 1, \cdots, n$ as given here have in fact the property of correcting the systematic bias estimated from the m sample trajectories for data source i, or more precisely, from the m computed travel times $c_{i1}, \dots, c_{im}$, and the m observed actual travel times $o_{i1}, \dots, o_{im}$, notice that in analogy to (1), we have that

$$\frac{1}{m}\sum_{k=1}^{m} \bar{p}_i c_{ik} = \frac{\bar{p}_i}{m}\sum_{k=1}^{m} c_{ik} = \frac{\bar{o}_i}{\bar{c}_i} \cdot \bar{c}_i = \bar{o}_i \tag{2}$$

For $i = 1, \cdots, n$, the trajectory data of source i is used for the calculation of $\bar{p}_i$. As has been said before, it will often not be possible to do this separately for every individual link and for every period of interest. Therefore, the approach followed here calculates the correction factors separately for each of L sets of links with identical constructional attributes.

Regarding the second point, it also does this separately for each of T sets of corresponding periods, respectively. Recall from Section 2.1 that, in order to extend the previous approach of self-evaluation to periodically computing systematic biases for each link of interest, a second assumption has to be made (besides the one that has already been made, i.e. assuming that actual travel times for individual vehicle trajectories can be used as a ground truth for the mean link travel times): it is assumed that it is possible to define corresponding periods (time slices) with typically similar traffic conditions. Based on this assumption, correction factors can be transferred from one (reference) period to corresponding periods.

More precisely, for $i = 1, \cdots, n$ and each data source i, for $l = 1, \cdots, L$ and each set L_l of links with identical constructional attributes, and for $t = 1, \cdots, T$ and each set T_t of corresponding periods, a separate estimation of the true travel times $\hat{v}_{lt}$ on the links in L_l for the periods in T_t is done, using trajectory data of source i (for an instructive example of corresponding periods see Figure 2).

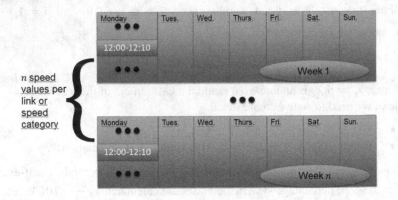

Fig. 2. Example for corresponding periods [own study]

Thereby $\hat{v}_{lt}$ is estimated as the mean trajectory travel time $\bar{o}_{ilt}$ for trajectories of source i on links in the particular set L_l, and during observation periods in T_t. In doing so, it is also assumed that the travel time on individual links along a trajectory can be determined without introducing a significant systematic bias. In other words, one assumes that a reintroduction of any significant systematic bias during the necessary arithmetic decomposition of the total trajectory travel time on individual links can be avoided by appropriate means (cf. [5]).

Then, separate estimations of the expected travel time μ_{ilt} for each data source i and the aforementioned links and periods are done, as the mean travel time $\bar{c}_{ilt}$ on links of trajectories of data source i, which are also in the particular set L_l, and observed during periods in T_t, as computed by the FCD system, using tracking data from source i. The final correction factor used for $i = 1, \cdots, n$ and each data source i, for $l = 1, \cdots, L$ and each set L_l of links with identical constructional attributes, and for $t = 1, \cdots, T$ and each set T_t of corresponding periods, is

$$\bar{p}_{ilt} := \frac{\bar{o}_{ilt}}{\bar{c}_{ilt}} \tag{3}$$

This is an estimator for $\frac{\hat{v}_{lt}}{\mu_{ilt}}$ (cf. our remark that p_i is really fixed, right before Eq. (1)).

Notice that the approach only uses the trajectories of data source i when calculating the estimator $\bar{o}_{ilt}$ for $\hat{v}_{lt}$. This is done in order to match the degree of data coverage on individual links during the computation of $\bar{c}_{ilt}$ for data source i, respectively. For this reason, there are n estimators for the true travel times $\hat{v}_{lt}$, namely $\bar{o}_{ilt}$, one for every data source $i = 1, \cdots, n$.

Then, finally, the y_i with $i = 1, \cdots, n$ are the *unbiased* measurements for data source n, that is, the *bias-corrected* realizations $y_i = \bar{p}_i x_i$ of the random variable $Y_i = \bar{p}_i X_i$ (indices l and t for the considered L link sets and T periods have been suppressed). The x_i with $i = 1, \cdots, n$ are the original biased measurements of data source i (for the considered period set of interest, respectively). Thereby, choice of an appropriate correction factor $\bar{p}_i$ is based on the fact that a correspondence of periods at the same time of day (TOD) has been defined, as well as a correspondence of links with the same constructional attributes. In other words, the correction factor $\bar{p}_{ilt}$ for the tth time slice and the lth set of links, is used for every period corresponding to t (i.e, for every period at the same TOD), and every link in the set of constructionally comparable links L_l.

Summarized, the approach followed here calculates the correction factors separately for each of L sets of links with identical constructional attributes, and for each of T sets of corresponding periods, respectively. Thereby it relies on the validity of the second assumption made (see above). It only remains to further illustrate the term "identical constructional attributes": To reduce the number of different cases that have to be considered and to be able to efficiently collect the needed reference data, traffic situations were categorized by the criteria used in Section 2.1, which had already yielded well-differentiated systematic biases.

To validate this approach, correction factors were determined for eight Wednesdays as one subset of the data pool, and then these factors were applied on the data for the remaining two Wednesday to test whether it is possible to effectively transfer the correction factors to other, corresponding time periods, and also if the selected separation criteria were good choices for the separation of traffic conditions.

These plots show that for the resulting corrected FCD (see Figure 3), the systematic bias was reduced dramatically in comparison with the uncorrected values (as presented before in Figure 1). Also the typical daily course of speeds is no longer visible and the average systematic bias per street category no longer deviates from zero as for the uncorrected results. This shows that the proposed assumption holds in this case and specific correction factors determined from the systematic bias of previous data can be applied to correct further results of FCD processing systems.

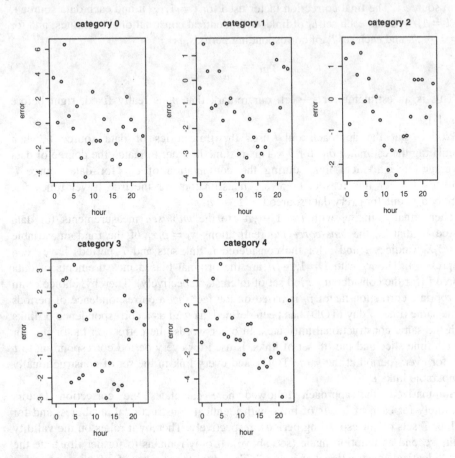

Fig. 3. Corrected FCD results by application of correction factors determined from a reference data pool [own study]

4   Conclusion

A new approach for automated bias-correction of traffic data has been developed, deployed and evaluated. Rather than basing the corrections on data from a few costly measurement campaigns, it bases its corrections on really large amounts of reference data which are not limited to specific parts of a road network. By combining data for similar traffic conditions, the required amount of reference data to generate correction factors can be collected within weeks. These factors are then applied automatically during online processing to generate corrected FCD results in real-time.

The clear dependence of the variance of the traffic data on the external factors that have been identified as separation criteria shows that these are indeed suitable to describe specific traffic conditions, and confirms the assumption that similar traffic conditions also result in similar systematic errors. While it cannot be expected that the systematic bias in FCD processing can be eliminated completely, e.g. due to small differences in traffic conditions between reference and application intervals, the results clearly show a significant overall reduction.

Acknowledgment. The research leading to these results has received funding from the European Union Seventh Framework Programme "SimpleFleet" (http://www.simplefleet.eu, grant agreement No. FP7-ICT-2011-SME-DCL-296423). The authors thank the taxi control center Taxi Berlin TZB GmbH for provision of GPS-data for the taxi-FCD system.

References

1. Brockfeld, E., et al.: Validating Travel Times calculated on the basis of taxi floating car data with test drives. In: 14th ITS World Congress, Beijing (2007)
2. Brockfeld, E., et al.: Validation of a taxi-FCD system by GPS – test drives. In: 17th World Conference on Intelligent Transport Systems, Busan (2010)
3. Reinthaler, M., et al.: Evaluation of speed estimation by floating car data within the research project DMotion. In: 14th ITS World Congress, Beijing (2007)
4. Kuhns, G., et al.: Self Evaluation of Floating Car Data Based on Travel Times from Actual Vehicle Trajectories. In: IEEE Forum on Integrated and Sustainable Transportation Systems, Vienna (2011)
5. Neumann, T.: Accuracy of distance-based travel time decomposition in probe vehicle systems. Journal of Advanced Transportation (2013)

Model of Incentives for Changes of the Modal Split of Traffic Towards Electric Personal Cars

Grzegorz Sierpiński

Silesian University of Technology,
Krasińskiego 8, 40-019 Katowice, Poland
grzegorz.sierpinski@polsl.pl

Abstract. Application of technology that uses electric drive opens up new possibilities in traffic. Previous models of modal split traffic usually included four types of movements (by car, by public transport, by bicycle and by foot). Personal car was then perceived as the least eco-friendly. The creation of new means of transport changed this situation. The article focuses on the problems associated with the development of transport systems in the direction of support electric cars. At the local level and national level in different parts of the world are accepted various types of incentives that will bring about changes of travel behaviour and increase participation of electric cars in the traffic. The article presents possible model the relationship between different types of incentives and determines barriers that must be overcome in order to improve the image of this means of transport. Example of using the proposed method was also briefly described.

Keywords: modal split, electric cars, sustainable development, alternative transportation.

1 Introduction

The development of transport in the 21st century necessitates measures which have been previously neglected or insufficient. Problems arising in transport systems related to growing number of trips, in particular using individual means of transport, result in severe congestion of city centres and consequently loss of time for travellers, higher noise levels, and fuel consumption and larger emission of pollutants to the environment (especially in locations where vehicles frequently stop and start) [21], [30]. Sustainable development is based on two basic assumptions [20]: the concept of needs – which translates into activities implemented only when needed – and the necessity to take into consideration limited non-renewable resources. Both concepts should be implemented with the view of contemporary and future generations. As regards the concept of needs, it is necessary to thoroughly study and analyse travels including defining origin and destination, motivation and frequency. Complete knowledge about the area in question, taking into consideration not only the situation created by the current system of transport, but also actual needs of people travelling, should enable developing appropriate solutions and adjust new technologies [27].

J. Mikulski (Ed.): TST 2014, CCIS 471, pp. 450–460, 2014.

Guidelines or recommendations regarding directions for developing EU transport systems included in consecutive White Papers and communications [1], [6], [28], [29]. In general, it is possible to distinguish two basic areas of initiatives:

- necessary changes in modal split, including public transport and growth of rail and intermodal transport, and
- changes of sources energy.

A comprehensive approach is needed using a variety of measures, including integration of planning, organization, policy and law. To promote change of modal split, people travelling need to be incentivised, and in long-term perspective a change of travel behaviour. This aspect (and barriers associated with it) has been widely described in the article. The second area of initiatives includes technologies that enable reducing noise, emissions to the environment, and reduce the use of non-renewable resources. One of recent documents defining the European strategy for the use of alternative fuels [6] of 24 January 2013 draws attention to threats related to the high oil dependence of Europe (in relation to mobility and transport). Alternative fuels listed in the document included LPG, natural gas (LNG and CNG), electricity, biofuels and hydrogen. In this particular case, apart from the development of infrastructure, (European) technical specifications, attention should also focus on public acceptance for those solutions.

The article focuses on the possibility of changing the approach to individual trips by using ecological vehicles, especially electric cars. Attention has also been drawn to overcoming barriers to promoting the development of transport systems on a larger scale. In the past, modal split models usually included four modes (individual cars, public transport, bicycle and travelling on foot). An individual car was then considered as the least ecological (or non-ecological) mode. The development of new modes of transport necessitated changes in this field. The article concentrates on issues related to the development of transport systems towards supporting electric individual cars. The article includes a proposal to extend the traditional approach of modelling by the procedure for selecting the optimal scenario incentives to support electric cars in cities. The article concludes with a calculation example using a genetic algorithm, as one of the options for implementing the described method.

2   Modal Split and New Ways of Travelling

Modal split results from choices made by people travelling. Subjective choices made by individuals lead to distributing traffic among various modes in a given area. From this point of view, modal split can be understood as an assessment of activities implemented at the level of a city, region or a country. The traditional modal split comprises four modes. These include travelling on foot, individual car, bicycle and public transport. In this particular group, individual car is the only mode which cannot be considered environmentally friendly. Thus, its share in the total traffic should be reduced. The development of technology and organization produced variations of those traditional modes. An example is the use of bicycles not as individual transport mode but a mode shared by many people using public bicycles (bike rental). The same applies to individual cars (that can be rented by users). The technological advancement enabled introducing vehicles with propulsion which significantly reduce impact on the environment (reduction of noise and emission of pollutants). While introducing solutions of sustainable transport and promoting alternatives to individual cars, it seems appropriate to promote a more detailed modal split. A detailed description of the model should include:

- travel on foot,
- other than foot:

    o individual transport   o public transport
    - private   ▪ bus
        > bicycle   ▪ tram
        > motorcycle/scooter   ▪ trolleybus
        > private car   ▪ metro
    - public   ▪ fast city train
        > city bike
        > city passenger car

Of course, availability of particular modes depends on their accessibility or infrastructure supporting them. It is still debatable how to determine position in the list presented above for the carpooling system (use of one car by more than one person travelling in the same direction).

A key issue is to differentiate vehicles in terms of their propulsion. It is important for at least two reasons. Firstly, it is the proportion of vehicles using conventional fuel as opposed to vehicles with non-conventional propulsion in overall traffic, which shows the advancement of the transport system and awareness among users. Secondly, defining the share of various propulsion types helps building of a transport system in a specific area promoting specific vehicles (e. g. electric cars).

3   Barriers to Larger Use of Electric Cars

New technologies as regards alternative fuels widened the variety of means of transport, including electric cars. This enabled reducing the negative impact of transport on the environment which does not require significant increase in using public transport. Electric vehicles offer high efficiency, and therefore one may travel cheaper than in the case of using a traditional car (using fossil fuel). Although this type of a car has several advantages, its use is too limited because people travelling are not convinced to this new solutions and motivation is poor at the level of the state. Table 1 lists issues that may be considered barriers for the desired use of electric cars in cities. Some barriers are apparent only, since an electric car is already suitable for its application in cities. Considering the range of an electric car (according to information of 2013), several of electric cars can travel 150-220 [km] on a single charging (cars using energy accumulated in package of batteries above 25 kWh).

Selected models with more powerful batteries can travel as much as 400-500 [km] [7]. While analysing distances in cities and possibility of recharging batteries at home, a distance exceeding 150 [km] is sufficient to cover average distances in a city (for instance, in Poland, commuting to work at distance of 20 km accounts for 70% of all trips [4]). This approach eliminates several barriers listed in table 1. Therefore, some of items on the list are only apparent issues as perceived by the general public (and this needs to be changed). A major barrier to overcome is the price of an electric vehicle. Financial incentives for those who decide to buy an electric vehicle might be a solution to the problem. Various countries have decided to apply some of the incentives below [8], [9], [17]:

- subsidising purchasing cost,
- discounts on or free charging during initial years of operation,
- possibility of using designated HOV lanes (high occupancy vehicles) or lanes for buses, and
- discounts on toll roads.

Table 1. Selected areas requiring changes to promote common use of electric cars in traffic

Barriers and limitations	Needs and opportunities
Lack or shortage of relevant infrastructure significantly reducing transport accessibility of electric cars.	The building of a large number of charging points in cities. Until 2020, it is planned to commence operation of 2.4 million slow charging stations all over the world and about 6000 fast charging facilities (from 0.5 to 2 hours).
High cost of buying electric car.	State subsidies for those purchasing such cars.
Different performance standards for parts of electric cars and charging systems.	Developing common (European) technical specifications.
Lack or shortage of information for electric cars users as regards trip planning.	It is necessary to expand existing and building new trip planners taking into construction need to charge electric cars – for short and long distance trips (exceeding travelling range several times).
Random location of charging points that could help integrating electric cars into transport chains.	Including the issue of charging points distribution in city and region development strategies to promote full integration within transport chain.
Lack of designation of electric cars in modal split (research and modelling).	Due to a specific nature of operation, it is necessary to distinguish this group of trips in traffic models.
Short travelling distance covered by electric cars without recharging.	Development of technologies improving technical parameters.

Source: own study based on [6]; [10], [11]; [23]

In Poland, incentives have been introduced on a local level only in the form of free parking for electric cars in paid zones (e.g. Gdańsk, Katowice, Toruń and Tychy [5]).

4   Proposed Support Model for Electric Cars

As mentioned earlier in the text, changes in modal split require a different approach to the transport system by people travelling. By using appropriate measures, it is possible to influence travel behaviour of selected transport network users. These activities may take two forms. The first one of them involves introducing restrictions for users of a specific mode. This includes fees for entering specific zones or parking, as well as total restriction of entry for certain vehicles. The second group of activities includes possible support for certain vehicles (most frequently proecological means of transport). In the case of public transport in cities, solutions include separate lanes for buses, specific shape of platforms, priority at signalized intersections, other solutions in transport telematics (including traffic information systems and others [18], [19]), and optimized routes[1]. Another environmentally friendly mean of transport is bicycle (as urban means of transport). In this particular case, cohesive and safe cycling paths, safe bike parks and urban bike rental may be used.

The article [23] presents proposed changes of selected traffic model elements, including function of utility. In this case, the majority of indicators result from specific qualities of a given route and they are related to time, distance, accessibility, weather conditions, cost, and behaviour of individuals and groups. Only one indicator reflected organizational and technical changes introduced.

The function, however, was applicable to one route only, rather than general conviction among people travelling. An important factor for people shaping transport systems is the possibility to estimate optimized solution regarding incentives to achieved desired results. Thus, modelling of various support schemes is needed. Appropriate selection of incentives, further referred to as the optimum incentive scenario, depends on a number of factors. Selecting an appropriate scenario can be defined by two sets A, B and a group of sets D_s described below.

$A = \left\{ a_i : a_i \in R^+, i = 1, \ldots, n \right\}$ is a set of functions describing n local conditions (attributes), including travelling behaviour. Particular elements in the set define a given area at a time t_0.

$B = \left\{ b_j : b_j \in \langle 0, 1 \rangle, j = 1, \ldots, m \right\}$ is a set of functions describing m incentives (measures, initiatives, and tools), facilitating decision making by people travelling as regards purchasing and using an electric car. Particular values in the set determine specific measures (e.g. subsidising price, free charging during initial period of operation, special privileges for users such as designated parking places, free parking, separate HOV lanes or lanes for buses, electric cars included in trip planners, etc.).

Thus, functions b_j assume values from the set $\langle 0, 1 \rangle$.

$D_s = \left\{ d_{si}(a_i) : a_i \in A, i = 1, \ldots, n \right\}$ (where $s = 1, \ldots, k$) is a family of sets of functions reflecting different levels of desired (target) results. D_1 is a set of functions defining the perfect (highest) level of results, whereas D_k corresponds to the lowest

---

[1] The selected initiatives are characterized in (e. g.): [2], [3], [13-16], [24-26].

of desired levels of fulfilling needs. In the case of electric cars, desired effects include, for instance increased number of such cars in the total number of cars registered, more electric cars in traffic, appropriate distribution of electric cars in city transport network – specific routes, reduction of noise and emission to environment within selected area, etc. Thus:

$$d_s : A \rightarrow R^+ \cup \{0\},$$ (1)

where $d_s(a_i) \in R^+ \cup \{0\}$ interprets desired values of results for attribute a_i at s level of meeting needs.

In longer perspective, a result of an appropriate configuration of values of set **B** (specific measures implemented) will lead to the change of values in **A**, namely a durable change in travelling patterns (2).

$$a' \rightarrow A \times B \rightarrow R^+ \cup \{0\},$$ (2)

where $a'(a_i, b_j) \in R^+ \cup \{0\}$ has interpretation of attribute a_i after applying incentive b_j. This leads to the set of functions **A'** which can be presented as a matrix:

$$A' = \begin{bmatrix} a'(a_1, b_1) & a'(a_1, b_2) & \dots & a'(a_1, b_m) \\ a'(a_2, b_1) & a'(a_2, b_2) & \dots & a'(a_2, b_m) \\ \dots & \dots & \dots & \dots \\ a'(a_n, b_1) & a'(a_n, b_2) & \dots & a'(a_n, b_m) \end{bmatrix}$$ (3)

Defining particular values in **A** and estimating values in **A'** to evaluate measures implemented is possible by using different studies. One of the ways is to determine the approximate impact of the taken activities by *ex post* study (including questionnaire surveys among people travelling [27], and using statistical analysis or telematics devices which collect current information for example about the structure of the traffic, the number of recharges electric cars, using dedicated lanes for this type of vehicle, etc.). By dividing an area into transportation sections [12] it is possible to obtain values of sets using a polynomial with multiple variables (4).

The advantage of this method is the ability to determine the actual effects for the area. The disadvantage is lack of optimum incentive scenario at start - iterative method for the selected area.

$$\left\{ a \in A : W(a) = \sum_{i_1, \dots, i_n \leq m \in N} \xi_{i_1 \dots i_n} \cdot x_1^{i_1} \dots x_n^{i_n} \right\}$$ (4)

where:

a – element of set **A**;

$\xi_{i_1 \dots i_n}$ – parameters of model.

$x_1 \dots x_n$ – indicators influencing specific element in **A**.

Another approach is to estimate the value of A '. This is possible using the experience of other (similar) areas, where adequate initiatives have been implemented to varying degrees. There is also another approach - genetic algorithms and fuzzy sets theory can be apply. In this case estimate based on a sufficiently large sample can provide answers both - in terms of successive "generations" (for example by taking the following activities after some time period) and the optimal configuration of incentives at each stage of the analysis (the proper selection of the full package of incentives).

Regardless of the method acquisition data for a set of **A'**, optimizing an incentive scenario involves finding a configuration of elements in **B** leading to maximum changes in **A** towards a direction defined by desired results in **D**. Maximum benefits can be defined by developing an indicator based on a difference between D_s and **A'**. The objective function at this case is to achieve a minimum values for the indicators.

The procedure requires an algorithm taking into consideration the current distribution of traffic flows in the transport network and inventory of transport infrastructure.

The possible configurations of a set of incentives **B** are limited by the possibility of financial, organizational and technical. Thus, to achieve the desired level of results D_1 is not always realistic. In this case, the proposed method also gives an opportunity to the efficient use of resources and supports decision-making on a limited budget.

5   Example

As an example, an analysis of possible changes in the behaviour of people traveling for a sample of 100 persons of a specific area was realized. Information about the initial status (original level of attributes) is based on a questionnaire. Reactions of particular groups of people to incentives are defined in two ways: some are based on a questionnaire and others require an application of the fuzzy set theory. A hierarchical structure of issues has been assumed as in Figure 1. The original status of set **A** was common for consecutive analyses. The set was modified in two ways: parallel and serial. Changes in the parallel system involved analysing the original set for various incentive structures (specific sets **B**). The second approach involved implementation of various scenarios for incentives **B** in consecutive steps (while taking into consideration modifications of original set **A** and modifications of individual's features, as well as time elapsing – in every case it was 1 year).

The example used elements of a genetic algorithm. Traditional transformations were adjusted to meet research objectives. It was assumed that:

- generation 1 (G_1) is the original (initial) set **A** (consisting of defined features for each person in form of chromosomes having structure as in figure 2)
- further generations comprised sets **A'** subject to actions taken (mutation through incentives **B** scenarios)
- drawing was performed by picking participants of consecutive mutations in the trial set with approximation to the Poisson distribution.

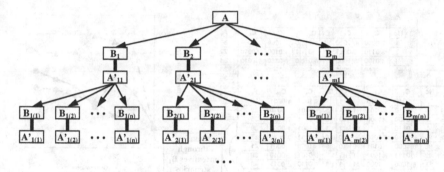

Fig. 1. Hierarchic structure of the research problem (plan of experiment) [own study]

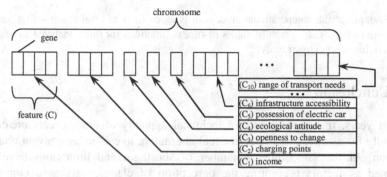

Fig. 2. Chromosome structure (part of features analyzed in the experiment) [own study]

An important element of genetic algorithms is crossing, which in this particular case, due to a specific nature of the issue, may take an overt form or can be implemented, for instance, by:

- exchanging random specimen with new ones due to time and possible fluctuation in an area concerned, and
- mutual changes and interactions with the environment (e.g. possibility of selling car, which results in changes to attributes analysed).

In the research involving a sample of 100 people, the value of a chromosome has been each time determined for a selected specimen. The total for the entire set defines the fitness function of population F. While analysing changes in consecutive mutations, as well as comparing values of the function in serial analyses, it is possible to determine the objective function as maximum $F_i \rightarrow max$. Figure 3 presents some results followed by a description of the calculation process.

More elaborate description of results extends beyond the framework of the article. Due to its general nature, the example shows the proposed method applied in practice only. The comparative chart (Figure 3) presents changes of the fitness function depending on incentive scenarios and influence of other factors in time.

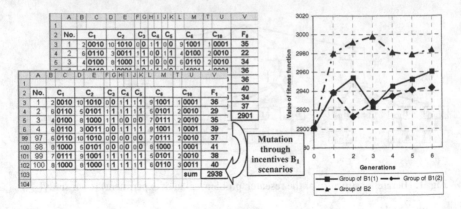

Fig. 3. Example of the computational process in practice (part of results: left – first mutation after incentives **B₁**; right – graph of values of fitness functions for three analyzed strategies of consecutive incentives) [own study]

6   Conclusion

In recent years, the improvement of technical capacity of electric cars created an opportunity for electric cars to become real alternative to cars using conventional fuel very soon. At the same time, a number of shortages and limitations have been highlighted as factors preventing the perception of electric cars as a convenient solution. Some of the issues mentioned include adjustment of transport infrastructure, organization problems, access to information for people considering this means of transport, integration with other means of transport into transport chains, changes in transport behaviour etc. It is necessary to adjust transport systems to needs of electric cars to include this particular mode in the future single European transport market (full integration in transport chains).

In the future, models of incentives can be used for developing scenarios for more effective use of electric cars in the traffic. The proposed procedure allows the use of many kinds of methods to obtain initial and intermediate data. The number of sets with desired results can be selected depending on various options of solutions applied. However, it requires defining indicators for specific areas due to cultural and social differences among travellers. For this reason, it is justified to examine the area more thoroughly.

References

1. Action Plan on Urban Mobility, SEC(2009) 1212 Brussels (September 30, 2009)
2. Autolib' Official Site, http://www.autolib.eu/ (data of access: April 7, 2014)
3. Celiński, I., Sierpiński, G.: A dynamic management of a public transportation fleet. LogForum 9(3), 135–143 (2013)
4. Central Statistical Office, http://www.stat.gov.pl/gus (data of access: April 12, 2014)

5. Cities which promote electric cars, http://www.samochodyelektryczne.org/ (data of access: April 7, 2014)
6. Clean Power for Transport: A European alternative fuels strategy, COM(2013), 17, Brussels (January 24, 2013)
7. Comparing the energy consumption of electric cars from 2013, http://www.samochodyelektryczne.org/ (data of access: April 07, 2014)
8. Electric Vehicle Incentives around the world, http://www.teslamotors.com/incentives/ (date of access: April 11, 2014)
9. Electric Vehicles in Urban Europe, http://www.urbact.eu/project (data of access: April 11, 2014)
10. EV City Casebook. A Look At The Global Electric Vehicle Movement. Organisation for Economic Cooperation and Development/International Energy Agency, Paris (2012)
11. Global EV Outlook. Understanding the Electric Vehicle Landscape to 2020 (2013)
12. Karoń, G., et al.: The investment program tramway development for the years 2008 ÷ 2011. Traffic Analysis. Research study NB-67/RT5/2009
13. Macioszek, E.: Modele przepustowości wlotów skrzyżowań typu rondo w warunkach wzorcowych. Open Access Library 3(21) (2013)
14. Macioszek, E.: The Influence of Motorcycling and Cycling on Small One-Lane Roundabouts Capacity. In: Mikulski, J. (ed.) TST 2011. CCIS, vol. 239, pp. 291–298. Springer, Heidelberg (2011)
15. Macioszek, E.: The Passenger Car Equivalent Factor for Heavy Vehicles on Roundabouts. In: Janecki, R., Sierpiński, G. (eds.) Contemporary Transportation Systems. Selected Theoretical and Practical Problems. The Development of Transportation Systems. Monograph, vol. 256, pp. 127–137. Silesian University of Technology, Gliwice (2010)
16. Mathew T. V., Krishna Rao K. V.: Introduction to Transportation Engineering. IIT Bombay, http://www.cdeep.iitb.ac.in/nptel/Civil%20Engineering/ (date of access May 19, 2013)
17. Menu Of Plug-In Electric Vehicle Incentives. U.S. Department of Energy (2013)
18. Mikulski, J.: Telematic Technologies in Transportation. In: Janecki, R., Sierpiński, G. (eds.) Contemporary Transportation Systems. Selected theoretical and practical problems. New Culture of mobility. Monograph no. 324, pp. 131–143. Publishing House of the Silesian University of Technology, Gliwice (2011)
19. Nowacki G. (ed.): Telematyka transportu drogowego. ITS Warszawa (2008)
20. Our Common Future. Report of the World Commission on Environment and Development (1987)
21. Pawłowska B.: Zrównoważony rozwój transportu na tle współczesnych procesów społeczno-gospodarczych. Wydawnictwo Uniwersytetu Gdańskiego, Gdańsk (2013)
22. Sierpiński, G., Celiński, I.: Use of GSM Technology as the Support to Manage the Modal Distribution in the Cities. In: Subic, A., Wellnitz, J., Leary, M., Koopmans, L. (eds.) Sustainable Automotive Technologies 2012, pp. 235–244. Springer, Heidelberg (2012)
23. Sierpiński, G.: Revision of the Modal Split of Traffic Model. In: Mikulski, J. (ed.) TST 2013. CCIS, vol. 395, pp. 338–345. Springer, Heidelberg (2013)
24. Sierpiński, G.: Theoretical Model and Activities to Change the Modal Split of Traffic. In: Mikulski, J. (ed.) TST 2012. CCIS, vol. 329, pp. 45–51. Springer, Heidelberg (2012)
25. Starowicz, W.: Zarządzanie mobilnością wyzwaniem polskich miast. Transport Miejski i Regionalny 1, 42–47 (2011)
26. Suchorzewski, W.: Opłaty za wjazd do obszarów śródmiejskich – sukcesy i porażki. In: Kaczmarek, M., Krych, A(eds.) Skuteczne zmniejszenie zatłoczenia miast, Poznań – Rosnówko, pp. 195–206 (2009)

27. Travel Survey Methods Committee (ABJ40): The On-Line Travel Survey Manual, http://www.travelsurveymanual.org/ (data of access: April 07, 2014)
28. White Paper: European transport policy for 2010: time to decide. COM, 370 (2001)
29. White Paper: Roadmap to a Single European Transport Area – Towards a competitive and resource efficient transport system. COM, 144 (2011)
30. Załoga, E.: Trendy w transporcie lądowym Unii Europejskiej. Wydawnictwo Naukowe Uniwersytetu Szczecińskiego, Szczecin (2013)
31. Mikulski, J. (ed.): TST 2011. CCIS, vol. 239. Springer, Heidelberg (2011)
32. Mikulski, J. (ed.): TST 2010. CCIS, vol. 104. Springer, Heidelberg (2010)
33. Mikulski, J.: Introduction of telematics for transport. In: Proceedings on 9th International Conference ELEKTRO 2012, Rajecke Teplice, IEEE Catalog Number CFP1248S-ART, May 21-22, pp. 336–340 (2012), http://ieexplore.ieee.org

Telematics for the Analysis of Vehicle Fleet Fuel Consumption

Wolfgang Niebel, Rüdiger Ebendt, and Günter Kuhns

German Aerospace Center (DLR),
Institute of Transportation Systems, Department of Traffic Management
Rutherfordstr. 2, 12489 Berlin, Germany
{Wolfgang.Niebel,Ruediger.Ebendt,Guenter.Kuhns}@dlr.de

Abstract. Within the European research project SimpleFleet, a telematics system for fleet management business intelligence was developed, delivering live or near-realtime statistics about individual vehicles or the entire fleet. This supports the fleet manager in ad-hoc decisions and in medium and long term improvements. The fleet vehicles (e.g. taxis, delivery vans) are equipped with an On-Board-Unit (OBU) for GPS tracking and data collection from other sensors, e.g., an engine on/off detector. These raw data are sent to a host system and database, being enhanced to Floating Car Data (FCD) using map-matching and routing. Beside other route-related information, consulted fleet operators expressed their interest especially in fuel consumption calculation. For this purpose the German EWS procedure was chosen, providing 2nd degree polynomial functions of the driven speed. Final results for the test in the Athens region are presented, including the comparison of two calculation approaches with different aggregation levels of driven speeds.

Keywords: Logistic services, Fleet Management, Floating Car Data.

1 Introduction

Project SimpleFleet makes it easy for small and medium enterprises (SMEs), both, from a technological and business perspective, to create web-based fleet management applications. For this purpose, a large data pool ("TrafficStore") comprising base data such as maps and traffic data from dedicated providers has been built. A simple interface provides a means to connect user-contributed data streams to this pool. An algorithmic framework dubbed "TrafficIntelligence" which includes map-matching algorithms, vehicle routing services and a statistics package utilizes the collected data and provides value-added services. SMEs are able to access the data and services by means of a web-based API, a Software Development Kit (SDK) wrapping API access for specific languages and environments and Application Frameworks for rapid application development for target platforms such as Web (JavaScript), and iPhone and Android mobile platforms.

To ensure a service development which addresses the real needs of the SMEs a Customer Advisory Board was set up. From their feedback it became clear that

J. Mikulski (Ed.): TST 2014, CCIS 471, pp. 461–468, 2014.

adding a sensor to measure the fuel consumption is possible, but too expensive, so most fleet managers would probably not pay for it. Instead they calculate the fuel consumption, based only on the recorded speeds. To overcome this vague approach a more sophisticated method was developed as described in section 2. Its implementation (section 3) was tested with field data from a member of the advisory board, B-K-Telematics. This telematics and fleet management service provider is settled in the urban area of Athens/Greece. Section 4 gives some results from that test. Detailed descriptions of the work are contained in [1].

2   Fleet Analytics Methodology

2.1   Input Data

Raw data is delivered by the original fleet management systems into the TrafficStore via the TrafficAPI. It contains series of time stamped geo-coordinates (traces) derived from the GPS functionality of the On-Board-Units. B-K Telematics provided the following additional information per GPS trace:

- vehicle type,
- engine on/off to identify stops, and
- engine on but stopped (which fleet managers will consider as a rather undesired state).

2.2   Basic Performance Indicator Computation

Basic performance indicators desired by the Customer Advisory Board comprise the kilometrage and number of stops.

Kilometrage calculation requires some pre-processing steps which are well-established within the field of Floating Car Data (FCD). These algorithms enhance the received geo-traces by map-matching and routing based on road network maps. Summing up the lengths of these trajectories yields the kilometrage.

A vehicle is considered as stopped when its engine is off. The most important attributes defining a stop include the identity of the vehicle, the time the vehicle stopped and the time the vehicle started moving again. Additionally, the position of the vehicle at the start time point and the position at the end time point of a stop are also considered as attributes of a stop. The data model used for storing vehicle stops for FleetAnalytics is simple and is realized using one relational table in a PostgreSQL database (DB). The population of the stops DB table is triggered from the FCD collection process. A database trigger defined on the INPUT_FCD_FLEET DB populates the stops table based on fact that there are two possible conditions for one vehicle:

- Condition A: If one vehicle is currently stopped, then its most recent entry in the stops table contains the start time point of the stop and a null value for the end time point.
- Condition B: If a vehicle is currently moving, then its most recent entry in the stops table contains the start and end time points of the last stop realized by the particular

vehicle. There is also the special case that no record is contained in the stops table for the particular vehicle. This case appears only once for one vehicle, at the first time it is encountered by the stops population process.

For a new FCD sample that is considered by the database trigger, the following actions may be realized:

- If Condition A is true and the FCD sample's engine status value is ON, then the end time point of the most recent record in the stops table, for the particular vehicle producing this FCD sample, is updated using the timestamp value of the FCD sample.
- If Condition B is true and the FCD sample's engine status value is OFF, then a new entry is stored in the stops table for this particular vehicle. The start time point of the record gets the value of the FCD sample's timestamp and the end time point is set to NULL.

2.3   Fuel Consumption Model

An appropriate fuel consumption model had to be chosen, for which the decision criteria were, i.a., suitability for the existing data range and format like vehicle type and speed, as well as its applicability in Europe. Within the EU FP7 project iTetris ("An Integrated Wireless and Traffic Platform for Real-Time Road Traffic Management Solutions"), literature regarding the models for pollutant emission and fuel consumption has been reviewed [2]. A lot of the therein found models turned out to be not suitable for SimpleFleet, as it became clear that a large amount of static parameters such as the engine displacement, and parameters modelling the processes within the vehicle's engine should not be expected to be available. At the end the German EWS sub-model for fuel consumption [3] was chosen.

It is particularly the ability of EWS to deliver continuous functions which makes an advantage over COPERT III [4] or HBEFA [5]. Nonetheless, it is possible to use both the (online) FLEET data of, e.g., EMISIA S.A. [6], and the most recent HBEFA publications to adapt the factors of EWS for a particular forecast period and for most European countries.

The dependency of fuel consumption k on

- (mean) velocity V [km/h]
- longitudinal slope s [%] (positive: ascending, negative: descending)
- considered year Y

is modeled by a multiplicative conjunction as

$$k=F(V)\cdot G(s,V)\cdot H(Y) \text{ [g/veh*km]} \tag{1}$$

The functions G and H are normed such that $G(s=0,V)=1.0$ for slope s=0%, and such that $H(Y=1990)=1.0$ for the base year . The respective empiric values represent mean values of the measurements for classes of engine displacement, gross vehicle weight, etc.

Note that the approach taken here is more general than necessary for some customers of SimpleFleet´s FleetAnalytics suite of software modules, since information about the longitudinal slope might not be at hand in the road network map. Due to $G(s=0,V)=1.0$, this is not a problem for the model.

Regarding function F, it is of note that the mean velocity V is used to distinguish between two patterns of driver behavior. One is the pattern of "normal range of travel speeds", the other is the "stop-and-go pattern". The first is always detected when V>20 km/h, and the latter is detected when V≤20 km/h. Fuel consumption in this case is the minimum of either a constant "stop-and-go factor" c_s or the calculated value for the "normal range of travel speeds". Written as a formula, we have that

$$F(V) = \begin{cases} c_0 + c_1 \cdot V^2 + \frac{c_2}{V} & \text{for } V > 20 \text{ km/h} \\ \min\left\{c_s, \left(c_0 + c_1 \cdot V^2 + \frac{c_2}{V}\right)\right\} & \text{for } V \leq 20 \text{ km/h}. \end{cases} \quad (2)$$

The values c_s, c_0, c_1, c_2 can be found in look-up tables [3] for each of the eight EWS vehicle classes, e.g., PO=**P**assenger car with **O**tto engine (petrol), LN=light duty etc., differentiated between urban roads and freeways. A final conversion from grams into liters can be applied if needed.

It could be proved by fleet mileage data for the year 2005 [6] that the Greek fleet's specific consumption (per vehicle) is a few percent less than the German fleet's (max. 10%). Therefore the EWS parameters were found to be eligible for use for Greece. Since no data for future fuel consumption in Greece was available, the respective trends in Germany were assumed to be valid again. HBEFA [5] data for fuel consumption is available from 1995 on until the year 2035. For each vehicle the relative change H(Y) was derived for the years 2014 to 2025 as stated in Table 1. It is noteworthy that for duty vehicles no decreases or even slight increase are expected between 2014 and 2025 according to these data.

Table 1. Correction factors H(Y) for the EWS vehicle types, exemplary years

EWS vehicle type ID (according B-K fleet vehicle type)		Year Y				
		1990	2014	2015...	2020...	2025
PO (passenger car)		1.00	0.77	0.76	0.70	0.64
LN (van 4X4 Pickup)		1.00	0.75	0.73	0.62	0.52
ZS (refrigerator truck)	urban road	1.00	0.89	0.89	0.91	0.92
	freeway	1.00	0.96	0.96	0.97	0.97

3   Implementation

A prototype of the FleetAnalytics suite of software modules has been implemented in Java by DLR. It operates on a test fleet of ~400 vehicles in Athens as provided by B-K Telematics. The implemented approach to calculate the fuel consumption is based on map-matched trajectories of the FCD data. The speed of an individual vehicle is derived from the time-stamped position reports of its trajectories. The trajectories are stored in a database where each trajectory consists of a chain of trajectory entries containing a timestamp, an edge identifier, the edge length, the edge speed and a flag that identifies motorways.

Because of the map-matched FCD data we now have information about the type of the road and can apply special formula constants for motorways to achieve better results.

In a nutshell the implemented algorithm should calculate:

- The sum of the fuel consumption of the whole day over all vehicles in liters.
- The travelled distance of all vehicles for the whole day as sum of kilometers.

Next, a description of the steps of the algorithm based on trajectories is given:

```
CONSTANT GRAMM_PER_LITER_DIESEL = 820    # gram per litre
Diesel
CONSTANT GRAMM_PER_LITER_GAS = 720;     # gram per litre
Petrol

Read all trajectories of one day

Read all vehicle type dependent constants and the annual
correction factor from the database for the EWS formula
with (c0, c1, c2, cS, cY)

Read all vehicle type dependent motorway constants and
the annual correction factor from the database for the
EWS formula with (cMW0, cMW1, cMW2, cMWS, cMWY)

FOR EACH trajectory DO
    get all trajectoryEntries for the trajectory

    FOR EACH trajectoryEntry(trajectory) DO
        # calculate travelled distance:
        travelledDistance = travelledDistance + trajecto-
ryEntry.length

        # calculate velocity
        velocity = trajectoryEntry.edgeSpeed

        # calculate fuel consumption in g/km (gram per km)
        IF (trajectoryEntry.isMotorway) THEN
            consumption = cMW0 + (cMW1 * velocity^2) + (cMW2
/ velocity)
            IF (cMWS < consumption) THEN
                consumption = cMWS
            END IF
            # apply annual correction factor
            consumption = consumption * cMWY
        ELSE
            consumption = c0 + (c1 * (velocity^2) + (c2 /
velocity)
            IF (cS < consumption) THEN
                consumption = cS
```

```
          END IF
          # apply annual correction factor
          consumption = consumption * cY
       END IF

       consumptionLiter = convertToLiter(consumption,
GRAMM_PER_LITER)

       fuelConsumptionSum = fuelConsumptionSum + consump-
tionLiter

    END FOR
END FOR

store in database: fuelConsumptionSUM and trav-
elledDistance
```

4   Experimental Results

To demonstrate the operation of the FleetAnalytics prototype, several statistics have been calculated, based on an exemplary week of fleet operation. The week chosen was from Monday the 3rd June until Sunday the 9th June 2013. The herein given statistics are for the whole fleet, rather than for particular individual vehicles, which is also enabled by the FleetAnalytics suite of software modules. The aggregated view should give a more interesting and more instructive experimental result. Fig. 1 gives the average fuel consumption per day and vehicle type, clearly revealing that the refrigerator trucks consume the most fuel on average. The two weekend days can also be identified by the absence of passenger cars (SUV). There seems to be no day-type dependencies of the specific fuel consumption.

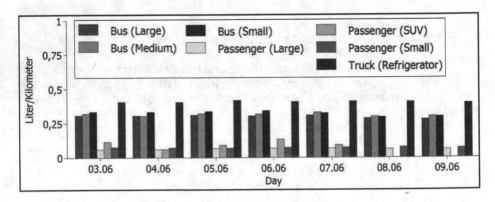

Fig. 1. Average fuel consumption per day and vehicle type in June 2013 [own study]

In Fig. 2, the distribution of the overall fuel consumption per vehicle type of the test fleet over daytime is depicted (limited to the period of interest; after 2:30 pm the overall level remains for another 3 hours and further decreases with time). We can identify an early consumption peak between 3 am and 5:30 am, i.e., before the morning rush hour. The other consumption peak between noon and 2:30 pm is also before the afternoon rush hour. Refrigerator trucks are very active between midnight and the first peak as well as after the first peak but cease operation even before noon. Passenger cars do not have a significant share in the overall consumption.

The velocity distribution in Fig. 3 shows a peak at 20 to 25 km/h, and a second one at 80 km/h, mainly for refrigerator trucks. This might be due to their speed limit which is lower than the limit for buses at 100 km/h. Another reason could be the more frequent usage of freeways.

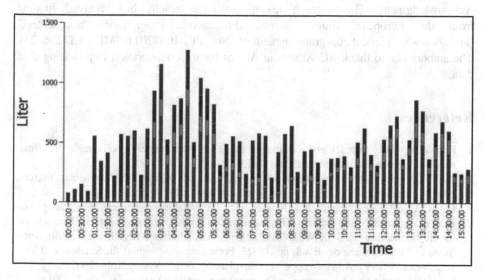

Fig. 2. Absolute fuel consumption per 15 minutes [own study]

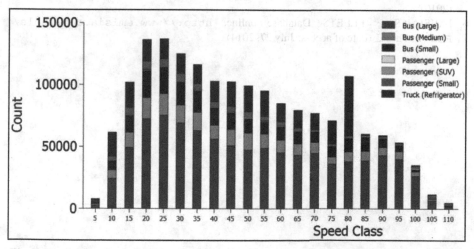

Fig. 3. Distribution of velocities by vehicle types, week from 03 June to 09 June 2013 [own study]

5   Conclusion

The software suite for the business intelligence of the project SimpleFleet has been described. The FleetAnalytics suite is capable of calculating important daily statistics for the tracked assets of connected fleet managers, such as the fuel consumption. It is now up to the companies to use this new tool and gain experience how to utilize it for improvements. Such an improvement could be Eco-Routing by including not only travel times but also fuel consumption (and therefore emissions) into their routing algorithms.

Acknowledgment. The research leading to these results has received funding from the European Union Seventh Framework Programme "SimpleFleet" (http://www.simplefleet.eu, grant agreement No. FP7-ICT-2011-SME-DCL-296423). The authors like to thank RC Athena in Athens for the collaboration in providing fleet data.

References

1. Ebendt, R. et al.: SimpleFleet – Democratizing Fleet Management, Deliverable 3.2: Business Intelligence (Confidential). Berlin (2013)
2. iTETRIS consortium: Deliverable D3.1 – Traffic Modelling: Environmental Factors, (2009), http://ict-itetris.eu (date of access: July 27, 2014)
3. Cerwenka, P., Dischinger, N., Klamer, M.: Anwendungsorientierte Ermittlung von Kraftstoffverbrauch und Schadstoffemissionen des Kraftfahrzeugverkehrs in Deutschland für die Neufassung der RAS-W (EWS). In: Wirtschaftlichkeitsuntersuchungen an Straßen – Stand und Entwicklung der EWS, pp. 15–23, Forschungsgesellschaft für Straßen- und Verkehrswesen (FGSV), Arbeitsgruppe Verkehrsplanung, FGSV Verlag Köln (2002)
4. EMISIA S.A., http://www.emisia.com/copert (date of access: July 27, 2014)
5. Infras: Handbuch für Emissionsfaktoren des Straßenverkehrs 1980-2010, Version 3.1. Bern (2010)
6. EMISIA S.A.: FLEETS Database online, http://www.emisia.com/tools/FLEETS.html (date of access: July 27, 2014)

Author Index